QABBALAH
THE PHILOSOPHICAL WRITINGS
OF
SOLOMON BEN YEHUDAH IBN GEBIROL

Qabbalah
The Philosophical Writing
of
Solomon Ben yehudah Ibn Gebirol

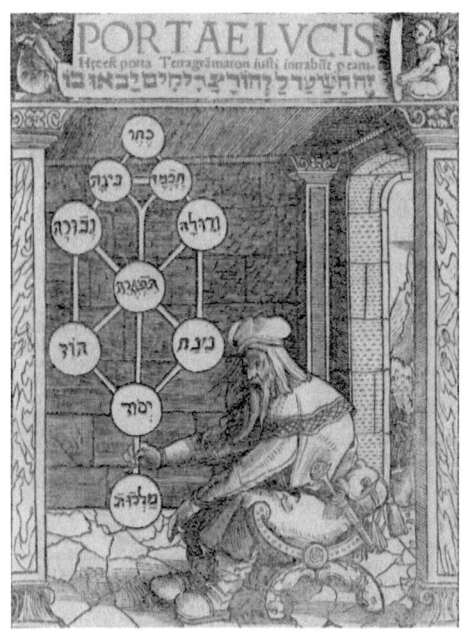

BY
Isaac Myer, LL.B.

Athens ‡ Manchester

Qabbalah. The Philosophical Writings of Solomon Ben Yehudah Ibn Gebirol

Old Book Publishing Ltd

Book Cover Design: Old Book Publishing Ltd

Copyright © 2011 Old Book Publishing Ltd
All rights reserved.

Title of original: Qabbalah. The Philosophical Writings of Solomon Ben Yehudah Ibn Gebirol or Avicebron and their connection with the Hebrew Qabbalah and Sepher ha-Zohar, with remarks upon the antiquity and content of the latter, and translations of selected passages from the same. Also An Ancient Lodge of Initiates, translated from the Zohar, and an abstract of an Essay upon the Chinese Qabbalah, contained in the book called the Yih King; a translation of part of the Mystic Theology of Dionysios, the Aeropagite; and an account of the construction of the ancient Akkadian and Chaldean Universe, etc. Accompanied by Diagrams and Illustrations.

Originally published in 1888

Copyright © 1888 Isaac Myer, LL.B.

ISBN-10: 1-78107-027-X
ISBN-13: 978-1-78107-027-7

EDITOR'S NOTE

Old Book Publishing Ltd takes care in preserving the wording and images of the original books. For this reason we have invested in technology that enables us to enhance the quality of such reproduction. This investment helps overcome problems encountered when reproducing old books, such as stains, coloured paper, discolouration of ink, yellowed pages, see-through and onion skin type paper.

This reproduction book, produced from digital images of the original, may contain occasional defects such as missing pages or blemishes due to the original source content or were introduced by the scanning process.

These are scanned pages and the quality of print represents accurately the print quality of the original book, though we may have been able to enhance it.

As this book has been scanned and/or reformatted from the original we cannot guarantee that it is error-free or contains the full content of the original.

However, we believe that this work is culturally important, and despite its imperfections, have elected to bring it back into print as part of our commitment to the preservation of printed works.

Old Book Publishing

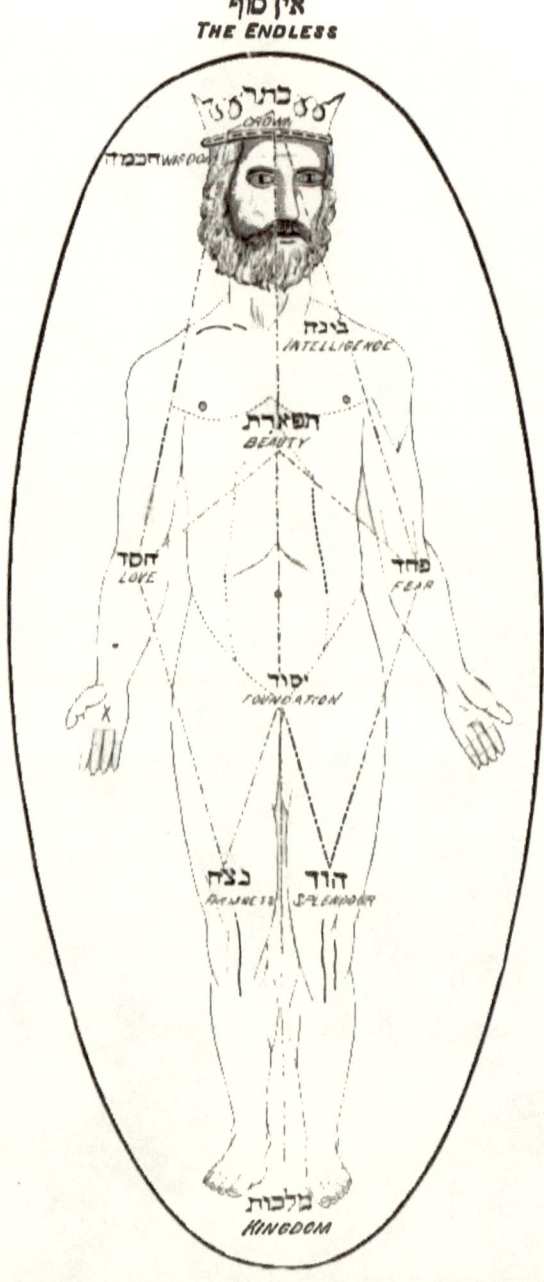

THE UPPER ADAM WITH AIN SOPH AND THE TEN SEPHIROTH.

QABBALAH.

The Philosophical Writings

OF

Solomon Ben Yehudah Ibn Gebirol

OR

AVICEBRON

And their connection with the Hebrew Qabbalah and Sepher ha-Zohar, with remarks upon the antiquity and content of the latter, and translations of selected passages from the same.

ALSO

An Ancient Lodge of Initiates,

TRANSLATED FROM THE ZOHAR,

And an abstract of an Essay upon the Chinese Qabbalah, contained in the book called the Yih King; a translation of part of the Mystic Theology of Dionysios, the Areopagite; and an account of the construction of the ancient Akkadian and Chaldean Universe, etc. Accompanied by Diagrams and Illustrations.

BY ISAAC MYER, LL. B.,

Member of the Numismatic and Antiquarian Society of Philadelphia; La Société Royale de Numismatique de Belgique; Corresponding Member of the American Numismatic and Archæological Society, Historical Society of the State of Pennsylvania, etc.

350 COPIES PUBLISHED BY THE AUTHOR.

PHILADELPHIA.
—1888—

Copyrighted by the Author,
ISAAC MYER,
AT
Washington, D. C., 1888.

All rights reserved.

PRINTED FOR THE AUTHOR
BY
MACCALLA & COMPANY,
NOS. 237 AND 239 DOCK ST.,
PHILADELPHIA.

TO
ALL EARNEST, UNPREJUDICED AND
INDEPENDENT, SEARCHERS
FOR THE
TRUTH,
THEOLOGIANS, PRIESTS AND LAYMEN:
THIS WORK
IS RESPECTFULLY
DEDICATED
BY THE
AUTHOR.

INTRODUCTION.

"God hath spoken once; two-fold is what I heard."

THE following pages are devoted to a short account of the life and writings of the philosopher, Solomon ben Yehudah Ibn Gebirol or Avicebron; proofs of the antiquity of the Zoharic writings and the Qabbalah, a condensed statement of some parts of the Qabbalistic philosophy, quotations from the Zoharic books, and various articles pertaining to the same, in Appendixes.

The investigation of the antiquity and content, of the Qabbalah and Zoharic writings, has been neglected by the learned, and, with the exception of a very few in England, Germany, Russia and France, has been almost wholly ignored by the writers of this century. To the student of the origin of religions or their philosophy, especially of the origin of the formulations, dogmas and doctrines of early Christianity; a study of the Hebrew Qabbalah and of the Zohar is of great value and importance, and has not received the attention it justly merits and demands. It is apparent from the many similarities in this Qabbalistic philosophy, to the doctrines in the New Testament and early Patristic literature; that both of the latter, most probably, have had a common germ and origin in the esoteric teachings of the Israëlites, as well as in the more open and exoteric teachings of the Hebrew Holy writings.

It was these striking similarities which struck my thought in the course of my reading, and caused an examination of the subject; the more the investigation proceeded the more manifest to me appeared many of these similarities, and the more satisfied I became, that a common origin existed. Many learned theologians have endeavored, without much success, to find these origins in the Talmud, but the latter treats almost entirely of the Ha-la'khah or Common Law, Customs and Ritual, considered essential to the outward life of the Israëlite; however it sometimes, gives in explanations, short Ha-gadic statements, which most probably, were taken from the Secret Learning, the ancient *Sod, i. e.*, Mystery, of the Hebrews; but one might as well study the English Common Law Reports and the Digests of the same, in order to ascertain the content of English philosophy, as to expect to find the full content of the inward esoteric metaphysics and philosophy of the ancient Israëlites, in the Talmudic writings. It was through the spirituality of the doctrines of the Secret Learning, that many of the ideas and dogmas, set forth by the Evangelists in the New Testament as those of Jesus and his Apostles, found so ready an entrance and acceptance, in the Jewish thought of their period.

The New Testament taken in connection with cotemporary writings, especially those of Philo Judæus, many of whose writings have reached our day; shows that the Jewish mind at the epoch of its formulations, was prepared to accept, without much questioning, many of its doctrines and conclusions. At that period, many of the Jews were daily expecting the appearance of a Messiah, coming to them through the generations from David; but all did not accept Jesus as that Anointed One, as that Messiah who was daily expected. It is in the study of the Jewish *Disciplina Arcana*, that we must hope to find the higher spiritual ideas of the cotemporaries of Jesus and the Apostles, and not in the outward law, ritual and forms, of the Pharisees; whose religious convictions stuck too much in the bark, and did not penetrate very deeply, into the heart and core of the tree of spiritual religious truth. But outside of the importance of the Qabbalistic philosophy to the theologian, to the philosophic mind; "Any form of speculation which has at any time powerfully influenced human thought, will repay the study which is spent in understanding it, and, sooner or later claim fresh regard. The variations of human nature are too limited, to place any of its developments wholly beyond the pale of interest."*

At the present time, the great foes to any rapid advance in the spirituality of religion, are materialism and formalism. The first tends to merge itself into agnosticism, pantheism or atheism; the latter, into the formuations in creeds and dogmas, and in ritualism. Like the formalism of

* Canon Brooke F. Westcott, Contemporary Rev., Vol. v, May-Aug., 1867.

the Pharisees in the time of Jesus, the second would see in the mere performance of ritual, the repetition of creeds or fixed forms, the letter of the law; and through mere attendance at the house of worship, a compliance with the true inner faith and requirements of real spiritual devotion. Against these phases of so-called religion, the free inward consciousness and liberty of the true spiritual and higher man, always rebels; the inner man, drawn by the Deity, desires to see, a worship from the heart, sentiment and soul, and not a mere formal observance of creeds and books, a mere repetition of words and genuflexions of the body as a saving Grace and a true road to Salvation. To such, the spiritualistic philosophy of the higher phases of the Qabbalistic system, when truly searched for, contemplated, and understood; opens her arms, and from its great height in the Unknown Essence of the Supreme Deity, the Eternal Boundless One, to its depth, in the lowest materialism of evil; gives an opportunity for the reception, and acquisition of the grandest and noblest ideas, to the highest and most subtile order of religious spiritual thought. The greatest Mystics of the past, be they John Tauler, Thomas A'Kempis (Hamerken), Saint Theresa, or Dionysios, the Areopagite, have all been under the influence of ideas which are fully included in those of the Qabbalistic philosophy. As to the materialists: "What are they finding, more and more below facts, below all phenomena which the scalpel and the microscope can show? A something nameless, invisible, imponderable, yet seemingly omnipresent and omnipotent, retreating before them deeper and deeper, the deeper they delve, namely; the life which shapes and makes. * * * More and more the noblest-minded of them, are engrossed by the mystery of that unknown and truly miraculous element in nature, which is always escaping them, though they cannot escape it."*

It is my desire to awaken a higher spiritual feeling towards the investigation of the Mysteries of Ancient Israël, in which, the Mysteries of the New Covenant lie hidden; which shall help to awaken in Christian Mysticism its fundamental elements, faith and belief in the True; to animate it to study the metaphysics of the great Fathers of the Church, especially the great Greek Fathers, the most erudite thinkers of the early Christian

---
*Kingsley. Pref. to Westminster Sermons, pp. xxvii–xxviii.

church; and establish the vast edifice of theology on deep philosophical principles and belief in the True, and not on man's alterable creeds and formulations: and by so doing; prepare a common centre for the re-union of all the, at present divided, religious sects. I also believe that such researches and investigations are calculated to pave the way to an understanding of the true principles in the primitive history of mankind, and be an assisting guide, in the dark labyrinth of myths, mysteries and archaic religions; and that they will place much, which is now uncertain, on a firm foundation and in a stronger and clearer light, and so prepare the way, for that which the Deity never intended should be separated, the union of sound reason and correct philosophy with true religion.

We cannot in this connection forbear quoting the words of a great German thinker: "Whenever in religion, or polity, or civilization, in art or science; the inner element is developed most strenuously in its outward productions and the spiritual earnestly sought after, be it with more or less modifications of existing institutions, there is progress at hand; for it is from within that life issues forth into the external, from the centre to the circumference. This therefore is the pathway which leads to life, that on which there are ever opening new outlets for the Spirit, and on which Genius, can unfurl its wings with god-like self-assurance. If this be true, the contrary result must also happen, wherever the external or material life is continually exalted,—wherever the symbol supersedes and stands more and more for the essence; a form of words or an external work for the mental act or for conscience; where the symmetrical superfices is accepted for the inner content, and the outer uniformity for vital unity, and appearances for truth. In every such happening the luckless future must be impending whatever be the aspect of the present. * * * When such a path is once entered upon, the necessity very soon becomes apparent, of treating the dictates of the common conscience as apostacy, of putting down conscientious objections as insubordination, and suppressing personal freedom as sedition. And then tyranny, either ecclesiastical or political, becomes a necessity, etc."*
To-day around us this latter feeling appears to be getting the upper hand,

* *Gott in der Geschichte* 1857–8, by Christ. Karl Josias Baron von Bunsen, Vol. iii, Bk. vi, c. iii, thesis 6.

there is too much desire for wealth and the gratification of the present and not enough of the Divine Afflatus. Too much of the spirit of Voltaire, Condillac and Descartes, and not enough thought of our future existence, nor of the feelings which animated the Qabbalists, true Theosophists and Mystics, of the past. We want more men influenced with the same feelings as were Savonarola, Tauler and Jacob Böhme.

In the Hebrew Holy Scripture, the visible or creation, is regarded as the manifestation of the Divine Glory or She'kheen-ah. The attributes of the Deity are therefore seen through His works, so St. Paul says: "For the invisible things of Him from the creation of the world are clearly seen, being understood by the things that are made, even His eternal power and glory." (Rom. i, 20.)

But the human mind obtaining its ideas in this matter-world, can never whilst existing in it, raise the veil to its full height nor thoroughly understand in their full purport, the mysteries concealed behind it. Even the words used in the most abstract sciences and in religion and philosophy, to signify the most perfect abstractness, have only a partially definite meaning, and in most minds, are vague and tinctured by the grasp of individual intellect, surroundings, modes of thought, imagination, experience; yes, even by the prejudices, dislikes and sentiments of thought, in the minds of those who use them; and so mar the tendency to the true, the abstract, and the real. There is an endeavor on the part of enlightened abstract thinkers to avoid this as much as possible, and they frequently seize upon foreign words and the "mixed modes" of one tongue, to express through them the pure simple ideas of another language, for in their new position these words are clear of the alloy of experiences and the mistakes caused by the senses of their old masters. The naturalism therefore of the Hebrew Old Testament has been largely merged into the Greek language, as a greater idealization and abstraction; first we see this in the Septuagint or Greek translation, and then, more thoroughly, in the New Testament, a fusion of Hebrew and Hellenic thought. We can imagine a language in its first beginnings, in which every act and operation of the mind, every idea and relation, was expressed by a matter-image or symbol, a language at once based purely on the senses and the material, its words only mental pictures like its written symbols, of which, the archaic Egyptian hieroglyphics may be considered as example; higher than this we can imagine a language with the world of mind and the world of matter distinct, but such cannot in this matter-world, exist. All language exists between two extremes and is passing continually from one to the other, it is never, no more than are the stars and the universe at anytime standing still.

The language and words in the Holy Scripture are intermediaries between the seen and the unseen, thoughts are the winged angels which partake of both the visible and invisible as did the angels of the Bible. They are spirits which may be clothed in the æther of man's breath and so become visible, but not always, for language cannot always define and formulate, those things which are within the veil; there are things we feel which we cannot formulate into words, the sigh of sorrow, the cry of despair, the exclamation of anger, the ecstasy of heavenly bliss, of love and hope and earthly happiness, are a few of the thoughts we can never formulate into words.

The nearest approach that man can make to the unseen, is that inner communion which works silently in his soul but which cannot be expressed in absolute language nor by any words, which is beyond all formulations into word symbolism yet is on the confines of it and the unknown spiritual world. This is conceptualism. We experience these feelings only in our hearts and inner thoughts, that which strikes our consciences as right or wrong comes unbidden to us and without any logical sequence, is like a dream. The more intensely man feels the highest intellectuality, the more thoroughly does his spirit enter into this spiritual communion and the more difficult is it to express to others, these emotions and this undefined consciousness, this converse with another world; formulate them, express them, in words; and we draw them down to a gross, dark and material plane. Silence, meditation, intercommunion with self, this is the nearest approach to the invisible. They are sublimations. Many of our ideas are only negations, the Highest Deity is clothed, as to Its essence and appearance, in darkness to the finite thought. Yet even these negations are affirmations and we only leave the opposition to the negation, a condition to our thoughts, of vagueness and uncertainty. "There is a spiritual body and there is a natural body," but this does not take us out of the material-world, a spirit can only be conceived of as something vague, dim, in opposition to matter, yet the inner motor of us, is spirit. The Deity and Its attributes cannot be defined, they are to us an absolute negation of all our so-called absolute knowledge, for all our absolute knowledge is based, raised upon, centred and carried on, through our matter-world knowledge and symbolism, *e. g.*, Eternity is not the past, present, future, these are in Time, Eternity can be conceived of, only as an absolute negation of all thought of Time, so only can spirituality by the absolute negation of all matter-world thought and matter-world existence. The Non Ego is the nearest approach to the invisible, the Ego is a manifestation.

From a want of knowledge of the Qabbalistic philosophy, the translations of many statements in both the Old and New Testaments are frequently erroneous, and this is especially evident in numerous of the asserted improvements in the revised versions, *e. g.*, Ephesians iii, 15, the older versions of which evidence the fact, that it is in agreement, with both the Qabbalah and Talmud, in the use of the words "family in heaven:" to signify, the Upper angels and spirits who are near the Deity; also Matt. vi, 13, where the desire to be delivered from the *Ye'tzer ha-rah, i. e.*, the evil inclination, which is asserted in the Qabbalah to accompany every human being through life, is referred to the Devil.

The reader may be sometimes startled by my statements, which may be at times contrary to his conventional religious ideas, as to this I can only say, that I have stated the subject as I have found it, and, as this is not a polemical work, do not criticize it.

The student of Assyriology and ancient Babylonian thought, will find many similarities between it and the ancient Hebrew Qabbalah. Both are Semitic but in germ derived, I think, from other sources. The student of archaic Hindu Aryan thought will also notice many similarities, especially in the Upanishads of the Vedas, in old Hindu Mythology, also in the Bhagavad-Gita and the Vedantas. Much of the mystery of the Practical Qabbalah will be undoubtedly discovered in the Tantras, but I have not as yet had an opportunity of seeing any of the latter.

The study of the Qabbalah in the disfigured condition which the powers of evil have succeeded in placing it, is one of extreme difficulty, and I have appreciated the full force of the words of the German historian I. M. Jost, when he says:

"Whoever desires to fathom all this, must give up the entire present and bring himself into a world of thought which stands absolutely alone.

* * * As the work of an elevated observing understanding accompanied by phantasy, she awakens admiration, and this, more on account of the purpose, * * * for the purpose declares, that the Kabbalah brings the soul of man into undoubted communion with God, which entirely sanctifies his thoughts and walk." (History of the Jews. Leipsic, 1859, p. 146.)

The Zohar is a very difficult book to translate, as it is full of strange words in Aramaic, Syriac, Hebrew and Chaldee; also, many formed from Greek, Persian, Sanskrit and Syriac roots: besides it has many dark and veiled suggestions and hints, which require explanations, as one proceeds with the setting forth of its system.

I also ask the indulgence of the critic for any errors in this new exposition of a difficult subject. Unable to find a publisher, because of the timidity of those engaged in the business of publishing resulting from their unfamiliarity with the subject, and fears for its financial success; I have been compelled at considerable expense and extra work, to take the risk of publishing upon myself and of getting a return for my outlay in printing, etc., and therefore became my own publisher.

No. 929 Clinton Street,
    Philadelphia, Penna.

TABLE OF CONTENTS.

INTRODUCTION.. . . . . .pp. vii–xiv
TABLE OF CONTENTS . . . . .pp. xv–xix
A SHORT DESCRIPTION OF THE PLATES. . . . . .pp. xix–xxiii
TABLE OF THE DIAGRAMS, ETC . . . . .p. xxiv

I.
IBN GEBIROL'S LIFE AND WRITINGS. .pp. 1–9

II.
THE SEPHER HA-ZOHAR; WRITINGS AS TO, ITS BIBLIOGRAPHY, Authors and Antiquity. . . . .' . . . . .pp. 10–54

III.
ANTIQUITY OF THE ZOHARIC WRITINGS, CONTINUED. OBJECtions to their Antiquity by Dr. Hirsch Graetz, Dr. Christian D. Ginsburg, and others, considered. Some quotations from the Zoharic Writings, elucidating passages in the Old and New Testaments. . . . . .pp. 55–100

IV.
FURTHER EXCERPTS FROM THE ZOHAR. PARABLES. EXPLANAtion of New Testament passages. The Basic element in Religions. Herbert Spencer cited. Ancient Chinese Taoism. Meaning of Idea, anciently. New Testament and Pagan writers on the Invisible and Visible. The Ideal and Real, etc.. . . . . .pp. 101–115

V.
PASTOR OF HERMAS, ETC., ON THE NATURE OF CHRIST. THE Teaching of the Twelve Apostles, on the Kosmic Mystery. The Oppositions and Harmony. Three Conceptions of Jesus . . . . .pp. 116–120

VI.

THE SECRET OF THE ACCOUNT OF CREATION IN GENESIS. Ex nihilo nihil fit. Doctrine of the non-annihilation of matter. Some Qabbalistic accounts of the Creation. The Heavenly Adam. Creation by the Word. The Zohar sets forth the circular movement of the Earth many centuries before Copernicus. Opinions of the Ancients on the circular movement of the Earth .... pp. 121–141

VII.

AN ANALYSIS OF THE ME'QÔR 'HAY-YÎM, OF IBN GEBIROL ... pp. 142–157

VIII.

THE THEORY AS TO ECSTASY. THE WRITERS WHO MENTION IBN Gebirol, or make use of his philosophy. The so-called Arabic philosophers............................ pp. 158–164

IX.

THE ANTIQUITY OF THE QABBALAH. BOOKS AND WRITERS IN which the Qabbalah is referred to. Letter of St. Jerome on the Divine Names. Connexion with early Christianity. Ancient thought, language, symbolism and tradition. High position claimed for the Qabbalah. The Ideal Man and the great Brotherhood of Humanity. Free-will, the Good and Evil. The Oppositions and Harmony. .... pp. 165–187

X.

SIMILARITIES IN THE WRITINGS OF IBN GEBIROL, THE ZOHARIC writings and the Qabbalah...................... pp. 188–218

XI.

THE HEBREW QABBALAH AND ITS ORIGIN. ITS CONTENT AND the problems it seeks to solve. From the Visible ascertain the Invisible. The several divisions of the Qabbalah. The four animals of the ancient Chaldean and Hindu religions and those of the Merkabah, their colors, etc. The Speculative Qabbalah. The Qabbalah of the Roman Catholic Church and of the Law. Curious par-

allels regarding the Serpent, the World-tree and the Seven
kings of Edom; in the Zoharic books and the Cuneiform
Tablets..pp. 219–236

XII.

FURTHER PARALLELS BETWEEN THE CUNEIFORM AND THE QAB-
balah. Account of the Akkadian and Semitic Babylonian
religion and temples and those of the Israëlites. Of the
Akkadian and Babylonian Cosmogony. Of the Demiurge.
The Dust Body of Man. Of Lil-ith. The Ancient
Zodiac..pp. 237–250

XIII.

OF AIN SOPH AND THE TEN SEPHIROTH..................pp. 251–273

XIV.

THE AIN SOPH AND THE SEPHIROTH CONTINUED. OF THE AYIN.
Views of the Ancients as to Ideas. Of the True and of
Illusion. Sound, color, rhythm. Quotations from the
Zohar as to the Sephiroth. The Prototypic Man. The
Sephiroth as between themselves. The Sephirothic Pillars.
Of Azriel and his writings. Analysis of his Commentary
on the Sephiroth.....................................pp. 274–288

XV.

THE SEPHIROTH AS BETWEEN THE DEITY AND AMONG THEM-
selves. The Prayer of Eliyah........................pp. 289–294

XVI.

OF THE MEANING OF THE WORDS SEPHIRAH AND SEPHIROTH.
Origin of the ideas as to the Sephiroth. Decadal division
of the Commandments and the Lord's Prayer........pp. 295–319

XVII.

THE FOUR WORLDS. OF PRANA. OF PAN AS THE MAKRO-
kosmos. Other ideas of the Makrokosmos. Asserted Origin of the Idea of the Four Worlds..................pp. 320–334

XVIII.

EXCERPTS FROM THE ZOHAR: AS TO THE MAN WITH THE HEAVY burden. Vicarious Atonement by the Messiah. The She-'kheen-ah. A formula of the Great Names. Original sin. Power of Satan. Free Will. The heavenly Mediatrix between God and man. Necessity of Repentance for Salvation. Eternal Reward and Punishment in the Future Life. Resurrection of the dead in the body. Judgment of the souls of the wicked, etc....................pp. 335–358

XIX.

EXCERPTS FROM THE ZOHAR CONTINUED. THE HOLY, WITH THE She'kheen-ah created the universe. Reason of the existence of Good and Evil. Of Metatron. Messiah ben Joseph and Messiah ben David. Description of, and the Triadic Idea as to, the Deity. The Names. Creation. Souls, spirits, etc. ....pp. 359–414

XX.

STRUCTURE OF THE UNIVERSE. STABILITY OF THE OPPOSITIONS. The Lower world like the Upper. The Makrokosm and Mikrokosm. The Upper Adam. The Makrokosm as the Great Tree, and as Man. Creation of Adam and 'Havah. Their condition before and after their Fall. Four ways of seeing the Deity. The permanence of Spoken Words. Love and Fear. Entire dependence should be on the Deity when man is in trouble. Paradise and Hell. Samā-el and Lil-ith, etc. The Angel of Death, etc. Coming of the Messiah and the Kingdom of the Supreme Deity upon Earth, etc. ....pp. 415–438

APPENDIX A.   AN ANCIENT LODGE OF INITIATES..........pp. 439–443
APPENDIX B.   SYNOPSIS OF THE CHINESE QABBALAH......pp. 444–447
APPENDIX C.   CONSTRUCTION OF THE AKKADIAN, CHALDEAN and Babylonian, universe........................pp. 448–455

APPENDIX D. MYSTIC THEOLOGY OF DIONYSIOS, THE AREO-
pagite ....pp. 456–458
APPENDIX E. THE DOGMAS IN THE NICENE CREED AND THE
Qabbalah.......................................pp. 459–460
APPENDIX F. ANTIQUITY OF THE HEBREW VOWEL POINTS..pp. 460–470
INDEX...p. 471, etc.

A SHORT DESCRIPTION OF THE PLATES.

No. 1. p. 45. This engraving is described on page 45 note.

No. 2. p. 45. This engraving is described on page 46 note.

No. 3. p. 116. This figure is a copy of one found in the ruins of an Egyptian Temple at Luxor, and represents the oppositions and harmony, under the form of two wings with a circle or globe between them. Similar symbols are frequently found on the walls and over the door-ways, of the ancient Temples of Egypt.

No. 4. p. 120. Represents *Arddha-nari*, a Hindu androgenic deity and is from a Hindu drawing. See Moor's Hindu Pantheon.

No. 5. p. 121. Is a representation said to be of the Vedic deity Indra but, I think, it is undoubtedly a representation of the three Upper Sephiroth and the efflux. Notice the position of the hands as 'Hokhmah and Binah.

No. 6. p. 141. Is a Qabbalistic portrayal of the universe, as if a species of armillary sphere, sustained by three hands, and inscribed with three Hebrew letters. א *Aleph*, stands for אמת *A'meth*, (E'meth) *i. e.*, Truth, ד *Daleth*, for דין *Din*, *i. e.*, Judgment, and ש *Shin*, for שלום *Shalom*, *i. e.*, Peace.

The saying in the Pirqé Aboth is: "Rabban Shim-on ben Gam-(a)liel (*circa* 164 A. D.) said: 'On three things the world stands; on Truth, on Judgment and on Peace.'" (i, 19.) These are a system of internal energies through which the world exists. So the heavenly bodies are kept in their places by חמדה '*Hem-dah, i. e.*, Desire, and אמונה *Amun-ah, i. e.*, Faith, which draw them to אהיה *Eh'yeh, i. e.*, I Am. Peace is an important word in the New Testament. (Eph. ii, 14; Micah v, 4; Rom. xvi, 20.) It is a Talmudic Name for God. "Everything is perfected by Peace." (Comp. Eph. iv, 3; Col. iii, 14; Col. iii, 15, with Zech. viii, 16.) With the Qabbalists, Peace = '*Hes-ed* Love or Mercy; Judgment = *Pa'had* Fear; Truth = *Ge'dool-ah* Greatness. These are severally made equivalent to the Ineffable Name, and therefore one to the other. *Sepher B'rith Menoo'hah, i.e.*, Book of the Covenant of Rest. (Amsterdam Ed., 1648, fol. 3*a*.)

No. 7. p. 142. A Hindu androgenic deity termed *Arddha-nari*. From a Hindu drawing. See Moor's Hindu Pantheon.

No. 8. p. 157. A Representation of the ancient Mexican Makrokosmos. To be found in Lord Kingsborough's great work on Ancient Mexico, Vol. ii, plate 75, which is copied from an Ancient Mexican MSS. in the Library of the Vatican. In Vol. vi, pp. 222-223 is a description of the plate. In a note is: "In a Missal entitled *Heures a l'usiage de Rome, 1498*, is the figure of a man with his principal viscera exposed, and from the heart, liver, etc., lines are drawn to the symbols of the ruling constellations. In the XV century astrology had the sanction of the Church."

The ancient Mexicans appear to have believed in 9 heavens, a Mexican king built a tower with 9 stories as emblems of the 9 heavens, in which to worship the Creator of all things. Their solemn dance also represented the motion of the heavens. *Ibid*. pp. 155-156. They also had a symbolism of colors. *Ibid*. p. 157 note. Consult as to the Mexican signs of the Zodiac. Transact. of the American Ethnological Society, 1845, i, 57-305; ii, 316. See also the works of Captain Dupaix, John L. Stephens, Charles Rau, Ed. S. Holden, Cyrus Thomas, Leon de Rozny, Désiré Charney, etc., on Ancient Mexico and Central America.

No. 9. p. 158. From an old Hindu drawing. This I think is intended to represent, the Sephirothic Tree rooted in the World-egg and floating on the Chaotic Sea.

No. 10. p. 164. Is a representation of the Egyptian Makrokosm and Mikrokosm from an ancient Egyptian picture.

No. 11. p. 165. This is an attempt to show the Ark of the Covenant in the Hebrew Tabernacle with the Cherubim and She'kheen-ah. We do not offer this as the actual. Modern discoveries have given to us somewhat different ideas.

No. 12. p. 187. A figure of Buddha probably under the Bo tree or Tree of the Sephiroth. The original of this is in possession of a friend in Philadelphia.

No. 13. p. 188. The decadal division of man.

No. 14 to 19. p. 218. Occult Qabbalistic representations of the Triad, No. 15 is also the Jewish priests method of holding the hands when giving the blessing. No. 16 is a Qabbalistic method of holding the hands.

No. 20. p. 219. Sephirothic Tree from the ruins of Carthage.

No. 21. p. 219. Sephirothic Tree from ruins in Scotland. As to both of these, see, The Early Races of Scotland, by Forbes Leslie, Edinburgh, 1866, Vol. i, pp. xvii, xix, 178, 181, plates iii, iv and vi, p. 46; also, Ancient Faiths embodied in Ancient Names, etc., by Thomas Inman, London, 1868, Vol. i, p. 79.

No. 22. pp. 228–229. The explanation accompanies the engraving.

Nos. 23 and 24. p. 236. Are representations of the method of holding the hands used by the Jewish Kohanim or Priests, in giving the blessings.

No. 25. p. 237. Copy of an intaglio signet of Babylonia. Talisman with the Triad, on sard. See p. 249 note.

No. 26. p. 249. Copy of an intaglio signet cylinder of Assyria with the Triad, on amazon stone. See pp. 249–250 note.

No. 27. p. 251. The Hindu Makrokosm from a Hindu drawing.

No. 28. p. 273. The Hindu Makrokosm as Krishna, with the Bull, Peacock and Crocodile.

No. 29. p. 274. The Hebrew letter *Shin*, a symbol of the Triad. Comp. *Supra* p. 366.

No. 30. p. 321. The Four Worlds of the Hindus. The Head, is the Upper Spiritual, Brahman *neuter*. The Breast, the creative or Soul Principle, Brahma. The Heart. The Stomach, vitality, Vishnu as

Krishna. The Navel, etc. Power of Generation and Destruction. Siva. Comp. figure 27 *Ante* p. 251.

No. 31. p. 322. Prana, the Hindu Makrokosmos, description is on pp. 321–323.

No. 32. p. 325. Pan, the Greek Makrokosmos. Description pp. 324–326.

Nos. 33 and 34. pp. 326–327. The Medieval Makrokosmos. We have engravings similar to figure 33, in our almanacs.

No. 35. p. 334. Hindu Qabbalistic symbol of the four worlds. The everlasting arms holding up the world. See my description in, The Path, Vol. i, p. 370 *sq.*

No. 36. p. 414. An occult representation of the Point, Ten Sephiroth, Four Worlds, Ineffable Name, etc.

No. 37. p. 438. Man as the dwelling of Brahma, the Creating-deity, a form of the Hindu Makrokosm. The original of this drawing was made by a Brahmin after the ideas in the Vedas. In it man is represented as in Brahma-loka, the city of the Creator-god, as the Mikrokosmos. A, is a water-fosse, extending around and between the walls of the fortress as if surrounding a citadel, this is to represent the outer man and the fluctuating passions of the soul, Bhut-atma. In this quarrel and surge, lashed by the storm-winds of evil, the waves of passion and the evil thoughts. There are 11 gates and draw-bridges; these are the 11 openings of the senses, they lead over the fosse. 1. The gate of the mouth. 2 and 3. The gates of the nose. 4 and 5. The gates of the eyes. 6 and 7. The gates of the ears. 8. The skin with its many openings. 9. The gate of the heart. 10. The rectum. 11. The lingam or yoni. B, is rejuvenation and immortality, in lake Behra near by is C, the phallic tree. Then comes the fortified city, Sabeh, to it belongs all within the wall line D. In Sabeh is Apradyat, the impregnable castle E. E, is inhabited, protected and illuminated, by the spirits of perception or Indra and Prajâpati. It has a second story F. This is the Intellect and Light out of atma, *i.e.*, soul. Above this is G, which resting on the wreath around the roof of the citadel F, is the radiating light-throne of Hiranyagarbha, *i.e.*, the golden embryo, which symbolizes the Primary Form. Here is seated H, Mansi or Brahma-sakti, the mistress of the Beauty of the Mind indeed Brahma himself, but considered as Brahma-Maya, mistress of the Imaginative-world. I, above her crown, is the Brahma-sun, the sun of Truth, illuminating all; but between her head and Truth, the veil of Maya or Deceptive Illusion intervenes and envelopes, everything Below.

No. 38. To face p. 439. This is an occult representation of the Makrokosm as if in the Noa'hic Ark, which contained in itself and preserved, according to the Hebrew Sacred Writings, the ancestors of all existing animal life, and therefore had a close resemblance to the Qabbalistic ideas as to the Upper Adam. In this engraving, the length centre would answer to the Ecliptic of the Zodiac with the Decans upon either side, together 30. The ten compartments of the Zodiac are given excluding Scorpio-Virgo, which is androgenic, and considering, the first of the last five, as if the tail of Scorpio; Scorpio taking up, as the ancient astronomers inform us, all that space from which the Balance was afterwards made. When the androgenic Scorpio-Virgo was separated and the Balance or Harmony made from Scorpio, and placed between Scorpio, *i. e.*, male, and Virgo, *i. e.*, female, then appeared the 12 constellations or signs, as we now have them. The ark is three stories high (perhaps to symbolize Heaven, Man, Earth). In the figure of the Man, notice the parting of the hair in the middle of the forehead and the arrangement of the beard, whiskers, moustache and the hair, on the back of the neck and shoulders. See *Ante* p. 370. Compare this with the statements in the Siphrah D'Tznioothah, Idrah Rabbah and Idrah Zootah, as to Ze'ir An-peen, *i. e.*, Small Faces. Note also the stigmata, and that נח $50 + 8 = 58$ *Noa'h* and חן '*Hen* $8 + 50 = 58$, *i. e.*, *Grace* (Salvation?), have the same number.

Compare, *Antiquitatum Judaicarum Libri ix*, etc., *auctore Benedicto Aria Montano, Hispalensi. Lugduni Batavorum*, etc., 1593, pp. 74–77. Plate L. The Rosicrucians their Rites and Mysteries, etc., by Hargave Jennings, New York, 1879, pp. 350–353, 368.

No. 39. p. 447. A representation of Brahma-Maya, Mahat-Maya or Brahma Viraj, the Great Androgenic Illusion Deity of the Hindus. See my Articles in, The Path, Vol. i, upon Hindu Symbolism.

TABLE OF THE DIAGRAMS, ETC.

Frontispiece. The Upper or Celestial Adam with the Ten Sephiroth.

Sephirothic Tree of Life with the Columns, etc......Facing p.	1
Diagram I. Table of the Sephiroth, in Circles, with the Ineffable Name ....p.	100
Diagram II. Table of the Divine Names and the Sephiroth with their Channels or Canals......p.	169
Diagram III. Table of the Sephiroth with the Channels, the Ineffable Name and the names of the Planets....Facing p.	251
Diagram IV. The Universe according to the Ptolemaic system.......p.	295
Diagram V. The idea of the Universe in the Middle Ages..p.	319
Diagram VI. The Universe according to the Akkadians, Chaldeans, Babylonians, etc......p.	448
A Formula of the Divine Names, etc......p.	342
The Ineffable Name reversed......p.	446
The Me'norah or Candlestick, and Chinese symbols.......pp.	446, 447

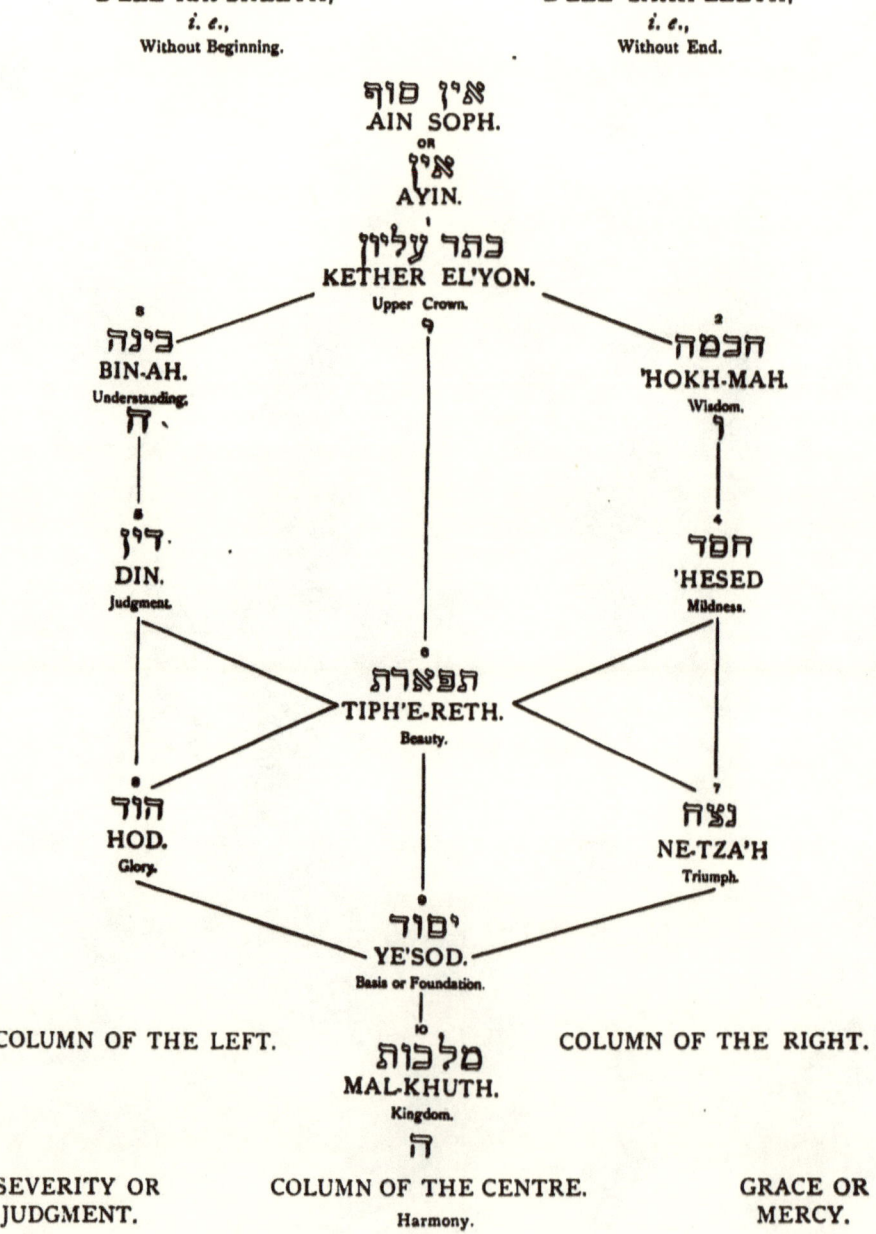

The Sephirothic Tree of Life viewed from the Back.

I.

IBN GEBIROL'S LIFE AND WRITINGS.

SOLOMON ben Yehudah Ibn Gebirol, of Cordova,* called by the Jews, Solomon the Sephardi, *i. e.*, Spaniard, the Hymnologist, and by acrostic from the initials of his name, Ra S H Ba G.; by the Arabs, Abu Ayyub Suléiman ben-Ya'hya Ibn Djebirol, and by the scholastics, Avicebrol, Avicebron, Avicembron, etc., was born at Malaga about 1021, educated at Saragossa, and died at Valencia, 1070. It is said, in a legend, that he was killed by a Mohammedan who was jealous of his great talents, that the murderer buried him under a fig tree, in the former's garden; the tree bore so much fruit, of such extraordinary sweetness, that the king, informed of the phenomena, made the proprietor of the garden come before him, and being pressed by questions, the murderer ended by avowing his crime, and expiated it with his life. Ibn Gebirol may be considered as the greatest philosopher of his century.

Towards the middle of the XIth century, Ibn Gebirol began to make himself known, as a philosopher and poet, notwithstanding the repugnance towards each other, which these two branches of human thought generally evince; so as rarely to be found united in the same individual. However in Ibn Gebirol's poetry are most profound philosophical meditations, and in his philosophical works are to be found traces of the rhetoric, lively imagination, and inspiration, of the poet. The philosophical works he wrote in Arabic, his poetry in Hebrew. In poetry, he occupied a first rank among the Jewish poets of the Middle Ages, and was, we think we are justified in saying, among all contemporary poets, the greatest poet of his time.

The Jewish poetry of the Middle Ages was much more elevated than

*NOTE.—A portion of this Paper was read by me, before the Numismatic and Antiquarian Society of Philadelphia, at its Hall, on March 4, 1886. A synopsis has been published in the Proceedings of the Society.

the Arabic; it was founded upon the magnificent imagery of the ancient Hebrew prophets and poets, was based on the memories of their wonderful past, the sufferings of the present, and the hopes of a more glorious future. It was more universal. The elegies of the Jewish writers of this period were full of a sombre melancholy, their hymns and prayers full of a profound religious sentiment, and a touching resignation; and their lessons of morality and wisdom, gathered in the midst of ruins and tombs, found a reverberation in the hearts of all men, at all times; because in them were thoughts, sentiments, and emotions, for men of all countries, and of all centuries. The vanity of terrestrial things is the ruling thought, which reproduces itself under a thousand forms, in the Jewish poetry of this period. Ibn Gebirol especially, always directed his regards towards heaven, the earth had not offered him many charms, happiness had flown from him without cessation, and a settled sadness, proceeding out of all he saw, made him refuse the most legitimate and purest joys. This melancholy is apparent in writings by him, when only 16 years of age.

The Kether Malkhuth or Crown of the Kingdom, was given by him the first place among his hymns, and he tells us in it, that it was written in his declining years. It is a hymn celebrating the only one and true God, and the marvels of His creation. The veil, which covers the mysteries of Nature, the poet seeks to fathom and unravel, by means of the scientific knowledge of his time. The task is divided between the spirit and the heart, between intelligence and sentiment, between knowledge and the imagination. It is not only a religious poem, but a poetical resumé of the Peripatetic, Oriental, Alexandrine and Qabbalistic cosmology; and in it he endeavors, in magnificent language, to unite religion and philosophy or the spiritual and physical, in a perfect harmony, so as to glorify and praise the only True Being.

We here give a few lines from it:

"Thou art God, and all creatures are Thy servants and adorers; Thy Glory is not diminished in any way, should they adore others than Thee, because their aim is entirely, to come nearer unto Thee; but they are as the blind, it is towards the Royal route that they direct themselves, but they have strayed from the right road; one has fallen into an abyss of destruction, the other fallen into a pit. They believed that they had wholly reached the desired aim, but they have labored in vain. But Thy true servants are as those travelers who, marching in the right road, turn neither to the right nor to the left, until they enter into the court of the palace of the King.

"Thou art God, who supports, by Thy Divinity, all the Things formed, and sustains all the existences by Thy unity. Thou art God, and there is not any distinction established, between Thy Divinity, Thy Unity, Thy Eternity, and Thy Existence; because all is only one mystery, and, although the names may be distinct, all have only one meaning. Thou art Wise, Wisdom which is the fountain of life, floweth out from Thee, and compared with Thy Wisdom, all the knowledge of mankind is foolishness. Thou art Wise, being from all eternity, and Wisdom was always nourished by Thee. Thou art Wise, and Thou hast not acquired Thy Wisdom from another than Thyself. Thou art Wise, and from Thy Wisdom Thou hast made a determining Will, as the workman or artist does, to draw the Existence from the No-Thing, as the light which goes out of the eye extends itself. Thou didst draw from the Source of Light without the impression of any seal, *i. e.*, form, and Thou madest all without any instrument." This theory of the Divine Will limiting the faculty of the Highest Deity, which, unlimited, produces only the Infinite, is largely set forth in his Me'qor 'Hayyim, *i. e.*, The Source of Life. This Upper Will is, we think, in the Ideal Man, the Adam Qadmon of the Qabbalists, and is in the Kether of the Sephiroth, *i. e.*, the highest point of the brain or head, of the Ideal Man. In the Kether Malkhuth, Ibn Gebirol also says: "Thine is the Might, in the mystery of which our contemplations are too feeble to stay." "Thine is the hidden Name, from the habitations of Wisdom." "Thine is the Existence, from the shadow of the light of which all existence came." "Thou art One, and the mystery of Thy Unity confounds the wise in heart, for they do not know what it is." "Thou art the Living One, and he who reaches to Thy mystery, findeth eternal delight, he eats and liveth forever." He illustrates the work of creation by the simile of "the extension of light which proceeds from the eye;" and he says: "The exalted Name which is girded with Might, is one in all Its forces, like a flame of fire in Its various appearances, like the light of the eye, proceeding from the blackness of the eye, one emanating from the other, like smell from smell, light from light."

Ibn Gebirol wrote poems and hymns as early as the age of 16 years, and a Hebrew grammar in verse at the age of 19. A writing called Choice Pearls, composed of moral maxims, is attributed to him. It is in 64 paragraphs. A Latin edition was published in Frankfurt on the Oder, in 1630, by Ebert, and it has been printed several times since in various languages. Another writing attributed to him, is, On the Soul, a Latin translation was made of it, by Archdeacon Dominic Gundissalimus, or Gundisalvi.* Gebirol says he wrote, a special treatise, "On the Will;" this is lost. In 1045 A. D., he wrote the ethical-philosophic work, called Tiqqun Middoth han-Nephesh, *i. e.*, The Correction of the Manners (Faculties, Qualities), of the Soul (or Vital Spirit, the Nephesh). In the latter work man is contemplated as the Mikrokosm, and viewed in his relation to the Makrokosm, the entire Universe, considered as the Great Universal Ideal Man or Adam Qadmon of the Qabbalah. In it, he quotes the Old Testament, the Talmud, Socrates, Plato, Aristotle, the Arabian philosophers, and especially the maxims of a Jewish philosopher called Chefez Al-Kuti.† In consequence of some personal allusions in this work, the author was obliged to leave Saragossa in 1046, and wandered about Spain, until he obtained recognition and encouragement, from Samuel ha-Levi ben Josef Ibn Nagréla, also called Nagdilah, and by the Jews, han-Nagid, *i. e.*, the Prince; the celebrated Prime Minister of Moorish Spain.‡

Before the voice of the Jewish prophets had ceased to guide that people, the Interpreters of the Thorah; *i. e.*, the Law, or Pentateuch, the Sages, Wise-Men, and Doctors of the Mishnah and the Talmud, had began their labors, and before the great Oriental Jewish universities and schools of Mesopotamia and Babylonia were closed, centres of Jewish thought were flourishing in the West, in Italy, France, and especially, in Spain.

* Munk, *Melanges, Philos. juive et arabe*, pp. 170-173.

† Steinschneider. Jewish Literature. Longmans. London, 1857, p. 101.

‡ See Lindo's History of the Jews in Spain, p. 50; also Publications of the Society of Hebrew Literature, London, vol. 1, pp. 1-12.

Rabbi Abraham ben David Ha-Levi, or Hallevy, of Toledo, Spain (d. 1180), in his Sepher haq-Qabbalah, written in 1160,* says:

"After the death of the last rector, 'Hiz'qee-yah,† Head of the Academy and Prince of the Exile, called the Rosh Hag-golah or Resh-galutha, the Academies were closed and no new Ge'onim appointed. But long before that time,‡ a ship sailing from Bari was captured by Ibn Romahis, commander of the naval forces of Abd-er-rahman al-Nasr (A. D. 912–961). In this ship, were four distinguished rabbins of the celebrated Babylonian Jewish school of Sura, these were R. 'Hushiel, father of R. 'Hananel; R. Moses, father of R. 'Ha'noch; R. Shemaryahu, son of R. El'hanan, and a fourth whose name is not given. They were sold as slaves; R. 'Hushiel was carried to Kairuan, (in Africa); R. Shemaryahu was left in Alexandria; R. Moses was brought to Cordova; he was there ransomed as a supposed uneducated man. In that city was a synagogue known by the name of Keneseth ham-Midrash, *i. e.*, assembly for study, and a certain R. Nathan, renowned for his great piety, was the head (or judge) of the congregation. The members held meetings at which the Talmud was read and discussed. One day when R. Nathan was expounding a Talmudic passage, he was not able to give a satisfactory explanation of it. R. Moses spoke, and at once removed the difficulty, and answered several other questions which were submitted to him. Whereupon R. Nathan thus addressed the assembly: 'I am no longer your leader; that stranger in sackcloth shall henceforth be my teacher, and you shall appoint him your chief.' The admiral upon hearing of the high attainments of his late prisoner, desired to revoke the sale, but the Khalif would not permit this, being pleased to learn, that his Jewish subjects were no longer dependent for their religious instruction on the schools of the East."

The knowledge of Ibn Gebirol, was undoubtedly fostered by the patronage and erudition, of the before-mentioned Samuel ha-Levi ben Joseph Ibn Nagréla, or han-Nagid, who was born about 993 A. D., died about 1055, aged 62 years. This great scholar, usually called Samuel han-

---

* Edition of Basel, 1580, p. 69*a*.
† Killed by orders of the Khalif.
‡ In the X century.

Nagid, *i. e.*, the Prince, supported Ibn Gebirol after his banishment from Saragossa in 1046. And our author has dedicated to Samuel many of his verses. Samuel han-Nagid was educated at Cordova, in Spain, in the Jewish school of that place, by R. 'Ha'noch, son of R. Moses of Babylonia, whom we have just mentioned, in the Talmud and the history of his people, and was taught Hebrew by R. Yehuda 'Hayyug, one the most erudite founders of Hebrew grammar. At the age of 20, owing to a revolution, he was obliged to quit his studies, for a fearful conflict between the Berbers, Arabs and Sclavonians, who composed the bodyguard of the Khalif, brought desolation on Cordova in 1013. Samuel escaped to the seaport-town, Malaga. Here he continued his former studies, and entered into others, applying himself especially to philology. He knew six languages; besides Hebrew, Chaldee or Aramaic, and Arabic, he understood Berber, Latin and Castilian. This evidences great application, mental power, and perseverance, for there was not at that time any method to facilitate the study of languages. The educated Arabs seldom knew Latin, and the Christians of Spain seldom acquired much knowledge of Arabic. In 1027 Samuel was appointed Grand Vizier and Minister of State to the Khalif Habus, the monarch of Moorish Grenada. For nearly 30 years he occupied this position in that kingdom. During this period he found time, to write several books on the Talmud, a Jewish history, and books on proverbs, maxims, prayers, poetry, a grammar, etc. He shared his riches with every disciple of Jewish erudition, not only in Spain, but in Babylonia, Judæa, Sicily, and Africa. He kept up a thorough correspondence with all the distinguished Jews of Syria, Egypt, Irak, and Africa, took the greatest interest in their studies, and was in close relations with the African authorities on Judaism. He also employed transcribers to make many copies of the Talmuds and Holy Scriptures, which he presented to poor students.

Can we wonder if we find, that Ibn Gebirol living under the influences and learning of so great a scholar, had at the basis of his philosophical knowledge, an acquaintance with the ancient Midrashim treating on the Sod or Mysteries, the Secret Learning, afterwards termed the Tradition or Qabbalah, and which we believe, were afterwards redacted into the Zohar and the Zoharic books? Is it surprising that we find him in his

Me'qôr 'Hayyîm, *i.e.*, Source of Life, and in the Kether Malkhuth, anticipating many of the statements subsequently to be found in the Zohar and Zoharic writings, if he received a knowledge of these ancient writings in their early, disconnected, Midrashic form, before they were collected and redacted in Spain? The Zohar and the books bound up with it, were accepted by the Jewish learned men, almost immediately upon their publication in MSS., as a verity, if not by the Qabbalist, R. Shim-on ben Yo'haï, at least, as containing an accepted ancient secret tradition, part likely coming through him. Everything points to this, and denies the authorship and forgery imputed by many critics, to R. Moses ben Shem-Tob de Leon of Spain, who only claimed in his writings, to be a copyist and redactor of older Qabbalistic works, and not their author. These strange, wonderful, weird writings, required more than one intellect to produce them, and contain a mine of ancient Oriental philosophical thought.

Ibn Gebirol's process of treating his philosophical system, however, differs from that pursued in the Zohar and the Zoharic books. The Zohar proper, is a running commentary on the Five Books or Pentateuch, touching at the same time, upon numerous problems of philosophical speculation of the deepest and most sacred import, and propounding many ideas and doctrines, with an acumen, worthy to proceed from the greatest intellects. It, and the Zoharic books, support their statements by continual references and quotations, from the Old Testament. Ibn Gebirol in his, "Source of Life" does not follow this course, and differs from almost all other Jewish philosophical authors of the Middle Ages, in not quoting Scripture; nevertheless, from their similarity, his writings, and the Zohar and Zoharic books, are most probably, offshoots from the same ancient roots.* The Zohar, and the fragments contained in it, were not made public in MSS., for over 225 years after Gebirol's death, but it does not follow that its secret traditional sources, were not open to the friend of that great Jewish scholar and patron of learning, upon whose shoulders fell the traditions, learning and mantle; of the Rectors of the Babylonian schools; the erudite and celebrated, Samuel ha-Levi ben Joseph Ibn Nagréla, also called Nagdilah, and han-Nagid, the Prince

* Munk, *Mélanges de Philos. juive et arabe*, pp. 275, 276.

of the Jews, and Grand Vizier, under two Mohammedan Khalifs, of Moorish Spain.

It was after his recognition by Samuel han-Nagid, and about 1050, that Ibn Gebirol wrote, in Arabic, his great philosophical work, Me'qôr 'Hayyîm, *i. e.*, Fountain of Life, called in Latin, *De Materia Universali* and *Fons Vitæ*, which is really a philosophical Qabbalistic work. He is, however, mostly known by his coreligionists, from his Kosmic Qabbalistic hymn, founded on Aristótle's *De Mundo*, and based on the Ptolemaic astronomical system: the Kether Malkhuth, the Royal Crown, perhaps not incorrectly, from its referring to the highest and lowest Sephiroth, Crowned Kingdom, which we have above mentioned. We shall refer hereafter in this essay, more especially to his Me'qôr 'Hayyîm and its connection with the wonderful Sepher haz-Zohar, or Book of Splendour, the text-book of the Hebrew Qabbalists. The Me'qôr is one of the earliest exposures of the secrets of the Speculative Qabbalah. It was first translated into Hebrew by Shem-Tob ben Joseph Ibn Falaquéra.* A MSS. of this translation was discovered by the learned Arabic and Hebrew, German scholar, Salomon Munk (b. 1802), one of the Librarians of the French Imperial Library, at Paris, in the *"Bibliothèque Impériale"* whilst redacting its Hebrew MSS. This, he found, was almost in the words of the Latin *Fons Vitæ*, attributed by the scholastics to Avicebron. After this he found in the same Library a MSS. in Latin of the *Fons Vitæ*. Afterwards in the *"Bibliothèque Mazarine,"* a second Latin MSS. of the same work, was discovered by Dr. Seyerlen, of Germany. M. Munk, in 1859, in his *Mélanges de Philosophie juive et arabe*,† published the Me'qôr 'Hayyîm, in French, from the Hebrew MSS. translation by Falaquéra, supplementing omissions by statements from the Latin MSS. We acknowledge obligations to M. Munk's work, for assisting us in this essay, as to the contents of Ibn Gebirol's philosophical writings.

Sometime between 1167 and 1186 R. Yehudah Ibn Tibbon, called "Father of the Translators," in conjunction with R. Joseph Ibn Qimchi, translated, from the Arabic into Hebrew, the writings of Ibn Gebirol

* B. *circa* 1224–1228. Was translating in 1264, and subsequently. He died after 1280.

† Paris. *chez A. Franck.*

for the Qabbalist Asher, son of Meshullam ben Yacob, of Lunel (d. 1170 A. D.). The name of Asher has been confounded with that of the great Qabbalist Azriel, and the translation may have been for the latter, who has given us, in his :—"Questions and Answers as to the Ten Sephiroth" one of the most scientifically philosophical expositions of these Qabbalistic intermediaries, between God and all the existences, ever published. Meshullam was teacher of the celebrated Qabbalist, R. Abraham ben David, junior, of Posquieres, France (d. 1198), called acrostically R A Ba D. In the XII century, Joannes Hispalensis, or, of Seville, also called Abendehut, perhaps the same as Ibn David and Andreas, whom Roger Bacon says, was the real Author of that, which Michael Scot, called the Wizard (d. *circa* 1290), published as his own writing; made a translation from the Arabic of some of Albenzubrun's (Ibn Gebirol's) works. Abraham ben David (called Ibn Daud by the Arabs, also called Ben Dior) ha-Levi, or Hallevy, the Elder ; of Toledo, Spain, who died a martyr in 1180; in 1160 A. D., in Spain, attempted with bitterness, a refutation of Ibn Gebirol's philosophy in his writing called The Sublime Faith, in which Abraham b. David tries to put the Jewish religion in accord with Aristotelianism. He wrote the Sepher haq-Qabbalah above mentioned. In 1209 the *Fons Vitæ*, of our author, and the celebrated book, *De Causis*, were interdicted by the University of Paris, as Aristotelian.*
In 1502 the Neo-Platonic Jewish Qabbalist, of the School of Count Giovanni Pico della Mirandola, R. Yehudah Abravanel, also known as Messer Leone Hebreo, and Leo Hebræus, is acquainted with our author, but only from Christian authorities, and calls him, Albenzubrun. Ibn Gebirol's writings are of great importance to Oriental scholars, from the assistance they render to the settlement of questions as to the authenticity, authorship, and authority of the Zoharic writings, the antiquity of the Qabbalistic philosophy, its earliest formulated ideas, and its origin.

* Haureau, *Philos. scholastique.* I, p. ii, p. 46, ed., Paris.

II.

THE SEPHER HAZ-ZOHAR, WRITINGS AS TO, ITS BIBLIOGRAPHY, AUTHORS, AND ANTIQUITY.

AS we have already stated, the Zoharic writings were not published as MSS. to the uninitiated, until some 225 years after the death of Ibn Gebirol; his writings, however, when compared with them, tend to confirm the opinion, that they have an older common source, and the learned German Jewish orientalist, Salomon Munk, is compelled to acknowledge, that after investigation, the Zohar, and the fragments bound up with it, entire, are neither the work of a simple cheat, nor a pure invention, but the editor or compiler used very ancient documents, among others, certain Midrashim, which we do not possess to-day,* and Falaquéra says, that Ibn Gebirol's Me'qôr 'Hayyîm, contains an antiquated or ancient system, going back to philosophers of the highest antiquity.† R. Moses Shem-Tob de Leon, who has been termed, by most of those opposed to these writings, their forger, expressly tells us, that he only edited and compiled them from the works of older writers, among others, from those attributed to the School of the Tannaite, R. Shim-on ben Yo'haï. A large room could be filled with the books written upon the validity or forgery of the Zoharic writings. In our time, Dr. Adolph Jellinek, Dr. Hirsch Graetz, Dr. A. Tholuck, Dr. Abraham Geiger, Dr. Leopold Zunz, S. D. Luzzatto, Dr. Christian D. Ginsburg, and earlier, the French ecclesiastic Jean Morin, Lewis Cappelus, Jacques Basnage de Beauval, Frederick Strunz, Gabriel Groddeck, Buxtorf, the Elder, Scaliger and Winder, among others, think they were written by R. Moses de Leon.

The learned M. H. Landauer was just as positive, that they were written by R. Abraham ben Samuel Abulafia. The erudite Samuel Cahen, in his Great French Bible, is sure that they were composed by a convocation

---

* *Mélanges de philos. juive et arabe*, etc., *par* Munk. Paris, 1859, pp. 275–6.
† *Ibid.*, p. 274.

of Christianized Rabbins, sitting together for the purpose, in a monastery in Spain, and employing R. Moses de Leon, to publish their work.

In favor of their antiquity, and that they were not written by Moses de Leon, in modern times, are, Franz Joseph Molitor, Dr. Adolphe Franck, Dr. D. H. Joel, Salomon Munk, Dr. J. W. Etheridge, David Luria, Dr. J. M. Jost, Dr. John Gill, M. H. Landauer, Ignatz Stern, Leopold Löw, John Allen, Jacob Frank, Joh. Ant. Bernh. Lutterbeck, Eliphas Levi (Abbe Louis Constant), Moses ben R. Me'na-a'hem Mendel Konitz, etc. Earlier, Raymond Lully, John Reuchlin, Pico della Mirandola, the learned Jesuit Athanasius Kircher, Dr. John Lightfoot, Giulio Bartolocci (de Celano), Augustus Pfeiffer, Valentine Ernest Loescher, Christian Knorr von Rosenroth, Henry Cornelius Agrippa, of Nettesheim, John Baptist van Helmont, Franz Mercurius van Helmont, Dr. Robert Fludd, Dr. Henry More, Buxtorff, the Younger, Rev. John Francis Buddæus, Dr. Johann Friedrich von Meyer, the Cardinal Ægidius of Viterbo, Christian Schœttgen, Rev. John Christopher Wolff, Jacques Matter, and many others.

Uncertain as to the author, but opposing the books, are many of the orthodox Jewish Talmudists, also the learned bibliographer M. Steinschneider, although he acknowledges a deficiency of thorough study upon the subject. R. Jacob Emden, named acrostically Ya Be T Z, started out to oppose them, using Morin's arguments. From the very excellent introduction of Dr. Adolph Jellinek (or Gellinek), to his German translation of Prof. Adolphe Franck's *La Kabbale*,* we condense the following: There are three names under which more especially the wonderful monument of the Qabbalah appears. I. Midrash of the Rabbi Shim-on ben Yo'haï. "This name," Jellinek says; "speaks for the genuineness of the work." II. Midrash va-Ye'hee Ôr, *i. e.*, "Midrash; let there be light!" So called because in some of the MSS. the explanation to the verse in Genesis i, 3, *Yehee ôr*, forms the beginning of the work, or which is more probable, because it leads the reader to the light imparted to him through this book. III. Zohar, *i. e.*, Splendour or Light, called so after Daniel xii, 3. This last name has become the governing one since the

---

* *Die Kabbala oder die Religionsphilosophie der Hebräer von Franck. Aus dem Französischen übersetzt, verbessert und vermehrt. Mit einer Abbildung : Leipzig*, 1844, 8vo.

compilation called Yu'hazin, which was published in Constantinople 1502 A. D. It is so called, either because it begins with the theme as to the light, or because the word Zohar frequently occurs on the first page. In the work itself it is also sometimes called by this name. (Comp. Raÿah Me'hemnah III, 153 b.) Mena'hem di Recanati of Italy, *circa* 1290–1320, commented upon it as undoubtedly genuine and calls it: The Book of Zohar, The Wonderful Book of the Zohar, Book of the Great Zohar. R. Isaac Ibn Minir (1330) terms it, the Midrash Haz-Zohar, also Midrash of R. Shim-on ben Yo'haï. Other early Qabbalists call it, Book of the Holy Zohar by R. Shim-on ben Yo'haï. The Zohar is also quoted by R. Moses de Leon, the alleged forger, in his other writings; it is referred to by name by Yo-seph ben Abraham Ibn Wakkar of Toledo (flour. A. D. 1290–1340), referring as a Qabbalist to the Ten Sephiroth, he recommends as reliable guides: the Talmudim, Midrash Rabboth, Siphra, Siphree, Bahir, Peraqim of R. Eliezer, the opinions of Nachmanides and Todros Ha-Levi Abulafia, also the Zohar, but says the latter has some errors.* The reason of this remark was, Ibn Wakkar desired to introduce Aristotelianism into the Jewish philosophy and found the Zohar in his way.† The Zohar is mentioned, with favor, by Todros (Theodorus) Ha-Levi Abulafia (b. *circa* 1204, died 1283 A.D., at Seville). We have not space in this writing to go fully into the subject, but it is certain that the Zohar was accepted as a correct exposition of orthodox Hebrew Qabbalism, immediately upon its publication, which universal reception is strong proof for the antiquity of its doctrines. Its opponents were almost universally Jewish Aristotelians, who therefore opposed the ancient Secret Learning of the Israelites, because it was more in accord with the Philosophy of Plato and Pythagoras, and indeed most likely originated from the same sources, the Aryan and Chaldean esoteric doctrine.

The book Zohar proper, is a Qabbalistic commentary on the Pentateuch, wherein the entire system of the Hebrew Qabbalah is compiled. It is written partly in Hebrew and partly in Chaldee or Aramaic, and is a mine of occultism, giving the mystical foundation of the Mosaic ordinances, poetical and philosophical views on the Kosmogony and Kosmol-

* Comp. The Kabbalah, etc., by Christian D. Ginsburg, London, 1865, p. 119 *et seq.*
† Compare Steinschneider's Hist. of Liter., Eng. ed., p. 114.

ogy of the Universe, soul, redemption, triad, sin, evil, etc.; mystical expositions of many of the laws and appearances in nature, *e. g.*, light, elements, astronomy, magnet, etc.; explanations of the symbolism of the Song of Solomon, of the construction of the Tabernacle, etc.; forming a complete Qabbalistic Theosophy. In its present form in the editions as hereinafter set forth, there are imbedded in the Zohar proper, the following independent works.

The books bound together and generically termed the Zohar are :—

1. The Zohar properly so-called. That is a running Commentary on the first Five books of the Old Testament, or the Pentateuch.

2. Siphrah D'Tznioothah,† Book of Mystery, Concealment or Modesty.

3. Idrah Rabbah, The Great Assembly (of the Threshing-floor).

4. Idrah Zootah, The Small Assembly (held in the house of R. Shimon ben Yo'haï).

* 5. Sabah D'Mispatim, The (discourse of the) Aged One in Mishpatim. (Exodus xxi–xxiv inclusive.)

* 6. Midrash Ruth, (Fragments).

* 7. Sepher Hab-bahir, Book of Brightness.

8. Tosephthah, Addendum or Additions.

9. Raÿah Me'hemnah, The Faithful Shepherd.

* 10. Haikhaloth, Mansions or Abodes.

11. Sithrai Thorah, Mysteries (Secrets) of the Thorah.

12. Midrash Hanne-e'lam, The Hidden Midrash.

* 13. Razé D'Razin, Secret of Secrets or Original Secrets.

* 14. Midrash 'Hazeeth, A Midrash to the Song of Solomon.

* 15. Ma-a'mar To-'hazee. Discourse (beginning with) Come and See!

* 16. Ye'nooqah, The Discourse of the Youth.

* 17. Pe'qoodah, Explanation of the Thorah or Law, (the Pentateuch).

* 18. 'Hibboorah Qadma'a, The Primary Assembly or Society.

19. Mathanithan, We have learned, or Traditionally received, (the Doctrines).‡

According to John Christopher Wolf, there are apparently two *editio princeps* of the Zohar—that of Cremona and that of Mantua. The

† Pronounced, Seeph'rah Detz'neeoothah.

‡ All of these are in the Sulzbach edition. The Mantua edition contains only those not marked with an asterisk.

Cremona edition is in folio, and is called the Great Zohar (Zohar haggadol) and is used by the more modern and Occidental Jews. It was published 1558-60 and is the one of the greatest authority among the Qabbalists. It contains all of the books above mentioned and was corrected by 'Hayim (b. Samuel) Gatino, and Vittoris Eliano. Vincensio Conti., pp. 400. The entire introduction, which is in Hebrew, is only a page and a quarter. There is not any introduction by Isaac de Lattes or others, as stated by many European bibliographers. The editions of Cremona and Mantua sometimes differ in the reading.

The other *editio princeps* is in quarto, in three volumes, and is called the Little Zohar. It is used more by the Oriental and ancient Italian Jews. It was published at Mantua by R. Meir b. Ephraim Da Padova* and Jacob b. Napthali. I vol., pp. 251 ;, II, 269 ; III, 300. It has an important introduction by Isaac de Lattes, dated 1558.

A Hebrew MSS. edition of the Zohar of as early as 1506, has been mentioned as now in existence.† Bartolocci also mentions a Venetian edition of about 1558, but it has not been found.‡ Likely several volumes of the Zohar appeared about 1558.§ The publisher of the Cremona edition, whom it would appear from an acrostic poem attached to it, may have been one Joseph Onkel (or Winkel) from Germesheim, in Germany, therefore most likely a German or of German descent, says in his preface, that he: "Executed this work under the most invaluable help and supervision of a highly learned Jew, unsurpassable in all the branches of knowledge required * * * so that this present edition should be the absolutely correct one, free from all errors and corrupt readings, which abound in the *various other editions heretofore* offered to the public. And besides, there are some on whom the spirit of men rests, who continually soar towards heaven ; these are the very wise men of Egypt, and others again who are pervaded with the heavenly light which gives wisdom ; both are equally competent in their sublime

---

* Jellinek, in his German edition of Prof. Franck's *La Kabbale*, p. 293, says it was by Asraÿisn.

† M. Steinschneider's Jewish Literature. London, 1857, p. 228. Jellinek's Franck, p. 294.

‡ *Bibliotheca Magna Rabbinica Pars*. IV, p. 446.

§ Comp. Steinschneider, Jewish Liter., p. 227.

sphere, and with the learning of both we have associated ourselves * * * . We must also make mention of some others thoroughly conversant with the spirit of the Zohar, who assisted us and thus were co-instrumental in issuing this work * * . In interesting these great lights in our enterprise and by making their unanimous judgment the sovereign rule, we have succeeded in the establishment of the *only correct version*, while other particular versions emanating from single sources, are not omitted, they are printed with Spanish Rabbinical types, whereas the usual square Hebrew type (commonly called Ashoorith) is adopted in general. And all the books, joined to the principal book, follow in proper order along with the text, so that they may easily be found in this succession: Tosephthah (Addition), Sabah (Senior), Siphrah D'Tznioothah (Book of Hidden or Secret Things), Ye'nooqah (the Youth), Pe'qoodah (Commandant or Statute), Midrash Hanne-e'lam (Midrash of the Hidden Thing), Midrash 'Hazeeth (Midrash on Canticles), Midrash Ruth, Bahir (Brightness), Ma-a'mar To'hazee (Treatise beginning with "Come and See!"), Rayah Me'hemnah (Faithful Shepherd), Haikhaloth (Halls). * * We determined upon a folio, and saved neither money, time or trouble, not even space, for the accomplishment of the work to perfection: not a word is missing of the various texts in existence, but it is properly marked, etc." Therefore we "need not fear the adverse opinions of our competitors, who would fain belittle our work and find fault with the execution thereof, and thus prevent the public from buying it, forgetting at the same time, that the purchaser of such a book will be able to judge for himself by examining it, and has certainly not the intention to place it into his library for self-adulation. Still we admit that all of us, as children of one Father, are liable to make mistakes in thousands and ten thousands; but theirs are the ten thousands and the thousands are ours, etc."

In 1623 the edition of Lublin was published in folio after the Cremona edition, by Levi b. Kalonymos, with a few notes by R. Nathan Spira. It follows the paging of the Cremona. I vol., pp. 132; II, 122; III, 146. Baron Rosenroth considers it most defective and inaccurate.* In 1684 the Sulzbach edition was published, edited by Baron Christian Knorr von Rosenroth, assisted by Dr. Franz Mercurius van Helmont, with types set

* Comp. his *Theatro. Anon Placciano*, p. 691.

by Moses Bloch, wherein with the book Zohar were intermingled, the Midrash Ruth, Extracts from the book Hab-bahir, Tosephthah or an Addition to some legal sections, Raÿah Me'hemnah, Hibboorah Qadma'a, Haikhaloth, Sithrai Thorah, Midrash Hanne-e'lam, Razé D'Razin, Sabah, Ye'nooqah, Midrash 'Hazeeth, Ma-a'mar To 'hazee, Mathanithan, Piqqoodin. Here and there are seen extracts from the books of Adam, 'Ha'noch (Enoch), Abraham, Solomon, R. Cruspedia, and R. Akibah, together with three treatises by R. Shimon ben Yo'haï, viz: Siphrah D'Tznioothah, Idrah Rabbah and Idrah Zootah. The text itself is in the square letters, but the various readings are from the writings of R. Isaac Loriah, R. Moses Cordovero, MSS. of the Wise-Men of the Earth, and from printed editions, together with corrections from the book Derekh E'meth, *i. e.*, Way of Truth, and are in round (Rabbinical) characters. Under the text are scattered explanations of the more difficult words, from the Commentary of Issachar Bär (b. Petachja) under the title of Imrai Beenah, *i. e.*, Words of Understanding. Within the open spaces of the columns, the pages of the prior Mantua and Cremona editions are carefully noted down: at the end there is subjoined an index of the Biblical expressions in the Zohar, explained here and there, which was published once in Cracow separately, 1647, 4to, under the title of Petha'h Ainayim, *i. e.*, Opening of the Eyes. The dissertations which in the former editions had been placed in a less suitable place, have herein been restored to one suitable, as also others which were omitted have been added. In the opening, after the new preface of R. Moses ben Uri Sheraga Bloch, the old introduction by Isaac de Lattes is to be found. The Amsterdam edition is first of 1714, 4to, of a small form, in three volumes and is after, and paged as, the Mantua edition. In the margin are the corrections from R. Isaac Loriah's book, Way of Truth, also passages from the Old Testament and an Index of places by Meir Cordovero, also explanation of difficult words from the Imrai Beenah, *i. e.*, Words of Understanding, by Issachar Bär (b. Petachja), which appear evidently to have been done after the example of the Sulzbach edition. Finally at the end of each volume are added those things which are wanting in the original Mantua edition, but are found in those of Cremona and Lublin. At the end of the third volume appears a good index to the Zohar, arranged according to the names of the letters of the alphabet (I, 251 pp.; II, 270; III, 299 + 10). Other editions have been published at Amsterdam, 1728, 8vo, with notes by Schal Bosoglio, 3 vols., 1740; 1772, 8vo; 1805, 8vo. This edition has been reprinted at Constantinople, 1736, Yonah b. Yakhob; Krotoschin, 1844–5, 8vo, edited by Bar Monash; *ibid.*, 1858, 8vo; Brody, Galicia, 1873, III vol. 8vo; Przemysl, Galicia, 1880–1, 4to; Wilna, Russia, 1882. An edition, with points, is now going through the press of Signor Elia Benamozegh, the great Qabbalist, of Livorno (Leghorn), Italy. A folio edition, with points, on vellum paper, in three volumes, with comments by Massud Alfassi and Moses Salum, also Livorno, 1872. Other editions of the Zohar have been published at Salonica, Koenigsberg, Zolkiew and other places.

Rabbi Shim-on ben Yo'haï lived in the period of the destruction of the second Temple, at Jerusalem, from about 95 to about 190 A.D. His whole life was spent in the study of the Hebrew Secret Science, since called Qabbalah, of which he has ever been regarded as one of the most eminent masters. A thorough ascetic, he lived in a world of his own, beyond the regions of ordinary life, in the full flood of a religious metaphysic, peopled with the creation of his imagination, and that which had been handed down to him by the preceding masters in the science. Feared by his co-religionists from his asserted connection with the spiritual world, contemplative and secluded in his disposition, evidently of strong will and religious feelings, and not understood by those around him, he was not an affable companion, but an uncompromising and strong opponent in carrying out that which he thought was right. In the reign of the Roman Emperor Antoninus, when the School at Jamnia or Jabneh was watched with the greatest suspicion by its Roman rulers, so much so, that its students were prohibited by the Jewish Patriarch from even taking notes of the lectures, R. Shim-on was rash enough to speak against the oppressors in public. It happened one day while he, Yehudah b. Illaÿ, and Yo-seh b. Haleftah were holding a rabbinical exercise in the congregation, the comparative characteristics of the Jews and the Romans arose; aware of the danger of the subject, Yehudah commenced with an eulogium of the Romans. But we will quote from the Talmud, (Treatise, *Shabbath*, fol. 33, col. 2.)

" Once upon a time R. Yehudah, R. Yo-seh, and R. Shim-on b. Yo'haï were re-united and sitting together discoursing, and near by was found a certain R. Yehudah ben Gerim. (This name signifies, says Rashi, descendant of the proselytes.) During the discourse R. Yehudah, speaking of the Romans, said: 'This nation is great in all that which it builds. See how it has constructed everywhere bridges, and markets, and erected public baths!' At these words R. Yo-seh kept silent; but R. Shim-on responded 'Yea, indeed; but it has not made anything which has not for an aim its own advantage, it has constructed the markets so as to draw thereto the lost women, the baths so as to refresh themselves, and the bridges in order to gather from them the imposts.' R. Yehudah ben Gerim went directly (to the authorities) and informed against them that which he had heard, and it reached the ears of Cæsar. The latter at once rendered an edict, that, 'R. Yehudah, who has exalted me, be raised in dignity, R. Yo-seh, who kept silent, be exiled to Sepphoris; R. Shim-on, who has held me in contemptuousness, must be seized and put to death.' Immediately upon hearing of this decree, the latter, accompanied by his son (El'azar), managed to conceal himself in the House of Study, to which his wife (some say a guardian) brought to them each day, a loaf (of bread) and a porringer of water. But the proscription which weighed upon him being very severe, R. Shim-on said to his son, 'Women are of a feeble character; it is then for us to fear that, pressed by questions (probably, the question, a mode of punishment,) our guardian may finish by denouncing us!' Upon these reflections they quitted that asylum and secretly stole away to another place, and concealed themselves in the bottom of a cave. There a miracle operated in their favour, God created a carob bean tree (St. John's bread tree) bearing fruit through all the year for their support, and a perpetual spring of water for their refreshment. To save their clothes they stripped themselves and laid them aside, except when at prayer, and at other times, to protect their naked bodies from exposure, sat up to their necks in the sand wholly absorbed in study. After they had passed twelve years thus in the cave, Eliÿah was sent to inform them that the Emperor was dead, and his decree powerless to touch them.*

* R. Shim-on b. Yo'haï was sentenced about 161 A. D. by Lucius Aurelius Verus, co-regent of the Emperor Marc Aurelius Antoninus, and dwelt in the cave about thir-

On leaving the cave, they noticed some people ploughing and sowing, when one of them exclaimed 'these people neglect eternal things and trouble themselves with those which are only temporal.' As they fixed their eyes upon the place, fire came and burnt it up. Then a Bath Qol was heard, saying: 'What! are ye come forth to destroy the world that I have made? Get back to your cave and hide yourselves.' They returned to it, and after remaining in it for twelve months longer, they remonstrated, pleading that even the judgment upon the wicked in Gehenna, lasted no longer than twelve months; upon which a Bath Qol was again heard from heaven, which said: 'Come ye forth from your cave.' Then they arose and obeyed it." *

Owing to those indiscreet remarks of R. Shim-on, the Jewish school at Jamnia was put under interdict, license was granted however to R. Yehudah, to exercise the office of preacher to the synagogue. After the death of the Emperor Antoninus, R. Shim-on re-appears as the founder of a school at Teqo'a, now called Tekû'a, a city of the tribe of Judah almost south of Jerusalem and Bethlehem; the prophet Amos was of this place, and Isaiah is said to be buried there.† About 300 magisterial sentences by R. Shim-on b. Yo'haï are recorded in the Talmud. The Idrah Zootah of the Zohar gives an account of his death and burial. He is said to have been buried at Meïron to the north-west of the Lake of Tiberias, and his monument still exists. At Ain-etam, a few miles north-west of Tekû'a, are the ruins of an ancient synagogue attributed to R. Shim-on, who is said to have built

---

teen years, until after the death of Lucius Verus in 169 A. D. During this time he and his son devoted themselves to the study of the oral Talmud, Asceticism, the Secret Learning and Mysticism. Before this, R. Shim-on had been sent as a delegate to Rome and found favour with the Roman government. Talmudic Miscel. by P. I. Hershon, London, 1880, p. 64 *et seq.*

* Comp. Talmud, Yerush. Treatise *She'bee-ith* ix, 1; *Menachoth.* fol. 72; *Me'ee-lah* 7 and 17; B'reshith Rabbah c. lxxix; Midrash Koheleth, x, 8; Midrash Esther, i, 9.

† The cave in which R. Shimon hid himself, may have been in the neighborhood of Tekû'a, where he was so appreciated and known that he founded his school. In its vicinity are numerous caverns and deep ravines; some of the former will hold hundreds of men, and can be defended by a few against any number. One has numerous intricate passages, and Tobler found in it a number of sarcophagi and inscriptions in the Phœnician character. Dict. of the Bible by Dr. Wm. Smith, New York, p. 3189-90.

24 on the Lake of Tiberias; at Tebarieh is another. Carmoly gives a drawing of his tomb.* When the disturbance which caused the suppression of the school at Jamnia had subsided, a new school, which became celebrated, was founded at Tiberias by Shim-on b. Gamaliel about A.D. 165.

Among the published books favoring the antiquity of the Zohar, we call the reader's especial attention to the two following books on the subject, although many others have been written to the same effect, one is by Konitz, the other by Luriah.† The first is "The Book, Ben Yo'haï, explaining the Hidden Things, in the sayings of the divine Than-nah Rabbi Shim-on ben Yo'haï, his memory be a blessing, which are written in the entire Babylonian and Yerushalemitic Talmud, and in (the books) Siphra, Siphree, and Thosephthah, in the laws, rules and narratives, in which occur the words of this sainted man, whether spoken of as R. Shim-on ben Yo'haï, or only as Rabbi Shim-on; and the distinguished position occupied by him, before he sojourned in the cave and after his leaving it; furthermore unassailable proofs, that the books: the Holy Zohar, Raÿah Me'hemnah, Midrash Hanne-e'lam, and the Tiqqoonim, are the literary works (of the school) of R. Shim-on b. Yo'haï; also refutations of the objections raised against that authorship, etc.; finally the decisions in matters of casuistry given in the Zohar, either independently of or in accordance with, the Talmud; by Moses ben R. Me'na'him Mendel Konitz of Ofen (*i. e.*, Buda-Pesth, Hungary), Vienna, 1815." This book is a large folio of 149 pages of two columns each, and is divided into seven Gates (*She'arim*), spread over the first 62 pages. As the book is in Rabbinical text and not easily obtained, we will give a short analysis of its contents. Gate 1. Whenever the name R. Shim-on simply, occurs in the Talmud, R. Shim-on ben Yo'haï is meant. Gate 2. R. Shim-on

* *Itinéraires de la Terre Sainte des* xiii, xiv, xvi et xvii *siecle*, etc. Bruxelles, 1847, p. 451.

† Articles showing the antiquity of the Zohar have also appeared in many other writings, books and periodicals, too numerous to mention now, but we cite *Kerem Chemed*, Vienna edition, 1836, T. ii, ep. 25; also a criticism on Dr. H. Graetz's positions in his History of the Jews, which might be made much stronger, written by Dr. Leopold Löw, late chief Rabbi of Szegedin, on the Danube, and published in the periodical *Ben Chananja, Monatschrift für jüdische Theologie*, vol. vi, pp. 725-733; 741-747; 785-795; 805-809; 821-828; 933-942. Szegedin, 1863.

was his name prior to going into the cave, after leaving it he was called, in addition, Ben Yo'haï. Gate 3. The reverence and sublime distinction shown and assigned to him throughout his life, substantiated by quotations from the Talmud. Gate 4. After leaving the cave, (*i. e.*, his ascetic life), his decisions were accepted by the Wise-men of the Talmud as final. Gate 5. Even the great Rabbenu Haq-qadosh bases his own decisions upon those of R. Shim-on, speaking in the latter's name. So also does R. Yo-'ha'nan (ben Zakkai), and more than 50 quotations are given from the Talmud, that "R. Yo-'ha'nan said, in the name of R. Shim-on b. Yo'haï." Gate 6. In which it is shown, that where R. Shim-on b. Yo'haï differs from the other Rabbins, the latter always submit to his opinion as final. This gate has 145 doors, in which 145 Talmudic passages are cited in support of this assertion. Gate 7. In this Konitz speaks of "the Holy Zohar" as the spiritual fruit of R. Shim-on ben Yo'haï, and refers to R. Yakob ben Z'vee (or Tze'vee, the initials of YaBeTZ) of Emden, as the assailant of the antiquity of the Zohar, and as author of the book *Mitpa'hath se'pharim, i. e.*, Wrapper of books,* out of which Dr. Graetz gets most of his objections to the Zohar.† Yabetz has borrowed largely from the objections made by Jean Morin, a French ecclesiastic, b. 1591, d. 1659 A. D., in a book published by the latter, first in 1631, and after his death with his *Exercitationes Biblicæ*, in 1669.‡ Yabetz gives 132 objections to the antiquity of the Zohar, in the above-cited book, which Konitz says he will refute, in the second part of his book which is called *Ma-a'noth u-Mitpa'hoth, i. e.*, Replies and Precious Wrappers. Gate 7th closes at page 149 and bears on its back§ the "Keys of the Gates," *i. e.*, an Index of the books quoted from, and matters treated of as above mentioned.

In Gate 1 many passages from the Talmud are quoted, evidencing that R. Shim-on ben Yo'haï before his entrance into the cave, the latter without doubt referring to his ascetic life, was called Rabbi Shim-on, and that after

* Written 1758–1763; published at Altona, 1768, 4to, 2 vols.

† *Geschichte der Juden*, vol. vii, pp. 73–94; 185, 186; 193, 194; 217–256; 326–328; 442–459; 487–507.

‡ Morin's anti-Massoretic zeal, "was not according to knowledge, as later investigations in the same field have abundantly proved." Kitto's Cyclop. Bib. Liter., ed. 1876, Vol. iii, p. 217.

§ pp. 150–2.

his re-appearance he is spoken of as "Ben Yo'haï," or "Rabbi Shim-on ben Yo'haï." In Gate 2, Full reasons are given for this change of names. Gate 3 Explains the difference between the ordinary Rabbi Shim-on prior to the time he passed in the cave, and the completed man, Rabbi Shim-on ben Yo'haï after leaving it. The interval, some twelve years, had served to endow him with a heavenly superiority and sublimity, of which the two Talmuds and the Midrash Rabbah give us striking instances. In the Talmud (Treat. *Shabbath* 33 *b*.) we are told, the prophet Eliÿah sent him word of the death of his persecutor, the Roman Emperor Antoninus. He is also said to have annihilated wicked men by his breath (*Ibid.* 34 *d*). In the Talmud Ye'rushalmi it is stated, a man was bitten by a serpent, through the mere prediction of R. Shim-on ben Yo'haï (Treat. *She'bee-ith*, ch. 9). Upon leaving the cave he had an apparition in the shape of a bird, and a Bath-Qol as to it (*Ibid.*). A prophecy and miracle in connection with the cemetery in Tiberias, is given (*Ibid.*). Konitz cites numerous other instances which we have not now space to give. Konitz says: "The wise men of the A'mora-im testify to his standing as exceeding that of the Men of the Great Assembly, and say: 'What distinction in the ages of the world is there between the age of R. 'Hiz'qee-yah and the ages of the Great Assembly?' The age of R. 'Hiz'qee-yah closes that of the Great Assembly and opens that of R. Shim-on ben Yo'haï." (*Be'-reshith Rabbah*, ch. 35. See also *Miz-ra-'hee* 58, c. 9 and 12.) Lastly, "The sages of the Talmud distinguished the rank of R. Shim-on ben Yo'haï above all the heads of the entire congregation of Israel, and said: 'All Israel is bound to interrupt the study of the Thorah, so as to read the She'mah and the Prayer of Eighteen Benedictions at the prescribed time, except R. Shim-on ben Yo'haï, the only one excellent from world to world, and from his learning (or study) he shall not pause for the reading of the Shemah, and the Prayer of Eighteen, for his whole life is exclusively devoted to heavenly interests, etc." *

---

* See Midrash She'moth Rabbah, middle of Chap. 52. Talm. Yerushalmi, Treat. *Be'rakhoth*, chap. 1. *Shabbath* 11 a. M. Schwab's French ed., vol. 1, pp. 15–16, 51–52. *Ibid.* vol. iv, p. 13. This shows the divinely sublime study and teaching, in which he was engaged, which was, the oral tradition as to the Secret Learning, the Sod or Mystery, afterwards called Qabbalah, *i. e.*, that received (by oral tradition).

It is also said of him in the Talmud "He saw the future by means of the Holy Spirit." (Talm. Ye'rushalmi: *Shabbath* 89; Babli: *Me'eelah* 17*b*.) Konitz also gives many passages from the Talmudim and Midrash Rabbah, containing R. Shim-on ben Yo'haï's sayings about himself, his visions, supernatural powers, etc., and the statements of others to the same effect, and as to the sternness, integrity, and severity of his character, so that he even deemed himself competent to pass an adverse criticism on King Solomon, and to rebuke his own mother for conversing too much on the Sabbath day. This is continued in many quotations to show how, living on earth, he was yet a citizen of heaven, unconcerned about earthly things, wholly ingrossed with the study of the Thorah, his thorough penetration with the spiritual life, and his identification with the ministering angels of God, who see His glory and carry out His will. In Gate 4, Konitz shows how the opinions of this great man, no matter how contrary to or against whom pronounced, always prevail, and that his decisions on all casuistic discussions and questions are considered as final, whenever his name is mentioned in full, which was only after his return from his ascetic life in the cave. He overwhelmed the celebrated R. Eli-ezer b. R. Yosé, with cutting reproaches for contradicting him, and is reported to have contradicted his Rabbi (Master) the celebrated Qabbalist R. Akeebah, and insisted he was right. He is quoted as explaining four things contrary to his teacher Akeebah. Gate 5, gives many instances to show, that even the great redactor of the Mishna, Rabbenu Haq-qadosh, gave his decisions in the name of R. Shim-on ben Yo'haï, and that the great scholar R. Yo-hanan b. Zakkai gives 62 decisions in Ben Yo'haï's name. Gate 6 has 145 doors, through each of which a Talmudic quotation is given, in corroboration of, that wherever a decision of R. Shim-on b. Yo'haï occurs, the sages of the Talmud lay down a binding law according to it. In Gate 7, Konitz introduces 1st. The book Zohar, a production of R. Shim-on ben Yo'haï, and his school; and 2d. A venerable man named R. YAkob BEn Tz'vee, the anagram of which is (YABETZ), who raises his voice 132 times in denunciation of this book, alleging it to be spuriously shouldered on R. Shim-on b. Yo'haï. In answer to which, Konitz replies with 132 very profound, learned, and convincing explanations and elucidations; among them are the following: The disciples say:—" All thy males shall appear before the face of Adonai Elohim."*—Zohar ii 38*a*, refers to R. Shim-on b. Yo'haï before whom all men must appear. The Gaon Yabetz is indignant at the words in the Zohar ii 38*a*: "What is the meaning of *pe'naï ha-a-don* YHVH, *i. e.*, 'the face of Adonai YHVH'† This is Rabbi Shim-on ben Yo-haï," and Yabetz called this "Blasphemy on the part of a later writer, and R. Shim-on could not have been the author, God forbid that he should have thought to put himself as God!" Konitz says:—"It seems to us that the proper meaning of the words quoted is: 'the face of the lord of YHVH,' that is, of the man whom YHVH has chosen, and so made him *adon*, *i. e.*, a lord of YHVH, as: 'the mountain of YHVH;' 'the Messiah of YHVH,' etc. Although not thoroughly grammatical according to the more modern grammar, in its position in the Zohar it is in accord with:—'R. Akeebah said to R. Shim-on: It may suffice thee to know that I and thy Creator recognize thy power,' (Talmud Ye'rushalmi: Treat. *Sanhedrin*, c. 1); so R. Shim-on himself says, 'I have seen the sons of the Upper-room, they are few, and if they are two, it is I and my son.' (Talmud Babli: *Succah* 45*b*, Ye'rushalmi: *Be'rakhoth* c. 9.) Midrash B'resheeth Rabbah (c. 35,) completes this with the words 'And if it is One, it is I, myself.' See also Rashi's Commentary on the Talmud, Treatise *Sanhedrin* 98*a*—from which it appears that Rashi had, through Qabbalah from his teachers, many sayings and sentences of the Zohar, orally delivered from Rabbi to disciple, from and after the existence of the school of R. Shim-on ben Yo'haï. (Comp. Konitz. Reply 24, which is on page 73, col. 1.)

As to the Gaon's objection to Zohar ii, 132*b*, Idrah Rabbah; viz.: "R. Shim-on said: 'I call the upper heavens and the upper earth as witness, that I see at present, what no son of man ever saw since Mosheh went upon the mount of Sinai the second time, for I see my face shining as brilliantly as the light of the sun when it descends as a healing for the world; as it is written:—'To you who fear My Name shall shine the Sun of Righteousness with healing in his wings' (Mal. iii 20, iv. 2). Yea more, I know that my face is shining, but Moses did not know it or understand it; for

---

* Exod. xxiii, 17.

† Exod, xxiii, 17. "The Master, the Eternal," Onkelos says "The Master of the world." Cahen's French Bible, Vol. ii, p. 105, note.

it is written 'Moses wist not that the skin of his face shone.'"* (Exod. xxxiv, 29.) and *Ibid.* 144a, "That is revealed to and by us, which was never revealed since Mosheh stood upon the mount of Sinai."† For the

* The idea of the face shining is a metaphor to express the celestial and spiritual expression of the countenance. Comp., however, as to "face" Kitto's Cyclop. Bib. Liter., Ed. 1876, v. ii, p. 2.

† We will here give, from the Zohar, the whole passage:—"Thus far go the words which are hidden (abstruse), and the clear and choice meaning in them (which is set forth in many particulars); blessed is his lot who knows and attends to those things and errs not therein! Because these words are only given to the Masters of the Masters, and Reapers of the fields, who have entered in and gone out again (*i. e.*, ascended steadily). As it is written (Hos. xiv, 10): 'For the ways of YHVH are right, and the just walk in them, but the transgressors shall stumble therein.' We have learned, R. Shim-on wept and raised his voice, and said: If with these our words, which are here disclosed, our companions were gathered up, to be within the assembly-room of the world to come, and are raised up from this world, it is all right and well; for they (the words) were not revealed to any one of the children of the world. Again he said: I come back to myself, for truly I have revealed in the presence of Atikah D'Atikin, *i. e.*, the Ancient of the Ancients, Hidden through all Concealment; but *I have not done so for my own glorification, nor that of the house of my father, nor for yours, my companions,* but solely, that men might not stray in His paths, nor yearn to enter shame-faced into the gates of His Palace, nor be destroyed by their own errors. Blessed is my lot with them in the world to come! We have learned, before our companions went forth from this place, *i. e.*, the Great Assembly of the Threshing-floor, R. Yo-seh bar Yakob, R. 'Hiz'qee-yah and R. Yez-zah died; and the companions saw that the holy angels took them away by that expanded veil. R. Shim-on spoke and was finally prostrated. He cried out and said: Perhaps, which the Holy One forbid! a decree has been pronounced upon us to punish us, *because of something which has been disclosed by us, which had not been disclosed since the day on which Mosheh stood upon Mount Sinai,* as it is written (Exod. xxxiv, 28): 'And he was there with the Lord (YHVH) 40 days and 40 nights, etc.' Why then do I tarry here; if on that account they were punished? He heard a voice saying: Blessed art thou, R. Shim-on, and blessed is thy lot and that of those companions who are with thee; for that has been revealed to (all of) you which is not revealed to the whole upper army, *i. e.*, the angels. Come and see! It is written (Josh. vi, 26) 'And he shall lay the foundation thereof in his first born, and with his youngest son shall he set up the gates of it,' much more so here, because with vehement and too much study they (the three dead companions) applied their souls at this time and they were accepted. Blessed is their portion, truly they have been taken up (when) in perfection; which was not the case with those who

argument that it was not possible that R. Shim-on would speak thus of himself, Konitz refers the reader to that which he has already said in Gate 3d, and concludes, "Our Rabbi's of both Talmudim, have placed R. Shim-on ben Yo'haï, above all the learned men, praised him and his character, and wonderful deeds in unbounded terms, revered him as they did the patriarchs Mosheh and Ahron, put him on a level with the prophets, and exalted him above the men of the Great Assembly, speaking of him in even more extended terms of veneration, than the Zohar represents him as having spoken of himself; does not this certify to the veracity of the above words in the Zohar?" (Comp. 66th Reply, p. 87, col. 2, p. 88, col. 1.)

In the Tiqqooneh Zohar 7a we read: "The masters (teachers) of grammar (*diqduq*, properly, subtilty, or accurate distinction) have established the Qamets, which is a long vowel." Which according to Yabetz is proof of the comparatively recent period of the production of the Zohar, the phrase "masters of grammar," belonging to a much later period than that in which R. Shim-on flourished, even to that of the Ge'onim, "the originator of this science having been a certain R. Yehudah 'Hiyug of Pas." In refutation of this, Konitz refers to what he has before said in Gate 3, adding: "Nearly in the above quoted language of the Zohar you will find it distinctly stated in the Talmud, that the vowels, far from being the invention of R. 'Hiyug and those who lived after him, are a Ha'lakha (*i. e.*, rule), given to Mosheh on Sinai.' Thus we read in the Talmud—Treatise

---

were before them. Why did they die? We have learned: When as yet the words were being revealed, the upper and lower of those of the chariot (merkabah), were in movement, and a voice sounded through 250 worlds because ancient words (matters of antiquity), were being revealed below. And before they could again gather their breaths (souls) by these words, their life went forth in a kiss, and they were wrapped up in that expanded veil, and the angels above carried them away. * * R. Shim-on said, how blessed is the lot of those three, and blessed is our lot on their account. A voice went out a second time and said: 'But ye who cleave unto the Lord (YHVH), your Elohim (God), are all alive to-day.' (Deut. iv, 4.) They arose and from every side a sweet odour proceeded. R. Shim-on said: Henceforth, I perceive, that the world will receive blessings because of us. And all their faces shone so that men could not look on them. We have learned: Ten went in and seven came out, etc." Idrah Rabbah. Zohar iii, 144 *a et seq.* Mantua Ed. Cremona Ed., col. 271–2.

Ne'dareem 37*b*—R. Yits'haq said: 'The reading of the scribes (*Miqrah So-phe'rim*, i. e., the manner in which words and sentences are to be pronounced), and the omitting by the Scribes (*Ittur So-phe'rim*, i. e., the omission of certain letters in writing and speaking), what is to be read (*Qe'ree*) though not thus written (*lo Ke'thib*), and what is written (*Ke'thib*) and not thus read (*ve-loh Qe'ree*) is a Ha'lakha to Mosheh on Sinai.' " * Instances of the *Miqrah So-phe'rim* are: Where to read, *ah-rets*, instead of *eh-rets*, *sha-mo-yim*, instead of *sha-ma-yim*, namely, where there is the accent (called) *Eth-na'htah;* as R. Nathan, author of the book A-rookh states; or where to read *Mitsreem*, Egyptians, or *Mits-rayim*, Egypt, etc., which early distinctions must certainly have been pointed out at the time by signs or marks. The *Ittur So-phe'rim*, chiefly refers to the use or omission of the letter ו (vav) as a vowel ו, oo; or וֹ, o, or as a consonant with the meaning of a conjunctive "and"; *e.g.*, Genesis xxiv, 55: "Let the maiden stay with you a year or ten months, *a'har*, *i.e.*, *then* (not '*and* then;' *a-'har*, and not *ve*' *a-har*, properly: *and* afterwards) she may go!" Another instance (previous to this), Genesis xviii, 5, "*then* or *afterwards* (*a-'har*, not *ve a-'har*, *and* afterwards or *and* then) ye may pass by." Again, Numb. xii, 14, "*then* (*a-'har*) she shall be gathered in (as it is quoted in the Talmud, though our version has *ve a-'har*). Further *a-'har* in Ps. lxviii, 26, and the omission of ו *and*, before *mish-pate-kha*, thy judgments. Ps. xxxvi, 7.† Note especially *Sanhedrin* 99*a*, where it is plainly said:—" And though one say, the whole Thorah is from heaven, *except* this *grammar* (*diqduq*)," the laws and rules of which are referred to in the Talmud as well as in the Zohar, as above quoted, as also other early books.‡ From the examination of which writings the difference may be seen between the *Diqduqeh Thorah* and the *Diq-duqeh So-phe'rim*, as it is stated in the Talmud, Treat. *B'khoroth* 30*b*. See also Rashi on Treat. *Succah*

* Scribes means here, the authorities on the correct reading and writing of the Holy Scriptures. As to the Scribes or So-phe'rim, see Kitto's Cyclop. Bib. Liter., Ed. 1876, vol. iii, pp. 783–792. Massorah. Ibid., pp. 103–105.

† Comp. Rashi on *Ze'ba-'him* 115*b*, '*Ha'geegah* 6*b*.

‡ Comp. the book *Beth Yoseph; Toor Ora'h 'Hayyim* § 142; Response of R Sh B A. (Adereth) § 43; Response of R. Yitz'haq b. Shaisheth, disciple of R. Nathan (author of A-rookh) § 284; Response of R. David b. Simrah of Saragossa, part iii, § 594 and § 643.

28a, viz: "This is what they (the Rabbins) say in the Talmud, Treat. *Shabbath* 37b, R. Nathan was a *master* of the work,* which means, he was *accurate, i. e., me'daqdeq = diqduq,* in his work." This is to show the application of the word *diqduq* to other things, in the sense in which it is originally used with regard to grammar. In favour of the antiquity of the accents is:—" The words in Nehemiah viii, 8, viz: 'And they were intelligent *in the reading (bam-Miqrah)'* " † are to be understood as referring to the *distinction of the sentences* indicated by *the accents*, which Rashi on Talmud, Treatise *Ne'dareem* 37a, properly explains, as " the pointing and accents." And we learn in *Massekheth, Treat. So-phe'rim*, c. iii, rule 7: "A Sepher (Thorah)‡ which is pointed and accented, must not be used for reading;" for, says the book *Beth Yoseph*§ in the name of R. Moses ben Na'hman (Nachmanides), a Sepher Thorah must be written in the same way that it was given on Sinai; and R. Ye'ru'ham writes: "For we have it by tradition that there is an *aim le'miqrah*, a mother to the reading, and an *aim le'massoreth, i. e.*, a mother to the tradition, and pointing would do away with the latter." In this connection the *points over* the letters of ten words in the Pentateuch are to be noted, the antiquity of these cannot be disputed. These points served to direct the attention of the reader to the respective word as requiring a definition, *e. g.*, Numb. ix, 10, where the ה of the word רחֹקָה *re'hoqah, i. e.*, distant, is so pointed as to indicate that the distance need not be large, etc. Konitz says: (Reply 119, p. 103, col. 2, Zohar 'Hadash 69a) "It is necessary to know that the Talmud was already in existence in the times of the The'na-im, and Rabbenu Haq-qadosh—Yehudah the Holy, redactor of the Mishnah—was himself a disciple of R. Shim-on ben Yo'haï, he, his companions and teachers, studied the Ge'marah, which was not completed, however, until a long time after it, *i.e.*, the Mishnah."

Yabetz asserts that the phrase "to become like an ass of burden carrying books," occurs in Zohar 'Hadash 77b, and is not to be found in any

---

* See quotation before given from Tiqqoonim 7a.

† Talmud, Treat. *Me'ghillah* 3a.

‡ A synagogue roll of the Law or Pentateuch, which is always written by hand without points, except as hereafter mentioned, on skin.

§ Comp. *The Toor Yoreh Dai-ah,* § 274.

other book except the *Sepher 'Hoboth Halle 'baboth, i. e.*, The Book of the Duties of the Heart, in the section "Gate of the Service of God," the author of which was the R. Be'haï b. Yosef Ibn Bakoda, or Pakoodah, of Saragossa—flour. *circa* A. D. 1050—who was almost a contemporary of R A B a D,* from whence, Yabetz asserts, R. Moses de Leon has copied the original and given it a Zoharic dress. Yabetz does not see its connection with one of the Fables of Æsop. Konitz (p. 104, col. 1, Reply 120) says:—"Rabbenu Be'hai, the author of the book *'Hoboth Halle 'baboth*, was nearly a cotemporary of R A B a D, the author of a commentary on the Sepher Ye'tzirah, and borrowed many things from the Zohar under the name of the *Midrash of Rabbi Shim-on ben Yo'haï*. The author of "the Duties of the Heart" undoubtedly borrowed his expression from the Zohar. There lived not much later also Rabbenu Be'hai b. Asher, flourished *circa* 1291 A. D., author of the book Be'hai on the Pentateuch, he wrote frequently in the name of his teacher, who had seen the book Zohar, and he also quoted from the Zohar, for instance on Exod. xxi, xxii, etc., calling it, the Zohar, the Midrash of R. Shim-on b. Yo'haï.† This also is the name by which it was called by the first Qabbalists, the authors of the A'bodath Haq-qodesh and of Be'rith Me'noo-'hah.

In Reply 87, and in 125, p. 106, col. 1, Konitz gives examples which show the existence of the vowel points now termed *Patha 'h*—and *Qamets* —and *Dagesh*, in the Talmud.‡ In Reply 126, p. 106, col. 2, he supports the use of the Hebrew tongue among the Aramaic writings of the Midrash Hanne-e'lam by giving analogous instances in the Talmud. In Reply 128, p. 107, col. 1, Konitz distinctly says: "All these books of the Zohar (*i.e.*,

---

* R. Abraham b. David of Beaucaire, in France, lived *circa* A. D. 1125, died 1199.

† He was pupil of the erudite R. Salomo b. Abraham b. Adereth, *circa* 1234-1310 A.D., acrostically called Ra Sh BA. Be'hai's commentary is of 1291 A.D. He quotes also Levit. xxi–xxii; comp. Zohar ii, p. 114, Rayah Me'hemnah, Zohar i, p. 46*b*. Salomon b. Adereth did not oppose the Theoretical or Speculative Qabbalah, like Maimonides he held it in great veneration. They both opposed talisman, amulets, and the Practical Qabbalah. See Joel, *Die Religions-philosophie des Sohar*, Leipzig, 1849, p. 61, n. 4.

‡ See on this subject:—Genesis with a Talmudical Commentary by Paul Isaac Hershon. London. 1883. p. 92, v. 4, ii; p. 16, n. 4; p. 17, n. 8; p. 99, n. 13; p. 185, n. 6; p. 200, n. 28; p. 207, v. 8; p. 242, n. 3; p. 311, n. 2; p. 374, n. 133; p. 452, n. 7. These are only a few which may be given from the Talmud.

the Zohar proper, and the Raÿah Mehemnah, Midrash Hanne-e'lam, also the Tiqqoonim and the Zohar 'Hadash) are the composition by either the Thannah R. Shim-on ben Yo'haï, or his son R. El'azar and their colleagues and disciples, and the disciples of their disciples, the bearers of the sheaves of their traditions. He, ben Yo'haï, is the celebrated Than-nah of the Mishnah, two Talmuds, the books Saphra, Siphree, and Tosephthah, under the name of R. Shim-on, disciple of R. Akeeb'ah, and colleague of R. Yehudah b. Illaÿ, and R. Yo-seh b. 'Ha'leftah. He is the author from their beginning and no one else, he the exalted and wonderfully endowed teacher of occult science, the distinguished Qabbalist and possessor of supernatural and miraculous powers, in which sublime capacities he appears in hundreds of instances in the Rabbinical literature, as is shown in the first Six Gates of this book." We would here say, R. Shim-on was never claimed in the Zohar to be an author of any part of it, but only taught the oral tradition as he received it, and it was written down afterwards. Then follow over a hundred parallel passages from the Talmud compared with those in the Zohar, from the sayings of R. Shim-on b. Yo'haï (pp. 107-114).

In the Zohar 'Hadash 77*b*, occurs a reference to two kinds of Phylacteries which Yabetz thinks, proves the late period of the entire book, although it may have been interpolated in that place only, as it was consequent upon a controversy, between the different opinions of Rashi (R. Solomon b. Yitz'haqi, b. 1040, d. 1105 A. D.),* and R. Tam (b. *circa* 1100, d. 1171 A. D.)†, concerning the arrangement of the Scriptural quotations in the Te'phillin or Phylacteries, from which dispute two kinds came into use, called, those of Rashi and those of Tam. Konitz says, as early as the Talmudic period (perhaps before), differences of opinion existed as regards the Scriptural passages to be used in the Phylacteries, which resulted in the Talmudic times in the use of two kinds. In the Talmud, Treat. *A'bodah Zarah* 44*a*, it is said: "R. She-moo-el b. R. Yitz'haq says: There is a spot on the head fit to have two kinds of Te'phillin to be placed on it." Which implies two kinds of Te'phillin then existed, based on differences between the religious

---

* As to this author, see Kitto's Biblical Cycl., Ed. 1876, iii, p. 643.
† *Ibid.*, p. 945.

leaders of Israel. It is also said in the Talmud, Treatise *Erubin* 95*b*, and later in the book *Toor Ora'h 'Haÿyim* § 34, that there is also such a place on the arm. These prove that two kinds were in use among the adherents of either one or the other opinion, whereupon R. She'moo-el b. Yitz-haq, in order to reconcile both opinions, pointed out that second "spot on the head," beside that already described by the Rabbins, to place the Phylacteries on, certainly including a second place on the arm, as is plainly stated in the before quoted book *Toor*. Konitz in this place (Reply 121, p. 104, col. 1) also quotes various other passages from the Talmud, and other authorities, even from Haÿ Gaon, who lived about 100 years before Rashi and Tam, in support of his confutation of Yabetz.

If the book Zohar, the Raÿah Me'hemnah, the Tiqqoonim and the Midrash Hanne-e'lam, were really the work of R. Moses de Leon, and he the originator of the words put into the mouth of R. Shim-on b. Yo'haï, his son, and the companions, he would have been careful not to have mentioned the names of A'mora-im who lived at a later period ; and if he was an eminent scholar and familiar with the words of all the The'na-im and A'mora-im occurring in the Babylonian and Ye'rushalemitic Talmud, in the books Saphra, Siphree, and the Midrashim, so as to be able to quote them fluently and correctly, how would the folly of quoting posterior authorities agree with his great learning? This naming of the later Rabbins testifies to the originality of these books, as being the original works of those very remote times, which embraced the period of all the authorities quoted therein, at the expiration of which they were completed.

All the Hebrew Sacred Writings, it is asserted by the sages of that people, were not completely penned and their canon fixed, until the lapse of a considerable time after the deaths of their authors, and the heroes mentioned therein, as is set forth in the Talmud*. They assert, the Pentateuch was completed by Joshua, Joshua was partly by him, but was finished by El'azar and Pin'has, after his death. Samuel was partly written by him, but finished by Gad and Nathan, the prophets. Isaiah was written by Hezekiah ('Hiz'qee-yah) and his assistants. Jeremiah, Kings and Lamentations, in part by Jeremiah and then by Barukh, his secretary. Ezekiel was

* We will give the names, with the usual spelling of the King James' Version.

written by the Men of the Great Assembly, who also wrote the Twelve minor prophets, Daniel and Esther. The Psalms were some by David and others by the Ten Elders, who lived before and with him, and also by others. Proverbs, Canticles and Ecclesiastes, were written by Hezekiah's Society; Job by Moses; Nehemiah by Ezra, and Ezra by Nehemiah. Chronicles partly by Ezra, was finished by Nehemiah, Ruth by Samuel, Esther by the Men of the Great Assembly. So also, the Mishnah, the Be'raÿ-tha, Talmud Ye'rushalmi, Talmud Babli, Masse'kheth Sophe'rim, Me'sekhtoth qe'tannoth (*i. e.*, Small Treatises), Saphra and Siphree, Tosephthah, Midrash Rabbah, Pirqé d'Rabbi Eli-ezer, Targum Jonathan, in much of their content, date far back of the time they appeared in completeness. It took centuries after the death of their authors or starters, before they were finished, and in them all were embodied many oral traditions of a far more remote time. So the Zohar was not completely written until about 80 years after the death of R. Shim-on ben Yo'haï, and its books, called Raÿah Me'hemnah, *i. e.*, The Faithful Shepherd, Midrash Hanne-e'lam, *i. e.*, Hidden or Secret Midrash, and the Tiqqoonim, *i. e.*, Rules or Regulations, were the work of succeeding A'mora-im, and were not finished for 200 years later, about the time of the completion of the Talmud Ye'rushalmi. The Zohar 'Hadash appeared 100 years later, *i. e.*, 300 years after the Zohar Haq-qadosh, at the time of the completion of the Babylonian Talmud. Besides these supplementary works, there are even some additions in the body of the book from later disciples, who in the fullness of the wisdom they received by tradition, did not hesitate to transmit their knowledge to successive generations, by giving it utterance and noting it, on the margins of the pages. As to the " Introduction (*Haqdamah*) to the Zohar;" the Hebrew term of which being a production of later times, it is necessary to know, that the Zohar has, as do even the Midrashim and other contemporaneous writings, the word "Opening" (*Pe'thee'hah*) instead of *Haqdamah*, *e. g.*, "R. 'Hiz'qee-ÿah patha'h," *i. e.*, opened or began, and later writers substituted the word *haqdamah*, *i. e.*, preface or introduction.

The reader must not forget that R. Shim-on b. Yo'haï did not write anything himself, his oral traditions were written down by his school, first by R. Abbah and then by others who came after him. Referring to the book *Shalsheleth Haqqabbalah, i. e.*, Chain of the Tradition, Konitz says, "We read: Some say of the book Zohar, that R. Moses de Leon was a very learned man, and made these expositions for mercenary purposes, suspending them on the great tree, R. Shim-on b. Yo'haï; which the book Yu'hazin gives at greater length in the Edition of Constantinople, (1566, A. D.)* How utterly unfounded these surmises are, shall be proved by draughts from the wine of the sainted rabbins, who lived before the publication of the Zohar in the XIIIth Century." To this he devotes:

Reply 130, p. 120, col. 2, and shows that the Zohar was known long before R. Moses de Leon. That R. Sa-adÿah Gaon—892–942 A. D.—was a great Qabbalist, knowing by tradition from his father and his teacher, the mysteries of the Pentateuch, which were in the Midrash of R. Shim-on b. Yo'haï, as they are now found in the Zohar, and the latter transmitted them to his disciples. The Zohar was made public about 300 years after this Gaon, not as a new production, but as a work of earlier days. Rab Tsema'h Gaon of Pumbeditha, son of R. Paltvï Gaon, was Gaon of Pumbeditha, 871–876 A. D., over 400 years before the publication of the Zohar, he laid down a rule in the Codex of the Jewish Ceremonial Law, the *Toor Ora'h 'Hayim*, in connection with the morning prayers, of which no trace can be found in the Talmud, and the Massekheth Sophe'rim has the very opposite, but we find the Zohar § *Te'rummah*, is quoted in the book Beth Joseph § 59, as his authority. R. Sar Shalom Gaon, an eminent Qabbalist according to 'Hayim Vital, decided that the custom of not studying the Law at the *Min'hah, i. e.*, Vesper time, was because the Talmud† says:—"All the schools are to be closed at the death of a 'Ha-kham, *i. e.*, Wise-man, in the city," and that in that hour Moses died. This usage is not mentioned in any of the text books, and to the contrary the death of Moses is said to have occurred on the *evening* of the Sabbath, but in the Zohar § *Te'rummah* 156*a*, we find a statement

---

* This refers to the account said to have come from Isaac of Acco, which has been left out all the editions since, until replaced by the Edition of London, England, by Filipowski. 1857, pp. 88 *et seq.* This account Dr. Graetz admits, Isaac of Acco evidently either did not write or did not believe, for the latter copied Zoharic passages in his subsequent writings.—*Geschichte der Juden*, vol. vii, p. 492.

† Treatise *Moed Qaton*, 22*b*.

of the custom, and the death of Moses on the *afternoon* of the Sabbath. So in the Targum Ye'rushalmi, usually called the Targum of Yonathan ben Uziel, which is said to have been written by a disciple of Hillel I., therefore about 50 B. C. to 10 A. D., are many statements evidently taken from the Zohar, or coming from the same mystical School, of which our author gives the quotations. So in the book Arookh by R. Nathan— b. 1030, d. about 1106 A. D.—which was finished 1101 A. D., about 200 years before the publication of the Zohar, are statements to be found only in the Midrash of R. Shin-on b. Yo'haï, which was one of the names of the Zohar before its redaction. Rashi (1040–1105 A. D.), a giant among the learned of his race, quotes and uses statements, the same as are in the Zohar, of which Konitz quotes numerous examples. The authors of the Thosaphoth also received from the Midrash R. Shim-on b. Yo'haï, as we find it now redacted in the Zohar. Maimonides even quoted from the Zohar in his *Ye'sodeh Hat-thorah*, *i. e.*, Cardinal principles of the Law. Nachmanides or R. Moses b. Na'hman—1200–1272 A. D.—was certainly acquainted with the Midrash of R. Shim-on b. Yo'haï. In this way Konitz proceeds, quoting from these authors and showing, that all the prominent learned men among the Jews of this period, were familiar with this Midrash of Shim-on b. Yo'haï, which has been since redacted into the book called the Zohar, giving among others the names of the celebrated R. Salomo b. Adereth (Ra SH B A), a disciple of Nachmanides; R. Abraham b. David (R A Ba D) d. 1198; Rabbenu Ye'ru'ham and many others; he brings numerous quotations from the two Talmuds, to show that the Midrash of R. Shim-on b. Yo'haï was known by the Rabbins of the Talmuds, and that the Zohar, containing the identical words and sentiments of those quotations, is only a later name for this Midrash. Rabbenu Hag-gadol, *i. e.*, the Great Rabbin, shows in his writings that he and his teachers must *have received—qibbel—*all the words of the The'na-im and A'mora-im, contained in the Zohar, in their purity, and all of his disciples were great Qabbalists. The book *Toor Ora'h 'Hayïm* is the statute book of orthodox Israel, and it decides according to the teachings of the Zohar. Konitz then quotes numerous laws and rules from this, and twenty-five other, thoroughly orthodox Jewish books, as in accord with the teachings in the Zohar, and enumerates the disciples of the authors of these books who were all great Qabbalists. On page 130, col. 1, line 51, after a quotation from Yabetz's book Mit-pa'hath Se'pharim, Part 1, fol. 4*b*, confirming the antiquity and sanctity of the Hebrew Qabbalah, he shows that in this very book, Part i, fol. 5*a*, Yabetz says:—"The Zohar is truly the adorning crown of the Qabbalists, as R. Yitz'haq Luriah has testified concerning it, who himself was a holy and divine man with the holy spirit resting upon him, and upon it—the Zohar—was his sublime and tremendous wisdom built and founded. God forbid that any one should doubt his words." Konitz then shows the distinctions between the Zohar and Talmud very fully, and among other things says: "Legislation on the Mosaic law and its traditions, pure and simple, is one thing; philosophical and metaphysical contemplation and discussion with regard to this written and traditional law, is another. The latter, entering into the spirit and hidden meaning, is for the initiated few, the former for the general masses. This explains the language and dress of each, circumscribed, nay merely fragmentary in the one; distinct, clear, elaborate, in the other; allegorical and speaking in parables here, plain and intelligible there. The Qabbalah and the Zohar allow a great margin to speculative thought, the Talmud deals with every-day life, and humanity under the Law; the former—the Qabbalah—starts from a spiritual point of view, contemplating a spiritual finality as regards the Law and its explanation, while the latter—the Talmud—is eminently practical in both its starting point and end, and having, in the face of the ignorance, want of perception and natural waywardness of the masses, nothing but the strict observance of the Law in all its details in view. This explains the hesitancy of the Qabbalistic Rabbins, to impart the mysteries of the Ma-a'seh Be'resheeth and Ma-a'seh Merkabah, to even the ordinary learned and certainly to the many, who were obviously unfitted for such knowledge; and thus we must understand and appreciate their advice to their disciples in general, not to give themselves up to these studies." In ancient times when education was much less diffused, the original Qabbalistic companions led an ascetic and holy life, separated from the unlearned and unwise, such a life being required, and lest this mysterious and occult science might prove injurious to all concerned; admission and initiation were required to be granted, but even these were only to a few wise, elect, discreet and worthy disciples, who had arrived at full years of discretion and were of known formed character. This period of ascertained wisdom and discretion was fixed at 40 years of age and over. At a very early date it was called by the The'na-im and A'mora-im, a "Science," as may be seen in the Talmuds Babli (*Be'rakhoth* 33a) and Ye'rushalmi (*Be'rakhoth* 85) and in other earlier books. The secrecy of this oral traditional "Science," is evidenced in the Talmud Ye'rushalmi : * " R. Shim-on b. Laqish said : On the Jordan the children of Israel received and accepted the 'hidden things' or the *nistaroth*, *i.e.*, mysteries.† Joshua said unto them, unless ye accept the *nistaroth*, the waters shall drown you. R. Levi said : In Yabneh this obligation was rescinded by a Bath-Qol exclaiming : Ye have nothing to do with the *nistaroth*." Yabetz again contradicting his own theories, says : " The words of the Zohar are the words of the living God, very profound, who can find them? It took even, as we know, R. Yitz'haq Luriah a long time of due and steady preparation until he reached his glory in this science, a small portion of which, he said in his dying hour, his disciple, R. 'Hayim Vital only possessed." ‡ This chapter of Konitz closes with a quotation from the Midrash Mishleh (Proverbs) according to which, one of the questions asked of every Israelite when his soul is before the judgment seat on high will be : " Hast thou *contemplated* (*tsa-pheetha*, *i. e.*, glanced at) the Merkabah? Hast thou *looked at* (*tsa-pheetha*) my Shee-oor Qo-mah—*i.e.*, Measure or Proportion of Stature?" Not : Hast thou learned or occupied thyself with this *Science ?* Because this *Science*—the Qabbalah—requires open eyes and open intellects, and not merely mechanical learning, as does the Law and its execution. In Reply 132 he shows that the teachings of the Zohar are in perfect conformity with passages in the four Toorim or four law books, by which the entire life of the Israelite is regulated in all its relations, citing from the Zohar, 90 quotations which are in the Ora'h 'Haÿim ; 31 in the Yoreh Daiah ; 6 in the 'Hoshen Ham-mishpat ; and 8 in the Eben Ha-ezer, in all 135. This followed by an index closes his book.

* Treatise *Ailoe ne-e'marim*, from whence it is quoted in Those'photh *Sotah*. 34a.

† Comp. Deut. xxix, 29. The idea of the Secret Learning belonging to the Sacerdotal Class, and the legal precepts which are revealed, appear in this verse. See next page.

‡ Book Mit-pa'hath Se'pharim, end of chap. 86.

Dr. Hirsch Graetz, although bitterly opposing Konitz and Luriah and everything showing the antiquity of the Qabbalah or the Zohar, is obliged to acknowledge,* that when Mohammedanism spread in the days of the Ge'onim—657–1038 A. D.—a book became known, the author of which, he says, was unknown, called: "*Nistaroth*† *a' Rabbi Shim-on ben Yo'haï*, *i. e.*, the Mysteries of R. Shim-on b. Yo'haï, in which among other things, R. Shim-on is stated to have complained: "In addition to our sufferings from the government of Edom (Rome, *i. e.*, at that period Byzantium), we shall also have to suffer from the Yishmaelites (Arabians)? To which Metatron, prince of the countenance, *i. e.*, the Angel of the Presence, answered: Fear not, son of man, for the Holy One, blessed be He! establishes the government of Yishmaël to save you from this wicked one (Rome), and He will place over them a prophet after His own Will, who shall conquer the land, and afterwards return it to Israel, etc." This book was most probably in existence some 600 years before the birth of R. Moses de Leon, but we do not admit the entire correctness of the quotation given by Dr. Graetz without seeing the original. We shall hereafter refer more fully to Dr. Graetz and his opposing school.

The learned Doctor disposes of Konitz with a stroke of the pen,‡ yet he is compelled to admit, that Yabetz's arguments are of little force,§ for the latter says, that the germ of the Zohar is very ancient, can be carried back to Moses, yea! even to a divine revelation. Dr. Graetz, although a man of great erudition, like many other theorists, bends his authorities to suit his hypothesis, but a thorough examination of the authorities cited by him, will frequently reveal to the student, an entire disproval of his formulations. He is apparently prejudiced, by a thorough antagonistic feeling toward the scientific and most elevated metaphysical philosophy of the Israelites, and has ignored many of the great writers upon the subject, notably Dr. Peter Beer, Dr. J. M. Jost, Dr. Leopold Zunz, Dr. August Tholuck, Salomon Munk, Ignatz Stern, D. H. Joel, N. Krochmal, and indeed, all those in any way favorable to the Qabbalah and Zohar. He dis-

* *Geschichte der Juden*, V. p. 490, n. 16. Comp. Jellinek's *Bet ha-Midrasch, Dritter Theil*, pp. xix, 78–82, and the Zohar, ii, 32*a*.
† See *ante*, p. 36.
‡ See his *Geschichte der Juden*, Vol. vii, p. 495.
§ *Ibid*, pp. 495–6.

poses of the antiquity and authorship of the Zohar with the pen of an autocrat, basing many of his ideas on those of Dr. Adolph Jellinek, of Vienna,* who is disposed to assert that it was entirely written, out of his own head, by R. Moses b. Schem-Tob de Leon of Spain, as before him did the Roman Catholic Jean Morin,† and as Yabetz started out to do, but changed his views as they became more enlightened by an examination of the subject. Dr. Graetz cuts away the bridge of historical continuity and separates by a vast abyss, all the Qabbalists of the XIIIth century, from all preceding Israelitish Secret Learning, Theosophy, and Mysticism. Dr. Jellinek does not go so far, but acknowledges a Qabbalistic knowledge in the Xth and XIth centuries, by R. She'reerah Gaon, Eliÿah ha-Zaken, R. Haÿ Gaon, R. Yekhutiel of the Babylonian School at Pumbeditha. One of the first Qabbalists in Spain, was R. Chasdaï (or Chisdaï) Ibn Shaprut ben Yitz'haq ben Ezra ha-Nazi or Nagid, *i. e.*, Prince or temporal head of the Jews in Spain. His Arabic name was Chasdai Abu Jusuf Ibn Shafruth. His father was Yitz'haq Ibn Shafruth, of Jaen. Chasdai lived in Cordova, Spain, in the time of the Khalif Abderrahman III who reigned 912–961 A. D., and his successor Hakem—961–976 A. D.—and was Grand Vizier of Moorish Spain—961–976 A. D.‡ We have not space in this writing, to give his doctrines, but will say they are in agreement with those we know of other early Qabbalists, *e. g.*, Haÿ Gaon and Ibn Gebirol. Then came Ibn Gebirol, Spain, Jacob Nazir, of Lunel, Abraham Ab-Beth-Din, Abraham ben David, of Posquieres, (Isaac) Yitz-haq, the Blind, of Beaucaire, Azriel and Ezra, Yehudah b. Yakar, Jacob b. Shesheth, which brings the Qabbalah, in Spain, down to 1270 A. D., and the period of Todros b. Joseph Hallevy Abulafia, Abraham ben Samuel Abulafia, the

* See, *Moses Ben Schem-Tob de Leon und sein Verhältniss zum Sohar, etc.* Von Adolph Jellinek. Leipzig. 1851. And *Supra*, p. 39, note.

† J. Morin's object was to prove that the Jews had falsified the Hebrew Old Testament, and that the only correct version was the Greek Septuagint. Modern scholarship has not adopted his views. See Kitto's Cyclop. Biblical Lit., Ed. 1876, Vol. i, p. 582. *et seq.*

‡ See, Pub. of the Soc. of Hebrew Liter. London. 1872. Vol. i, pp. 63–112. Also Carmoly's *Itinéraires de la Terre Sainte des* xiii, xiv, xvi, *et xvii siecle* etc. pp. 1–111. Jellinek's *Auswahl Kabbalistischer Mystik*, second part, pp. iii–v. Also the book Khusari or Cosri, of R. Yehudah Hallevy. David Cassel's ed., Leipzig. 1869. Also the ed. by H. Hirschfeld, Leipzig, 1886, 2 Thle.

learned Nachmanides, and other Qabbalists about the time of the appearance in public of the Zoharic MSS. Into Germany Dr. Jellinek traces it from the Jewish Universities of Babylonia. Haÿ and Ibn Gebirol also, he says, used the expression *Hokhmath haq-Qabbalah, i. e.*, Wisdom of the Qabbalah. Dr. Jellinek also asserts the great influence of R. Azriel b. Mena'hem of Valladolid, b. *circa* 1160, d. 1238 A. D. The book Ye'tzeer'ah, Dr. Jellinek admits, was known in the Xth century, we note here, that St. Agobard, b. *circa* 800, d. 840 A. D., notices this and other mystical Jewish books;* which takes it before and into the beginning of the IX century. Jellinek also gives a short account of mystical Jewish sects before Saadÿah Gaon—892–942 A. D.—taken from Shâhrestâni,† who flourished *circa* 1090–1125 A. D. According to Dr. Graetz's hypothesis, the Qabbalah sprung up as a new thing, from the school of R. Abraham b. David, of Nismès, and Beaucaire, called Rabad; whose teacher was a certain Jacob Nazir, of the XIIth century.‡ And that this school sprung up in opposition to the newly asserted philosophy of Maimonides, which was considered as Aristotelian. Maimonides, however, was very favorable to the Speculative Qabbalah, as will appear from his book Moreh Ne'boo-kheem, and especially from his writing "Introduction to the Talmud," where " in the fourth place" speaking of Rab Ashi and his great undertaking, the drawing up of the Babylonian Talmud, he also speaks in the highest terms of the Hebrew Secret Learning and Science, afterwards generally called in Europe, the Qabbalah. In another writing his words are :—" If I had acquired this species of knowledge (the Qabbalah) sooner, I would have given the world so many a production more." §

* See Basnage's Hist. of the Jews, Taylor's English trans. of 1708, pp. 598–99.

† See *Beiträge zur Geschichte der Kabbala, von Adolph Jellinek*. First and Second Parts. Leipzig, 1852. *Adolph Jellinek und die Kabbala, ein Literatur-Bericht von* Dr. J. M. Jost, Leipzig, 1852. *Thomas von Aquino in der jüdischen Literatur, von Adolph Jellinek*, Leipzig, 1853, and *Auswahl Kabbalistischer Mystik*, by Adolph Jellinek, Leipzig, 1853, *Erstes Heft*, p. 27 *et seq.* and notes.

‡ Comp. *Auswahl Kabbalistischer Mystik*, by Adolph Jellinek, Leipzig, 1853, Part i, pp. 1–6 and notes; Karpeles, *Geschichte der Jüdischen Literatur*, Berlin, 1886, Vol. ii, p. 669 *et seq.*; Graetz, *Geschichte der Juden*, Vol. vii, p. 73 *et seq.*

§ See Jerusalem, A treatise on Ecclesiastical Authority and Judaism, by Moses Mendelssohn. Samuel's English Ed., London, 1838, Vol. ii, p. 306.

The Qabbalist Shem-Tob b. Abraham Ibn Gaon—b. 1283, d. 1332—in his *Migdal Oz, i. e.*, Towers of Strength, to Maimonides' "Yad," at the beginning, says: "I testify I have seen in the book * * * written on old and yellow parchment, this expression: 'I Moses bar Maimon, when I dived into the hidden recesses of the chariot, conceived that it referred to the end, *i. e.*, redemption of Israel.' And his words coincide with those of the true Qabbalists."* Maimonides opposed only the Practical Qabbalah.† The law of historical continuity is disposed of Dr. Graetz, in a way much more astonishing, than any of the alleged miracles asserted to have been performed by the Practical Qabbalists. Dr. Graetz has an axiom in this connection, which it would be well to keep in mind whilst considering his critical views:—"Criticism needs not to be more scrupulous, than the adherents of the Kabbalah to vindicate for it an old age."‡

The book *Kadmooth haz-Zohar*, by David Luriah, of Buchau, in favor of the Antiquity of the Zohar, is a small 8vo of 44 double pages. It is partly in Rabbinical and partly in square Hebrew letters, and is excessively rare and valuable in Europe. The title is "A Treatise speaking Righteousness and Rectitude. Antiquity of the Sepher Haz-Zohar, the origin of which is from very ancient times. Its faithful source from R. Shim-on ben Yo'haï and his disciples, his holy words and accumulation of lights, sparks of majesty to those who fear God and think of His Name. The basis (of it) in the Talmudim and the controversies of the Ge'onim. Divided into Five branches, planted in a row, to send forth beautiful

---

* Cited by Dr. Graetz, *Geschichte der Juden*, Vol. vii, p. 234, note 3.

† Jerusalem, by Mendelssohn, above cited, p. 297, and the Moreh Ne'boo-kheem, *i. e.*, The Guide of the Perplexed, English edition by Dr. M. Friedländer. London. 1885. On the Ma-a'seh B'resheeth (Gen. i *et seq.*) Vol. i, 7, xvii, xxx; ii, 141; iii, 1. Ma-a'seh Merkabah, Vol. i, 7, 116, 124, 271; ii, 141; iii, 1 *et seq.* Mysteries of the Thorah, Vol. i, 3, 111-129, 274; ii, 169-170, 219-222; iii, 1. Compare with these citations, the learned notes by Salomon Munk in his magnificent Arabic and French edition of the Moreh. There are many other places extending throughout the Moreh, showing the favorable tendency of its writer towards the Speculative Qabbalah and his opposition to the Practical Qabbalah.

‡ *Geschichte der Juden*, Vol. vii, pp. 446-447.

twigs. Written by David Luriah (of Buchau)." Julius Fürst* says, it was published at Johannisburg in 1857.

The Branches are, I. Proof that R. Moses de Leon did not compile the Zohar. II. The Ge'onim in Babylonia cite from the Zohar and Midrash Hanne'elam, under the name of, Midrash Ye'rushalmi. III. The Zohar must have been compiled before the completion of the Talmud. IV. Proof that a great part of the Zohar, was written in the period of R. Shim-on b. Yo'haï and his pupils. V. As to the Aramaic language of the Zohar. Branch I. This he divides into three arguments. 1. From that which appears in Moses de Leon's book, *Sepher Has-shem, i. e.*, Book of the Name, and from the book Pardes and other writings of R. Moses Cordovero, it is evident that R. Moses de Leon did not write after the style of the Zohar, and in many places contradicts it. 2. It is evident from his book *Nephesh Hah-'hokhmah, i. e.*, Vital Soul of Wisdom, called also *Sepher-Ham-mishkal, i. e.*, Book of the Balance, in which he quotes from the Zohar, that de Leon either mistook the sense of the Zohar or had an incorrect edition of it. In but few places does he follow the drift of the Zohar, and in his style and manner, he follows the words of the antecedent and contemporary Qabbalists. He has, however, mixed some words of the Zohar with his own, without crediting the source, but he often contradicts the Zohar. Luriah gives quotations proving this. 3. From the contents of the books written before the time of R. Moses de Leon, or by his contemporaries of greater age and standing, who quote passages from the Zohar, the greater antiquity of the latter cannot be questioned. The earlier Ge'onim quote from the Zohar, as the Midrash Ye'rushalmi. David Luriah cites many proofs from early books to support this, his third proposition. He shows that there are in the book *Ô'tsar hak-Kabod, i. e.*, Treasure of Glory, by R. Todros (Theodorus) ha-Levi or Hallevy (died 1283, nephew of R. Më-ir Hallevy), quotations from books in the name of Midrash, which quotations are to be met with only in the Zohar. In the time of R. Moses de Leon, Todros was an old man, and his standing was such, that he certainly would not have quoted as an ancient Midrash, a book newly written by R. Moses de Leon, his contem-

* *Biblioth: Judaica*, Vol. iii, p. 332.

porary.* The Zohar was also cited under the name *Nistar ve'ne-e'lam*, *i. e.*, The Mysterious and Hidden Midrash, by the author of the book, *Migdal Oz, i. e.*, Towers of Strength. Its author was a contemporary of R. Moses de Leon. The celebrated Italian Rabbi Recanati, living in Italy, cites in his Commentaries on the Pentateuch and in his other writings, many passages from the Zohar. He was a contemporary of R. M. de Leon. The last named frequently quotes passages which are now to be found in the Zohar, as from "the earlier sages," also as from the *Sithrai hat-Thorah*, *i. e.*, Secrets of the Thorah. Recanati writing in Italy, cites other and frequently the same passages, as from "the earlier sages," and from the *Sithrai hat-Thorah*. These facts tend to prove the existence of a book on the Mysteries of the Thorah, prior to Recanati, Moses de Leon, R. Shalomo ben Adereth, or Ra SH B A, and other contemporaries, from which they quote.

Branch II. In this Luriah asserts and shows by proof through quotations, that the earlier Ge'onim—657–1038 A. D.—discussed Qabbalistic matters under the name of "Midrash Ye'rushalmi," which were in the language and content of the Zohar, that these were simply quoted as from the A'mora-im—220–540 A.D.—or from ancient sources without any especial reference, which were the words of the Midrash Hanne-e'lam of the Zohar, which though now in the Zohar only in some sections, was undoubtedly written, at first, on the whole Pentateuch. It can be satisfactorily shown, that the Ge'onim had a Midrash Ne-e'lam, by tradition in the Aramaic tongue, in the form and character of the present Zohar and Midrash Hanne-e'lam. This Branch is divided into, 1. What exists of the explanations of the Ge'onim in other ancient works, under the name of "Midrash Ye'rushalmi." 2. What is published of the same by Luriah. 3. What is discussed in other ancient writings under the name of Ye'rushalmi, without mention of the Ge'onim, but which justify the supposition of transposition from the Ge'onim, and that they have quoted as Ye'rushalmi, the contents of the Midrash Hanne-e'lam in the Zohar. 4. What in the writings of the Ge'onim—657–1038 A. D.—is simply quoted from the A'mora-im—220–540 A. D.—or from very ancient

* We shall find Todros again referred to when we come to the account by Isaac of Acco (Acre, Palestine).

sources, etc., without any special reference; which also may be unhesitatingly ascribed to the Midrash Hanne-e'lam. The early Ge'onim discussed Qabbalistic matters, under the name of a secret book apparently called "Ye'rushalmi," referring to, as named therein, many of the companions, whose names are now to be found in the Zoharic writings, as authority for what is therein decided. The language, content and sages referred to, are mostly those to be found in the Midrash Hanne-e'lam in the Zoharic writings, and are not to be found in the Talmudim and other Midrashim outside of the Zohar. This secret book was from the earlier Ge'onim, or other even earlier sources. Haÿ Gaon, b. 969—d. 1038 A. D., and other Ge'onim often quote from the Midrash Ye'rushalmi, Haÿ also quotes from the *Noosa'h Ye'rushalmi, i. e.*, copy or transcription of the Ye'rushalmi, and this quotation is not to be found in the Talmud Ye'rushalmi nor in any of the Midrashim, but we find it in the Zohar, Para'shath *Te'rummah* (Exod. xxv–xxviii), in the Aramaic language, and the Gaon Haÿ translated it into Hebrew; this may explain why he says: "*Noosa'h Ye'rushalmi*," i. e., a copy or version, Ye'rushalmi; which he uses to signify, that it was translated into his own language. Luriah cites other Ge'onim, who quote from the "Ye'rushalmi," matters which are now to be found only in the Midrash Ne-e'lam of the Zohar. He then shows by quotations from ancient books, that much was taken in early times from the Midrash Hanne-e'lam or Secret Midrash, which is now among the Zoharic books. There is good reason to believe that the book Zohar, the contents of which were considered more profound and sublime than those of the Hanne-e'lam, was not even mentioned by name, it being quoted from, in phrases only understood by the initiates; *e.g.*, "thus we learned," or, "in the name of the ancient ones they said," without mentioning it as a book, so that the uninitiated should remain in ignorance of its existence, and only that, which they deemed proper to be known, should be made known. The very meaning of the name, Siphrah D'Tznioothah, of the Zoharic writings, is: that it is the book kept modestly or secretly from the gaze of the public. It was doubtless known at this period, not in writing but only orally. The Babylonian initiated Jews were very strict in keeping secret from the uninitiated, the theosophical traditions or Secret Learning, which they had inherited from their ancient masters and the successors of those masters. We will give an instance: Rab She'reerah Gaon* having been asked a question regarding the book Shee-oor Qo-mah, *i. e.*, Proportion of the Height, a very mystical book, as it is found in the Bo-rai'toth of the Pirkqeh Haikhaloth, *i. e.*, Halls, of R. Yishma-ël, said: "This matter cannot possibly be explained in its particulars, but merely (by hints) in an abstract way; for R. Yishma-ël has not originated this matter, nor does it come from any human mind. Besides, God forbid! that man should speak of the Creator, as if He had bodily members and dimensions. The 'Proportion of the Height' are matters of a Qabbalah, superior to the conception of mankind, of which not anything more mystical can be said, for not any likeness can give a description of Him, only the sages, familiar with this profound and sublime science, can occupy themselves therewith. But they are strictly prohibited from delivering these secrets and mysteries to any man, except he possess the characteristics and qualifications imparted to us. Even not a summary, how much less any particulars, shall be revealed to any one; for with regard to this matter, and to *what is below it of the Ma-a'seh Merkabah, i. e.*, Chariot Throne,† our sages have said: ‡ R. 'Heeyah said: It is not permitted to impart the summaries, *Ra-sheh P'raqim, i.e.*, Headings of the Chapters, except to an Ab Beth Din, *i. e.*, the head of a court of justice, whose heart is solicitous (careful) within him, as regards matters inferior to all these. R. Immi said:§ It is not permitted to impart the Mysteries of the Thorah, except to a 'counsellor, cunning artificer, and skillful orator' (Is. iii, 3), (properly "skillful orator" *nabon la-'hash* means to one who understands in *la-'hash, i. e.*, silence or secret), to him it is permitted to impart generalities, he will understand them, and will be enlightened from heaven in the hidden recesses of his heart. As is said in the Midrash: || *Nabon la-'hash, i.e.*, a skillful orator, is he who draws his

* B. 930, d. 1000 A. D., was one of the last Ge'onim of the University of Pumbeditha, in Babylonia. He was Gaon from 967 to 997. His father was 'Hanina Gaon and his son was Haÿ Gaon, Co-gaon with him from 987. Haÿ was full Gaon from 997 to 1037 A. D.

† Comp. Ezekiel i, 10.

‡ Talmud, Treatise *'Ha'geegah* 13. § *Ibid.*

|| Also in the Talmud Treatise, *'Ha'geegah*, which is here called Midrash in the sense of *de 'rashah, i. e.*, exposition.

inferences and conclusions from teachings received, in silence, *i. e.*, secret, such a one is worthy of receiving Mysteries of the Thorah, given him *in silence, i. e., in secret.* Therefore the sages imparted one to the other, the knowledge of physiognomy and the lineaments of the features,* which

No. 1.

No. 2.

*The Zohar treats on physiognomy quite fully. Human countenances are divided into four primordial types of faces such as appeared at the Chariot Throne or *Ma-a'seh Merkabah* of Ezekiel's vision, chap. i, 10–the face of a man, lion, ox and eagle, and it says: our faces resemble these according to the rank which the soul occupies in the intellectual or moral worlds. "Physiognomy," it says, "does not consist in the external lineaments, but in the features which are mysteriously drawn within us. The features of the face vary, following the form which is impressed on the inward face (or presence) of the spirit. The spirit only produces all those physiognomical peculiarities, which the Wise know: and it is through the spirit that they (the features) have any meaning. When the spirits and souls go out of Eden, *i. e.*, the Place of the Supreme Wisdom, they have entirely a certain form which later reflects itself in the face." It then treats of the different forms of forehead, face, etc., and their indications. Comp. on this Zohar ii, 71*b*, 75*a*, 73*b*. In the Neurological System of Anthropology, etc., by Dr. Jos. R. Buchanan, Cincinnati, 1854, Part iv, on Sarcognomy, a curious theory is advanced, in regard to the sympathy existing between the different parts of the human body and the inner spiritual man, and that one may judge of the inner man from the outward shape. We give two Hindu symbolic pictures, which are of interest in this connexion, from Niklas Müller's *Glauben, Wissen und Kunst der alten Hindus, Erster Band, Mainz,* 1822. Tab. I, figures 112 and 113; and refer the reader to figures 12 and 110 on the same plate, and Tab. II, figure 59. Compare also Dan vii, and *La Clef des Grand Mystères suivant, Henoch, Abraham, Hermès Trismégistus, et Salomon, par Eliphas Lévi (l' Abbé Alphonse Louis Constant).* Paris, 1861, p. 443 *et seq.*

No. 1. Is a Brahma image, with its four principles, and four wings encircled three times by Ananta or Shesha, the Serpent of Eternity. In this we find the prototype of the symbols of the Divine perfection as in the symbols of the Merkabah, *i. e.*, Chariot Throne, and of the four Evangelists. The four figures represent the four Vedas. Here we have the Eagle of St. John, the all-piercing eye, also the sublimated ether, the spirit; the Bull of St. Luke, the all-generating, also the sublimated water or humidity ; the Lion of St. Mark, the symbol of unrestrained strength and potentiality, the sublimated fire; and the Human Face, the symbol of St. Matthew, the fruition of the Intellect of the Supreme Brahman, *neuter.*

are partly communicated in: 'this is the book of the 'generations of man,' (Gen. v, 1) and partly in the next verse: 'male-female created he them.'" This is the answer of Rab She'reerah Gaon, Head-master of this great Babylonian Jewish school, which Nachmanides quotes in his Commentary on the Thorah, adding these words: "We have not been able to reach that far."* So the Babylonian Rabbenu Hag-gaon Abraham,†

No 2. Is similar to the former, only that the five potentialities of Brahman, *neuter*, are given in animal types. Man is the symbol of wisdom, the Lion of strength, the Eagle of ubiquity, the Bull of the generative potentiality in its highest idea, and the Goat as sensual affection. The animals have wings to signify their divine character, the human figure as the symbol of Brahman, is surrounded by a halo. We also refer the student to the valuable article in Kitto's Cyclop. Biblical Liter., Ed. 1876, i, pp. 484–493; Handbook of Christian Symbolism, by W. & G. Audsley, London, pp. 97–110; *Histoire et Théorie du Symbolisme Religieux avant et depuis le Christianisme*, etc., par *M. l'Abbé Auber*, Paris, 1870–72, 4 vol., 8vo; Symbols and Emblems of Early and Mediæval Christian Art, by Louisa Twining, London, 1852, 4to; Christian Art and Symbolism, by R. St. J. Tyrwhitt, London, 1872; *Œuvres de Saint Denys l'Aréopagite traduites du Grec en Français*, etc., par *l'Abbé J. Dulac*, Paris, 1865, 8vo, p. 390–1, 385, 328. St. Dionysius does not appear to know of the creatures we have named as symbolical of the four evangelists. St. Dionysius has done much, through his writings, to bring into early orthodox Christianity the doctrines of the Hebrew and Jewish Qabbalah. St. Synesius—flour. *circa* 370–413 A. D.—surnamed the Philosopher, in his writing, On Dreams—404 A. D.—also shows considerable knowledge of the Qabbalah. Jerome Cardan has written a long commentary upon the "Dreams." The doctrine of sympathy between the spiritual man, his body, etc., and all parts of the universe, as the affinity between the Makrokosm and Mikrokosm, was taught by the learned among the archaic Hindus, Chinese, Egyptians, Chaldeans, Hebrews, Greeks, etc., and by Moses, Pythagoras, Plato, Aristotle, the Qabbalists, Neo-platonists, etc. It appears in a number of places in the New Testament. It is the doctrine of the Paradigmatic Celestial Ideation, or the Perfect Upper Heavenly Man and the visible Terrestrial realization. The Perfect Kingdom or Place, of the Deity, the Celestial and Heavenly Government, and its imperfect shadow, the visible universe in its entirety. The Ideal Kingdom of God and the Kingdom of the visible matter-world. Compare also the Moreh Ne'bookheem, Vol. iii, p. 1 *et seq*., i, c. lxxii.

* These matters are further enlarged upon in the Zohar § Yithroh. *i. e.*, Exod. xviii to xx, and in the Zohar 'Hadash in the same place, and in the Tiqqoonim, *i. e.*, Rules (or Regulations) of the Zohar, Tiqqoon. 70. The Tiqqooneh Zohar was edited and printed as early as Novem. 9, 1557, 4to, Mantua, by Jacob b. Naphtali, and compiled by Imm. di Benevento after an MSS.

† Quoted by Luriah, p. 12, note 1.

says: "And as they imparted these secrets, only to persons considered worthy by *virtue of the signs mentioned*, we will tell you that we deem you worthy in our heart, but we cannot impart them to you before you have lived *the life of a recluse for fully three years;* in the meanwhile we pray that heaven may enlighten your eyes, etc." The initiated only imparted Qabbalistic matters to men personally known to them as discreet, intelligent and worthy of such a distinction, and then only under promise of secrecy. The same idea is in the Zohar § Yithroh.,* that every feature, of the (man's) face, shows whether he may be initiated or not, into these sublime divine secrets, and into matters of magic,† concerning which the Gaon Rab She'reerah, writes: "Under penalty of excommunication, it is forbidden to reveal these matters except to reliable persons, and only to such whose physiognomy speaks in their favour." So as to the pronunciation of the Ineffable Name YHVH, the Shem Hamme'phorash or Tetragrammaton, pronounced only by the High Priest on the Day of Atonement, She'reerah says: "It was delivered by Qabbalah only to the Heads of the College," not to all, but only to the Heads of the *Ye'sheebah*. It appears, from his "Responses," that Haÿ Gaon imparted some of this Secret Science to a trusted few of his contemporaries, who lived at a great distance from Babylonia, and most probably this included parts of the Zohar and the Hidden (*Hanne-e'lam*) Midrash. As it is stated in the beginning of the Tiqqooneh haz-Zohar‡ that the book Zohar has existed from immemorial time at Fez in Africa, § we may assume that it most likely came there from the men who imbibed a knowledge of it from Rab Haÿ, the Gaon of the sages of Chirvan, on the Caspian sea, and from Rab Nissim and the other great theosophists of the Babylonian schools, who obtained their knowledge from very old sources, either Semitic or the archaic Aryan Wisdom religion of Central Asia. This secrecy accounts for any differences in the first published versions

* Comp. Zohar ii, 71*b*, 73*b*, 75*a*.

† Magic had a very different meaning in early times, from that which it has acquired since the Middle Ages, in the minds of most modern readers. Comp. Franz von Hartman's, Black and White Magic, 2nd Ed., London, 1886.

‡ Amsterdam Ed., 1718, by Prophos.

§ Some writers state, that originally the complete Zohar was more than a camel's load. Most of it has been lost or destroyed.

of the Zoharic writings, and also for the late period at which the learned world had any knowledge of these secret and revered writings. Further, as regards the name "Ye'rushalmi," by which the Zoharic writings are called, though several of the earlier sages used to call the Midrashim thus, the Ge'onim did not, but called them by their respective names; they also did not call the actual Talmud Ye'rushalmi, by that name, but "Talmud of the *B'nai Ma-arbah, i. e.*, Talmud of the Sons of the West" or "Talmud *ehretz* (land of) Yisra-el," with but few exceptions. The Talmud Ye'rushalmi was edited, by the pupils of R. Yo'ha'nan ben Eliezer (d. 279), in the school of Tiberias, on Lake Gennezareth, 45 miles north of Jerusalem, and not in the latter city. It was not compiled into its present written form until the latter half of the IV century A. D. The Babylonian Talmud, or the Babli, was composed principally in the V century, from old oral sources, by Rab Ashi bar Simaï (d. 427 A. D.), Head Master of the Academy at Sora. He did not complete it. Its final redaction was by R. Yosseh, the last of the A'mora-im, and really belongs to the VI century A. D. The Talmuds are compends of the Halakha, and written legal digests of the oral common law or customs and ritual, of the Israelites; they were not compiled as exponents of their religious metaphysical or natural philosophy. The Babylonian is four-fold larger than the Ye'rushalmi, and is called *ShaS** by the Jews, who prefer it to the Palestinian. The latter, which is shorter, also more difficult to understand, has been preferred by Christian Orientalists, but the Babli is the most important.

The The'na-im were altogether from Palestine. In the time of R. Yo'-ha'nan, Jerusalem was not a seat of learning for the Palestinian Jews, but Tiberias was. R. Shim-on b. Yo'haï's school was near Jerusalem,† this would account for the productions from that school having the name, "Midrash Ye'rushalmi." Luriah asserts through quotation, that the Zohar was known to R. Ne'hunÿah, the pious, of Jerusalem, who delivered a great many Qabbalistic discussions, which were arranged for him since the days of the The'na-im, and these were the Zohar, and when he brought the Zohar and Qabbalistic Midrashim along with him from Jerusalem, they obtained the name, "Ye'rushalmi." The book Bahir, is also

---

* The initials of *Shishah Se'darim, i. e.*, Six arranged books.

† *Ante*, p. 19.

called "Yerushalmi," in a commentary written by the great Qabbalist R. Azriel (or Ezrah), pupil of R. Yehudah, son of R A Ba D, on Canticles.* Recanati quotes sentences as from "Ye'rushalmi" and at first thought they were in the Talmud Ye'rushalmi, but they were in the book Bahir, which he afterwards discovered. The Bahir was called thus because it came from Palestine and Jerusalem.

Branch III. Luriah in this, shows by quotations from older writings, that the ideas in the Zoharic writings were in existence long prior to the redaction and publication of the Talmudim. He gives these statements with great care and exactness, quotation after quotation, but they are too extensive to give in this writing.

In Branch IV, Luriah gives logical inferences so as to show, that the origins of many portions of the Zohar were contemporaneous with the period of R. Shim-on b. Yo'haï. He cites the prediction as to the sovereignty which is to arise for the "Sons of Yishmaël," the Arabs, after 400 years, and that they should then have possession of the holy land. Omar, Khalif of the Arabs, conquered Jerusalem and the holy land about 637 A. D.—397 of the fifth thousand. This was 569 years after the destruction of the second Temple, which took place 173 before the close of the fourth thousand of years, and Luriah shows this statement is a proof of the antiquity of the Zohar. He also says: in the Zohar § *Shemoth* (Exod: 1 *sqq*) 6*c*, we read: "R. Eliezer b. R. Shim-on, said: A Roman king will conduct to and lead over the land of Egypt a government of severity, and appoint armed princes over it." This actually occurred in the days of R. Eliezer b. R. Shim-on, who was contemporary with Rabbi; viz: when Antoninus, the Roman Emperor waged war against Egypt. The Talmud says,† that one of Joseph's treasuries was shown to Antoninus ben Asverus‡ after the conquest of Egypt, in the days of Rabbi and R. Eliezer b. R. Shim-on.§

Luriah says, those who object to the antiquity of the Zohar, say,

* P. 20*d*, Altona Ed. It has been incorrectly ascribed to Nachmanides.
† Treatise *Pe'sa'him*, c. x, p. 119.
‡ L. Aurelius Verus, b. 130 A.D., Emperor with M. Aurelius, of the Roman Empire, 161 to 169 A. D.
§ Comp. the book *Me'khiltha*, in the Para'shah of the Song on the Red Sea, 87.

4

that the modern author went cunningly to work in shaping matters of the past, and described them as if going to happen in the future, the authors of the Zohar had not any such deceptions in view, if such attempts had been in their minds, then, if modern, they or he, would surely have been more careful in wording and quoting that which subsequently appears in the Talmud. "And the great men, says Luriah, who at and after Moses de Leon's time, read and understood the Zohar with reverence, did not discover the forgery, not even that in his endeavors to strengthen his own inventions, he (M. d. L.) overdid it to his own injury; but it was reserved to the modern quarrelers to discover the fraud and expose it, but no fair-minded man or impartial thinker, will agree with them." He asserts, that the period of the The'na-im (200 B. C. to 200 A. D.) prior to the close of the Talmud, was the age of the birth of the Zohar, that it is highly probable that the very essence of the Zoharic writings was prepared during their time, and during and after that of R. Shim-on b. Yo'haï, by his disciple, the Babylonian writer R. Abbah, as will be shown hereafter. But there are also discussions in the book Zohar, which took place in the school of R. Shim-on b. Yo'haï* by his pupils and the pupils of his pupils, at the time of the A'mora-im; which are quoted by the scholars as the "Learnings in the Beth-Hammidrash of R. Shim-on b. Yo'haï," and these received in some parts slight additions by subsequently initiated Wise-men. Luriah says "This occurs in all the books of the The'na-im, which we now possess, and is especially evident in the Zoharic book, Midrash Hanne-e'lam; the majority of the authorities therein cited being of the A'mora-im, it surely dates from those times, (which were prior to the closing of the Talmud.)" The Gaon R. Abraham, called by the Jews, our great Rabbi, says, "this was his opinion." Luriah then gives numerous authorities proving his assertions.

Branch V. Concerning the Aramaic language in the Zohar. As to this, he says, the modern quarrelers argue, that in the times of the The'na-im, matters relating to the Thorah were written in the Hebrew, like the Mishnah, Thosephthah and all the Midrashim of the Thorah; the Aramaic having been in those days the vernacular, which was not used in re-

* Likely that at Tekû'a; *ante*, p. 19.

ligious writings, and especially not, in writing the Mysteries of the Thorah. This branch also treats of the style, diction and tenor, of the Zohar and Zoharic books. He says, it is evident from the Zohar, that the writer who took down R. Shim-on b. Yo'haï's oral teachings, was Rabbi Abbah. The Master R. Shim-on says in the Idrah Zootah * " R. Abbah shall write;" and at the close of the Idrah Zootah is: "R. Abbah said: I wrote, believing to have to write much, etc.," and also in the Zohar,† "I wrote from the sacred lamp (*i. e.*, R. S. b. Y.), etc." ‡ This R. Abbah was a Babylonian, and as such, thoroughly conversant with the Chaldee or Aramaic language, as all the Babylonians were; consequently he wrote the Zohar in his own language, which was also that used by the Wisemen of Babylonia, who occupied themselves in these matters, and who much more than those of Palestine gave attention to mysticism. The Babylonian Jews also gave considerable attention to the Practical Qabbalah.§ He was the same R. Abbah, who is mentioned in the Zohar as a

* Zohar § *Ha-a'zeenu*, *i. e.*, Deut. xxxii, p. 287*b*.

† Para'shath, *Mishpatim*, *i. e.*, Exod. xxi–xxv, p. 123*b*.

‡ The Idrah Zootah, says: (Zohar, Mantua Ed., § *Ha-a'zeenu*, Vol. iii, 287*b*; Cremona Ed., part iii, fol. 140, col. 557 *et seq.*); when the companions were gathered together in the house of R. Shim-on, and he arranged his words of departure, he, R. Shim-on, said:—" Now this is my arrangement concerning you, *R. Abbah shall be the scribe, and my son El'azar shall set forth my views*, but the others shall meditate in their hearts. R. Abbah arose from the place behind him, and R. El'azar his son sat down in front of him. He said to him: Arise, my son, for some one else shall sit in that place, and R. El'azar arose. R. Shim-on having veiled his head, sat down, began and said." Further, " R. Abbah, said: Scarcely had the sacred lamp finished the word 'life,' when his words ceased. But *I was writing, and thinking I was to write more*, heard nothing. I did not however raise my head, because the light was too much, and up to this time I had not been able to look in that direction. I trembled therefore, when I heard a voice," etc. (*Ibid.*, Mantua Ed., fol. 296. Cremona Ed., col. 599.)

§ Comp. Layard's Discoveries in the Ruins of Nineveh and Babylon, etc. New York, 1853, pp. 509–526. Bowls similar to those mentioned, may be seen in the Metropolitan Museum of Art, New York City. *Essai sur la propagation de l'Alphabet Phénicien dans l'ancien monde, par* François Lenormant. Paris. 1875, Vol. i, pp. 271 *et seq.*, and Wessely in The Expositor, No. XXI, Sept., 1886, 3d series, pp. 194–204. On the Spread of Jewish-Christian Ideas among the Egyptians, which shows the early Ebionites gave attention to the Practical Qabbalah.

Babylonian, and as superior to R. 'Heeÿah, but he is of course not the R. Abbah of the Babylonian Talmud. R. Abbah was especially selected by R. Shim-on b. Yo'haï to write down his words, because of his attainments as a student and a master, both in the Qabbalah and the Chaldaic language, a language spoken and understood by all the students of the occult science, the Divine Qabbalah. Abbah's father-in-law appears to have been a resident of the Babylonian city called Tarsha, which was also called Sora, in which was a celebrated Jewish Academy of Science and seat of Theosophical Secret Learning. It was the residence of many of the friends and companions of R. Shim-on and his colleagues. The colleagues or companions in Babylonia, were, as is stated in the Zohar, very careful to conceal the mysteries of the Secret Knowledge, the Qabbalah, under a peculiarity of language, terms and phraseology, and by symbols, so that they could study and converse on the mysteries in even a public assembly, in a language and by methods understood by the initiates, and adapted to conceal the precious mystical doctrines, from the mental grasp of the uninitiated, the ignorant and foolish masses around them, and so keep their pearls from the swine, who would have trampled them under their feet, and then perhaps, have turned and destroyed the masters in the Secret Science.* This is frequently set forth in the Zohar, and its justice and wisdom must be appreciated even to this day, by the learned. The open revelation of R. Shim-on b. Yo'haï's wisdom was too sublime for the general public, to be given in an open language intelligible to everybody; this appears in the Talmud.† R. A'keebah, the master of R. Shim-on, said to the latter: "It may suffice that I and thy creator know thy power," which means, it is not advisable to reveal thy doctrine and great wisdom to the public. Hence R. Shim-on chose R. Abbah to do the writing, and as to whom in another place in the Zohar he says; ‡ "Abbah! Abbah! loosen the knot and consign this to thy bag." Loosen the knot wherewith thou hast already tied fast the mysteries received, and receive also this additional mystery, to

* Comp. Matt. vii, 6; Acts xiii, 45–52; John xvi, 12, 25, 29; Mark iv, 2, 11, 12, 33, 34; Luke viii, 10; Matt. xiii, 34, 35.

† Treatise *Sanhedrin*, c. i.

‡ Comp. Para'shath *Pe'qudeh*, Exod. xxxviii sqq.

hide it among the rest, in thy collection. This systematic secrecy became a line of guidance to the companions in Babylonia, and they transmitted it to the generations of Ge'onim who came after them, binding them to strictly observe it in all the times to come. The Zohar is written in the Aramaic, the Targumatic language, and the Targums themselves are mystical; to intimate that it is not delivered for a revelation of its contents to mankind in general, but is covered in its appearance, as it really is, and is in the dress of the lower degrees, that of the "*a'horayim*, *i.e.*, the hinder or back part, as distinguished from the face or front, the Sacred or Hebrew tongue; in other words, the doctrine contained in the Zohar is the manifestation of God by the exterior or visible word, but the divinely mystical and concealed, is to be ascertained and read between the lines of the same.* As the Gaon R. Abraham, called the Great Rabbi, states in his Commentary on the Siphrah D'Tznioothah, at the end, "Even in our age we have only been able to reach to the heel of the World of 'A'see-yah, *i. e.*, the World of Action or Making, the lowest; hence the great number of skeptical adversaries, etc., and whatever we speak in regard to Adam Qadmon, *i. e.*, the Primordial Ideation Adam, and of A'tzeelah, *i. e.*, World of Emanation, of Bree-ah, *i. e.*, World of Creation, of Ye'tzee-rah, *i. e.*, World of Formation, and of A'see-yah, continually takes place in all the Worlds of the universe; and so all the investigations are in conformity therewith and merely investigations of the extreme *a'hora-yim*, *i. e.*, back, and not clearly defined; hence the parabolical and allegorical language, which the opponents (the uninitiated) do not in any way understand." The same is in Daniel. Its beginning is in Hebrew, like all the writings of the Prophets, till chapter ii, 4, where "the Chaldeans spoke to the king in Aramaic," for that which follows are the words spoken in the presence of the king, the words of the kings and the dreams are written in Aramaic, in the tongue in which they were spoken. So in Ezra iv, v and vi, the words of the kings being there literally quoted, all matters connected therewith are in Aramaic. In Daniel, the words of the Prophet are in Hebrew, as was usual with the words of all the Prophets, except

* Comp. Exod. xxxiii, 23. A similar word in Latin, is *Tergum*, the back, that opposite to the face or front.

in the vii chapter, where Daniel's dream is related in Aramaic, the recital of the dream over, the language again is in Hebrew. This Luriah explains, as in full accord with that which he has before stated. Another reason for the Aramaic may be, the Siphrah D'Tznioothah and the Idroth Rabbah and Zootah, contain the fundamental principles of the entire Qabbalah, being, as it were, the Mishnah of the Zohar, and their very starting point is in Daniel, and in the verse "The Ancient of Days did sit, and his garment was like white snow, and the whiteness of the hair of his head like pure wool." These words being the basis of these three books are, so to speak, the text of the whole, and as they are in Aramaic, the whole structure, in conformity with this basis, is in Aramaic also, hence the Aramaic language of the Zohar. The Qabbalistic matters are discussed in other books in Aramaic, as in the *Sepher Ham-maggid i.e.*, the Reporter to the Beth Yoseph, and in the book *B'rith Me'nu-'hah, i.e.*, Covenant of Rest, so in many other books. Much more is said by David Luriah which space prevents our giving, but until the writings of Luriah and Konitz are fully disproved, most of the contents of the Zohar and Zoharic books may be considered, as indeed is evident from a comparison of their style and content, with the Sacred Books of other Oriental peoples, to be very ancient.

The language of the Zoharic writings sometimes elevates itself to much grandeur of thought, but in other places it descends to sentiments and ideas which reveal puerility, and alongside of ideas which by their simplicity and enthusiasm, take rank with the highest period of Hebrew intellectuality as we find it in the Old Testament, is a knowledge which approaches the ignorance of its lowest period. In its contents we will however, discover much in accord with the Archaic Oriental thought-world, especially that of Mesopotamia, Persia, India, Egypt and China, as we now have their ancient literature in fragments. The two Talmuds do not mention the Zoharic writings by name, but frequently refer to the Secret Learning and to ideas, which we find in them; so also many of the formulations to be found in the Talmudim are to be found in the Zoharic writings.

III.

ANTIQUITY OF THE ZOHARIC WRITINGS, CONTINUED. OBJECTIONS TO THEIR ANTIQUITY BY DR. HIRSCH GRAETZ, DR. CHRISTIAN D. GINSBURG AND OTHERS, CONSIDERED. SOME QUOTATIONS FROM THE ZOHARIC WRITINGS, ELUCIDATING PASSAGES IN THE NEW AND OLD TESTAMENTS.

WE will now cite from some additional authors upon the subject: "The Zohar of which the rays enlighten the world, which contains the most profound mysteries of the Thorah and Qabbalah, is not the work of R. Shim-on ben Yo'haï, although it has been published under his name; but it is from his words that it has been redacted by his disciples, who themselves intrusted to other (subsequent) disciples the care of continuing their task. The words of the Zohar, from them, are most conformable to the truth, written as they are by men who have lived sufficiently late to know the Mishnah, and all the decisions, and precepts of the Oral Law. This book was not divulged until after the death of R. Moses ben Na'hman, or Nachmanidés,* and R. Asher, who have not known it." †

A dispute has arisen as to the versions of the Yu'hasin. Franck ‡ used the version of Cracow. A version was printed in 1566 at Constantinople.

---

* Flourished *circa* 1200–*circa* 1272.

† Sepher Yu'hasin, *i. e.*, Book of the Genealogies, pp. 42–43, translated from the French, as given by Franck, *La Kabbale*, p. 92. The author of this book was R. Moses Abraham b. Samuel Zakut or Sacuto. He was living at Saragossa in 1492. Compare Jerusalem and Tiberias, by J. W. Etheridge. London. 1856. pp. 451–2. *Lehrbuch der jüdischen Geschichte und Literatur von David Cassel*. Leipzig. 1879. pp. 330, 397, 449. *Geschichte der jüdischen Literatur von Gustav Karpeles*. Berlin. 1886. p. 863, *sqq*. John Christ. Wolf, *Bibliotheca Hebræa*, Vol. i, p. 104 *et seq.*

‡ *La Kabbale*, p. 92, etc.

E. Carmoly * takes Franck to task for not using the edition of 1566, and gives an alleged version of that edition in French. † Dr. Hirsch Graetz ‡ gives a version in Hebrew, from the reprint of the Constantinople edition, by Filipowski, London, 1857, of this Dr. Christian D. Ginsburg,§ gives a very one-sided and mutilated translation. Dr. Graetz's quotation in Hebrew, is much more extensive and favorable to the antiquity of the Zohar, than Carmoly's French translation. Since then, Heinrich Ellenberger has taken Dr. Graetz to task for his unfair arguments against the Qabbalah and the Zohar,‖ and among other things, says: " The appeal by Dr. Graetz to the Sepher Yu'hasin, where it says: p. 42: ' He (Shim-on b. Yo'haï) has not made the Zohar,' is not tenable, for in the following sentence it, the Sepher Yu'hasin, says: ' But his disciples, his son, and the disciples of his disciples, were the authors according to the tradition descended to them!'" The whole passage quoted by Dr. Graetz from the book Yu'hasin, ed. 1857, London, is one of the main points against the antiquity of the Zohar, yet Dr. Graetz is compelled in his history to say :¶ "How the credibility of Isaac of Acco has contented itself with these evidences, cannot be decided, as the end is missing. *Apparently he was in the end convinced of the genuineness of the Zohar, as he wove into his (book) Me'-irath Enaÿim, i. e., Enlightenment of the Eyes, many Zoharistic ideas.*" In the statement above cited Isaac of Acco is alleged to have said: that R. Moses de Leon told him at Valladolid in Spain, under oath, that he, de Leon, had the book Zohar in MSS. at his home in Avila, and would show it to him there. R. Moses de Leon started for his home, but on the way, died at Arevolo. Then Isaac goes to Avila, where he meets a relative of de Leon, but evidently an enemy, named R. David Rafon of Corfu, who says: " R. M. de Leon is a spendthrift, who earns a great deal of money from his writings, but

* *Itinéraires de la Terre Sainte des xiii, xiv, etc., siècle. Bruxelles.* 1847. p. 272 *et seq.*

† *Ibid.*

‡ *Geschichte der Juden,* vii, p. 490 *et seq.*

§ The Kabbalah, etc. London. 1865. pp. 90–91.

‖ *Offenbarung, Kabbalah, Magnetismus und Spiritismus, etc.* Buda-Pesth, 1880, p. 19.

¶ Work cited, vii, p. 492.

makes up the Zohar out of his head, and he treats his wife and daughter badly." Finding de Leon had died, Isaac, with the assistance of a wealthy man, R. Joseph di Avila and his wife, tries to surreptitiously get the MSS. of the Zohar, from the widow and daughter of de Leon, but is not successful. He then leaves Avila and goes to Talavera, and at that place meets " R. Joseph Hallevy, son of Todros, the Qabbalist," and asks him about the Zohar. The latter says: " Know thou and believe, that the Zohar by R. Shim-on ben Yo'haï was in the hands of R. Moses, who copied from it for whomsoever he liked," and tells Isaac, how he, Joseph, had conclusively proved this fact. Isaac then goes to Toletola (Toledo) where he "learned from some of the scholars, that they had seen an old man and prominent disciple of R. Moses de Leon, of the name of R. Jacob, who testified by heaven and earth, *that the book Zohar, of which R. Shim-on b. Yo'haï is the author—*" This ends the statement. It must be noted that it commences " R. Isaac of (the city of) Acco (in which the Jews were massacred 1291 A.D.) was in Novara, in Italy, after the capture of Acco, from which he escaped, where he heard that there was in Spain a Rabbin in possession of the book Zohar; and having written a Qabbalistic book himself, he was anxious to see the Zohar *written by R. Shim-on b. Yo'haï, and R. El'azar, his son, in a cavern.**

"*If it is written in the Ye'rushalmetic idiom, he says, it is genuine*, but if in Hebrew not." Then he, Isaac, went to Spain. "At last I learned that Moses Nachmanides had sent the book (Zohar) from Palestine to Catalonia to his son, but the wind carried it (the ship) to Aragonia (some say to Alicante) where the book fell into the hands of R. Moses de Leon." We must not forget, Moses de Leon, born 1250, died 1305. Carmoly says: "Here is what we find in the edition of Constantinople, year 5053 A. M., 1293 A. D. I do not cite the page because the first edition is not paged, the spoken of R. Moses de Leon was living at the time (1293)." † The statement in Yu'hasin also refers to a period after de

---

* This statement of itself is curious, there is nothing in the Zohar to show that it was written in a cavern. The cavern was only the place in which they studied and hid themselves during the Roman proscription. The next statement is equally strange; indeed, the whole passage in Yu'hasin bears the appearance of untruth.

† Carmoly says M. d. Leon died 1293. *Itinéraires*, etc., p. 278.

Leon's death, 1305-1293 = 12 years. How does this accord with the account?

Isaac of Acco was a disciple of Nachmanides, and wrote little treatises on the miracles he performed as a Practical Qabbalist, by means of the transposition and combination of the letters of the Hebrew alphabet, which system he alleged he had learned from angels, who came to him with revelations of mysteries. He has had much to do with that part of the Practical Qabbalah, which asserts that wondrous results will follow from the use, by the adepts, of the Hebrew holy Names of the Deity.*

Of the book "Yu'hasin," edition of Constantinople, 1566, Jost says:† "It is more complete than the Cracow and Amsterdam editions, *but incorrect, and to be used only with the greatest circumspection.*" Concerning the reproduction of Acco's story in the Mitpa'hath Se'pharim, by Yabetz, which we have before mentioned, R. Azulaï in his *Ma-a'rekheth Se'pharim*, 2nd part of the book, of which the 1st is called *Ma-a'rekheth ge'dolim*, and above cited; p. 20a, heading Zohar, says: "In looking over the contents of the Mitpa-hath Se'pharim, which I recently received, I was astonished to find, that the Than-nah (R. S. b. Yo'haï) should be asserted as not the author of any part of the Zohar, whereas our 'lions of the Thorah,' R. Moses d. Cordovero and R. Yitz'haq Luriah, most strenuously contradict this, and are followed by many exalted saints. Therefore it seems to me, that also the Rabbi (Yabetz) himself was aware of the contents of the Zohar to be truth and perfection, but in *his zeal against that accursed set of transgressors of the statutes of the Beth Din, which 'clings to the various expressions of the Zohar in a false and lying way,' he chose to oppose it, in order to crush them,* for God's sake!" which view seems indeed very plausible. As regards the re-publication of Isaac of Acco's story by a R. Elikom of Se'mila, in his book Rabiyah, at Ofen (Buda Pesth), 1837, we may remark that it contains alterations which suffice to show little dependence can be placed upon it. If we take the account from Yu'hasin, we have the following results:

1. R. Isaac of Acco, believes in the antiquity and authenticity of that part of the Zohar written in Aramaic, and that it comes from R. S. b. Yo'haï, and his school.

* See *Ma-a'rekheth ge'dolim*, by Azulaï, 47*b*.
† *Allgem. Geschichte d. Jüdischen Volkes*, Vol. ii, p. 420.

2. He was familiar with the existence of the book whilst in Novara, about 1291 A. D., during the life-time of M. d. Leon, and from the statement just formulated, appears to have had knowledge of the Zohar in Syria.

3. He goes to Spain, to inquire how this book by R. S. b. Yo'haï has become known in his time.

4. Among the conflicting statements was also that of the alleged spuriousness of the book.

5. He meets R. M. d. Leon in Valadolid, *who, on his oath*, assures him that he, M. de L., possesses the original book of the Zohar, and was *perfectly willing to show it to him*, when he would visit Avila. This was shortly before M. d. Leon's death (1305 A. D.), *at which time* the Zohar was so well known, and so thoroughly studied in countries foreign to Spain, that the belief in M. d. Leon's authorship stands on a par with the statement in Yu'hasin, that he wrote it under the guidance of the *Shem ko-theb, i. e.*, the Writing Name, or the angel superintending writing.

6. The old man, R. David Raphon Ke'robo or Daphon Korpo, or Rafon of Corfu, who knew so much as to be able to say, "that the book Zohar does not anywhere exist," is an imaginary figure in the story.

7. The trick that Isaac endeavored to play on the widow and orphan, with the aid of R. Joseph the rich man of Avila and his wife, is weak, and seems to have too many women mixed up with it.

8. Is it possible that the very M. d. Leon, who, according to this account, neglected his wife and daughter, should have taken them into the secret of the fraud he was daily committing, to get money to spend and throw away upon himself without giving them any support?

9. If the wife and daughter did disclose this secret, why did they not show the MSS. *written by M. d. Leon himself?* Why did the astute rich man and the deceitful Rabbi not ask for it, so that they might be sure of the forgeries and expose them?

10. Who has ever seen this large MSS.? Where is it?

11. The ending of the account in Yu'hasin is very strange, very suspicious. The whole story is only hearsay, weak, and crumbles into nothing, like the other futile objections made against the antiquity of the Zohar.

It is alleged by those who say that Moses de Leon forged the Zohar, that the five books undoubtedly written by M. d. L., do not show any literary merit, that he does not in any of them enter into the depth or spirit of the Qabbalah, that he was even deficient in a knowledge of the Talmudim. That M. d. L. traveled very much in his life, having lived in Guadalah, Vevira, Valladolid and lastly in Avila; that he was a great spendthrift, and very fond of worldly enjoyments, and he was so poor that he was continually compelled to write for his daily bread. M. d. L. first wrote the *Shushan Ha-edooth, i. e.*, Lily of the Testimony, 1285; then the *Sepher Ha-rimmon, i. e.*, The Book of the Pomegranate, 1287; three years later, 1290, the *Nephesh Hah-'hokhmah, i. e.*, The Soul of Wisdom, also called, *Sepher Ham-mishqal, i. e.*, The Book of the Balance, which has been published in Basle, 1608. *Sepher Sheqel Haq-qodesh, i. e.*, Book of the Sacred Shekel, 1292. *Sepher Has-sodoth, i.e.*, Book of the Secrets, *Mishkan Ha-edooth, i. e.*, Tabernacle of the Testimony, 1293. He appears to have also written a *Sepher has-Shem.** These were written in Hebrew, but the Zohar and Zoharic books are mostly in the Aramaic. Here we have numerous books written by this alleged superficially learned man, and this ignoramus has also, it is said, the ability to write the immense and very learned book on the Secret Learning, the Zohar, and the other books bound up with it. The books we have quoted as by M. d. L. were written by him, between 1285 and 1293, the period when the opponents of the antiquity of the Zohar say, the author was living a reckless life, traveling from place to place. Let us admit he was one year preparing the first book, it then took nine years for him to write these works in Hebrew, the language in which the Jewish learned men of this period usually wrote, the exception being the Arabic. They never wrote books at this time in Aramaic, but understood it as the language of the Talmudim. The Zohar is a voluminous work, larger than all the books admitted to be by M. de Leon put together, and they took nine years for their composition, and it would have taken, had he the ability to have written it, twelve to fifteen years

* Comp. Pardes Rimmonun by R. Moses Cordovero, fol. 110a, col. 1, in *Sha-ar has-Shemoth, i. e.*, Gate of the Names, and *Sha-ar hat-Tsinnoroth, i. e.*, Gate of the Channels or canals.

to have written the Zohar. M. d. L. died 1305, and he would have to have begun it about 1290. Then he did not only write it in this time, but according to Drs. Graetz, Jellinek, and Ginsburg, he "copied and sold it, to rich and learned men at a high price." Now the art of printing was not yet invented, yet a book written in Avila, in Spain, and then secretly copied only by the author, for sale, occupies a prominent place in the libraries of the rich and learned of other cities of Spain, Italy and even Germany, at almost the same time. The rich were all ready to pay M. d. L. money for his uncertain forged wares, the learned were too credulous and too ignorant to discover his fraud, and expose the forger. What a slur upon the learning of the Rabbins of the XIIIth and XIVth centuries, who were led astray by this prodigal, this unlearned and inferior writer, who was of such bad reputation and of such an equivocal standing in the learned world around him! The opposers also strangely assert, that all passages where the name of "Moses" is expressed or mysteriously indicated, are evidence that M. d. L. *wanted the intelligent reader to understand, that he, M. d. L., was the author of Zohar*, and yet wanted to pass it off as the genuine work of R. Shim-on b. Yo'haï. The learned historian, Dr. J. M. Jost says:* "The passion for systems aroused by the school of Aristotle, and the production of many works on the philosophy of ethics and theosophy by the Rabbis in general, seized the minds of the adherents of Occult Science very vividly, especially during the Crusades. The Kabbalah began to be written down, and the book Zohar, *in its present form*, a production of the XII century, represented the Kabbalah more extensively in the usual way. The difficulty in the understanding of the symbols and the terms therein, excited the activity of many Rabbins, especially of Spain and France." He also says:† "Whether the books, referred to in the Zohar, be merely fictitious is not decided; the work contains the most sublime symbolism and develops in a very inferior language, and through an excessive amount of symbolization of the Jewish Laws, as well as of visible nature, *an uncommonly profound religious doctrine, which it was the intention to protect by that thick veil.*"

Another writer, Gedalyah ibn Yachia ben Don Yosef, of Imola (*circa*

* *Geschichte d. Jüdischen Volkes*, ii, p. 293.
† *Ibid.* p. 123.

1523-1588), in his *Shalsheleth haq-Qabbalah, i. e.*, Chain of Tradition, begun at Ravenna, 1549, says:* "Towards the end of the year 5050 of the Creation (1290 A.D.), several persons existed, who asserted that all the parts of the Zohar, written in the dialect of Yerusalem (the Talmudical dialect), were the composition of R. Shim-on ben Yo'haï, but that all which are in the sacred language (pure Hebrew) ought not to be attributed to him. Others affirmed that R. Moses ben Na'h-man (Nachmanides), having made the discovery of this book (the Zohar) in the holy land, sent it to Catalonia (in Spain), from which it passed into Arragon and fell into the hands of R. Moses de Leon. Finally several others have thought that this Moses de Leon was a learned man, who found all these commentaries in his own imagination, and that in order to draw by it great sums from the learned, he published it under the name of R. Shim-on ben Yo'haï and his companions. They add that he acted thus, because he was poor and weighed down with expenses." †

"As for me," says the author, Gedalyah, "I think that all these opinions have not any foundation, but R. Shim-on ben Yo'haï and his sacred society have really said all these things and besides many others; only they were not able to have the same conveniently written down at that time, but after having been disseminated a long time in several copies, they were finally collected and put in order (redacted)."

"This is not a matter to be surprised at; because it was in this manner that our master, Ye'hudah, the Holy, has redacted the Mishnah, from different manuscripts which had been before this, scattered to the four quarters of the earth. It was also in this manner that R. Ashi has composed the Gemarah."

* Ed. of Amsterdam, fol. 23 *a* and *b*.

† This may have been partly taken from the account said to have been given by Isaac of Acco and published in Yu'hasin, originally to be found only in the ancient edition of Constantinople, which is exceedingly rare. It had been left out of all subsequent editions, until Filipowski reintroduced it in 1857, in his London edition, pp. 85–95. Comp. Landauer's objection to this record. *Literaturblatt des Orients*, 1845, Vol. vi, col. 711 *et seq*. Dr. Graetz is compelled to acknowledge that Isaac of Acco: "Was in the end convinced of the genuineness of the Zohar as he wove into his Me'-irath Enaÿim, *i.e.*, Enlightenment of the Eyes, manifold Zoharist ideas. His writings in which the above record was originally imparted, appear to have been lost." The whole account by

The learned Dr. S. M. Schiller-Szinessy, Reader in Rabbinic and Talmudic, in the University of Cambridge, in his late able essay on the Midrashim,* which we have only at this moment seen, says: "The nucleus of the book (Zohar) is of Mishnic times, R. Shim'eon b. Yohai was the author of the Zohar in the same sense that R. Yohanan was the author of the Palestinian Talmud, *i. e.*, he gave the first impulse to the composition of the book. But R. Mosheh of Leon, on the other hand, was the first not only to copy and disseminate the Zohar in Europe, but also to disfigure it by sundry explanatory interpolations." "The Zohar was begun in Palestine late in the IId or early in the IIId century A. D. and finished at the latest in the VIth or the VIIth century. *It is impossible that it should have been composed after that time* and before the Renaissance, as both language and contents clearly show." This view is also indorsed in The Speaker's Commentary. It says,† among other things, the language shows that the Zoharic writings were composed in Palestine, but in the Jerusalem Talmud § *Synhedrim* iii, 9, *Ed. princeps* iii, 10, it is forbidden to carry books belonging to Palestine unto places "without the land." The Zoharic writings were without doubt sent by Nachmanides—flour. 1267—to his son and to his disciples in Spain. On one of Moses de Leon's MSS. now in the Cambridge University Library, he, M. de L., endorses "And I adjure every one who should deeply study this book, or who should copy it, or read it, that he do not blot out my name from my property (inheritance), for *I have* composed it." Is it likely, says Dr. Szinessy, after such vanity he would have written the Zohar and ascribed it to any one else? The Doctor also terms him, an "inferior cabbalist."

In the Zoharic writings it is rarely R. Shim-on who speaks, the Qabbalistic doctrines come from the mouth of the companions, who after his

---

Isaac of Acco has the appearance of a forgery, but Dr. Graetz slaps at the Qabbalists by saying: "Possibly the Kabbalists destroyed them." (Dr. Graetz, *Geschichte der Juden*. Vol. vii, p. 492.)

* Encyclop. Britannica, 9 Ed. Edinburgh, 1883, Vol. xvi, p. 286 *et seq*.

† The Holy Bible according to the authorized version (A. D. 1611), with an Explanatory and Critical Commentary, and a Revision of the Translation by Bishops and other clergy of the Anglican Church. Edited by F. C. Cook, M.A., Canon of Exeter, Chaplain in ordinary to the Queen, etc. New Testament, Vol. iv, p. 388.

death, again reunite themselves, to communicate to each other their recollections, and to instruct themselves reciprocally in the Qabbalistic Secret Science. To themselves they apply the Scripture verse " How beautiful it is to see the brothers remain united."*

The companions always have before them the Holy Writings of the Thorah, when either rising up or lying down. †

The great critic R. Azzarÿah Min Ha-adomim *dei Rossi* or *Rubeis*, " of the red ones," of Ferrara—flourished 1513–1577 A. D.—author of *Me'or Ainaÿim, i.e.*, The Light of the Eyes,‡ followed the teachings of the Zohar as regards the antiquity of the vowel points. He knew the book Yu'hasin, for in his book *Me'tsareph l'keseph, i. e.*, The Refiner of Silver, § i, ch. 2, he says: " The book *Shalsheleth Haq-Qabalah, i. e.*, Chain of the Tradition, *i. e.*, Qabbalah, was published at the time of the *Sepher Yu'hasin*, which came from the great city Constantina." Dei Rossi saw the untruthfulness apparent in the statement in the book Yu'hasin, as to the modern composition of the Zohar, and therefore did not follow it.

The erudite Rev. Dr. Peter Allix,§ and the Rev. Thomas Maurice,‖ also favour the Zohar as an early book. We refer the reader to the writings cited or which will be hereafter cited, also to the work of Joel, *Die Religionsphilosophie des Sohar*, Leipzig, 1849; the

---

* Ps. cxxxiii, 1. Zohar iii, 59*b*.

† Zohar, Part I, fol. 115*b*. The following additional writers favour the antiquity of the Zohar: J. Satanow, in his, *Kontros Sepher haz-Zohar, i. e.*, Folio of the Book Zohar, Berlin. 1783. J. Hamburger. *Real-Encyclopädie für Bibel und Talmud*, etc. Part i. 1870 Strelitz in Mecklenburg. ii. 1883 in same, Supplement, Leipzig, 1886. Be'hai ben Asher, pupil of R. Solomon b. Abraham ben Adereth (1234-1310 A. D.), acrostically RaShBA, who in his Pentateuch Commentary of 1291 A. D. quotes many passages under the name of Midrash of Rabbi Shim-on b. Yo'hai, which may be found in the Zohar. Comp. Lev. xxi, 22, and Zohar iii, p. 114. Raÿah Me'hemnah. In the beginning of his Commentary, he says: " And in the Midrash of R. Shim-on ben Yo-hai I have seen ' And a bird ' this is Michaël, ' upon the earth ' this is Raphaël. Compare Zohar i, p. 46*b*, and many other places.

‡ Mantua, 1574-75. See Kitto's Cyclop. Biblical Liter., Ed. 1876, iii, pp. 702-3.

§ The Judgment of the Ancient Jewish Church against the Unitarians in the controversy, etc. 2nd ed. Oxford, 1821.

‖ Indian Antiquities, etc. London, 1800, Vol. iv.

learned Jesuit Athanasius Kircher's *Œdipi Ægyptiaci, Romæ*, 1653; *Tomus Secundus, Partis Prima*, pp. 209–400; Dr. I. M. Jost's *Geschichte des Judenthums und seiner Secten*, Leipzig, 1859, Vol. iii; and especially to the greatest work on the Qabbalah of this century, the *Philosophie der Geschichte oder über die Tradition*, in four volumes, Vol. i, 1st ed. 1827, 2nd ed. 1857; Vol. ii, 1834; Vol. iii, 1839; Vol. iv, Part i, 1853, 8vo. Münster, by the learned Roman Catholic Franz Joseph Molitor. The fault of Molitor is, that he follows too closely the school of the Modern Qabbalah, that of Yitz'haq Luriah, Cordovero, etc., and not that of the school of the early Qabbalah and the Zohar, which is that in the greatest accord with the New Testament, and writings of the Fathers of the Christian Church. Baron Christian Knorr von Rosenroth's great work, the *Kabbala Denudata*, 1677–1684, is of value to the student, who has mastered the rudiments of this philosophy. He also follows too closely the Modern Qabbalah. There are a great many other works we can refer to, but will not weary the reader by a list.

Dr. Christian D. Ginsburg* has attacked the age and authenticity of the Zohar, in thirteen objections, in which are condensed those of Graetz, Beer, Jellinek, Steinschneider, Geiger, M. Sachs, Yabetz, Morin, etc., etc. We will take up his objections *seriatim*.

I. The first has been partly answered by Konitz and our note to page 25 *ante*.† Shim-on b. Yo'haï did not write the Zohar, it was the production of his school, and because the disciples termed him in one or two places *Boo-tseenah Ke'doshah*, *i. e.*, the sacred light, that is not evidence against the general authenticity of the Zoharic writings. Similar phrases are very usual in Oriental imagery and are frequent in both the O. T. and N. T. Compare Works of Rev. John Gregorie. 4th ed. London, 1684, p. 109 *et seq.*, and Kitto's Cyclop. Biblical Liter., ii, 832 *et seq*.

II. That the Zoharic writings mention the Hebrew vowel points. If the Zohar was not completely finished until about the VIth or the VIIth century, by the school of R. Shim-on b. Yo'haï, ample time

---

* The Kabbalah, its Doctrines, Development and Literature. An Essay, by Christian D. Ginsburg, LL.D. Read October 19th, 1863; reprinted, London, 1865. Also Kitto's Cyclop. Biblical Liter. II, pp. 699–703. Encyclop. Britannica and other works.

† See our synopsis, *ante* pp. 23–26.

existed to put into it the results of the centuries previous. The subject of the origin of the symbolism of the Hebrew vowel points, in the form we now have them, is one of much difficulty, has caused great disputes among the learned for centuries, and is not yet settled. The result we think may be summed up: 1. All Hebrew writing must have been in some way vowelized from its commencement in the very earliest period. It is, as are all the Semitic languages, written in consonantal form, and the vowels, which are the life and soul of it, are necessary to every language. The difficulty has been, that so far very ancient examples of pointed Hebrew have not been found in any old MSS. dating before 916 A. D. nor any monuments of it before the VIth century. It is asserted by Dr. Ginsburg, that the Rabbins of the school of Tiberias invented the vowel points, and that they were introduced for the first time by the Karaite R. Mocha, of Palestine, whom, he says, flourished *circa* A. D. 570,* to facilitate the reading of the Scriptures for the use of his students. We think that they only applied and propagated, but did not invent the points.† The subject is one of so much difficulty and of such a length, that we will put it in an Appendix. See however, *ante* pp. 26–30.

III. The Zohar in the Rayah Me'hemnah, *i. e.*, Faithful Shepherd; § *Qe'doshim*, Part iii, 82*b*, has nearly the same words, as are in the Kether Malkhuth of Ibn Gebirol, which forms part of the Polish Jewish Service for the evening preceding the day of Atonement,‡ as follows: "And moon and sun remained like a body without a soul, the master over them having darkened their lights." Zohar. The Kether Malkhuth merely says, "But there is a master over them darkening their lights."§ Dr. Ginsburg quotes Michael Sachs ‖ to show this, but he might also have stated that the context of the Zohar is complete without these words, indeed they appear as an addition out of place. If appropriate here, and Moses

---

* Others say, 780–800 A. D.

† Comp. *Des points-voyelles dans les langues Sémitiques par Moïse Schwab*, in *Actes de la Société philologique, tom. viii, fasicule 4, année 1877.* Paris, 1879, § v, p. 201–2. Also Pinsker in Liqqute Kadmoniyoth. Vienna, 1860, pp. 42–43 and Appendix.

‡ See *ante* p. 2 *et seq.*

§ See Dr. D. H. Joel. *Die Religions-philosophie des Sohar, etc.* Leipzig, 1849. p. 63.

‖ *Die Religiöse Poesie der Juden in Spanien*, Berlin, 1845, p. 229, Note 2.

de Leon was the author of the Zoharic writings, with intent to deceive, would he not have turned these words into the Aramaic and made them part of the original?

The Rayah Me'hemnah, only a fragment bound up with the Zohar proper, has been considered as one of the later books, and to have been originally written in Hebrew and then translated into the Aramaic. We have shown Ibn Gebirol lived 1020–1070 A. D., and had means of access to the original Qabbalistic authorities, and we shall hereafter show, that much in his philosophical writings is in accord with that set forth in the Zoharic books. Admitting however, that the redactor of the Zoharic manuscripts published with the Rayah a marginal note, it is evident that it was not intended to deceive, for it was given in the Hebrew and the rest of the Rayah is in Chaldaic, nor is a mere interpolation, admitting that this is one, any evidence of modern authorship. Gebirol lived over 225 years before the giving out to the uninitiated of the Zoharic writings. Ibn Gebirol even alludes to the Qabbalah *E'eyooneth*, *i. e.*, the Speculative or Theoretical Qabbalah in his Tiqqoon Middoth han-Nephesh, A. D. 1045, and Haÿ Gaon—987–1038 A. D.—alludes to the Qabbalah *Ma-a'seeth*, *i. e.*, the Practical Qabbalah.*

IV. The Zohar† quotes and explains the interchange, on the outside of the Me'zuzzah,‡ of the letters כוזו במוכסז כוזו KhVZV Be'MVKhSZ KhVZV instead of יהוה אלהינו יהוה YHVH ELoHENU YHVH introduced into Spain from France, at the end of the fifth Thousand *circa* 1240. This is an instance of the permutation or transmutation of letters according to the old system of Hebrew exegesis called *Ab-bag-gad*,§ which was known even in the time of the Old Testament, and hence was

* Landauer in the *Literaturblatt des Orients*. 1845. No. 13.

† Part i, 18*b*; 23*a*.

‡ The Me'zuzzah is a piece of parchment upon which is written; Deut. vi, 4–9; xi, 13–21, it is then put into a hollow cylinder or reed, which is affixed to the right hand door-post of every door, in the dwelling-houses of the Jews. Comp. Kitto's Cyclop. Biblical Liter. Ed. 1876. s. v. Mezuza, pp. 152–3.

§ Comp. Ginsburg, work cited, p. 50 note, and p. 54–55. Kitto's Cyclop. Biblical Liter., Ed. 1876, Vol. i, p. 258. *Bibliotheca Magna Rabbinica*, Pars. iv, p. 230 *et seq.* Historical and Critical Comment. on Ecclesiastes by C. D. Ginsburg, 1861, p. 30 *et seq.* Molitor. *Philos. der Geschichte oder über die Tradition*, Münster, Ed. 1857. Vol. i, p. 55 *et seq.*

not any innovation by the French Rabbins, who were in the XIIIth century, antagonized by the Spanish Rabbins, and not likely to influence the latter's religious teachings. In the cited places in the Zohar* where these letters occur, the Me'zuzzah is not spoken of at all; and where the Me'zuzzah as a Biblical commandment is spoken of in the Zohar,† there is not any allusion to these letters. How the above statement came into the learned Doctor's mind we do not see, however he has cited an authority which we have not at hand.

V. Another objection is that the Zohar‡ says: "The She' kheen-ah is light and light belongs to fire, *whence* it is that the house of meeting is called *Esh Nogah, i.e.*, a shining fire, or, brilliant light." In the original there is a transposition of letters, and without an understanding of this, the logical "whence" cannot be understood, it may be explained as follows: She' kheen-ah, in Hebrew שכינה reads in the Zohar שכינתא *She' khintah*, and the "house of meeting" is in Hebrew בית הכנסת *Beth hak k'neseth*, and reads in the Zohar בי כנישתא *Bai k'nishtah;* hence the transmutation of She'kintah and K'nishtah, *i. e.*, שכינתא and כנישתא, from which *Esh nogah, i. e.*, shining light, as a name for the latter in consequence of its being of the nature of the former. So it says in the Tiqqooneh haz-Zohar 6*a*: "The 'house of prayer' of above is '*Esh nogah*' and 'My house' below, is, a meeting house." Compare Isaiah lvi, 7, "Mine house," ביתי *Baithee* shall be called a "house of prayer," in Hebrew בית תפלה *Beth Te'-phillah*, and in the Zohar בי כנישתא *Bai k'nishtah*. We must take note of the former explanation here. Compare also Jerem. xxiii, 29. Dr. Ginsburg has not followed this out. The objection is based on the idea that the word *Esh nogah* (*Esnoga*) is a Portuguese word, a corruption of the word Synagogue, and therefore a mistake in the Zohar, coming from Moses de Leon, as a Spaniard and the author of the Zohar; but the Portuguese word for synagogue is not *Esnoga* but *Synagoga*, and in Italian *Sinagoga*. The word *Esnoga*, however, is a *Portuguese Jewish* term for the Jewish "house of prayer," and as such, it passed over to and is used also by the Portuguese *Christians*. In the same manner the

* Part i, p. 18*b* and 23*a*.
† Part iii, 263*b* and 269*b*. Deut. vi, 9; xi, 20.
‡ Part iii, 282*a*. The Ra*y*ah Me'hemnah

German Jewish *Schule*, and the Italian *scuola*, *i. e.*, school for synagogue (the synagogue being really a school for the adult, the *Beth, hammidrash*, *i. e.*, House of Learning or School for Learning, anciently, so *Schule* and *scuola*) passed over to and is used by, the Christians of Germany and Italy, to designate a synagogue. But in correct German, synagogue is *Synagoge*, in Portugal and Spain *synagoga*, and in Italy we have *sinagoga*.

VI. "The Zohar, Part ii, 32*a*, mentions the Crusades, the momentary taking of Jerusalem by the Crusaders from the Infidels, and the retaking of it by the Saracens."*

In the IVth Branch of Luriah's book cited,† he shows from statements in the Zohar,‡ "after four hundred years shall exist (or rise) a sovereign of the sons of Yishmaël (the Arabs), etc., and it shall be given to him as his portion (or, he shall have possession of) the holy land." Omar, king of the Arabs, conquered Jerusalem and the holy land in 397 of the fifth thousand (4397 A. M. equals 637 A. D.), this happened 569 years after the destruction of the second Temple, which occurred 173 years before the close of the fourth thousand of years, hence there is 569 years between the destruction and that conquest, why did the Zohar say 400

---

* The Crusades were:—1. 1096: Jerusalem taken by assault, July 15. 1099: Godfrey de Bouillon, King of Jerusalem.

2. St. Bernard's, 1146, headed by Conrad II and Louis VII. Jerusalem lost to the Crusaders, 1187.

3. Frederick Barbarossa. Philip II, France; Richard I, England, 1188-1190. Fruitless.

4. Henry VI. Successful 1195 to 1197.

5. That of Pope Innocent III, 1198. Baldwin of Flanders, attacks the Greeks and takes Constantinople (Byzantium), 120?.

6. 1216: Frederick II obtains Jerusalem on a truce of 10 years.

7. St. Louis (the IX of France), 1248, defeated and taken prisoner at Mansourah, April 8th; 1250, ransomed; truce 10 years.

8. 1270, by the same, who died at Carthage, Aug. 2, 1270. Prince Edward (after Edward I), of England, at Acre, 1271. In 1291 the Sultan takes Acre and the Christians are driven out of Syria.

† Comp. *ante* p. 49.

‡ Part ii, end of § *Vayera*, 32*a*, and compare what we have said *ante* p. 49.

years? Moses de Leon, if he wrote the Zohar, could have placed a correct prediction in it, as the time of conquest, 637 A. D., was well known in his day. Luriah says: The fact is, the passage in the Zohar dates from the time of R. Shim-on ben Yo'haï and his companions. At that time about 100 years had elapsed since the destruction of the second Temple, hence there remained up to the Arab conquest 469 years, which was taken at the round number 400 years. Those who endeavor to prove the late writing of the Zohar from these facts, Luriah calls upon to explain the other prediction in the same passage, "the holy land shall not be delivered (or, remain) to the children of Edom," *i. e.*, the Christians.* Would it have been difficult during the last centuries for the Christian powers to have combined and conquered the holy land from the Turks, had it not been intended by God that they should not have it? We can also say, would it not have been in accord with a writing by De Leon, to have, from the evident to him growing power of the Christian sovereigns, predicted such in the future? Luriah says, it is evidently providential that the sons of Yishmaël (the son of Abraham) reign over Palestine, and that the Christian powers of Europe should fail in reconquering and holding the holy land. Luriah says, the rest of the Yishmaëlitic empire, and the conquest from them by the branch of the Son of David, is mentioned in the *Pirqeh d' Rabbi Eliezer*, which was written before the compilation of either of the Talmudim.

The same idea is in the Mysteries of R. Shim-on b. Yo'haï.† In *La Kabbale*,‡ Prof. Franck, alluding to the adverse criticisms as to the antiquity of the Zohar and its authorship, says:§ "Several critics have thought that they observed, under the name Ishmaëlites,

* Edom at one time meant pagan Rome, then Byzantium, the capital taken for the whole of the Eastern Roman Empire, then the Christians and modern Catholic Rome. To this day, the people of Central Asia call the Sultan at Constantinople, the Sultan of Rome.

† See Jellinek's *Bet ha-Midrasch. Dritter Theil*, p. xix *et seq.*

‡ *La Kabbale ou la philosophie religieuse des hébreux, par Ad. Franck, professeur-agrége a la faculté des lettres de Paris, professeur de philosophie au collège royal de Charlemagne.* Paris, Librairie de l' Hachette. Rue Pierre-sarrasin, 12, 1843.

§ P. 98 *et seq.*

a reference to the Mohammedan Arabs, whom all the writings published by modern Jews designate under the same name * * *. Here is that which a disciple of R. Shim-on b. Yo'haï claims to have heard from the mouth of his Master: 'Woe upon the moment in which Yishmaël saw the world, and received the sign of circumcision! For what did the Holy One, whose Name he blessed! do? He excluded the children of Yishmaël (*Be'nai Yishmaël*), from the heavenly union, and gave them a portion below in the holy land on account of their circumcision; thus the children of Yishmaël are destined (or appointed, *ze' mee-nin*) to rule over the holy land, when it is vacated (or empty, *raiqna-ÿah*) by all Israel, a long time, inasmuch (or, in proportion) as their circumcision is also empty (*raiqna-ÿah, i. e.*, empty, imperfect); and they will prevent the children of Israël (*Be'nai Yisraël*) from returning to their place, until the merit of the children of Yishmaël (v. s.) shall be exhausted. And the children of Yishmaël are destined (*ze' mee-nin v. s.*) to arouse terrible wars in the world, and to have the children of Edom (*Be'nai Edom*) gathered together against them, waging war against them, one part at sea, another on land, and another near Yerusalem; and they will prevail one over the other, and the holy land shall not be delivered to the children of Edom " (Zohar ii, 32a).

In order to understand the meaning of these lines, continues Franck, it suffices to know, that the Jewish authors, *i. e.*, those who wrote in Hebrew, originally indicated by the name of Edom, pagan Rome, afterwards Christian Rome and all Christian nations. As this passage cannot refer to heathen Rome, the idea was to speak of the war of the Saracens against the Christians, and even of the Crusades prior to the capture of Yerusalem." So far Franck.* Franck is evidently inclined to ascribe this to the interpolation of a later writer, for he finds R. Shim-on ben Yo'haï's teachings to be in the Zohar.

In the commentary by Abravanel, on Isaiah lxiii, 6, is: " Rabbi Yishmaël† says: The children of Yishmaël will wage three awful wars *in the latter days*, as is said in Isaiah xxi, 15, ' They flee from the sword.'

---

* *Ibid.* 99–100.

† Who was a contemporary of R. Akeebah, the master of R. Shim-on ben Yo'haï.

The first war will be on land, as is said* 'from the drawn sword'; the second will be at sea, according to† 'And from the bent bow;' and the third will be in the *Ke' rakh gadol Shebba-Romi, i. e.*, in the great city of the Roman Empire, as it is said‡ 'and from the grievousness of war.'" That the Zoharic version, substituting Jerusalem for Rome, is very similar to this early prediction of R. Yishmaël is quite apparent to the mind, but in the latter, the reference also is apparently to Catholic Rome, or at least Byzantium, for it is "in the latter days;" *i. e.*, it is at the time of the redemption of Israel and her restoration to the holy land, that these three wars are to occur. The Zohar may refer to pagan Rome or to Byzantium, the Holy City of the Greek Church, but not necessarily to the Mohammedans, for in the days of R. Yishmaël the Mohammedans did not exist. The "children of Yishmaël" were the asserted descendants of Abraham through the son of Hagar; the "children of Israël" the descendants of Abraham through Isaac. The Mohammedans as "children of Yishmaël" do not appear in history until centuries, some 500 years, after R. Yishmaël's prediction, why apply the Zoharic prediction necessarily to the Crusades? The empire of Yishmaël is mentioned in the Talmud, which was redacted long before Mohammedanism; it says: "It is good to live under the government of Yishmaël."§ The name has been applied to the Turks in Europe since 742 A. D., but long before Mohammed, the Yishmaëlite, the name "children of Yishmaël" designated all the asserted descendants of Yishmaël, son of Abraham. This fact must be kept in view by the student, for a proper understanding of the Zoharic passage. Dr. Ginsburg makes this error, he quotes the Zohar as saying, "descendants of Ishmael, *i. e.*, the Mohammedans," assuming the Zoharic reference to be to the followers of that religion, calling them by the latter name no less than three times;|| also always saying: "the descendants of Ishmael" instead of "children of Yishmaël" as it is written in the Zohar, his object apparently being, to convey the idea of a more recent period in the history of this branch of Abraham's children.

---

* *Ibid.*   † *Ibid.*   ‡ *Ibid.*

§ Treatise *Shabbath*, 11a.

|| The Kabbalah, its Doctrines, etc., p. 87 *et seq.*

He also translates "the children of Edom" as "the Christians." But this does not necessarily follow, "*Be'nai Edom*" now means Christians, it was originally a Jewish designation of the Pagan Romans, for we may read in Abravanel's book, *Ma-ye'nai ye'shoo-ah*, *i.e.*, Fountains of Salvation, and R. Liva's *Ne-tza'h Yisraël*, *i. e.*, Victory of Israel, that the words of Rab in the Talmud* refer to the kingdom of Edom, *i.e.*, Rome. In the Midrash *Vay̌-yiqrah Rabbah*,† "Edom" is mentioned in connection with the vision of Daniel (vii, 7), on which the commentary *Mathnoth Ke'hunnah*, *i. e.*, Gifts of Priesthood, says: "He (Daniel) saw the dominion of Edom exceeding the other three."‡ Ibn Ezra, says:

"There were few people believing in that man (Jesus) who was taken for a deity; but when Rome, at the time of Constantine,§ who renewed the whole religion and put the image of that man on his banner, believed in him, there was nobody in the world keeping the new law except a few Edomites, therefore Rome is called, the kingdom of Edom." These quotations show the antiquity of the names "children of Yishmaël" and "children of Edom," and that the first was applied to the Arabs long before their becoming followers of Mohammed, and the latter was first applied to the pagan Romans. Further, the passage quoted by Dr. Ginsburg, is only a fragment selected to attack the antiquity of the Zohar. The following is a translation of the whole passage:∥

"Rabbi Yoseh and Rabbi 'Heeyah were walking together, said R. Yoseh to R. 'Heeyah: Why art thou silent? a road can only appear straight by (a conversation on or an explanation of) matters of the Thorah. R. 'Heeyah aroused himself and wept. He began and said: We read in Genesis (xi, 30), 'And Sarah was barren, she had no child.'

---

* Treatise *Sanhedrin*, 98*b*.

† Ch. 13, p. 2, col. 2.

‡ Comp. Exposition of the Thorah by R. Be'haī, Gen., 36*b*; *Be'raisheeth Rabbah*, 15*b*, and § 16; fol. 40*d*, 41*a*, § 43, fol. 59*a*, and § 65. *She'moth Rabbah* (Exodus) fol. 124*c*, § 35.

§ This is evidently a reference to Byzantium, as Rome, it was then in the Eastern Empire, and is to the Greek Church.

∥ Zohar ii, 32*a*. Brody and Amsterdam editions, which follow the Constantinople and Mantua editions.

Woe on account of this; woe upon the time when Hagar gave birth to Yishmaël! Whereupon R. Yoseh said to him: Wherefore, did not she (Sarah), herself afterwards bear a son, a holy branch? Said R. 'Hee-yah to him: Thou shalt see it as I see it, and so I have heard it from the mouth of Rabbi Shim-on (b. Yo'haï), and I cried—Woe upon that time! For since Sarah was childless, 'she said to Abraham: Go in, I pray thee, unto my maid,' (Gen. xvi, 2), in consequence of which, Hagar succeeded in replacing Sarah, her mistress, and having a son from Abraham. And Abraham said (to God): 'O that Yishmaël may live before thee!' (Gen. xvii, 18.) And though the Holy One, blessed be He! had given him assurance about Yitz'haq, Abraham clung to Yishmaël, until the Holy One, blessed be He! answered him,[*] 'As for Yishmaël, I have heard thee!' Afterwards he (Yishmaël) was circumcised and admitted into the holy covenant, until Yitz'haq went forth into the world. Now, Come and see! 400 years had the guardian-angel of the 'children of Yishmaël' thus existed, when he (the angel of Yishmaël) asked the Holy One, blessed be He! saying: Has he, who is circumcised, a share in thy Name? He answered him: Yes. He then said to Him: Yishmaël is circumcised (and at his thirteenth year), why has he no part in Thee like Yitz'haq? Said He to him: Because the latter has been given the sign of the covenant according to the rules, and the other one is not so. And not only this, but the sons of Yitz'haq are joined to Me at the proper age of eight days, while the sons of Yishmaël remain distant from Me a long time (13 years). Said he to Him: Though this be so, should he, because of his having been circumcised, remain without a good reward? Woe upon the time, when Yishmaël was born in the world and was circumcised!" With this "Woe" begins the portion we have before quoted; read in this connection, the "Woe" has quite a different meaning and bearing, from that of a first sentence of an exclamation and peroration, uttered by the writer of the Zoharic passage, as those opposed to the antiquity of the Zohar desire it to appear. Further the paragraph does not end where the fragment quoted by Dr. Ginsburg apparently ends "and the holy land shall not be delivered to the children of Edom," it goes on: "At that time, *a people from the extremes of the world shall*

[*] *Ibid.*, 20.

arise against the guilty Rome, and prosecute a war against her for three months, and many peoples shall be gathered together there and fall into its hands, until *all the children of Edom* shall be gathered against it from all the ends of the world,* and then the Holy One, blessed be He! will arise over them, according to, and in fulfillment of, Isaiah (xxxiv, 6) 'For YHVH has a slaughter in Bots-rah.'"

What has such a war to do with the crusades? Bots-rah means Rome.† "The great city in the Roman Empire" is to be visited by *Tohoo vab-Bohoo*, in the Messianic time. This "great city" is Bots-rah, so says Abravanel in his *Mash-mee-ah ye'shoo-ah, i. e.*, Herald of Salvation, fol. 17c. All the best Hebrew commentators agree upon this, that Bots-rah means Rome, and it is against Rome that the Zohar says, a destructive war is to be waged simultaneously with that predicted war "in the holy land, both on land and at sea, and near Yerusalem, as a great slaughter (or *Ze-bah, i.e.*, sacrifice), to YHVH, etc., to seize the corners of the earth, etc." The Zohar terminates this prophecy with "And He will destroy the children of Yishmaël from it (the holy land), and break every superior army (or strength), and there shall not remain a superior army (or strength) over a people in the world, *except the army (or strength) of Israel alone.* This is the meaning of the Psalm (cxxi, 5) 'YHVH is thy keeper, YHVH is thy shade upon thy right hand.'" This ends the quotation of which the adverse critics Ginsburg, Graetz, etc., have only used a small portion, applying the mutilated fragment to an event in history with which, when the whole passage is read in full, the paragraph quoted by them has not any connection, or is it a fact, that after the Crusades, the armies of the contending nations were annihilated and those of Israel alone preserved? How about the great slaughter at Rome at the time of the war of the Crusades in the holy land, *previous to the victorious preservation of Israel?* But our critics have apparently not seen and have not given any attention, to these questions which may be founded on the final portion of the prediction. Further, the Zohar has

* Evidently not the Crusades.

† Comp. Ibn Ezra on Is: xxxiv, 6, and Amos i, 12; R. D. Qim'qee on Is: lxiii, 1. Abravanel on the same, and on Is: xxxiv, 6, and Jer. xlix, 13. Targum Jonathan on the latter verse. In the Talmud, Treatise, *Pe'sa-'him*, 118b.

not exhausted this subject in the place before quoted; if we consult the III Part* we will find the relative position of Israël and Yishmaël, in the symbolical Sarah and Hagar, as mistress and maid. is there discussed, and the conclusion reached, that though the position of the mistress (Israël) may, under the temporary prominence of the maid (Yishmaël), be pitiable, in the future the mistress will be restored to her former eminence. The essential parts of this last reference are: "We have learned elsewhere: Once, during a walk with his disciples, R. Shim-on said to the latter: I see all the nations above, and Israel beneath all of them, what is the reason? It is because the King has dismissed the Matronitha, and given her place to her maid. Therefore it is said: "For these things the earth is disquieted, etc.,† 'for * * an handmaid that is heir to her mistress.' What does 'handmaid' mean? It is the alien crown, the first-born of which the Holy One, blessed be He, killed in Egypt, as it is written: 'Even unto the first-born of the maid-servant that is behind the mill.' (Exod. xi, 5.) Formerly she sat behind the mill, and now that maid-servant is heir to her mistress. R. Shim-on wept and said: The King without the Matronitha cannot be called 'King;' the king who joins the hand-maid of the Matronitha—where is his dignity? There is, however, a mystery in the matter, explained by the fact, that a voice is appointed to announce to the Matronitha and to tell her; 'Rejoice greatly, O daughter of Zion! Shout O daughter of Yerusalem, behold, thy king cometh unto thee, he is just and having salvation, lowly and riding upon an ass.'"‡ (Zechar. ix, 9.) * * "And again, we have learned elsewhere: That maid-servant is appointed to rule over the holy land below, as the Matronitha used to do formerly, and now it is the maid-servant who has become heir to her mistress over all; but the Holy One, blessed be He! has resolved to return the Matronitha to her place as heretofore. The king rejoices on account of his return to her and his separation from the maid-servant, and the Matronitha is

---

* p. 69a of the Brody or the Amsterdam Ed.· Parashath *A-ha'rai Moth*, fol. 31, col. 3-4 of the Cremona Ed.

† Comp. Prov. xxx, 21-23.

‡ Interpreted by most Hebrew commentators as referring to the Messiah, who, from a Hebrew, and consequently Zoharic, point of view, still is to come.

overjoyed at her reunion with the king; hence: Rejoice greatly, O daughter of Zion, etc.," as above. This portion, from the Zohar iii, 69a, explains and completes the other portion from ii, 32a. The *Mysterien des R. Simon ben Jochai** undoubtedly written long before the Crusades, appears to refer to the same subject.† We think these remarks dispose of the adverse criticism.

VII. Dr. Ginsburg has made use of writings by Drs. Adolph Jellinek, B. Beer, and Zuckerman, formulated by them in their futile endeavors to show the modern time of the authorship and content of the Zoharic books. We will hereafter give these, and it will be seen that they all differ among themselves, and that history does not support their statements as applied to their theme. Dr. Ginsburg says :‡

" 7. The *Sohar* records events which transpired A.D. 1264. Thus on Numb. xxiv, 17, which the *Sohar* explains as referring to the time preceding the advent of Messiah, it remarks, 'the Holy One, blessed be He, is prepared to rebuild Jerusalem. Previous to the rebuilding thereof He will cause to appear, a wonderful and splendid star, which will shine seventy days. It will first be seen on Friday, Elul = July 25th, and disappear on Saturday or Friday evening at the end of seventy days. On the day preceding [its disappearance, *i. e.*, October 2nd] when it will still be seen in the city of Rome, on that self-same day three high walls of that city of Rome and the great palace will fall, and the pontiff ruler of the city will die.' (*Sohar* iii, 212b.) Now the comet here spoken of appeared in Rome, July 25th, 1264, and was visible till October 2nd, which are literally the seventy days mentioned in the *Sohar*. Moreover, July 25th, when the comet first appeared, actually happened on a Friday; on the day of its disappearance, October 2nd, the sovereign pontiff of Rome, Urban IV, died at Perugia, when it was believed that the appearance of the comet was the omen of his death, and the great and strong palace (היכלא רברבא) Vincimento, fell on the self-same day, October 2nd, into the hands of the insurrectionists."

* Jellinek's *Bet ha-Midrasch*, etc., *Dritter Theil*. Leipzig. 1855.
† See *ante*, p. 37.
‡ The Kabbalah, etc., before cited, p. 88.

The portion referred to is Numbers xxiv, 17, and reads in full as follows :*

"I see him, but not now. These words were partly fulfilled in that time, and partly afterwards, and partly (they will be fulfilled) in the time of King Messiah. We have learned, the Holy One, blessed be He! resolved upon rebuilding Yerusalem, and will cause to appear a fixed star scintillating in 70 flaming channels, and 70 shining beams, in the centre of the firmament; and 70 other stars will borrow their light from it. And it is to shine and flame seventy days; on the sixth day it will be seen on the 25th day of the 6th month, and on the 7th day, it will disappear at the expiration of 70 days. On the first day it will be seen in the (or, *one*) city (of the Empire) of Rome;† and on that day the three principal walls of Rome and the great temple (or, hall), will fall, and the ruler of that city will die, thus that star will be extended to be seen in the world. And at that time, mighty wars will be waged in all the four sides of the world, and no faith (faithfulness) will be found among them, and in the middle of the world. When that star shines in the middle of the firmament, a great king will arise and rule in the world, and proudly look down upon all the kings, and make war in two directions and be victorious over them. But on the day of the disappearance of the star, the entire holy land will quake in 45 miles circumference round about the spot where the Temple stood. And *a cave from beneath the earth will be opened*, and a fire will burst forth from it, with a bright conflagration (or general burning). And from that cave a large and powerful bird ‡ will grow supreme and rule over the world, and to him the government shall be given, and the exalted saints will disappear as naught before him. And thus King Messiah will be revealed in all the world, and to him the government will be given; and on his appearance, the children of the world will meet with trouble after trouble, and Israel's adversaries will grow strong; thus the spirit of the Messiah will

* In the Brody and Amsterdam editions, iii, § Balak, p. 212*b*; in the Cremona ed. § Balak, fol. 98, col. 3.

† In the Cremona Edition, "Rome" is omitted.

‡ One version says עוף *oph*, *i. e.*, bird, doubtless meaning *a great angel*, another says ענף *anaph, i. e.*, branch.

be aroused against them, and he will make an end of the guilty Edom, and all the land of Edom he will burn in fire. Thus it is written: 'And Israel shall do valiantly.'." (Numb. xxiv, 18.) Or as this passage says in full, 'And Edom shall be a possession and Sëir also a possession as his enemies (the enemies of Israel), and thus Israel will do valiantly.' And at that time the Holy One, blessed be He! will resurrect the dead of his people, and make death forgotten among them, and thus 'the right hand of YHVH does valiantly; I shall not die but I shall live' (Ps. cxviii, 15). 'And Saviours shall come upon Mount Zion,' etc. (Obadiah i, 21.) 'And YHVH shall be king over all the earth, etc.'" (Zechar. xiv, 9.)

Now from this quotation in full from the Zohar, it is evident that the prophesying writer had in view a very distant future, in which *all* these particulars *were to be fulfilled*, and that *all of them had to come to pass for the verification of the prediction;* so that the occurrence of one or two of the events indicated, could not be looked upon as satisfying the requirements of the whole. The number 70 is prominent therein, and is in the manner of Daniel (ix, 24) and other places in the Old Testament, in which 70 is a prominent figure; the 6th and 7th day, *i. e.*, the Sabbath eve and Sabbath day, terminate the Hebrew week and complete in themselves the end, content, and object, of all the days of the week; and so they do as regards the ten weeks = 70 days; the 6th month ends the civil year, and the 25th of that month is not a more definite number than 70 is, but as all these events are to happen in the *future*, the date as to month and day, may be considered as gratuitously admitted and made use of, in the same sense, as if the 25th of the 6th month, *i. e.*, Elul, of the year. *The Zohar does not fix it.* But some of the critics adverse to the antiquity of the Zohar assume to find in the above quoted Zoharic passage, or a garbled statement of part of it, a reference to incidents which have occurred in past history, if not in one century, then in another, from one or two minor items therein, admitting of a forced interpretation, on the ground of similarity. They point to three or four different events, in as many different periods, in which these things are said to have happened; and although each differs from the other in his surmises, their followers accept their various distorted and differing statements instead of rejecting them, and indeed the entire criticism founded thereon ; on the ground of its uncertainty, apparent bias and forced construction. Instead of this, among others Dr. Ginsburg, seizes on the various statements and endeavors to formulate from them a most plausible one against the Zoharic writings, and exclaims, Here is the unassailable evidence, "that this Thesaurus of the Kabbalah is the production of the thirteenth century."* He states as if an uncontroverted fact, that "the Sohar (Zohar *sic*) records events which transpired in 1264 A.D.," and then endeavors to support this by a mutilated fragment of the above quotation, intermixed within the quotation marks, with statements not in the original. This writer in this and in other places in his work on the Qabbalah, seems to speculate upon the credulity and want of expert knowledge of the subject, in the reader, using garbled and detached fragments from the Zohar, to evidence its being a modern book of the XIIIth century, and everywhere showing an evident bias against it. We call attention, among others, to the mistranslation of *yomah qadma-ah, i. e.*, "on the first day" by "On the day preceding [its disappearance, *i. e.*, October 2nd]," the verse concluding "thus that star will be extended to be seen in the world" for 70 consecutive days.

Dr. Adolph Jellinek's statement is : "As many scholars still ascribe to this book (the Zohar), a great antiquity, I will show there is mentioned in it the date of August 22nd, 1280. We read Zohar iii, 212*b* as follows: ' God is prepared to rebuild Jerusalem, and shall let a wondrously bright star be visible—which shall be seen for seventy days. It shall be visible on Friday, the 25 of Elul, and disappear on Saturday, at the end of seventy days. On the first day (*i. e.*, 25th of Elul), it shall be visible in Rome†—and on that day three high walls and a great temple shall fall and the Regent shall die.' This passage is made plain from the following calculation : In the year 1280, Rosh 'Hodesh Elul (the new moon of Elul) happened on Sunday and Monday—on the 29th of July—consequently the 25th of Elul = 22nd day of August fell on Thursday, on the evening of which the star became visible—the seventy days of which

* Dr. Ginsburg, work cited, p. 85.

† In the Cremona Edition of the Zohar, Rome is omitted, probably from regard to the Censorship. This reference in the MSS. was probably to Pagan Rome, the Zohar has however, been printed in the time of Catholic Rome.

ended Friday evening—which evening is counted in the day following, *i. e.*, Saturday, and on Thursday, the 25th of Elul, 1040 (?5040) A.M., or the 22nd August, 1280, Pope Nicholas, III, died in Rome. His successor was Martin IV, whom Abraham Abulafia endeavored to convert the following year."*

In January, 1856, Dr. B. Zuckermann,† referring to this statement by Dr. Jellinek, says: "On the one side are those who ascribe great age to the Zohar, on the other those who claim for it a late origin. The proofs are taken by the respective sides, either from external marks or the dates alluded to in the Zohar itself, as to the latter, they are not anywhere given in such an unequivocal manner as not to admit of various constructions. They have therefore to be confirmed by other well-known historical facts, and without a full confirmation of them, the door is open to hypothesis, and even the latter is subject to limitation. From such statements we must be able to deduce the facts under investigation in a plain manner, if not with mathematical certainty, at least with some probability. If an historical mark is given, at the very least the most important *indicia* must find an explanation, if they are to lead to a result. If we only take one solitary instance out of it, without considering the rest, then the hypothetical construction is founded on a very feeble basis and soon crumbles." Dr. Zuckermann then cites the Zoharic passage given by Dr. Jellinek, and continues: "Several facts are asserted: 1st. The rebuilding of Jerusalem. 2nd. The appearance and disappearance of certain natural phenomena. 3rd. The falling of three high walls and a great temple. 4th. The death of a ruler. The explanation of Dr. Jellinek does not mention in what relation the year 1280 stands to the rebuilding of Jerusalem; and it further omits the phenomena of Nature." Dr. Zuckermann then advances a new hypothesis, and says: "In the year 4127 A.M., 367 A.D., the 25th Elul, fell on Thursday. In this year mention is made by three authors, Hevel, Lubinczki and Casius, of the appearance of a comet (in splendour) like the light of the planet

---

* *Bet ha-Midrash*. Leipzig. 1855. Vol. iii. Introduction pp. xxxvii–xxxviii.

† Frankel's *Monatschrift für Geschichte und Wissenschaft des Judenthums*. Vol. v. Leipzig. 1856. p. 27.

Venus, which was visible in the daylight.* About this time the Roman Emperor Julian, the Apostate, issued a commandment for the rebuilding of the Temple in Jerusalem, and as history tells us, many labourers went there, and when the construction was commenced, it was prevented by the sudden falling of several walls. Further commands of the Emperor were now looked for, but he fell in battle against the Persians. Here upon comparison the date corresponds, as the 25th Elul fell on Thursday, and the most important event, the natural phenomena, is without doubt that in relation to Jerusalem, it and the death of the Roman emperor about this time are ascertained, the objection is, historians give the date of the death of Julian as in the year 363 A. D. This could be met, in that in the (book) Zemach David by David Gans, it gives 367 as the year, and the author of the Zohar, whoever he may be, might have taken the same date, therefore with greater justice the year 4127 A.M. or 367 A.D. could be used for the explanation of this passage."

In the same year Dr. B. Beer, noticed these† statements of Dr. Jellinek and Dr. Zuckermann, and says of the latter, that he admits Julian was dead when the comet mentioned appeared—Julian died far from Rome, June 26, 363 A.D., the comet appeared 367 A.D.—so that we have to go to the very uncertain source of David Gans, to suppose that both events occurred at the same time, and that such an exact designation of the days, as it has been assumed we find in the Zohar, is not likely to refer to the time of Julian. Either the Zohar is older than the IVth century or it is, as some critics suppose, a great deal later, and therefore this allusion to an occurrence a long time past is not to be thought of. The walls of the Temple of Jerusalem did not, according to the accounts, fall, but flames broke out of the ground and prevented the prosecution of rebuilding. The passage in the Zohar must be taken in its true spirit, it is not expressed that 'just at that time' Jerusalem shall be rebuilt, in the introduction it is said, that some (of that which is narrated) will occur in this time, some later and some, only in the days of the Messiah. Dr. Beer, seeing that the old are without

* As Venus sometimes is. Myer.

† Comp. Frankel's *Monatschrift für Geschichte und Wissenschaft des Judenthums*. Vol. v. Leipzig, 1856, pp. 158–160.

support, now advances a new theory, saying: "According to my view the passage refers neither to 1280 or 367, but to 1264. In the last mentioned year, the great comet became visible from the end of July to the 2nd of October, especially in Rome, which comet is again expected in our days. It showed itself magnificently with a sabre-like tail 100° long, and appeared on the same day on which Pope Urban IV died—Compare scientific appendix to the Official Leipzig Gazette, of 17th January, 1856, p. 19.—It was believed that this large comet was a precursor of his death. At the time, there occurred several insurrections and fights in and about Rome, the insurgents looked for the flying Pope in Orvieto, and the large and firm castle of Vincemento fell finally into their hands, the Pope had to be carried away in a sedan chair to save his life, became sick on the road and died on the 2nd day of October.* After his (the Pope's) death, a relaxation in the Roman Catholic belief took place, even the festival of Corpus Christi, introduced by him, fell into oblivion. The cardinals were a long time choosing a successor, the Ghibellines seriously thought of wresting from the Papacy the temporal power. The Latin Empire a short time before had fallen into the hands of the Greeks, in Germany no Emperor existed, and great confusion reigned; not long afterwards Jerusalem was wrested from the Christian crusaders. The comet disappeared October 2nd, if we count back seventy days, then it first became visible the 25th of July. This day in 1264 fell on Friday. The 2nd of October, 1264, when the comet was seen for the last time, fell on Thursday, therefore it had disappeared on Friday evening. On the 2nd of October, when it was yet visible, the strong castle fell into the hands of the insurgents, whereby *possibly* some walls might have fallen yet this is not mentioned, and Pope Urban IV died." So Dr. Beer.

Now we say, against this statement, the great comet of 1264 was discovered July 14th, some say July 1st, 1264.† The duration of visibility

---

* Muratori, Hist. of Italy. Part viii, p. 72. Hist. of the Popes. iii, 235. De la Gournerie, *Rome chretienne tome* i, p. 425, and other authentic sources, especially Raumer. Hist. of the Hohenstauffen's. Part iv, p. 491. Ed. 1824.

† See *Cometographie*, 4to, Paris.

was three months. Some say four months. Its tail was 100° long.* It was seen in China on the 26th July, and was visible four months. † Watson says the comet of 1264 was first seen about July 1st, and attained its greatest brilliancy, in the latter part of August and beginning of September, and that it was last seen the evening of the 3rd (2nd ?) of October, the date of the death of Urban IV.

Urban IV had declared a holy war against Manfred, king of Sicily. The papal army at first was successful, but finally Manfred was victorious and laid siege to Rome. His army was composed almost entirely of Saracens. The Pope retired to Orvieto, fifty miles from Rome. This was in 1261. He was afterwards driven from that city by the citizens, and although sick, was transported in a litter as far as Perugia, where he died October 2nd, 1264.‡

We have now seen that three attempts, all differing, made by Drs. Jellinek, Zuckermann, and Beer, to prove a modern date for the Zohar, from the passage cited, are not warranted by historical data. The comet appears to have been visible according to some astronomers as early as July 1st, the latest say July 17. Chinese and European observers noted it. The duration was either ninety or one hundred and twenty days. Pingre says the latter. The day of the death of Urban IV appears to be fixed, but not the exact day of the appearance and disappearance of the comet, all astronomers agree it was visible not only during the seventy days mentioned in the Zohar, but for a longer time. If the Zohar was written after these facts, why did it not state the facts as they had actually occurred? Does anything given, support an hypothesis as to any of the dates given by the three writers mentioned? What as to the rebuilding of

*Chamber's Astronomy. Bk. iv. c. 6. p. 338. c. 3. p. 308. Cometic Orbits, etc., by Edward J. Cooper. Dublin. 1852. pp. 14-15, 37, 68, 173. *Memoires de l'Academie*, by Pingre. Paris. 1760. pp. 179-203. Delambre. Vol. 3, p. 418.

† Cooper, work cited, 68. Zach's Correspondence, Vol. 5, p. 342. Philos. Trans. Vol. 10, p. 209-210. Also Treatise on Comets, by James C. Watson, Philadelphia. 1861. pp. 86-88, 90-94, 95, 96.

‡ Life and Times of the Roman Pontiffs by Artaud de Montor. Eng. Trans. New York. 1867. pp. 435-438. Bower's Hist. of the Popes. Dublin. 1768. pp. 353-361. Complete Hist. of the Popes of Rome, &c., by Louis Marie de Cormenin. Eng. trans. Philadelphia. 1851. Vol. ii. p. 6-8.

Jerusalem, the advent of the Messiah, the appearance of the star for seventy days, the disappearance on Thursday, October 2nd, 1264, not Friday or Saturday, at the end of seventy days, the falling of the three high walls of Rome, and of the great palace, (of Rome)? Is it not likely that the prophecy is a false one or is yet to be fulfilled?

It may be interesting to the reader to know that the idea of a new star to appear in the heavens, to precede the coming of the Messiah is very ancient; the *Aggadoth Meshiach, i.e.*, Messiah Haggadoth, commences:—
"'A star shall come out of Jacob.' There is a Ba'raï-thah in the name of the Rabbis: As to the heptad (seven) in which the Son of David cometh:—in the first year, there will not be sufficient nourishment; and in the second year the arrows of famine will be launched; in the third great famine; in the fourth, neither famine nor plenty; in the fifth, great abundance, and the star shall shine forth from the East, and this is the Star of the Messiah. And it will shine from the East for fifteen days, and if it be prolonged, it will be for the good of Israel; in the sixth, will be sayings (voices) and announcements (hearings); in the seventh, wars, and at the close of the seventh, the Messiah is to be expected."* A similar statement is in the Apocalypse of Elijah.† Also the Chapters about the Messiah; ‡ and, The Mysteries of Shim-on ben Yochaï, § where we read of a Star in the East, to appear two years before the birth of the Messiah.

So also the Zohar says, *concerning the appearance of the Messiah.* R. Shim-on (b. Yo'haï) lifted up his hands, wept, and said: "Woe to him who shall live to see the time (of the Messiah)! salvation to him who shall live to see it! For when the Holy Blessed One shall come, to consider the Unfruitful One, He will see, who has remained true to her, who is still found by her, and what have been the individual deeds of each one: but He will not find any just one, as it says:—'And I looked, and no helper was there.' (Is. lxiii, 5.) And then affliction upon

---

* From the *Aggadoth Meshiach, i. e.,* Messiah Haggadoth; cited in Dr. Adolph Jellinek's *Bet ha-Midrash.* Leipzig. 1855. Part iii, p. xxviii, 141–143.
† *Ibid.*, pp. 65–68.
‡ *Ibid.*, pp. 68–78.
§ *Ibid.*, pp. 78–82.

affliction will come upon Israel. 'Happy lot to him who shall live to see that time!' Because he who is persistent in the faith shall attain to the joy of the King. Of that time it says: 'I will refine them as silver is refined, and try them as gold is tried.' (Zech. xiii, 9.) After those tribulations have been poured out over Israel, and after the nations, together with their kings, shall have taken common counsel over the same, and have devised many pernicious precepts, in which all will coincide, so that such distress shall follow, that the last (distress, on account of its severity), shall cause the first to be forgotten; then a pillar of fire shall appear, which shall, for forty days, reach from heaven to earth, and be visible to all the nations of the earth. On this day will the King, the Messiah, come forth from the Garden of Eden, from the place called גן צפור, *qan tzippor*, *i. e.*, the Bird's Nest, and will appear in Galilee. And on the day of his arrival there, the whole world shall tremble, and all the children of the world shall hide themselves in the holes and caves, because they cannot any more think of salvation. As to this it says: 'And they shall go into the holes of the rocks, and into the caves of the earth, for fear of YHVH, and before the Glory * of His Majesty, when He arriveth to terrify the earth' (Is. ii, 19). '*For the fear of YHVH*,' that is the trembling of the whole world, '*Before the Glory of His Majesty*,' that is, the Messiah; '*When He ariseth, to terrify the earth*,' that is, when he (the Messiah) shall arise and appear in Galilee. For the reason, that Galilee was the first destroyed of the provinces of the holy land, he will therefore first reveal himself in it. From thence he will stir up war against the whole world. After the expiration of the forty days, in which will be visible before the eyes of the world the pillar of fire, reaching from earth to heaven, and the Messiah shall have revealed himself, there shall become visible a star from the East, shining in all colours † beside seven other stars surrounding it. From all sides they will carry on war with it, three times a day for seventy days, which all the inhabitants of the world will see. But the Star (in the East) will

---

* The She'kheen-ah.

† The Old Testament, Bileam, son of Beor, says: "I shall see him, but not now; I shall look upon him, but not nigh. There will come a Star out of Jacob, And a Sceptre will rise out of Israel, etc."

fight against the others, with beaming sparks of fire, flaming and sparkling, and will force itself against them so violently upon all sides, that it will swallow them every night, but eject them again every morning, so as to renew the war before the eyes of the entire world. This shall continue for seventy days. After these seventy days shall expire, the star with the Messiah shall become invisible for twelve months. Then shall the pillar return as before, and the Messiah will hide himself in it, but (the pillar) itself shall be invisible. After twelve months the Messiah, hidden in the pillar of fire, shall be taken into heaven, where he will receive power and the Crown (Kether) of the Kingdom (Malkhuth). But when he again descends, then that pillar of fire will again become visible before the eyes of the world. Then the Messiah will reveal himself, and many nations will gather themselves to him, and he will cause war on the whole world. About this time that the Holy Blessed One shall stir up His power against the nations of the world; the King, the Messias, will become known in the world, and all the kings of the world will mutually band together, to fight against him. But also many nations, descended from the rejected Jews, shall come up united with them (the nations) to carry on war against the Messiah, the King. Then for fifteen days the world shall be in darkness, in which a great many of Israel shall die."*

This refers to "the latter days." The reference has therefore been applied to the coming of the Messiah. The celebrated astronomer Kepler formed a theory, that Jupiter and Saturn were in conjunction in the Zodiacal Constellation of Pisces, the Fishes, and the fish is the astrological symbol of Judea, in the latter half of the year of Rome 747, and were joined to Mars in 748. This would be about six years before the commencement of our common era. Wieseler† has applied the theory of Kepler, in conjunction with a discovery that he has made from Chinese astronomical tables, which show that in the year of Rome 750, a comet appeared in heavens, and was visible for seventy days.‡

* Zohar ii, fol. 7, col. 2, Amsterdam Ed.; *ibid.* ii, fol. 53, Sulzbach Ed.

† *Chronolog. Synopse der 4 Evangelien.* Hamburg. 1843.

‡ Compare Kitto's Biblical Cyclop., Ed. 1876. Vol. iii, pp. 890–891. Rev. Wm. Hale's Chronology. Lond., 1830. Vols. i, 74; ii, 199–209. Cahen's Great French Bible. Vol. 4, p. 122, Note 17. Our Christian era was introduced by Dionysius

"The King, the Messiah, shall appear in the land of Galilee. A star in the eastern heaven, shall swallow (or absorb) seven stars in the north, and a flame of black fire* shall hang in the heavens for sixty days, and there shall be wars towards the north carried on in the world, two kings perishing in the north in these wars. Then all the nations shall combine together against the dominion (palaces) of Jacob, in order to expel it from the world."†

VIII. In this objection Dr. Ginsburg says: "The *Sohar*, in assigning a reason why its contents were not revealed before, says that the 'time in which R. Simon ben Jochai lived was peculiarly worthy and glorious, and that it is near the advent of the Messiah,' for which cause this revelation was reserved till the days of R. Simon, to be communicated through him. Yet, speaking elsewhere of the advent of the Messiah, the *Sohar*, instead of placing it in the second century when this Rabbi lived, *forgets itself*, and says—'When the 60th or the 66th year shall have passed over the threshold of the sixth millennium (A. M. 5060–66 = A. D. 1300–1306) the Messiah will appear' (*Sohar* i, 116a, 117b; comp. also iii, 252a); thus showing that the author lived in the XIII century of the Christian era."

The numbers 6 and 7 were favored by the ancient Rabbis as alluding to the sacredness of the Sabbath eve and the Sabbath day. If Dr. Ginsburg had looked a little further in the paragraph, from which he takes the quotation just given, he would have found: "In every six‡ of the sixth

---

Exiguus, a Roman abbot in the VIth century (525 A.D.), and came into general use two centuries later, during the reign of Charlemagne. This put the nativity of Jesus as happening upon December 25, 754 *Anno Urbis*, *i. e.*, after the founding the City of Rome. The early patristic writings distinguish between the Conception or Annunciation, with which they identify the Incarnation, and the Nativity (Matt. i, 18). Since the time of Charlemagne, the two appear to have been used synonymously. Comp. Ideler. Chronology, ii, 381 *et seq*. Gieseler. Church History. New York. 1857. Vol. I, 59 *et seq*. This date is wrong by at least four years. Jesus can therefore be considered as having been born A. U. 750 or B. C. 4, and likely earlier. See Hist. of the Christian Church by Philip Schaff. New York. 1882. pp. 111–127, and Gieseler. Church History last above cited.

* Black fire is visible light, as distinct from "white fire," diaphanous light.

† Zohar i, fol. 119, Amsterdam Ed.; *ibid.* i, fol. 74, Sulzbach Ed.

‡ ו Vau (V) = 6, separated from the ה Heh (H) of יהוה *i. e.*, YHVH during Israel's dispersion.

thousand (year) the ה increases in strength until it recovers its former degrees, and then in the six hundredth year of the sixth (thousand) the gates of Supreme Wisdom will be opened, and so shall the fountains of the lower wisdom (*i. e.*, Malkhuth, *i. e.*, the Kingdom), and the world will be suitably fitted to enter into the seventh (thousand), like a man who prepares himself on the sixth day at sunset, to enter into the Sabbath. So also here, and thy token* is to be found in Genesis vii, 11, viz: ' In the six hundredth year of Noah's life, etc., were all the fountains of the great deep broken up, and the flood-gates of heaven were opened.' "

A little further on R. Yo-seh approving of the interpretation above given by R. Yehudah, " as a very ingenious observation on the two letters ה (H = 5) and ו (V = 6 of יהוה *i.e.*, YHVH)," reminds his hearers of the well-known fact, " *that the time of Israel's redemption is known only to God, and is entirely dependent on Him and also dependent on their good or bad conduct*, according to Isaiah lx, 22. ' I YHVH will hasten it in its time.' *If they are worthy* ' I will hasten it ! ' *If they are not worthy*, ' In its time.' "

This conclusively shows, that the Rabbins of the Zoharic writings did not attempt to determine the time of the advent of the Messiah, and that the remarks upon the letter ו = 6, in connection with the time of the redemption of Israel, are to be considered only as complete at the close of the six thousand of the years fixed, but not at a definite period. This shows that the remark that " the Sohar, instead of placing it in the second century when this Rabbi (S. b. Y.) lived, forgets itself, etc." is incorrect. The Talmud, Treatise *Sanhedrin* 97a, supports our view: " *The disciples of the house (or school) of Eliÿah teach*, the world is to exist *six* thousand years, *two thousand* years of which are to be desolate,† *two thousand* years blessed with the Thorah, and *two thousand* years of the time of the Messiah ; but on account of the multitude of our sins, there have passed away from them that many that have passed :—" on which Rashi comments: " 172 years before the completion of the 4000 years the Temple was destroyed, and at the termination of these 172 years, the 2000 years of the Thorah (*i. e.*, 4000 years of the world) were completed, etc. But as

* Which may be used by thee to rely on, because of its being a Biblical verse.

† *To-hoo, i. e.*, without the Thorah, says Rashi, in his Commentary.

regards the 2000 years of the Messiah, these last ought to have come immediately after the expiration of the 2000 years of the Thorah, and the Kingdom of Wickedness ought to have ceased, and with it, also the servitude of Israel. Our manifold sins, however, have caused the Messiah not to appear at the end of 4000 years, and of the third 2000 years there have already passed away those which belong to the past, and he is still prevented from coming." The same passage is in the Talmud, Treatise *Abodah Zarah 9a*. Rashi on it, says: "The world is destined to stand *six thousand* years according to the number of *the days of the week*, but the seventh day is the Sabbath, and in the 7000th year, the world shall rest. The first 2000, etc;" as above. The Zohar says the period of R. Shim-on was "near the advent of the Messiah,"* and the Talmud describes the 2000 years following the period of the Thorah, as *the Messianic period;* consequently "the Zohar does—*not*—forget itself," when speaking of the emancipation of Israel as to happen at a favourable moment, *prior to the expiration* of the 2000 years of the Messianic period, which period is still in existence, nor is the Zohar mistaken in mentioning the Messianic period as that near which R. Shim-on lived. The Temple was destroyed A. D. 70 + 172 = 242 A.D. as the completion of the 4000 years according to Rashi. R. Shim-on lived *circa* 190 A. D., therefore near 242 A.D., the beginning of the Messianic period of 2000 years, the last third of the 6000 years of the world's standing at any period of *six*, or *sixty* or *six hundred* days or years, which the Zohar terms an "outpouring of heavenly wisdom upon the world," and which the Talmud calls: "the emancipation of Israel." St. Paul and the early Christians were also daily expecting such a second advent, and the whole orthodox Christian and Jewish world are still expecting every day an advent, the last of a Messiah, the first of a second coming of Christ. How this Zoharic statement shows that the Zohar was written in the XIIIth century we do not comprehend.

IX. This includes several objections which will be answered more fully in the body of this writing. The doctrine of transmigration of souls is undoubtedly very old among the Jews, we note especially the Levirate

* We adopt the reading "of the Messiah" although this word does not occur in the passage quoted.

Marriage, and it is mentioned, either positively or inferentially, in a number of places in the New Testament as if an undoubted tenet. We also refer the reader to Dr. Ginsburg's own note, on his work cited, page 43. The Midrashim and Talmud are not altogether silent about it. St. Jerome says: "*Hæc impia and scelerata doctrina olim in Ægypto ana Orientis partibus versabatur, and nunc absconditè, quasi in foveis viperarum apud plerosque versatur, illarumq partium polluit puritatem, ana quasi hæreditario malo, serpit in paucis, ut perueniat ad plurimos, etc.*"* Showing us that it was an *esoteric doctrine among the early Christians, but was considered as traditional and intrusted only to the select few.* Origen believed in it. See his writings which are full of it. It existed for centuries before the time of Jesus among many of the Oriental peoples, and is notably to-day to be found among the followers of the Buddhistic and Brahminical religions.

X. Objection is answered in the general statements in this book.

XI and XII. These objections have been and will be further answered, in this book.†

XIII. *If* the Zohar contains passages which are similar to those which M. d. Leon has in his own writings, it is only evidence that he copied them from the original Zoharic MSS., which he then had in his possession. The passage quoted from Ps. xlvi, 8, by M. d. Leon, is correctly quoted, and is also to be found in the MSS. cited in Dr. Kennicott's large work: *Vet. Test. Hebr., Cum. variis Lectionibus.* Oxford, 1776–80. 2 vols., folio, in a number of MSS. cited by him, and in Rossi's *Varia Lectiones* to the Hebrew Bible,‡ also in the edition of the Psalms, in Hebrew, published by Elia Benamozegh in Livorno, in these Elohim is in both Ps. xlvi, 8, and Ps. xlxvi, 5.

In the Commentaries on the Pentateuch, by the great Qabbalist Elia

---

* *Epistol. Hieronymous ad Demetriadem, de seruanda virginitate. Hieronymi Stridonensis, Opera omnia quæ extant, etc.* Paris. *1546. Tom. i, p. 22, E.*

† *Ante*, pp. 56 *et seq.* and in other places.

‡ See *Biblia Hebraica a Benj. Kennicotto;* and *J. B. de-Rossi*, by Christopher Doederlein. Halle. 1818.

Benamozegh of Leghorn,* are statements favorable to the antiquity of the Zohar, we here give some of them in a condensed form, adding some comments of our own.

Genesis xxxvii, 36, is: Joseph was sold by the Yishmaëlites to Potiphar *se'ris Par-oh, i. e.*, a *se'ris* of Pharao," *i. e.*, a prominent officer of the household, who by the ancient custom of archaic Oriental countries, was a sâ-ras, *i. e.*, eunuch;† in the Syriac, *sa-ri-so*. So the Talmudists use the verb מסרס *me'sa-res*, to geld, emasculate, eradicate, in the meaning of the kindred verb שׁרשׁ *sha-raish*, to pull up by the roots, to extirpate.

Onkelos—flourished *circa* 50 B.C.—10 A.D.—says, in his Targum as to this: *rabba d' Phar-oh*, a prince of Pharaoh, leaving undecided the question, whether he was an eunuch or not. However, in the East, a sense of importance, dignity and eminence, was connected with being an eunuch, and *the Zohar looking upon celibacy as a meritorious thing, if its motive be a spiritual one*, calls the *Talmidai 'Hakhameem, i. e.*, Disciples of the Wise, those who occupy themselves with the study of the Word of God, *sâ-ri-sim, i. e.*, eunuchs. This designation is never found in the Talmud, but we find it in the New Testament, Matt. xix, 11–12, spoken of as if an esoteric thing. This passage in the New Testament, can only be thoroughly understood from a Zoharic point of view.‡ It is quite evident, that the Zoharic passage which uses the term under discussion, in the same secret sense which underlies it in the words of Jesus, must have been in existence in his time if not before, and the Zohar cannot be assumed to have copied it from Matthew. Most likely Jesus of Nazareth and Shim-on b. Yo'haï received many of their teachings from the same school, that of the Secret Learning, which accounts for the fact that the Zoharic writings have so many points in common with the New Testament, Philo and the early Patristic literature.

* *Le Pentateuque avec comment. aim le'miqrah, i. e.*, mother to the reading, *et aim le'massoreth, i. e.*, mother to the tradition; *illustr. et recherches philol., critiques, archéol. et scientif. par Elia Benamozegh.* 5 vol. *Livorno.* 1862.

† Comp. Is. lvi, 3, 4, 5; Dan. i, 3, 4, 7, 11, 18; II Kings xx, 18; I Kings xxii, 9; II Kings viii, 6; Ibid. xxv, 19, etc. Kitto's Cyclop. Bib. Liter., Ed. 1876, iii, 358; i, 848–9.

‡ Comp. Josephus. Antiq. iv, c. 8, § 40.

The Church Father Origen followed this text literally.* Indeed this Father adopted many of the opinions of the older Qabbalists.

Exodus ii, 6, 10. The Hebrew periodical *Bikku-reh Ha-ittim, i. e.,* The First Fruits of the Times, Ed. Vienna. 1829. p. 18, says: "As to the opinion that Moses occurs in the ancient history of Egypt under the name of Typhon, we are unable for the present to examine into the correctness of; we will however say, that Typhon was said to be *red haired* (Artapanus, Eusebius *Prep. Ev.* Ed. Paris, Vol. ii, p. 35), but we do not know from what source it has been taken, that Moses was red." If the writer had consulted the Zohar, he would have found, Vol. i, p. 28, *B'sar d'Mosheh soomaq, i. e.*, the flesh of Moses was deep red, and to it refers the saying: The face of Moses was like the face of the sun. Nowhere else in Hebrew literature does this or a similar statement occur. The statement is a proof in favour of the asserted fact, that the Egyptians embodied the life of Moses in the history of their Typhon, and also shows the remote age from which the Zohar obtained its ideas.

Leviticus xxiv, 15. "Whosoever curseth his God, shall bear his sin." Josephus,† Philo Judæus and the Essenians, who were all under the influence of the Secret Learning, agree in this, that this law also prohibits men reviling the gods of the heathens. Strange to say, the Zohar, and no other Hebrew writing, explains this passage in the same way,‡ it distinctly states that whosoever curses strange gods, which "God has imparted to all nations," § shall bear his sin. The same idea is in Ecclesiasticus xxi, 30, not to curse Satan "lest one would forfeit his own life." So in Jude, verses 8-10. Michael dared "not bring against him (Satan) a railing accusation, but said: the Lord rebuke thee."‖ Here is an instance of similar interpretations by these authorities and the Zohar,

---

*Mosheim Institutes of Eccles. History, etc., by James Murdock, D.D., 11th Ed. London. 1880. IIId century, ch. ii, p. 93, N. 3. Smith's Dict. Greek and Roman Biog. iii, pp. 46-55. Kitto, work cited, i, 849.

† Antiq. Bk. iv, c. viii, § 10, and *contra.* Apion Bk. ii, § 34.

‡ Zohar iii, p. 106*b*.

§ Deut. iv, 19.

‖ Comp. Zech. iii, 2. II Peter ii, 10-12. Comp. The Speaker's Commentary, before cited, N. T. iv, pp. 251-2 and notes; also Jude. 9.

from which we conclude, that the Zoharic ideas were in existence at the time of these authorities, most likely all being part of the Secret Tradition. Even the Talmud has been influenced, for we read:* "Satan appeared one day to a man who used to curse him daily, and said to him: Why dost thou this? Consider that God himself would not curse me, but merely said: 'The Lord rebuke thee, Satan!'"

We know that many parts of the Qur'ân, especially that regarding the Pentateuch and its interpretations, were delivered by the Jews to Mohammed, who likewise prohibits the cursing of strange gods in the Qur'ân. Is it reasonable to suppose, that the Zohar borrowed from the New Testament and the Qur'ân, for the benefit of the most secret and philosophical, and in some cases, the most pious and bigoted, of the Church of Israel, which is distinguished in the Zohar as, the *very beloved daughter of YHVH, His only beloved one?* The New Testament borrowed from the Traditional Secret Learning, the Metaphysical side of Judaism, and the Qur'ân borrowed from the Jewish Secret Tradition and the Old and New Testaments.

Numbers xii, 1. "He (Moses) had married an Ethiopian woman." The very rare and ancient book *Dibreh hajyamim l' Mosheh, i. e.,* The Chronicles of Moses, and Josephus in his Antiquities,† from whom Irenæus cites in his Fragments, relate in the History of Moses, that he was a general of the Egyptians against the Ethiopians,‡ whom he conquered, and that he married the king's daughter, none of which is in the Old Testament. Nor does the latter make mention of the father of Moses, called Amram, as having been a judge in Israel, a prophet, and a seer of visions; as Josephus does in his first chapter of the Antiquities. Neither do we find this in the Talmud or the Midrashim, but it is in Maimonides, who lived in Egypt, and it is in the Zohar. The Zohar never copied it from Maimonides, and it is doubtful from Josephus, whose writings were not known among the Jews for many centuries after, and when known, in comparatively recent times, were not considered as an authority of much weight. We must look for the Zoharic statement as belonging to the age,

---

* Treat. *Kiddusheem,* p. 81.
† Bk. ii, c. x.
‡ Comp. Acts vii, 22.

when such traditions were in the custody of the initiated in the Sacred Secret Learning, the source of which was undoubtedly ancient. They were among : "The secret things belonging unto YHVH our Elohim." (Deut. xxix, 29. Numb. xi, 16–17, 24–30. Exod. xxxv, 31, 32.)

Deuteronomy vi, 8. "And thou shalt *bind them for a sign upon thine hand*, and they shall be *as frontlets between thine eyes.*" This law was considered by the ancient Israelites as literally to be followed, hence was the custom of wearing of the phylacteries or tephillin. Choirilos of Samos, (lived about 468–405 B.C.), in his Epos "Persica," in which he immortalizes the victory of the Athenians over Xerxes, writes of the Jews in the Persian army "And behind them came a numerous host of people, distinct from all other people in their bearing and wearing apparel. Their language is like that of the Phœnicians, and they inhabit the mountains of Jerusalem." This "wearing apparel" by which they were distinguished, undoubtedly refers to the phylacteries, "the sign upon the hand" and the "frontlets between the eyes," and "the fringes on the borders of the garments." * These were constantly worn by the males of the Israelites prior to the destruction of their Temple by the Romans. Subsequently the Rabbins limited the wearing of these external symbols of distinction, to the time and service of the morning prayer, and the former literal application of the Law was soon entirely forgotten. The Zohar, however, corroborates the statement by Choirilos, mentioning,† that "R 'Heeyah and R. Yo-seh met a man in the garments prescribed by the Thorah, and carrying arms (weapons) below them." This is also a proof of the antiquity of the book; for unless this R. 'Heeyah and R. Yo-seh lived in the very remote times, they hardly would have mentioned this incident which was lost and unknown, shortly after the destruction of the Temple, and is not mentioned in the Talmud.

II Timothy iii, 8. "Now as *Jannes and Jambres withstood Moses,* so do these, etc." Comp. Exod. vii, 11, 12. The Talmud speaks of two Egyptian magicians : "Yo-haneh and Mareh ;" and in the Zohar we have them as : "Yonos and Yombros." Champollion-Figeac in *Égypte Ancienne*, p. 100 *et seq.*, mentions two magicians by the name of : *Nécepso*

* Numb. xv, 38, 39.
† Zohar i, 204*b*.

and *Petosiris*, who lived in the time of Sesostris (*i.e.*, Rhameses II), from which two names the above two Talmudic names are perhaps a translation: "*Pet-Osiri*" means sacred to Osiris, as "*Poti-phera* or *Pete-phe're*" means, sacred to Phe'ri; so *Yo-haneh* means, the favorite of God (יוחני Yohaneh = יוחנן Yo-hannan or Joannes, Greek), and *Necepso* has been considered the same name as Ne'kho* (Pharao Necho) which occurs in Jeremiah.

We see the Zohar differs from the Talmud in the names. The two magicians who rose against Moses existed, and what the Talmud† says of them is also true.‡ The Zohar mentions them twice; first as two magicians§ and then as Bala-am's sons.|| A marginal note to the first quotation, suggests them to be the same as the Yo-haneh and Mamreh of the Midrash *She'moth Rabbah*, ch. ix, 73c—and so they are. From all which we deduce.

1. That the authorities of the Midrash, Talmud and Zohar, gathered from ancient trustworthy sources, that which was also gathered from such sources and not rejected, by such men as Paul, Pliny and Eusebius. The latter two of whom had not any dealings with the Rabbins.

2. Placing the two names according to the Midrash and Talmud, *i. e.*, *Yo-haneh* and *Mamreh*, on one side, and the other two of the Zohar, *Yonos* and *Yombros*, with the readings of Paul, Pliny and Eusebius, on the other, the comparison will result in showing the correctness of the Zoharic version in opposition to that of the Midrash and Talmud.

3. The Zohar not agreeing with the Midrash and Talmud regarding these two names, had either not seen or known them from these as its sources, or it would not have deviated from such great authorities in Judaism (first, because the matter does not involve any question of such moment as to add any importance to it as a difference of opinion; and second, because in agreeing with the Talmud, the Zohar would have had

---

* *Ibid.*, 102.

† Treat. *Sanhedrin*.

‡ Comp. Eusebius *Prep. evangel, livre* viii, ch. ix, *liv.* ix, ch. xxvii; Pastoret, *Histoire de la legislation Egypte*, ch. xix; Pliny, the elder, in *Historia naturalis, lib.* xxx, c. i. He calls them, *Jamne* and *Jotape*.

§ Zohar ii, 191.

|| Zohar iii, 194, also fol. 90, col. 2.

the benefit of the undisputed authority of the former). Consequently the Zoharic statement is of greater antiquity than the Talmud and Midrash. The Zohar in the main, agrees with the other statements, but it is not probable that the writers of it knew of them, or even if they did, they would not have copied from them as their sources. It, the Zohar, received the tradition from the more ancient sources, at the time when the names had not yet been corrupted, and were as yet even without the Talmudic adjustment of *Yo-haneh* and *Mamreh*. The Zohar does not endeavor to give them a Hebrew or Aramaic appearance, *it leaves them in the original Egyptian garb and shape, because it had them from an original source, prior to the Talmud.* So says Benamozegh. This apparently insignificant item, is a strong piece of evidence for the antiquity of the Zohar.

These names occur in other ancient Rabbinical literature as Yo-hanna and Mamreh, and as Yanes and Yambres, even as Yoannes (*i.e.*, Yohn = John) and Ambrosius. The latter in the *Shalsheleth Haq-qabbalah*, fol. 13*b*. The Targum known as that of Yonathan ben Uzziel from a pre-Talmudic time,* invariably has, Yannes and Yambres,† the Zohar, also pre-Talmudic, always, Yonos and Yombros; the Midrash *Vaÿ-yosah*, like the Talmud, Yohaneh and Mamreh. The latter are evidently *Hebraized*, from the original Egyptian Yanes and Yambres or Jannes and Jambres, as Yonathan and St. Paul have it, whereas the Zoharic version may be ascribed to the predilection of the Syriac language for the vowel *o* instead of *a*. As to Champollion-Figeac's *Nécepso* and *Petosiris*, they designate the position of the two magicians rather than signify the names of the bearers. Pliny's *Jamne* and *Jotape* are undoubtedly a Latinized corruption; compare Jamnes of the Vulgate. As to their having been Bala-am's two sons, see the Targum of Yonathan in Numbers xxii, 22, where " his two boys," (*ne'arav*) is taken in the sense of " *his two sons.*" This also accounts for the statement in Ambrosius: ".*Jamnes et Jambres fratres erant Magi.*"

The names of the magicians who opposed Moses, are also mentioned in

---

* Most probably of the time of Jesus. Kitto's Cyclop. Biblical Liter., ii, 304. See however, *ibid.*, iii, 954 *et seq.*

† Comp. Exod. vii, 11, i, 15, and Talmud, treatise, *Sanhedrin*, c. 9.

the Gospel of Nicodemus, formerly called, the Acts of Pontius Pilate, (c. v, 5) as Jannes and Jambres.

Apulius makes mention of Joannes, a great magician mistaken by Pius for St. John. In the book *Dibreh haÿ-yamim l'Mosheh*, Chronicles of Moses, fol. 56, they are called Yanne and Mamre, and are said to have been the two sons of Bala-am.

Numenius Apamensis, a Greek philosopher of the Platonic-Pythagorean school, lived in the IInd century of our era. He preceded Ammonius Saccas, and belonged probably to the age of the Antonines. He is mentioned by Clement of Alexandria, Origen, Theoderet and Eusebius. In his book on the Good, Numenius relates the history of Moses and mentions by name, Jannes and Jambres as the magicians, which is also stated by Aristobulus in his book dedicated to Ptolemy Philometer.*

Gen. v, 24. "And *Enoch walked with God*, and *he was not, for God took him.*" The ancient Rabbins of the Talmud and Midrashim disagree in their descriptions of '*Ha-nokh* (Enoch) the son of Yê-red; some even place him among the wicked, whilst others rank him with the pious, and a third class place him as intermediate between both. The *Pe'siqthah* pronounces him a "Saint who entered Paradise alive," so does Ben Sirach, and in the Targum Onkelos are two versions of the passage we have above quoted, apparently contradicting each other and yet both confirmatory of the opinion of Enoch's transportation into eternal life. One reads: "And he *was*, for the Lord did not let him die," and the other "And he *was not*, for the Lord did not let him die." Josephus says: "And indeed as to Eliÿah, and as to Enoch, who was before the Deluge, it is written in the Sacred Books that they disappeared, but so that nobody knew that they died." †

In the Midrash *Pirqeh R. Eliezer*, ch. 8, it says: "'Ha-nokh trans-

---

* See Talmud, Treatise *Menachoth*, fol. 85a, Origen *contra*. Celsus. Bk. iv, c. xi. Eng. Ed., vol. ii, p. 218. Eusebius Pamphilus *Præp. Evang.*, Book ix, 8; especially upon this subject. Kitto's Biblical Cyclop. Ed. 1876, ii, p. 464, and the authorities there cited. Apocryphal New Testament. Rev. Dr. Peter Allix, in his: Judgment of the Jewish Church against the Unitarians, also the valuable article by the Rev. John Gregorie, in his works before cited. London. 1684. pp. 61–63.

† Antiq. ix, 2.

mitted the knowledge of computing the seasons to Noah," and the Book of 'Ha-nokh is referred to, as that of which it is said, Gen. v, 1; "This is the book of the generation of Adam." The Zohar (Part I, 36*b*) says: "'Ha-nokh had a book which was identical with the 'book of the generation of Adam;' this is the mystery of wisdom." It is frequently and elaborately quoted in the Zohar. In the 14th and 15th verses of Jude, is a reference which is in the Book of Enoch we now have. Enoch was quoted by the Fathers of the Christian Church, but from the VIIIth to the XVIth century it was lost sight of. Jellinek* gives several '*Ha-nokh* pieces. The book was in existence at the time of Jude and up to 300 A.D.; it disappeared about the VIIIth century and re-appeared about the XVIth. These facts tend to show, as the Zohar frequently quotes, 'Ha-nokh, that it, the Zohar, most probably was not written between the VIIIth and XVIth centuries, it is therefore, from this evidence highly probable, that the Zohar was written before the VIIIth century A. D.†

Exodus iii, 1. "The *mountain of God*, Horeb," Moses and Eliÿah alone, says the Zohar, came down together to learn and teach the Mysteries of the Thorah. This Qabbalistic sentiment, says Benamozegh, found its application in Mark ix, 4, 5; Matt. xvii, 3, 4.

Exodus xiv, 30. "And Israel *saw the Egyptians dead* upon the seashore." In that hour, says the Zohar, the patron-prince (*sar*) of Egypt was reduced from his prominence and made *prince of the Gai-hinnom* (*sar shel gai-hinnom*). Not stated anywhere else in Hebrew literature, but verified by modern Egyptologists, who tell us that Egypt gradually lost her pre-eminence after the downfall of the XVIIIth dynasty, under which the Exodus took place. It is known that Osiris was the patron-prince of Egypt, and became *the prince of the Gai-hinnom, i. e.*, the abode of the dead, by the name of Serapis. It would appear that the Zohar had knowledge of this part of ancient Egyptian mythology, by tradition.

Exodus xx, 18. "And *all the people* saw *the voices* (or sounds, *qo-loth*)." In the Zohar ii, 81*b*, "voices" are interpreted as the "Sephi-

* In his *Bet ha-Midrasch*.

† As to the Book of Enoch see: The Book of Enoch translated from the Ethiopic with Introd. and notes, by Rev. Dr. Geo. H. Schodde. Andover. 1882.

roth," hence they "*saw*" them, and *did not* "*hear*" them. Note R. El-azar's words there. Philo says: "Likewise when the Thorah was promulgated on the Mount Sinaï, it is not said, that the voice had been '*heard*,' but according to the text, it had been '*seen*' by all the assembled people," in a spiritual way.*

Table of the SEPHIROTH, in Circles.

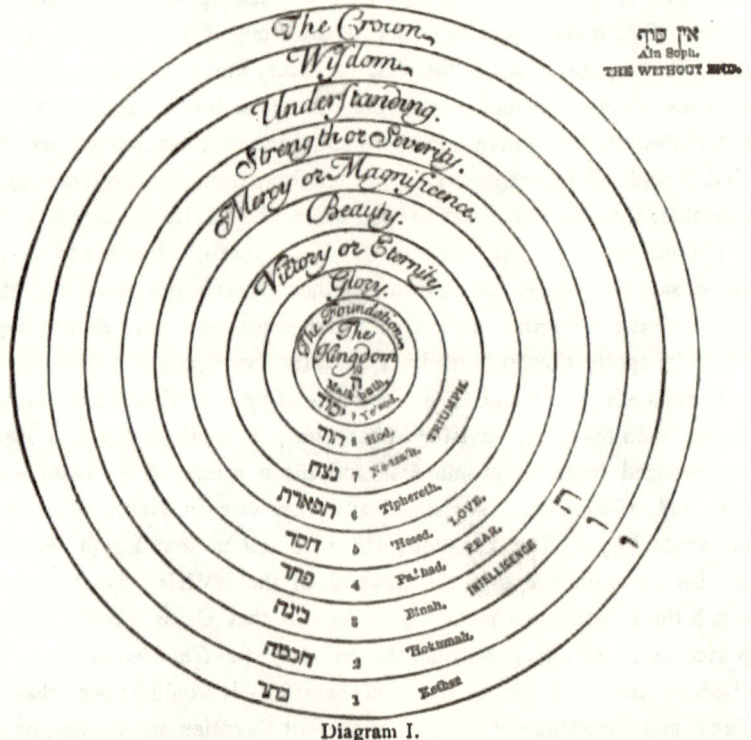

Diagram I.

The above diagram will give the reader, some idea of the arrangement and names, of the intermediaries between the Upper and Lower worlds, termed by the Qabbalists, Sephiroth. We shall explain them more fully hereafter.

* Comp. Philo. Of the Migration of Abraham, Bohn's Ed., Vol. ii, p. 53 *et seq.;* Franck, *La Kabbale,* p. 314, 315.

IV.

FURTHER EXCERPTS FROM THE ZOHAR. PARABLES. EXPLANATION OF NEW TESTAMENT PASSAGES. THE BASIC ELEMENT IN RELIGIONS. HERBERT SPENCER CITED. ANCIENT CHINESE TAOISM. MEANING OF IDEA, ANCIENTLY. NEW TESTAMENT AND PAGAN WRITERS ON THE INVISIBLE AND VISIBLE. THE IDEAL AND REAL, ETC.

AS an introduction to the Siphrah D'Tznioothah is the following parable: "What is the Book of Mysteries? It consists, said R. Shim-on ben Yo'haī, of Five Chapters, contained in a grand palace and filling the whole universe. If, replied Rabbi Yehudah, they contain the fundamental ideas, they would be the most excellent of all things! And so they are, replied R. Shim-on, for the initiated; but he who is unacquainted with that book, is in this respect like a mountaineer who has always dwelt in the wilds of the mountains, and who is a stranger to the usages of civilized life. He sows wheat, but is accustomed to partake of the same, only in its natural condition. One day this barbarian came into a city, and whilst there, good bread, a food until then unknown to him, was placed before him. He asked: What does one do with this? He was told that it was bread to eat. He took it and tasted it with pleasure. He then inquired, of what material is it made? It was answered that it was made of wheat. Afterwards a person offered to him a fine cake kneaded in oil. He partook of it, and again asked: And this, of what is it made? He was told of wheat. Finally one placed before him, the royal pastry, kneaded with oil and honey. He again addressed the same question as at first and obtained the same reply. Then he said: At my home I am in possession of all these things, I partake daily of them in their root, and cultivate the wheat from which they are made. In this crudeness he remained a stranger to the delights which one draws from the wheat, and the (derived) pleasures are lost to him. It is the same with those who stop at the general principles of knowledge, because they are ignorant of the delights which one may draw from the further investigation and application of those principles."*

The Qabbalah holds, that there is a hidden, secret meaning, concealed under the words of the Hebrew Holy Writings, and the Zohar supports this idea:† "Woe, it says: to the man who sees in the Thorah, *i. e.*, Law, only simple recitals and ordinary words! Because, if in truth it only contained these, we would even to-day be able to compose a Thorah much more worthy of admiration. For if we find only the simple words, and we would only have to address ourselves to the legislators of the earth, to those in whom we most frequently meet with the most grandeur. It would be sufficient to imitate them, and make a Thorah after their words and example. But it is not so; each word of the Thorah contains an elevated meaning and a sublime mystery. * * The recitals of the Thorah are the vestments of the Thorah. Woe to him who takes this garment for the Thorah itself! It is with this meaning that David has said: 'O YHVH! open my eyes, to the end that I may contemplate the marvels of Thy Thorah' (Ps. cxix, 18). David wished to speak of that which is concealed under the vestment of the Thorah. There are some foolish people, who seeing a man covered with a beautiful garment, carry their regard no further, and take the garment for the body, whilst there exists a still more precious thing, which is the soul. The Thorah also has its body. There are some of the commandments that one can call the body of the Thorah. The ordinary recitals therein mingled, are the vestments by which the body is covered. The simple take notice only of the garments or recitals of the Thorah, they know no other thing, they see not that which is concealed under the vestment. The more instructed men do not pay attention to the vestment, but to the body which it envelops. Finally, the Wise, the servitors of the Supreme King, those who inhabit the heights of Sinai,‡ are occupied only with the soul, which is the basis of all the rest, which is the Thorah itself; and in the future time they will be prepared to con-

*Zohar ii, 176a, Mantua Ed.
† III, fol. 152b, § *Beha-alothe'ha*.
‡ Num. xi, 24 *et seq.;* Exod. xxiii, 9–11.

template the Soul of that Soul (*i. e.*, the Deity,) which breathes in the Thorah." It also says: "If the Thorah was composed only of ordinary words and recitals, as the words of Esau, Hagar, and Laban, as those which were pronounced by the ass of Bala-am, and by Bala-am himself, wherefore would it be called, the Thorah of Truth, the Perfect Thorah, the Faithful Witness of God? Wherefore would the Wise esteem it more precious than gold or pearls? But no; in each word (of the Thorah) is concealed a more elevated meaning; each recites to our understanding, other things than the events which it appears to contain. And that superior and most holy Thorah is the True Thorah."* Origen uses almost the same language, saying: "If we take our stand on the literature (according to that which seems good to the Jews or to the crowd generally), let us receive what has been written in the Law, and if we do this, I blush to say and confess that God has given us such laws; for the laws of man will appear to be more elegant and reasonable. Compare for example the laws of the Romans, Athenians or Lacedemonians."†

He also says: "What man who has any understanding will suppose that the first, second and third day (of Creation), and the evening and the morning, had been able to exist without a sun, and moon, and stars? And that the first day was as it were, also without a sky? Where can we find a mind so foolish as to suppose that God acted like a common husbandman, and planted a paradise in (the Garden of) Eden, towards the East; and placed in it a Tree of Life visible and palpable, so that one tasting of the fruit by the bodily teeth obtained life? And again that one was a partaker of good and evil by masticating what was taken from the tree? And if God is said to walk in the paradise in the evening, and Adam to hide himself under a tree; I do not suppose that any one doubts that these things figuratively indicate certain mysteries, the history having taken place in appearance, and not literally. Cain also, when going forth from the presence of God, certainly appears to thoughtful men as

---

* Zohar iii, fol. 149*b*.

† Homil. vii, in Levit. See also to the same effect: The Writings of Origen. Clark's Edinburgh Ed., 1869, Vol. 1, pp. 315, 316. Huet. *Origeniana*, p. 167. Philo, Bohn's Ed., i, p. 422. Davidson, Sacred Hermeneutics, Edinburgh, 1843, p. 99.

likely to lead the reader to inquire, what is the presence of God, and what is the meaning of going out from Him," etc., etc.*

A charming allegory in the Zohar also sets forth the same ideas. "Like unto a beautiful woman hidden in the interior of a palace, who when her friend and beloved passes by, opens for a moment, a secret window, and is only seen by him; then again retires and disappears for a long time: so the doctrine shows herself only to the elect (that is, to those devoted to her with soul and body), but also not even to these always in the same manner. In the beginning, deeply veiled, she only beckons to the one passing, with her hand; it simply depends (on himself) if in his understanding he perceives this gentle hint.† Later she approaches him somewhat nearer, and whispers to him a few words, but her countenance is still hidden in the thick veil, which his glances can hardly penetrate.‡ Still later she converses with him, her countenance covered with a thinner veil.§ After he has accustomed himself to her society, she finally shows herself to him, face to face, and intrusts him with the innermost secrets of her heart.‖ He who is thus far initiated into the Mysteries of the Thorah, easily comprehends, that all those profound secrets, are already based upon the simple sense of the word and are in harmony with it, from which (the literal sense of the word) not a single yod is to be taken or added." ¶

Origen in his writings, also admits of the three meanings, an historical,

---

* Origen's works, Clark's Ed. cited, i, 315 *et seq.*, Bk. iv, c. 2. Huet *Origeniana*, p. 167. The Talmud al o holds to a spiritual or hidden meaning in the Hebrew Holy writings, under their letter. Treatise *Sanhedrin* 99*b*. In the Christian Church at present this idea is carried to a great length. See, among others, the curious statements in the writings of Dr. Christopher Wordsworth, Canon of Westminster, especially his Comment. on Genesis and Exodus. London, 1864, p. 52.

† This is the species of interpretation of the Holy Scriptures called: Remez, *i. e.*, indication, hint, known meaning.

‡ The species called: D'rash, *i. e.*, allegorical exposition.

§ This is the Haggadah, which is written in enigmatical language.

‖ This is the species called, Sod or Mystery, *i. e.*, the Secret of the Thorah or Law; the 'Hokhmah, *i. e.*, Wisdom *par excellence*, the Secret Learning or Qabbalah. The ordinary and usual intelligence of the words, etc., was called Pashut. The whole together forms the word PaRDeS, *i. e.*, Paradise, the Intellect.

¶ Zohar ii, fol. 99, § *Mishpatim*. Comp. Matt. v, 18; Luke xvi, 14.

a legislative or ethical, and the mystical sense. The first he compares to *somatikos, i. e.,* the body, the second to *psychikos, i. e.,* the soul, the third to *pneumatikos, i. e.,* the spirit. These corresponding to the Platonic notion of the component parts of the man, *soma*, body ; *psyche*, soul ; *pneuma*, air or spirit. Origen* speaks of these in almost the very words of the Qabbalah.† The learned Franciscan, Nicolas de Lyra, b. *circa* 1270, d. 1340 A. D., forerunner of the Reformation, and an erudite commentator on the Bible,‡ adopts the four Jewish modes of interpretation פרדם PaRDeS = סוד *Sod*, secret, mystical ; *D'rash*, allegorical, *Remez*, spiritual or moral, and פשט *Pashut* literal. In his first prologue, he says : " The letter teaches the things which are done, the allegory those which you believe, the moral the things which you are to do, the anagogical (the mystical interpretation), that to which you tend." § The word PaRDeS, *i. e.*, Paradise or the Intellect, covered the same ground in the mind of the Jewish exegetists.||

Matt. v, 22, " Whosoever shall say, Thou fool, shall be in danger of hell fire."

The Zohar says :¶ " R. 'Hiz'qee-yah, said : He who calls his fellow-man *wicked*, him they will bring down to the *Gai-hinnom, i.e.*, hell fire, and they bring him down לעלעוי *le'il-oÿ*, literally ' to his ribs,' *i. e.*, by scourging him on his bare skin, or by subjecting him to want and starvation, until he is nothing but a skeleton. The above quoted verse from St. Matthew, comprises the Talmudical meanings. The Talmud says :** " He who calls his fellow-man *wicked yored immo le'haÿÿav*," *i. e.*, he goes with him to his life, or, he may, or will, punish him to his very life, even injuring him in his means of earning a living. On these words Rashi commenting, says : " It seems hard to me, that the 'Hakhameem,

---

* Clark's Ed. cited, Vol. i, p. 294-315. Homil. v, in Levit.

† Compare Davidson, Sacred. Hermeneutics, p. 97.

‡ *Postillæ perpetuæ in universa Biblia ;* first printed at Rome 1471-5 in 5 vols.

§ Compare Kitto's Cyclop. Bib. Lit., Ed. 1876, iii, pp. 869-70.

|| Comp. Talmud Ye'rushalmi, French Edition, by M. Schwab, Paris, Vol. i, Introd. Talmudic Miscel. by Hershon, p. 75, § 33.

¶ § *Mishpatim*, Part ii, p. 122a.

** Treatises, *Baba Me'tzeeah* 71a, *Kiddushin* 28a, *Ke'tubboth* 90a, *Yomah* 75a.

i. e., Wise-men, should have permitted Israël to take revenge and retaliate." The termination וי *oÿ* of לעלעוי *le'il-oÿ, i.e., to his ribs*, answers to the Hebrew יו *av* of לחייו *le'haÿ-yav, i.e., to his life*, both meaning *his* with the noun in the plural; the first ל in both words means *to;* hence there remains in the word of the Zohar עלי *ill-a*, which is the same as the Hebrew צלע *tzelah, i.e., rib*. This has been asserted as an error of Moses de Leon, who did not understand the Talmudic sentence and the word *le'haÿ-yav*, but thought it was derived from לחי *le'hee, i.e., the cheek or jaw-bone*. The Zoharic critic, however, did not himself apparently know that *le'il-oÿ, i. e., to his ribs*, is not derived from לוע *lo-ah, i. e.*, jaw or cheek.

II Peter ii, 4. " For if *God spared not the angels that sinned, but cast them down to hell,* and *delivered them* into *chains of darkness*, to be *reserved* unto *judgment*." It has been generally held that this statement applies to Genesis vi, 4, and that the angels referred to are those called בני האלהים *B'nai ha-Elohim, i. e.*, Sons of Elohim, but no account is to be found in Genesis of any punishment of the offenders, and it is the punishment that is especially dwelt on in the Epistle of Peter. Reference is made to them in the Book of Enoch.* The parallel passage is Jude vi. "And (the) angels which kept not their own dignity (principality, dominion), but forsook their proper habitation, he hath kept in everlasting bonds under darkness, unto the judgment of the great day."† From such passages as Ephesians i, 21, we can see, that the celestial world was conceived and spoken of by the Apostles, as arranged according to the dignity of its inhabitants.‡

The Zohar states: " R. Yitz'haq began and said: 'What is man that thou rememberest him' (Ps. viii, 4). This was said at the time when it came into the Will of the Holy One to create man. He called before Himself many hosts of the upper angels and said unto them: 'I wish to create man.' Then they replied: 'Man will not continue one night in his glory' (Ps. xlix, 12). Then the Holy One stretched forth his finger and burned them. After that he called other hosts before him, and said unto them: 'I wish to create man.' And they said before Him 'What is man, that

---

* vii, 1, 2; x, 6, 15; xxi, 6; cc. 1–36.
† Comp. Gen. vi, 2; I Pet. iii, 19; Tobit vi, 14.
‡ Comp. Col. ii, 18.

Thou rememberest him?' 'What is the good of this son of man?' And He said unto them: 'This man shall be in our image so that his wisdom shall be superior to your wisdom.' When Elohim had created man, and man had committed a sin, and gone forth as a culprit, there came Uzza and Azaël and said to the Holy One, 'We have cause of complaint (literally an opening of the mouth, accusation) against Thee. Here is the son of man whom thou hast made; he has sinned before Thee.' And He said unto them: 'If you had been among them, you would have done worse than they.' What then did the Holy One? He threw them down from the holy position that was theirs, even from heaven. * * *
After YHVH had thrown them down from their holy place, even from heaven, they erred after the women of the world, and caused the world to err. Here is a subject worthy of our meditation. Surely it is written 'He maketh His angels spirits,' (Ps.,civ, 4) and surely these were not the angels? How could they exist upon the earth? Come and see! All these angels above do not exist and cannot exist, except in the Upper Light that shines unto them and preserves them, and if this Upper Light is cut off from them they cannot exist. How much less can those whom the Holy One has thrown down, and from whom that Light of Above has ceased? For their glory was altered, and when they came down and the air of this world obtained rule over them, they were changed into another (lower) degree. Here is an explanation. The manna that came down to Israël in the wilderness sprang originally from the dew above,* which comes down from the Ancient One, the Hidden of all the Hidden Ones. And when it comes down its Light shines through all the (created) universe, and from it is fed the field of the apples, and the upper angels. But when it came down here below and the air of this world had rule over it, it became congealed and its splendor was changed, becoming only like coriander seed† and nothing more. How much more so with the angels. When they came down the air had power over them, they were changed from their former degree in which they had been. What did the Holy One then do? He saw that they were misleading the world, so He bound them in iron chains in the mountain of darkness. In what place do they sit? In

---

* Song of Songs v, 2.
† Num. xi, 7.

the depths of the mountains He placed Uzza, and cast darkness into his face, because at that time when the Holy One bound them, Uzza hardened himself and rebelled against the Highest. So the Holy One threw him down into the abyss up to his very neck and cast darkness into his face. Now Azaël, who did not harden himself, the Holy One placed near his fellow, but let the darkness be light to him."* Again, the Zohar says: " They, the spirits of Light and Darkness, dive into the great sea, and when they have arrived at the chain of Uzza and Azaël, they rouse them, and these spring into the mountains of darkness and think that the Holy One is going to cite them to judgment." †

In Luke viii, 31, we have the devils saying: "They besought Him that He would not command them to go out into the deep," (the abyss).

The basic element of most of the ancient, and to this day, of many of the modern religions of the world is, the *idea* of a perfect invisible universe above, which is the real and true paradigm or ideal model, of the visible universe below, the latter being, the reflection, simulacrum or shadow, of the invisible perfect ideal above. This idea was fully understood by the Ancient Egyptians, as was shown in their deities Nut or Neith, the Upper World, Shu or Mâ, the Intermediary, and Seb, the Earth. In India, the same idea is fully set forth in the esoteric books of the Vedas, called the Upanishads. It is The Supreme Ideal Brahm which is the only True. It manifests Itself first in Brama, Vishnu and Siva, past, present and future, time, and through these in the visible, the last being Maya or Illusion. The temples of most of the archaic peoples of Asia and of Egypt, were intended to be visible copies of the heavenly Temple, the starry firmament called *Templum*, and the same idea is visible in those of the Hebrews. Philo and Josephus, represent the Temples of the Israelites, as typical of the visible universe, and this was based on an invisible universe. The archaic heathen free-masons had for their special deity, Jupiter Megalistor, or, the Jupiter of the Universe.

*Zohar, Ed. of Zolkiew, iii, 208a. The Spihrah D'Tznioothah and the Idroth have much upon the angels called B'nai ha-Elohim.

† Zohar, i, 9b.

"And the temple of God was opened in heaven, and there was seen in his temple the ark of his testament." *

The idea of the Upper ideal but *real* and *true*, and the Lower *apparently* real, but in truth *changeable* and *untrue*, goes through the entire Apocalypse of St. John, is in St. Paul, and in the Epistle to the Hebrews.

The Zohar also says: "All that which is found (or exists) upon the Earth, has its spiritual counterpart also to be found on High, and there does not exist the smallest thing in this world, which is not itself attached to something on High, and is not found in dependence upon it. When the inferior part is influenced, that which is set over it in the Superior world is equally (influenced), because all are perfectly united together."† We can compare this with the doctrine to be found in the New Testament. ‡ And an old Jewish Commentator has said: "Know that we have to make a separation between those that are hidden from us, and those (things) that are manifest to us." § The Talmudic maxim is: "If thou wilt know the invisible have an open eye for the visible."

"All that which is contained in the Lower World is also found in the Upper (in prototype). The Lower and Upper reciprocally act upon each other." ||

"All that which is on the earth, is also found above (in perfect prototype), and there is not any thing so insignificant in the world, that does not depend upon another above: in such a manner, that if the lower moves itself the higher corresponding to it moves towards it. As to the number therefore of the different species of creatures, which are enumerated below, the same number is to be found in the upper roots. ¶

* Rev. xi, 19. Comp. *ibid.* 1–2. Exod. xxv, 8, 9, 40; especially Heb. viii, 5, ix, 1. Acts vii, 44; I Chron. xxviii, 12, 13; Ezek. xi. Compare The Speaker's Commentary, on these verses.

† Zohar, i, ¿ *Vaya'hee*, fol. 156, col. 6, 158*b*, 205*b*.

‡ Matt. x, 29–31; Luke xii, 6–7.

§ Recanati in his *Taamey ham-Mitz'voth*, *i. e.*, Meaning of the Commandments *ad init.*

|| Zohar, ¿ *Vaya'hee*, fol. 156, col. 2.

¶ Sepher *Shephathal*, fol. 11, col. 2. Comp. Matt. x, 29, 30, 31; Luke xii, 6, 7; Matt. xviii, 10.

This is also the view of R. Yitz'haq Luria. "All the creatures in the world have each a superior above. This superior, whose inner pleasure it is to emanate into them, cannot impart efflux until they have adored."*

According to the Qabbalah, the emanated in its inner being, does not in reality proceed from the emanating one; that which is produced is only an appearance,† and the real (or true) nature remains in the inner upper one.

"From the Great Light of the being of Ain Soph and its A'tzeeluth, after It had emanated the A'tzeeluth from Itself, nothing was withdrawn: Its powers which expand and reveal themselves, are affixed and interwoven in It, and in Its being."‡

A curious idea of the Qabbalists is, that as to emanation stated in the book, Nobeleth 'Hokhmah:

"The Qabbalists say, that the entering into existence of the worlds, happened through delight, in that Ain Soph, rejoiced in Itself, and flashed and beamed from Itself to Itself; and from these intelligent movements, and spiritual and divine scintillations, from the parts of Its being to Its being, which are called delight, Its sources have spread themselves toward the outside, as seeds for the world, etc." These movements are called the Upper Ziwug.§

The soul has its origin in the Supreme Intelligence, in which it is asserted, the forms of the coming existences already can be distinguished from each other, and this Supreme Intelligence can be termed the Universal Soul. From thence, if it is a masculine soul, it passes through the principle of Grace, the Expansion (Right side); if a female, it impregnates itself from the principle of Justice, the Concentration (Left side), finally it is born into this world in which we live, through the union of the King and Queen who are, as regards the generation of the soul, like the human species in the generation of the body.|| So the soul is as-

---

* Sepher *M'bo Sha-arim*, near the end.

† Similar to the idea of Maya or Illusion of the Hindu philosophy.

‡ Sepher *Shephathal*, fol. 25.

§ Comp. *The Eme'h ha-Mele'h*, i. e., Valley of the King, fol. i, in *Shaar Shashuah* (the Delight). *Sheber Joseph*, fol. 61.

|| Zohar iii, fol. 7.

serted to descend here below, and so, it is asserted, it is restored to the bosom of the Deity when it has fulfilled its mission, and adorned by its virtues, is prepared for heaven; and raising itself by its own action and the assistance of the Divine Love, which it incites by that which it feels, to the highest degree of emanation, to the *real existence*, thus places itself in harmony and affinity with the *ideal form*. This is what the Qabbalah undertakes to support, with what basis we do not know.* "In that manner, says the Zohar,† life is drawn at the same time from on High and from Below, the source renews itself, and the sea always full, distributes its waters in all places."

This idea of the perfect invisible and the reflection or imperfect visible, Herbert Spencer places among the primitive ideas of mankind.‡ We find these ideas in the archaic literature of China. Dr. De Groot says:

" The Tao-teh-King, *i. e.*, The Book of the Perfection of Nature, attributed to Laou Tsz', contains the following principles: There was a time when Heaven and Earth did not exist, but only an unlimited Space in which reigned absolute immobility. All the visible things and all that which possesses existence, were born in that Space from a powerful principle, which existed by Itself, and from Itself developed Itself,§ and which made the heavens revolve and preserved the universal life; a principle as to which philosophy declares we know not the name, and which for that reason, it designates by the simple appellation Tao, which we may nearly describe as the universal soul of nature, the universal energy of nature, or simply, as nature. Tao manifested itself in Heaven and Earth, with which it is, so to say, One. If man reaches to purity and rest, he

* See the Pardes Rimonim, fol. 60–64.

† I, fol. 60–70.

‡ The Principles of Sociology, 3d Ed. New York. 1886. Vol. i, c. viii, § 53, p. 105 *et seq.*

§ Compare: "The Holy One, Blessed be He! created and destroyed several worlds before the present one was made, and when this His last work was nigh completed, *all the things of this world, all the creatures of the universe, in whatever age they were to exist, before even they entered into this world, were present before the Deity in their true form.* Thus are the words of Ecclesiastes to be understood 'What was, shall be, and what has been done, shall be done.' "—Zohar iii, 61*b*. Comp. the Sayings of the Jewish Fathers, by Charles Taylor, p. 70, note 36, end.

will be not only one with the Heaven and Earth, the former being the ideal of purity and the latter of passivity or rest, but his entire existence even, may be absorbed into the great principle Tao. Purity and rest or peace, imply the return into the maternal breast, into that principle which is the source and foundation of all felicity. We have to attain purity, through the exercise of virtue, and repose, by freeing ourselves from the anxieties of the world and the inquietude of the human spirit. These principles will be able to conduct, following the manner of their application, perhaps to a moral epicurianism or a moral asceticism, and at the same time to the belief in the possibility of acquiring immortality. This is the superior part upon which has been constructed the entire system of Taoism." * Of the writings of Laou Tsz' the celebrated French Sinalogue Pauthier, has said: "Human wisdom cannot ever use language more holy and profound." †

The Asiatic Journal says: "By the Chinese, man is considered as a mikrokosm; the universe is man, on a large scale: this is all we find positively stated upon the subject. Human reason is the reason of the universe. The holy-man, or sage by eminence, is like the great pinnacle, and spirit. He is the first of all beings. His spirit is one with the heavens, the master work of the Supreme Reason, being perfectly unique." (Asiatic Journal, No. xxxvi, New Series, Dec., 1832, p. 306.)

Dr. Medhurst quotes from one of the disciples of Laou Tsz': "What is there superior to Heaven and Earth, and from which Earth and Heaven sprung? Nay, what is there superior to Space and which moves in Space? The great Tao is the parent of Space, and Space is the parent of Heaven and Earth, and Heaven and Earth produced men and things * * * The venerable Prince (Reason) arose prior to the Great Original, standing at the commencement of the Mighty Wonderful, and floating in the ocean of Deep Obscurity. He is spontaneous and self-existing, produced before the beginning of the void, commencing prior to uncaused existences, per-

---

* *Annales du Musée Guimet. Tome Onzième et Douzième. Les Fêtes annuellement célébrées à Émoui* (Amoy) *Étude concernant la religion populaire des Chinois, par J. J. M. De Groot, etc. Traduite du Hollandais, etc.,* Paris. Ernest Leroux, éditeur *1886*, 2 vol.; Vol. ii, p. 692 *et seq.*

† *Ibid.*, p. 695.

vading all Heaven and Earth, whose beginning and end no year can circumscribe." *

Laou Tsz' (b. *circa* 604 B. C.) in his Tao-teh-King, by Dr. Williams translated, Canons of Reason and Virtue, ch. xlii, says: "Tao produced one, one produced two, two produced three, and three produced all things." † An examination of the writings of this ancient Chinese philosopher and their comparison with the Qabbalah, will show many points of similarity. ‡

The Chinese believe, as do many other peoples, that each created being or thing has a double. §

The "*ideas*" of these early thinkers, especially Plato, were not intellectual "ideas" or conceptions, as we, in our day, usually understand the word, idea, they were more properly specific essences or the absolute realities of things; this the Pythagoreans meant by their Real-forms, of which the material forms are only the illusions, and are nothing but fleeting, changeable images. This was the view taken by Aristotle and Plato. The latter sought to consider them as *entities, noumena*, of which all individualities were only the *phenomena*. Philo also says: "God, intending to make a visible world, first formed an intelligible one; that so having an incorporeal and most god-like pattern before him, he might make the corporeal world agreeable to it."

Still Plato has some thoughts which evince that they are like our ordinary ideas, as, *e. g.*, goodness, justice, beauty.

The idea of the visible declaring the invisible, is very old, and in the Psalms we find it beautifully described: " *The heavens declare the glory of Elohim ;* and the firmament showeth His handiwork." ||

---

*Cited in The Middle Kingdom, etc., by Prof. S. Wells Williams, LL.D. New York. 1883. Vol. ii, p. 214.

† *Ibid.*, 210.

‡ Comp. Dr. Williams' work cited, pp. 206–217, 246.

§ Herbert Spencer, The Principles of Sociology, Vol. i, c. viii, §§ 53, 57, 58; c. xiii, § 96. *Musée Guimet.* Tome Douzième, p. 621 *et seq.*, pp. 648–49.

|| Ps. xix, 1 ; see also *ibid.*, viii, 1 ; c. xiii, 4 ; xxxiii, 6 ; lxviii, 4 ; lxxxix, 11 ; Prov. iii, 19.

Xenophon says, "The Supreme God holds himself invisible, and it is only in his works that we are capable of admiring him." *

Plato tells us, God the eternal, the Chief Ruler of the universe and its creator, the mind alone beholds; but that which is produced we behold by sight. † So Cicero, "Though you see not the Deity, yet by the contemplation of his works, you are led to acknowledge a God." ‡

And St. Paul, speaking of Christ, says: "For *the invisible things of him from the creation of the world are clearly seen,* being understood *by the things that are made,* even his eternal power and Godhead." § "For *in him we live, and move, and have our being; as certain of your own poets have said,* For we are also *his offspring.*" (Acts xvii, 28.)

The type and anti-type of the first and second Adam is to be found in the Rabbinical writings. In reading the first and second chapters of Genesis, a distinction was made by the learned of the Israëlites, between the higher Adam, *i. e.,* the Adam Qadmon, or first Paradigmic Ideal Man,—who was *the Light of the World, and had created and had control over, all the things,* spiritual or material, and who was mystically referred to where it is said, they two shall be one flesh; and the inferior (the terrestrial) Adam, *who was lord only of the visible creation,* who had only "the breath of life" but not "the living soul." ||

The Zohar says: "Man, *i. e.,* the Spiritual Man, is both the import and the highest degree of creation, for which reason he was formed on the sixth day. As soon as the Man was created, everything was complete, including the Upper and Lower worlds, for everything is comprised in the Man. *He unites in Himself all the forms.*" ¶ This is a reference to the Primordial Celestial Ideation Man, the Adam Illa-ah or Adam Qadmon,

---

* Memorabilia, Bk. iv, c. 3.

† Timæus.

‡ *Disp. Tusc.*, Bk. i, c. 28.

§ Rom. i, 20. Comp. Origen's works, English Ed., Vol. ii, 129.

|| Christian Schœttgen, *Horæ Hebraicæ et Talmudicæ in Universum Novum Testamentum,* etc. Dresden and Leipzig. 1733. Vol. i, 512–514, 670–673. Schœttgen gives this in explanation of I Cor. xv, 45, and Rom. v, 12.

¶ Zohar iii, 48*a*.

not to the terrestrial Adam made of dust. The first is called the Bolt or that which unites Heaven and Earth, the Invisible and Visible. It is He:

"Who is the *Image* of the *Invisible God* (Elohim), the *first-born of every creature. For by him were all things created, that are in heaven, and that are in earth, visible and invisible,* whether they be *thrones,* or *dominions,* or *principalities,* or *powers,* (*i. e.,* the Sephiroth): *all things were created by him, and for him.* * And *he is before all things,* and *by him all things* consist (*exist*). And *he is the head of the body, the Church:* who is the beginning, the first-born from the dead; that in *all* (*things*) *he might have the pre-eminence.* For it pleased *the Father that in him should all fullness* (*the pleroma*) *dwell.*" † "Are not five sparrows sold for two farthings, and not one of them is forgotten before God. But even the very hairs of your head are numbered. Fear not therefore: ye are of more value than many sparrows." ‡

"Now unto the King eternal, immortal, invisible, the only Wise God (Elohim), *be* honor and glory for ever and ever. Amen."§

The Mohammedans say, the first thing God created was a pen. "Indeed the whole Creation is but a Transcript, and God when He made the World, did but write it out of that Copy which He had of it in His Divine understanding from all Eternity. The Lesser Worlds (Mikrokosmos) or Men, are but transcripts of the Greater (the Makrokosmos), as Children and Books are the copies of themselves." ||

---

* Comp. Schœttgen, work cited, i, pp. 662, 807–8; also Plato's Timæus.

† I Col. 15–19. Comp. Schœttgen, work cited, i, 807 *et seq.,* 812.

‡ Luke xii, 6–7. Matt. x, 29–31. Comp. Schœttgen, work cited, i, p. 103 *et seq.*

§ I Tim. i, 17. See also Heb. i, 3, xi, 27. I Cor. xii, 12. To the student who may wish to be *learnedly informed* on the *origin of Christianity,* we especially recommend, in connection with a study of the Qabbalah, the learned work of Christian Schœttgen, *Horæ Hebraicæ et Talmudicæ in Universum Novum Testamentum, etc.*

|| The works of the Rev. Mr. John Gregorie, etc., 4th Ed. London. 1684. To the Reader. Compare for further knowledge upon the content of chapters iv, v, The Jewish and Christian Messiah. A study, etc., by Prof. Vincent Henry Stanton, Edinburgh 1886, and the writings cited by him, pp. xi–xii; also, A Hist. of the Jewish People in the time of Christ, by Dr. Emil Schürer, Edinburgh, 1885, and the works cited by him; also, St. Synesius, on Dreams.

Figure 3.

V.

PASTOR OF HERMAS, ETC., ON THE NATURE OF CHRIST. THE TEACHING OF THE TWELVE APOSTLES ON THE KOSMIC MYSTERY. THE OPPOSITIONS AND HARMONY. THREE CONCEPTIONS OF JESUS.

IN the Pastor of Hermas (*circa* 138 A. D.) the Holy Spirit, the Jewish She'kheen-ah, which came to live in Christ, that is, the *Divine Nature* of the Christ, is at once the *Holy Spirit above all* and the *true Son of God* before the Creation of the Universe, and the *author* of the Universe. He is identified in Hermas with the arch-angel Michaël, who is the Great Angel of Israël, and is Metatron, the Presence Angel of the Covenant. Above all and infinitely superior to all other angels. The writers of the New Testament call Christ the *first-born* of Creation.* Justin Martyr, says, the Son of God is an angel; † as also do Clement of Alexandria, (Pedag. Bk. i, c. 7) and Origen *contra* Celsus, (Bk. v, 53, *ibid*. viii, 27). Lactantius (*Inst. div.* Bk. ii, c. viii) makes *the Word*, the *first-born brother of Satan*, and *the first of all creatures*. According to Hermas, the Son of God is the Thorah. ‡

The Teaching of the Twelve Apostles, chap. xi, has this curious expression. "And *every* approved *true prophet doing (what he doeth)* with reference to *the Kosmic mystery of the Church*." What is the meaning of "the Kosmic mystery of the Church?" Clement of Alexandria uses the same expression of Christ, "being not Kosmic, he came to men as Kosmic." (Strom. vi, 15). There is an *archetypal Church* and its "Kosmic"

---

* Colos. i, 15; Heb. i, 6; Apocal. iii, 14.
† I Apol. 6 and 63; Tryph. 93, 34, 56, 60-61.
‡ *Le Pasteur a'Hermas*. Paris, 1880, pp. 88-93.

manifestation; (Heb. ix, 1) so the Qabbalists say, to every "Upper Mystery" corresponds a mystery in our, the "Lower" world, which is the *Kosmos*.

By the Hebrews the Church of Israel was called the mystic Bride, but among the early Christians the Church of Christ being considered as the true Israel; the ancient prophets may be said to have acted and spoken with reference to the "Kosmic Mystery," which in our "Lower" world, is the counterpart of the *celestial mystery* of Christ and the *Christian* Church in the "Upper." As the Kosmic sanctuary or temple, was a pattern of the Heavenly or Upper, so a "Kosmic Mystery" is, a spiritual idea symbolized in the matter-world. The Zohar says רזא דעלמא עלאה *râ-za de'alma illa-ah, i. e.,* a Mystery of the *Upper World* (Exod., fol. 90*b*, end). So a few lines further it says, "On this אנכי *a-no-khee, i. e.,* I, depend mysteries of Above and Below רזין עלאין ותתאין *rázin illa-in u-te'tha-in.**

The pseudo-Clement of Rome, writes: "God made man male and female. The male is Christ: the female, the Church." The Qabbalists called the Holy Spirit, the mother; and the Church of Israel, the Daughter. Solomon engraved on the walls of his Temple, likenesses of the male and female principles, to adumbrate this mystery; such, it is said, were the figures of the cherubim.† This was, however, not in obedience to the words of the Thorah. They were symbolical of the Upper, the spiritual, the former or maker, positive or male, and the Lower, the passive, the negative or female, formed or made by the first.‡ The oppositions, the positive and negative, conditioned by the harmony, govern, as far as man can ascertain, throughout the entire universe. In it everything is in motion, in opposition, yet held in combination. This applies to the mental as well as the physical world, and from

---

* The Teaching of the Twelve Apostles, with illustrations from the Talmud. Two lectures * * given at the Royal Institution of Great Britain, by C. Taylor, D.D., Master of St. John's College, Cambridge. Cambridge, 1886. See pp. 82–91, 104, 133 and notes. This book is also termed, the Didaché or Teaching. See also The Oldest Church Manual called, the Teaching of the Twelve Apostles, etc., by Philip Schaff. New York. 1885. 201–202 and notes.

† I Kings, vi. See Talmud Babli. *Yomah*, 54*a;* Exod. xxxvii, 9.

‡ Comp. Taylor's Didaché, cited, 84 *et seq.*

these oppositions, controlled by the peace or harmony, proceeds the new productions. The ancients knew this and placed it among the zodiacal signs. Scorpio, the male or positive, is in opposition, to Virgo, the virgin, the negative, but between is Libra, the scales or balance, the harmony. The idea is set forth throughout the ancient Qabbalistic book Ye'tzeer'ah. It is especially noticeable in our own earth, through the difference of sex and the tendency to unification, by which the existence itself is preserved. Among the Qabbalists, this necessity to continued creation and existence, is called the Balance, and the oldest book of the Zoharic writings, the Siphrah D'Tznioothah, treats especially upon this subject, but its explanation is continued in the Idroth. The D'Tznioothah begins: " We have learned (by oral tradition): that the Book of Mystery, is the book which describes the equilibrium of the Balance. Before the Balance existed, Face could not view Face,* and the primordial kings died, (comp. Gen. xxxvi, 31 *et seq.*) and their sustenance was not found, and the earth was desolate until the Head, the Delight of all Delights, prepared, perfected and imparted the garments of costliness. This Balance hangs in the Place (*Maqom*) which is No-Thing (*Ayin*). In the same were brought into equilibrium those who did not yet exist. The Balance exists through the At-tee'qah, *i. e.*, Ancient One. Is not held anywhere and is invisible. In it, ascended, and in it, do ascend, things which were not, which are, and which will be. In the Concealed of the Concealed, there is formed and prepared, the representation of a cranium † full of crystalline dew, a membrane of air. Transparent and hidden filaments of pure wool are hanging in the Balance.‡ And they manifest the Good Will of Good Wills through the prayers of the lower ones, by a look of the open eye which never sleeps and is always watching. The Providence below by the light (or eye) of the Providence above," etc.

---

* The Parzuphim, Intellectual, Moral and Material Worlds, of which more hereafter.

† The immense cranium is the representation of the Makrokosm, the arched firmament above and surrounding us, called Heaven. The Makrokosm is usually represented as an immense man, but sometimes as an immense head, the head of man containing the intellectual part of man.

‡ Hanging threads of pure wool, are a symbol among some of the Orientals for the efflux of wisdom and vitality.

There seem to be three conceptions of Jesus in the N. T.

I. As a prophet favoured with a full flow of the Holy Spirit. This we find in the Synoptics and Acts of the Apostles. We must, however, distinguish passages, where the name Son of God, is given metaphysically, they are Mark xiii, 32; Matt. xi, 27, with Luke x, 22; and Matt. xxviii, 19. The recitals of the miraculous conception also tend to put the son of Mary outside of humanity.

II. As a Great angel, the instrument of the Creation of all the Things,* abased momentarily in the position taken by him as Redeemer, then raised to the Throne of God in recompense for this sacrifice. †

III. The Johannic theology, the most metaphysical and mystical of all, which makes Jesus a being positively participating in the *Divine Nature*,‡ who descends upon our earth without any loss of glory,§ but full of grief, and this glory is again found in him after his death, which is for his glorification,|| as that which it was before, his death.¶ St. John makes no allusion to the eternity of the Son, but solely to his pre-existence through affinity with the world, and he affirms frequently the inferiority and subordination of the Son to the Father. The first Christians believed in their time, in an impending return of Jesus in a second advent, as the Christ, and the hope of a reign of 1000 years for the elect. This has not a little contributed to the success of early Christianity and the enthusiasm of the then faithful. It is to be found in the N. T. in many places.** The idea of the immediate second advent of Jesus as the Christ and as the Messiah coming in the glory of Malkhuth, *i. e.*, his Kingdom, is therein fully set forth.†† The same idea runs through all the Apocalypse, which was

---

* I Cor. viii, 6; Col. i, 16; Heb. i, 2, xi, 3.
† II Cor. viii, 9; Phil. ii, 5–11; Heb. ii, 6–11, 17, iii, 3; Apocal. v, 9.
‡ Gospel i, 1.
§ *Ibid.* i, 14.
|| *Ibid.* xii, 23–28; xiii, 31, 32.
¶ *Ibid.* xvii, 4, 5.
** Comp. Matt. xvi, 27–28; Mark viii, 38, ix, 1; Luke ix, 26–27.
†† See Matt. xxv, 64; Mark xiv, 62; Matt. xxiv, 3–36; compare Mark xiii, 1–32; Luke xxi, 5–33; I Cor. xv, 51–53; I Thess. iii, 13, iv, 13–18; II Thess. ii, 6; Acts ii, 15 *et seq.;* Rom. xvi, 20; I Cor. vii, 26, 29, x, 11; Philip. iv, 5; Heb. i, 2, ix, 26, x, 25, 27; James v, 4, 8, 9; I Pet. i, 5, 20, iv, 7, 17; I Epist. John ii, 18, 28, especially Apocal. xi, 15.

written about 68 or the beginning of 69 A. D. In it are references as to the 1000 years*, and the vanquishing of Anti-Christ.†

* Apoc. xx, 4-5.

† *Ibid.* xix, 11, 21. See in this connection I Cor. xv, 23-28; and The Hidden Wisdom of Christ and the Key of Knowledge or the History of the Apocrypha, by Ernest De Bunsen. London. 1865. 2 vols. The Angel-Messiah of the Buddhists, Essenes, and Christians, by Ernest De Bunsen. London. 1880. Compare also the Keys of St. Peter, by the same author; Harnack on, The Pastor of Hermas, Vis. ii, 4, 1; Exod. xxv, 9, 40; xxvi, 30; xxvii, 8; Numb. viii, 4.

Figure 4. Arddha Nàri, the Hindu Androgene.

Figure 5.

VI.

THE SECRET OF THE ACCOUNT OF CREATION IN GENESIS.   EX NIHILO NIHIL FIT.   DOCTRINE OF THE NON-ANNIHILATION OF MATTER.   SOME QABBALISTIC ACCOUNTS OF THE CREATION.   THE HEAVENLY ADAM. CREATION BY THE WORD.   THE ZOHAR SETS FORTH THE CIRCULAR MOVEMENT OF THE EARTH MANY CENTURIES BEFORE COPERNICUS. OPINIONS OF THE ANCIENTS ON THE CIRCULAR MOVEMENT OF THE EARTH.

WE have referred to the ancient Asiatic idea, that above the earth, in the heavens, existed a true and perfect ideation of everything created in the universe, visible or invisible. That this perfect ideal, true and real paradigm, was in opposition to yet in harmony with, its imperfect shadow, the changeable—by man considered, real—universe, but the really, untrue and unreal. The unseen universe was a Makrokosm, to the visible, and the latter was, in comparison with the former, a Mikrokosm, the latter was also as to the inferior copies of it in the descending scale, a Makrokosm, and yet when compared with the higher beings of which it was a copy, it was a Mikrokosm, and this was so in the ascending or descending scale depending on position. This view is shown in both the New and Old Testaments, which are Semitic and Oriental books. The Qabbalah holds fully to this idea. It also claims, that the first account of the Creation in Genesis, referred exclusively to this ideal world and to an ideal man. The ten "saids"* or desires, under the Will of the Deity, made this perfect ideal paradigm of the universe. In the first account in Genesis, there is not any Garden of Eden, not any Eve, and the Ideal Man is created as an Androgene but in the similitude of Elohim. The ten "saids" are divided, seven are given to the lower creation, three to the upper, the male-female. The account begins with the lowest and goes up to the highest, the invariable procedure of the Qabbalists. The vitality of this Man is to be supported on strictly vegetarian principles, animal death is not contemplated. We have not space at this time, to go into an extended analysis of this first account, we have many new views of it in writing, and an analytical examination of it which is very curious.

We now advance for the consideration of the reader some thoughts we have worked out, as to the account in Genesis, in connection with modern scientific physics. It will be noticed in reading the first account of the Creation, that in the first place it is Elohim, which creates the duality, *i. e.*, heaven and earth, the active and passive, positive and negative. The action of the positive or active, upon the negative or plastic, produced, by the Deity's wish, Light; but this was not fire or even daylight, it was the white, hidden fire, which permeates all things and becomes visible through friction, the result being black fire or visible light. We may call this white fire the energy of attraction, electricity, etc. Its comprehensive name we do not know. It exists as the affinity, vitalization and bond, of all the atoms. The key of this chapter of Genesis is the number four. This is the number of the letters of the Tetragrammaton or Ineffable Name. Arranging the numbers of the days in this form:

*As to the ten "saids" see: The Sayings of the Jewish Fathers, etc., by Charles Taylor. London, 1877. p. 92, and notes.

and reading the account of the Creation in the first and second chapters of Genesis, we have the following result:

I. 1. The creation of Light, the hidden principle of attraction. Force or vital energy, the bond of all the atoms.

II. 4. The creation of the sun, moon, planets and stars, in the firmament of heaven.

III. 2. The division of the firmament in the midst of the waters, the crystalline sea of the sky. The crystalline sea under the firmament, was divided from the waters, the crystalline sea above the firmament.

IV. 5. The waters still cover the earth. The lower have their crystalline sea and its fish, the birds which float in it; the fish are also created to inhabit the lower waters.

V. 3. The dry land now appears and vegetation sprouts forth.

VI. 6. The animals appear and finally, the androgenic Man, created in the similitude, image and likeness of Elohim, which is to reproduce, through a copy of itself, its own species.* On the seventh day appears the rest point in the centre. "Elohim ended His work." Then comes the account of "the generations," by YHVH Elohim to be created materially. The earth was covered with a mist or nebulous matter. In the second account of the Creation, the terrestrial man is "formed of the dust of the ground, and has breathed into his nostrils the Nephesh, *i. e.*, breath of life, and becomes a living soul." The Garden of Eden, the Neshamah or intellect is then planted, and the man is put into it; man has however, as yet no knowledge of good or evil, the Rua'h or ethical spirit was not yet in the man, and the power of judgment of the good and evil did not yet exist in Adam. The terrestrial Adam, like its predecessor, the perfect paradigm or Celestial Man, was yet an androgene, and whilst in this condition all the creatures are brought before man and named, but "for Adam there was not found an help-meet." Then YHVH Elohim creates, from Adam's side, woman. The latter however existed in Adam, in potentiality, from the first. The serpent, which " was more subtile than any beast of the field which YHVH Elohim had made," now appears and a dialogue ensues, it will be noticed that neither the woman

* The Androgenic being, as the first human existence, appears in nearly all the ancient religions.

or the serpent use the Ineffable Name YHVH. After eating of the fruit of the tree of the knowledge of good and evil, having made conscience and the ethical, part of themselves, the still small voice of YHVH Elohim appears to them in the intellect, to accuse them. We cannot for want of space continue this subject, but it will be noticed, that the creation follows a philosophical sequence.*

Not only does the Qabbalah repudiate the adage *ex nihilo nihil fit.*, *i. e.*, "From nothing nothing is made†" that is, nothing can come from nothing, but it does not believe in the absolute annihilation of anything which has ever existed. "There is not any thing new under the sun."‡ "Not any Thing," says the Zohar: "is lost in the universe, not even the vapour which goes out our mouths, as all things, it has its place and its destination, and the Holy One, blessed be It! makes it concur to Its works; not anything falls into the void, not even the words and the voice of man, but all has its place and its destination."§ This is one of the most mysterious of the doctrines of the Qabbalah, and the Zohar makes it proceed, from the lips of an unknown aged man, who is immediately interrupted, by several of the companions exclaiming: "Old man! what hast thou done? Would it not have been of greater value to have kept silence? Because now thou art carried away, without any sail and without any mast, upon an immense sea. If thou desirest to mount thou wouldst not be able, and in descending, thou wilt meet an abyss without

---

* As to the Celestial Adam compare: The Sayings of the Jewish Fathers, by Charles Taylor. London, 1877. pp. 70, n. 36; 72, n. 37.

† See Lucretius *De Rerum Natura*, Bk. i, 151–265. The ancient Hindu philosophical system, termed *Sankhya*, holds to the same idea; Indian Wisdom, etc., by Prof. Monier Williams. London, 1875. p. 89 *et seq.*

‡ Comp. Eccles. i, 9, 10.

§ Zohar, Part ii, fol. 100*b*, § *Mishpatim*. Comp. As to the ancient Hindu idea of non-annihilation; Indian Wisdom, before cited, pp. 62–63. As to the Eternity of Sound; *Ibid.*, pp. 110, 111. For the curious theory in regard to the latter, see; Christianity contrasted with Hindu Philosophy, etc., by Prof. James R. Ballantyne. London. 1859. pp. 177–195. The statement of this author as to America, on page 193, exhibits so much prejudice and ignorance, that we have great doubts as to his truthfulness, in many of his statements.

any bottom."* The companions then cite to him, the example of their Master—R. Shim-on ben Yo'haï—who, reserved in his expressions, would not venture upon that sea, without being careful to have a means to return, that is, R. Shim-on would conceal his thoughts under the veil of parable or allegory. Shortly after, however, the same principle is set forth plainly: "All things of which this world is composed, spirit as well as body, will again enter into the Principle, and into the root from which they went out."† "The Holy One, blessed be It! is the commencement and end of all the degrees (Sephiroth?) of creation; all these degrees (Sephiroth?) are marked with Its seal, and we cannot denominate It except through the unity; It is the sole Being in spite of the innumerable forms with which It is clothed." ‡

The Qabbalist Abram ben Dior, says: "When they (the Qabbalists) affirm, that All Things have been drawn from No-Thing, they do not wish to speak of nothing properly to say, for never can being come from Non-being, but they understand by Non-being, that, which one can conceive of, neither by its cause or its essence; it (the No-Thing) is in a word, the Cause of Causes; it is It whom we call the Primordial Non-being, because It is anterior to the entire universe; and we understand (by the Adam Qadmon or Celestial Man or Adam) not only the material objects, but also Wisdom, (*i. e.*, the Word) by which the Universe has been founded. If now it is demanded: What is the *essence of Wisdom, and pursuant to what mode is it contained in the Non-being*, or in the Supreme Kether (Crown), nobody will be able to respond to that question, for, *in the Non-being, there is not any distinction, not any mode of existence*.§ They also will not be able to comprehend how Wisdom is found united to Vitality (or Life)."‖

* Zohar, *Ibid.*

† Zohar, Part ii, fol. 218*b*.

‡ Zohar i, fol. 21*a*.

§ We shall frequently apply in our translations, the *neuter*, It, to the Supreme Deity, instead of using He, which indicates the *masculine* gender. The Deity not having any sex. If we depart from this in any place, it is in deference to usual and familiar Bible quotations, which use the masculine gender, or where such a distinction is important for the more complete understanding of the subject matter.

‖ Comment on Sepher Ye'tzeer'ah, see Rittangel's Edition, p. 65 *et seq*.

Notwithstanding the idea of the non-annihilation (and absolute non-destruction of matter) except by the decree of the Deity, who is the Principle of the oppositions and of the harmony, the tendency in nature, to dissolution, death and change, as well as to vitality, life, and the building up into new forms, is apparent throughout the Qabbalah. This is shown in the ideas of the angels and of the demons or shells.

If we look at the principles of this metaphysical religious philosophy in one of its simplest forms, we shall see that in each of all the objects of nature, the Qabbalists recognize two distinct elements; one is the interior, incorruptible and life-giving principle, which reveals itself in the spiritual, *e. g.*, in vital energy or the Form; the other, is the purely exterior, plastic and material, which is considered as inert and without life or vitality, always tending to dissolution and a return to its original atoms. These two are considered as existing, in all the created, in a greater or less degree. The first as a symbol of Blessing and life, the latter as a symbol of Curse and death. The first, is the Qabbalistic hierarchy of the angelic host and good spirits, the latter, that of the demons or *K'lippoth*, *i. e.*, shells and evil spirits. The Deity has created both the good and the evil, and one is absolutely necessary to the existence of the other (Isa. xlv, 7). It considers that each human being is accompanied throughout its life on earth and is influenced spiritually, by two spirits, the good and the evil.* These are the oppositions, but the Free Will of the individual is the harmony, by which he *exercises the Divine Power of Judgment*, and accepts the one or the other as his master. This idea is in the Talmud and especially in the Zohar, also in the celebrated Qabbalistic book, called the Sepher Ye'tzeer'ah or Book of Creation. The latter says (Mishnah, ii, § 1): "Twenty-two letters: three mothers, seven double and twelve simple ones. The three mothers, אמש (*i. e.*, א Aleph, air, מ Mem, water, ש Shin, fire) their basis, the vessel (*i. e.*, the scale-pan or receptacle of a balance or scales for weighing) of purity, and the vessel (scale-pan) of guilt, and vibrating between each, is the tongue of the Law." That is, the index hand of the Balance.

* See; The Sayings of the Jewish Fathers, by Charles Taylor, pp. 142–145; 51; 76–78; 96, n. 11; 99, n. 21; 111, 112. Comp. Ephes. iv, 22, 23; Luke xi, 21–26; Ps. xxxvii; Deut. iv, 9.

The Zohar also says: "Until Elohim created the universe, It was alone, and then it went forth from Its Will to create the universe."* "At the time that the Holy One: Praised be Its Name! desired to create the universe, it (the universe) was present before It in the Idea."† "Before the At-tee'kah D'At-tee'keen, *i. e.*, the Ancient of all the Ancients, had prepared the Royal Form, the Crown of Crowns, there could be neither beginning nor ending. Then It first spread out a carpet (veil, or tapestry) before Itself, and in this inscribed the Crowns (*i. e.*, the Worlds)."‡

"When the Unknown of the Unknown wished to manifest Itself, It began by producing a point; as long as that luminous point had not gone out of Its bosom, the Infinite was still completely unknown and diffused no light."§

This emanated point is the Kether or Crown, the first Sephirah, which crowns the Ego or I, abstract thought, simple thought, the innate consciousness of being or existence. "It is the Principle of all the Principles, the Mysterious Wisdom, the Crown of all that which there is of the Most High, the Diadem of the Diadems." || The point represents the Infinite distinguished from the finite, and its name in the Scripture signifies, "I am," *i.e.*, אהיה, *Eh'yeh*, because it is the existence in Itself, the existence considered in the point of view, that analysis cannot penetrate it, and to which not any qualification is permitted and which absolutely does not admit of any. Above Kether is the Ayin or *Ens* (אין) *i.e.*, *Ain*, the No-Thing. "It is so named because we do not know, and it is impossible to know, that which there is in this Principle, because it never descends as far as our ignorance and because it is above Wisdom itself."¶ This view was held by many of the early Church Fathers.** It is fully set forth in the writings of the pseudo-Dionysius, the Areopagite, especially in his

* Zohar, i Part, 29*a*.
† Zohar, ii, fol. 96*b*.
‡ Zohar, iii Part, 128*a*. For a representation of this veil in Hindu symbolism, see my essays upon that subject in *The Path*, New York, 1886.
§ Zohar, i, fol. 2*a*.
|| Zohar, iii, fol. 288*b*.
¶ Zohar, iii, fol. 288*b*.
** History of Christian Doctrine, by Prof. Henry C. Sheldon. New York, 1886, Vol. i, pp. 53–63; 187–194.

Mystic Theology, and in his Divine Names. This writer is an acknowledged authority in the Roman Church, and is in many of his statements, fully in accord with many of the doctrines of the Qabbalah. With this description of the Deity, among the great metaphysicians, the philosopher Hegel coincides. The Zohar alluding to the Ego, also says: "This was the Light which Elohim created before everything."*

The Deity may be considered from four points of view, following each other: 1. As the Ain Soph, the Without End, the Eternal which is neuter, is above man's comprehension and to man's thought is as the No-Thing. 2. Eh'yeh, the I or, I Am, abstract thought. 3. YHVH, It, who was, and is, and will be, therefore in Time. 4. Elohim, the Deity in Nature, therefore used in connection with the Qabbalistic ideas as to the She'kheen-ah, the Matroneetha, Metatron, Adonai, Malkhuth, etc.

"Before Elohim manifested Itself (in the Universe), when *all Things* were yet concealed in It, It was the least known among all the Unknown. In that condition the Supreme Deity has not any other Name than that which expresses interrogation (*i. e.*, Who?). It began (the Creation) by forming an imperceptible point; † this was Its own Thought; then It turned Itself to construct with Its own thought, a mysterious and holy Form ;‡ finally It covered this (Ideal) Form, with a rich and shining (visible) garment; that is, the entire universe, of which, the name necessarily enters into the Name of Elohim."§ The Divine Name in Kether is Eh'yeh, *i. e.*, I Am. The grandest and most elevated designation of the manifestation of the Supreme Unknown to man's mind, Deity; the

---

* Zohar i, 31*a*, 32*b*.

† The first Sephirah Kether or the Crown, represented by the letter Yod ּ = 10. This Sephirah represents the entire content of abstract simple thought or idea, *i. e.*, *Ma'hshabah, i. e.*, imagination or idea, which being in It, is called, the crowned Thought. Kether is the Ego or I, that is consciousness of existence, and contains in germ, all things.

‡ The totality of all the Sephiroth, the Mikrokosm to the Deity, the Makrokosm to mankind and creation, the Adam Illa-ah or Heavenly Adam, the Celestial Adam or Upper Man, also called Adam Qadmon, the Archetypal Primordial Ideation Man in whom were the perfect models of all forms.

§ Zohar i, fol. 1 and 2; ii, fol. 105*a*. Comp. Franck, *La Kabbale*, p. 177, note 1; Ginsburg's Kabbalah, p. 12; also Joel, *Relig. Philos. Sohar.*

ego coming from the *Non-ego*, from the No-Thing because it is impossible for man's intellect to know the Supreme God in Its essence. Above all manifestations of the Supreme Deity, man can only express himself as to the unknown, by, Who? To which question no clear, formulated reply ever comes.

As this subject is quite difficult, and is also tersely stated in the philosophy of Ibn Gebirol, we will endeavor to explain it to the reader. In the introduction to the Brody edition of the Zohar, at the beginning, is an explanation of this Qabbalistic theory of the formation of the word Elohim, which word is translated in the English version of the Bible, God, although in the Hebrew Sacred Writings, our Old Testament, the word holds an inferior position to יהוה, YHVH, which is translated into English from Adonai, *i. e.*, Lord, its Hebrew equivalent. This introduction says: R. El'azar quotes from Isaiah xl, 26, "Lift up your eyes on high, and behold, *who* has created *these* things." If you "lift up your eyes on high," R. El'azar continues, "you will behold (that it is) *who** (that) has created all *these* things," (that) it is our pronoun Who? which is an interrogative, and thus alludes to something hidden and unknown, which thus symbolizes and represents, the original Creator of *all things* in the upper world, as *Who?* But as to the *things below*, from which a superior and higher knowledge cannot be derived, the exclamation "What, מה *Maah*, doest thou know!"† is to be applied to them. "*What* doest thou know, O son of man? *What* canst thou see? *What* hast thou been able to search? *Everything* is hidden from thee, as *it was before!*"

And with reference to this mystery it is said: "*What* is my witness for thee, *what* shall I liken unto thee?" ‡ Which means when the (first) Temple was destroyed, a voice (or, Bath Qol) exclaimed: "*What*, מה *Maah* —is my witness for thee?" it (What) testifies with reference to thee daily from the earliest days (when heaven and earth were created); as it is said: "I call *heaven and earth to witness* against you this day."§ "*What*, מה *Maah*, I shall liken unto thee?" says the Holy One, blessed

---

* According to the original מי Mi, pronounced Mee, *i. e.*, Who.
† Job xv, 9.
‡ Lament. ii, 13.
§ Deut. iv, 26.

be It! By all that is comprised in "*What*," I have crowned thee, O daughter of Jerusalem, with sacred diadems and made thee ruler over the world, as it is said: "This is the city, of which they say; it is the crown of beauty."* They called thee "Jerusalem built as a city to be associated with."† "*What* I shall equal unto thee,"‡ in the way thou art situated, not visited by multitudes as formerly, when the holy people came in sacred sections, hence "thy breach is great like the sea."§ And if thou wilt say that thou art without help and health, I assure thee, that, "*Who ?* (מי *Mee*) can heal thee ;"‖ surely, the Supreme Degree, hidden from thee, whereby everything exists, shall heal thee and lift thee up.

"*Who ?*" (מי *Mee*) points "to the *end* of heavens," *Above*, and *What ?* (מה *Maah*) "to the *end* of heavens," *Below ;* and this is the inheritance of Jacob, which represents the axis around which the entire spheres of the universe revolve from end to end ;¶ from the first, upper, or original end מי Mee, *i. e., Who ?* to the lower or latter end מה *Maah, i. e., What ?* because it is in the midst.**

"And with regard to מי *Mee, i. e., Who ?* created *these*," said R. Shim-on: "El'azar, my son, stop thy words, and the hidden mysteries unknown to men shall be revealed." Whereupon El'azar was silent. Then R. Shim-on, with tears in his eyes, said: "El'azar, what is the meaning of '*these ?*' If thou shalt say, the stars and planets, truly, they are constantly visible, and they were created by מה *Maah, What ?* (not by *Mee, Who ?* see *ante*): As it is said : 'By the *Word*, (*i. e.,* the Targumic *Memrah,*) of YHVH were the heavens made.'†† But as regards hidden things, the reference '*these*' is not applicable, for '*these*,' *i. e.,* the stars and planets, are open to the sight of man, and consequently *are not in-*

* Lament. ii, 15.
† Ps. cxxii, 3.
‡ Lament. ii, 13.
§ *Ibid.*
‖ *Ibid.*
¶ This is taken from Exod. xxvi, 28, where the "*bar*" בריח (*Bar-ia'h*) is spoken of as "reaching from end to end," and it is applied here as just stated, *Bar-ia'h,* meaning in the rabbinical language *axis.*
** Comp. Exod. xxvi, 28, beginning.
†† Ps. xxxiii, 6.

cluded in the *hidden things Above.* This mystery was however not revealed until on a certain day, when I was at the shore of the sea, and the prophet Eliÿah came to me and said: 'Rabbi, doest thou know the (hidden) meaning of, *Who* (מי *Mee*)—created *these?*' I replied to him: '*These* are the heavens and their hosts,' *i. e.*, the angels, the *work* of the Holy One, blessed be It! for it becomes the son of man to behold them, and bless It, according to ' For if I see thy heavens the *work* of thy fingers, moon, stars, etc.'* 'O YHVH our YHVH! how excellent is thy Name in all the earth.'† Said he to me: 'It was a mystery with the Holy One and revealed in the supreme place of learning, and here it is: At the time when the 'Mystery of all Mysteries,' willed to reveal Itself, It made in Its head a little point which became a *thought* (idea), wherewith It designed all the Forms, carved out all the Engravings, and in that way shaped a mysterious and sacred Lamp (Light) of every Form, which mysterious Light among the holy ones, is a profound construction going forth from the (abstract) *thought*, and is called, מי *Mee, i. e., Who?*‡ The very beginning of the construction whether visible or invisible, is profound and mysterious, by its name (מי *Mee,*) Who?

Now intending to reveal Itself and assume a Name, It encompassed Itself with dazzling Light and 'created *these*'§ which is *Ele'h*, the beginning of the word אֱלֹהִים ELoHim, *i. e.*, God, and thus was created the Name, Elohim, by the previous creation of אלה Ele'h, *i. e., these*. And those who trespassed by the worship of the Golden Calf, exclaimed on the ground of this mystery, אלה *Ele'h, i. e., These* thy Elohim! O Israel!|| (Exod. xxxii, 4.) And as מִי *Mee, i. e., Who*, is here combined with אלה *Ele'h, i. e., these,* we have thus the Name אֱלֹהִים Elohim (made of the letters of these two words) resulting and established forever, and on the basis of this mystery the world exists!' Whereupon Eliÿah disappeared, and

---

* Ps. viii, 3 *et seq.*

† *Ibid.*, 9.

‡ The two consonants "י" and "מ" are the initials of מַחֲשָׁבָת זֹה, *i.e.*, the thought of God.

§ Which is in Hebrew אלה *Ele'h*.

|| By this play of words the sin of that idolatry is to be looked upon as merely a mistaken view of Elohim, God.

I did not see him any more; from him, however, I have communicated to you the revelation of the great mystery." When R. Shim-on finished, R. El'azar and his friends bowed down before him visibly affected and said: "If we had come into the world merely to hear this, it would have been sufficient!" Said R. Shim-on: "The heavens and their hosts were created by מה *Maah*," *i. e., What?* which is evident, from "For if I see thy heavens, etc., how (מה) excellent is thy Name, etc., who givest thy glory upon (or, above) the heavens* which are above the earth by that Name, since It created Light to Its Light, enveloped one in the other, and made it ascend by the Supreme Name. And as, 'In the Beginning created Elohim,' that is the Supreme Elohim, for מה *Maah, i. e., What?* was not yet in existence, nor was it until the letters of אלה *Ele'h* were changed from *above* to *below;* I now ask: When did It adorn her thus? At the time when all the males appeared before It,† then the ה (*h*) of מה *Maah, What?* disappeared, and the י yod, came into the place of ה (*h*) and was (מי *Mee*) *Who?* and it adorned itself with garments of the males for the reception of every male in Israël.

'*These* אלה, *i.e., Ele'h*, I remember!' ‡ I remember or mention with my mouth and 'shed' my tears. 'As my soul wills it,' in order to move those letters and 'guide them' from above to the house of Elohim, to be like Elohim himself, 'by the voice of joy and praise, a feasting multitude!'" R. El'azar said, referring to the foregoing: "Without any sound or voice, *i. e.,* in silence, It built the celestial and terrestrial temple, hence the truth of the adage (Talmud Babli, *Me'ghillah* 18): 'If a word costs *one* Sela, silence is worth *two* (Selas).' 'A word costs one Sela,' when we have aroused ourselves and have said it: 'Silence is worth two,' in that which we do quietly; thus the two worlds (the Upper and Lower), were created at the same time." In accordance with which

---

* In Hebrew תנה הוד על השמים, the final letters of which four words, to wit: הכלם reversed constitute the word מלכה, Queen, an allusion to the Supreme Wisdom, as: Queen of the heavens.

† "Before the face of the Lord," *i. e.,* האדון *ha-adon*, YHVH, who is called אדון, Adon, *i. e.,* Lord, according to Joshua iii: "Behold the Ark of the Covenant of the Lord ארון Adon, *i. e.,* Lord, of all the earth.

‡ Ps. xlii, 4.

R. Shim-on said: "This completes the meaning of Isaiah xl, 26; '*Who? bringeth forth* in numbers *their hosts*.' The two divisions of the *Above* and the *Below*, one of which (the Upper) arises under מי *Mee, i. e., Who?* and the other (the Lower) under מה *Maah, i. e., What?* And they needed corresponding designations; the first is designated by '*Who? bringeth forth* (in numbers *their hosts*),' being known as such and none other like, It, and the latter, the lower degree or created universe, is indicated by '*Who? bringeth forth, bread from the earth;*' both (of the '*Who?* bringeth forth, etc.)' *are* however only, *One.* 'In numbers' of two myriads, which exist together and support the innumerable *multitudes.** 'All of them,' whether numbered or not, 'He (It) calls *by name*' not by *their names*, but by *His* (*Its*) *own Name;* 'through the fullness of Power' (potentiality or potency), *i. e.*, the Highest Degree, from which, all powers and mysteries emanate the 'greatness of might' peculiar to the Upper world. 'Not one man faileth' of all the number (neither Above or Below), they all proceed from *one source* and *exist after one image.*" So R. Shim-on interpreted "Lift up your eyes on high, and behold *Who* created *these* things, *Who bringeth forth their host* in number! he called them *all by their name*, through the greatness of his might and fullness of power, not one (man) faileth."

The Zohar says: "It has been handed down: When Resha hivrah, *i. e.*, the White Head, proposed to Itself to superadd an ornament to Its ornament (or, willed to, manifest Its excellency); It appointed, prepared and produced, a spark (scintillation) from the splendour of intense Light (or, the Cardinal Lamp). It breathed on it and it cooled down (or, was reduced to form); and Resha hivrah's, *i.e.*, the White Head's, Will went on, and the spark (scintilla) was extended into 370 currents (or, sides). And the spark existed and remained (intact), and a pure air (azoth) came forth rolling forward on every side, and there was extended and going forth, a firm (or hard) cranium (the firmament) on four sides (the four cardinal points of the compass). And in that pure air (of the appearance as it were of a skull) the spark (of vitality) was absorbed and taken up and included "*in it*"† (or "by it"). "By it" do you think? No, but it

---

* Ps. xlii, 4.

† בָיה *baih*, which in Egypt meant, soul or spirit.

was hidden "in it" (the cranium, the luminiferous æther, the hard skull). And therefore that cranium was expanded on its sides, and that air (azoth) is the most hidden thing of the At-tee'kah Yo-men, *i. e.*, Ancient of Days. In the Spirit, which is laid up in that cranium, are expanded fire on one part (or, side), and air (æther) on the other (part or side). And the subtile air (azoth) exists above it on this, and the subtile fire (the white hidden fire) on that, side.* What is the fire in this place? But indeed it is not fire, but that splendour which is included in the subtile air, it (the Luminiferous Æther?) shines into 270 worlds * *. In that cranium distills dew from Resha hivrah, *i. e.*, the White Head, from which it is always full, and by that dew the dead will be brought to life. And that dew has in itself two colours from the side of the Resha hivrah; there is whiteness (absolute transparency) within it, *i. e.*, the dew, which comprises every whiteness and it is entirely white. But when they, the two colours, abide in the head of Ze'ir Anpen (*i. e.*, the short Face, the Mikrokosm) redness appears in it, just as in a crystal (*bdellium*), which is white (or transparent), a red colour flashes in the white colour, etc."†

The Zohar says: It is handed down; Before At-tee'kah D'At-tee'keen, *i.e.*, the Ancient of all the Ancients, the Concealed of all the Concealed, had prepared the institutions (or, royal forms) of the King, *i. e.*, the Ze'ir Anpen (or, Short Face) ‡ under certain members, limbs and degrees, (or, Sephiroth); and the Diadem of Diadems (*i. e.*, the various wrappers—or, folds—by which the redundance of Light might be enveloped), there was not as yet any Beginning nor Ending, *i. e.*, there was no imparting and reception. Time had not yet begun to exist. It, the At-tee'kah, therefore engraved, *i. e.*, made empty a space (void or vacuum), into which It might impart Its efflux, and institute proportions in Itself (in as many modes as the Light of Its wisdom could be received, whence arose the gradation of the worlds), and It expanded over Itself a certain veil, *i. e.*, produced a certain nature, through which Its Infinite Light might be modified and imparted, which was the first Adam, *i. e.*,

---

* This hidden or white fire, shines night and day and yet is not ever seen, answering to vital force, energy, electricity, etc., of which we have as yet but little knowledge.

† Idrah Rabbah, Zohar, Cremona Ed., col. 256; Mantua Ed., col. 135.

‡ The Heavenly Adam, Adam Illa-ah or Adam Qadmon.

the Celestial Adam, Adam Illa-ah or Qadmon; and It, the At-tee'kah D'At-tee'keen engraved in it, and by a certain proportion distributed Kings and their forms, *i. e.*, all creatures under the condition of their own especial activity; by which they might be known and loved, but they did not remain.* This is that which is said: "And those were the Kings such as reigned in the land of Edom, before a King reigned over the sons of Israel.†

The primary Kings preceding the primary children of Israël. (By the children of Israël are here meant, the Sephiroth of the restored world.) And all those which were engraved and did not stand firm, are called by their names, *i. e.*, were divided into fixed classes. "Nor yet did they remain fixed, until It modified them (so that the Lights from the vessels, *i. e.*, the Sephiroth, went upward and the vases were left empty and became shells, and It set them down in rest from before them) with a diminished Light.‡ All those loose formations were certainly called by certain names, but they were not able to exist (keep themselves up), hence It put them out of sight, and caused them to completely disappear.

After some time It, At-tee'kah, looked contemplatively upon that minute sketch (or veil) and formed on it according to Its own Forms. And thus it is handed down: It proposed to Itself (or, it was Its Will) to create a Thorah (Law) (*i. e.*, the letters of the alphabet, from the transpositions of which thenceforth, the Thorah was written, perhaps meaning a plan or sketch); a Thorah hidden for 2000 years, and when It had produced it, the Thorah immediately addressed it (saying): "It who wishes

---

* Here is hinted at the Fall of the creatures, partly in a condition of quietude as (inert) matter is, partly into a state of inordinate motion, such as that of the evil spirits, etc. Matter is now considered by physicists as always in motion.

† Gen. xxxvi, 29. A strange statement in Genesis, Saul was first king of the Israelites.

‡ Another translation is: " It caused sketches and outlines to appear in Its imagination (own substance?) and then spread a veil (tapestry, carpet or cloth) before Itself, in which It engraved (hewed or incised) and marked, the kings and their limits and (royal) forms, but they did not have any duration;" to this alludes the mention of, "the kings who ruled prior to the kings of Israël," Gen. xxxvi, 31 *et seq.* (*i. e.*, the primitive kings and the primitive Israël).

to arrange and appoint other things should be first arranged Itself in Its proper Forms."

It is handed down in the Siphrah D'Tznioothah, that At-tee'kah D'At-tee'keen, the Ancient of all the Ancients, the Concealed of all the Concealed, arranged Itself into members and prepared Itself (for future recognition). And it might as it were, be said, It is to be found (*i. e.*, as far as It could be known), and yet is not found, for It could not be clearly known, but It was arranged nor yet was It known to any one, since It is the At-tee'kah D'At-tee'keen, *i. e.*, the Ancient of all the Ancients. But It became known through Its conformations (or, revealed) as a certain Old Man of Old Men, the Ancient of the Ancient, a Concealed One of the Concealed, and by Its symbols (manifestations) It became known and yet It did not become known.*

The Zohar also says: " The indivisible point (*i. e.*, the Absolute) not having any limits and not being able to be known, on account of Its energy and Its purity, spread Itself outwardly, *and has formed a canopy* (or, *veil*) which serves to veil this indivisible point. This canopy, although of a Light less pure than the point, was still too bright to be regarded; and it in its turn spread outwardly, and that extension served It for Its vestment; it is thus that all is made through a movement which always descends, it was thus, in a word, the universe was formed."†

Another passage teaches, of the voice which goes out of the Spirit and identifies itself with it in the Supreme Thought, that this Voice is, at the

---

* We have not any knowledge of Its Absolute Essence, and as far as this Essence is concerned, the Supreme Deity does not exist in Its Essence for man's thoughts because beyond them. To human intellect It is as if *Ayin*, *i. e.*, No-Thing, and It can be described only negatively. To manifest Itself to us to a certain extent, the Supreme Deity made the alphabet, numbers and other forms, it is only through these that the materially and fleshy enveloped, spiritual man, can have any knowledge of God. Man can only conceive of the invisible, through the openings in his flesh called senses, by means of the visible. The Zohar says: It is the Lord whose dress is white (transparent), and so also is the appearance of the veil of Its face. It sits upon a Throne of sparks (scintillations of Light or Flames) that it may subdue them, etc. Zohar, Cremona Ed., fol. 61, col. 243. Mantua Ed., fol. 128, *et seq*. The reader will especially note the distinction between "the Ancient of *all* the Ancients" and "the Ancient of the Ancient."

† Zohar. Part I, fol. 20*a*.

foundation, no other thing than the water, air and fire, the North, South, East and West, and all the Energies of nature,* but that all these elements and forces are blended in one sole thing, that is, in the Voice which goes out of the Spirit. By this the Qabbalists intended to inforce the idea that the universe was created by the Will, *Memrah*, *Logos* or *Word*, Wisdom, of the Invisible Absolute Unknown Supreme Being.

The Zohar also says: "We have learned: Before the Forms of the Holy King, the At-teek, were prepared, It built worlds and made Forms for their preservation, but the female principle was not joined yet with the male principle, called 'Grace,' therefore they could not exist until that was done." This is the hidden meaning of (Gen. xxxvi, 31 *et seq.*) "And these are the kings which ruled in the land of Edom," the place, where all Judgment is found, and which was fit for existence only upon the appearance of "Grace." Up to that time we read repeatedly in that chapter "and he died," until we read: "And in his place ruled Saul from *Re'hoboth han-nahar*," *i. e.*, Understanding with its fifty gates, which shine and illumine the six sides (pillars) of the world.† We have learned: Judgment was on all except one, who continued after them to exist; and this "Saul from *Re'hoboth han-nahar*," is one side (pillar) which extends and came forth from *Re'hoboth han-nahar*. Proper duration only came with the last, "Hadad," *i. e.*, Supreme Grace, which resides in the excellency of productive man, who is worthy of the Holy Ghost. We read further.‡ "And the name of his wife was Mehetabel," the mentioning of the name of the wife points to the degree of perfection above explained,§ the daughter of Matred, *i. e.*, the assiduous worker under the influence of "Strength," the daughter of Mezahab, *i. e.*, the female principle together with the male, Mercy or Grace, and Judgment or Strength.||

---

* Zohar, Part I, fol. 246*b*.

† That is, the positive and negative poles of the three dimensions, Length, Breadth and Depth.   ‡ *Ibid*.

§ The positive and negative principles, Grace and Punishment, good and evil, male and female. The productive Man. The Balance. Compare in the Zodiac, Scorpio and Virgo, and between them Libra, the Harmony.

|| Zohar iii, 142*a*. The Idrah Rabbah.

We also read in it: Because of the constitution of Man in Its Elohim's likeness, the Man, *i. e.*, the Perfect Primordial Ideation Man or Adam, comprises (in itself as the similitude of Elohim) All Things and admits All Things to settle (be contained or arranged) in it. And because that constitution of (the Perfect Man) Adam was not at that early time found, they (the Primitive Kings of Edom. Gen. xxxvi, 31 *et seq.*), could not exist nor settle down: and they were made an end of. What were they made an end of, notwithstanding that they were included in the Man? They were made an end of so far as they were taken away from that previous formation, until the complete formation of Adam came forward.* But when that likeness (of the Perfect Adam) came, All Things were reduced to shape (were combined) and turned in another condition, etc."†

Man gives, in his own spiritual action, an example of the existence of the potentiality and energy of the Deity throughout the universe. A painter, say Raphael, makes a picture, or a sculptor, say Michael Angelo, carves a figure, these artistic creations or works, contain a part of the potential spiritual energy or force of the spiritual man, the real man, who within the matter body, does the work. We call this genius or artistic power. That is, by the vital, energetic arrangement of the particular atoms which produce the shape, colour or effect, a part of the spirit of the artist goes into his work, and is, so to say, crystallized or embodied with the atoms which he combines or arranges in the picture or figure produced by him. This work is not the result of the matter-man but of the spiritual man, acting by means of the material man's hands, eyes, etc., as his tools or instruments. It is entirely by the action of the spirit that man originates and stamps his work, and enables other men, who have knowledge, at sight, of this spiritual stamp of the artist, upon looking at the latter's result-

* This refers to the Ideal Adam, the Adam Illa-ah or Qadmon, who is also Ze'ir Anpen, *i. e.*, the Small Countenance, the Celestial Man as the producing male and female, no longer an androgene. These kings of Edom were the pre-Adamite androgenic kings.

† The primitive kings were now carved out anew, from the likeness of the Perfect Ideation Adam, who was at first an Androgene, but who had been separated into the two sexes, and returned to a new existence. Zohar, Cremona Ed., col. 256. Mantua Ed., fol. 135.

ing work, to say, thousands of years after the dissolution of the artist's material form, that such a picture, figure, etc., was by this or that, man. This applies to all the works of man, even to his handwriting, so with the Creator, It has stamped into the entire universe a part of Its spiritual potentiality and energy, and as to that much exists in it, but the universe is not the Deity, any more than the picture, statue or handwriting, are the man himself.

The Zohar, iii, 9*b*, refers to the different races of men, which, it says, do not all descend from Adam, and we especially call attention to the fact, that many centuries before Copernicus wrote his work on the "Revolution of the Heavenly Bodies," which was about 1542 A. D., the Zohar stated, as to the cosmography of the Universe, that: "In the book of Hammannunah, the Old (or, the Ancient), we learn through some extended explanations, that the earth turns upon itself in the form of a circle; that some are on top, the others below; that all creatures change in aspect, following the manner of each place, keeping however in the same position, but there are some countries of the earth which are lightened, whilst others are in darkness; these have the day when for the former it is night; and there are countries in which it is constantly day, or in which at least the night continues only some instants."* It also says, race differences are to be ascribed to climate. Very singular is the close: "These secrets were made known to the men of the secret science but not to the geographers."† Where the first knowledge of this came from it is difficult to say. The Church Father Lactantius—*circa* 290–325 A. D.—writes: "It is an absurdity to believe, that there are men who have their feet above their heads, and countries, in which all is inverted, in which the trees and plants grow from the top to the bottom. We find the germ of that error among the philosophers, who have claimed that the earth is round."‡ St. Augustine holds to the same view.§ Aristotle says that: "Almost all those, who affirm that they have studied heaven in its uniformity, claim that the earth is in the cen-

---

* Zohar iii, fol. 10*a*.
† *Ibid.*
‡ Works, Bk. iii, c. 24.
§ *De Civitat Dei*, Bk. xvi, c. 9.

tre, but the philosophers of the Italian School, otherwise called the Pythagoreans, teach entirely the contrary. In their opinion, the centre is occupied by the fire, and the earth is only a star, which by a circular movement around this same centre, produces night and day."* Aristotle opposed the Pythagorean idea and the Greeks, Romans, and Arabs followed him. The Italic sect founded by Pythagoras, and the Ionic by Thales, brought from either India or Egypt, the idea of the movement of the earth about 600 B. C.

The following Greek philosophers believed in the rotundity of the earth: Pythagoras of Samos, Anaximander, Nicetas of Syracuse, Heraclides of Pontus, Aristarchus of Samos, Séleneus and Ecphantus. Heraclides and Ecphantus only admitted the movement of the earth upon its own axis, or the diurnal movement. The Pythagoreans held, that each star was a world having its own atmosphere with an immense extent surrounding it, of æther.†

Their ideas were considered visionary and not accepted as correct, by the learned of their time. In India at a very early period the astronomer, Arya-bhata (said to have lived, A. D. 476), held to the opinion that the earth revolved upon its own axis, but all the later Hindu astronomers opposed his views. It is not yet known whether any Hindu held to the theory of the earth's revolution around the sun. The Egyptians and Chinese may have arrived at that truth, and we know at a very ancient period, the Chaldeans calculated with certainty eclipses of the moon, and very closely approximated the time of eclipses of the sun. Maimonides‡—1190 A. D.—holds that the earth has the form of a globe, that it is inhabited at both extremities of a certain diameter, that the inhabitants have their heads towards heaven, and their legs toward each other, yet they do not fall off. §

*De Cælo, Bk. ii, c. 13.

† Comp. Aristotle de Cælo, Bk. ii, c. 13. Seneca, Quæst. natur., lib. viii. Freret, Academ. des Inscript., tom. xviii, p. 108.

‡ Moreh Ne'boo-kheem. Eng. Trans. Vol. i, p. 336.

§ Dr. Schlegel, Uranographie chinois, pp. 55, 196, 494 et seq., gives the great antiquity of 18,000 years, to the Chinese astronomical sphere. Comp. Annales du Musée Guimet. Tome Douzième, by J. J. M. De Groot. Paris, 1886. p. 436 et seq. Ibid., Tome Onsième, p. 368 et seq.

Pythagoras held, everything in the universe has been made, not through the virtue of numbers, but following the proportions of numbers. The Book of Wisdom holds to the same as regards our Universe.*

In the theory of the Mystic numbers, the unity is called the monad. It is the first ring in the chain of existences, and one of the qualifications which the ancient philosophers have given the Divinity. Its symbol is the mathematical point. From this simple being emanates the duad, represented by 2 and also by the line of geometry. This is the emblem of matter or the passive principle and is the image of the contrasts, because the line, which is its type, extends itself indifferently towards the right or left. 3 is the mysterious number figured as the triad, by the equilateral triangle. It is the emblem of the attributes of God, and reunites the properties of the first two numbers.†

* *Wisdom*, xi, 20. "Thou hast ordered all things in *measure* and *number* and *weight;*" and "made the world, of matter with form." *Ibid.* 17. "For in the greatness and beauty of the creatures *proportionately*, the *maker of them is seen*." *Ibid.* xiii, 5.

† Comp. Mart. Capella in *de Nuptûs Pholologiæ et Mercurii*, also the 30th chapter of Anacharsis.

Figure 6.

Figure 7. Arddha Nâri, the Hindu Androgene.

VII.

AN ANALYSIS OF THE ME'QÔR HAŸ-YÎM, OF IBN GEBIROL.

THE system set forth by Ibn Gebirol, in the Me'qôr 'Haÿ-yîm or Fountain of Life, although Aristotelian in its form, is yet contrary to the doctrines of the Stagirite. The object of the writing is, to set forth ideas of form and matter, in connection with the Deity; and singular to say, in many of its propositions it is in accord with the writings of the early Christian Theosopher, the pseudo-Dionysius, the Areopagite, (who is not later, and most probably much earlier, than 532 A. D.), as well as with the Zohar and Zoharic books. Four influences are shown in the Me'qôr: 1. Gebirol's theological belief. 2. Arabian peripateticism. 3. Oriental philosophy, more especially that of the so-called school of Alexandria. 4. The Hebrew Qabbalistic philosophy, which had been brought into Spain from the Jewish Babylonian schools, being, however, not thoroughly Semitic in origin, but having an Aryan germ. The following is a *resumé* of the Me'qôr.

It conducts us to the ideas of a Universal Form and a Universal Matter, embracing all things, except the Supreme Deity. Soul and other created things are equally only one matter. The work is divided into five books. In Book I, he says: Man's desire is towards knowledge, its final attainment should be, to obtain wisdom as to the final cause of all that which is, viz: God. Doing this to the end, that man obtain the Supreme Good, and that everything be in subjection to the Will of the Sole Supreme Being. Psychology ought to be taken for the point of departure from all philosophical studies. From the Supreme Will movement has emanated, through movement all things are generated, and the work of the human soul ought to be, to lead itself to affinity with the superior world, from which it draws its origin. That knowledge man attains through meditation and contemplation, and by practising pious exercises. The proof of this is, that all in potentiality is destined to pass into action. Man, however, as the finite, cannot know the Infinite, in Its essence.

Metaphysical science should have for its aim: 1. Abstract knowledge of matter and form. 2. Abstract knowledge of the Divine Will or Creative Word. 3. Abstract information of the first substance, or God. The last, man can only know imperfectly. He cannot reach to it by philosophical speculation. The Will of the Deity is the highest knowledge to which man can reach, it is the First Efficient Cause, it has in its essence, the Form of All Things, and is the harmony between God and the universe. The latter emanates from it. Creation is not a necessity, but a free act of the Supreme. He gave to it the perfection He desired to give it. Matter manifests itself in different hypostases proceeding from the simple to the composite. We can begin with the Will, Desire, Wisdom or Word, (Logos), of the Unknown.

The essence of the universe, in general, is passive, but it conducts us to some knowledge of that Will, which emanates, embraces and sustains, all the existing. This passivity embraces an Universal Form and an Universal Matter. These are, however, to be considered as purely ideal. They are that which carries and that which is carried; from these, we proceed upward to the third, the Will, and downward to the material universe. The destruction of form results in chaos.

He then defines matter and form, and endeavors to prove the existence of an Universal Matter and an Universal Form. The former has but one existence, that through itself; has only one essence, in that it bears (supports or carries) the diversity, and gives to all its essence and name. The knowledge of this we obtain through reflection, and by sublimating the forms, one after the other, and in passing from the visible to the invisible, until we reach one last form, in which we are not able to recognize any other, and it is by this means we shall find the absolute idea of the Universal Matter, *e. g.*, beginning with the celestial sphere, we can sublimate the ideas until we come to the last, which is one that exists by itself and carries all these forms. That is the Universal Matter; above this we find only the First Efficient Cause, the Will which is intermediary and from the Supreme Deity. The diversity in the beings, whether spiritual or corporeal, resides only in the form. The Universal Matter embraces all the spiritual and corporeal worlds. The potentiality or faculty, *to become*, exists in all that which is, outside of the Highest Deity, who is the Absolute Being, always in action. That Matter receives from the Will, that existence, unity, and substantiality, which constitute the Universal Form. The Universal Intellect is a direct emanation from the Will, and contains all form and universality. The second hypostate is the Universal Soul. It manifests itself in the Makrokosm (*i.e.*, the whole Universe), also in the Mikrokosm (*i.e.*, Mankind), under different forms.

The Universal Form is founded in the Universal Intellect. It has properties by which we recognize it in all that which exists: 1. That of the quality of *to be*, reached through its action on other things, and subsisting in them, because if the form were not carried by them, they would be chaotic matter. 2. That of perfecting the essence of the thing which bears it, and giving to that thing its existence, because it is only through its form that the thing is. Matter is only *to be*, in potentiality, the Form of All Things is, *to be*, in action. Having in a general way established the Universal Matter and Form, he seeks to base it on analysis. He calls this the particular method, it consists in the consideration of things evident to our senses, and individual things; going up, through them, to the spiritual and general. Animal existence and that of plants and minerals, are composed of matter and form, the same as the artificial things, *e. g.*, a statue. The last are composed of a particular matter and an artificial form. The four elements have each a particular form, but also have a common form, that of element in general, for the particular forms of the elements do not exist of themselves, they are only accidents; they are to the elements, that which the particular form is to the substance. All nature resolves into the four elements, and these resolve themselves into something, which is the substratum of their general form. They are qualities, and a substratum is necessary to unite these qualities, *e. g.*, generation, is the result of the mixture of positive and negative or opposing elements; if a subtile substratum did not precede substance, the latter would proceed from non-substance. Beyond all usually called matter is the most sublimated general substratum, this is the Universal Matter. Above the elements are the heavens, but they also possess quantity and corporeality, and from thence we may conclude, that they have form and matter. They have not the qualities of the elements, and have not generation or destruction. The form of the heavens is, therefore, different from the elemental form. There are four species of matter: 1. Particular or artificial, *e. g.*, bronze. 2. Particular or natural matter, *e. g.*, that coming from the mixture of the elements. 3. General natural matter, *e. g.*, that which is the element of the elements. 4. Matter of the heavenly spheres or orbits.*

The II Book treats of the place in the universe, of the Universal Matter which is the substratum of its corporeality. We reach this by sublimating from ordinary corporeality, color, etc. In sensible bodies that which is visible and gross, serves to carry that which is more subtile; sublimating this, we arrive at the sole substratum, the Universal Matter. Above all the forms of the existences is that of the Intellect, which embraces everything by its knowledge, because its substance is the most subtile and penetrating of all things. In the bond of the forms we pass insensibly from the visible to the invisible, from the matter-world to the spiritual world. The forms evident to the senses can be considered as the images of the intelligible intellectual forms, the spiritual existences, and

* This may mean of the Sephiroth.

through the visible world one can form some judgment of the spiritual and invisible world. The sensible forms are the symbols, which retrace in the soul the intelligible forms; as the letters in a book bring back to the reader the thoughts of the writer, which they carry and conceal. It is through the substance which bears the nine categories, which he afterwards more fully describes, that we ought to begin our researches for that which is not evident to the senses. Our author then endeavors to establish a perfect parallel between the superior and inferior world. The Will (*ra-tzon*) of the Supreme Deity emanates all forms, and makes them penetrate to the lowest extremity of matter, and it draws together all the existences dependent upon it, and puts them in harmony and equilibrium, by a wise distribution of the forms. The substance upon which this Will acts, is Space thought of in its most sublimated abstractness. The other simple substances are solely and only, in their causes, and are not in any corporeal place; together, they reside successively one in the other, and together, in the Divine knowledge. The lower the existences descend from the abstract or simple to the composite, the less sublimated and grosser they become, and the higher they are, the more clear and subtile. There are two Spaces, a corporeal and a spiritual; the first is a shadow or image of the latter, as the inferior world is only an image of the superior world. He says much as to the divine Will, and that everything comes from, lives and moves, in it. After having spoken of the Absolute Unity above all number, and its passage into the lower Unity, that of number, and thence into multiplicity, our author gives examples of his views, by approximation. In his system he formulates four universal matters, placed in, yet above, each other, sublimating the more, the higher they ascend. 1. The absolute Universal Matter, or that embracing at the same time, the spiritual and corporeal worlds, in the most abstract sublimation. It is the substratum of all existing outside of the Unity's. 2. The corporeal Universal Matter, the sublimated element of all the elements, or that which serves as the substratum to the forms of corporeity and quantity, and which permeates at the same time the celestial spheres and the sublunary world. 3. The Universal Matter common to all the corporeal celestial spheres. 4. The Universal Matter of the sublunary world, that of the elements, and seat of the contingencies, and which he calls the general natural matter. To each of these corresponds an Universal Form, and the Forms as the Matters, particularize and corporify themselves, in the measure that they descend in the scale of existences. Forms in general, are of two kinds—one, constituting the essence of all things, is common to all which has directly issued from the Divine Will, the other, limited more and more, varies in each degree in the ladder of the existences.

In the III Book, he undertakes to prove the existence of intelligible simple substances, which are intermediaries between the First Efficient Cause, the Will, and the substance of the corporeal. The system of Gebirol is based on the unity of form and substance, and the latter, is matter qualified to receive all forms, qualities and accidents. He asserts two species of proof to demonstrate the existence of such substances. The first is founded on the absolute contrast or opposition, existing between the abstract Deity and the corporeal universe. One is the First Efficient Cause, most subtile and most noble, the other gross and vile; one is eternal, nay, above eternity, the other falls within the limits of time. The Supreme Deity is Absolute Unity, the physical world, absolute plurality. The universe, however, draws its existence from Absolute Unity in spite of the abyss which separates it. It is necessary that this abyss be bridged by something intermediary, which resembles on the one side, the one existence, the Supreme Deity, and on the other, the two existences, Matter and Form, and which shall serve to bind all together. Man as the Mikrokosm (*ha-olam haq-qatan*), is an image of the Universe, and the whole Universe forms one sole individual (the Makrokosm), which is the prototype of the inferior; as in man, the Mikrokosm, *i. e.*, the little world, the Intellect, Spirit or *Neshamah*, which is the most simple, subtile, and sublime, of all the substances, is not attached to the corporeal body, but the animal soul, *Nephesh*, and the ethical spirit, *Ru-a'h*, are intermediaries between them, through the inferior faculties of the animal soul: so in the Makrokosmos, the Great World, *i. e.*, the whole Universe; the Great Paradigmatic Perfect Man; there are the divine Will, and nine intermediaries or categories,*

---

* This is evidently a reference to the Ten Sephiroth which form in their totality, the Adam Qadmon. Comp. the Me'qôr, Bk. III, §§ 5, 8, 30, 44.

through which the Absolutely Existing who is above number, is attached to Its corporeal universe. The activity of the First Efficient Cause is to make proceed, or create, out of the No-Thing, Some-Thing; but the substance which contains the categories being composed of the most simple, abstract, sublimated, elements, has not gone out or separated, from the No-Thing, but its energies or rays extend. The latter are under a dependence which comes through the divine Will. It is then necessary, that there be an intermediary creation going out of the Absolute No-Thing. Our author, however, admits, that it is an absolute impossibility to demonstrate by metaphysics, the connexion of the matter-world, with the Absolute Being of the Supreme Deity. The simple substances communicate their essence, without any kind of diminution, and the Absolute Unity emanates through yet is immanent in them. Their action consists in the gradual and successive communication of form, which has its primitive source in the Will. This is by the Will's rays and faculties, but not by any diminution of its essence. As evidences of such an emanation without diminution, he refers, to sight, through the eye, and to the rays which proceed from the sun. Its first cause can be sought for, only in the Superior Faculty and First Agent, who made All Things, put all in movement, and acts upon all that, which is susceptible of receiving Its action. All the simple substances obey Its action, and act by and through It, whenever they find matter which has been deposited to receive Its action. All the impressions come from the simple substances. The First Efficient Cause, however, is the first emanation, which renders necessary the effusion of all the substances one into the other. The more the substance is simple, subtile, and abstract, the more it possesses the power of penetrating. The rays of the sun become perceptible to our vision, only when they touch a corporeal substance, and the thickening of the same causes the shadow. The impressions which the composite substance receives, become evident only, because the matter which receives them, is essentially in contact with the corporeal. The emanations of the simple substances only become evident, when in contact with the corporeal substance. We can recognize that all the forms exist in the Will, in germ, in a more simple sublimated manner than in the Universal Matter. The simple substances on the one side are receptive and passive, on the other side active; they receive the forms from the higher and communicate them to the lower. The substance which carries the categories is purely corporeal and receptive and not any action emanates from it. The forms, evident in themselves, such as quantity, shape, color, etc., are in the essence of the simple substances, and Ibn Gebirol tries to show, that all the categories, which are solely applicable to the corporeal, have their analogues in the world of the spiritual substances. In it, he asserts, are the prototypes of all the categories, which come to corporify themselves in the corporeal universe. From this alliance between the spiritual and corporeal substance is born a form, which in its entirety, is neither one nor the other, because in general, when two opposites are united, a third is born, which is neither of the two opposites, thus results a triad. Gebirol says: " If thou comparest the spiritual form to the light which exists in the substance of the sun; the form, spread upon matter, to the light which exists upon the surface of a body; and the color to the corporeal form, which is found, in potentiality, in the corporeal matter (because color is found in a body, in potentiality), thou wilt find, by the comparison of these different forms, that the corporeal form, which exists in potentiality in the body, manifests itself to our senses, when the form, emanating from the spiritual form, comes to join itself to it, the same as color, which exists in potentiality in a body, manifests itself for the senses, when the light emanating from the light of the sun, comes to join itself to it. So then, thou wilt find, that the form which emanates from the spiritual form, coming to spread itself over matter, manifests itself to the senses, when it joins itself to the corporeal form, which exists in potentiality in matter, because the two (forms) become one, the same as the light spread upon the surface of a body, manifests itself in the senses, when it joins itself to the surface of the body and which itself identifies with the color." Besides the Will and the nine categories, he makes the simple substances or intermediaries, three. 1. The Universal Intellect. 2. The Universal Soul. 3. Nature or energy, which is more directly in affinity with the corporeal world, which it more immediately produces and governs. This is based on the idea of the triadic incorporeal in man. The intellectual or rational, the vital, and the vegetative spirits, in the human being, the rational being the highest, the vegetative, the lowest. The inferior substances cloth the light of the superior to them, and all cloth the Light of the First Agent.

The Universal Soul being considered as like the particular soul, is viewed as vegetative, vital, and intellectual or rational. The impression of the superior is shown in the inferior, *e.g.*, nature, the lowest of all substances, produces by the movement of attraction, transformation, retention, and expulsion. In the vegetative soul originates generation and growth, the vital produces sensibility and locomotion of body, and in the intellectual soul (*nephesh ham-me'dabbereth*) thought is produced. The Intellect above it, produces the perception of intelligible things (Form), without time, space, or proof of anything, because being in perfect completion, it perceives all in the true essence. A substance both moving and being moved, like the Kosmic mind, souls, and nature, must be physico-spiritual (*ruchni gashmee*). The substance of the nine categories, is rather physico-passive, and not at the same time intirely active-passive. As they descend they thicken, are enfeebled and in shadow, and the density hinders them from rapid motion and penetrating into other things. Whether the categories (*sugheem*) can be inferred as from the spiritual, is answered by the axiom,—" You can conclude from the visible as to the invisible, from the compound as to the simple." The body of man, as the Mikrokosm, resembles that of the Makrokosm, or Great World, the Universe, both in its course and construction. The forms of the purely spiritual substances become visible, through the resistance of matter against the intrusion of that which is more subtile, the latter therefore, is retained on the exterior and assumes a kind of density. By the union of the spiritual and physical substances a new form, neither totally spiritual or totally physical arises. The Divine faculty is an extreme perfection, that cannot be enfeebled; but the gradual enfeeblement of the forms in the substances results from the fact, that the light of the Divine faculty, when concentrated in itself leaves these substances more or less in shadow (or image). Like sunlight penetrating different media, the change is not to be attributed to its essence, but to that of the thing which receives its action, and which cannot be manifested except by partaking of its qualities; but it partakes of these in different gradations; because the further that the thing is from the source of the Divine faculty, the less it receives the former's action. The higher existences yearn after the Divine potentiality (*b'hishtokek hak-kokhoth ailav*), the lower are in the shadow (*v'hayah hash-shafal tzail*). The Divine power never decreases. The mediative substances also never decrease in power. They impart without any loss, like the sun, etc. The inferior world is an image of the superior, and an analogy exists between the different parts of the two worlds. To arrive at a true knowledge of the simple substances, man must throw off the bond of matter, and by meditation transport himself into the intelligible world, and so seek to identify his essence with that of the higher substances; when in that condition, man does not recognize anything of the world of the senses. In that condition, man will find the evident bodies in comparison with the intelligible substances, extremely insignificant, and see, that the corporeal world is borne by the intelligible world, as if it were a ship on the sea, or a bird in the air. Ibn Gebirol thought he resolved the connection between the Infinite and the finite, by establishing, that the simple substances and the Will, are neither wholly the one or the other, that the Will or Desire of the Supreme Deity, is infinite in its essence, but through its action, is in affinity with the finite, and that this action began at the instant of the creation, or rather emanation, of the Universe. The intellect has had a commencement, has been emanated or created, whilst its action, falls not in time but is eternal and infinite. He then, to show the bonds existing between them, sets forth the meaning we can infer, in his saying, that the simple substances, are from and in the orbits or spheres which environ each other, and which themselves wholly surround the composite substances, and these are evidently those which the Qabbalists term the Sephiroth, and which, he calls, spheres or circles. Properly they should be called, orbits. The essence of the Will, he admits, is however impenetrable to man's intelligence, and we arrive at a knowledge of it only through ecstasy, which puts us into the world of the Divinity. We know the essence of the Will, only through the actions which emanate through the intermediary of the Will.

The IV Book.—This book treats of a subject of much importance, that is, that all the simple substances are composed of form and matter. St.

Thomas Aquinas, Albert the Great, and other celebrated scholastics, consider Avicebron, as the first, who has attributed matter to the soul and all other simple substances, and that doctrine has been regarded by them as the principal point of Gebirol's system. Gebirol goes back to the idea of the bonds, existing between the superior and inferior worlds, the superior being a prototype of the latter. The simple substances have an affinity and all form one sole unity; they are distinguished only through the matter they carry, which is more or less subtile; as it approaches or recedes from the first source of all perfection. Simple when in affinity with the corporeity which is underneath them, composite relatively to that which is above them, *i. e.*, the Will or first agent, which is Absolute Simplicity. An effect is weaker than a cause, and junction is possible only through a similarity. The simple substances, as between themselves, are different; this is the result of form, form is the realization of their existence, to the latter, matter is indispensable. Matter has not any real existence and is without form.* Most of this book is composed of demonstrations, too numerous to be given in this writing, but he asserts that all the Universe, which is outside of the Supreme Deity, from its superior extremity to its inferior, is yet in one continued unity, in which the Deity is immanent yet transcendental. The Highest above All Things is an Absolute Unknown Unity, the emanator of the created is a different Creator getting all potentiality from the former. The latter is the One in number. There is therefore a two-fold *Ens*. Matter, in its greatest abstraction, is only being in potentiality, or, the simple power, *to be*. The word designates at once that simple faculty in all its abstractness, that ideal potentiality, which has not yet passed into action, and which is not yet clothed with any form, either spiritual or corporeal. Matter is also the composite matter, which may be spiritual or corporeal, and lastly, it is that which holds the medium between them, that is, the elementary matter and that of the spheres. This is the abstract matter of the corpo-

* " The powers (potentialities) of matter we know and recognize in every phenomenon of creation; the absolute matter in none." Prof. Faraday, London and Edinburgh, Philos. Journ., 1844. See also, "Curious Things of the Outside World," etc., by Hargrave Jennings, London, 1861, Vol. ii, 32, 33. " Solar Light and Heat," by Z. Allen. New York, 1879, p. 166.

reity, that of the latter in potentiality. In the higher world there is a two-fold *Ens*, quality and that which bears it. Substratum is matter, quality is form. Our author has some remarks as to the affinity which exists between the *to be*, and numbers, and shows the number 3 is the root of all things, because Form represents the Unity, and Matter the Duad, and together with the Will, the bond, results a Triad; and his reasoning recalls that of the Pythagoreans, especially the statements of the Arabian authors, upon the numbers of Pythagoras. In the idea of *to be*, are the necessary, possible, and impossible, or, Creator, created, and non-being. Intellect, *Neshamah*, represents the monad, the ethical soul, *Ru-a'h*, the duad, the vital soul, *Nephesh*, the triad, and Nature, the tetrad. All the existing are constituted after the nature of numbers, which are considered as entities, and all are dominated by the intellect, the same as all the numbers are comprised in the unity. The Highest Abstract God is the indivisible, metaphysical unity. The Will is a production, a secondary and divisible unity, the One, the unity of number, which is in direct affinity with multiplicity. This secondary unity, the One of number, is an immediate emanation of the unity above all number, the Absolute Divinity. The Universal Form in itself is a Perfect Light, which weakens in the measure it penetrates into matter, just as physical light terminates after passing through several, more or less, transparent bodies. The first Light is the creative Will, the efficient faculty, which passes into the Universal Form, the potentiality to act. Matter is the principle of unity, Form, of multiplicity. There is Universal Matter and Form; the former corresponds with unity, the latter with two-foldness, hence not unity, but the Triad is at the root of All. The Light in the Universal Matter, or in the Universal Form, is insignificant when compared with the Light in the Will. There are three forms. 1. That which exists in the essence of the Will; this however in reality is not form. 2. Form which is in action or reality and is attached to matter, *i. e.*, the Form of the Universal Intellect. 3. The Ideal Form, the abstract of all matter and which is virtually attached to matter. The other forms are contained in the Universal Form. If the Will is an efficient cause, it has in its essence, the form of all the things, because it is certain that the form of every effect exists in its cause, or better, the effect (itself) exists in its cause through the form which it has. Things therefore exist in the essence of the Will only for so much as they are its effects. The effects of all of these may be included under the term movement. The principle of this, not even the most subtile bodies bears within itself. All motion comes therefore from above and is beyond all composite things.

Creation with Gebirol is only the impression of Form in Matter, an impression emanating from the Will. Creation keeps within bounds the Universal Matter and Universal Form. All the rest emanate from these. Creation does not happen in time, but precedes it and is in eternity.

The V Book.—In this the theme is, the Universal Matter and Universal Form considered in themselves. These are the culminating points of the whole work, and should serve as the ladder to rise to a knowledge of the Will. Of the Will our author says, he would treat in another writing; but this is now lost. In this Book, Gebirol sets forth the Will or Divine Word, as the intermediary and bond of the Universal Matter and Form. Yet they also are bound together and exist in the Divine, for they were born simultaneously. The Will is one, the Matter and Form two, together the triad, but they have never been separated, and different from the knowledge in man, knowledge in God passes from potentiality to action, without the intervention of any time, all in the action of the Deity is instantaneous. The knowledge of these things, he says, is the most elevated, man as a finite being, can attain. The Form and Matter are as an open book, they are the pages upon which are traced the lines of letters. Those who know how to read that book, acquire the highest knowledge. The highest Intellect is without form, and therefore is enabled to conceive all the other forms, which are contained in the Universal Form. The Matter peculiar to the Form of the Intellect (*Sè-khel*), receives its form from the Will. Matter is a spiritual power, existing without Form by itself, and the Form is a light which gives everything its characteristics and stamp. The Form, is in the knowledge of the Supreme, yet separate, from whence it gets united with Matter. The Will (Memrah or Logos), is a Divine faculty which emanates from the Deity and penetrates the whole universe; it has been called, the Creating Speech or the Divine Word; it is the first source of the movement which has created and vivified all, and communicates itself successively to all parts of the spiritual and corporeal world as a vitalizing energy. From it, the Universal Form emanates. The movement through the Will is not the movement of physics, that is, the movement in inferior substances. The movement through the Will is an energy and faculty which determines itself, freely in itself, and communicates itself to the spiritual world, to which it gives knowledge and life. From this Will the Universal Form emanates. We call to the attention of the reader, that this Will or Word was most likely in the mind of our author, the speech ("said") of the creation, repeated ten times in Genesis, Chapter 1, which indicates the Will and Desire of God, the Divine Potentiality, and manifests itself freely in the work of our Creation.

We say God is in everything, because through and by Its Will, Desire, or Word, Creation came into being and still exists. God's Will is always in everything in potentiality and action. This Will or Word is the action of the Absolute manifested. Creation is like the word spoken by man, as far as it enters the ear of the hearer; it creates spiritual forms in the latter. So the Creator has spoken the Word, the intent and meaning, of which became manifest in matter. Saadya Gaon (927–942 A. D.) had already written, that the "He said" of Genesis, meant "He Willed" or "Desired." To know, and to will, are the two sides of the Deity, one latent, the other active. The Absolute Supreme is the thinker, thought, and object of thought; with the Deity all of these are instantaneous. The Will acts beyond time, produces motion without being itself moved; Universal Matter is like non-existence, Form is existence. Every existence tends towards the higher, the first Unity, to obtain perfection. Reward is for the pious soul in after life, punishment for the wicked; this refers only to the thinking, intellectual soul, *Neshamah*, but not to the *Nephesh*, or animal soul. In the Kether Malkhuth the pre-existence of the soul is referred to. The whole universe is one complex, the lower emanates from the higher, and is its image, but the Divine potentiality is active in each. Love and yearning for the original source of being, and the desire of Divine perfection, are the principles of motion, common to all the created. The extent of attainment is various and depends on their capacities. The emanations take place dynamically; forces, scintillations and rays issue from the categories, but the essence of the Supreme Unity, which is transcendental to yet immanent in them, never decreases. These are the intermediaries which are neither absolutely limited, nor absolutely endless, but like the Will they partake of each, yet are still, in their kind, different. They are evidently the Sephiroth of the Qabbalah. The same view is in Philo, iii, p. 185 *et seq.* The Will is infinite in its essence, but in its action, beginning with Time, it is finite. The *spiritus mundi* is, on its created side, finite, but its actions also being beyond Time, it is infinite.

That Will, Memrah or Logos, has been considered by the Jewish theologians, as a first hypostasis of the divinity, putting in direct affinity and bond, the first and absolute substance, the Supreme Unity, with the universe; but really, at the foundation, the Will, Desire or Word, as a Divine attribute, is inseparable from the Divinity, and is, as far as we can in this world know, the Divine Essence.* Ibn Gebirol's distinction is purely ideal. This book may be summed up in three propositions: 1. All emanated or created things, that is, all beings outside of the Supreme, have matter and form. 2. All movement and vital energy in the universe emanates from the Divine Will. 3. This Will is a Divine faculty, which as the Divine Word or Speech, emanated, or immanently created, and since has always penetrated and kept in existence, the whole universe. Gebirol holds that the simple, abstract, highest unknown Being, corresponds to Who? What? to 2, How? to 3, Why? to 4. The Universal Perfect Soul is the Makrokosm, Humanity is the Mikrokosm. The energy of the universe begins at the highest celestial sphere, called by Gebirol, the environing sphere, but does not begin, as with Giordani Bruno and Spinoza, in the Absolute Deity as a first substance. Our author's idea of the Supreme Deity is similar to that of Ain Soph in the Hebrew Qabbalah, and he takes refuge in the idea of the Will as the first expression, of the unnumbered, unknown, primal Supreme Deity above all number; the Will being the unit of number, and the simple abstract idea; and the Supreme

---

* NOTE.—See John i, 1–15, Prov. viii, Ps. xxxiii, and the writings of Philo Judæus. The Targums of Onkelos and Jonathan ben Uzziel, etc., by J. W. Etheridge, London, 1865, as to the Memrah or Word, the Logos. Also writings of Rev. Peter Allix before cited, and Jacob Bryant on Philo. Cambridge, 1797.

Deity being unknowable and above all finite number and idea. He holds that one can only reach to the unknown Supreme Deity through the ecstatic condition. Such is a short resumé of the Me'qôr Haÿ-yĭm.

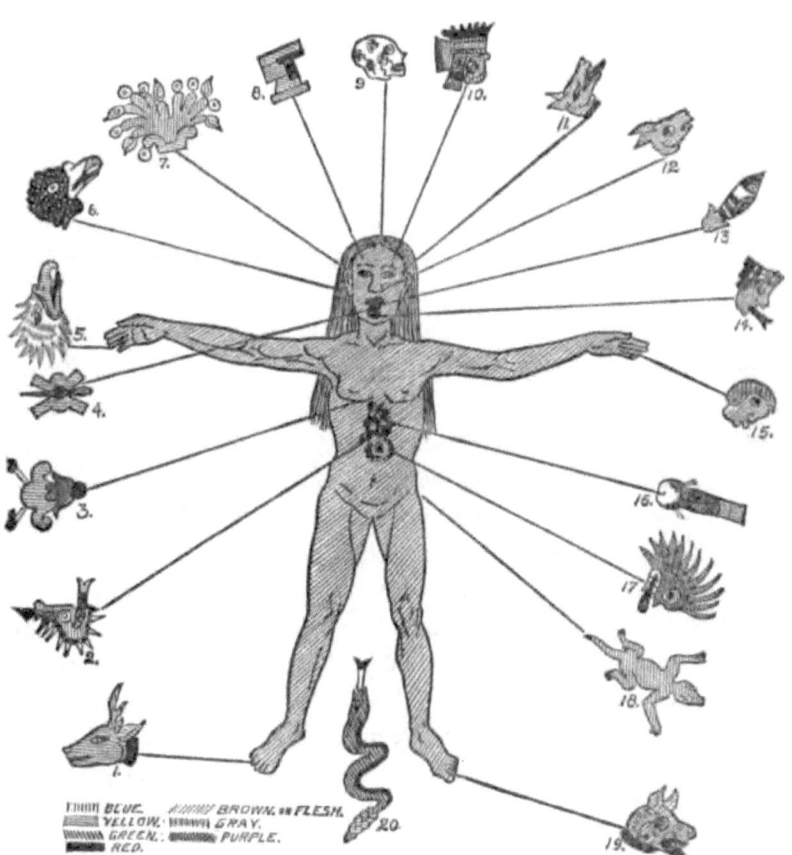

Figure 8.—The ancient Mexican androgene or makrokosmos, with the ancient Mexican signs of the Zodiac, from an archaic, aboriginal, Mexican MSS. in the Vatican Library.

Figure 9.—Hindu Tree of the Sephiroth.

VIII.

THE THEORY AS TO ECSTASY. THE WRITERS WHO MENTION IBN GEBIROL, OR MAKE USE OF HIS PHILOSOPHY. THE SO-CALLED ARABIC PHILOSOPHERS.

THE doctrine of ecstasy as understood by the ancients was: The soul was regarded as an emanation from the Divine Intelligence, but being in a finite body, as if in a prison, it could only have a knowledge of finite things; for instance Plotinus held knowledge and existence are identical, therefore human intelligence to comprehend and know the Divine Intelligence, must become as if the Divine Intelligence, arriving at that, the same plane, it is no longer an emanation from it, but is an identification with it. In a word, the human soul must lose its personality, and this is reached only through ecstasy. When in this condition, the human soul is assumed to be separated from individual consciousness, freed from its fleshly prison, and absorbed into the Divine Intelligence from which it emanated. The captive soul goes back to its parent, the Supreme Deity. Among the Mohammedans this is the effort of the Sufi; the Hindus, the Yogin; the Buddhists, the Sçraman. It was the doctrine of the Neo-platonists, and probably of many of the Hebrew prophets. The early Qabbalists held this view, as also did Philo Judæus, also the Apostle Paul, who was frequently in trances. The same idea is apparently in the Didaché or Teaching of the Twelve Apostles, and is fully set forth in the pseudo-Dionysius, the Areopagite. Many of the Early Fathers of the Christian Church, believed in it, and a thorough examination by the student, of the real meaning of the "Gift of tongues" of the New Testament, may reveal to him that it contemplated a similar idea.* Gebirol was obliged to admit an emanating or creating Deity, a manifestation of the Unknowable Supreme Unity, but, with him, this is the impression of the Universal Form on Universal Matter, both of which emanate from the Will. This preceded Time, is Eternal. With the Qabbalah, he also insists upon a superior ideal paradigm, after which the universe has been formed, and which is in affinity with the latter, through the orbits or spheres. This is the Qabbalistic doctrine of the Adam Qadmon or Adam Illa-ah, the Makrokosm, and the totality of the ten Sephiroth. The doctrine of numbers and letters as entities, enters into his system, and considered as sounds, we must admit, they stand on the border land of the spiritual and physical worlds; from the spirit they resolve into a physical element, the breath, and are the symbols indispensable to the communication of thought, and, indeed, are to us, the best possible outward and also receptive, form of the spirit.

Gebirol must have known the celebrated Qabbalistic Sepher Ye'tzeerah, *i. e.*, Book of Creation, rather Formation, as he evidently quotes from it (Bk. II, § 27): "It is wherefore it has been said that the construction of the world was made through the inscription of numbers and letters in the air." The Ye'tzeerah reads: Edition of Mantua, c. i, § 10; c. ii, §§ 2 and 3—"Two, it is the breath (air or azoth) which comes from the spirit, in which It has engraved and sculptured the 22 letters. * * The 22 letters It has graved, sculptured, weighed, transposed and combined them, and It created through them, the soul of all that which is created and all that which has been created. * * * The 22 letters, which are the foundation, are engraved in the voice, sculptured in the air, and fixed in the mouth, in five places (organs of speech), etc." R. Saadyah Gaon in his writing—Bodleian Library, MSS. cod. Poc. No. 256—upon this Qabbalistic book, essays to make this its fundamental doctrine. Ibn Gebirol's quotation is important for the completion of his system. Comp. *ante*, p. 141, note. The method of the Ye'tzeerah is analytical, that of the Zohar is based on the analytical-synthetical process. The former uses the letters and numbers as the principles of all the things, the latter uses the inner forms of thinking, the ideas. The Ye'tzeerah is very old. See

*Comp. Dr. Schaaf's Hist. of the Christian Church. New York, 1882, pp. 224 to 245.

ante, page 39. It was doubtless the book mentioned in the Talmud.*

Among the Jewish writers, whose writings we now have, the first who mentions Ibn Gebirol, is Moses Ibn Jacob ben Ezra, of Granada, who lived in the first half of the twelfth century (d. 1138); he eulogizes our author.† In his Arugath hab-Bosem, *i. e.*, Garden of Aromatics, he borrows much, either from Ibn Gebirol, or from the same sources. "The Active Intellect," he says, "is the first among the creatures of the Most High; it is a faculty emanating from the Will, a simple, pure and scintillating substance, which bears in itself the forms of all the existences. The human intellect is a composite faculty, in affinity with it (the Active Intellect). * * * Man is called the Little World (Mikrokosm), and the universe, the Great World (Makrokosm), because the Mikrokosm greatly resembles by its composition, derivation, and creation, the Makrokosm." Also, "The rational soul only subsists in the body, through the intermediary of the spirits, which are placed between the two; because the one being subtile and the other gross, the soul can exist in the body only through an intermediary bond. It is the same with the universe, I desire to say, that the simple and sublime substance, cannot (directly) unite with the body of the world; this last is the substance which carries the ten categories." These ten categories may refer to those mentioned by Aristotle, but most probably, to the ten orbits or spheres of the universe, as the ten Sephiroth. Haÿ. Gaon (died 1038 A.D.) knows the Sephiroth, and Gebirol wrote an elegy upon Haÿ. Gebirol in his writings evidently intends the Sephiroth, although he speaks of them, as the First Agent and the nine categories, but he also refers to the circles, orbits, or spheres as Intermediaries.‡ The celebrated Abraham Ibn Ezra, in his Bible Com-

---

*Comp. Hershon's Talmudic Miscellany, before cited, pp. 57, 234, 329. Treasures of the Talmud, p. 42. Genesis with Talmudic Comment., p. 287, before cited. Ad. Franck, *La Kabbale*, p. 74 *et seq.* The Talmud Babli, treat. *Berakhoth*, folio 55. Schawb's French Ed., i, p. 453–4, says of Be'tzaleel (Ex. xxxi, 2, etc.), "R. Yudah said in the name of Rab. That man knew the mysterious combination of the letters, by which heaven and earth were created, etc."

† See *Geschichte der Jüdischen Literatur von Gustav Karpeles*. Berlin, 1886, p. 504 *et seq.* Munk, *Mélanges des Philos. juive et arabe*, p. 263, etc.

‡ Book II, § 1, § 2, § 12, § 23, § 27. III. §§ 1–2, 4, 7, 8, 9, *et seq.*, § 41. IV, § 1, § 8. Saadyah Gaon, in his Comment on the Sepher Yetzirah—MSS. of the Bodleian

mentaries on Isaiah, also eulogizes Gebirol, cites some of his allegorical explanations, and apparently knew the Me'qôr 'Haÿ-yîm. He speaks of the creating Will and identifies it with the Divine Wisdom, and the Divine Word.* It also appears, from some passages of the book Khozari of Yehudah ha-Levi, that he knew of similar ideas to those in the Me'qôr, and most likely obtained them from the Qabbalistic philosophy. He does not however, mention Gebirol or his writings.†

In 1160 A. D. Abraham ben David ha-Levi, attacked Gebirol bitterly in his book, called:—The Sublime Faith, which is Aristotelian in its tendency. This writing apparently discredited our author with his co-religionists, and the popularity of peripateticism, through the writings of Ibn Sina (Avicenna), and perhaps, the revelations in, and the mysticism of, the Me'qôr 'Haÿ-yîm, may have contributed to their forgetfulness of his philosophy. The Me'qôr did not suit, the positiveness of Maimonides (1135-1204 A.D.) and his school, and the rapid advance of the Maimonic tendency and Aristotelianism, soon caused the philosophical writings of this great Jewish philosopher to be forgotten by his race. Only one Jewish philosopher of the thirteenth century, the erudite Shem Tob Ibn-Falaquera (*circa* 1264 A. D.), in his Commentary upon the Moreh Ne-boo'kheem of Maimonides, cites from Gebirol frequently, and has appreciated his philosophical work, which Falaquera says: "Contains an antiquated system, going back to philosophers of the highest antiquity." We find however, although not mentioned by the Qabbalists, from the similarity of their statements, that either they drew from him, or that both drew, which we think our writing shows to be more probable, from a common ancient source, the Secret Learning. The Speculative Hebrew Qabbalah is an abstract science, based undoubtedly upon the Secret Learning, as we shall hereafter mention. It assumes the unveiling of the secrets of crea-

Library, Cod. Poc. No. 256, refers to the ten Sephiroth. He lived *circa* 927-942 A. D. Philo appears to have had an idea of them. See his treatise, On Monarchy; especially pp. 185-6.

* For Commentaries in English, see Transactions of the Society of Hebrew Literature. London. See, same series, Essays on Writings of Ibn Ezra.

† For the Khozari, comp. D. Cassel's Ed. Leipzig. 1853. Also, Warsau Ed. of 1880, with two commentaries; and H. Hirschfeld's, Breslau, 1885.

tion and physics termed by it, Ma-a'seh Be'resheeth, and of the essence of the Deity and God's connection with the universe, or religious metaphysics, which it calls Ma-a'seh Merkabah, *i. e.*, the Chariot-Throne.

Under the name of Avicebron, Avicembron, Avicebrol, and Albenzubrun, Ibn Gebirol held, in Christian Europe, a position as one of the greatest philosophers of the Middle Ages; and his philosophical writings were largely used by the scholastics. He was thought by many, to be an Arab or Saracene. The learned orientalist, Jourdain, in his Critical Researches as to the age and origin of the Latin Translations of Aristotle;* tells us, one can surely know the philosophy of the thirteenth century, if he will analyze the *Fons Vitæ* of Avicebron, and the book *De Causis*, which does not appear to have been known to Gebirol. The ideas in the *Fons Vitæ* caused great disputes in the Christian schools. As early as the middle of the twelfth century, Archdeacon Dominic Gunsalvi, with the aid of a converted Jew, named Jean Avendoth, translated into Latin, the Me'qôr 'Haÿ-yîm. It has been asserted, that from this, and the book *De Causis;* Amaury de Chartres and David de Dimant, drew doctrines, afterwards condemned by the Roman Church as heretical. The *De Causis*, was probably a production of the twelfth century. Its contents are aphorisms borrowed from Proclus, but it was incorrectly ascribed to Aristotle.† Adelard of Bath, Bernard of Chartres, Alain of Lille and others, professed doctrines very similar to those of Gebirol, and in both church and synagogue, learned men of this period, became theosophists and mystics.‡ Gebirol's philosophical work, was used by Guillaume de Auvergne, Bishop of Paris in 1228 (d. 1249), Albert, the Great (b. 1200, d. 1280), St. Thomas Aquinas (b. 1225, d. 1274), Duns Scotus (b. 1265, d. 1308). Later, the unfortunate philosopher Giordano Bruno (b. 1550, burned 1600 on account of his philosophy), and the Neoplatonicians of Italy as late as the sixteenth century, cited from Avicebron's philosophical writings. The schoolmen, no more than the Jews

---

* Paris, 2d ed., p. 197.

† See B. Haureau's *De la Philosophie Scholastique*, Paris, 1880, Bk. I, part 2, p. 46. The doctrine attributed to Amaury, may be condensed in the formula: *Omnia unum, quia, quicquid est, est Deus*, Ibid. Vol. I, p. 403 *et seq.*

‡ Vacherot, *Histoire Critique de l'École d'Alexandrie*, Bk. III, p. 117 *et seq.*

of the thirteenth century, appear to have had much knowledge of the author whose works they used. Most of the scholastics thought him to be an Arabian Mussulman, Guillaume de Auvergne believed him to be an Arab, but as he had written a book *De Verbo Dei Agente Omnia*, believed that he professed Christianity.* Without doubt his Qabbalistic ideas largely influenced the Mediæval mystics. The Dominican St. Thomas Aquinas, as a Nominalist, opposed our author's philosophy. The fiery Franciscan Duns Scotus, the Realist, who recommended the most revolting violence, so as to force the Jews into the bosom of the Roman Church, without knowing our author was a Jew, embraced his doctrines.†

A few words as to the philosophers, who wrote in Arabic, that which has been incorrectly called, the Arabian philosophy, and who preceded Ibn Gebirol. These men lived in the Orient, some in Central Asia, their systems were based on Greek thought, expressed in Semitic language, modified and influenced by the so-called Oriental philosophy. With the exception of Al Kendi, its originators were not Arabs, nor did they come from the seat of the khalifate in the East. They were Persians or Turks, but they were fostered however, under Saracenic or Arabian dynasties. They were influenced by Aristotelianism viewed through an orientalized Platonism, and by Hindu, Persian, and Chaldean philosophy, and their offshoot Neo-platonism and Neo-pythagorianism. Al Kendi (b. *circa* 812, d. after 861 A. D.) was surnamed by the Arabs, the philosopher *par excellence*. His place of birth is unknown, his father was Governor of Koufa, under the Khalifs, Al-Mahdi, Al-Hadi, and Haroun al-Rashid. He studied at Bassora and Baghdad, and became celebrated under the Khalifs Al-Mamoun (813–833 A. D.) and Al-Mo'tacem (833–842 A. D.) by his writings on philosophy, medicine, mathematics, astronomy, politics, music, etc. In 861 he was yet living.

Abu-Naçr al-Farabi, called in Latin, Alpharabius (d. 950 A. D.), was a Persian. Guillaume de Auvergne, Albert, the Great, and Vincent de Beauvois, made much use of his commentary upon the Logic of Aristotle. Abu-Ali al-Hosëin ben-'Abd-Allah Ibn Sina, called by the scholastics

---

* Jourdain, work above cited, 2d ed., p. 299, Note 2.

† Comp. Haureau, work above cited, Bk. II, p. 327 *et seq.* Duns Scotus, *Opera, de rerum principio*, quæst VIII, No. 1 and art. 4, No. 24, 30, 31, 32, art. 5, 38.

Avicenna, was of Persian origin, and born 980, died A.D. 1037. The Me'qôr Haÿ-yĭm, appeared shortly after the publication of his Al-Shefa, *i. e.*, Cure or Healing, a vast Encyclopedia of the Philosophic sciences, in 18 volumes; composed about 1000 A. D. There is not anything to show that Ibn Gebirol had knowledge of it. Al Ghazali, was a native of Khorasan (b. 1058, d. 1111 A. D.). The first so-called Arabian philosopher in Europe was Ibn Gebirol (1021-1070 A. D.). The first Mohammedan Arabic philosopher, was Abn Becr Mo'hammed ben Ya'hya, surnamed Ibn-al-Çayeg, commonly called Ibn Badja, known to the scholastics as Aven-Pace or Avempace (b. 1100 at Saragossa, d. at Fez 1138 A. D.). He was Aristotelian, and followed the writings of Ibn Sina. After him were the Spanish Moors, Ibn Tofail, (b. *circa* 1100, d. 1185 A. D.) and Ibn Roschd, called by the scholastics Averroes (b. 1126, d. 1198 A. D.). These were as ignorant of the writings of Gebirol, as the Jews appear to have been. Gebirol is not even mentioned by the learned Moses Maimonides, (from the acrostics of his name frequently called Rambàm—1135-1204,) but Maimonides from his own writings, appears to have been in agreement with much of the tone of Gebirol's philosophy. The Mohammedans of this period did not read works written by Jews.

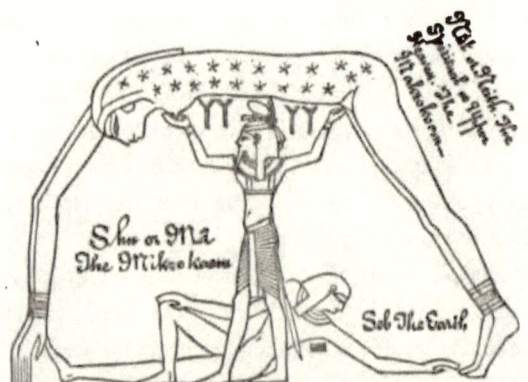

Figure 10.—The Egyptian androgenic intermediary, Shu or Mâ, with the Makrokosm, and Seb the Earth.

Figure 11.—The Ark of the Covenant, Cherubim, and the She'keen-ah.

IX.

THE ANTIQUITY OF THE QABBALAH. BOOKS AND WRITERS IN WHICH THE QABBALAH IS REFERRED TO. LETTER OF ST. JEROME ON THE DIVINE NAMES. CONNEXION WITH EARLY CHRISTIANITY. ANCIENT THOUGHT, LANGUAGE, SYMBOLISM AND TRADITION. HIGH POSITION CLAIMED FOR THE QABBALAH. THE IDEAL MAN AND THE GREAT BROTHERHOOD OF HUMANITY. FREE-WILL, THE GOOD AND THE EVIL. THE OPPOSITIONS AND HARMONY.

THE origin and antiquity of the Qabbalah have been enigmas to the most erudite orientalists, for centuries. The Qabbalists claim, that their most important doctrines are of most remote antiquity, in which we think they are right; but we do not go as far as some, who say, they were first taught by the Deity to a select company of angels, and that after the Fall, by the direction of the Deity, they were taught by these angels to Adam and Eve, to give the protoplasts the means of exercising their Free Will, and by it to return to their first nobility and felicity.

These say, from Adam, the Secret Oral Doctrine passed to Seth, and from Seth to Noah. Josephus perhaps refers to this learning in his book on the Antiquities of the Jews.* From Noah it passed to Abraham, the

* C. ii, § 3, Whiston's Edition.

friend of God; he emigrated, after having a knowledge of it, to Egypt, there he taught part of it to the learned of the Egyptians. And thus the Egyptians obtained some knowledge of it, and the Eastern nations were enabled to introduce it into their philosophical systems. Moses, who was learned in all the wisdom of the Egyptians (Exod. ii, 10, Acts vii, 22), obtained knowledge of it in the land of his birth, he studied the Qabbalah and devoted all his leisure hours to it, during the forty years' wanderings in the Desert, and during that time received further instructions as to it, from the angels. By the aid of this mysterious science he was enabled to solve the difficulties, which arose during his management of the Israelites. In the first four books of the Pentateuch, he has esoterically laid down the principles of the Secret Doctrine, from the fifth, Deuteronomy, they were withheld, therefore the Qabbalists call the first four, the man, the fifth, the woman. He initiated the Seventy Elders into the mysteries, (Numb. xi, 24 *et seq.*; Exod. xxiii, 1–11), and they transmitted them from mouth to ear, by the *Thorah Shebbe'al Peh*, *i. e.*, "the law which is by the mouth." The reader will note, seventy is the number of the Hebrew word, Sod, *i. e.*, Mystery, also of Wine, and the expression, wine of the Thorah, means secrets of the Thorah. It is also to be noted that seventy-two, six for each of the twelve tribes, were not initiated. In the chain of the initiated were David and Solomon, who had an extensive knowledge of the Qabbalah, and many of its doctrines may be discovered by the initiates, in their writings. Isaiah, *circa* 763–713 B. C., Daniel, 167–165 B.C., and Ezekiel, *circa* 594 B.C., also had considerable knowledge of the Qabbalah. Until the time of R. Shim-on ben Yo'haï, not any one had dared to impart the Secret Teaching by writing. He lived about 95–190 A. D., near the time of the destruction of the Second Temple, and fearing from the dispersion of the initiates, that the Secrets of the Qabbalah might be lost, he instructed certain of his disciples to write part of it. This has been done, largely through hints, symbols and aphorisms. Many of the doctrines of the Qabbalah, more or less veiled, may be found in the Hebrew Old Testament, and especially its Greek version called, the Septuagint, in the writings of Aristobulus, 170–150 B. C., the Apocrypha, especially in Jesus, the son of Sirakh, *circa* 290–280 B. C., some say; 190–170 B. C.,

the New Testament, the Targums, the oldest of the Sibylline Oracles which are Jewish, these appeared *circa* 140 B. C.; The Psalter of Solomon, *circa* 63-48 B. C.; the Assumption of Moses, *circa* A. D.; the Ascension and Vision of Isaiah; the Book of Jubilees, *circa* 100 B. C. to 70 A.D.; Testaments of the Twelve Patriarchs, *circa* 70 A.D.; Apocalypses of Barukh and IV Esdras, *circa* 81-96 A.D. (Ezra, the II. Esdras of the English Apocrypha. The Vulgate differs.) And in the books attributed to Hermes Trismegistus and 'Hanoch (Enoch); and especially in the writings of Philo Judæus, and Josephus, and in the most archaic of the Midrashim, that have survived their general destruction; also in the Apocryphal New Testament, especially the Epistle attributed to St. Barnabas, the scholar of St. Paul, which if not by him is very old, and is quoted by Clement of Alexandria, Origen, St. Jerome and Eusebius.*
They are in the Pastor of Hermas,† which was highly esteemed by Clement of Alexandria, Origen, Irenæus, Tertullian and Eusebius, and was at one time ranked as canonical; and also in the early Patristic literature, especially in the writings of Justin Martyr, Clement of Alexandria, Origen, St. Synesius, and the pseudo-St. Dionysius, whose hierarchy of angels is triadic, and in accord with the Ten Sephiroth.‡

* Comp. Kitto's Cyclop. of Bib. Liter., Ed. 1876, Vol. I, p. 300 *et seq.* and Apocryphal New Testament. Philadelphia, p. 145, *et seq.*

† Kitto, *Ibid.*, II, p. 283 *et seq.* Apoc. New Test. *Ibid.*, p. 197 *et seq.*; also *Le Pasteur d'Hermas.* Paris, 1880.

‡ The arrangement according to Dionysius is—

1. Seraphim.	4. Dominations.	7. Principalities.
2. Cherubim.	5. Virtues.	8. Archangels.
3. Thrones.	6. Powers.	9. Angels.

In a writing of the Syriac Church, called; the Testament of Adam, which is not later than 300 A. D. and probably much earlier, and which lies outside of Greek and Latin Christianity and is "an interesting monument of an almost unknown world of ancient creeds." Dict. of Christian Biog., by Smith and Wace, i, p. 38. Which has a connection with the book, the Conflict of Adam, which may be much older than the N. T. *Ibid.* 34 *et seq.*;—we have a celestial hierarchy like that of Dionysius, beginning with the 9. Angels, 8. Archangels, 7. Principalities, 6. Sovereignties, 5. Virtues, 4. Dominations, 3. Thrones, 2. Cherubim, 1. Seraphim. See *Fragments du Livre Gnostique intitulé Apocal. d'Adam ou Penitence ou Testament d'Adam, publié d'apres deux ver.*

The works of Dionysius have had great influence in the Roman Church, especially with the Mystics. St. Jerome—*circa* 331–420 A. D.— mentions the ten Divine Names, in almost the same order given in the Qabbalistic writings,* and follows many Qabbalistic explanations.

---

sions Syriàque par Mons. Ernest Renan, *Journ. Asiatique*, Paris, 1853. 5th *Str. tom. ii*, pp. 427–471; also his *L'église chrétien*, 1879, p. 529 sq. Also *Bulletin de l'Athénée Oriental de Paris*, 1881, p. 191, and note. *Ibid.* 1882, p. 50 *et seq.*

In the hierarchy of the Roman Catholic Church we have three divisions, the Princes of the Church, the Bishops and Priests, arranged into nine orders, viz:

1. Cardinal Bishops.
2. Cardinal Priests.
3. Cardinal Deacons.
4. Archbishops.
5. Bishops.
6. Co-adjutor Bishops.
7. Rector Priests.
8. Ordinary Priests.
9. Deacons.

We find nearly all the divisions mentioned in Dionysius in St. Paul; see Col. i, 16; Rom. i, 38, 39; Ephes. i, 21, iii, 10, 15; I Peter iii, 22, and other places, the balance in the Old Testament. The angelus bell in the Roman Church rings every day 3 times, and each time 3 times $3 = 9$, for the celestial hierarchies, and then a number of times for the spirits on earth.

* His epistle to Marcella, is as to the ten Mystic Names (*decem nomina mystica*) by which the Hebrews designate God. We here note that this fragment resembles the ten Names of the Deity—applied to the Ten Sephiroth by the Qabbalists. The following is a translation:

"St. Jerome to Marcella:—Thou mayest read in the xc (xci) Psalm, 'Who abideth in the help of the Highest, shall dwell under the shelter of the God of Heaven,' I would say that (in this quotation) with the Hebrews, for the 'God of Heaven' is placed (substituted) שדי, *i. e.*, *Shaddai* (the Almighty); this (word) Aquila interprets as *ikanon* (*i. e.*, the warlike, brave, powerful or strong), and we may accept its meaning for our purposes as robust or all-sufficient, and that this (Name) is one of the ten Names by which God is known (or called) among the Hebrews. Therefore as thou hast asked most earnestly that I should demonstrate to thee, these many Names with their interpretation, I will do what thou askest. The 1st Name of God is אל *El*, which is in the Septuaginta (translated) *Theon*, *i. e.*, God. Aquila explaining the etymology of it, *ischuron* (*i. e.*, interprets it), as the 'strong.' Then (2d) is אלהים *Elohim*, and (the 3rd) אלהי *Elohai*, which he translates as meaning the word, God. 4th, צבאות *Tsabaoth* which the Septuaginta (translates) 'Of the Forces (or Powers, *virtutum*),' but Aquila, would translate it, of Hosts (the Energies or Forces were considered by the Hebrews, as the Hosts of heaven, the angels, doing the Deity's Will.) 5th. עליון *El'yon*, which we call, the High. 6th. אשר אהיה *Eser Eh'yeh* (*i. e.*, 'I shall be who I shall be'), of which we read in Exodus (iii) thus:—'Who is, sent me.' 7th. אדני *Adonai* (or Adanoi) which we always term, Lord. 8th. יה (*YaH*) which is placed only as to God (in the expression of the tetragrammaton

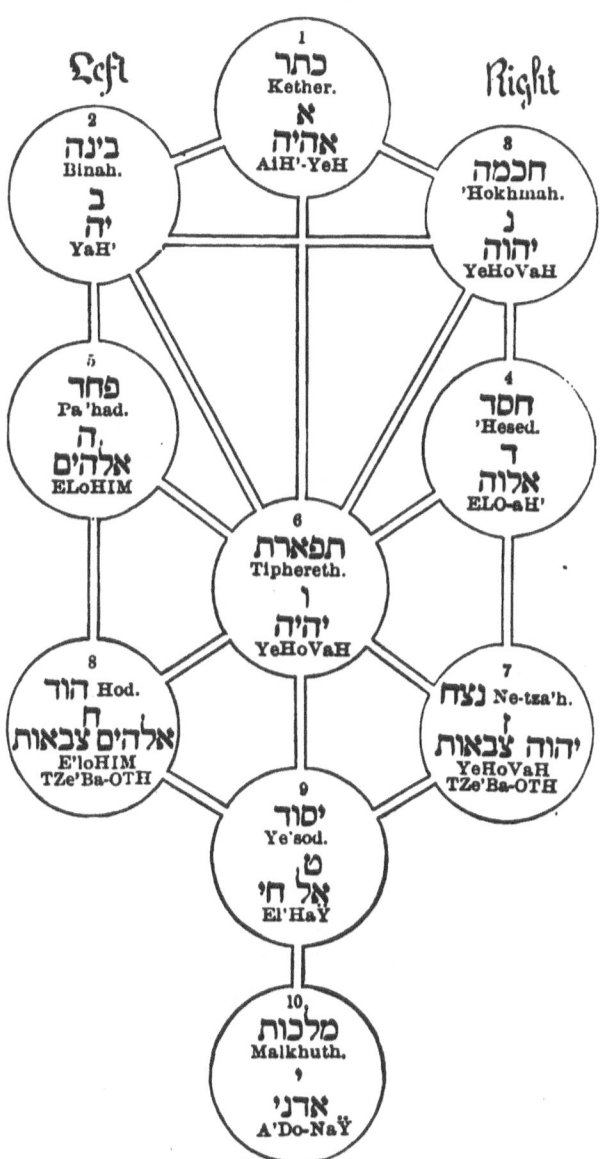

Diagram II. The Divine Names and the Sephiroth.

Many similar ideas were borrowed by the School of Alexandria and the Neo-platonicians; probably coming through the Aryan branch, the Hindus, at least the profound Norwegian scholar, Christian Lassen, presents a strong argument for the Neo-platonic doctrine having originated in India.*

The Gnostics, Manichæans and other, so-called heretical, sects of their time, have also borrowed from the Qabbalah. Earlier we find many of the Hebrew Qabbalistic ideas in the Aryan writings, in the Vedas, especially their Upanishads, in the Bhagavadgîtâ, the Tantras, etc. Among the Chinese, in the Yih-King, the writings attributed to Laou Tze', and other secret philosophical books. We may also find many of them in the Zend and other early Persian writings,† in the cuneiform texts of the early inhabitants of Mesopotamia, Chaldea, Babylonia, and Assyria; on the monuments and papyrus of Egypt, and among the remains of the archaic Buddhists and Dravidian races, of India, among others in the cave temples of Ellora, Elephanta, and the Sanchi and Amravati topes.

Name of the Deity usually יהוה YHVH), and which in (the word) *allelu-YaH* is sounded as the final syllable. 9thly. The Tetragrammaton, which they thought *anekphônhêton*, *i. e.*, the Ineffable (Name, not to be spoken,) and it is written with these letters יהוה *Yod, Heh, Vav, Heh*, as to which indeed those not learned upon this (subject) on account of the similitude of the elements (letters), are accustomed when they find them in Greek books, to read (as if Greek letters and pronounce them) PIPI. 10th. That which above is called שדי *Shaddai* (Almighty) and is not interpreted in Ezekiel. But we ought to know that *Elohim* is of the common number, (*i.e.*, singular and plural) and that one God may be thus called, and many; by a similar way 'heaven' is also designated, and also 'the heavens,' *i. e.*, שמים *Sha'mayeem*. From whence and often interpreters vary, for an example of which, we have in our language Athenas, Thebas, and Salonica." *Epistol. Hieronymous*, cxxxvi, *ad Marcellam. Opera omnia, etc., Paris, 1546. Tom. iii, p. 31, A. and B.* Benedictine Edition, xxv, *Tom. i, p. 131.* Comp. Hist. of the Jews, by Basnage, trans. by Taylor London, 1708, p. 198 and diagram. Kircher's *Œdipus Ægyptiacus, Tom. ii*, p. 213 *sq.* Jerome in several of his writings speaks of certain Hebrew traditions upon Genesis, which make Paradise or, as the Jews call it, Eden, more ancient than the world. Compare the little work *Quæstiones sive traditiones hebraïcæ, in Genesim.* Edition of Paris, *Tom. iii, p. 65, A. B. C., etc.* That in parenthesis is not in the original, but inserted by me for the more correct understanding of St. Jerome.

* See his, *Indische Alterthumskunde.* Leipzig. 1858. Vol. iii, pp. 353–441.

† *La Kabbale*, p. 353 *sq.*

It is extremely probable that many reminiscences of them are in Thibet, in the possession of the Buddhists.

Among the Medieval Christian scholars who have agreed with the Hebrew Qabbalists, that their doctrines came from the Patriarchs, and especially from Moses, are, Raymond Lully, Archangelus Burgonovensis, the Prince Giovanna Pico della Mirandola, William of Postel, John Reuchlin, John Stephen Rittangel, Paul Ricci, Julius Conrad Otto, Henry Cornelius Agrippa von Nettesheim, Rev. John Francis Buddæus, Dr. Henry More, Rev. John Lightfoot, the learned Jesuit, Athanasius Kircher, Claudius Duretus, Christian Knorr, the Baron von Rosenroth, Franz Mercurius van Helmont, Peter Galatinus, Johann Rhenferdius, Augustus Pfeiffer, etc., etc. It largely influenced the Medieval Mystics, especially Paracelsus, Jacob Böhmen, Henry Kuhnrath, Oswald Crollius, Dr. Robert Fludd and the Rosicrucian Society, also the two Van Helmonts, Henry Cornelius Agrippa, the Abbot Johannes Tritheim, Valentine Weigel, Dr. Jerome Cardan, and Franc Giorgio Zorzi (Franciscus Georgius, surnamed Venetus); and it has also influenced, Cardinal Nicolas Cusanus (Cusani), Cardinal Ægidius of Viterbo, Pope Sixtus IV, Marsilius Ficinus, Theophilus Gale, Ralph Cudworth, Sir Isaac Newton, Baron Leibnitz and Barukh (Benedict) Spinoza, later, Schopenhauer, Hegel, Shelling and other German philosophers. Sir Francis Bacon studied the writings of Dr. Fludd the Qabbalist, and Sir Isaac Newton those of Jacob Böhmen; and the great Leibnitz became much interested in its study, through Baron von Rosenroth. Upon the Practical Qabbalah, Abbe de Villars (nephew of De Montfaucon) in 1670, published his celebrated satirical novel, The Count de Gabalis, upon which Pope based his Rape of the Lock.* Qabbalism runs through the Medieval poem, the Romance of the Rose, and permeates the writings of Dante.

Among those who ascribe it to the Egyptian metaphysics and philosophy, are, Jacques Basnage de Beauval, who has written upon it, in his History of the Jews, chiefly basing his assertions on the learned, but frequently erroneous, writings as to the Qabbalah, of the erudite Jesuit, the Rev. Athanasius Kircher in his, *Œdipi Ægyptiaci, Tom. Secund. Romæ*, 1653.

Of those who say it came from Chaldean sources, from which they

* The Count de Gabalis, in English, was reprinted in England in 1886, at Bath.

claimed Plato and Pythagoras obtained their systems, are Richard Simon and Paul Berger. Among those who claim it came from Gentile philosophy, are John George Wachter, Joachim Lange, and the Rev. John Christopher Wolff, who also claims a great antiquity for it. The Rev. Jean Morin, as we have before shown, and Lewis Cappellus opposed it, especially the antiquity and doctrines of the Zohar. The learned German historian of philosophy, Johann Jakob Brucker, has written much to prove that it was brought from Egypt to Palestine, by R. Simeon ben Shetach, about 100 years before the Christian era, but really appears to know very little about it.

John Frederick Kleuker, in his prize essay on the Qabbalistic philosophy, says it is akin to the Secret Teaching of Orpheus and Thales, and certainly came from Pythagoras. He also, with Reuchlin, thought that the Secret Science was derived from the Patriarchs, and much cultivated in ancient times in Chaldea, in which latter idea he is probably correct. Osiander agrees with Kleuker; C. G. Bretschneider, Adolphe Franck,[*] and some others, think it is to be found in the ancient doctrines of the Persians, and Jacques Matter, seems to agree with them. Wilhelm G. Tennemann, the German historian of philosophy, sides with Brucker. Steiger confesses in his works its great importance, but does not investigate it. Roth, in his writing on the Epistle to the Hebrews, says he will write a special treatise upon it, but has not done so. Augustus Tholuck favors the ideas of Jean Morin. Among the modern Jews, Munk, Jost, Stern, Leopold Low, David Luriah, Dr. Schiller-Szinessy, and Konitz, among many others, favor its antiquity, Dr. Hirsch Graetz, Dr. Leopold Zunz, Dr. Michael Sachs, Dr. Abraham Geiger, we think as Talmudists and for sectarian reasons, oppose it. The great German Hebrew bibliographer, Dr. Moritz Steinschneider, says, its history has not yet been written by any one. Dr. Adolph Jellinek started out in opposition, but a thorough examination of his *quotations*, tends to show its antiquity. Dr. Jellinek deserves much praise for his labour upon the subject. Elia Benamozegh of Livorno [Leghorn], Italy, whom we have previously men-

---

[*] Franck in his *La Kabbale*, shows a similarity to the Qabbalistic philosophy in the writings of Philo. The latter certainly has in his writings much of the Qabbalistic philosophy, and in many places is in accord with the Zohoric writings.

tioned, one of the greatest Qabbalists now living, also a learned Talmudist, favors its antiquity. The above are only a very few of those who have given the subject attention.

The subject has much importance both from its content, and in the history of human thought; in the words of a learned writer on the Hebrew Qabbalah, "A doctrine, which has more than one point of resemblance to the doctrines of Plato and Spinoza; which, by its form, elevates itself sometimes, as far as the majestic tone of religious poetry; which has taken birth upon the same land * * as Christianity; which, during a period of more than a dozen centuries, without other proof than the hypothesis of an antique tradition, without other apparent motive than the desire, to penetrate more intimately into the meaning of the Holy Books, has been developed and propagated in the shadow of a most profound mystery,"* certainly has some claims upon our attention.

In the words of the distinguished German philosopher, Frederich Wilhelm Joseph von Schelling,† the Qabbalah "contains ruins and fragments, if you will much distorted, but nevertheless remnants, of *that primitive system which is the key to all religious systems*, and those do not speak falsely, who say: that the Kabbala is the transmission of a doctrine which existed alongside, but outside, of the original (Holy) Writings, and which was revealed, and therefore was also revealing, as a more comprehensive, but secret and not universally communicated, system. Very gratifying to the scholar, must be the announcement just made (1815) in Vienna, of a Jewish-Rabbinical work that is to appear, which promises to collect the didactic opinions of Ben Yo'haï, the author of the Zohar, a work as important as it is famed, from the original sources. Would that a Jewish, or some other scholar, find enough support, to be able to edite the whole Zohar and open up other sources! It is almost sad to see how scholars have turned wholly in their essays from the real sources. In Egypt's very dark and insoluble hieroglyphics, the keys to the archaic religions have been sought, now nothing is spoken of save India's language and wisdom, but the Hebrew language and writings, especially those of the Old Testament, in which the roots of the doctrines and even

---

* Preface by Prof. Franck in *La Kabbale*. Paris, 1843.
† *Ueber die Gottheiten von Samothrace*, etc. Stuttgart und Tübingen, 1815, p. 108.

of the languages, of all the ancient religious systems, even to details, are clearly recognizable, lie uninvestigated. Very much is it to be wished that these most reverend of monuments, should soon pass from the hands of the mere Theologians into those of the purely historical investigator, when we may dare hope, that they will obtain the same unstinted reverence, and also be considered as sources of at least as much importance, as the Homeric poems and the accounts by Herodotus."

With the appearance of Jesus, the Jewish thought-world became divided. The Secret Doctrines were mostly under the guidance of a spiritual faith of a high intellectual order; the Pharisees, had made the Jewish religious life, one of form and ritual, and had destroyed most of the inward spiritual life of the Hebrew religion. Many of the higher spiritual teachings of the Secret Doctrine were at this time, absorbed into the formulations which resulted in the firm establishment of Christianity. In the words of an erudite scholar of the Anglican Church:

"The germ indeed of the Cabbalistic doctrine regarding Shechinah, and so forth (*i. e.*, Metatron), may probably have existed in the time of St. Paul and St. John, and *the inspired writers may have been aided by these forms of thought, in setting forth the Christian Revelation,* just as St. John was by the Jewish-Alexandrian doctrine of the Logos."* Which latter is also found in the Qabbalah, and Philo is one of the early exponents of both.

The connection and relation of the invisible to the visible, must in the most archaic times, have attracted the attention of human beings. To the advanced thinkers, it must have appeared that in the treatment of the Primal Cause, two things must be considered, the Primal Cause *per se*, and the relation and connection of the Primal Cause, with the visible and unseen universe. Both are still to us, as creatures sure to die, of more profound importance than anything else, and both are to our intellectual comprehension in this matter-body, of the most intricate and difficult nature. The Arabian peripateticians, in order to give an explanation of this most abstruse subject, were obliged to step into the mazes of the Chaldean, Persian, Hindu, and the generally called, Oriental

* The Jewish and the Christian Messiah, etc., by Vincent Henry Stanton. Edinburgh, 1886, p. 130.

philosophy. The Hebrews, at an early day did the same, and most probably designated the Primal Cause, at first by the triadic שדי Shaddaï, the Almighty, subsequently by the Tetragrammaton, יהוה YHVH, symbol of the Past, Present and Future, and also the equivalent for the really highest name of the Deity אהיה Eh'yeh, *i.e.*, I Am. Against the unnecessary pronunciation of יהוה the Third Commandment was made, and an Israelite always uses אדני A Do Na Y, (Adonaï) Lord, in place of it, hence the rendering "Lord" in the English version, whilst the lowest designation, or the Deity in Nature, the more general term Elohim, is translated, God. In the Qabbalah the Name יהוה YHVH, expresses a He and a She, two persons in one Deity, *i. e.*, the Unity of the Holy One, blessed be Hû, *i. e.*, He, and His She'keen-ah. See also the Jewish Liturgy, for Pentecost, also the daily "In the Name of Unity, of the Holy and Blessed Hû and His She'keen-ah, the Hidden and Concealed Hû, blessed be YHVH forever." Hû is said to be masculine and YaH feminine, together they make the יהוה אחד *i. e.*, One YHVH. One but of a male-female nature. The She'keen-ah is always considered in the Qabbalah as feminine.

In what men now term the ancient, but which in reality was the younger world, man stood in a far simpler position and one more consonant to nature, than he does at present in civilized life. Then the natural accord and affinity of the written to the oral, of theory to practice, was more correctly observed. Then the intent of the written or symbolical compilation was, to present to the mind of the reader only the most fundamental points of the object in hints. Sentences were simple, terse and didactic. Some of the early languages as written, commencing in ideograms, never went beyond the syllabic; *e. g.*, the Akkadian, Assyrian, Babylonian, Egyptian, Chinese. Others advanced to the consonantal but never have reached the vowel or true alphabet. These were the Phœnician, Hebrew, Syriac and Arabic. No Semitic tongue has been written with alphabetic vowels. The Aryan race have always introduced vowels into their written language and are a true alphabetic race. The early writing comprised more especially the essence, and fundamental *indicia* of knowledge, and its symbols were incomprehensible to the uninitiated. Tradition preceded the use of symbolic writing, and was after its introduction necessary to explain it. And tradition, both before and after the introduction of ideograms and other symbols, *e. g.*, letters of the alphabet, was made part of all subsequent writing. Written tradition gives us a lasting efflux and influx within comprehended time, and presents to the eye, in fixed, understood symbols, the imperishable tints of the transiently passing and everflowing word and language, as a constant, fixed presence; it is therefore the most certain means for preserving in a permanent form, the ever tending to be lost, oral tradition, through a more fixed symbolism than the sound of the spoken word, by also giving the sense of the eye, an opportunity to fix the hieroglyphic symbol, in the sensorium of the human brain. Yet even the written compilation is, like everything in the matter-world, constantly changing in its spiritual content, in its inner and spiritual shades of meaning, and even in its method of spelling, etc., with the progress of human thought. It is at its best but a deduced picture, made by the writer of a reality, as human life gives it to him in his mind, and it is wholly deficient in all absolute concrete precision and individual specification. Human thought, therefore, when written, even in its most perfect form, is always to a great extent ambiguous, and subject to every species of explanation, misrepresentation and change, from the original spiritual meaning and intent of the writer and his time, and besides, is seen in the mirror of different receptive minds, under different meanings, apprehensions and reflections. It is therefore an absolute necessity of writing and of human life and intelligence, that a vitalizing oral or spoken word, be the constant companion and interpreter of the otherwise dead written symbols, the original meanings of which, are ever subject to be changed by the slightest inflections and emphasis of the human voice and by progressive thought. The written symbol itself, is absolutely dead, and without such a constant living oral tradition, to infuse into it, energy, vitality and life, and give it concrete value, would not be of any use to mankind. This energetic vitality exists not only in the pronunciation but also in the emphasis, intonation, inflection, etc., which thought naturally takes in our minds even when mentally reading to ourselves. In the archaic periods of the world's history, knowledge was more attached to practical life, and abstract theoretical knowledge did not exist, then it was the ability to do, and that educated the whole character and individuality of the man. Teacher and pupil, stood more in the relation of father and son, and master and servant, as is the case in India to-day between the *Guru* or Brahminical master and his scholar. The pupil remained long in his position of pupil, and was obliged to tame the natural, uncultivated animal man, before he could be advanced to and before he could mentally grasp, the true sublime earnestness for intellectual contemplation, the pure inner love for study for its own sake, the thorough impregnation of the whole spirit of the disciple with the genius of the subject, without which permanent success, intellectual or otherwise, is not ever possible or assured. The earnest apprentice, became gradually assistant, and finally master, and only then had the right to instruct others. If of sound discretion, good judgment, and intellectually receptive, as a reward, the disciple was at last made an initiate, one of the innermost, a companion or *mystæ*, and then was taught something of the esoteric as well as the exoteric teachings and traditions of his predecessors, and continued them to those who followed him who were deemed worthy. Thus the orally traditional in religion, philosophy, science and art, the real, inner, intelligible to the intellect, spirituality of the whole; was taught and faithfully handed down and preserved, among the initiates and intellectual workers; and to all the ignorant and uncultivated, that higher spirituality remained inaccessible and closed. Each religion, philosophy, science, art, had its *disciplina arcana*, which in fact largely exists to-day, in the technical methods and language of the religious, scientific and art worlds.* This was the real meaning of mystery: the mystery, the inner spirit, was not an unrevealed knowledge; it was revealed, but only unto the man, who showed sufficient intellect and discretion to enti-

* The learned of the ancients, especially the Orientals, concealed their philosophy and religious metaphysics, to an extreme scarcely comprehended by the learned of our day. A similar method of secrecy has been used by some scientists to a very late period, *e. g.*, Leibnitz published in the *Acta Eruditorum* of Leipzig, his scheme of Differential Calculus, in such a way as to hide both the method and object from the uninitiated, but was subsequently detected by the great mathematicians James and John Bernouilli; Newton hid his invention of Infinite Series, by a transposition of the letters which make up the two fundamental propositions into an alphabetical order. Algebra, as far as it was understood by the Arabian school, extending to quadratic equations, was known to and hidden by some Italians for 300 years as a secret.

tle him to it, and who consecrated himself to it, with his whole soul, heart, and undivided love. The more intelligent men of antiquity drew a veil of secresy over its more profound metaphysical ideas, granting access only to those found worthy and capable of appreciating and comprehending, the boon granted them by such consecration and initiation. This is fully exemplified in the remarks of Jesus: " Give not that which is holy unto the dogs, neither cast ye your pearls before swine, lest haply they trample them under their feet, and turn and rend you" (Matt. vii, 6). Jesus spoke to the people (the uninitiated) in parables, which he *explained in private* to his disciples (Comp. Matt. xiii). For this cause, and the interruptions from wars, revolutions, and persecutions, most of the ancient thought has perished. In our time, reflection threatens to absorb amongst the learned, the actual life and vitality of intellection, and to lead everything back to a dead, dry, abstract knowledge of idea only, and believes it can educate man by theory alone. The practical is merged in the theoretical, the connection between the writing and the oral word has been deranged, and but little is left to the vitality of oral repetition and instruction. In ancient times the written word was only the symbol, the oral practical instruction, transmitted by word of mouth through the master to his pupil, was the true secret treasure. If human intellectual culture as an entirety rested more upon oral tradition, we would find, that that which is of the highest and greatest import to mankind, namely: religion, beside the plain symbolism of the written letter, has and must have, to be of any value, a living, vitalizing oral teaching, which is explanatory and makes it a living thing; and must have an esoteric higher disclosure, of which the written word, is only the bark or rind. The sacred oral primitive teaching, oral long before it was placed in symbolic writing, has left its traces among all the races of the Orient. It has come more especially to us, through the Oriental books, which we have adopted as our religious mentors, termed by us the Old and New Testaments. The first, the Sacred Writings of the Hebrews; the second, written by Jews, but based on a fusion of Israelitish and Hellenic thought. It is therefore of the greatest importance for those interested in Christianity, which was largely formulated and kept alive by the writings of St. Paul, those by the writer of the Epistle to the Hebrews, those usually attributed to

St. John, and some of those by St. Peter; to investigate the Secret Doctrine of the Hebrews, termed at first Sod or Mystery, subsequently Secret Learning, and afterwards the Qabbalah, especially the speculative branch, as in it will be found, that an intimate connection exists between the New Testament ideas and the Israelitish secret philosophy. The system of the Speculative Qabbalah, appears to Occidental thought, which has been largely formulated and built up, on Greek philosophical modes and methods of thinking, and is unused to the Oriental systems; which are frequently based on parables, allegories and other figurative language; and which is also written, in a veiled form and given in hints, to preserve it from the uninitiates; frequently *bizarre*, strange, perhaps at times, absurd. It is therefore quite difficult to reach the Aristotelian formulations, and those in accord with Western methods of expression, in setting forth the Oriental Secret Philosophy. It also requires an unbiased mind in the student, which can proceed without bigotry and with discrimination, delicacy, and especially impartiality, both analytically and synthetically, and see similarities, make comparisons, and give a perfectly fair opinion as to the merit or demerit, of the content of the Oriental secret traditions: which are not only of great abstruseness, but have been most frequently misrepresented, misunderstood, or misjudged, by even their most ardent votaries. We claim, that a thorough study of the Hebrew Speculative Qabbalah in its connection with the Oriental books of our own religions, and the systems of other Oriental peoples; will give it a much more elevated position, show that a much greater value is in it and a much greater antiquity, than has been heretofore accorded it, and consider all investigations made by unprejudiced, acute, and unbiased minds, of a sound logical tendency; as a great advance towards a more thorough and correct knowledge of the origin and germs of many ideas now existing in religion and philosophy. To deny this fact, without a more thorough and unprejudiced examination than the Qabbalah has heretofore received, would be to display an ignorance of the past intellectual nature and progress of mankind, and of ideas, upon which, we have based some of the most advanced knowledge in modern thought and religion; and indeed of the whole history of the antique intellectual world and its subsequent development. The elements of this Secret Tradition in religion and philosophy, are only to be found in a fragmentary form, in all the writings, which we now have of the ancient Eastern thought-world. The Qabbalah asserts, that intellectual culture, as the educational institution of the fallen protoplasts, began with a Divine Revelation, and consists of a continued from this, series of traditions. These have been, through the influence of the Kingdom of Obscuration and Evil, acting on the Free Will of mankind, more or less shattered and disfigured. The traditions passing through the prior generations, have been the educators of the succeeding, and largely dependent on the organic development etc. of the preceding, the subsequent have advanced or retarded, the transmitted results of the past; the totality being, great thought waves passing through the spirituality of all humanity from its beginning. From time to time, the great love and mercy of God has exerted a more immediate influence, upon this great energetic vitalized organic process, this great stream of life coming down from the first living beings; giving it a new and fresh advancement, a new flight, through a new revelation, by which, the totality of the inspired knowledge upon our earth has been increased and extended. More frequently individual minds, influenced from the Above, announce and make plain, the till then only obscurely recognized truths, or invent some useful and beneficent contrivance, whereby humanity is advanced, benefitted and its general condition ameliorated; on the other side, for the fulfillment of the unknown, but wise, purposes of God, the opposition, the spirits of Darkness and Evil, are permitted to try and to retard, the liberty of advance in the stream of humanity, to attempt the destruction of the Divine Tradition, disfigure the Truth, shatter Goodness, Peace and Harmony, and have a scope given them to exercise deception and evil, and to destroy or retard the beneficial inventions, arts and sciences, useful and salutary to mankind, and so keep back progress and advancement.

Man, although considered by it to be of divine origin, is not looked upon by the Qabbalah, as an absolutely independent being, who from his own absolute innate volition and autonomy of being and intellect, can independently originate by and through himself. All his knowledge, it holds, he receives only by the permission and through the efflux from the spiritual, outside of himself. Unconditioned, objective, within produced, and autonomatic existence and knowledge; exist solely in the Supreme Deity, who is the only Real, True and Absolute, and the originator, and preserver of All Things; who through the Absolute Idea or Perfect Paradigmatic Form, produces the same, and who is immanent in, yet transcendental to, All the created Things, spiritual or material. The entire universe is not the Place or Abode of the Supreme Deity, nor Its Glory or Content. The Qabbalah looks upon mankind as one great totality of human existence, whose beginning was the celestial androgenic protoplast called the Heavenly Adam. Humanity is considered by it, as one great universal brotherhood, as a great spiritual energetic vitality, called the Mikrokosm, and in this slumbers the idea of the higher Makrokosm, the Heavenly or Celestial Man or Adam, the Primordial Perfect Paradigm, or Adam Qadmon, the Perfect Model of all Form and of the first terrestrial Adam, who was as to it, the Mikrokosm. In this Great Paradigm the Qabbalah asserts, are all the forms, the perfect ideals of the emanated or created existences, it might therefore be termed the Idealized Form, or, the Form which contains all the perfect ideas in their origination. Yet the Makrokosm no more than the Mikrokosm, could have come into existence, nor its existence be preserved, without having been made by and receiving without cessation, the continued efflux of the Eternal Absolute, the Unknown Ain Soph or Endless, the Ayin or No-Thing. It holds that the bond and limit of a necessary material symbolism, developed in letters, numbers and proportions, binds and keeps man's thoughts, within the limits of the matter-world expression of them, and prevents his ever absolutely raising, whilst in that matter-world, the veil, or obtaining a perfect knowledge of the created spiritual world. This is set forth in Oriental Metaphor, with great precision in Exodus (xxxiii, 12–23). Man in his matter-form cannot elevate himself to a full comprehension of the Eternal Absolute and see the Supreme Deity, face to face. To man in this world the back of the Deity, the visible universe is shown. The Deity is always enshrouded in Its Glory, Its She'keen-ah, and man cannot penetrate unaided, the obscurity and thick darkness in which God dwells (Ex. xix, 9; II Sam. xxii, 10–12; I Kings viii, 12; II Chr. vi, 1; Ps. xviii, 14), nor find the true method of reconciliation with God and re-attain his lost felicity, through his own unaided efforts and powers. Man has not a perfect autonomy; and the oppositions in his spiritual nature are too strongly opposed, to permit the balance or harmony between them, to become evident to his senses without Divine assistance. A Divine Mediator therefore becomes, according to the Qabbalah, a necessity; a something must exist which shall continually draw man from his animal nature toward his spiritual, and enable him to comprehend within himself, an intellectual and spiritual consciousness of himself, without which, he would not be able to raise his ideas above the mere animal or matter-world existence in which he lives, and would be like an ordinary animal (Ec. iii, 18–22).

This Divine Mediator is symbolized in the Qabbalah by the Sephirah 'Hokhmah, Wisdom, the Son of Abbah, the Father, who is symbolized by the Sephirah, Kether, Absolute Idea, the Crown of all. 'Hokhmah is the Word, Memrah, or Logos, the third hypostasis of the Triad, yet the Qabbalah considers it, in a mysterious way, in the Sephirah Binah, the Holy Spirit or Immah, the Mother; and in Kether, the Father, and they in it. The Triad is One. This is also expressed in the Qabbalah in another way; Kether, the Crown or Father, the harmony of the first three Sephiroth; Tiphereth, Beauty, the harmony of the second three; and Malkhuth, the harmony of the remainder and indeed of all the Sephirothic decade, are considered, as forming a triad which represents the whole decade, and in this triad is the full content of all the Sephiroth and the Heavenly Adam. Sometimes the Qabbalah expresses this, in the idea of Ayin, No-Thing, the A'reekh An'peen, *i. e.*, the Long in Visage or Countenance, and the Ze'ir An'peen, *i. e.*, the Short in Countenance, the latter two also respectively termed, the Makroprosopos and the Mikroprosopos. The reader will observe on the II Diagram, the Holy Name of Kether is, AiH'YeH (Eh'yeh), *i.e.*, I Am; of Binah, YaH; of 'Hokhmah, the Tetragrammaton YHVH, called Adonai, *i.e.*, the Lord. In the Zohar, where the question is the meaning of the verse: "Let *us* make Man in our image, after our likeness (similitude)." Gen. i, 26, it says: "There are two persons of the Deity, one in heaven, and one which descended upon earth in the form of Man (*i. e.*, the Adam Qadmon), and the Holy One, praised be It! unites them. There are three Lights in the Upper

Holy Divine united in One, and this is the foundation of the doctrine of Every-Thing, this is the beginning of the Faith, and Every-Thing is concentrated therein." (Zohar iii, Beginning of § *She'meneeh*, fol. 36a). In another place the Zohar says: "Two persons are in the Divinity, and a third, emanating mutually from them, is associated with them, and so now there are three, but if three, yet It is only One; this is the mystery of the Scriptures, where it says: Hear O Israel YHVH, our Elohim, is one YHVH" (Deut. vi, 4).* In this verse YHVH stands twice and Elohenu (Elohim) once. Twice YHVH are the two persons in the Divinity, and Elohenu, is the third person which mutually flows from them.† The Man after the Fall, was not any longer the same being as when first created in the spiritual similitude of Elohim, the fault of the terrestrial Adam, had even affected the Celestial. His copy, the terrestrial Adam, was controlled by the Deity, yet was permitted a certain liberty, or Free Will, through which he yet had sufficient power to conduct himself so as work out his future redemption, or continue in his degradation. To help him, he was granted divine assistance if he would call for it, to prevent the absolute dominion of the evil powers. Man to-day, as an individual, is only a concatenation of the being-hood of all precedent human life, his thought is the result of internal, as well as external agencies, acting upon his spirit, and his so-called wisdom, is the result of example, inherent qualities and revelation. His capacity is doubtless influenced, to an extent, by the precedent spirituality of his race; and its power of receptivity, retention, merger and expression; he is tinctured by the precedent chain of existences, and is subject to laws not yet comprehended by humanity. Empty and helpless, he is yet endowed with a feeling full of presentiment, and with a longing for a more perfect realization. Endowed by the Deity with the power to reproduce a copying ideality, man can follow actively, that

---

* "And Jesus answered him, The *first* of all the commandments *is*, Hear O Israel; The Lord (YHVH); our God (Elohim) is One Lord (YHVH)." Mark xii, 29. This is the famous Jewish Declaration of Faith, still used every day, called the Shemah.

† Zohar iii, § *She'lakh Lekha*, fol. 162a. We have numerous extracts in MSS. from the Zohar to the same effect, but have not space for them in this writing. The same idea is in Ibn Gebirol. See *supra*, and in Philo., Vol. i, pp. 61 *sq.*, 219 *sq.*

which the Deity produces originally, creatively, and by an efflux, from and out of Its own autonomy, from Its fullness of mercy, grace and love for Its creatures. The real man, the inner spiritual man, is simply a receptacle for the impregnation and birth of ideas, an activity only acting through a conditioned receptivity, yet with certain amount of liberty, but not a perfect autonomy. His spirituality contains the susceptibility, content and living ability, to produce spiritual and material births, but to be able to produce, requires an outside spiritual impregnation and permission from the Deity. Each human being for its formation and development, presumes others preceding it, who have been to a certain extent developed and educated, so the first human pair had a spiritual, developed educator, the Deity, and from this educator, has proceeded in the chain of existences, all subsequent education. The Qabbalah does not recognize in the Good and Evil, two independent, autonomatic, opposing powers, but both are, according to it, under the power of the Supreme Absolute Deity. It asserts that the Evil springs out of the Good, and only originated from a diversion of the latter. Evil exists, for God's own wise purposes, by the sufferance of the Absolute One, who gives us the blighting cold, frost, and night, and also, the beneficent and blessed day-light, warmth, and sunshine. Man therefore partakes of two regions, that of the external, visible, matter world, that of Evil and Darkness, and that of the internal spiritual higher world, that of Goodness and Light (Comp. Is. xlv, 6, 7).

The German philosopher Hegel, holds that a thing can only *exist* through its opposite, *that the thing and its opposite must arise together, and that eternally, as the complements of a unity;* white is not without black, nor black without white, good is not without evil, nor is evil without good. This is the doctrine of the Siphrah D'Tznioothah and the Sepher Ye'tzeer-ah. At the very beginning of the life germ, dissolution and death oppose its vitality and endeavor to destroy it, and the whole existence of man in this world, is a continual struggle to preserve his vitality. Isaiah says, in his magnificent language: "I am YHVH, and there is none else, there is not any Elohim beside Me. I girded thee, though thou hast not known Me; that they may know from the rising of the sun, and from the west, that there is none beside Me. I am YHVH, and there is none else. I form light and create darkness; I make safety and I create misfortune; I YHVH do all these things" (xlv, 5–8). The widow's son, Hiram Abiff of Tyre, cast for the Qabbalistic Temple of King Solomon, two high pillars or pylons of bronze, their capitals were of pomegranites and lily work. The lily, most likely the lotus, an emblem of life, white or male, on the right side, the pomegranite, emblem of fecundity and plasticity, red or female, on the left side. The first was called Ya-kheen, the latter Bo-az. These columns represented, Understanding, Binah, ה, and Wisdom, 'Hokhmah, ו, and between them was the Temple of Kether, ׳, the Father. Here we see symbols of the Former, the Harmony, and the to be Formed. All energy must have resistance, all light must have darkness, all projecture or emanation, a hollow or excavation to receive efflux, affirmation supposes a negation; if the first androgene had not been separated into male and female, the result would have been entire sterility, as was the result as to the Seven Kings of Edom described in Genesis and the Qabbalah; and the Balance not existing, the forms did not and could not, exist, and the emanation of the existences could not proceed and be manifest. The dogma of the Balance being recognized and the application of its consequences having been made universal; by the law of analogies, there becom eevident to us the great secrets of affinity and aversion, of natural sympathy and antipathy, as discoverable in animal magnetism, homeopathy, love, moral or political influence, etc. This law of analogy, carried out to its utmost extent in the harmony of the equilibrium which springs out of the opposites, is that which governs under the Deity, the entire physical, spiritual and moral universe. This agent, is the universal alkahest, the universal law of vitality and life, by which the animated beings, and the atoms of which the universe is composed, become magnetized, polarized and held together, and is the foundation of Free Will. It is the Temple standing between Ya-kheen and Bo-az which together with them, forms the Sacred Triad and the Sacred Triangle. In the Hebrew alphabet א Aleph = 1, the leader of the letters, is the male, it is the letter of the Sephirah Kether, it is the Alpha of the Greek alphabet. ב Beth = 2, and is that of the Sephirah Binah, the female; and from these result ו Vau = 3, the Sephirah 'Hokhmah or Wisdom, the Word or Son, yet the three are an unit. They form

YHV of the Ineffable Name. In the Cubical Holy of Holies were the right and left Cherubim and above them the She'keen-ah, a Holy Triad. The female is *taken from Adam* but not produced by him, she existed in the androgenic man from the beginning, so all the human organs are disposed of in twos, and the anatomy of the female life organs shows, that they are those of the male, reversed. The Zodiachas Scorpio, the male, and Virgo, the female, but between these oppositions, is Libra, the Balance or Harmony. The Divinity has two essential bases for Its existence, Necessity and Liberty, but above all is Its independent autonomy, Its Harmony. To manifest truth we must have doubt, destruction is regeneration, Evil is essential for the ascertainment of and existence of, the Good. Error is necessary for the manifestation of Truth, the decay of death gives us immortality. We prop ourselves on that which resists. The shield of Satan stopped the progress of the spear of Michael and prevented his destruction, Satan is necessary to bring out in the contrasts, the goodness of the former, and is as necessary, as a base is essential to the standing of a column. The Satan of Genesis and Job is not a fallacy. The entire universe is balanced upon two opposing forces which produce the equilibrium and harmony of All and so maintain it. The opposing centripetal and centrifugal forces make that harmonious movement, which is the path of all the stars and the life of all the universe. These opposing energies are in all physics, all religion, all philosophy, all intellect and are everywhere, except in the Deity, who is entire and perfect harmony. The ancient Greek represented these forces, by Eros, Desire or Love, and its opposition by Anteros or Aversion. In science we have the phenomena of polarity, in the heart, arterial and veinous motion, and also the spiritual law of sympathies and antipathies. Even the disciples of Zara-thrustra, although supposed to have only the Light or Good and the Darkness or Evil for their deities, had yet a higher, a harmony in which both merged and rested, known as Zervane Akerane or Endless Time. The harmony is represented by the circle, by the serpent, an emblem of both Satan and Wisdom, with its tail in its mouth. In the physical universe it is the luminiferous æther, the vital caloric, the electro-magnetic azoth. It is the ambient fluid which penetrates, permeates, vitalizes all Things, the ray detached from the glory of the sun, fixed by the weight of the atmosphere and crystallized by the central attraction, to our earth. In the words of the erudite Yehudah ha-Levi (A. D. 1140): " There is not any life without motion, nor motion without inspiration, no inspiration without struggle, no struggle without opposition, oppositions are everywhere essential, but the Divine power conciliates every opposition " (Sepher Khozari, Part iv, § 25).

Figure 12.—Copy of a sacred bronze statuette plated with gold, of Buddha and the Tree of the Sephiroth, from Burmah.

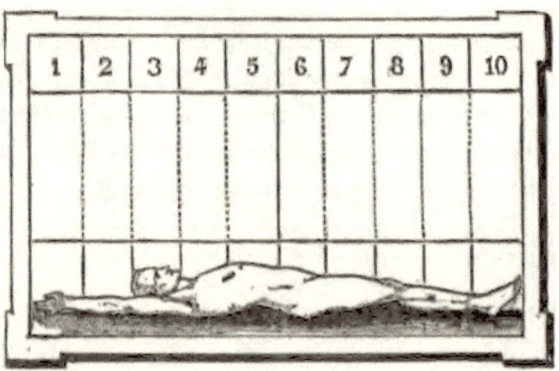

Figure 13.—A correctly proportioned man divided into the decade, each tenth, being the length of his head.

X.

SIMILARITIES IN THE WRITINGS OF IBN GEBIROL, THE ZOHARIC WRITINGS AND THE QABBALAH.

WE will now give some quotations and references, to prove similarities exist between the Zohar, the Qabbalah and those writings of Ibn Gebirol, which have come to our day, similarities, we think, more frequent, close and precise; than *any heretofore given* from the writings of Moses de Leon, by those who assert the Zoharic books were forged by him, and we claim these are strong evidence of a knowledge in Gebirol, as early as 1050 A. D., of much that is in the Zoharic writings. This would be about 250 years before the time, it has been alleged, De Leon forged the Zoharic books. The student is also referred to our resumé of the Me'qôr 'Haÿ-yîm.

Ibn Gebirol teaches that all the Forms, reunited in the Will, compose an Unity of number, the One; above which, is the Supreme Unknown Absolute Unity, without number. The Will, the One, subsequently emanated, multiplied and particularized Itself, gradually however, and thus emanated and produced the Intelligible World, and ultimately, the World of Action, that of the Senses. The Zoharic writings contain this idea and also, as we have shown, that an analogy exists, between the

Ideal prototypic and the Sensible, Worlds. This is archaic Qabbalistic doctrine as we have already shown. The Superior World in several places in the Zoharic writings, is asserted to be, the positive or male, the higher spiritual, the former; and the Inferior World, to be, the negative, plastic, matter or formed. (Comp. Zohar ii, 144*b*, i, 159*a*. The same idea is in the Book of Enoch.)

The different manifestations of existence from the Ayin or No-Thing, follow each other without interruption, surrounding themselves and mutually using, form and matter, for their development. The Zohar says: " When Elohim wished to make the world, It made go out a concealed Light, from which afterwards, went out and rayed all the manifested Lights, from that first Light, formed and spread themselves, the other Lights which formed the Superior World (A'tzeel-ah). Afterwards, the Superior Light in it, spread itself, and gave birth to light without brightness, and thus formed the Inferior World. * * * That light without brightness, by its bonds with the Superior (World) produced all the celestial armies (Hosts of Angels), according to their numerous species, as it is written: 'How numerous are thy works O YHVH!' (Ps. civ, 24). All that which is found on earth can also be found (has its spiritual counterpart) on high, and there does not exist the smallest thing in this world which is not also itself attached to something on high, and does not find itself under its (the higher) dependence. When the inferior is influenced, that which is set over it in the superior world is equally (influenced), for all are perfectly united together."* Everywhere Ibn Gebirol insists upon this doctrine, and that such a connection, exists between the Intelligible world and the Sensible world, or, Idea and Matter. (Comp. the Me'qôr iii, § 21, *et seq.*, and many other places.) A doctrine of the Old and New Testaments is, that there is a heavenly ideal or prototype of all existing in the visible universe. This is also in Philo and the Talmud (see *ante*, p. 108 *et seq.*), and from it results the idea, that we must arrive at our knowledge of the invisible through a contemplation of the visible. These doctrines are also in Gebirol (Me'qôr

*Zohar, i, ¿ *Vaya'hee*, 156*a*. Comp. i, 158*b*, 159*a*, 162*b*, 205*b*; ii, 144*b*. Comp. Matt. x, 29; Luke xii, 7, 6; Acts xvii, 28; I Cor. xii, 12; Matt. xviii, 10; *ante*, p. 109, *seq.*

'Haÿ-yĭm, i, § 1 *et seq.*; ii, § 10, § 25, § 30; iii, § 21; iv, § 8, § 23). The Zohar (i, fol. 158*b*) says: "The words YHVH! YHVH (Exod. xxxiv, 6) indicate (by repetition) two worlds, the one manifest, the other occult, it is wherefore there is between the two words the disjunctive sign. These two worlds however are together and form one unity" (Comp. Zohar, i, 159*a*, 162*b*; ii, 144*b*). The intermediary between the two Worlds, the bolt which unites them is the decade, which is always looked upon, as in one totality and unity, and as forming in that unity, the Great Ideal or Heavenly Adam, also termed, the Adam Qadmon, the Man from the East; in whom is contained the Tetragrammaton יהוה YHVH, the Ineffable Name.

Gebirol, the Qabbalah and the Zohar, assert, that "the lower world is made after the higher world (its prototype), and that of everything in the former there is, as it were, an image in the latter, still all are one" (Zohar, ii, fol. 20*a*).

Gebirol also says: the higher soul is the prototype from which all human souls emanate, they having thus been in their real form already in the divine idea. The Zohar (ii, fol. 96) says: "Also all human souls, before coming down on earth, were present in the divine idea in the same form, which they afterwards had in the world."*

The Zohar (i, fol. 19*b*–20*a*) comparing the universe to a nut, the kernel or almond of which is enveloped in several rinds or shells, says: "It is even thus with the entire universe, superior and inferior; from the mysterious superior point, as far as the extremity of all the Degrees (Sephiroth), all form one whole; of which the parts are formed, one in the other, insomuch that they serve as shells, the one to the other. The first point (the Sephirah Kether, the Ego or Will) was an interior and incommensurable Light, so that we are not able to know its splendour, subtility and purity, until (we reach) that which has developed itself by expansion.

---

*Comp. Franck, *La Kabbale*, p. 228 *sq.*; Zohar, i, 91*b*, 96*b*; ii, 96; i, 245*b*; iii, 61*b*, 104*a* and *b*; ii, 73*b*. The doctrine of the pre-existence of souls is in the Book of Wisdom, viii, 20. Josephus tells us the Essenes believed in it; Wars, Bk. ii, c. viii, § 11, Whiston's ed. Philo holds to the same idea; On the Giants, i, pp. 330–331: On Dreams, ii, pp. 321–322. So does the Talmud, treat. '*Ha'geegah* 12*b*; *Yevamoth*, 62; *Avodah Zarah*, 5; *Niddah*, 13; and the B'resheeth Rabbah, § viii.

That expansion of the point, becomes a temple or palace,* enveloping this same point, that is, the Light which we cannot know because of its great splendour. But that palace (Sephirah) which serves as the envelope of that occult point, is itself an incommensurable Light, without containing equally the same subtility and splendour, as the first concealed and occult point. That sphere is again extended through a new expansion (forming) a first Light, an expansion which serves as an envelope of that subtile sphere (which is) clear and altogether interior. The portions of existence continued thus to develope, the one from the other, and to envelope themselves the one in the other. So that they each and in totality, served as mutual envelopes, and that they (relatively the one to each and to all the others), are as the kernel and the shell, but yet all are one in totality, because that which is one envelope, is at the same time, a kernel for another degree. All absolutely occurs the same in these inferior regions; and man in this world is made after that resemblance, being (composed) of a kernel and a shell, which are the spirit and the body. Such is in general the order of the universe." Ibn Gebirol has the same idea (see, the Me'qôr Haỹ-yîm, Bk. ii, § 1; iii, § 41, etc.). With the Zohar the "superior point," as the germ emanating from the Supreme Unknown Deity, contains, as does the Universal Form and Matter of Gebirol, both the spiritual and the corporeal worlds intact. Gebirol attributed a species of matter to everything beside the Supreme Deity, so many of the Qabbalists consider the Supreme Deity as alone the pure, simple, and absolute spirit, without any tincture of even spiritual matter; and that all other existing, even the highest spiritual existences, which were the Supreme Deity's energies, forces or angels, doing Its Will, had a substance of some species. Philo Judæus holds the same view. Gebirol thus defines the Will or Desire: "The Desire is the executor (worker) of everything and mover of everything, and the simile is the creation by the creator, blessed be He! of the Things (*i. e.*, the formation of form) for the Primal Source, is the Desire. And the Desire is the Divine force (or

* The word Palace is used to indicate the different Degrees of Existence or the Expansion of the Sephiroth, from the highest world A'tzeel-ah, to the lowest, A'seey-ah, which have been presented as the spheres or orbits continued and contained, one in the other, as it asserts the Sephiroth are. Comp. the Me'qôr, iii, § 41.

energy) working in the elements and formations, and lying together, in them." The great Qabbalist Azriel has the same view, he says: "The Thought, which comes from Ain Soph, is both the essence and the reality, within the limitation which includes everything connected with thought or contemplation on earth; which can come into existence by speech, and be known through any creation; whatever comes within limits has dimension and is physical, for whatever can be taken hold of (comprehended) by the thought of the heart, is called, a body. The metaphysicians say, every man has a limit, and we daily see, that everything, even the air, has limit, space and measure."

The Kether Malkhuth says of the angels: "Some of them sheets of flames, and some of them breathing winds, some of them composed of fire and water, some Seraphim and some Cherubim." So the Zohar (§ *Va-yeek'reh*, p. 9), of the angels, says: "Some of them flaming fire, some of them water, some of them wind." The B'resheeth Rabbah (300 A. D.) says: "The flame of the turning sword, according to which He makes His messengers, *i. e.*, angels, of winds, His servants of flaming fire turning, since they turn sometimes into men, sometimes into women, sometimes into winds, sometimes into angels."

The Zohar also says: "Come and see! Thought is the principle (or beginning) of all that which is, but it is at first unknown and contained in itself. When thought begins to spread itself, it arrives at that degree in which it becomes spirit (or, where the spirit rests or lives), reaching to this point, it takes the name of intelligence (Binah, understanding), and is no more, as before, contained in itself. The spirit in its turn developes itself, in the bosom of the mysteries by which it is yet surrounded, and from it goes out a voice, which is the reunion of all the celestial choirs; a voice (word) which spreads itself in distinct speech and articulate words, because it comes from the spirit. (This refers to 'Hokhmah, Wisdom, or, the Word.) But in reflecting on all these degrees, we see that the thought, intellect, that voice and that word, are only one thing, that thought is the beginning (principle) of all that which is, and that not any interruption can exist in it. The thought itself is bound to the Non-Being and it is not ever separated from It. Such is the meaning of these words: YHVH is One and His Name is One." (Zohar i, 246*b*). This is a most important passage of the Zohar.

From the bosom of this Unity, the Thought, Consciousness, or Ego; two parallel principles proceed in apparent opposition, but which in reality are inseparable; one is female, passive, negative, called Binah, Understanding; the other male, active, positive, called 'Hokhmah, *i. e.*, Wisdom. "All that which exists, all that which has been formed by the Ancient, whose Name is holy, can only exist through a male and female (principle)." (Zohar iii, 290a.) That is the subjective and objective, coming into the matter world and comprehensible in it.

The Zohar (ii, 179) says: "Upon the one side, the sublimity of the Divine Existence, the contrast between Creator and creature, does not seem to admit of the idea of a special supervision on the part of the Supreme Holy One, May It be blessed! especially as the possessor of infinite knowledge and felicity, cannot stand in any relation to unclean-matter; but on the other side, the admirable order and regularity throughout nature, presume a reasonable intention; which manifestly purposes, through every single member, to advance the plan of the whole, and points to an uninterrupted Providence and Government of the Universe." This idea runs through the Me'qôr Haÿ-yĭm. The Zoharic idea is; that the Deity has given definite laws to nature, and the immediate and direct causes, are effective according to these laws; but this efficacy is not ever independent of the Divine Will, which extends to the smallest change and action in the realm of nature; and each natural effect, coincides with just so much of the Divine intention, as flows from the Omnipotence and Will of the Deity. The Qabbalah calls this, the coalescing of the Deity with the Universe, or the spiritual elements of the worlds (*Ru'ha ye'sod ha-Olamah*), by means of the Ten Sephiroth; the Deity acting upon the whole content of the Universe, as it were, by an efflux through channels or canals, and thus remitting Its Will to all natural energies and forces. The Zohar teaches, an unceasing, in the Will of the Deity, conditioned, and through Its co-operation never dispensed with; potential activity in nature, by means of and through the Sephiroth; in which, though on the one side distinct from the Primitive Supreme Being, the Deity is always present; this is also in the Modern Qabbalah as taught by Luriah and Cordovero. A miracle or change in the regulated course of nature, takes place, only when the Deity undertakes a change in these high organs, the

Sephiroth, the *Kaileem, i.e.*, Vessels; by decreasing their number, weaking their potentiality or, *vice versa*, increasing it. It is understood however at the same time, that this Divine co-operation, as it is only a norm of the activity of nature, is as it were, a natural law, which we do not understand. It also holds, that the Divine Will does not in any way abolish human Freedom of Will. The Zohar says that the Deity is completely separated from Every-Thing, and is transcendental; yet is not separated, for the Deity is also immanent in Every-Thing. The Deity emanates the Universe, has a form, and yet has not any form; by Its form It is manifest and potential, yet It has none as It does not in any way inhere in the Universe. "The Holy One, praised be It! gave heaven and earth, definite laws, as is written: ' He hath made a decree, which they shall not pass away' (Ps. cxlviii, 6), but still It has not given them real freedom; as a master who has fully liberated his servant, and left him, to his own free will; but It gave them laws, which always depend upon Its concealed Will. And the Holy One, praised be It! rules them according to the might of Its own Sacred Will, which makes itself known through the Holy One's sacred Vessels."

In the Qabbalah, the original principle, symbolized by Kether, is called, Abbah or Father, and that which flowed out, the Son.* This original principle, is also called, *Ra-tzon, i. e.*, Absolute Will, or *Ra-tzon al col R'tzoneem, i. e.*, the Will above All Wills.† The Father is also called, *Baal ha-Ra-tzonim, i.e.*, Master of the Will, when considered as the originator, and as on the side towards the Ain Soph. But in so far as by Baal, can be understood, the possessor who is held by a matter, *e. g.*, *Baal chay*, a living being, possessor of life: the Son, is called *Baal ha-Ra-tzonim*. In the Tiqqooneh Zohar (V. Beginning, p. 15*a;* xviii, 36*b*) we find: "In the beginning was the Will of the King, in the light of the Quadrant (probably meaning; the four points of the compass, as the four quarters of the universe). When the Messiah measured therein, there went forth a mysterious line, which is referred to by the nebulous spark of matter, etc."

Further the Zohar says: "In the beginning, was the Will of the King,

* *Sepher Shephathal*, fol. 9. Comp. Mark xiv, 36. Rom. viii, 15. Gal. iv, 6.
† *Sepher Shephathal*, fol. 51. Comp. Exod. iii, 14.

prior to any existence which came into being, through emanation from this Will. It sketched and engraved the forms of all Things, that were to be manifested from concealment into view; in the supreme and dazzling light of the Quadrant. And there went forth, as a sealed secret, from the head of Ain Soph; a nebulous spark of matter without shape or form, a centre of a circle, neither white nor black, neither red nor green, in fact without any colour; but when It took the measure of the structure to be erected, It made the colours to give light therein (Above), and one beam of the Supreme Light went forth for the production of colors Below—and thus the sealed secrets of the Ain Soph, It partly opened, etc."*

The Zohar holds; that no Thing can exist in which the Deity is not immanent to a certain extent, yet all together (all-Things) do not in any way, include the Deity; who is transcendental to and above all, of the spiritually and materially emanated or created.† Gebirol has the same idea. He also says: "The emanation which produced the creation of the universe, is like water gushing out from its source and spreading over everything near." (Me'qôr ii, § 27; v, §§ 64, 71.) The Zohar often uses this simile, *e. g.*, "Thus life is drawn from Below and from Above, thus the source renews itself, and the sea always full, spreads its water everywhere." (Zohar iii, 290*b*, Idrah Zootah, and in many other places.) The first source with Gebirol is the Will or Wisdom, which the Zohar calls, "the Source of Life." Gebirol, says: "Thou art wise, Thy Wisdom is the Source of Life which springs from Thee, etc." (Kether Malkhuth. Comp. Zohar ii, 261*a*.)

The Zohar often uses this simile (Comp. Zohar iii, fol. 7). In the Kether Malkhuth is: "Wisdom, is the fountain of life." The Zohar says: "The seventh palace, the fountain of life, is the first in the order from above, etc." (ii, 261*a*.)

* Zohar, Cremona ed., i, fol. 56. Comp. Joel, *Relig. Philos. Sohar*, p. 312, etc.

† The doctrine of emanation has been asserted to be in the Old Testament, and it is claimed by some writers to be set forth among other places, in the following verse; " And he said. The Lord is come from Sinai, and has appeared from Seir to us, and has hasted out of the mount of Pharan, with the ten thousands of Kades (in the Hebrew, *saints*); on his right hand were his angels with him." Deut. xxxiii, 2. See the Septuagint. Brenton's English Trans., London, 1844. Comp. Cahen's Great French Bible, Vol. 5, p. 153 and note.

The Kether also says: "It (the Will) draws from the source of Light without a pail (bucket) and effects everything without a vessel." (Comp. Me'qôr iii, § 15). The Will or Divine Word, holds a high position in the Zohar: (see ante and Zohar iii, 17*b*; i, 65*a*; ii, 268*b*).

Both have the doctrine of the pre-existence and reminiscence of the soul, which we also find in Plato. The Zohar says (iii, 61*b*): "The souls knew everything they learned on earth prior to their coming into this world." Franck's *La Kabbale*, p. 242. Gebirol says: "Thou askest, Wherefore the soul becomes deprived of the impressions of knowledge, so that she has need to be instructed in order to remember? Know then, the soul was created with the True knowledge, from which it follows, that she possessed in herself the knowledge which is proper to her. But when the soul unites with substance (matter) and confuses herself with it, by the mixture and union, she is removed from the perception of these impressions; they remain concealed in her, because the darkness of the substance covers her in such a way, as to obscure its light, and the substance dulls her: she then becomes as if a transparent mirror to which has been applied, a muddy and thick substance, etc." (Meqôr, v, § 65.)

The "higher soul," according to Gebirol, is the prototype, from the treasury of which all human souls proceed; they all having previously been there in their Real and True Form in the Divine Idea. (Comp. the Kether Malkhuth and the Me'qôr in many places.) The same idea is set forth with great distinctness in the Zohar (ii, fol. 96*b*): "All human souls before coming down on earth, were present in the Divine Idea in the same form, that they were to have in this world:" (comp. Franck, *La Kabbale*, p. 228 *sq.*). So the human soul was divided, by the Zohar and Gebirol, into three divisions, as we have above mentioned, these were the Neshamah, Intellect; Rua'h, Mind or Reason; and the Nephesh, Animal life. (See Meqôr Haÿ-yîm iii, §§ 27–30; Comp. Franck's *La Kabbale*, p. 232.) Gebirol holds that the temporal union of the two superior principles of spirit, *Neshamah*, and soul, *Rua'h*, with the senses; that is, life itself, the *Nephesh;* must not be considered an evil, he did not see in life a lowering down, but a means adopted by the Deity for the education of the soul, a salutary trial. The task of the soul is to elevate matter, "to teach the body, the right path for the prevention of evil." (Kether Malkhuth). He sees in life, an opportunity for the exercise of the man's Free Will to work out his salvation. "Who can repay," he says, "Thy love, in giving the body a soul to vivify it; that her light might guide and instruct it, and deliver man from evil. * * * Thou hast tried me in the pit of captivity; Thou hast purified me from my abundant wickedness; but hast not consumed me. I am also conscious that it is for my benefit that Thou hast tried me, and in faithfulness Thou hast afflicted me; and in order that it may be well with me in my latter days, hast Thou brought me into this trial of troubles:" (see, the Kether Malkhuth). The Qabbalists have the same idea, they "consider it a necessity for the soul, a necessity inherent in its finite nature, to play a *rôle* in the universe; to contemplate the spectacle which the creation presents to it, so as to have the consciousness of itself and its origin; in order to re-enter, without absolutely confusing itself with it, into that inexhaustible source of Light and Life, which they term the Divine Thought." (Franck, *La Kabbale*, p. 236.) The Zohar says (i, fol. 62a): "The breath, Nephesh, and the spirit Neshamah, are united together; whilst the soul, Rua'h, depends upon the conduct of the man. * * * If the man purifies himself, he will receive the assistance of the holy soul which purifies and sanctifies it; if he does not purify himself, he possesses the breath and the spirit, but not the holy soul." This union is to be obtained, it says, on the man's side by his piety and study of the Holy Scriptures; on the other side, by assistance from on high. The three souls united, it frequently terms; the three faculties. (Zohar iii, 24*b*; 46*b*; 70*b*). The Qabbalists do not see in life a lowering down from a higher degree to an exile, as did the Gnostics, and as the Talmudists do in the Pirkey Avoth (Comp. Sayings of the Jewish Fathers, before cited, pp. 56–57), but consider its abode on earth as a means of trial and education. If the soul remains pure during this trial, "She obtains," says Gebirol, "God's pleasure, and may anticipate the joys of the last day; for then endless happiness will be her portion, then she will enter into the palace of the King, etc." The same idea is in the Zohar, and is (i, fol. 245*b*. Franck, *La Kabbale*, p. 236 *seq.*) given in a most beautiful parable which we have not space to repeat. The doctrine of metempsychosis or transmigration of souls, is in both. The

Kether Malkhuth reads: "If she (the soul) be pure, then shall she obtain favour, and rejoice in the latter day; but if she hath been defiled, then shall she wander for a time in pain and despair (*tanood b'she-tzeph ke-tzeph*), and in all the days of her uncleanliness she shall dwell alone, an exile, banished; she shall not touch any hallowed thing, nor come into the sanctuary, until the days of her purification have expired." The Zohar (ii, 199*b*) says: "All souls are subject to revolution (metempsychosis *a'leen b'gilgoolah*) but men do not know the ways of the Holy One; blessed be It! they are ignorant of the way they have been judged in all time, and before they came into this world and when they have quitted it, etc." (Zohar ii, fol. 99*b* sq. Franck, *La Kabbale*, p. 245 *et seq.* See *ante* pp. 90–91.)

The Kether Malkhuth, speaking of the eclipse of the sun, says: "And when in conjunction with the sun at the end of the month; if the dragon be between them, and they are both in one line; the moon appeareth before the sun as a black cloud, and intercepteth its light from every eye. That those who view her may know, that the Kingdom doth not belong to the host of heaven and their armies (*i. e.*, the angels), but that there is a Lord above them, who darkeneth their light." The Zohar says: "And the moon and sun remained like a body without a soul, the master over them having darkened their lights." (Zohar, Raÿah Me'hemnah, iii, 82*b*, § *Qado-sheem*.)

The Qabbalah in presenting the earthly man, as the Mikrokosm or inferior copy of the prototypic Heavenly Adam, asserts the existence of four divisions or worlds; which are to be found in a greater or less degree in each; basing this assertion on Isaiah (xliii, 7). "For I *b'ree-ah, i. e., created* him for *My Glory*, I *ye'tzar, i. e., formed* him, yea I *a'seey-ah, i. e., made* him." On these words of Isaiah, Ibn Ezra (b. 1088–89, d. 1176) in his Commentary on this passage, tells us, with disapproval, that Ibn Gebirol saw the Mystery of the Universe, that with him; "My Glory" stood for the Kosmic dynamos, which dwelt with God, and in the verse were intended the three Worlds called: B'ree-atic, Ye'tzeer-atic and A'seey-atic, which follow the A'tzeel-atic world; (see Trans. of the Soc. of Hebrew Literature. Comment of Ibn Ezra on Is. xliii, 7. Comp. Philo, On Dreams, ii, pp. 292–343, especially §§ iii and viii.) We hope to have space further on, to give further information on the Four Conditions or Worlds.

Gebirol's Supreme Unity above all number, who is unknowable to the mind of mankind, is evidently the *Ain Soph* of the Qabbalah and the Zoharic writings, termed also in them *Ayin* or No-Thing. Its first emanation is called, *Abbah* or the Father, and is the Will of the Zohar and Gebirol. It is the Unity of number, and among the Sephiroth it is the first, and as we said before, is called, Kether or the Crown. It is considered as the One or the Harmony, Consciousness or Abstract Thought, the Ego, the Content of all the subsequent Sephiroth. The first emanation from *Kether*, the Will or Father, is the Sephirah *Binah* (Bee'nah), the Universal Intellect or Understanding, which is Gebirol's first emanation, Universal Matter. It is also termed by the Qabbalah *Immah*, the Mother, and is considered as receptive, negative, feminine, plastic, and to receive form. The Universal Matter is with him the feminine or receptive principle. "Everything existing," says the Zohar (iii, 290*a*), "can only be the work of the male and female (principles)." The Zohar and Gebirol both hold, that everything must be of Form (male) and Matter (female).

The second emanation from *Kether*, is the Sephirah (this word is pronounced Seph'ee-rah) '*Hokhmah*, Wisdom, the Word, also called, the Son ; the united complex of all forms. It is the male principle and that which gives existence to Every-Thing, by giving Form to the Universal Spiritual or other Matter. (Me'qôr, v, §§ 11–12.) The Zohar says : " For it ('*Hokhmah*) generates all Things ;" also ; " By means of the Thirty-two paths by which '*Hokhmah* is spread throughout the universe, it ('*Hokhmah*) gives Every-Thing existing, shape (*i. e.*, form) and size." (Zohar, iii, 290*a*.) It is the Universal Form of Gebirol, "giving existence to Every-Thing by emanating and producing (the Form of) Every-Thing." (Me'qôr, v, § 12.) For " Everything existing can only be the work of the male and female (principles) : " (Zohar, Siphrah D'Tznioothah. Beginning). Form corresponds to the male or positive, Matter to the negative or female. *Kether* being called in the Qabbalah, Father, and *Binah*, Mother, '*Hokhmah* is termed, the Son, sometimes, " the Son of Elohim (God)." This Sephirah is the *spiritus mundi*. From 'Hokhmah, Wisdom, proceed all the balance of the Sephiroth, the first six of which are called, the Sephiroth of Construction or Building, and refer to dimension, *i. e.*, to Length, Breadth and Depth, and their positive and negative poles, and so to the six days of Genesis i. The last Sephirah Malkhuth, *i. e.*, Kingdom, the 7th and 10th, is the Harmony of all, the seventh day, the Sabbath or day of rest.

These first three Sephiroth are called by the Qabbalists, *Olam ha-Moos'kal;* the Intelligible or Intellectual World. Gebirol places the Will, Universal Matter and Universal Form together, as a triad above all other emanations and this would be their abode. He tells us "the Triad is the root of Every-Thing."

"Descended two Ancient ones; the Supreme Ancient One came between them, saying: We were three, now in our connection we are One;" (Tiqqooneh haz-Zohar, *Tiqqoon,* No. xxi, beg.)

"And they make known, that in the vision of the closed eye, three are one; so also: YHVH, our Elohim, YHVH, are one; three variations of forms which are one." (Comp. Zohar, ii, 43b.)

"And since the Holy Ancient is expressed and impressed by three, so also all the lamps that receive their light from the Holy Ancient are triadic." (Zohar, iii, 188b.)

The second triad of the Sephiroth, is called, *Olam ha-Moorgash,* the Moral or Sensuous World. It is represented by Gebirol's, Soul of the World or Universal Soul, emanating from the *spiritus mundi,* and which he divides into the Intellectual or Rational, the Vital and the Vegetative. (Me'qôr, iii, § 24 *sq.*) They are the male or positive principle, '*He-sed, i.e.,* Grace or Mercy, also called *Ge'doolah,* Magnificence, and the negative or female principle; *Pa'had, i. e.,* Punishment, also called *Din* (*Deen*), *i. e.,* Judgment, and *Ge'boorah, i. e.,* Rigour or Severity. These two, unite in *Tiph'e-reth, i. e.,* Beauty. According to our Gebirol, all human souls proceed from this Qabbalistic World, and each human being has, spiritually, the same Triadic division, as we have mentioned, termed *Neshamah, Rua'h* and *Nephesh.**

* The word *Nephesh* is to be found in Genesis ii, 7, *ha-adam l'ne'phesh haÿ-yah, i. e.,* to man the breath of life. *Neschamah* and *Nephesch* are not the correct English spelling.

Tiph'e-reth, says the Idrah Zootah, is, "the highest manifestation of ethical life and perfections, the sum of all goodness, in short, the Ideal." This Triad is Gebirol's Universal Soul, from which the human souls proceed. (Comp. Franck, *La Kabbale*, p. 228 *et seq.*)

The next, third, Triad of the Sephiroth is called *Olam ha-Moota'bo*, or the Material World, it apparently accords with Gebirol's, Spirit of Nature; with him it occupies the last degree of the simple substances, and is the intermediary of the Material World; through the energies or forces of the Deity, and the contraction and expansion everywhere evident. It is the Qabbalistic *Tzim'tzum*, and the multiplication. These Sephiroth are called, *Ne-tza'h, i. e.,* Triumph, the male or positive, sometimes termed Victory; and the female or negative, called, *Hod, i. e.,* Glory or Splendour; by which two, sometimes termed by the Qabbalists, the arms of God; the Zohar intends the centripetal and centrifugal energies and potentialities, in the entire universe.

The Zohar says: "All the energies, forces and increase in the universe, proceed through them." (Zohar, iii, 296a.) These two opposite Sephiroth unite in one harmonious principle, symbol of the principle of all generation, *Ye'sod, i.e.,* Foundation or Basis. Together they represent the Deity as the universal power, creator and generator of all the existences. Ibn Gebirol calls it *te-bang, i. e.,* nature, the Qabbalists, *Olam Ha-mool-bang, i. e.,* the Natural World. It is the *natura naturans* in contrast to the *natura naturata*, the Material World. (Comp. as to Gebirol's views on the above, the Me'qôr, v, §§ 38–40; iii, §§ 32, 33; iv, § 31; v, § 18.)

The last Sephirah, *Malkhuth* (Mal-khooth) or Kingdom, the Abode of the She'keen-ah, does not in the Zohar and Qabbalah, represent any new attribute, but symbolizes the harmony of all the others, and the kingdom of that harmony, over the entire universe. Its name is also, She'kheen-ah, the Divine Presence or Glory of the Deity, which sometimes visibly manifests itself in the universe. "It is the sum total of the permanent emanating yet immanent activity, of the totality of the entire Sephiroth, and is Elohim's (God's) presence in Its creation." As such it is apparently the same as Gebirol's Divine potentiality, which he says: "Is dominant in all the existing," penetrating all by virtue of the Deity's everywhere-acting Will-power, and not leaving any vacuum within, but establishing harmony everywhere and in all the existences. Here is the idea of an Ideal Perfect Kingdom, which is in perfect prototype in the highest world and which is to come on earth in the future, in perfection; and in which, the Messiah or Christ, is to govern over all the just or pious; which idea is to be found running through the entire Old and New Testaments.

This Sephirah symbolizes the feet of the Heavenly Adam which rest upon the world (comp. Ezek. xliii, 7). The head of this Adam reaches up to heaven. The Name of the Deity in this Sephirah is Adonai, *i. e.*, Lord, the equivalent for the ineffable Name YHVH. It may be, to the ideas clustering around this Sephirah, that St. John alludes, when he says in the Apocalypse; that when the 7th angel sounded his trumpet, there followed great voices in heaven, and they said: "*The Kingdom (Malkhuth) of this world is become the Kingdom (Malkhuth) of our Lord (Adonai) and his Christ (anointed One): and He shall reign forever and ever.*"* And the four and twenty elders which sit before God, on their thrones, fell upon their faces, etc." (Apoc. xi, 15–16. Comp. Ibid. i, 1–8; x, 7.) This grand, sacred and most mysterious, text, which we have italicized, the foundation of Bible teachings, is said to have been; on account of its mystery and holiness; omitted from some of the, printed, Douay editions of the N. T. We here note that the Ineffable Name YHVH, is frequently written by the Qabbalists crowned with 24 *taggin*, *i. e.*, crowns, each crown having three indentations equaling together 72, the number of the Elders of Israel, and of the Name of 72.†

---

* Note here, the Qabbalistic verse of the *Pater Noster*, "For thine is the Kingdom (*Malkhuth*) and the Power (*Ge'boorah*) and the Glory (*She'keen-ah*) for ever. Amen." Matt. vi, 13. Which is left out of the new authorized version of the English Church. In the Teaching of the XII Apostles (90–100 A. D.) it is: "For thine is the Power and the Glory for ever." C. viii, 2. See The Oldest Church Manual called the Teaching of the Twelve Apostles, etc., by Dr. Philip Schaff. New York, 1885, pp. 84, 189. The Teaching the Twelve Apostles with illustrations from the Talmud, etc., by Dr. C. Taylor. London, 1886, p. 64 *sq.* The Mysteries of Magic, etc., by Arthur Edward Waite. London, 1886, pp. 283–4.

† See, Kircher's *Œdipi Ægyptiaci, Tom. Secundus*, p. 267 *et seq.* One of the Qabbalistic formula of the Name of 72, is the Ineffable Name יהוה arranged in the form

Malkhuth is also called the Queen, the Matroneethah and the Matron. It represents the World of Matter. Its symbolic sphere is that of the moon, its symbolic color, blue, its ancient metal, silver. It was also called, the Church or Congregation of Israel, the Daughter, the Bride of the Spouse, the She'keen-ah, *i. e.*, the Glory or Real Presence of the Deity, the Sabbath or Rest day, the Harmony. It is considered by the Qabbalah, as the executive energy or power of the Sephirah Binah, the Holy Spirit or Upper Mother. Its color is also, blue. Blue is a symbolic colour of the Virgin in the Roman Church, who is usually covered with a blue robe, as a red or yellowish-red robe is usually portrayed around Christ. The Sephirah Tiph'e-reth is called, the King, and all the existences proceed from the Union of the King and Queen. The potencies of the Sephiroth are represented by the harmonies, *i. e.*, *Kether*, the Crown, *Tiph'e-reth*, the King, and *Malkhuth*, the Queen. The first affects the Neshamah, *i. e.*, the Spirit, the head, the second, the Rua'h, the Soul, the heart, the Nephesh, the animal life or materiality, is in the third triad.*

We have shown, *ante*, p. 159, that Gebirol evidently knew the ancient Qabbalistic, Sepher Ye'tzeerah, and the Zoharic writings have much the same thoughts as those contained therein, although set forth in a

---

of the Tetrad of Pythagoras, which latter is very ancient and signifies the decade. It is arranged thus:

•	1	'	=	10
• •	2	The Ineffable	יה	= 15
• • •	3	Name, thus	יהו	= 21
• • • •	4		יהוה	= 26
	——			——
	10			72

The sacred Tetrad of the Pythagoreans appears to have been known to the ancient Chinese. (Comp. *Einleitung in das Berständnik der Weltgeschichte, von, Aug. Gladisch*, etc. *Die alten Schinesen und die Pythagorees*, Posen, 1841, p. 82, *et seq.* See also upon the Tetrad, the valuable writing, *Pythagore et la Philosophie Pythagoricienne*, etc., by A. Ed. Chaignet, Paris, 1873, Vol. ii, pp. 96-128 and other places.)

* Comp. in this connection, the writings of Candlish, Davidson, Stanton, Drummond, Schürer, Edersheim, Hausrath and others, who have written on the Messiah and the coming Kingdom of Heaven upon our Earth, with the teachings of the Zohar and Qabbalah upon this Sephirah.

different manner. With the Qabbalists, the Deity is above but not completely outside of the numerals and letters; as entities, they constitute the 32 paths of that Wisdom, which is almost synonymous with the Will, Word and Holy Spirit, which are with them a Triad yet a Unit. With them, the vitalizing efflux of Elohim is in Every-Thing (see *ante*, p. 141, note).

We do not know that Ibn Gebirol wrote any Commentaries upon the Old Testament, at least not any have come to our day; but his explanations of certain texts, as cited by other authors, prove that he was fond of allegorical interpretations. Ibn Ezra (b. *circa* 1088, d. 1176 A. D.) cites him, in his Commentary upon Genesis (xxviii, 12). He states, that following Ibn Gebirol; the ladder which Jacob saw in his dream, signified the Superior (or rational) soul; "the angels of Elohim" which mount and descend thereon, are "the abstract thoughts of Wisdom," which attach themselves at the same time, both to a spiritual or superior subject, and also to the corporeal and inferior. Gebirol defended the opinion of Saadyah Gaon, that it was not intended in Genesis, to attribute in reality the faculty of speech to the serpent; and Ibn Ezra, in the Commentary above cited, also quotes the following mystical and allegorical meaning of the facts set forth in Genesis ii and iii, as by Gebirol: "'Paradise' is the superior world, the word 'Garden' designates the inferior world, it is full of a crowd of creatures (men), who are the plants; the River of Paradise, is the first matter, mother of all the corporeal; 'the four heads' or branches, of the River, designate the four roots, or elements; 'the man' (*i. e.*, Adam) who names all the animals, is Wisdom. Havvah or Eve, is the spirit of the living (the power of vitalization), which gives movement, and all that follows from it. 'The Serpent,' in the meaning of divination, is desire (comp. Gen. xliv, 5, to tempt, to incite). 'The Tree of Knowledge,' is carnal gratification, the power of which comes from 'the Garden' (desire or lust, comes from vegetation, or the products of the dust in the Garden, therefore the serpent of desire is to eat dust "all the days of (its) life"). The growth in the dust, is the seed of the woman, which causes the end (destruction) of that which comes from 'the dust;' and the end of the living (creature), is where the vegetation begins (*i. e.*, the final end of the earthly man, is his return to the ground or dust; from which vegetation, the life of the animal, proceeds). 'The clothes of skin,' is the body,* driven away from 'the Garden,' to cultivate the soil, from whence the terrestrial man was taken. 'The Tree of Life,' is the higher knowledge, which is: 'A Tree of Life, to them that lay hold upon it.' (Prov. iii, 18.) 'The Cherubim' are the angels. 'The flame of the sword,' refers to the sun. From this mystery it appears, that the higher intellectual soul, has its place at the Throne of Glory (She'keen-ah), where it delights in the glorious and tremendous Name of Elohim." (Comp. Kether Malkhuth.) This passage evidently considers Wisdom, doubtless the Higher Wisdom, as a separate potency; and the human body is a later condensation of the original body, which was first composed of Light. Gebirol therefore places the corporeal body as a minimum when comparing it with the spiritual body.

The Zohar calls Wisdom, the Divine Word, which announced and finished creation, and says; that it is the foundation of all spiritual and physical life. It calls Wisdom, the Upper Paradise or *Eden illa-ah*.† This Superior Eden, the Wisdom or the Ancient, is in the Zohar "a Form comprising all forms." (Zohar, *Ibid.*, 288a.) The idea of Wisdom as the creating power, is in Proverbs, Psalms, St. Paul, St. John, Sirakh, Wisdom, and other places in the Old and New Testaments. The Qabbalists and many of the Talmudists make *B'raisheeth, i. e.*, of Gen. i, 1, *Be' Raisheeth, i. e.*, through Wisdom, *Elohim barah, i. e.*, God created.

The Sephirah 'Hokhmah or Wisdom, as the Word; the *Logos* of Philo and St. John, and the Chaldaic, *Memrah;* has similar ideas clustering around it, as do the *Vach, i.e.*, Word, of the Hindu, Rig Veda; *Honover, i. e.*, Word, of the Persian, Zend Avesta; *Wisdom*, of the Proverbs of Solomon and of the later Book of Wisdom; and the *Avalôkitês'vara*, or

---

* "The flesh of man is a garment," etc. (Zohar i, 20b.) "When man is taken away, he rids himself of those garments in which he was dressed; the (garments of) skin in the which the Son of Man was dressed." (*Ibid.* 76a.) The learned Qabbalist Yehudah b. Salomo Charisi, or, al-Charisi (1170–1230), of Toledo, Spain; also compares the body of man to a garment, which the soul takes off at death; and to a prison, from which, at that time, the soul is liberated. He says: "On the day it takes off the body, it puts off its ornaments, and rids itself of the garments of its captivity."

† Comp. Zohar, iii, Idrah Zootah, "The higher Wisdom is also called, the higher Eden."

Kwan-Yin, the *Sakti* of *Amitâbha*, *i. e.*, boundless light, of the later Buddhists.

Ne'bo, the god of Wisdom of ancient Mesopotamia and Babylonia, was originally the deity of the visible universe, who was the *bolt* or *binder*, of its several parts together. (See *ante*, pp. 115; 190.) He was "the bond of the universe," the "overseer of the angel-hosts of heaven and earth." The *ziggurrat* or planet tower of his Temple at Borsippa, was called; "the house of the seven bonds (planets) of heaven and earth." The tower of the seven planets, or stations, attached to his house; was in seven stages, each of the astrological colour of the planet to which it was devoted. Ne'bo was therefore at one time evidently a god of all the heavenly bodies. His special planet in Babylonia was Mercury; that of Merodach, his father, who anciently was the Sun-god, was Jupiter; his mother was Zarpanitu, the Moon-god. Ne'bo is the Semitic *Nabiu* or *Na'boo*, a prophet or proclaimer, the נביא of Exod. iv, 1–17. Ne'bo was in Borsippa, considered the supreme god, the creator of the universe.

Moses, the Great Prophet, died and was buried, on mount Ne'bo. Ne'bo was also adored as the god of wisdom and prophecy, by the Canaanites, Moabites, and Assyrians, and in Palestine in general. Bo, Bod, Boden, or Buddha, in China, Fo; is the ancient Buddhistic god of Enlightenment and Wisdom; his early worshippers, the aboriginal or Dravidian races of India, erected the Great Topes of Amravati and Sanchi, in Hindustan, to him. His especial day among the Buddhists and Brahmins was our Wednesday, which among the ancient Akkadians was, the day of Ne'bo, and it is to this day, in India, the day of Buddha. His name is in Wo, Wod, Wo'den, of the Scandinavians, from whom our name Wednesday comes. He is the Thoth of the Egyptians, the Hermes of the Greeks, and the Mercury of the Romans, who named our Wednesday, after him; and it is on the fourth day, Wednesday, that Genesis tells us; the planets, etc., were created as *signs*, for the wise. The Word or Wisdom, represents, the Creator of the Universe and the Mediator between the Holy One and Its creation. In the Qabbalah it is called, the Upper Wisdom; to distinguish it from the Sephirah Malkhuth, Kingdom, the Lower Wisdom, the manifested She'keen-ah or Glory of the Deity. It is the Son of the Sephirah Kether, the Abstract Thought, the Ego or

Consciousness of existence; and is the representative of the Association of the Abstract Ideas which constitute Wisdom, and is looked upon as the Former and Maker, of the existing content of the Universe. Without such Association of Ideas, the human mind could not comprehend. It is used almost synonymously, in many places, by Philo and St. John; by the first of the Messiah, by the latter of Christ; and by the Targum of Onkelos, as Wisdom, the Creator of all. In the Targum Ye'rushalmi on Genesis i, 1, it is said: "In (By) *be-'Hohkmah*, Wisdom, the Lord created." This view also supported by Maimonides in his Moreh Ne'boo-kheem (*circa* 1190 A. D. Comp. S. Munk's French trans., ii, pp. 232, 236; English Ed., ii, p. 143 *sq.*) The Targum above cited, also says: "And the *Memrah* (Word) of the Lord created man in Its likeness, etc." The first word of Genesis *B'raisheeth*, usually translated "In the beginning;" has had various meanings assigned to it. Maimonides, says; it should be read as: *Be-Raisheeth, i.e.,* by the *Principle*, and that the verse should be translated: "*In* (or, By) *the Principle, Elohim (God) created the height and the depth of the universe.*" *Principle* meaning the Upper Wisdom, "a beginning not temporal." The learned Beausobre says: * "There is yet a reflection to be made upon that matter. It resolves itself upon the explanation of the word *Raisheeth*, which is at the commencement of Genesis, and which; if we believe the ancient Jewish interpreters; *does not signify, the Beginning,* but the active and immediate *Principle* of all Things. Thus instead of translating: 'At the beginning, God created the heaven and the earth:' they translate: 'God made the heaven and earth by the *Principle*,' that is; according to the Targum of Jonathan, '*By Wisdom.*' Maimonides supports the view; that only this explanation, is the literal and true one. It at first passed among the Christians. We find it not only in Chalcidius; who remarks that it came from the Hebrews; but also in Methodius, Origen, and in Clement of Alexandria; who is more ancient than either. * * * The latter says, there is only one God, who has made the *Principle* of all things; signifying in that way, his first-born Son. St. Peter (II Pet. iii, 5–6), who has very well understood, that word

---

* *Histoire critique de Manichée et du Manicheisme par M. De Beausobre, A. Amsterdam, 1734.* Vol. ii, Bk. vi, ch. i, p. 290–1. Comp. Bk. iv, c. vi, p. 89.

(*i. e.*, Wisdom), says: 'God has made the heaven and earth by the Principle.' That principle is that which is called, Wisdom, by all the prophets.

The Christian philosophers adopted this explanation for two reasons. I. They found the Trinity of the divine persons at the head of the (Hebrew) scriptures. God, the Father, created the universe, but he created by the *Principle* (Logos, Wisdom), which is His Son, and the Holy Spirit inflamed and animated nature. It (the Holy Spirit) was borne upon the waters, says Moses: 'That explanation,' St. Augustine says: 'gives me so much the more pleasure, as in that way, I find the Trinity established at the head of the Holy Book of Genesis.' II. The aforesaid explanation favored the sentiment of the Christian philosophers, who believed in the pre-existence of the Intelligible world, because, if by *Raisheeth* is understood the *Active Principle* of Creation, and not, the Beginning; then it has no more than said; the Heaven and Earth were the first works of God. And Moses has only said, that 'God created the Heaven and Earth by the *Principle*,' which is His Son. It is not the epoch, it is the immediate Author of Creation, which it teaches. St. Augustine has also said: 'The angels have been made before the Firmament, and even before that which is reported by Moses; God made the Heaven and the Earth by the *Principle;* because by this word *Principle* is desired; not to express that the Heaven and Earth, were made before all things, since God had already made the angels precedently; it means to say: that God has made all things by *Wisdom*, which is His *Word*, and which the scripture has called, the *Principle*.'" St. Paul (I Cor. ii, 7, 8) says: "But we speak the *Wisdom* of God, *in a mystery*, even the *Hidden wisdom*, which God *ordained before the worlds* unto our glory. Which none of the rulers of this world knew: for had they known it, they would not have crucified the Lord of glory." This *Hidden Wisdom* is Christ (I Cor. i, 21–24; Col. ii, 3), "who of God, *is made unto us Wisdom*, and Righteousness, and Sanctification (Holiness) and Redemption." (*Ibid.* 30–31.) "Wherein He hath abounded towards us in all *Wisdom* and *Prudence*." (One of the names of Binah, Understanding, the *Rua'h ha-Qadosh, i. e.*, the Holy Spirit.) (Eph. i, 8). "I *Wisdom* dwell with *Prudence;* and the Knowledge of discreet Thoughts do I discover." (Prov. viii, 12.) "Christ in whom are hid all the treasures of *Wisdom* and *Knowledge.*" (Col. ii, 3.) "Now ye are the body of Christ, and members in particular." (I Cor. xii, 27; compare the whole chapter with I Cor. xv.) St. Paul referring to Christ as the Son, says: "Who is the image of the invisible God, the first born of all creation; for *in him were all things created, in the heavens and upon earth*, things visible and things invisible, whether *thrones*, or *dominions*, or *principalities*, or *powers;* all things have been created through him and unto him, and *he is before all things, and in him all things consist.* (exist?) And he is *the head of the body*, the Church, * * that in all things he might have pre-eminence. For it was the good pleasure *of the Father* that in him should all the fullness dwell, etc." (Col. i, 15–20.) Compare with this, there is a Heavenly Adam and an Earthly Adam. (I Cor. xv, 45–49, 22–28 and I Cor. xii.) "His Son * * by whom also he made the worlds." (Heb. i, 2.) "We understand that the worlds were formed by the Word of God, so that things which are seen, were not made of things which do appear." (*Ibid.* xi, 3.) "For thy Almighty hand, that made the world of *matter, without form.*" (Wisdom, xi, 17.) "And by his *Memrah* was the world created." Targum of Onkelos to Deut. xxxiii, 27. "The world was made by him," *i. e.*, the Word. (St. John i, 10.)*

Ibn Gebirol, says, in his Kether Malkhuth: "Wisdom is the fountain of life." The Zohar says: "The seventh palace, the fountain of life, is the first in the order from above, etc." (Zohar, ii, 261*a*.)

To account for the construction of the world, Gebirol introduced simple

* Compare with these: Eph. i, 18, 21; iii, 9, 10; Col. ii, 3; Rom. xvi, 25–27; Jude 25; James iii, 17; Prov. viii, ix; Hebrews, St. John and, Philo: iii, 95, iv, 391–2; Book of Wisdom, xviii, 14–15; i, 4, 5; and Sirakh xxiv, 3–9; Targum of Onkelos to Deuter. xxxiii, 27; Book of Enoch, Schodde's English trans., p. 208, c. 84; p. 137; c. 48, 50; c. 49 and other places; Apocryphal New Test., p. 174; Epist. of Barnabas (*Ibid.*) iv, 7; v, 12. The Conciliator of R. Menasseh ben Israel, etc., London, 1842, p. 6. Basnage, Hist. of the Jews, Bk. iv, c. v, § vii, English trans., p. 288, col. 2. Kircher's Œd. Ægypti, Vol. ii, c. ix, § iv, p. 309. Anacalypsis of Godfrey Higgins, Vol. i, pp. 73, 75–81, 122, 235, 250, 264–5, 308, 338, 348, 469, 511, 564, 769, 803, 806–7, etc., as cited in index Vol. i, p. 862. Hidden Wisdom of Christ, by De Bunsen, i, p. 430. Targums by J. W. Etheridge, London, 1862, i, pp. 157, 160, 162. Bertholdt's Christology, p. 131. As to the Talmud, Hershon's Genesis, etc., p. 79; Hershon's Talmudic Mis., p. 104. Heb. Mis. Society, Hebrew Liter., London, i, p. 40, note.

substances between the Godhead and the physical world, he does not actually use the term Sephiroth, but his idea of the highest and simple substances, evidently refers to them; he also speaks of the spheres in the same way as Philo (Philo, iii, 185–6) and the Qabbalists. The spheres, or properly the orbits, of the planetary and astronomical universe, were doubtless those which entered into the idea of the Sephiroth. This was an ancient idea. And we think we may assert; that the simple substances of Gebirol refer to the orbits, called in his time, the spheres of the planets, and to other ancient astronomical divisions of the heavens. He speaks of the sensible spheres which emanate from the intelligible spheres. (Me'qôr, iv, § 8.) Of the corporeal spheres emanating from the spiritual spheres. (*Ibid.*, § 1.) That the simple substances are called spheres or circles. (*Ibid.*, iii, § 41; ii, § 1, §§ 3, 4.) His nine categories evidently refer to these spheres. (*Ibid.*, §§ 11, 12, 23; iii, §§ 1, 2, 8, 17, 36, 41; iv, §§ 1, 8; v, 67, and other places.) The potential energy of the Deity; penetrates all, surrounds all, and acts in all, through all eternity. (*Ibid.*, iii, § 14; iv, § 23, § 29.) With Gebirol, the body of man as the Mikrokòsm, corresponds to the concrete body of the perfect ideal vitality of the universe, the Great Ideal or Forming Man, the Makrokosm (*Ibid.*, iii, § 44, § 6).

The connection between the Highest and the Lowest; through the surrounding orbits, spheres or coatings, supposed to surround our earth; was a very ancient idea, and is a reminiscence of the archaic astronomical religious philosophy; of the Akkadians, Chaldeans, Assyrians, Babylonians, Hebrews and Hindus, with some of these peoples, going back thousands of years before the Christian era. Philo evidently has this in his mind. (See his works, iii, pp. 177, 184–186, 190, 196; ii, 138, 208. Comp. his treat. On Fugitives, ii, 320–326, 136–139, and other places.)

The Qabbalah frequently uses instead of the word Sephiroth, the word *kaileem*, *i. e.*, vessels, for the intermediaries, and thus indicates the indirectness of their activity. Gebirol in his Kether Malkhuth says of the Will, the emanation proceeding immediately from the Absolute: "He (It) draws from the Source of Light without a pail (or bucket) and effects everything without a vessel." (Comp. the Me'qôr, iii, § 15.) Instead of Sephiroth, he often uses, orbits or spheres, but generally, "categories." He tells us, the potentiality of the Holy One, is more visible in some of the simple substances than in others. (*Ibid.*, iii, §§ 32, 33.) The same idea is in the Zohar and other Qabbalistic books, where this greater or less potentiality; is sometimes called, Parzupheem, *i. e.*, Faces (Visages or Aspects).

Referring to the idea of the divine power being weaker in some of the simple substances than in others, depending on the distance from the source. "How is it possible," he asks, "that the divine power should weaken, alter, or materialize itself; and that the action of the First Agent show itself, more in certain substances than in others, seeing that it is the perfect completeness of all power, perfection and faculty?" and he evades this by answering: "It does not depend on the giver but on the recipient; for at a great distance from the source, the receiving matter, is less apt to receive the abundance, from the Forms of Light streaming into it." (Comp. Me'qôr, iii, §§ 13, 32.)

In the Kether Malkhuth, he says: "Thyself, thou art the Being, who from the *shadow of thy Light* hast made the generation of all that which is." We may sum up Gebirol's propositions to be; that the Infinite Light, which at first filled all, retired itself into itself, that is, the Infinite rays retired into a centre or point, and left Space, the Abyss, which is a species of shadow or vacuum; afterward, the Divine Light gradually communicated itself with more or less energy, into the Space or Abyss; according to the receptibility of matter, and to the proportion of vitalizing energy, which the Divine Will wished to impart to it. This is also a condensed statement of the Zoharic cosmogony, and the Qabbalistic theory of *Tzim-tzum, i. e.*, expansion and contraction, or the symbolism used by it, to set forth philosophically, the centrifugal and centripetal motion or energy; which, under the direction of God, made and maintains, the universe. According to the Qabbalah the Light of the Infinite Being, the Ain Soph, *i. e.*, the Endless One, the nevertheless to man's finite thought No-Thing or Non-Ego, originally filled All; and in order to manifest Itself, this Unknowable in its Essence Deity, made Space, and in Space It developed or created gradually, through an emanation in which It was immanent yet transcendental. At first It concentrated Itself in Its own Essence, and that caused Space or a place for the universe to be constructed in, this was the Abyss; It afterwards filled this Space successively and in different gradations or degrees, with Its vitalizing Light.*

The Great Qabbalist, Moses Cordovera (1522–1570 A. D.) in his *Pardes Rim-monim, i. e.*, Paradise, or Garden, of Pomegranites, fol. 55a, says: "Elohim (God) is the prototype of all being, and all things are in Him, in their purest and most complete Form; so that the perfection of the created, consists exactly in the existence, in which they find themselves (in affinity) with the original source of their being; and in proportion to the distance of their departing from the Deity, they will sink down from that perfect and sublime condition." The Qabbalists hold, like Gebirol, the Supreme Deity alone, is absolutely simple; and that all the other simple, intelligible substances are composed of Form and Matter. Joseph Chiquitilla, an erudite Qabbalist, says: "Know that in all created things, superior and inferior, there is not anything absolutely simple. The Supreme Deity alone is pure simplicity, and a Unit without any multiplication; but, among all the other beings, comprising therein even the separate and superior intelligences which we call angels, there is not one who is simple and without multiplicity. * * * They bear an occult matter, simple and superior, which does not resemble our matter, etc." (see his *Sepher ha-Nik-kood*, fol. 3c.)

In the system of Gebirol, as in that of the Zohar, and of almost all the most archaic Eastern religious philosophy, the Triad holds a most important position as the principle of the universe. Our author says: "The Triad is the root of everything" (Me'qôr, v, § 56, § 30; iv, § 32, §§ 17–20, 8). The Qabbalah and Zohar develope the Sephiroth in the Triadic form, and the antient Akkadians, Chaldeans, Babylonians, Hindus, Chinese, and Persians, arranged their heavens and deities in Triads. In the Qabbalah each of the opposites, together a dualty, are united by a harmony and make a triad, and together, they constitute but one unity. The Idrah Zootah (Zohar, iii, fol. 288b) says: "The Ancient, whose Name be Blessed! has Three Heads which are yet One Head. And as the Ancient is designated by the number three, so also, all the other

---

* Franck, *La Kabbale*, p. 186. Zohar, Idrah Rabbah. See Joel, *Relig. Philos. Sohar.*

lights (Sephiroth) with their scintillations, are comprised in the number three."

The idea that the Triad is the root of everything, is in a great number of places in the Zohar, we have the quotations but not space to now insert them. The Triadic idea of the Deity is also in Philo, but he says, it is a great mystery not to be given to the uninitiated.

As to the creation out of nothing (*creatio ex nihilo*) Gebirol appears to agree with the Qabbalists. He compares creation to the water going out of its source (Maqôr, v, § 64) and to the impression of a form in a mirror (*Ibid.*, § 71; ii, § 27) God "has produced existence out of the No-Thing." "Thou drawest forth," he says, "the Light from its source, but not by any human means; and hast produced all, without the means used by man. Thou hast arranged and fixed, and purified and cleansed; and called unto the nonentity (? No-Thing) and it was dis-placed, etc." (Kether Malkhuth). The Qabbalists admit the objection to *ex nihilo nihil fit*, and declare the universe emanated from No-Thing, by the potentiality of the Divine Will, and the Desire or Word. They however say: "If the world came into existence, the nothing is meant as the No-Thing, *i. e.*, it came from a spiritual source, which was not *a Thing* in any sense which we can apply to *a Thing*." This No-Thing is the 'Cause of Causes,' the Ain Soph, the Endless, or the Ayin, *i. e.*, the No-Thing.

The optical metaphor of the light, visible or invisible to the eye; plays a most important part in the Zohar and in Ibn Gebirol's philosophy. The former says: "Come and see. There are four lights! Three of them are concealed and one is revealed, etc. In the eye there are three colors, which are revealed and marked therein, and none of them are guarded; for they exist (stand), in the light that does not shine, etc. And regarding this secret, close thine eyes and turn thine eye-balls; and those colors that are in that light and that are not guarded, will be revealed, etc." (Zohar, ii, 23*a*. Comp. Talmud, treatise *Yevamoth*, 49*b*). Ibn Gebirol says: "Thou art wise; and being the architect of unbounded might, hast from Thy own Wisdom imparted an immediate Desire (*Chephetz*) to draw the emanation of existence from non-existence; * * * as the ray of light which comes forth from the fountain of vision (the eye), illumines obscurity, etc. * * * Thou drawest forth the light, which comes forth from the eye, and attracts from the source of light but not by human means.

And Thou hast hewn out and engraved,

And spoken to the non-entity (the No-Thing) and it unfolded (was opened or displaced);

And to the existence, and it was fixed;

To the universe, and it was expanded." (Kether Malkhuth.) Ibn Gebirol says: "How wonderful are the words of the philosophers about sense of the eye-sight when they say; that the soul (*nephesh*) has spiritual colours which appear in the motions of the eye-lids." (Comp. his *Tiqqooneh Middoth han-nephesh*, 4a.) "The Deity made formations in the light of above, etc.; When he measured out the Messiah, It made colors to shine inside, etc. It opened and did not burst (or split) its air (the azoth). It did not make Itself in anyway known, until by emanation from this opening, a point was lighted, etc." (Zohar, i, 15a.) "Thou art the Light which is hidden in this world, but which shall be revealed in the Celestial World; for on the mount of the Lord, shall it be seen." (Kether Malkhuth.) Human vision is also mentioned a number of times with like purpose in the Me'qôr. (Comp. v, § 62 and other places.) Moses Cordovero uses the same simile: "The Holy One may he be Praised! Who is the girdle of energy, who is One, and in whom all the faculties form only One Unity: similar to the flame of the fire, which contains different colors, and of the light of the eye, which goes out of the pupil; these faculties emanate one from the other, as the odor emanates from odor, and light from light," (*Pardes Rimmonim*, § 4). Haÿ Gaon (969–1038 A. D.) and Ibn Ezra (b. *circa* 1088, d. 1176 A. D.), use the same imagery from the human power of sight. In the Hindu mythology the eye of a deity never winks. (Indian Wisdom, by Monier Williams, p. 16, n. 2.) The Zohar in the Idrah Rabbah says; the eye of Providence, like those of a fish, has not any lids, but is always open: (see in this connection, The Path, New York, March, 1887). The Zohar uses the Light as an illustration of the Mediator between the Ideal and the Real. " Let Light Be! all that came forth, is so by this mystery, etc." (Zohar i, 16b.) The eye is also used in the Zohar to explain the Divine illumination of man. (*Ibid*. ii, 23a and b.)

In the Tiqqooneh haz-Zohar (Tiqqoon, 70), is this beautiful allegory of the soul as it manifests itself through the light of the eyes: " 'In the beginning Elohim (God) created : ' This is the soul when it emerges from the bosom of its mother, and it is taught of it ; ' And the earth was void and in confusion and darkness was upon the surface of the abyss ; ' for its eyes were closed. Has it opened its eyes? ' And Elohim said : Let light be !' After this man is gathered in from this world, and what is written about the soul ; ' And Elohim said : Let the water be gathered from beneath the heaven to one place, and let the dry land appear !' When the soul is taken from the man, the body remains ' dry land.' "

Ibn Ezra in his short Commentary to Genesis, says: "I will now explain to you the mystery of the venerated and awful Name, and the mystery of the angels; and I will make a simile for you, from the light of the soul which comes forth from the eye. Know then that the eye consists of seven degrees, and that the inside one, is the white point. And behold the light is not a body (substance), and the light of the soul, requires another light from the outside, etc." It was held by the ancient anatomists and philosophers, that in seeing ; an intellectual force streamed out of the eye, which came in contact with the objects observed, and returned them to the eye. This was "the light of the soul which comes forth from the eye." In Gerson ben Salomo's writing, *Sha-areh has-shamayeem*, *i. e.*, Gates of Heaven: the coatings of the eye are called *chutanoth*, *i.e.*, shirts or epidermis (in optics, *tunica*) or *me'hitzoth*, *i. e.*, separations. Gerson and Samuel Çarça, quote the component parts under different names. Three are fluid, seven, solid, together ten : viz:

1. The crystal, *i. e.*, the vitreous humor. This includes the lens.
2. The sapphire, *i. e.*, the aqueous humor. Çarça calls it, "the icy" from *kera'h*, ice.
3. The tasteless fluid, *i. e.*, the albugineous humor. Çarça calls its, "egg white" from *be'tzah*, an egg.

The seven solid parts (separations, shirts or degrees) are :

1. The net, *i. e.*, the *retina*. Çarça calls it, the "cobweb."
2. The epidermis, *i. e.*, the *tunica vasculosa*. Çarça says, "epidermic."
3. The hard one, *i. e.*, the *tunica sclerotica*.

4. The dish-like separated web, *i. e.*, the iris. Çarça says, "the bread-like."

5. The grape-like, *i. e.*, the *tunica uvea*.

6. The horney, *i. e.*, *tunica cornea*.

7. The conjoining, *i. e.*, the *ligamentum ciliare*. Çarça says, "the net-like."

The arrangement of the points of the compass, elements and metals, in the Zohar (ii, 24*a* and *b*), are:

North	East	South	West
Fire	Air	Water	Earth
Gold	Bronze (or Copper)	Silver	Iron

After this the internal connection between the twelve is shown. It then says, "Come and see! Fire, air, water, and earth, are all united with each other, and conjoined, one with the other, and there is not any void (vacuum) between them, etc.; as it is taught in the Holy Writings; 'And from thence it separates and becomes four heads.'" That is the four principal streams of Eden. Gebirol has a similar idea in the Kether Malkhuth, and says: "Thou didst form the globe of the earth, divided into two parts, one half dry land, and one half, water. Thou didst encompass the water with the elementary sphere of air. * * * Thou didst also encompass the air with the element of fire.* These four elements have but one foundation (element,) and their source is one, from which they emanate and are ever renewed; and from which they are separated and become four branches or heads."† The Great Man seen by Nebuchadnezzar in his dream (Daniel ii) was composed of these metals, but his feet were part iron, and part pottery (clay or earth). It was most likely intended as a symbol of the Makrokosm, the Great Universal Heavenly Man, composed of the Four Worlds of the Qabbalah, through which it, as the intermediary, extends.

* This refers to the hidden, elementary fire or vitalizing energy, which permeates everything and holds the universes together. The elementary air, is the azoth, perhaps the same as the *akasi* of the Hindu philosophy, or, the luminiferous æther, of modern physics.

† Comp. Dr. Jellinek, *Beiträge zur Geschichte der Kabbala*, 2 Vol., Leipzig, 1852, p. 38.

In his Commentary on Daniel (xi, 20) Ibn Ezra, says: Ibn Gebirol was among those who had calculated the epoch of the coming of the Messiah, and founded it upon astrological theories. Ibn Ezra is himself, at this place, referring to a great conjunction of the superior planets Jupiter and Saturn. Ideas upon the time of the coming of the Messiah, are in the Zohar. (Comp. *ante*, 77 *sq.*)

Our author also makes use of the poetical figure: "He supports the world like a bunch of grapes," which is in the Siphrah D'Tznioothah of the Zohar (ii, 179*a*): "They hang on It like grapes in a bunch." He refers to the elementary, hidden invisible fire, so does the Zohar. In his poem called "Forget thy Sadness," he says:

> "That day He wills thy flight
> Like a bird to her nest."

Bird is a Hebrew term for angel, the Bird's nest, is heaven. This idea of bird and angel, is in the book of Ecclesiastes (x, 20) and the Talmud. In the Zohar the Bosom of God is called, "the Bird's Nest." "When the Messiah shall be made perfect, through the instrumentality of the righteous; he will enter the Garden of Eden, into that place which is called the Bird's Nest." (Zohar, ii, 8*b*, comp. *ante*, p. 86.) "And that is what the (biblical) passage says: 'Like a bird that is flying from its nest,' and that is the soul from which the She'kheen-ah does not move away." (Rayah Me'hemnah, Zohar, iii, 278*a*.) "About the Holy One, Blessed be It! And his She'kheen-ah, the verse says: 'Like a bird that is flying from its nest, etc.' This is also that which is written, 'Also the bird found a house, and the sparrow a nest for herself.'" (Tiqqooneem to Zohar Chadash, 72*d*, Amsterdam edition.) Gebirol also says, in the Kether Malkhuth: "Thine is the Might, in the Mystery of which our contemplations are too feeble to stay." Only if "Might" is used as a technical term for *Mysticism* does the mentioning of "Mystery" get a proper sense. R. Yekhutiel says: "All thoughts rise in vain to reach it," *i. e.*, this Mysticism. "Thine is the hidden Name from the habitations of Wisdom." (Kether Malkhuth.) Knowledge or Wisdom, the Gnosis, is used in the same way by Hay Gaon. "Thine is the existence, from the *shadow* of the Light of which, all existence came." (*Ibid.*) The symbolism of Light in the theory of the Creation is also in Hay.

Ibn Gebirol's poem on "The Thirty-two Paths;" shows the extent to which he occupied himself with the Qabbalistic Sepher Ye'tzeer-ah. Haÿ also took the Ye'tzeer-ah as the basis of his Gnosis. Comp. as to these last statements, Dr. Jellinek's, *Beiträge zur Geschichte der Kabbala*, Vol. ii, p. 26 *et seq*.

In looking at the writings of Philo, Ibn Shaprut, R. Haÿ Gaon, R. Yekhutiel, Ibn Gebirol, Azriel and the Zoharic books, and many statements in Maimonides; we can see such an affinity between their writings, that it evidences the antiquity of the Qabbalistic philosophy; and that they all drew from a common and much more remote source. Our essay is only an attempt, to show the similarity of the philosophy of Ibn Gebirol with that of the Qabbalists preceding and succeeding him; and with that in the Zohar and Zoharic books; all drawing their ideas from the ancient Sod, Mysteries or Secret Learning, which was delivered orally in its fullness; and as to which, only hints were noted in the old secret manuscripts as aids to the memory. These are a few of the points of resemblance between the ideas of Ibn Gebirol and the Zohar and Qabbalah, many others exist, which we have not had the time and place, to insert in this writing; the student can follow up our ideas.

Numerous similarities exist between the content of the Zoharic and other early Qabbalistic writings; and the translations from the cuneiform terra cotta tablets found in the ruins of Assyria and Babylonia. Showing that the ancient Babylonian religion influenced the Qabbalistic philosophy, and that much of the Zoharic writings came through the Babylonian Jews.

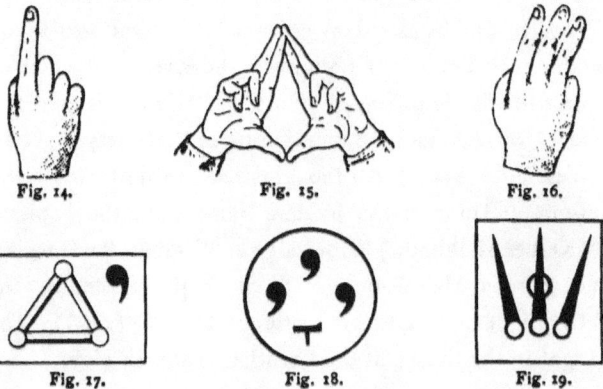

Fig. 14.   Fig. 15.   Fig. 16.

Fig. 17.   Fig. 18.   Fig. 19.

Figure 20.

Figure 21.

XI.

THE HEBREW QABBALAH AND ITS ORIGIN. ITS CONTENT AND THE PROBLEMS IT SEEKS TO SOLVE. FROM THE VISIBLE ASCERTAIN THE INVISIBLE. THE SEVERAL DIVISIONS OF THE QABBALAH. THE FOUR ANIMALS OF THE ANCIENT CHALDEAN AND HINDU RELIGIONS AND THOSE OF THE MERKABAH, THEIR COLOURS, ETC. THE SPECULATIVE QABBALAH. THE QABBALAH OF THE ROMAN CATHOLIC CHURCH AND OF THE LAW. CURIOUS PARALLELS REGARDING THE SERPENT, THE WORLD—TREE, AND THE SEVEN KINGS OF EDOM; IN THE ZOHARIC BOOKS AND THE CUNEIFORM TABLETS.

The predominating influence shown in the writings of Ibn Gebirol, is that of the ancient Qabbalistic philosophy; as far as it had been received, developed and not lost, up to his time, in Judaism. Long before his time, indeed we believe many centuries before the Christian era, there was in Central Asia, a "Wisdom Religion;" fragments of which subsequently existed among the learned men of the archaic Egyptians, the ancient Chinese, Hindus, Israelites and other Asiatic nations; as a secret metaphysical philosophy, and also as a secret physical philosophy. These together, were ultimately formulated among the Hebrews and Jews, under the designation; Secret Learning or Sithrai Thorah, *i. e.*, Secrets of the

Thorah, also, Rasé Thorah; Sodoth Thorah, and simply, Sod, *i.e.*, Mystery. Sometimes this was called; 'Hokhmah, *i.e.*, Theosophy or Wisdom, *par excellence*, also, PaRDeS, *i. e.*, Paradise, Gan Eden, the Garden of Eden, or Bliss, the Place of departed souls, the Place in which was the pure intellectual perception of the Deity. Therefore we have its derived form as a term for, intuitive intellectual and metaphysical speculation, and an inner true perception of God. The idea is in Philo Judæus.* It was divided, as we have mentioned, into two main branches. I. Physics, or the philosophy as to Creation, termed Ma-a'seh Be'resheeth; the principal occult book of which, is Genesis. II. Religious metaphysical philosophy, termed, Ma-a'seh Merkabah (or the work of the chariot-throne).† Its theophany is to be found running through the Hebrew Sacred Writings, especially those of the prophets Isaiah, Ezekiel, Daniel, and in Proverbs and Psalms, and is older than Chronicles. (The beginning of Chronicles is *circa* 535 B. C.) It is mentioned as secret, in Sirakh, which was written about 290–280 B. C.‡

'Hokhmah as Theosophy, was distinguished from 'Hokhmath Yavonith, *i. e.*, Grecian Wisdom, and Lashon 'Hokhmah, Secret Technical language. Based upon the content of the above-mentioned Secret Learning, we have, Qabbalah, *i. e.*, an esoteric doctrine received by oral tradition, which is also called נסתרה חכמה 'Hokhmah Nistharah, *i.e.*, Secret Wisdom, because it was only handed down, through esoteric oral tradition: by

---

* Bohn's English Edition of Philo, iv, p. 286, *et seq*. We shall always cite this edition unless we specify Mangey's Greek Edition, or some other; as it is more accessible to most readers. The Zohar speaks of a heavenly Paradise, of Light; and an earthly Paradise, of Darkness. (Schoettgen, Hor. Heb., i, p. 1096.) Both refer to the Intellect.

† The pattern of the chariot-throne to be put in the Temple of Solomon, is given by YHVH to David (1 Chron. xxviii, 18–19); and earlier to Moses (Exod. xxv, 18–22). Philo refers to this as existing in heaven. Comp. also 1 Sam. iv, 4; 1 Kings vi, 23 *et seq.;* Rev. xi, 19.

‡ See Sirakh xxxix, 8, and other places; M. Steinschneider's Hist. of Jewish Lit., London, 1857, p. 51. Philo, ii, p. 324 *et seq.;* iii, p. 177 *et seq.;* ii, 215 *et seq.* He also refers to the spiritual world as the chariot, the driver of which was the Logos, Word or Will, of the Deity. *Ibid.,* i, 167, 393. Compare Maimonide's Moreh Ne'bookheem, Arabic and French Ed. by S. Munk, English Ed. by Dr. Friedlander, on these subjects.

the initiated to new initiates, and is indicated to them, in the Holy Writings; by signs, hints, and symbols, hidden and unintelligible to the uninstructed in the mysteries. From the Hebrew initial letters of the latter name ח׳ן, it was also designated as, Grace. Qabbalah expresses reception, or receiving *per se*, differing from Massorah, in that the latter, implies receiving and transmitting, without esotery. The School of Alexandria, had much knowledge of the archaic Qabbalah in its fullness, that intellectual centre of the ancient learned world; having adepts in its population, who still had knowledge of the archaic "Wisdom Religion," of the Orient. This great Greco-Egyptian city received influences from learned Chaldeans, Jews, Hindus, Chinese, and Egyptians, as well as Greeks and Persians. We therefore find the writings of Philo Judæus of Alexandria, full of the same philosophy which is in the Zohar and the other early writings that have come to us; which set forth the archaic metaphysical doctrines of the Qabbalah especially as to ideas: (see *e. g.*, Philô., iii, 184 *et seq.*).

The Qabbalah most likely, originally came from Aryan sources, through Central Asia, Persia, India and Mesopotamia, for from Ur and Haran came Abraham and many others, into Palestine. We know that the Hebrew Genesis and many parts of the Old Testament, are tinctured with Aryan, Akkadian, Chaldean and Babylonian thought, and that Isaiah, Daniel, Ezra, Jeremiah, Ezekiel and other learned Israelites; were under the influence of Persian and Chaldean learning. We find several references to the wisdom of "the Sons of the East," in the Hebrew Sacred Writings. (Comp. Kitto's Bib. Cyclop., Ed. 1876, Vol. i, p. 336 *sq.*) Communication between the ancient nations of Asia, was much more general than has been usually thought by the learned of our day.

Before the time of Moses, the priests or prophets of the Hebrews, were not a distinct and exclusive class of men. The patriarchs occupied both positions and offered their own prayers and sacrifices. Moses changed this, confining the gift of prophecy to an initiated chosen few, the Seventy Elders (Num. xi, 16 *et seq.*; xii, 1–16); as he also did the priesthood to the Sons of Levi, but with Moses himself, YHVH spoke " mouth to mouth * * * and not in dark speeches." The prophets come prominently forward in the time of Samuel, but up to 800 B. C. they do not appear to have left any written prophecies. About 100 years after the return from the last Babylonian Exile, the prophets as a profession, appear to have entirely ceased in Judaism. Tradition is, that Haggai, Zekhariah and Malakhi were the last. The later prophets read and studied the writings of those who preceded them, and also undoubtedly obtained oral traditional knowledge from their predecessors.

In the ancient Secret Learning were teachings as to the Deity, Its essence and Nature, Names, attributes, revelation, and the spiritual world; also teachings as to magical arts, the exorcism of evil spirits, healing by the use of the Names of the Deity, by laying on of hands, talisman, etc., such perhaps as existed among the Chaldean priests;* black magic or necromancy and the Practical Qabbalah. It also contained secret doctrines, as to the creation and governance of the world by the Deity and the spiritual energies, the angels; and their relation to it, to man and to nations; the interpretation of the Hebrew Sacred Writings, original sin, sacrifice, atonement, forgiveness, redemption, retribution, the Messiah and his Kingdom on our earth; accounts of the Heavenly Jerusalem and its Temple; doctrines as to the soul, hell, death, heaven, the resurrection from the dead, the judgment day, the kingdom of heaven, the future world, etc., etc. These doctrines were kept secret to prevent any misconception and misuse of them, by the unlearned and unmetaphysical minds; who would, perhaps, have been led away by them from the truth; and in uneducated minds, they certainly would have tended to produce heterodoxy from the formal Hebrew religion. From such incapacity and heterodoxy, and from the Jewish mind becoming influenced by Persian and Hellenistic thought; after the conquests by Alexander the Great and his successors; and the arising of the School of Alexandria, orthodox Judaism had much to fear.

This apprehension finally became formulated into: " Do not discuss the Ma-a'seh Merkabah even in the presence of one pupil, except he be a wise and intelligent man, and then, only the headings of the chapters

---

* Comp. F. Lenormant's Chaldean Magic, London. Lectures on the Origin and Growth of Religion, etc., of the Ancient Babylonians, by Dr. A. H. Sayce, London, 1887. The Hibbert Lectures.

are to be given him."* Such a student also had to be not under forty years of age. Also "Do not discuss the Ma-a'seh Be'resheeth in the presence of two."†

The problems which the Qabbalah seeks to solve are those which present themselves to all thinkers. How are we to grasp and represent to ourselves, the transition and connection of the Infinite with the finite, the Invisible with the visible, and spirit with matter? How proceeded from Unity, the multiplicity. From a pure Intelligence a so different, varied and material many? In what position does the Creator stand to the created, so that we can rightly speak of the Providence and world-government by the Deity, notwithstanding the infinite abyss between them? How, correctly, can any name be imputed, any attribute ascribed to, or any imagination portray any idea of, the Deity? How is the idea, that man has been made in the similitude of Elohim (God), consistent with man's weaknesses and faults? How, with the conception of a perfect, just and merciful Deity, can be reconciled the existence of the imperfect and the evil? What was the Divine intention through the manifestation of the creation? It asks: Is the universe made of nothing, or out of an eternally original existing subtile matter, which may be thought of as the no-thing? Was the Deity before the universe, and eternal? Has the Deity, as a complete Being, through an inclination of Its Will, created the universe? If so, can the Deity be considered perfect, for has not something new arisen out of It? If the Will of the Deity did not emanate or create the universe, then we come to chance, which is contradictory to the wisdom shown in and throughout, all the works of nature? Is the Deity All-Knowing? Does the Holy One know before the birth of men who are to be virtuous, and who will sin? Why does the Deity permit sin and evil? If the Holy One is the All-good, why is there evil? Why the sufferings of the innocent and the escape of the guilty? Is the universe eternal? These are some of the questions which arise in the thoughts of man and which the Holy Scriptures do not answer.

*Talmud Babli, treatise *Ha'geegah*, 11b. Comp. Maimonide's Moreh Ne'bookheem, English Ed., i, 7, and note pp. 8, 68, 116, 124 *et seq.* See *ante*, p. 40, note.

† Talmud Babli, *Ha'geegah* 11b, Maimonide's Moreh, i, p. 68, and in other places.

The Hebrew Qabbalah bases itself upon the Hebrew Holy Writings as the foundation of all the revealed Will of God, as the source of all wisdom and knowledge, and asserts, that the Deity's Will is above all philosophy. The Qabbalah offers, to explain the Holy Writings so as to clear away all obscurity and difficulties in the way of understanding them, and endeavors to do this, by trying to ascertain the hidden and subtle meanings contained under the visible symbolic letter and word. In the Hebrew Practical Qabbalah, she endeavors to find this in the order of the chapters, the manifold Names and attributes of the Deity, in the composition of the Holy Writ, its letters, words, their numerical value, larger and smaller size, uneven forms, sound signs, signs of accentuation, etc. This brings into play, deep investigations in regard to the doctrines delivered therein as to the creation, of the relation of the unseen Deity to the visible manifestations of Its potency, as also to the invisible, and as to the government of the universe and this earth; also, regarding the revelations by the prophets and their workings upon man's thoughts, as a means for his sanctification and higher destiny. So in the reading of the Hebrew Holy Writings; in every letter, word, and form of the same, in every period and stroke thereof, in the practice of every observance, in every view therein of the Deity and of nature, etc.; the Hebrew Qabbalah teaches the whole is as a symbolic picture, and from this arises in the mind an infinitely extended view, producing and extending, a greater and more exalted ideality. She acknowledges the obligation of a moral law; the doctrine that through the sin of Adam, entire humanity descending from him, has degenerated; and that man must continually, through his individual work, and in himself, with Divine assistance; atone for his transgressions and sins, and endeavor to better himself. Must repent and humiliate himself by continual penances and chastisements; but she also teaches the dignity of human nature and admits Free Will. Out of the retirement of the Highest, in the manifested central point, the monad; she developes the Will, and from the Highest emanates the Holy Spirit and also Wisdom, or the Word; the first-born Son, the Heavenly Primordial Man, the Celestial Adam, the executor of the creation, the totality of the ten celestial spheres (orbits); in which, the Highest is immanent, yet as to which, the Highest is also transcendental. The whole of the created from its very beginning, is formed by the Qabbalistic philosophy; into one Great Ideal Man, a Makrokosmos, a Great World, of which the terrestrial Adam was a copy; and who, with his descendants, are as a Mikrokosmos or Little World. Man she teaches, is in continual danger from unclean spirits which surround him, and who are ever seeking to seduce him to sin and fasten themselves to his soul; but by a perpetual struggle and conflict, he can, with the Deity's assistance, banish them or render them harmless; opposing them through an incessant remembrance of the behests of the Holy One; and she asserts, that by God's assistance, the regenerated man will appear before the Deity at last, clean and spotless.

Among the cardinal doctrines of this theosophy are, those intended to solve the grand problems, relating to: 1. The Nature of the Supreme Being, as the unity or trinity. 2. The Cosmogony of the universe and its connection with the Deity. 3. The creation of angels and man. 4. The destiny of man and the universe. 5. The investigation of the meaning and import of the Revealed. 6. The unity of the Holy One. (Ex. xx, 3; Deut. iv, 35, 39; vi, 4; xxxii, 39.) 7. The incorporeality of the Deity. (Ex. xx, 4; Deut. iv, 15; Ps. xiv, 18.) 8. The eternity of God. (Ex. iii, 14; Deut. xxxii, 40; Is. xli, 4; xliii, 10, 11; xliv, 6; xlviii, 12.) 9. The immutability of the Highest. (Mal. iii, 6.) 10. The perfection of the Deity. (Deut. xxxii, 4; 2 Sam. xxii, 31; Job xxxvii; xxxviii; Ps. xviii, 31.) 11. The infinite goodness of the Holy One. (Ex. xxxiv, 6; Ps. xxv, 10; xxxiii, 5; c, 5; cxlv, 9.) 12. The creation of the universe and this earth, in time, according to God's free will. (Gen. i, 1.) 13. God's moral government of the universe, special providence, and creation of man in God's similitude (Gen. i, 27), and the doctrine of Rewards and Punishments; as set forth in all parts of the Holy Writings. 14. The emanation and nature of the soul. 15. The nature of angels, demons and the elementary spirits. 16. The transcendental meaning and symbolism of numbers, colours, letters, etc. 17. The balancing or equilibrium of the oppositions, etc., etc.

The theories of the Qabbalah usually proceed from the lowest to the highest and it reasons largely by analogy. Its fundamental principle is, to go from the visible to the invisible. Its maxim is:—"If thou wilt know the invisible, have an open eye for the visible," or in the words of

Mena'hem Reccanati, in his *Taamey ham-Mitzvoth, i. e.*, Meaning of the Commandments *ad init.*, "Know that we have to divide, between those that are hidden from us, and those things that are manifest to us." In the words of the same writer:—"The perfection of the work points to the perfection of the master." (*Ibid.*) All things of which we have knowledge appear to make a gradual transition from the lower to the higher, and *vice versa*. The idea is set forth in the Hebrew Holy Writings, and in Exodus, (xxxiii, 18 to end.) Moses said to the Deity:—"Let me see, I beseech thee, thy Glory." To which the Deity is said to have replied:—'I will make all My Goodness pass before thy face, and I will proclaim My Name, YHVH, before thee; and I will be gracious to whom I will be gracious, and I will show mercy on whom I will show mercy.' But also, said:—"'Thou canst not see My face; for no man can see me, and live.' And YHVH said: 'Behold, there is a place by Me, and thou shalt stand upon a rock. And it shall come to pass, while My Glory passeth by, that I will put thee in a cleft of the rock and I will cover thee with My hand while I pass by. And then I will take away Mine hand, and thou shalt see My *a'hoor, i. e.*, My back; but My face shall not be seen.'" That is, I will show you "My back," *i. e.*, My visible universe, My lower manifestations, but as a man still in the flesh, thou canst not see My invisible nature. So proceeds the Qabbalah.

The Qabbalists divide their system into two main divisions, included in the Work of the Creation and that of the Chariot Throne. The first is the Theoretic (*Iy-yooneth*); the second, the Practical (*Ma'aseth*). The first named may also be divided into three branches. I. Symbolical. II. Dogmatic or Positive. III. Speculative or Metaphysical. The first has a peculiar and very ancient system of exegesis coming under the heads of Temoorah, Gematria, Notarikon, Atbash, Albam, etc., which in this writing we have not space to explain. The second comprises all those beliefs and mystic dogmas engrafted on Judaism during and after its connection with Babylonia, Chaldea, Assyria, India and Persia. It was adopted in substance by the Pharisees, Essenes, Nazarites, etc., and existed probably before the formulations of the Speculative. It treats of angels and demons and their hierarchies and divisions, of the departments in Paradise and Hell, the transmigration of souls, etc. Many of its ideas have come from Aryan and Chaldean sources. Exodus (xxiv, 10) gives a partial description of, and the visions of Isaiah, Daniel and Ezekiel, further portray, the Deity as seated on a throne surrounded by angelic creatures and winged animals; and those given by the latter, have a close analogy with those shown in the art of Mesopotamia, Persia and India. Ezekiel's vision; which is also further carried out in the Apocalypse, and of which traces may be found in the vii chapter of Daniel and earlier in Isaiah; is more especially called by the Qabbalists the Merkabah or vision of the Chariot-Throne, and is considered by them, as a representation of the Court of the Deity, in which, God is surrounded by the angelic ministering hosts. The statements in the cited Hebrew Bible authorities, are at the foundation of the religious metaphysics of the Ma-a'seh Merkabah.

The ancient followers of the Ma-a'seh Merkabah, may have been the Rekhabites, Rekhab means a chariot, and this Israëlitish sect was held in high estimation by YHVH. (See Jerem. xxxv; II Kings, x, 15, 23; I Chron. ii, 55; II Sam. iv, 2; v, 6; Neh. iii, 14.) They were of the family of the father of Moses, and adopted the latter's religion.* There were undoubtedly certain saintly sects at a very early period among the Hebrews, at the time of if not before Moses, and later they came more especially into notice in the times of Judas Maccabæus. They were asserted to have power to perform miracles, exorcise evil spirits, etc., and it was through these most likely, that the fragments of the Sod and the Secret Learning have, as Qabbalah, come to our day. (Comp. Kitto's Bib. Cyclop. i, p. 475 *et seq.*)

In archaic Chaldea we find the protecting genii, which were those apparently in the mind of Isaiah, and the same symbolical animals support the Merkabah or Chariot-Throne of YHVH in Ezekiel: we also find a somewhat similar statement in Daniel vii. Among the Chaldeans, were the *Kirub* (Cherub?), the *Sed* or *Alaph*, which was sacred to Nebo, a bull with a man's face; *Nergal* or *Lamas*, a lion with a man's face; *Ustur*, after the human likeness, and the *Nattig*, with the head of an eagle. Above these were the heavenly angels, the *Igigi*, and the earthly good

* Judges i, 16; Exod. xviii, 9 *et seq.*; Numb. x, 29–32; Judges iv, 11, 17; *Ibid.* i, 16; I Sam. xv, 6. Comp. The Angel Messiah, by Ernest de Bunsen, London, 1880, pp. 11, 12, 86–87, 300–3; also Smith's Dict. of the Bible, Title, Rechabites.

spirits, the *Anúnaki*. The Hebrews were frequently in captivity in Chaldea. Among these were those *circa* 732, 599, 588 B. C. Returns were made in 536 and 458 B. C. The Assyrian, the language of Babylonia, is more closely related to the Hebrew than to any other Semitic Tongue. The Jews derived much of their knowledge from the libraries, learned men, and literature of ancient Chaldea; and they pointed to the valley of the Euphrates as the primæval cradle of their race and of humanity. Like the Phœnicians, they held, that their ancestors came from the great alluvial plain of Babylonia. (Hibbert Lectures 1887, 40 *sq.*) There were two periods when the Jews came under the influence of the Akkadian and Chaldean thought; one before the conquests and the other, during and after. (See also the erudite essay on the Cherubim, in Kitto's Cyclop. of Biblical Lit., Ed. 1876, i, p. 484 *sq.*)

In the Zodiacal signs, we have Taurus, the Bull; Leo, the Lion; Scorpio which as a good emblem was symbolized by the Eagle, and as an evil emblem, by the Scorpion or by the Goat, or as a winged snake partaking of the nature of each. There is also portrayed Aquarius, the water-man. In the Qabbalah we have the four worlds of Ezekiel's vision; A'tzeel-ah, the Deific form, the abode of Adam Qadmon, the World Spirit; B'ree-ah, the Throne, the abode of the great angel Metatron; Ye'tzeer-ah, the Firmament, the abode of the Spiritual Hosts; A'seey-ah, the place of the Ker-u'beem and the abode of the spirits united with the corporeity.

Figure 22.

The accompanying engraving is from Niklas Müller's work on the

Old Hindus, cited *ante*, p. 45, note; and represents Yotma or Yotna nephew of Maya, Illusion, father of Prakita (feminine) the Passive Principle, Primary Creation or Nature. This figure typifies, the metaphysical ideas of the Veda's and the philosophic systems of the Hindus. It portrays a lion's head with the horns of a bull, as the head of the Serpent Ananda. In its mouth is Ananda's tail. The latter is represented as the Time-serpent who is eagle-winged. From the open mouth proceeds *vach*, the cow, image of Prakita the great motherly preserver through the Deity, she is also speech and the mother of the Vedas. Bees, the carriers of the honey of the goodness of the Deity, rapidly detach themselves from the breast of the cow. Here we also have, as in the symbols mentioned *ante*, p. 45, note; the lion, for fire; the bull, for water; and the eagle, for air; united as the usual Oriental symbol of the divine potentiality. To be noted is the emanation of the sweetness from the mouth of the lion or strength, which calls to mind Samson's riddle, and also causes us to think of the mystic bees and honey of the ancients; of their Melissa's, Aristæus's, etc. Bees appear to have been considered by the Greeks as emblems of purity, and as the symbol of nymphs, who are sometimes called Mellissæ, as were also priestesses in general, especially those of Demeter, Persephone and she of the Delphic Apollo.

We may gather from Josephus, that four of the mystical colours of the Jewish Church, were typical of the four elements. These colors were Blue, Purple, Scarlet and White, the fifth mystical color Gold, he says; was typical of "the splendor by which all things are enlightened." Jerome (*Epistola ad Fabiolam*, written at Bethlehem 396 or 397 A. D.), also speaks of this ancient Jewish Tradition. They can be arranged, we think, according to the following table:

1. Gold,   Splendor,   Sun,   The Man.
2. Blue,   Æther,   Air,   The Eagle.
3. Purple,   The Great Crystalline Sea
                 surrounding the Earth. Humidity,   The Bull.
4. Scarlet,   The Hidden Fire, Warmth,   The Lion.
5. White (Linen), The Earth,   Atomic Matter,   The Goat.

Comp. *ante*, p. 45, note. The Bull is a symbol of the Sephirah 'Hesed, *i. e.*, Grace or Mercy; the spiritual Water or humidity. Hence Baptism.

The Lion symbol of force, energy, justice, wrath, fire; is a symbol of the Sephirah G'bur-ah, the spiritual fire. Hence lights, coals of fire and incense. The Eagle is a symbol of the Sephirah Tiph'e-reth, the spiritual Æther or Air. Hence the use of the voice and sound in hymns and prayer. The Angelic Man is a symbol of the Sephirah Malkhuth, the Kingdom, Government and Harmony; the spiritual Earth. Hence the products of the earth, the wine and bread, of both the Israëlites and Christians.

The four animals are also in the Apocalypse, c. iv, and the five colors appear to be referred to therein. "God doeth all things in *number*, and *measure* and *weight:*" says the Book of Wisdom, xi, 20. (Comp. II Chron. iii, 10–14, and Josephus, Whiston's Edition, v, p. 387.) "The Religion of Jesus is the flower, of which the Jewish Church is the bud, and the Patriarchal the stem."* With the first Christians the celebration of the Mysteries of the Faith was accompanied by the burning of 7 lights, (symbols of the Sephiroth?) with incense, the Trisagion, and the reading of the book of the Gospels; upon which was wrought, both on covers and pages, the winged man, lion, bull and eagle. The animals of the Merkabah of Ezekiel.

The third, the Speculative or Metaphysical Qabbalah is the one to which we will now give attention. It is a system of oriental philosophy explaining the connection between the Deity and the created, and tending to harmonize monotheism and the Hebrew account of the creation of all things, spiritual or material; with the fundamental principle of ancient philosophy *ex nihilo nihil fit, i. e.*, From nothing, nothing can come. It explains the existence of moral and physical evil by ascribing it to the grossness of matter, asserting that in the assertion of only one absolutely perfect principle the existence of evil would be incomprehensible. The doctrine of emanation, which existed in the archaic Aryan religious philosophy, was based upon the idea that all the created were effluxes from the Divine Light, and that the further away they were from the source, the nearer they approached the evil, matter and darkness, in that the latter two were the abode of evil. This is a doctrine not only of the Persians, the Hindus, the Qabbalah, and the School of Alexandria, but of Ibn Gebirol. Commencing with the indivisible, perfect, infinite unity, the

* Hutching's Lect. On the Person and Work of the Holy Ghost, p. 53.

Absolute Unknown Cause of All Causes, the Ain Soph, the Eternal All above All, a manifestation thereof comes freely through Its Will, which thus becomes the First Cause, the Cause of Causes. In this the Unknown Absolute, above all number, manifested Itself through an emanation in which it was immanent yet as to which it was transcendental. It first withdrew Itself into Itself, to form an infinite Space, the Abyss; which It then filled with a modified and gradually diminishing Light or Vitalization, first appearing in the Abyss, as the centre of a mathematical point which gradually spread Its Life-giving energy or force throughout all Space. This concentration or contraction and its expansion, being the centripetal and centrifugal energies of creation and existence, the Qabbalists call *Tzimtzum*. The Will of Ain Soph then manifests Itself through the Ideal Perfect Model or Vitalizing Form, first principle and perfect prototype in idea, of all the to be created, whether spiritual or material. This is the Mikrokosm to the Ain Soph, the Makrokosm as to all the created. It is called the Son of Elohim, *i. e.*, God, and the Adam Illa-ah or Adam Qadmon, the Man of the East or Heavenly Adam. A similar figure is in Daniel (vii, 13, 14), but there it is a totality of "the people of the saints of the Most High."* Such a figure is also in the first chapter of Genesis and is in Ezekiel, and most likely is referred to in the vision in Daniel, of the Great Man (Dan. ii, 31 *et seq.*) made of metals, etc., symbolical of the Four worlds of the Qabbalists, of which more hereafter. The Adam Qadmon or Heavenly Adam is composed of a decade of potentialities or energies, termed the Ten Sephiroth, always considered as together they are a unit and the entire content of the Adam Qadmon, whose head is in the highest created heaven and whose feet rest on the lowest created matter, and who is the content of the Ineffable Name YHVH. From these came most likely the Intermediaries and Powers of Philo which are like the Sephiroth,† and the Æons of the Gnostics.‡ The earthly man, a spirit covered with matter, lives in the lowest

---

* *Ibid.* 27. Comp. The Jewish and the Christian Messiah, etc., by Vincent H. Stanton, Edinburgh, 1885, pp. 109, etc., 240.

† See Philo iii, 184, etc.

‡ Comp. on this the works of Matter, King, Mansel, Burton, etc., on the Gnostics, also Beausobre on the Manicheans and the writings of Rev. John Francis Buddeus.

of the Four worlds, and is the *Olam Qatan* or Mikrokosm, for whatever the Heavenly Adam contains, is also in the earthly man, but in an imperfect degree. The earthly man has the Nephesh, the living soul or vital principle, the *animo;* also the Rua'h, his conscience, the power of judgment or mind, the *spiritus;* and an intellectual spirit, the Neshamah or *animus*. The last is considered a part of the Deity and as pre-existent and immortal. According to the Qabbalah, man is also composed of a good and an evil principle, and a harmony, his liberty or Free Will, and it depends on the latter, as to which shall be his master. After death comes judgment and retribution on his spirit according to man's works, the Neshamah being immortal.

The Roman Catholic Church claims to be the possessor of a Secret Tradition or Qabbalah, which is asserted as coming down orally through the Church, from Christ and the Apostles; and from this it formulates many of the dogmas and mysteries of its faith. The science of the Law as administered in our Courts of Justice is divided into two branches; the Written and the Oral. The first is termed Statute Law, the latter, the Common Law. The Common Law is deposited in the breasts of the Judges and by a legal fiction, is assumed to be of great antiquity, and is delivered orally, or, only for convenience, is put in writing in the opinions; it also is based on precedent traditions presumably oral, which are however generally to be found in the written or printed books of Law Reports: when a new subject arises, *e. g.*, telephones, telegraphs, steam engines, etc., which are not provided for in the written Statutes or precedents in the Reports: the Judges apply the Oral Law to them out of their skilled legal reason, based on an approach to precedents. This is a species of Qabbalah. The Common Law, as administered to-day, is paralleled in Judaism, by the Talmudic Law in contrast to the written Pentateuch usually termed, the Thorah or Law.

We call the attention of the reader in this place to a coincidence of agreement in the Zoharic writings, with the most ancient terra cotta tablets of Babylonia. In the Siphrah D'Tnioothah, (c. i, § 16 *sq.*) referring to the creation and primeval chaos, we read:

"*B'raisheeth barah elohim ath hashshama'yem v'ath haa'retz, i. e.,* 'In the beginning the God(s) created the heavens and the earth'; (the meaning of which is;) the six (Sephiroth of Construction,) over which *B'raisheeth* stands, all belong Below. It created six, (and) on these stand (exist) all Things. And those depend upon the seven forms of the Cranium up to the Dignity of all Dignities. And the second "Earth" does not come into calculation, therefore it has been said: 'And from it, (that Earth) which underwent the curse; came it forth,' as is written (Gen. v, 29): 'From the Earth which YHVH cursed.' 'It (the Earth) was without form and void; and darkness was over the face of the Abyss, and the spirit of elohim (or, spirit of the God(s)) was breathing, (*me'-racha'pheth, i. e.*, hovering, brooding over, moving. Comp. Deut. xxxii, 2) over the waters.' Thirteen depend on thirteen (forms) of the most worthy Dignity. Six thousand years hang (are referred to) in the first six words. The seventh (thousand, the millennium,) above it (the cursed Earth), is that which is strong by Itself. And it was rendered entirely desolate during twelve hours (one entire day, one whole period of various periods, of time :) as is written ; 'It was without form and void, etc.' In the Thirteenth, It (the Deity) shall restore them (as from the 'beginning';) through 'Mercy' (or, Grace), and everything shall be renewed as before ; and all those six shall continue, because it is written : *barah, i. e., created*, and then it is written: *hay'ethah, i. e., it was*, for truly, 'It was'; at the end of the 'shapelessness and void and darkness.' And YHVH alone will be exalted in that day.*

"The engravings of the engravings,† under the form of a long serpent, extended hither and thither, the tail (of the serpent) is in its head, the head, backwards of the shoulders, it twists, it is wrathful (or, trespassing) and it is angry (mutters, hisses). It watches and hides itself. Once, in a thousand short days, (? years or periods of time) ; it is manifested. It has a protuberance on its scales. A sapphire in * * * * * it has. Its head (however) is broken in the waters of the Great Sea, as it is writ-

---

* For terseness and want of space we are obliged to leave out our many explanations and long notes to these passages, so that as they appear in print, they are somewhat unintelligible.

† The engraved or excavated, which always leaves a hollow place, are the inferior or plastic, in contradistinction to the superior things which fill the emptiness of the excavated; with the form.

ten: 'Thou hast broken into pieces the *heads* of the *Dragons* in the Waters.' (Ps. lxxiv, 13.) There were two (male and female, positive and negative, whence the text of the Psalm says "Dragons"). They were reduced to one, for the word *thanneenim* (in the Psalm) is defectively written: (*nim* sing., not *neem* plural). It is also said (in the Psalm) *heads*, as it is written; (Ezekiel i, 22): ' And a similitude over *the heads* of the *animal*, the firmament.'" (Where "animal" is in the singular, and *the heads*, in the plural. The first to denote the *race* of the angels; the latter, to signify the *species or numerous individuals*.) Another reading is: "He made sketches and outlines of His creation in the shape of a serpent, long and darting in all directions; and the tail was in its head, and the head was seizing its hinder parts. It is twined backwards, and is full of fury and anger. Once in a thousand years, a revolution in its joints takes place, a violent commotion by the exertion of its fins, and its head is broken in the waters of the ocean. As it is said: (Ps. lxxiv, 13) 'Thou breakest *the heads* of the *dragons* in the waters.' There were two dragons (serpents,) *thanneenim* תנינם, spelled in full with two ׳׳ *yo-den*, they were turned into one, in *Ibid*. 14, where there is spoken of: ' the *heads* of *Leviathan, i.e.*, one.'" "And elohim said: *Ye'hee ôr i.e.,* Be Light! and Light was. This is the meaning of that which is written: ' For *Hoo* (or, *Hu*), *i.e.*, *He,* said, and *vaÿ-ye-hee, i.e., it was.'* (Ps. xxxiii, 9.) *He* (*Hoo* or *Hu*) is by himself (alone)." The Siphrah D'Tznioothah (c. v, § 33 *sq.*) also says: "The Serpent which runs with 370 leaps. It ' leaps over mountains and hastily runs up over hills' as it is written. (Song of Songs, ii, 8.) The serpent holds its tail in its mouth with its teeth. It is perforated on both sides. When the Perfect One (or, the Arch-Angel Metatron?) is raised up, the serpent is changed into three spirits, etc."

These passages are important in the Qabbalistic hieroglyphics, we have (Zohar ii, 34*b*) also: " R. Shim-on (b. Yo'haï) said: The (account of the) work of the beginning, the companions study and understand it; but the little ones (the perfect initiates) are those who understand the allusion to the work of the beginning, by the *mystery of the serpent of the Great Sea.*" (*i. e., Thanneen, Leviathan.*) As to this Leviathan as the symbol of the visible creation, comp. Zohar i, 35*b*, Talmud, treatise, *Bava Bathra*. In India, Vishnu as Krishna, steps upon and crushes the head of the *Kolinagha*, *i. e.*, the serpent of the *Kali* age, and thus illustrate the victory of Eternity over perishable Time. Perhaps Gen. iii, 15, has some reference to this. This reference to the "serpent of the Great Sea" is also explained by the ancient cuneiform tablets. Ea or Oannes, was the ancient Akkadian god of the abyss or deep; the Great Crystalline Sea of chaos, of *Bohu*, *i. e.*, emptiness or primeval Space. He was also the deity of Wisdom, the culture god of primitive Babylonia. His symbols were the fish, the serpent of the Great Sea, the antelope and the gazelle. This gives us some insight into the passage quoted, and also into Gen. iii, 1, which gives to the serpent, the possession of *greater subtility* than any wild beast created by YHVH Elohim. (See especially in this connection: The Hibbert Lectures, 1887, by Dr. A. H. Sayce, London, 1887, pp. 279–283; 116–118; 133–139; 262; 200; 374 *sq.*; 391 *sq.*) The Akkadians and Chaldeans, believed the world to be encircled, by this great serpent of the sapphire crystalline heaven sea, with seven heads, perhaps the seven stars of the Great Bear, perhaps the seven planets. (*Ibid.*, pp. 282–3.) It was the "bond" or "rope of the universe" which held together the heavens and the earth, the "golden cord" of Homer. (Iliad viii, 19 *sq.*) It was also called the bar or bolt holding heaven and earth, together. (Comp. *ante*, p. 115). Note in this connection, the Great Azure Dragon of the Chinese.

Another similarity to statements in the same Zoharic book is the sacred tree of the Akkadians and Chaldeans, which suggests to our thoughts, the Tree of the Sephiroth; which was frequently portrayed by the Qabbalists, as an ordinarily formed tree. It also suggests the Ygg-drasil of Norse mythology, the world-tree, whose roots were in the death-world and whose branches rise into Asgard, the heaven of the gods. With the Babylonians, the sacred-tree was the "tree of life," the world-tree; the roots were in the abyssmal deep, its seat was the earth, which stood midway between the deep and Zikum, *i. e.*, the primordial heavens above. Zikum rested upon its overspreading branches. Within it was the holy house of Davkina, *i. e.*, the Great Mother, and of Tammuz, the Sun-god, her son. The fragment of a very old bilingual hymn reads:—

1. "(In) Eridu (the garden of Eden?) a stalk grew over-shadowing; in a holy place did it become green;

2. its root was of white crystal which stretched towards the deep;
3. before Ea (the deity of Wisdom) was its course in Eridu, teeming with fertility;
4. its seat was the (central) place of the earth;
5. its foliage (?) was the couch of Zikum (the primeval) mother.
6. Into the heart of its holy house which spread its shade like a forest, hath no man entered.
7. (There is the home) of the mighty mother who passes across the sky.
8. In the midst of it was Tammuz, *i. e.*, the Sun-god.
10. (There is the shrine?) of the two."

(Hibbert Lectures, 1887; by Dr. A. H. Sayce, p. 238, etc.) The Siphrah D'Tznioothah (c. v, § 31 *sq.*) also says: "The Tree which has been rendered mild, remains in the interior. In its branches dwell birds, *i. e.*, angels, and therein they make their nests. Under it, animals having power (men?) seek shelter. This is the tree which has *two* narrow paths for going upon. And it has *seven* columns around it, and *four* splendors are rolled (revolve) around it on the *four* sides."

Important explanations of the curious passage, (Gen. xxxvi, 31–39:) as to the seven Kings of Edom; to which is attached, as early as Genesis, the statement of kings having reigned over the children of Israel; are in both the Zoharic writings and the cuneiform. (Comp. The Hibbert Lect., 1887, by Dr. A. H. Sayce, pp. 53 *sq.*, 181 *sq.*, 373 *sq.*, 54 *sq.*, 209, 203 *sq.*: with the Siphrah D'Tznioothah and the Idroth.)

Figure 23.

Figure 24.

* *Kether ke'hunnath malkhuth*, *i. e.*, Crown of Priesthood and Royalty.

† *Me'romam*, *i. e.*, Exalted.

Figure 25.

XII.

FURTHER PARALLELS BETWEEN THE CUNEIFORM AND THE QABBALAH. ACCOUNT OF THE AKKADIAN AND SEMITIC BABYLONIAN RELIGION AND TEMPLES AND THOSE OF THE ISRAËLITES. OF THE AKKADIAN AND BABYLONIAN COSMOGONY. OF THE DEMIURGE. THE DUST BODY OF MAN. OF LILLITH. THE ANCIENT ZODIAC.

WE gather from the various writings upon the religions of the ancient peoples of Mesopotamia, especially from the Hibbert Lectures for 1887, by Dr. A. H. Sayce the well-known reader of the cuneiform, the following facts. The priests of ancient Babylonia delivered the philosophy of their religion esoterically. (Hibbert Lect., pp. 4, 16, 141, 142.) The true pronunciation of the Divine Names was kept carefully concealed from the uninitiated.* Names and their true pronunciation were considered of great value. (Hibbert Lect., pp. 113 note, 305-6, 385. See further as to the value of the Ineffable Names among these nations, also the Egyptians, Journ. of the Royal Society of Literature, 1865, p. 274 *sq.*) As in the Practical Qabbalah, numbers possessed great value with the ancient people of Babylonia.† The angels

---

* *Ibid.*, pp. 4, 141-2, 113, 302 *sq.*, 353-4, 405. Comp. Chaldean Magic, by F. Lenormant, Eng. Ed., pp. 19, 29, 41-44, 104-5, 108.

† Chaldean Magic, F. Lenormant, Eng. Ed., pp. 41-42, 25-6, 113, 117. The ancient civilization of Mesopotamia was likely I, Kushite; II, Turanian; III, Semitic. *Essai sur un monument mathématique chaldéen*, etc., by F. Lenormant. Paris, 1868, p. 160 *sq.* See also as to the wonderful discoveries at Tel-loh, the beautiful work: *Découvertes en*

were termed Igigi, *i. e.*, "spirits of heaven." This name was expressed ideographically by the determinative of divinity followed by "twice five" $= 10$. Jensen in *Zeitschrift für Assyriologie* I, 1, has endeavored to show the Anúnaki "spirits of earth" or gnomes, were denoted by the numeral 8, the Igigi by the numeral 9. He would connect them with the *rîbu* or "the great divine princes." It is said in an old hymn, that Ea, the demiurge, the reflection of the Upper Ea, Wisdom; gave the names to the angels. (Hibbert Lect., p. 141.) The number appropriate to each of the gods is on a tablet (K. 170) in the British Museum, viz: I. Assur "Kings of the gods" is without number. In Babylonia this deity was Ilu (El). II. Oannes (Ea or Hea) the wisdom deity was $60 = 1$. III. Bel $= 50$. IV. Bel Dagon $= 40$. V. Sin (moon-god) $= 30$. VI. Samas (sun-god) $= 20$. VII. Bin or Ao $= 6$. VIII. Merodach (effaced). IX. Istar (deity of Venus) $= 15$. X. Samdan $= 50$. XI. Nergal $= 12$. XII. Nebo (Wisdom) $= 10$. (*Essai sur un document mathématique chaldéen et a cette occasion sur le systêm des poids et mesures de Babylone*, by François Lenormant, etc., Paris, 1868, pp. 6, 118, notes p. 2 *sq.*, 115. As to Ilu, Text, p. 10, and note 16, notes pp. 90 *sq.*, 98–99. Trans. Soc. Biblical Archæol. 1880–82, p. 370 *sq.*) The beginnings of Semitic Chaldean culture arose with prior Turanian, probably black skinned, races; termed by Assyriologists for convenience, Akkadian and Sumerian. Monuments, terra-cotta tablets and engraved signets of these peoples, containing symbols and statements, some said to be from before 4000

Chaldée, par Ernest de Sarzec, etc. *Ouvrage accompagné de planches*, etc., 2 Vol. Paris, 1884 *sq. Glyptique Orientale, par* J. Menant, Paris, 1883, Vol. i, 211 *sq. La Stèle des Vautours, étude d'archéologie chaldéenne*, by Léon Heuzey, Paris, 1884. *Les rois de Tello et la période archaïque de l'art chaldéen*, Paris, 1882. *Un nouveau roi de Tello*, Paris, 1884. *Les fouilles de Chaldée*, etc., Paris, 1882. All by M. Heuzey, to be found in *Revue Archéologique*, Paris, for 1882, p. 271 *sq.*, 1884, p. 109 *sq.*, 1881, p. 257 *sq.* The Kushite population inhabited the lowlands and alluvial plains in the Southern part. They came from Bactriana, the country of Kush. Ancient Hist. of the East, by F. Lenormant, etc., 1871, Vol. i, p. 57 *sq.* They have been termed Sumerians. The Akkadians occupied the Northern and mountainous part. We can only rank them among the Turanian *races*. The Semites subsequently overrun the whole country, which they appear to have obtained by conquest. These different people effected different phases in the religion of the entire region.

B. C., have reached our day. The earliest yet found were excavated at Tel-loh in 1876 to 1881, by M. de Sarzec, and are in the Louvre at Paris. At Tel-loh has been found the cubit of 20.63 which is that of the Egyptian pyramid builders of the IV and following two dynasties.* The writing of the early Turanian inhabitants of Tel-loh the ancient Zirgula, as found by M. Sarzec, had scarcely emerged from the ideographic into the cuneiform and has a vertical direction like the Chinese method. There is not anything to show that the Semite had come into the land. Magnificent figures have been found at Tel-loh, sculptured in green diorite, one of the hardest stones, which they brought from the quarries of Sinai. Upon these are most beautifully engraved inscriptions. Some of the figures are in a seated position in the archaic Egyptian style. They have the neck, right shoulder, side and arm bare, like the archaic representations of Buddha, *i.e.*, the enlightened or wise (one). (Compare the Hindu Pantheon by Edward Moor, London, 1810, Pl. 70.) Buddha is frequently represented in these with wooly hair and thick Ethiopian lips (*ibid.*, pp. 231-2, 243, 249-255), and is so sculptured in the archaic cave temples of Elephanta, Ellora, etc.; (*ibid.*, pp. 242-246,) supporting our view that the early people of Southern Mesopotamia were the race now called Dravidian in India; the race which built the great Buddhist topes of Sanchi, Amravati, etc.; millenniums before the appearance of Sakhya Mûni. One of the most wonderful ancient statues now in existence, is that of King Kheprên of the IV Egyptian dynasty, who built the second great pyramid of Gizeh: it is now in the Museum of Bulâq. This statue is carved out of green diorite and represents the monarch seated in almost the same position as those found at Tel-loh. This shows that the Egyptians worked the quarries of diorite at Sinai, and sculptured in it, as early as 4000 B. C. It is to be noted that the bronzes found at Tel-loh do not contain tin, which is to be found in those of the Chaldeans. The early Chaldeans carried on commerce with many places, notably with India. Dr. Sayce shows that the name of Mosheh (Moses) has a connection with the name of the Babylonian sun-god, as the "hero" or "leader." (Comp. that said by us *ante*, p. 93.) The name was especially, that of the Assyrian

* The Assyro-Babylonian cubit was 21.6. Hibbert Lect., p. 33 *sq.*, p. 137.

god Adar, the deity of the scorching sun of mid-day (Hibbert Lect., p. 46 *sq.*). The Akkadians, as we have stated as to other ancient peoples, considered the heaven or sky as the counterpart of the land upon which they lived. Their first astronomical observations were about the time that the vernal equinox first came into the Zodiacal sign of Taurus, the Bull. This would be *circa* 4312 B. C. The eagle symbolized the meridian sun. The orders of priests were divided into high priests, those attached or bound to certain deities like the Hebrew Levites; anointers or cleaners; the *kali* "illustrious" or "elders;" the soothsayers, and the *makhkhu* or "great one," in which Prof. Delitzsch sees the Rab-*mag* of the Old Testament. The temples were provided with "abysses" or "deeps," large basins filled with water, like "the sea" made by Jedidiah or Solomon, for his great temple at Jerusalem. The temples had a great court and an inner court, which was walled as a square; in the latter was built the *ziggurrat* or high sacred tower.* The temples were mostly constructed with the points of the angles facing the four points of the compass, but the Great Temple of Bel-Merodach at Babylon, differed from the others, its sides facing the four cardinal points. In the extreme end of the temple was the "holy of holies," concealed by a veil or curtain from the eyes of the profane; here at the beginning of the year, "the divine King of heaven and earth, the lord of the heavens, seats himself, etc."; here Herodotus says, was the golden image of the god, with a golden table in front, like the Hebrew table for the shew bread, and upon this food appears to have been placed. There also appears to have been in some of the temples, a little coffer or ark with two engraved stone tablets in it. The Akkadians and Chaldeans kept a Sabbath day of rest every seven days, they also had thanksgiving days and days for humiliation and prayer. There were sacrifices of vegetables and animals, of meal and wine, there were even vicarious sacrifices of human beings for sin, by the Akkadians (pp. 78, 365-6). The number seven was especially sacred (p. 82). There were sacred trees with seven branches and some of ten, like the decadic tree of the Sephiroth.† They had clean and unclean animals

* As to these, see Proc. Soc. Bib. Archæol., Feb'y 2, 1886, Vol. viii, p. 83.

† The Cuneiform Inscrip. and the Old Testament, by Dr. Eberhard Schrader, London, 1885, p. 18 *sq.* See engraving at the end of this chapter.

and pigs and reptiles were unclean. In the temple of Baal, the Babylonians had two altars, Solomon also had two in his temple, one for larger the other for smaller offerings. (I Kings, viii, 64.) The great temple of Babylon had a great tower in eight stages, called ; "the house of the seven spheres of heaven and earth," and also; "the house of the foundation stone of heaven and earth." The temple of Solomon also appears to have had such a tower. Arias Montanus, writing before A. D. 1593, portrays such a tower as part of Solomon's temple.*

The great temple of Babylon existed from, probably long before, 2250 B. C.† Its "holy of holies" was within the shrine of Nebo, the prophet god of wisdom. The ancient Babylonians had an intercessor between men and the gods, this was the benevolent deity called, originally by the Akkadians, Silik-mulu-dug or Silik-mulu-khi, the "God amongst the gods," the one who watches over mankind.

> "The merciful one amongst the gods
> Generator who bringest back the dead
> to life,
> Silik-mulu-khi, king of heaven and earth." ‡

Subsequently known in Assyria as Marduk, and in Babylonia as the god Merodach "the merciful." He was the only son and interpreter of the will of Ea (Hea), the Akkadian great deity of wisdom. "Thou art Merodach, the merciful lord who loves to raise the dead to life," says an old hymn on one of the tablets: the same idea is applied to Samas, the sun-god. § Nebo, in the Semitic Babylonian *Nabiu* or *Nabû*, was the "proclaimer" or "prophet," he made known the

---

* *Antiquitatum Judaicarum*, etc., by *Benedicto Aria Montano, Hispalensi, Lugduni Batavorum*, 1593, p. 93 and plate P, see also Kitto's Cycl. of Bibl. Liter., Ed. 1876, iii, p. 975. For depicted restorations of the ancient Temples and Palaces of Mesopotamia, see the magnificent folios of M. Victor Place and Sir Austen Henry Layard. The five great folios of Paolo Emilio Botta should also be consulted.

† For a description of it and its tower, by George Smith, see Hibbert Lect., 1887, p. 437 *sq*. Prof. Rawlinson has written a description of the Tower of Borsippa.

‡ Chaldean Magic, by F. Lenormant, p. 190 *sq*., and other places.

§ Hibbert Lect., pp. 98–99, 100–1, 106–7. For the idea of the immortality of the soul among the archaic Turanian and Semitic peoples, see: *Revue Archéologique*, Paris, 1882, p. 45 *sq*.

desire of Merodach. Nebo was the deity of literature and science, his especial day was our Wednesday, and he was the god of the planet Mercury, the Wisdom-planet.* He was probably originally the deity of the entire universe, a creator-god. (*Ibid.*, pp. 116–119 note, 120, 209 notes.) The ancient divine powers of Babylonia were at the same time beneficent and malevolent. Good and evil, as in the Qabbalah, were not in absolute opposition, the latter was the complement and minister of the good (*Ibid.*, p. 205–6), and where the Semitic faith existed in all its purity, Satan was the accuser or adversary but yet an angel of the Deity, who was creator of both the good and evil, light and darkness.† Dr. Sayce also gives an account of the winged bulls, lions, eagle-headed cherubs, scorpion men, etc., ‡ and thinks they were totem survivals from an immense antiquity.§ The Akkadians considered the heavens and earth as primordial powers or *Zi*, maintaining an eternal struggle with chaos. All things were made and their highest divinity was a creator; but with the Semite, the heavens and earth were carved out of a preexistent chaos, and were begotten. The Semitic Baal was a father. With the first, the *Zi* spirit of the earth and the *Zi* spirit of the heavens were the first creators, the first gods. The spirit of the moon for instance was a deity separated from the visible moon, it was identified with the creative energy of the moon which manifested itself in the motion of the moon and even the motion was spiritualized still higher. The creative deities together, represented the order and law of the universe embodied in *sabba* fate, to which all submit. This may have been represented by Ilu or El the supreme deity.||

The Chaldean historian Bêrôssos, whom we only have through Greek

* See *ante*, p. 206. Hibbert Lect., 1887, pp. 113–115.

† *Ibid.*, pp. 346, 347. As to Satan and Ahriman (Angra-Mainyus of Ancient Persia) see Proc. Soc. Biblical Archæol., Vol. ix, p. 365 *sq.*)

‡ Hibbert Lect., pp. 279, 289–291.

§ *Ibid.*, pp. 278–9, 290–1, 393, 401.

|| The Cuneiform Inscrip. and the Old Testament, By Dr. Eberhard Schrader, I, p. 11 *sq.*, 23–5. Chaldean Magic, by F. Lenormant, Eng. Ed., pp. 113–114. *Recherches sur la Glyptique Orientale, par M. Joachim Menant, Paris, 1886, seconde partie, p. 17 sq.* Menant gives numerous representations of this deity. See also M. Félix Lajard's *Culte de Mithra.* Also *ante* p. 238.

sources, says: that he obtained his knowledge from a document said to have been written by the deity Ea or Wisdom; that there was a time when all was darkness and an abyss of waters, in this lived hideous strange beings, which were the product of an androgenous principle and which were androgenic. There were men with two heads, one that of a man, the other that of a woman. They were androgenic in their organs, etc. A woman named Omoroka, Chald. Thalatth (read, Thavatth) in Greek, Thalassa (the sea) but equivalent to the Moon; presided over them, etc. * This account of the ancient universe being peopled with strange creatures can be carried back to terra-cotta tablets of at least 600 B. C. (Hibbert Lect., p. 372) and such creatures are portrayed on the very ancient signets. (See the works of Lajard, Smith, Sayce, Menant, etc.)

In the Babylonian cosmogony as in the Hebrew, the watery abyss, termed by the former the Great Sea-serpent or dragon Tiamat, is the first source of all things. The latter is also named Tiavat, and is the Thavatth of Bêrôssos, and the *t'hom* or *tohoo* " deep," of Genesis. In Assyrian its contracted form is *tamtu*, *i. e.*, the deep sea. The word is Semitic but of Akkadian descent. The old Akkadian deity of Wisdom, Ea or Hea, was a sea or water-god who lived in the Great Crystalline Sea of which he was the lord, and who was called: "mighty bond of heaven and earth." The Great deep or abyss, with the Sumerians was the mother of Ea or wisdom, and of all the gods. This "deep" rolled not only around the world, but above the firmament of heaven, consequently the mother of Ea was not only known as Apzu, the deep, but also as Zikum or Zigarum, the upper heaven, which is described in one tablet, as: "the mother that has begotten heaven and earth." But it was not the existing heaven that is referred to; Zikum was the primordial prototypic abyss out of which both the heaven and earth were produced. Possibly an old myth may have related that she was torn asunder when the present world was made, the upper half of her becoming the sky, the lower half the earth. This at least is what we may gather from the story of Bêrôssos.† It is said that among the priest-kings of Tel-loh, from

---

* See Cory's Ancient Fragments, Ed. 1876, p. 4. Hibbert Lect. 1887, pp. 369–70. For an account and engravings of the ancient androgene of the Akkadians, Chaldeans and Babylonians, see Menant's *Glyptique Orientale* before cited, Vol. i, p. 111 *sq.*

† See Dr. Sayce, Hibbert Lect., p. 375 *sq.*

which place the earliest cuneiform tablets we now have come to us, she was honored as Bahu. The Hebrew Genesis says that before "Elohim carved out the heavens and the earth * * * * darkness was upon the *face of the deep*," also "the earth had been *Tohoo* (waste) and *Bohoo* (emptiness, void)." This was Bau or Bahu of the Babylonians, and the Baau of the Phœnician historian Sankhuniathon (Cory's Ancient Fragments, etc., London, 1876, p. 4). The Phœnician cosmology also began in an abyss of waters in which the germs of all Things were begotten and the ancient Hindu does the same. With the ancient inhabitants of Babylonia, Davkina, the earth, lay upon the watery abyss as the wife of Ea, the Wisdom or the Word.* In the Hebrew Genesis we have a reference to the watery abyss above the visible sky, to the "Waters above the firmament." The sky was thought of as a created thing which floated on the surface of the Great Ocean stream, as did the earth. The visible sky was but another form of Davkina, "the lady of heaven, whence the oracular voice (the thunder) is created;" she was "the queen of the oracular voice of the deep," who was in Assyria, symbolized by the falcon, perhaps the eagle, and from this may have been derived the symbolism of the eagle as the upper air. (Comp. *ante*, p. 229 *sq*.) Zi-kum was the primordial abyss "the spirit of the lower firmament," then we have the visible heaven and after this the earth. Zi-kum parallels likely, Bahu the Great Mother, the Void of the Old Testament. Tohu, or t'hom being chaos. It may perhaps be admissible to assert, Zi or Zi-kum was the spirit of the Deep, Tohu active energy, Bohu resisting energy, Khosee inertia or rest, the result of the last preceding two when combined.

In the later or Semitic period, a new idea appears, Merodach the sun-god of light, has a struggle with Tiamat considered as the evil dragon of darkness, which ends in the defeat of the latter; but with the early Akkadian philosophers of Eridu, there was not anything unholy in the watery abyss, the home and mother of Ea or Wisdom, the primal source of this deity's wisdom and of his goodness to mankind; for them from the Great Sea, Oannes or Ea brought knowledge and art to man. But in the Semitic account, the abyss is the chaotic opposition to the present order

---

*See Chaldean Magic, by F. Lenormant, pp. 114, 44, 104. Comp. Hibbert Lect.

of nature and is evil. One of the tablets graphically describes the fight between Bel and the Dragon.*

Of the Assyrian idea, we have a cosmological poem, but only the fragments, part of these say:

"(Bel) prepared the (seven) mansions of the great gods;
he fixed the stars, even the twin-stars to correspond to them;
he ordained the year, appointing the signs of the Zodiac over it; †
for each of the twelve months he fixed three stars,‡
from the day when the year issues forth to the close.
He founded the mansion of the god of the ferry-boat (the sun-god);
that they might know their bonds,
that they might not err, that they might not go astray in any way.
He established the mansion of Mul-lil and Ea along with himself.
He opened also the great gates on either side,
the bolts he strengthened on the left hand and on the right,
and *in their midst he made a staircase.*§

---

* For a translation of it, see Hibbert Lect., 1887, p. 379 *sq.* The figures on a cylinder seal, which most probably portrays this fight, may be found in Sabæan Researches, etc.; by John Landseer, London, 1823, p. 87. This book has engravings of a number of important signet seals, some showing the sacred tree and balance, pp. 263, 260, 288, 361, 41. For other representations: see, *Les pierres gravées de la haute-Asie. Recherches sur la Glyptique Orientale, par M. Joachim Menant.* Paris, 2 vols., 1883, 1886. Also *Collection M. de Clercq. Catalogue méthodique et raisonné. Antiquités Assyriennes. Cylindres Orientaux, etc., Paris. Ernest Leroux, éditeur,* 1885 *sq.* The Chaldean Account of Genesis, etc.: by George Smith, new edition, by Dr. A. H. Sayce, New York, 1881. *Introduction a l'étude du culte public et des mystères de Mithra en oriènt et en occident, par* M. Félix Lajard, etc. Paris, 1847. Text and Plates: especially Plates xxxii, fig. 2, xxxiii, fig. 4, xxv, 5. *Recherches sur le culte, les symboles, les attributs et les monuments figurés de Venus en orient et en occident, par* M. Félix Lajard, etc. Paris, 1849. Text and Plates. Also the folio works of Botta, Victor Place and Layard, and the Photographs of Assyrian Antiquities in the British Museum, by Stephen Thompson, London, 1872.

† Schrader and Oppert translate: "He ordained the year, *established decades for the same.*" Cuneiform Inscrip. and the Old Test. by Dr. Eberhard Schrader, before cited, p. 15–16.

‡ Comp. Gen. i, 14–19.

§ Gen. xxviii, 12.

He illuminated the Moon-god that he might watch over the night, and he ordained for him the ending of the night that the day may be known, etc." *

In the Qabbalah reference is made to the seven androgenic kings who were first made, who were imperfect and were destroyed.†

In the ancient Library of Nineveh a tablet was found, which gives an account of the chaotic universe which in the main agrees with the statements of Bêrôssos, as we now have them, as to the then existing chaotic creatures, it also says: " In the midst of the mountains they grew up and became heroes and increased in number. *Seven kings, brethren, appeared* and begat children. 6000 in number were their peoples, etc." (Hibbert Lect., pp. 372-373.) The god Ner or Nergal, the deity of death, was deputed to destroy these (*Ibid.*, also p. 313). This tablet may date from about 2250 B. C. (*Ibid.*, pp. 374, 23 and note, 390.)

The cosmological tablets also state that the present creation was preceded by another. (*Ibid.*, p. 390.) The Zohar also says the same.‡

Among the earliest of the highest triadic deities of the Akkadians are Ana, Mul-lil, and Hea or Ea, these became later Anu, Bel and Hea or Ea, under them Samas, the sun-god; Sin, the moon-god; and Istar, the god of the planet Venus. These were followed by the spirits or deities of the other, then known, planets. With the Akkadians each object and power of nature had its *Zi* or spirit. The Akkadians formed their deities into triads, usually of males, the Semites also had triadic deities but introduced sex. At the head of the Semitic Babylonian deities was Bel, the Father of all. With them, all the upper deities together composed a heavenly family, outside of this were the hosts of heaven, ministering spirits and servants of the heavenly family. All the rest of the universe belonged to the adversary and his legions, to evil. The primitive Semitic Chaldeans appear also to have believed in a resurrection and an existence after death. See *ante*, p. 241 note. Compare writings on the Izdubar legend.

Dr. Sayce has shown that the general tendency of the Semitic Babylo-

* Hibbert Lect., p. 389.

† Zohar: Siphrah D'Tznioothah, beg. Idrah Rabbah, 128*a*, 135*b*. Idrah Zootah, 292*b*. *La Kabbale*, p. 205 *sq*.

‡ Franck's *La Kabbale*, p. 205 *sq*.

nian mind was towards attaching a weaker or feminine reflection, *paneem*, *i.e.*, face, to a masculine deity, the two however being thought of together as one in content. The Israëlites do not appear to have been an exception to this early Semitic tendency* and the Qabbalists trace this feminine reflection in Elohim or the She'keen-ah, the visible glory of the Supreme Deity upon the earth. The Akkadians appear to have made their triads of deities, of both males and females, but the Semites appear to have always made their feminine deities mere reflections of the male. (Hibbert Lect., 1887, pp. 110–111, 176–177, 112, 194, 346.)

Dr. Sayce gives (Hibbert Lect., 1887, pp. 104 *sq.*, 304–5), a translation of a cuneiform terra-cotta tablet which shows that the ancient Akkadians believed in an upper Ea, deity of wisdom, and a lower Ea, a creating demiurge, which was a reflection of the upper Ea or Wisdom, this idea has a similarity to the accounts in the Qabbalah of Ze'ir Anpeen and of the Adam Qadmon or Adam Illa-ah. In the great work of M. Félix Lajard† are copies from signets, etc., showing Ea, the upper wisdom and Ea, the demiurge. The tablet we have just before mentioned also refers to the fifty sacred names of Ea. The Qabbalah also refers to "the fifty gates of understanding," as to which it says, even Moses, the highest prophet only reached to the forty-ninth.

Indeed the conception of a creating deity is a distinguishing feature of the very early Akkadian religion of Babylonia. (*Ibid.*, pp. 142–144.) In a hymn of the time of Sargon of Akkad, likely 3750 B. C.: we read; "The divine man on behalf of his son attends thee :" (p. 172). "The man, the son of his god, has committed sin, etc." St. Luke iii, 38, says, Adam was "the son of God." (Comp. the Zend Avesta as to the first divine man, Yima-Kshaêta.)

The Akkadian Mul-lil means "the lord of the ghost-world," and has a connection with a "dust-storm" or a "cloud of dust," which was applied to ghosts, whose appearance was thought of as similar to a dust-cloud, and whose food was supposed to be dust. The Qabbalists hold

---

* See that said by us, *ante*, pp. 128, 175. Note what is said by S. F. Dunlap in ; Sod, the Son of Man. London, 1861, ii, p. xix.

†*Introduction a l'étude du culte public et des mystères de Mithra en orient et en occident par* M. Félix Lajard, etc. Paris, 1847. Atlas of Plates. Pl. xxxi. Pl. xxxii.

that Adam was first created with a spiritual body, which is described in the O. T. as "of dust," and that our present body was the coats of skin given after the Fall. We read in ii Genesis: "YHVH Eloheem," *vay-ye'tsar* וַיִּיצֶר (with two yods) *eth ha-adam* APHAR *meen*, etc., "*formed the man* (of) *dust* from the ground." Which may be explained by the *dust* meaning the spirit body.

We also have in the archaic cuneiform tablets, the *Lilatu* or Lilith, the female night demon of the Practical Qabbalah (Zohar ii, 255–9, i, 35*b*) originally "the handmaid of the ghost; *Lil* was in Akkadian "a cloud of dust," and the form of the *incubus* or Vampire ghost was like "a *dust-cloud*." It was thought of as male-female. The Semites made from this, *lillum* male and *lilatu* female. As *lilatu* represented *kel-lilla*, "the handmaid of the ghost," it subsequently became confounded with *lilâtu* "the night" and became the female night-demon, the vampire who sucked the blood of her sleeping victims. It is in the Old Testament. (Is. xxxiv, 14. See Hibbert Lect., 1887, pp. 103, 145–146. Chaldean Magic, by F. Lenormant, Eng. ed., pp. 31, 38.)

Lillith in the demonology of the Israëlites was called *Agrath bath Machlath*, *i. e.*, female leader of demons. Myth makes her the wife of Adam by whom she had Ka-yin and Hurmin (Ahriman?). She was considered the mother of many demons and the Practical Qabbalah has much to say about her. She is described in the Talmud as a beautiful and seductive woman, having long wavy hair. *Bath Machlath* is said to mean, "a dancing" woman, a dancing movement being ascribed to demons. See Proc. Soc. Bib. Archæol. 1887, p. 226.

We think that the Zodiacal constellations were at first ten and represented an immense androgenic man or deity, subsequently this was changed, resulting in Scorpio and Virgo and making eleven, after this from Scorpio, Libra, the Balance was taken, making the present twelve.* The old boundary stones of Babylonia *circa* 1120 B. C. have symbols of Virgo and Scorpio but none of Libra. They also have the Bull, a large

---

* Comp. Seyffarth, Trans. Acad. Science of St. Louis, Vol. i, No. 3, p. ix. Sod, by S. F. Dunlap, i, p. 153 *sq.;* ii, xvii *sq.* The Rosicrucians, their Rites and Mysteries, etc.: by Hargrave Jennings, Ed. 1879, pp. 47, 50, 62, 171, 297–309, 350 *sq.*

dog for the Lion, a dipper for Aquarius, etc. ; also the houses of the planets, with their symbols.

The early inhabitants of Babylonia appear to have had three degrees of religious initiation,* the Qabbalists apparently had the same number as did also the early Christian church in its esoterism. The foregoing parallels are but a few of those which exist and are open, to the student who especially devotes himself to the investigation.

We also call attention to the fact, that the Jewish names of the months and many of the names of the angels and evil spirits, in the Qabbalah, the Apocrypha and the Talmud, are based on the ancient Chaldean language. In the Practical Qabbalah this also appears in many of the names of the demons, *e. g.*, the *Maskim*. Comp. Chaldean Magic, pp. 8 ; 17 *sq.;* 191. †

Figure 26.

* Mon. J. Menant, *Recherches sur la Glyptique Orientale,* Paris, 1883, i, pp. 129–143.

† The engraving (Figure 25) at the head of this chapter is important, it is taken from an impression of an old cornelian or sard signet, having a Phœnician inscription. The original signet is conoidic in shape with an elliptical semi-convex base. It is pierced near the apex for the purpose of inserting a string or wire. The engraving is on the base, and upon the two sides, which are slightly convex. On one side is a worshipper, probably a priest, standing before three differing upright *asheras* or columns, likely representing the androgenic moon deity Sin and the separate male and female principles. On the other side is a man dressed in the military costume usual with the Assyrians, also a crescent moon, to which he points. Behind him is a human lion or demon-headed figure such as we often see depicted on the Assyrian monuments, his arm uplifted, the hand holding a weapon, as if about to strike. It may be Nergal. See

Layard's Monuments of Nineveh, 1st Series, Pl. 82, for a similar figure. On the base of the signet is a representation of the divine Triad, perhaps the supreme deity Ilu of the Babylonians, or Assur of the Assyrians, and the Upper Triad contained in it. Beneath this is a kneeling figure with both hands raised similar to the Egyptian picture we have given *ante*, p. 164. There are also two *asheras*, the male and female principles. The engraved letters are very primitive. It is from the collection of Rev. Dr. W. Hayes Ward. Comp. the American Journ. of Archæology, ii, p. 156. In Lajard's *Culte de Mithra*, Pl. xxxii, fig. 3, is another representation of the Triadic deity from a red jasper veined with green, signet. It is engraved with old Phœnician letters, and from a collection of J. Robert Steuart. Cylinder signet, Figure 26, is portrayed in, Discoveries in the Ruins of Nineveh and Babylon, etc.; by Sir Austen H. Layard, New York, 1853, p. 153. It was found at the foot of one of the colossal human-headed bulls at the entrance to the Assyrian palace of Kouyunjik. It is of that translucent green feldspar termed, amazon stone. Mr. Layard thinks it is the signet seal of Sennacherib, which would fix it as of *circa* 705 B. C., but this is far from certain. It also contains, a representation of the triune deity. The engraving on this hard stone is very graceful, minute and beautiful. Compare upon this triadic representation of the deity: The Babylonian and Assyrian cylinder seals of the British Museum, by Theo. G. Pinches, in the Journal of the British Archæological Association. Read June 3, 1885. Pl. Nos. 3 and 4. No. 4 is another signet representing the triadic deity and also has an archaic Phœnician Inscription. Comp. C. W. King on, Antique Gems. London, 1872, pp. 44, 52. *Empreintes de cylindres Assyro-Chaldéens*, etc.: by J. Menant. Paris, 1880, pp. 49–50. *Symboles Antiques employés en Assyrie, et conservés dans les livres supposés a tort propres a la Chine, exprimant le nom du Dieu Supreme, Dieu du Ciel, et celui des trois personnes de la trinité Chrétienne*, by M. le Cher de Paravey. In *Annales de philosophie Chrétienne, Tomes vii et viii, 1853.* Comp. *Les Achémenides et les Inscriptions de la Perse*, by Joachim Ménant. Paris, 1872, p. 84 *sq.* and Hibbert Lect., 1887, pp. 192–3.

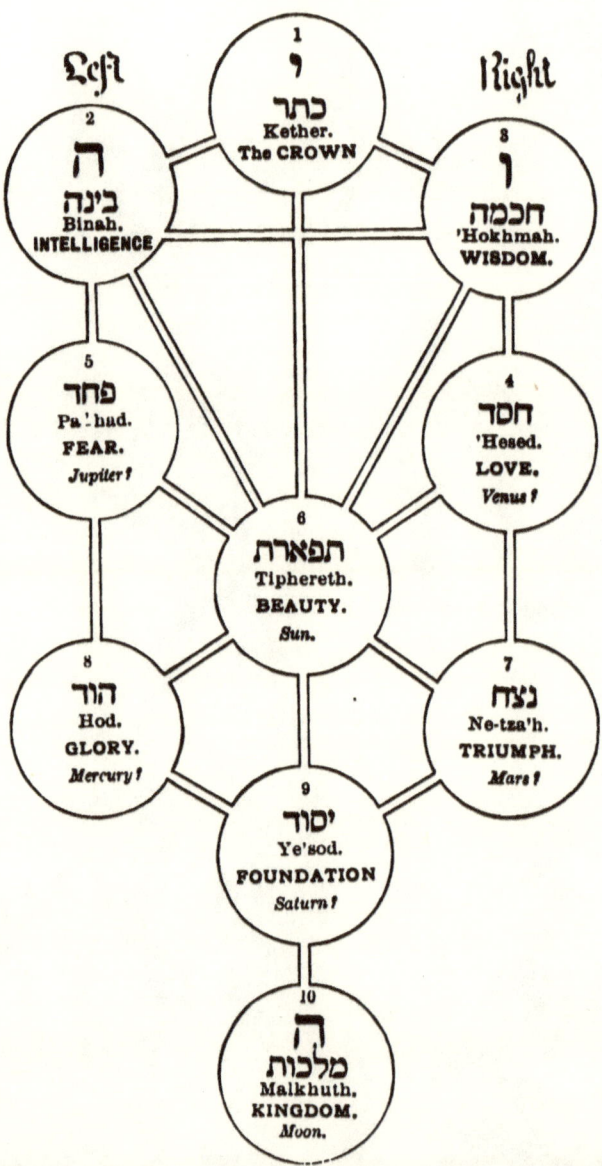

Diagram III.—The Sephirothic Tree of Life, the Ineffable Name, and the Orbits of the Planets.

Figure 27.

XIII.

OF AIN SOPH AND THE TEN SEPHIROTH.

THE Ten Sephiroth or Intermediaries, between the unknowable and invisible Deity and the, to man's mind, knowable, visible and material; were portrayed, to assist the comprehension and memory of the disciple, in different diagrams.

We shall not have in this writing, space to devote to a full exposition of the ancient origin, meanings, colours and symbols, of the Ten Sephiroth. Compare with this the Diagrams showing their arrangement. The following is cited as of interest. R. Isaac of Akko, says: " Illustrations delivered orally, served to explain the mystery of the Unity of the Ten Sephiroth in themselves, which is always concentrated in Ain Soph, from Ain Soph to the Ain Soph. * * * * * . Remember that some of the Qabbalists compare it (the Unity) to a chain forming an uninterrupted unity by its joined links; others, to *various waters issuing from one source,* and separating into many rivers, which become (again) united in the ocean; from whence they return again, from beneath the earth, to their former divisions; and so on in an uninterrupted unity; others compare the matter of the union of Mercy and Severity; to a *precious stone** which unites in itself, the various peculiarities of other precious stones of different qualities (colours?) and still remains a perfect unity; others, take as an illustration, the unity of the different colors in *the flame proceeding from a burning coal*, in which, both flame and coal, constitute a unity; and then again, there is the simile of *a bunch of grapes*,† in which both bunch and grapes are one. I have furthermore heard from the mouth of the most prominent of our learned men, the metaphor of *the tree with its roots* (the Ten Sephiroth) in the earth and its numerous branches, twigs, leaves, veins, fruits, and their rinds and kernels, which all are derived from each other, and yet all draw from the marrow of the tree, and thus all collectively form a complete and unbroken unity, from the roots to the very top of the tree, because they all are of, and point to, one and the same essential source."‡

These illustrations of the relations of the Ten Sephiroth to the Ain Soph, many of which are very old, may be found in the Zohar. The figure of the bunch of grapes is in the Siphrah D'Tznioothah at the end and is also in the writings of Ibn Gebirol. Another illustration is through the sparks produced by steel from the flint, which are always hidden in the latter as a potency and unity, and brought into visibility only by friction.§ Sometimes they were shown as a series of circular lines or concentric circles, one inclosing the other, as we have given in Diagram I, *ante*, p. 100. Sometimes they were arranged in columns and triads, as given by us in Diagrams II and III. In the latter two they are presented as if one was looking at the back, the *a'hoor*, as opposed to *paneem* the face. The perpendicular line on the Right, is termed,

---

* Sapphir, a pearl, or bdellium, a crystal; in both of which, play the colours of the rainbow, especially the white and red. One is transparent white, the other the ordinary white, but in each, like in the opal, colours play.

† A golden vine and grapes were over the doorway of the Temple of Jerusalem, built by Herod.

‡ From The Sepher *M'erath Ainayeem, i. e.,* Enlightenment of the Eyes, on Deuteronomy vi.

§ Comp. *Beiträge zur Geschichte der Kabbala,* von Adolph Jellinek. Leipzig, 1852, p. 81.

Active, Male, Positive and the column of Grace or Mercy; that on the Left, is called, Passive, Female, Negative, and the column of Rigor, Justice or Punishment; the Centre line is termed, the column of Harmony or the column of the Centre. The Right was the column called Yakheen; the Left, that called Bo-az; the Centre, the Harmony; that of the Holy Temple. King Solomon placed the first two pylons before his Temple to symbolize the opposing principles through which, with the Harmony, the universe exists. The Sephiroth are also arranged as in the Diagram given in the Frontispiece; in which they are applied to the different members of the Adam Qadmon, of this we give a face-view: they were also arranged as a tree having its roots in heaven, the trunk and branches being the several Sephiroth, and in several other symbolic forms. The arrangement as in the IInd and IIIrd Diagrams, was called *Ets 'Haÿ-yim*, *i. e.*, the Tree of Life or simply *Etieen*, the Tree. In the form as given of the Adam Illa-ah in the Frontispiece, they were called Anpeen, Parzu-pheem or Ano-pheem, *i. e.*, the Faces. These are all referred to in the Zoharic writings. The Modern Qabbalists have added to the circles given in the Diagrams I, II and III, channels or canals, to indicate all the affinities and effluxes between and in them, as a unit or totality. We have shown these connecting channels in II and III.

It must be especially kept in mind, that in the Qabbalah the Ten Sephiroth are always thought of as a totality, a second divine unity, that of number, yet as inherent in the Supreme Absolute Ain Soph in which number does not exist; and that they are always considered in this one totality, as forming the Adam Illa-ah, the Heavenly Adam or Adam Qadmon, the World of Perfect ideas. Philo evidently refers to this, iii, pp. 184–6, 178 *et seq*.

OF אין סוף AIN SOPH OR אין OR AYIN (A'y-een). The Endless, Boundless, or No-Thing; made Its existence manifest through the efflux, emanation and development, of the entire universe spiritual and material; this was by and through the medium of the Ten Sephiroth or Upper Intelligences. Ain Soph is called, At-tee'kah D'At-tee'keen, *i. e.*, the Ancient of All the Ancient, also At-tee'kah Ka'doosha, *i. e.*, the Sacred Ancient, and is considered as sexless and as the Non-Ego or Not I. A symbol of Ain Soph is the human eye closed. Ain Soph manifested Itself by the efflux of Its vitalizing energy or force, which the Qabbalists call Light. Comp. Gen. i, 2. This being a product is not equal to the Ain Soph. This Light is boundless on the side which produces it and is then called *Ain Soph Or*, but it is bounded on that side by which it emanates or produces, it is then simply the Light. "It (Ain Soph) is so named (Ayin, *i. e.*, No-Thing) because we do not know, and also it cannot be known, what was in this principle (the beginning of all Existence) as this, to our understanding, yea, even by our Wisdom! is unattainable." (Idrah Zootah, Zohar iii, 288*b*.) "Therefore the Sacred Ancient is called No-Thing, since the No-Thing hangs on It."* The French Qabbalist l'Abbe Alphonse Louis Constant, writing under the name of, Eliphaz Levi Zahed,† correctly says: "The Kabbalists have a horror of all that which resembles idolatry; they give however to God a human form, but it is as a purely hieroglyphic figure. They consider God as the intelligent, loving and living Infinite. He is for them neither the totality of the existences, nor the abstraction of Existence, nor a Being philosophically definable.

The Deity, with them, is in All, yet is distinct from All and is greater than All. Even Its Name is ineffable: and yet this Name only expresses the human idea of the Deity's Divinity. That which God is in Itself is not given to the comprehension of man. God is the Absolute of faith but the Absolute of reason is the Existing. The Existing is through itself and because it is that which is. The reason of the being-hood of the Existence is because, it is the Existence. We can ask: Wherefore does something exist, that is to say: Why does such or such a thing, exist? But we cannot, without being absurd, demand: Wherefore is Existence itself? That would be to assert Existence before Existence." In another place‡ he says: "We do not discuss an article of faith, we believe it or do not; but it is faith because it escapes the examination of our knowledge. * * * I will believe when the truth of the dogma has been scientifically proved to me. That is to say; I will believe when I shall have nothing more to believe, and when the dogma shall be destroyed as a

---

* Zohar iii, 288*b*, Comp. Graetz, *Geschichte der Juden*, Vol. vii, p. 240. Philo. i, 134; iii, 184–186, 467; iv, 260. See *ante*, p. 118.

† *Histoire de la Magie*, Paris, 1860, p. 105 *sq*.

‡ *Ibid.*, p. 183 *sq*.

dogma, by becoming a scientific theorem. That is to say in other words: I will believe in the Infinite only when it shall be explained, determined, circumscribed, defined; in a word, when it is finite. I will believe then in the Infinite when I shall be sure the Infinite does not exist. I shall believe in the immensity of the Ocean when I shall have seen it put into bottles. But, my good friends, as to that which we have clearly proved and made you comprehend, you no longer believe it, but know it. * * * The truth of science proves itself by exact demonstrations; the truth of religion proves itself by unanimity of the faith and the sanctity of its works. * * * The proof of the faith is in the works."

The celebrated German philosopher Hegel, uses almost the same words, saying: "All begins through Pure Existence, inasmuch as it is, as well as Pure Thought, that undetermined simple immediate Existence; for the first beginning cannot be another thing * * * . But that Pure Existence is only the purest abstraction; it is an absolutely Negative term, which can also, if we would conceive of it in an immediate manner, be called, Non-Being." *

From Ain Soph, flow out or emanate, *she'phah*, the Ten Sephiroth as a totality. The decade by the Qabbalah is considered as a perfect number, the total essence of all numbers, 0-1 ends with 1-0. "The number ten is an all-embracing number, outside of it none other exists, for what is beyond ten, returns again to the units." †

Ain Soph is considered in the Qabbalah as an Absolute Indivisible Unity, above all unity of number. "Thou art One but not in the numbers, thought cannot comprehend anything of Thee. In Thee no-Thing exists which can be imagined neither shape nor form." ‡ In Ain Soph, says the Zohar; "there is neither white nor black nor red, etc. There is absolutely not any colour, *i. e.*, divisibility. (Zohar, § *B'resheeth*, fol. 15.) The immanent diversity is not denied. "Before the universe was

---

* Comp. *Encyclopédie des sciences philosophiques*, §§ 86–87.

† Sepher Pardes Rimonim, *i. e.*, Paradise of Pomegranites, by Moses Cordovero, fol. 11, col. 3; comp. Philo. i, pp. 440–444, 12 *sq.*; ii, 175 *sq.*, pp. 231–2; iii, pp. 92, 140, 270.

‡ Prayer of Eliyah in the Tiqqooneh haz-Zohar. Comp. Philo. iii, 184–186, 95, 467 and many other places.

made, the Most Blessed One and Its Name were One." "Before the Most Blessed One made its world, It was, and Its Name was hidden in It." (Zohar, Midrash Ha-Neelam, § *Acharay Moth*, fol. 40; Zohar Chadash, fol. 11; comp. Zech. x, 12.)

As It measured the dimensions, It made colours (*i. e.*, divisibilities, in order to shine and be manifest) in the interior light of the Candlestick. From thence proceeded a stream, from which the colours (diversities) colour themselves Below, which are concealed in the concealments of Ain Soph." (Zohar, § *B'resheeth*.)

Creation is termed by the Qabbalah, the Shadow or Reflection of the Upper World, in the latter, is everything Below, in perfect *Zure, i. e.*, prototype. The Sepher Ye'tzeer-ah says: "It formed from the void, the perceptible (essential) and made the No-Thing, Some-Thing." (c. ii Mishna, 5.) Further: "It (the Deity) made a reality out of No-Thing, called the Non-entity into existence, and hewed as it were, colossal pillars from intangible air (*i.e.*, azoth or æther)." "The point in the creation, is called; the Shadow." (*Sepher Emek ha-Melekh, i. e.*, Valley of the King, fol. 12.) "In like manner, the creation is also called, the wife (passivity, the plastic principle) of the A'tzeel-oothic World, *i. e.*, that of the Deity. (*Sepher 'Hadreth Melekh*, fol. 88, col. 2.) "This (the Upper) is the male, the other, is the female, world." (Zohar, § *Theroomah*, fol. 127, col. 2.) "When the Unknown of all the Unknown, wished to manifest Itself, It began by producing a point, as long as that Light point did not appear through its energy, the Infinite was still completely unknown and did not spread any Light." (Zohar i, 2*a*, 15*a*.)

כתר *Kether, the Crown*. The first efflux or emanation of Ain Soph, the Non-Ego, was the Light, usually termed by the Qabbalah, Kether, *i.e.*, the Crown. This symbolizes Abstract Thought, individual Consciousness of being, the Ego or I. Within this Sephirah, the manifested Light of Ain Soph in the germ as a first manifestation, the unit; is asserted to be contained in full content and perfect Harmony, all that has been emanated, all that is, and all that man can possibly know upon this earth. Kether is considered as sexless yet as androgenic and containing the sexes, as the entire content of the positive and negative and their harmony. It is called Abbah, *i. e.*, Father, and is "the living (manifested?) God *the pillar and ground of Truth."* (I Tim. iii, 15.) Its letter is Yod ' = 10, but it contains in its full content the Ineffable Name YHVH, which is the content of the principles of Mercy or Grace as well as of Punishment and Rigor, and also signifies the past, the present and the future, and is we think referred to in the Apocalypse in this last connection. (Apoc: i, 8, 11; xxi, 6; xxii, 13.) But the special Name of the Deity considered by the Qabbalah as most applicable to Kether, is the Great Name, Eh'yeh, *i. e.*, I Am. (Exod. iii, 4.) Kether represents the Desire and Will of the Deity. "Kether is the principle of all the principles, the Secret Wisdom, the Most Exalted Crown, with which all crowns and diadems are adorned." (Zohar iii, fol. 288*b*.) It is even held as the Absolute Existence itself by some of the Qabbalists, but we think as the Ego, it is in contrast with the Non-Ego, which is Above, and is therefore to be accounted Below. Qualifications of Kether are not possible in man's intellect, yet it is perceptible to his thought in that it represents consciousness of being-hood. It is wholly united as the one in number, in an indivisible point the circumference of which is every-where and the centre of which is no-where. It is therefore termed in the Qabbalah, not only I. Kether, but also II. *Ne'-qood-ah Rai'shan-ah*, *i. e.*, the Primordial Point; III. *Ne'qood-ah Pe'-shoot-ah*, *i. e.*, the Smooth Point, because when Ain Soph desired to manifest Itself, It first made a point. (*ante*, p. 127.)

This is explained as follows; the Ain Soph at first was filling All and then made an absolute concentration into Itself which produced the Abyss, Deep, or Space, the Aveer Qadmon or Primitive Air, the Azoth; but this is not considered in the Qabbalah as a perfect void or vacuum, a perfectly empty Space, but is thought of as the Waters or Crystalline Chaotic Sea, in which was a certain degree of Light inferior to that by which all the created were made.

This idea of Kether as the representative of Existence, the Being or the Absolute manifested, if we consider it from the point of view just taken, constitutes a Perfect Form and Individuality, and this the Qabbalah calls IV. At-teek, *i. e.*, the Ancient of the Ancients, the Ancient, the Aged, and V. the At-teek Yo-meen, *i. e.*, Ancient of Days. (Dan. vii, 9 *sq.*) This name must not however be confounded with At'teek-ah D'At'teekeen, the Ancient of *All* the Ancients, who is Concealed. Kether is called the At-teek, because it is the oldest and first emanation from Ain Soph compared with whose splendid Light, Kether as manifested, is only as the Darkness and but a Shadow and a Reflection. This Sephirah is also termed VI. Resha Hiv'rah, *i. e.*, the White Head, because it is the Light in which are all colours, *i. e.*, the diversities, conceptions, and definite models, of all the existences in germ or absolute totality. As the Head of the column of Harmony, or, of the Centre, of the Sephirothic Tree; it is called VII. A'reekh An-peen or Appayeem, the Great Aspect, the Long in Visage or Face, also called, the Long Suffering, and VIII. the Makroprosopon, which has the same meaning, because it contains all the qualifications, intellectual and moral attributes; and because the totality of all the Ten Sephiroth, in germ, are contained in harmony in it, and so it represents, IX. the Adam Qadmon and X. the Adam Illa-ah, the Primordial and Heavenly Adam. We note however of A'reekh An-peen as in Kether, that the Qabbalah says of the A'reekh, in it is all Right side, the side of Mercy and not of Punishment. The remaining nine Sephiroth are known as Ze'ir An-peen, the Short in Visage, the Young One, the Son of A'reekh An-peen. In it is Right and Left side. "The first, says the Zohar, is the Ancient, beheld Face to Face, it is the Supreme Head, the Source of all Light, the Principle of all Wisdom, whose definition is, the Unity." (Zohar, iii, fol. 292b, 289b.) The A'reekh is then the One (1), the unity of number, and the second unity of Ibn Gebirol's philosophy. The symbol of Ain Soph is the O or circle beyond and above all number, which is also of as much importance in all numerical calculations, as the nine digits. Kether is also called XI. *Rûm Ma-aleh*, *i.e.*, Inscrutable Height, because it is the highest of all the Sephiroth and proceeds, by emanation, immediately from the Unknowable Ain Soph. The Zohar therefore, commenting upon: "Go forth, O ye daughters of Zion, and behold the King of Peace with *Kether*, *i.e.*, the Crown." (Song of Solomon iii, 11) says: "But who can behold the King of Peace, seeing that It is incomprehensible, even to the heavenly hosts? But he who sees *Kether*, the Crown, sees the She'keen-ah, *i. e.*, the Glory of the King of Peace." (Zohar ii, 100b.) Kether is also called XII. '*Hokhmah illa-ah*, Heavenly Wisdom, to distinguish it from the Sephirah 'Hokhmah, which is simply called, Wisdom.

In the angelic order, Kether is represented by the celestial beasts of the vision of Ezekiel the 'Haÿ-yoth haq-Qadosh, *i.e.*, the Holy living creatures, of the Merkabah or Chariot-Throne. The Kerubim of Ezekiel and St. John. These are in the Zodiac as Taurus the Bull, Leo the Lion, Scorpio and the Eagle, and Aquarius the Man. Scorpio as a good emblem is symbolized by the Eagle, as an evil by the Scorpion, as a good or evil by the Eagle winged Serpent. (See *ante*, p. 228.) Philosophically, Kether represents, the content of the simple abstract idea of individual consciousness or being-hood, and therefore contains the entire emanated spiritual or material, existing outside of the Unknowable Ain Soph yet in which, the Ain Soph is both immanent and transcendental, in germ. Its symbol is the human eye, open. Ibn Gebirol calls it: "The Form of all forms in the Highest Potency." Kether is likely, the One Head in which are Three Heads. "The Ancient, says, the Zohar; Its Name be praised! Has Three Heads which are yet One Head. And as the Ancient is described by the number Three, so also the other Lights, *i.e.*, Sephiroth, with their illuminations (Lights, the other Sephiroth), are comprised in the number Three." (Zohar, Idrah Zootah iii, 288*b*.) Kether represents the stage of developing existence, termed, the Universal, and is to be referred to the dimension of Length. In the three-fold division of the spiritual in the corporeal body of man, Kether represents the Neshamah, the immortal spirit in man. The symbolic colour of Kether, says the great Qabbalist R. Azriel; "is like the concealed Light." The Light that is wrapped in Darkness.

From Kether, the one, the germ and harmony, the I, Ego, individual consciousness and knowledge of being-hood and existence, therefore in Time; emanates the two oppositions, the female and male, the negative and positive principles. We think that the first emanation from the Ego or Abstract Thought, was that of Mind, the Sephirah Binah, to which the Abstract Thought became wedded, the result being the Word or Wisdom, the Son, or the Association of Ideas in the Mind, without which, Wisdom or the Word, would not be manifest to mankind. The letter of the Ineffable Name יהוה in Binah, is the second ה, the special Name applied by the Qabbalah to Binah, is יה YaH, a feminine Name, and it is on the Left Column, to the Sephiroth of which, the feminine

Name Elohim is applied. It is placed by many writers on the Qabbalah as the Third emanation of Ain Soph, but we are inclined to the view that it is the Second. Comp. Philo i, p. 3, § iii.

The old Qabbalists in writing down the Secret Learning frequently misplaced letters, words, statements, etc., the proper position, meaning, etc., of the same being taught orally to the initiate. This is evident in many places in the written books of Judaism outside of the Mystical writings, and is especially evident in the Synagogue Rolls. Compare in this connection what we quote from the Zohar, *ante*, p. 192, which supports our opinion. With Philo, the Logos or Word proceeds directly from the Deity, so in the doctrines of Gentile Christianity coming as it does through Jewish thought and Jewish Christianity; the Son proceeds directly from the Father, yet in the account of the Incarnation of the Word, the Holy Spirit is placed as the medium.

AS THE SECOND SEPHIRAH WE PLACE BINAH (pron. Been-ah) בינה. Binah is the abstract idea of the Intellect, *nous* the Mind or Understanding, emanating from Kether or Consciousness of existence. It is considered as feminine, negative and passive; and receives and absorbs, the impression of the simple abstract ideas from the androgenic Kether into itself. It is called the Upper She'keen-ah or Glory, and *Immah illa-ah, i. e.*, the Heavenly Mother; *Immah*, the Mother; *Rua'h haq-Qadosha, i. e.*, the Holy Spirit, etc. It is written "Thou shalt call Binah by the name of Mother." Prov. vii, 4. (Zohar iii, 290*a*.) Malkhuth, the tenth (or seventh) Sephirah, is sometimes called, the Lower Mother, Lower Wisdom and simply, the She'keen-ah. The letter of the Tetragrammaton in Binah, is the second, the ה (Heh) = 5. "Binah, in it are engraven, the ways of the letters; in the original image of all details and species, etc. The (imprinted) forms of all species and their details; the (imprinted) form of every herb, etc.; and so also of the minerals, etc. And the ways of these images are contained in the three letters of the Holy Name." * The latter part doubtless refers to יהו the three letters of the Tetragrammaton which are the symbolical letters of Kether, Binah and 'Hokhmah. In the Modern Qabbalah, that of Yitz'haq Luriah, Moses Cordovero, etc., to escape

* Comment. to the Sepher Ye'tzeer-ah ii and iii chapters, by R. Abraham b. David (RaBaD) of Beaucaire (d. 1198) fol. 8, 9.

the consequence of the Christian Trinity in the Sephiroth, they make proceed from 'Hokhmah as the Father, assuming Kether to be the Ain Soph, and Binah, the Mother; a Son whom they call Da-ath, *i. e.*, Knowledge or Science. The most Ancient Qabbalah does not know such an emanation, and it is not one of the Sephiroth. The Triad of the Ancient Qabbalah is Kether, the Father; Binah, the Holy Spirit or Mother; and 'Hokhmah, the Word or Son; which three are distinguished from all the other Sephiroth and are called the Upper Three or the Holy Sephiroth and together form the Intellectual World, and govern the head. They are the Three Heads which are One Head, and are reunited in Ain Soph. Sometimes they compare the Three Heads to the brain which, without losing its unity, is divided into three lobes; and by means of the 32 pairs of nerves springing from them, spreads itself through the whole human body. "Every-Thing, that existeth, says the Zohar (iii, 290*a*;) every-thing which At-teek: Blessed be Its Name! has formed, can endure only through the male and female (principles.)" The Modern Qabballist Yitz-haq Luriah, says of this, that it means in the intellectual, the subject and object, of the understanding. Binah is the Greek *nous, i. e.*, mind, and as the feminine or passive principle is placed on the Left side of the Sephirothic Tree. Its symbol is the brooding dove. It represents the dimension of Depth. The Universal spiritual passive matter of Ibn Gebirol is paralleled by Binah. In the Qabbalah matter always corresponds with the female passive principle, to be influenced by the active or male, the forming. The symbolic colour of Binah according to R. Azriel, is sky-blue.* From its union with Kether, out which it is emanated and to which it returns, proceeds 'Hokhmah, *i.e.*, Wisdom, the Word or Son, the Logos, called the "First-born," which is also looked upon as emanated from and as returning to, the androgenic Kether, the Father or Harmony.

'HOKHMAH חכמה, *i. e.*, WISDOM: we place as the Third Sephirah,

---

* The colour of the Great Crystalline Sea, the Sky, is blue; the color of the robe of the Virgin Mary in the Roman Church is blue, and she stands, as depicted in its symbolism, above the Sphere of the Active Intellect which was that of the moon, crowned with the stars of heaven. As to this Sphere compare the notes of Solomon Munk to his great Arabic and French edition of Maimonides, the Moreh; before cited.

but it is generally termed by the Qabbalists, the Second. The Modern or Lurian School calls it, the Father, but Abbah the Father, by the ancient Qabbalah, is Kether and 'Hokhmah is the Son. This Sephirah, we assert, proceeds from Kether the Father and Binah the Mother, for mysteriously, each is in the other. It is the representative of the Association of Abstract Ideas in the Intellect, its result being Wisdom or Knowledge. It is also called by the Qabbalah, "the Only begotten Son," "the first born Son of Elohim," etc. 'Hokhmah is the Word, the Greek *Logos*, and the *Memrah* of the Targums. By it, says St. John, all things were made that were made. According to a Talmudic explanation of Genesis i, 1, *B'resheeth, i. e.*, beginning, should be read *Be-Raisheeth, i. e.*, Through Wisdom, the universe was emanated.* The letter of the Tetragrammaton in 'Hokhmah is the third, that is ו (Vav) = 6. "By means of the 32 paths, Wisdom is spread throughout the universe, it gives to every-thing form and measure." (Zohar iii, 290*a*.) The 32 ways are generally assumed by the Qabbalists to consist of the letters of the Hebrew alphabet, which are 22, and the ten numbers or decade, together equaling 32. 'Hokhmah is the positive or male principle and is at the head of the Column of Benignity, Mercy or Grace, in the Sephirothic Tree. It parallels the Universal Form of Ibn Gebirol. "Wisdom generates all Things," says the Zohar. (Comp. St. John i, 1–15.) It is the Greek *Sophia*. From it emanate the seven other Sephiroth, the first six of which are called those of Construction or Building. R. Azriel says: the symbolic colour of 'Hokhmah is yellow, perhaps a yellowish red would be more correct. This is the symbolic color in the Roman Church of the robe of Christ.

The first Sephirah Kether, as we have stated, is the unit in number and is the harmony of all and the content of all, the created. It emanates the potentiality and energy it has received by immediate efflux from Ain Soph, to the separated passive and feminine Sephirah, Binah the Holy Spirit, and from the union is produced 'Hokhmah, the Word or Son,

---

*Comp. Prov: viii; St. John i, 1–13; Ps. xxxiii, 6, 9, and other places; Sentiments of Philo Judeus concerning the Logos or Word, etc.: by Jacob Bryant, Cambridge, 1797. Christology of the Targums, by R. Young, London, 1853. The Targums by Etheridge, London, 1865, Vol. i. The Moreh Ne'book-eem of Maimonides, and what we have said *ante*, p. 206 *sq*.

which is on the active or male side; or it may be assumed, that both were emanated at the same instant and that each exists in the other. The letter of Kether is י (Yod), of Binah ה (Heh), together YaH, the feminine Name. (Comp. *ante*, p. 175), the third letter, that of 'Hokhmah, is ו (Vav), making together, יהו YHV of יהוה YHVH, the Tetragrammaton, and really the complete symbols of its efficaciousness. The last ה (Heh) of this Ineffable Name being always applied to the Six Lower and the last, together the seven remaining Sephiroth; and finding its resting place in the last, Malkhuth or Kingdom, the 10th Sephirah; the Harmony of all the Sephiroth. The first three Sephiroth as we have above mentioned, are called; the Holy Upper Sephiroth, and together form a Triad which is a Unit and which is considered in the Qabbalah, in its content, as the most sacred of all the Sephiroth, as including all the balance—and is termed, the Upper Holy Triad, also *Olam ha-Moos'kal*, the Intellectual World or Condition.

The Zohar says: "The At-teek-ah Qadosha, *i. e.*, the Holy Ancient, Its Name be Blessed! exists with Three Heads, which together form only One (Head) and that Head is Itself, which is the most elevated among the highest things. And because the At-teek-ah Qadosha, Its Name be Blessed! is represented by the Three, all the other Lights (Sephiroth) which enlighten us by their rays, are equally comprised in the number Three." (Zohar, Idrah Zootah, iii, 288*b*.) Another statement is: "There are Three Heads engraved one within the other, and one above the other. In this number, first count the mysterious Wisdom, that concealed Wisdom which is not ever seen without a veil. The Mysterious Wisdom, is the supreme principle of all other Wisdom. Above that first Head is the Ancient, whose Name be Sanctified! that which is the most mysterious among the mysteries. Finally comes the Head which dominates all others; a Head which is not a Head. What it contains none know nor can know; because it escapes our knowledge and our ignorance. It is for that reason that the Ancient, whose Name be Blessed! is called Ayin, *i. e.*, the No-Thing." "Each point of matter has three directions, viz: Length, Breadth and Depth; there does not exist any-Thing Below, whose root, *i. e.*, perfect prototype, is not above. Therefore it is necessary, that these three have a spiritual root in the first point Above, they are therefore called in their spiritual nature in the primitive Upper Point; Kether, 'Hokhmah and Binah." (*Sepher Shepathal*, fol. 49, col. 3.) The Four-lettered Ineffable Name is considered as triadic and signifies the past, present and future. Before the revelation of this Name, the Deity was known as שדי Shaddai, *i.e.*, the Almighty, the Powerful One, the principle of Wrath and Punishment and not of Mercy, and therefore the Deity not to be loved but feared. In this Name, ש the symbol of fire, and also of the triad, is the first letter. In the word Messiah, ש is in the middle, but in the word Jesus, the letter of fire and punishment is reversed and placed last. In Jesus as in יהוה the yod, comes first. Ibn Gebirol says: "The Triad is the root of every-Thing." It is in germ in Kether, the Will of Gebirol. Philo holds it to be a great mystery* and even Maimonides hints at it. In early Christianity the Trinity was likely an esoteric doctrine, it is not in the Pastor of Hermas and the African, Tertullian, appears to have been one of the first of the Fathers who refers to it by name, and then as if not generally accepted. It however appears in Matt. xxviii, 19 and the Teaching of the XII Apostles. The subject requires a thorough separate treatment for which we have not space in this writing. The Triadic idea, we think undoubtedly existed in the Secret Learning, Philo who lived in beginning of our present era (*circa* 20 B.C.–40 A.D.), holding to the same view; but as a matter of course it was not the Trinity as it has been formulated in Christianity by Athanasius and the Greek fathers. Some of the theologians of the Middle Ages appear to have desired to prove that the Greek religious metaphysical definition was in the Jewish thought. "If thou art attentive to that most excellent Name of the Deity: (That is the Tetragrammaton or four-lettered Name יהוה YHVH), as found explained in the Mystery of Mysteries, thou beholdest, a Name of three letters, though of four symbols, one of them a twin, being written twice, (that is, the ה, Heh.) If anybody examines them, he can see that the very same Name, represents both one and three, truly each pointing to a oneness of the substance, so that it shows certainly the Trinity of persons." † And the writer goes on to say, that the first and second letters יה form YH (YaH), the second and third הו (HV), and the third and fourth וה (VH); joined they form the one Name YHVH.

* Philo i, pp. 219 *sq.*, 61.
† *Pugio Fidei*. Leipzig, p. 707, by Petrus Alphonsus, b. 1062 A.D.

"And this is the mystery of the three sacred Names which teach the *Unity of three and the Trinity of One*, by the allusion of Wisdom, Reason, and Knowledge, and that all three are One. This is also alluded to in the mystery of time, which is past, present and future, just the same; whence thou seest that the three souls or lives are one-threefold." (Abraham Abulafia.) "It is said, Elohim created Man in His image and likeness and perfected him in the Supreme Form, as it is stated 'And Elohim created man (Adam) in His image.' Much has been sought and defined on this subject of the mystery of man's creation in the image of Elohim, and we find in the Mysteries of the Thorah (Sithrai Thorah), that the *intellectual form* of man is called Adam, *i. e.*, Man, for the skin, flesh, and bones are merely the garment of the man; and for this reason it is written, (Job x, 11): 'Thou hast clothed me with skin and flesh and interwoven me with bones and sinews.' If skin and flesh are the clothing, look for man within the clothing! Observe, his completion is the result of three arrangements united; with reference to which I am going to reveal thee a most profound and sublime secret, according to that which is said in the *Sithrai Thorah*. In Ezekiel i, 26, we read; 'And upon the likeness of the throne, was the likeness, as the appearance of a man upon it, above.' What means the likeness of a man? Three degrees united in one, and they are the Mystery of the Supreme Truth. Thus man here on earth, is man, only by the union of *three* things which together constitute man, viz: spirit (Neshamah) soul (Rua'h) and the breath of life (Nephesh), and they really make the perfect man in the likeness of above, by the mystery of the three degrees united as one, for they are the likeness of man (Adam). Such is man during his life on earth; and when he dieth, the man is not dead, he is only stripped of his clothing." *

At the end, the same says: the trinity of Wisdom, Reason and Knowledge, correspond to the three Names; YHVH, our Elohim, YHVH: in the passage, Hear O Israel, etc.: called by the Israelites the *She'mah*, citing for this the book of Rab Ham-m'noonah Saba, which is also mentioned in some of the oldest books bound up with Zohar. R. Moses de

---

* *Sepher Shekel haq-Qadosh, i. e.*, the Holy Balance, by R. Moses de Leon, said to have been written in 1292. Third gate of the Basis of the Parts, *sha-ar ye'sod ha-Kha'lokeem*.

Leon also says: "These three lying at the well;" again: "The mystery of their order is, three in the mystery of three, each within and above the other, according to the order of the tree on its roots and in its order, which are also the mystery of three."*

Abraham Ibn Ezra in his book Zakooth, allegorized the three fundamental vowels; *'Holem,* *'Heerek,* and *Patha'h gadol,* as a trinity of the modes of motion, upwards, downwards, and in a circle. Joseph Chiquitilla, or Gikitilla, has also developed the application of this vowel-allegory to mystical objects.† The great Qabbalist R. Azriel said, that the benedictions in which mention is made of the Deity's government, are thus formulated: "Blessed art thou, O *Lord* our *Elohim, King* (Ruler) of the world."‡

This shows that the Qabbalists have not based their system only upon the principle of *shepha, i. e.,* emanation, nor upon the unity of substance only, but that they have assumed an identity of thought and of existence, of the ideal and the real. The world was to them only the expression of the Ideas or Absolute Forms of the Intellect.

Moses of Cordova, although of the modern Qabbalistic school understood the Ancient Qabbalah when he said; "The first three Sephiroth, viz: Crown, Wisdom and Intellect, ought to be considered as the sole and same thing. The first represents, Knowledge (the Gnosis) or Science, the second that which Knows, and the third, that by which it is Known. In order to explain that identity, it is necessary to know that the knowledge of the creator is not that of the creatures; for with the latter, Knowledge is distinct from the subject of the Knowledge and leans upon the objects which, in their turn, are distinguished from the subject. It is that which we describe by the three terms: thought, that which thinks, and that which is thought of. On the contrary the creator is Itself wholly at the same time, Knowledge, that which Knows, and that which is Known. In effect, Its manner of knowing does not consist in the appli-

---

*Compare De Leon's *Sepher ha-Rimmon, i. e.,* Book of the Pomegranite, and his *Avodath haq-Qadosh* 123a. Cracow ed. *Beiträge zur Geschichte der Kabbala,* von Adolph Jellinek. Leipzig, 1852, 2d part, pp. 53–56 and 69, etc.

† See Jellinek's work, last cited.

‡ *Ibid.,* p. xvii.

cation of Its thought to the things which are outside of Itself; It is in Itself Knowledge, and in Itself Knowing, and in Itself that It Knows and perceives all that which is. Not anything exists which is not united in It and that It does not find in Its own substance. It is the type (רפוס *typus*) of all being, and all things exist in It under their purest and most perfect form; in such a manner, that even the perfection of the creatures is in that existence, through which, they find themselves united to the source of their being; and in the measure (or proportion) that they are removed from It, they fall from that condition which is so perfect and sublime. It is thus that all the existences of this world have their form in the Sephiroth and the Sephiroth in the source from which they emanate." (Pardes Rimonim, Paradise of Pomegranites, fol. 55*a*.)

Aristotle, Averrhoes and Maimonides, had preceded Cordovero in this idea, the latter says : "The Holy One, Praised be It! knows exactly and recognizes Its true real being; but it does not know a way of knowledge separated from Itself, as we conceive a thing; for we are not identical with our knowledge, on the other hand the creator, whose Name be Praised! is with Its knowledge, as with Its life, absolutely one and the same. Were we to think otherwise, and desire to distinguish the divine substance from its knowledge or life; we should affirm several Godheads, to wit: God, God's life, and God's knowledge; and thereby fall into polytheism. Thou mayest say therefore: God is the Knowing One, the Known, and also Knowledge itself, God is all in One, etc."*

The three Sephirothic hypostases contain and unite in themselves, every-Thing that is, and are themselves united in the Ain Soph, the Attee'kah D'At-tee'keen, the Ancient of all the Ancients; for It is in every-Thing and every-Thing is in It, and yet to the finite comprehension of man, the Ain Soph is Ayin, *i. e.*, No-Thing. They are also united and merged in the White Head, the At-teek or Ancient, which is the first unit of number, the One, so that although described by the triad they are nevertheless the unit. The unity of the first manifestation, that of exist-

* See Maimonides, *Yad ha-chazakah, i. e.*, The Mighty Hand, also called Mishna Thorah. The first name is in allusion to Deut. xxxiv, 12, and because the work consists of 14 books. יד YaD=14. Comp. *Yesod ha-Thorah,* C. ii. Halak. 10. Joel. *Relig. Philos. Sohar,* p. 8, and notes.

ence and being-hood, and the triad of the intellectual manifestations, the ideas in it; are the resumé of All that which is, to man's comprehension. Symbolically they are applied entirely to the head of the Makrokosmos, and may also refer to the three lobes of the human brain, the seat of thought, which together make one brain.

The Upper Sephiroth are called by the Qabbalists, *Olam ha-Moos'kal*, *i. e.*, the Intellectual World. They together are the highest, most subtle and refined of all the Sephiroth. We can parallel them to Ibn Gebirol's Will, Universal Matter and Universal Form. (Comp. also the Moreh Ne'boo-kheem of Maimonides, i, 228 *sq.* Munk's edit. and notes.)

From the third Sephirah 'Hokhmah, Wisdom or the Word, whose letter ו equals 6, emanate the six following Sephiroth. These are considered as the efflux of the potentiality, energy and executive power, of Ain Soph and the Upper Sephiroth, through the Son or Word. The Qabbalah therefore calls the six sides of the entire universe, the six days of building. They are the representative of the Special as the Upper are of the Universal.

IV. OF THE SEPHIRAH חסד 'HESED, GRACE OR LOVE. We will now refer to the second three Sephiroth, which answer to the triad of Ibn Gebirol's soul of the world, which according to him emanated from the *spiritus mundi*. According to the Zohar, from the breast of 'Hokhmah, the Word, the Divine Son; emanated six principles or Sephiroth, called: *Sepheeroth hab-Been-ÿan*, *i. e.*, Sephiroth of Construction.* They symbolize the dimensions of matter, be it an atom or an universe, viz: Length, Breadth, Depth, and the positive and negative poles of each of

* "This (our) universe consists of six dimensions: Above, Below, and the four sides, in the mystery of Ze'ir An-peen, which contains six sides, etc." See *Sepher Ets ha-'Haÿ-ytm*, *i.e.*, the Tree of Life by Haÿ-ytm Vital of the Lurian School, fol. 26. "Therefore there are six working days, for the six sides of Ze'ir clothe themselves in them. But the Sabbath is Malkhuth, the wife" (passivity or rest). (Sepher *P'res Ets ha-Haÿ-ytm*, fol. 3, col. 3.) "As the Upper Mother has brought forth six (an allusion to the ו = 6 of 'Hokhmah, Wisdom, the Son), so the Lower Mother, brought forth six vessels of both, Genesis, says: 'For in six days YHVH made heaven and earth.'" Tiqqooneh ha-Zohar, fol. 22. At the Feast of Tabernacles, the Israëlites waved branches of trees before, to each side, behind, above the head and towards the feet; to signify the three dimensions, Length, Breadth and Depth, and their negatives and positives, together six.

these. The dimensions are only known through their extensions, the positives and negatives, and the six-sided cube symbolizes them. The upper three are as follows: on the Right or male side, is 'Hesed, *i. e.*, Grace. It is also called Love, Mercy, or Compassion. This is the side of the active principle and that of Life and Vitality.

This Sephirah is sometimes termed Ge'dool-ah or Greatness, also Magnificence. It is considered as the Right Arm of the Makrokosmos and as giving life. As Mercy it would be proper to have the color white as its symbol. R. Azriel holds to this. It is questionable as to its symbolic planet, if the androgenic Venus, its color should be green, its metal copper, according to the ancient Chaldaic and astrological ideas.

V. OF THE SEPHIRAH פחד PA'HAD. On the Left or female side, that of Rigor, Punishment, Fear and Severity; is the Sephirah termed Pa'had, *i. e.*, Fear; Deen, *i. e.*, Judgment or Justice; Ge'boor-ah, *i. e.*, Judicial Strength or Power.

This is the side of the Passive principle, that of Death and Corruption. It represents the Left Arm of the Makrokosmos which symbolizes Death. Its planet is Jupiter. Its metal, according to the archaic Chaldaic and astrological idea would be tin. R. Azriel, says: its color is red. The general opinion of the Qabbalists is, that it represents Punishment. Jupiter however generally appears among the Jews, as Gad, and to have been considered a lucky planet.* The Chaldean astrological color was orange. The usual astrological color was, sometimes reddish-purple, or a violet, also a reddish-green and a dark blue.

If the latter two Sephiroth, which are called; "the two arms of God," remained separated, some of the Qabbalists assert, the world could not exist, indeed they do not act separately for Judgment is not without Mercy. (Zohar iii, 143*b*.) They may perhaps be considered as the representatives of the expansion and contraction, the centripetal and centrifugal energies between the poles of the dimensions, acting under the Will of the Deity. From the first are considered to go out the virile and male souls, from the second, the female souls.

* Comp. Unheard of Curiosities concerning the Talismanical Sculpture of the Persians, etc., by James Gaffarel, trans. into English. London, 1650, pp. 323–6, 292.

VI. OF THE SEPHIRAH תפארת TIPH'E-RETH. The two Sephiroth, last mentioned, unite or merge in a harmony or common centre, Tiph'e-reth, *i. e.*, Beauty. It symbolizes the heart and is therefore looked upon as a great centre, and next to Kether, the head. Its symbol in nature is the sun, which was considered by the ancient oriental thinkers, as the heart of the universe; the Qabbalah considers Tiph'e-reth as the heart of the Heavenly Adam, and asserts that it rules over the heart of the earthly Adam or man. Tiph'e-reth is the seat of sentiment and affection and is considered as the expression and result of, all the ethical qualities and affections and the sum of all Goodness. These three Sephiroth are the representatives of all ethical life and perfections. They apparently coincide with the Universal soul of Gebirol, with its separation into the Neshamah, Rua'h and Nephesh. In the Sephirothic Adam, the first three correspond to the Neshamah, the Spirit; so the three we have just mentioned correspond to Rua'h, the Conscience or Ethical, called the Soul. R. Azriel says, the color of Tiph'e-reth is white-red or pink, perhaps a yellow-red. The white and red, may refer to its different aspects. According to the ancient Chaldaic astrological system, its metal would be gold, its color yellow or yellow-red, that of gold. The second triad is called; *Olam ha-Moor'gash*, *i. e.*, the Moral, Ethical or Sensuous, World.

The three Sephiroth next following, are of a dynamic nature; they represent the Deity as the Foundation, Basis or General Potentiality of all Things, the Energy and producing Principle of all existence.

OF NE-TZA'H נצח TRIUMPH. The first, which is on the Right side, is called: Ne-tza'h, *i. e.*, Firmness or Victory, sometimes Eternity. It represents the Right leg and thigh of the Makrokosmos. Its symbolical planet is probably Mars. Its color would therefore, according to the ancient Chaldaic astrology be red. Its metal, iron. R. Azriel says its color is, whitish-red.

OF HOD (pron. Hoo'd,) הוד SPLENDOR. The second is termed, Hod, *i.e.*, Splendor or Glory. It represents the Left leg and thigh of the Makrokosmos. It is probable that its symbolic planet was Mercury; if so, astrologically according to the ancient Chaldaic system, its color should be blue; its metal, quicksilver or mercury. R. Azriel says its color is reddish-white. "By Triumph and Glory, we comprehend extension, multiplication and force; because all the forces which were born into the universe went out of their bosom, and it is for this reason, that these two Sephiroth are called; the armies (hosts) of YHVH." (Zohar, iii, 296a.) The two unite, merge, centre in and go out of, a harmony or common principle, called Ye'sod.

Of Ye'sod (pron. Ye'soo'd,) יסוד Basis or the Foundation. This Sephirah is sometimes termed by the Qabbalists the Hidden or Mysterious Sephirah. It signifies the androgenic generative principle. It is the root of continuing existence, the link in the chain of the existences. "Every-Thing shall return to its Foundation, from which it has proceeded. All marrow, seed and energy are gathered in this place. Hence all the potentialities which exist go out through this." (Zohar, iii, 296a.) These three attributes together, constitute only one side of the Divine Nature, namely: that which the Holy Scriptures, calls: "YHVH Tze'ba-oth." All vitality and life the Qabbalah considers as based on Ye'sod, the source of all emanated and existing Things. Its planet probably was Saturn, the color of which according to the ancient Chaldean astrology, is black. R. Azriel, says: white—red—whitish—red—reddish—white. Its metal by the ancient Chaldean system, would be lead. This people and the Hebrews, considered it as the oldest of the planets. Its spirit was feared by both nations, and it was considered by both, as a star of ill-omen. The Assyrians called it, "the slow moving one."*

The three last mentioned Sephiroth, answer to Ibn Gebirol's triad, called; Nature. Ne-tza'h and Hod, are understood by the Zoharic writings, to be expansion, multiplication and potential energy, and that all the energies, forces and increase, which have at any time emanated into the universe proceed through these; "Therefore these two Sephiroth are called: the armies of YHVH." (Zohar, iii, 296a.) The Qabbalists call them, when united with their harmony Ye'sod; *Olam ha-mutbang*, *i. e.*, the Natural World; also, *Olam ha-Moota'bo*, *i. e.*, the Material World. "It can be designated in a modern formula *natura naturans* contrary to *natura naturata*, the material world."

* Comp. in this connection; Unheard of Curiosities, before cited, pp. 292, 315, 319, 330.

Of Malkhuth (pron. Mal'khooth,) מלכות Kingdom or Dominion. This is the 7th or 10th Sephirah. It represents the harmony at the end, as did Kether at the commencement, of the entire Heavenly Archetypal Adam. It symbolizes the feet upon which the Adam Illa-ah rests and stands, in connection with and upon our world, the soles resting upon our earth, the head reaching into heaven. (Comp. Ezek. xliii, 7.) The Divine Name attached to this Sephirah is Adonai, *i. e.*, Lord, the equivalent of the Ineffable Name YHVH. Its letter is ה which completes the name YHV. It is also termed the Queen for it is the She'keen-ah. (See *ante* p. 201 *sq.*) It is also called '*Hav-ah*, *i. e.*, Eve. "It is the mother of all the living and of all Things, and all Things which exist here Below, went from her bosom and are blessed by her." (Zohar, Idrah Zootah, near the end.) This Sephirah represents the Concrete, and is the energy and executive power of the Upper Mother Binah, the Holy Spirit, the Abstract Intellect. Malkhuth is the She'keen-ah, the Real Presence of the Deity in the Church of Israël, the Glory which hovered over the Ark of the Covenant, the female or reflection of Ze'ir An-peen, and is the creating spirit. It is also called, the Bride of the Spouse. It represents the Sabbath or 7th day, the close of the Construction or Building of the Universe, the Rest Day or Harmony of All. Its angel is Metatron, the Great Angel of the Covenant. The sum total of all the angelic forces or ministering energies. The angel as to whom the Deity said to Moses "My Name is in him," beware of offending him. The letters of the name Metatron = 314, and those of Shaddai, the Almighty = 314, having the same number value, by the Talmudic and Qabbalistic rule called Gematria, they are considered as equal. It is to be noted that Shaddai was the deity to be worshipped in Fear, and YHVH in Love. The latter was the Merciful One. Metatron is also the one to be feared. Ex. xxiii, 20–23; xvi, 10; xxxiii, 2.

Malkhuth does not represent any distinct attribute but is the sum total of all the Sephiroth, and the Divine Government over the universe, the absolute Kingdom, the totality therefore unity, of all the Sephiroth over the entire universe. It is similar to Ibn Gebirol's Divine Power, which he says; is predominant in all the existences, penetrating them by virtue of the potentiality of the Will and not leaving any vacuum, but establishing perfect harmony among them. It is also considered as the sphere or orbit of the Moon, that is of the Active Intellect.* Its color is like the light reflecting all colors. The transparent light of the universe around us in which are all the prismatic colors.

Many of the Qabbalists claim, that the first chapter of Genesis applies only to the Prototypic or Upper Adam, who was androgenic and made in the image and likeness of Elohim. That the repetition of the expression "said" or desired, three times therein applied to the Man, refers to the three spiritual natures of the Upper Adam which his copy, the earthly Adam had from his creation. The last male-female creation, they say, referred to the world-nature necessary for the mundane existence of man and its continuance. The Upper Adam is not made of "the dust," and indeed the second account expressly says, the plants, *i. e.*, man, were not yet on the earth and the terrestrial man did not yet exist. The entire earth was enveloped in a thick mist. Afterwards the earthly man was made of " the *dust* of the ground" and "the breath of life," the Nephesh, was "breathed into his nostrils," or *face*, by YHVH Elohim, only then the dust-man "became a living soul." A Garden of Eden, according to the first account, did not exist for the Upper Man. The Qabbalists say, the Garden or Paradise was pure abstract human thought in which was planted, the tree of the Good and Evil and also therein was the tree of vitality, of life.

* As to the different spheres, consult the valuable Notes of Solomon Munk, to his magnificent edition of Maimonide's Moreh in Arabic and French.

Figure 28.

Figure 29.

XIV.

THE AIN SOPH AND THE SEPHIROTH CONTINUED. OF THE AYIN. VIEW OF THE ANCIENTS AS TO IDEAS. OF THE TRUE AND OF ILLUSION. SOUND, RHYTHM, COLOR. QUOTATIONS FROM THE ZOHAR AS TO THE SEPHIROTH. THE PROTOTYPIC MAN. THE SEPHIROTH AS BETWEEN THEMSELVES. THE SEPHIROTHIC PILLARS. OF AZRIEL AND HIS WRITINGS. ANALYSIS OF HIS COMMENTARY ON THE SEPHIROTH.

THE Zohar (Idrah Zootah iii, 288*a*) says: "The Ancient of the Ancients, the Unknown of the Unknown, has a form yet also has not any form. It has a form through which the Universe is maintained, It also has not any form as It cannot be comprehended. When It first took this form* It permitted to proceed from it (Kether) nine brilliant Lights, which illuminating through it (Kether) spread upon all sides a brilliant light. Let us think of a light which is elevated and which spreads its rays in all directions: if we desire to grasp these rays, it will be impossible, as we will perceive they all proceed from the one light. Just so the Holy Ancient is an elevated (Absolute) Light, but completely hidden and incomprehensible in Itself, and we can conceive It only through Its manifestation in these diffusing Lights (the Sephiroth) which are however on the one side, only partly visible, and yet on the other side, are partly concealed. *These (in their totality) constitute, the Holy Name YHVH.*" "It is the Ancient of the Ancients,† the Mystery of the Mysteries, the Unknown of the Unknown. It has a form which

---

* Kether, the Crown. The Will in Ibn Gebirol.

† Not "the Ancient of ALL the Ancients," who is the Ain Soph.

appertains to It, since It appears (through it) to us, as the Ancient Man Above All, as the Ancient of the Ancients, and as that which there is the Most Unknown among the Unknown. But under that form by which It makes Itself known, It however still remains the Unknown. Its vestment appears white and Its aspect is that of a veiled face. It is seated upon a throne of fiery sparks which submit to Its Will. * * * . From Its head It shakes a dew, which awakens the dead and makes them re-born into a new life. It is because of this that it is written: 'Thy dew is a dew of the light.' It is that dew, which is the nourishment of the Holy Ones of the Highest Order. It is the manna, prepared for the Just (Pious) in the life to come. This dew descends unto the field of the sacred fruits (the saints). The aspect of this dew is white as (the whiteness of) a crystal, the color of which contains all colors * * * . The length of the Face, from the top of the head is that of three hundred and seventy times, ten thousand worlds. It is called the Long in Aspect (the Makroprosopos, or, A'reekh An-peen) for such is the Name of the Ancient of the Ancients." *

The name Ayin, (A'y-een) No-Thing is said to come from Job (xxviii, 12) "And *Wisdom, where* (מאין *mai-a'y-een*, literally: from no-thing) shall it be found? and *where* is the place, of *Understanding?*"† The passage was only used by the Qabbalists to help the retention, by the memory, of the doctrine as to Ayin. The same system was used by the Rabbins in the Talmudic teachings. Beyond man's comprehension is the *no-thing* because man's mind only comprehends *the things*. Ayin does not mean, nothing in the sense of the absolute negation of everything, if it did *mai-a'y-een* could not be translated *where?* This interrogative *where?* to the mind of the questioner at once implies a negation of *there*, and conveys the idea of a not-knowing and the prompting of a question, which may admit of an explanatory answer; thereby proving that the *Where?* points to an idea which on account of its apparent unreachableness, unknowable essence and real invisibleness; is to the questioner immediately as if a *no-thing*, but to the questioner only, for in reality an *absolute nothing* or negation within the reach of man's comprehension is impossible

* Zohar iii, fol. 128a.
† See, Cahen's Great French Bible, note to this verse.

and is entirely beyond his (limited) thought. The idea altogether excludes the idea of a some-thing (otherwise it would be within his reach) and refers to the absolute no-thing, in abstract and absolute endlessness and incomprehensibility, which exists and rules as the Supreme Deity; therefore the Qabbalists claim, that "the highest degree" of the Godhead is to man as Ayin that is, not even an idea. This word Ayin is more properly a definition than name, and comes within the sphere of theosophical science, intimately connected with the spirit of Divine wisdom, and breathes in the Mosaic writings even above Eh'yeh and YHVH and God's attributes; yet comes within the sphere of the Old Testament. Ayin is *non ens* but not absolutely *non est*, and far from asserting a description of the Deity as non-being, is abstractly to say, the Supreme is not a being (*ens*) among known existing beings, but is a *no-Thing* among the world of Things; the Supreme is the uncreated as far as man in the matter-body can know, is a non-something, opposed to and far above, the created some-thing, which is physically and spiritually the Hebrew *yaish*, Chaldaic *eeth*. The phrase *yaish mai-a'y-een*, *i. e.*, Some-thing out of No-thing, is the meaning of creation *ex nihilo*.

Thought in the ancient world was realistic. Ideas must have a real existence, they were not mere form and opinions which might be changed, this thought is especially evident in archaic Greek philosophy and it was this that Parmenides and Plato sought to change. With Plato, in the Parmenides, came the new thought that every subjective must have an objective. See *ante*, p. 113. Ideas are only a material symbolism acting in our minds. Realism is not the true, nor is nominalism the true, the nearest approach to what is pure ideality is conceptualism. But even conceptualism is inferior to the infinite subtilety of language and thought, for unformed ideas float in our minds which are too subtile even for conception, which are only intuitions, and which cannot find any mental symbolism nor absolute formulations, nor any means of visible expression.

The matter-world is perpetually changing and is therefore neither the True nor the Real; it presents to us nothing but uncertainty and mere appearance, is the Hindu *Maya* or Illusion. But the prototypic ideals are the True and the Real and are like the motionless shadows cast upon running water, they resist the force of change and motion, and afford a true basis for the understanding of the things. This conception is Oriental but also that of Pythagoras and Plato. (Comp. Aristotle's Metaphysics i, 6.) This highest ideal world was called by the Jews, the Heaven of Heavens.

How are we to bridge this chasm between the Real divine and the Un-Real human, the absolute ideas and the ideas in us? This is the stumbling block of Kant, Hamilton and Plato, as it is of all philosophy. The Theosophists and Mystics have endeavored to solve it through the ecstatic condition, but how successfully is for the reader to judge.

> " A hair, perhaps, divides the False and True,
> Yes: a single Alif were the clue—
> Could you but find it—to the Treasure-house
> And peradventure, to the Master too."

The Hebrew Qabbalah teaches, that sound is the inner soul of color, and that the rhythmus is the inner spirit of all life, and for this reason, the lower life by its conformity with the rhythmic motion of the upper heavenly life, is drawn towards it and is merged in its prototype; because similar affect similar, in a peculiar, unknown or magical manner. For this reason not only among the Israëlites but in the culte of all the Pagan nations, the play of colors and the sounds of music act in accord; this is clearly set forth in the ancient books of the Chinese. So we have the 7 colors, 7 in the musical scale, also 7 vowels, all apparently in affinity.

The Zohar also says: "' To whom then will ye compare Me, or to whom shall I be equal? Says the Holy One' (Is. xl, 25). Among all the creatures, although created in my similitude, there is not one like Me. I can even destroy the form, in which I may show Myself to the world, and reproduce the manifestation of Myself, repeatedly in many different (forms). No other Deity is above Me, who can destroy My form. Therefore it is said in the Scripture; 'Our Rock (Deity) is not like their rock (deity), our enemies may judge for themselves.' (Deut. xxxii, 31.) But should some one say: It is said: 'Ye have seen no manner of similitude,' (Deut. iv, 15;) to him can be answered: In this one form, we have seen YHVH, of which it is said of Moses, 'the likeness of YHVH shall he behold' (Num. xii, 8), but not under any other similitude; with justice the prophet, says: 'To whom will ye compare Me?' To whom will ye compare YHVH? What form shall represent the Supreme?

(Is. xl, 18.) Because form is not an attribute of the Supreme in Its Place (*Ma-qom*, *i. e.*, Abode or Reality), but the Holy One has condescended to govern the universe and to spread Its Glory (She'kheen-ah) over all the created (therein), It therefore appears (through the She'kheen-ah) to each one, according to his (that man's), comprehension, insight, and imagination. This is the meaning of the verse: 'Through prophetic images and representations' (Hosea xii, 10). Elohim (God) therefore speaks in the above text, as if saying: Although I represent Myself to you, in your own form, yet you cannot compare me to any Thing. Before the Deity had created any form in this (our) universe, before the Holy One had brought forth any image, It was alone, without form, and without any similitude whatever, who can conceive of the Supreme Deity as It was before the creation, for It then was formless? It is therefore prohibited to represent the Supreme Holy One under any kind of image or under species of form, yea even by Its Holy Name, by a letter or by a point. To this refer the following words: 'Ye saw no manner of similitude on the day that YHVH spake with you' (Deut. iv, 5). That is, ye saw not anything, that ye could represent under any kind of form, or species of image. But after the Deity had emanated the form of the Upper Man (Adam Illa-ah), It used the same, as a chariot (Merkabah), so as to descend (through it); It desired to be named after *this form, which is the Sacred Name YHVH*. It desired that it be known, according to Its attributes, according to each attribute separately, and It permitted Itself to be called: 'Elohim of Mercy;' 'Elohim of Justice (or Righteousness)'; 'Almighty One'; 'Elohim of Tze'ba-oth'; and the 'Existing One.'* The Deity intended thereby, that Its attributes (qualifications) be recognized by its creatures and that it be known, how Its Mercy and Compassion extended throughout the entire universe, as well as Its potentiality (energy and power). For if It had not diffused Its Light upon all Its creatures how could we know the Deity? How could be accomplished, that which is written (Is. vi, 3): 'The world is full of Its Glory?' Woe to the man who even compares the Holy One with Its own attributes, much less with those of man himself, who came from the earth and who falls into corruption. We must consider the Deity as exalted above

* Comp. with this the 13 Middoth. Exod. xxxiv, 5–8.

all creatures and all attributes, but beyond that which the attribute expresses we cannot conceive of the Supreme. If we divest the Deity of all these things, if we leave (to It), neither an attribute, nor an image, nor a form, the remainder is like a far stretching ocean ; for the waters of the ocean in and for themselves, are boundless and formless, and it is only when they spread themselves upon the earth, that they assume an image or a form (*Dimyon*). We can now make the following calculation: the *source* of the water of the ocean and the flume or stream of water proceeding from the source, so to spread itself further, are *two*. A great reservoir is then formed, just as if a huge hollow or excavation had been dug; this reservoir is called, ocean, and is the third. This unfathomable depth, ocean, then divides into seven streams, resembling seven long *Kailem, i. e.*, Vessels (or Vases). The source, the flume or stream, the ocean, and the seven streams (*Kailem*) together make *ten*. And if the Master breaks these vessels which he has made, the waters return to the source, and then remain only the fragments of these vessels, dried up and without any water. It is in this way, the Cause of All Causes, emanated the Ten Sephiroth. Kether, the Crown, is the source from which streams forth an unceasing infinite Light: hence the name Ain Soph (the Endless, or Infinite) by which the Highest Cause is designated : for It (in its Supreme Absoluteness) has neither form nor formation and there is not any means whereby to comprehend it or in any way know it. Hence it is written 'Seek not out the things that are too hard for thee, neither search the things that are above thy strength.' (Ecclus. iii, 21.) The Deity then emanated a vessel, as small as a (mathematical) point, like the letter ׳ (Yod) which is filled from this source (*i. e.*, the Ain Soph) by the Divine Light. This is the source of Wisdom, nay it is Wisdom itself! This was the Sephirah 'Hokhmah, after which the Supreme Cause, allowed Itself to be called: 'Wise God.' After this It made a great vessel resembling the ocean, this is called (Binah) Intelligence (or Understanding): hence comes the name 'Intelligent God.' But it must, however, be understood in this connection, that the Deity is Wise and Intelligent through Itself alone, for Wisdom does not of itself deserve its name through itself, but only through the Wise One, who has filled it with the Light which flows from Itself; just so Intelligence is not comprehended through itself, but through the Being who is intelligent, and fills it with Its own substance. The Deity needs only to withdraw Itself and Intelligence would be dried up and useless. This is also the meaning of the words 'As the waters run out from the sea, (perhaps, lake) and the bed of a river becomes dry and parched up.' (Job xiv, 11. Comp. Is. xix, 5.) The ocean is finally, divided as if into seven streams, and the seven costly Vessels (*Kailem* or the Sephiroth) are produced, which are called: '*Hesed* Mercy or Grace, and *Ge'dool-ah*, *i.e.*, *Grandeur; Ge'boor-ah* (Judicial Strength); *Tiph'e-reth* (Beauty); *Ne-tza'h* (Triumph or Victory); *Hod* (Glory); *Ye'sod* (Foundation or Basis); and *Malkhuth* (Kingdom). Therefore (answering to these attributes or Sephiroth) the Deity is called: the Great or Merciful; the Mighty; the Glorious; the God of Victory; the Creator, to whom all Glory appertains and Space belongs, and the Foundation of all Things. Upon the last attribute all the others are based, as well as the totality of the worlds. Finally, the Deity is also King of the Universe, for everything is in Its power; It can diminish the number of the Vessels, and increase in them the Light which streams from them, or reduce it, just as it pleases the Holy One. For these Vessels, It made subordinate to them and for their use, a Throne, which has four feet and six steps, together ten. (Note. This is the second world, Beriah, or B'ree-ah, see hereafter.) Subordinate to this Throne for its use, the Holy One created, ten Hosts of Angels, finally It created Samāel and his hosts, which are used by the Angels as clouds, upon which they descend to earth, or, as if horses, upon which they ride. So it is said in the Scripture: 'Behold YHVH rides upon swift clouds, coming to Egypt, and the gods (elohim) of Egypt tremble before Him.'"*

The Zohar calls the First World *D'yook-nah*, *i. e.*, form or image. It is that of Adam Illa-ah, the Celestial Prototypic Adam or Man. The Second World *Kur'sey-ah*, *i. e.*, the Throne. The Third World *Mala'hay-ah*, *i. e.*, the Angels, and the Fourth, our Matter-World, *Galgooleem*, *i.e.*, the Planetary World also that of the *Q'lippoth* or Shells.

The Universe as an entirety, is looked upon by the Qabbalah as the vestment or "garment of God." The Zohar tells us; "When the Hidden of all the Hidden, willed to manifest Itself, It first made a point

* Is. xix, 1. Zohar ii, 42*b*–43*a* ⸲ Bo.

(Kether, the first Sephirah also called A'reekh An-peen), shaped it into a Sacred Form (*i. e.*, the totality of all the Sephiroth, the Adam Illa-ah, or Adam Qadmon) and covered it with a rich and splendid garment, that is the universe." *Ibid.*, i, 2*a*.) Ibn Gebirol starts out with this idea in the commencement of his Me'qôr 'Haÿ-yîm.

The idea of a first ideal or prototypic androgenic Man is of great antiquity in the metaphysical religions of the Orient, and we think, may be found in the oldest writings of the Akkadians, Babylonians, Chaldeans, Hindus, Chinese and Egyptians: even in the Greek philosophy, especially in Plato, and in Philo Judæus and St. Paul, and there are images of the Great Man in Daniel and Ezekiel. (In Plato see the Symposium. Prof. Jowett's Plato, i, pp. 506–9. Geo. Burges' Plato, iii, pp. 508–14.) It appears also among the aborigines of America. (Comp. Plates *ante*, pp. 120, 142, 157, 164.)

It must also be noted that each Sephirah of this trinity of triads is also considered as containing within itself a triad, viz:

I. It has its own absolute characteristics;—Therefore is the Special.
II. Is passive and receiving that from above;—Therefore is the Concrete.
III. It is active and emanating to that which is below;—Therefore is the Universal.

The Zohar (iii, 288*b*) says: "Just as the Holy Ancient is represented by the number three, so all the other lights (Sephiroth) are of a threefold nature." However within this triad in each Sephiroth is a unit, and in this trinity of triads, there is also a trinity of units in the totality of all the Ten Sephiroth. Three of the Sephiroth; Kether, Tiph'e-reth and Malkhuth, constitute, as we have seen, the uniting links or harmony between the three pairs of the oppositions, the male and the female, or the positive and negative; and thereby are produced, the Intellectual, Ethical, and Material worlds in unison as a triad; and these three Sephiroth together, form the Middle Pillar of the Sephirothic Tree or Diagram. From the important positions they occupy, each of these Sephiroth is considered, as representing the World or condition of which it is the harmony. The division is perpendicular in three Columns or Pillars.

I. That on the Right, known as the Active, Positive Male side, or Pillar of Mercy (*Sithrai Yemeen-ah amoodah D'Hesod*); is composed of the three Sephiroth on that side which are usually called, Wisdom, Mercy, Firmness.

II. That on the Left, is the Passive, Negative, Female side, or Pillar of Judgment (*Sithrai D'samalah amoodah D'Deenah*), representing the principle of Rigor or Punishment. It is composed of the three Sephiroth on that side, usually called; Intellect, Judgment (also Fear) and Splendor.

III. The four Sephiroth in the Centre of the Tree or Diagram, representing Mildness (*Ra'ha-mayoon*), composed of the harmonies of the triads, is called the Middle Pillar (*Amoodah D'amzoothah*).

I. Kether, the Crown, the Brain; is used to designate the Intellectual World, and represents, the Neshamah, the Spirit.
II. Tiph'e-reth, Beauty, the Heart; is used to designate the Ethical world. It is called the King or Holy King and represents Rua'h, the Soul.
III. Malkhuth, Kingdom, which unites and merges in itself all the Sephiroth, is used to represent the Material World, instead of Ye'sod, Foundation, which is termed, the Hidden or Suppressed Sephirah. Malkhuth in this capacity is called, the Queen (*Malkhoothah*) or the Matron (*Matro'neethah*). It represents Nephesh, the Animal Vitality or Body. The energy, potency, and power of all the Sephiroth, are therefore considered to be, in Kether, Tiph'e-reth, and Malkhuth; but Malkhuth, the Queen, the She'kheen-ah, contains all in harmony.

Kether, the Crown, is the representative of the manifested spiritual substance of the Absolute. Is the Unity in number, the Supreme One. Tiph'e-reth, Beauty, the highest perfection of life and ethics, has its representative in the planetary world in the spirit or energy of the Sun, whose light gives vitality and preservation to all the created on this earth. It is the representative of the Ideal Beauty or Goodness.

Malkhuth, Kingdom, is the re-united action of all the Sephiroth, the Real Presence of the Deity in the midst of Its creation; the She'kheen-ah or Glory of YHVH Elohim, of Adonai, the Lord, and is the immanent energy of all the emanated Things. Its representative in the planetary world is the Moon. These three constitute the column of the Middle, a Triad.

The Crown is always A'reekh An-peen, the Great Face or Long in Aspect.

Beauty, is the Holy King, or, the King.

Malkhuth, Kingdom, is the She'kheen-ah, the Queen, the Matro'nee-thah, the Divine Presence. Its representative is the spirit or energy of the Moon, of the planet which obtains all its light from the Sun; the ruler of the lowest planetary sphere in connection with the earth. The existence on this earth the Qabbalah holds, is only a reflection or image, of the great Ideal Beauty or Goodness in the Above.

As to the active energies of the King and Queen, whom the Qabbalists frequently term, *the Two Faces*. (Zohar, iii, fol. 10*b*.) These form an androgenic principle whose constant endeavor is to shed upon the world new life and kindnesses and preserve and perpetuate, under the Will of the Supreme Deity, the work of the original creation. The reciprocal affinity of the Two Faces, operates in two ways, sometimes it is from Above to Below, then the existence and life go out of the Highest World affecting the objects of nature; sometimes on the contrary, it goes from the Below to the Above, that is from this, our world of illusion, change and unreality, to the real and true and Absolute, Above; and takes back to the Highest, the existences entitled to such a return.

One of the earliest writings after the period of Ibn Gebirol, which sets forth the system of the Qabbalah philosophically; that has escaped the general destruction of the Hebrew writings in the Middle Ages, is the Commentary on the Ten Sephiroth, by R. Azariel òr Azriel ben Mena-'hem, perhaps, ben Solomon; also called by some of the Jewish authors of the XIII century, Ezra. He was born in Valladolid, Spain, *circa* 1160 A. D. and is said to have died in 1238, aged 78. He was distinguished as a Philosopher, Talmudist, Qabbalist, and Commentator on the Hebrew Holy Writings, and he tells us, that he travelled much in search after the Secret Wisdom. He is said to have been a pupil of the celebrated Qabbalist R. Yitz-haq the Blind, and master of the erudite Qabbalist R. Moses ben Na'hman (Nachmanides) called by the Jewish authors, acrostically, RaMBaN. Azriel wrote a number of works, some of which have reached our day in MSS., others, which were printed at an early date. The one we are most interested in is his: *Sha-aloth u-th'shooboth al eser Sephiroth, i. e.*, Explanation of the Ten Sephiroth in Questions and Answers. In the edition of Warsaw of 1798, at the end, is: "He who wishes to become wise must turn towards the South," *i. e.*, towards the Sephirah Tiph'e-reth, Beauty; symbolized by the spirit of the Sun, the potency of the South. "He who desires to become rich must turn towards the Sephirah Tzad-dek, Righteousness; which is the potency of the North, and a memorial sign for thee is: The Table is in the North, the Candlestick in the South. 'And to my maker I will ascribe (give) righteousness,' (Job xxxvi, 3,) refers to the saying: 'The She'kheen-ah is in the West,' which means that the West is *avver-YaH*, *i.e.*, the æther (azoth) of Adonai (the Lord), and *Or YaH*, *i. e.*, the 'Light of the Lord,' and that is the She'kheen-ah. As to the question whether (in this wisdom) there is a giver and a receiver, the (position and work of the) Cherubim may answer, for they appear like man and wife and such is the love for you which comes from the Holy One, Blessed be His Name! We read (Job xxiii, 13) 'And his soul desireth her and he acts' and in Isaiah vi, 3, 'And one calleth to the other' which the Targum translates: 'And they receive one from another.' At times each doeth for himself, at times they do alike, at times one doeth the work of the other, and at times they reverse their work. (Job, xxiii, 8–10.) With reference to which the Rabbins say: Great is the power of the righteous (just) for they turn the quality of Severity (Fear or Rigor) into the quality of Mercy (Grace), but the wicked do the contrary and where there is a lacking the work is cut off, and such an one is called *Tumtum*, *i. e.*, stopped up. Concerning such an one it is said: (Job xxvi, 9,) 'He closed the Face of the Throne, He spread His cloud over it'; and it is also written: (Prov. xxv, 2,) 'The honor of Elohim (God) is to conceal a thing.' And these things are proceeded with in the fourth wake of the night and in the fourth wake of the day of their festival. So far the words of R. Azriel which he received from Moses ben Na'hman." Azriel tells us when he first expounded in Spain, the Secret Wisdom which had been taught to him through Tradition, he was derided by the philosophers under the influence of Aristotelianism, who only held that to be true which could be expounded and proved, logically. For their instruction, he therefore endeavored to give the Secret Wisdom a logical dress. Azriel belonged to that Qabbalistic system which was expounded by the School of Gerona.*

The following is a translation of the condensed analysis of the, Commentary on the Sephiroth, as made by Dr. Jellinek according to Spinoza's form of Ethics.†

Definition I. By the Being who is the originator and governor of all Things, I understand the Ain Soph, *i. e.*, an infinite Being, unlimited and with Itself absolutely identical, united in Itself; without attributes, will, intention, desire, thought (idea), word or action. Answers 2 and 12.

Definition II. By Sephiroth, I understand the potencies emanating from the Absolute Ain Soph, emanating as the by quantity limited entities, which like the will, which without changing its nature, wills the different objects that are the possibilities of the multifarious Things. (Ans. 3 and 9.)

Proposition I. The primary cause and governor of the world is Ain Soph, who is as well immanent as transcendental. (Ans. 1.)

Proof (a). Each effect is the result of a cause, and every thing that has order and is according to a design (plan) has a governor. (Ans. 1.)

Proof (b). Everything visible is limited, whatever is limited is finite, whatever is finite is not absolutely identical; the primary cause of the

---

* He is known to us principally by "The Commentary on the Ten Sephiroth by way of Questions and Answers" which first was made known in the Derekh Emoonah, *i. e.*, Path of Holiness, by Meier Ibn Gubbai, Padua, 1563, and the Avodoth haq-Qadosh, *i. e.*, the Service of Holiness, called also, The Vision of the Lord, Mantua, 1545; subsequently it is to be found in "A Collection of Qabbalistic Treatises," by Gabriel Warschawer, Warsaw, 1798. It was republished, Berlin, 1850. Comp. also Dr. Hirsch Graetz, *Geschichte der Juden*, vii, p. 448 *sq.* and Dr. A. Jellinek's *Beiträge sur Geschichte der Kabbala*. Leipzig, 1852, Vol. i, pp. 62–66, ii, 32 *sq.*

† See *Beiträge*, etc.; just cited, Vol. i, p. 61 *sq.* The statement in, The Kabbalah Unveiled, etc.; by S. L. Mac-Gregor Mather, London, 1887, p. 38, as far as it implies the origin of the subject matter as by Dr. Jellinek is not correct, Mr. Mather is also incorrect (p. 15) in his statement as to the books contained in the Zohar; δ and ε, 26 and 27, are not in it. Nes*ch*amah and Nepes*ch* used by Mr. Mather are German, in English, the extra c is not necessary.

world is invisible, consequently is unlimited, infinite, absolutely identical, *i. e.*, it is the Ain Soph. (Ans. 2.)

Proof (c). As the primary cause of the world is infinite, so nothing can exist outside (without, or extra) to It; consequently It is immanent. (Ans. 2.)

Scholion. As the Ain Soph is invisible and exalted, so also is it the root of both faith (belief) and of unbelief. (Ans. 2.)

Proposition II. The mediaries between the absolute Ain Soph and the material world, are the Sephiroth.

Proof. As the material world is limited and not perfect, therefore it cannot proceed directly from the Ain Soph; still the Ain Soph must exert Its influence over it, for in the opposite case Its perfection would cease. Consequently the medium must be the Sephiroth, for they in their intimate connection with the Ain Soph are perfect, and in their severance, imperfect. (Ans. 3.)

Scholion. As all that exists originated by means of the Sephiroth, so there is an upper, a central (higher), and a lower, degree of the material world. (See below, Proposition VI.)

Proposition III. The mediating Sephiroth are ten.

Proof. Each body has three dimensions (length, breadth and depth), each one of which repeats the other ($3 \times 3 = 9$); and if we add thereto the relation of Space in general, the result will be the number ten. As the Sephiroth are the potencies of all that is limited, there must be ten. (Ans. 4.)

Scholion (a). The number ten does not stand as a contradiction of the absolute unity of the Ain Soph, as *one* is the basis of all numbers, plurality proceeds from unity, the germ includes the development, just as fire, flame, sparks and the color, have one basis, although each is different from the other. (Ans. 6.)

Scholion (b). Just as all cogitation or thought and even the mind as a cogitated object, is limited, becomes concrete and has a measure; although thought abstractly proceeds from Ain Soph; so the attributes of the Sephiroth are, limit, measure and concretion. (Ans. 7.)

Proposition IV. The Sephiroth are emanated and not created.

Proof I. As the absolute Ain Soph is perfect so also must the Sephiroth proceeding therefrom be perfect; therefore they are not created. (Ans. 5.)

Proof II. All that is created decreases through abstraction; the Sephiroth do not decrease, for their activity never ceases; consequently they cannot be created. (Ans. 5.)

Scholion. The first Sephiroth was in the Ain Soph as a dynamis (power) before it became a reality; then the second Sephirah emanated as a potency for the Intellectual World; later the other Sephiroth emanated for the Moral World and the World evident to our senses, *i. e.*, the Material and Natural World. But this does not imply a *prius* and *posterius*, or a gradation in the Ain Soph, but just as an ordinary light contains, as in an unity in itself, the lights kindled from it which also give light sooner or later and differently, so the Ain Soph embraces all in a unity. (Ans. 8.)

Proposition V. The Sephiroth are both active and passive (*maqabel v'meth-qabal*) emanating and receiving in themselves.

Proof. As the Sephiroth do not abolish the unity of the Ain Soph, so each one of the preceding receives from its predecessor and imparts to its successor, *i. e.*, is at the same time both active (imparting) and passive (receptive). (Ans. 11.)

Proposition VI. The first Sephirah is termed Rûm Ma'a-leh, *i. e.*, Inscrutable Height; the second 'Hokhmah, *i. e.*, Wisdom; the third Binah, *i. e.*, Understanding; the fourth 'Hesed, *i. e.*, Love; the fifth Pa'had, *i. e.*, Fear; the sixth Tiph'e-reth, *i. e.*, Beauty; the seventh Ne-tza'h, *i. e.*, Firmness; the eighth Hod, *i. e.*, Splendor; the ninth Tzad-dek Ye'sod Olam, *i. e.*, the Righteous are the Foundation of the World; the tenth Tzad-dek, *i. e.*, Righteousness.

Scholion (a). The first three Sephiroth form the World of Thought (Idea); the next three, the World of Soul; the last four, the World of Corporeity; they therefore correspond to the Intellectual, Ethical and Material, Worlds. (Ans. 10.)

Scholion (b). The first Sephirah stands in relation to the Soul in so far as the latter is termed Ye'hedah, *i. e.*, Unity; the second, in so far as it is named 'Haÿ-yah, *i. e.*, the Living; the third in so far as it is named Rua'h, *i. e.*, Spirit; the fourth in so far as it is named Nephesh, *i. e.*,

Vital Principle; the fifth in so far as it is named Neshamah, *i. e.*, Soul; the sixth acts upon the blood; the seventh upon the bones; the eighth upon arteries and veins; the ninth upon the flesh; and the tenth upon the skin. (Ans. 10.)

Scholion (c). The first Sephirah is like the hidden (concealed) light; the second like the blue of the firmament; the third like the yellow; the fourth like the white; the fifth like the red; the sixth like the white-red; the seventh like the whitish-red; the eighth like the reddish-white; the ninth like the white-red-whitish-red-reddish-white; the tenth like the light reflecting all the colors which display light. (Ans. 9.)*

Scholion (d). The gradation of the Sephiroth is as follows:

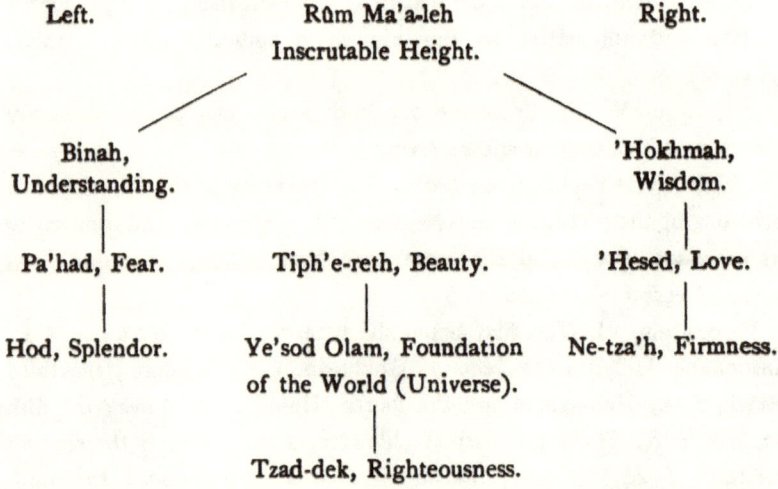

This system of the Speculative Qabbalah, R. Azriel argues to prove, was contained in the Old Testament.

The noticeable features of this early catechism of the Qabbalah, are:

I. The different names and arrangement of some of the Sephiroth. II. That Sephirah is the metaphysical category of number. III. The decade of the Sephiroth is based upon the idea of Space with its three dimensions, Length, Breadth and Depth. IV. The metaphysical idea of limit he uses in explanation of the concretion of the potencies of numbers.

* This may refer to the colors of Ze'ir An-peen of the Idroth.

XV.

THE SEPHIROTH AS BETWEEN THE DEITY AND AMONG THEMSELVES. THE PRAYER OF ELIÏAH.

VITAL questions early arose among the Qabbalists as to the Sephiroth, among these were: What is their affinity as between themselves? What is their affinity with the Deity? The Zohar strongly implies that they are the Names of the Deity; for the Names of the Deity are the only content in our minds of our ideas as to the Deity, and if the Deity could not be named, the Deity could not be known to or grasped by man's mind for the entirety of the Divine Names are only symbols of the Deity in the matter-world. If intelligent it must be assumed that the Deity has intellect; if wise, Wisdom; if active, Energy or Power, etc. The second question has caused more dispute. Some considering the Deity as immutable saw in the Ten Sephiroth only *kailem* vessels, organs or instruments; of the Divine potentiality, energy and action; creatures of a superior nature but wholly distinct from the Holy One.

R. Azriel, before mentioned, holds they were not created but emanated, and although mediums, when separated, were not of value and were contained in Ain Soph. In his third Introduction to Canticles, he says: "And He made them (the Sephiroth) measures (qualities) and organs, subjecting them to limits;" in his Commentary, p. 27*b*, he says; "The measures were completed and became organs." His idea was, that the power of the Sephiroth came by emanation and existed, by it and immanation, through the potency of the Ain Soph in each and all; when that was withdrawn they all became as empty shells or vases. In other words they were not essential attributes and did not destroy, the unity of Ain Soph.

The learned Mena'hem Reccanati of Italy, is also a representative of this School. Many others completely identified the Ten Sephiroth with the Divine Substance, considered them as עצמוּת essences; and held, not anything comes from nothing. The Ain Soph, with them, is the total assemblage of all the Sephiroth. The author of the writing; The Shield of David is a representative of this school. Between the two is a third, those who without considering the Sephiroth as only instruments or tools, do not wish to identify them with the essence of the Deity. The Absolute One, they say; is immanent in all the Sephiroth and reveals Itself through them, but does not entirely dwell in them, they can never include the Infinite. Each Sephirah has a well-known name, but the Supreme Holy One has not any definite Name which expresses all the Deity really is. By this they endeavor to escape any reflection upon any asserted forgetfulness on their part, of the immutability of God. We must admit, the Sephiroth have not any positive reality, nor have they any existence peculiar to themselves, they only represent, symbolically, the limits within which as ideality and spiritual potentiality and energy, the unknowable to man's mind Supreme Essence, chooses to manifest Itself to man's intellect; they are only the different gradations and degrees of obscurity, in which, the Divine Light, has been willing to veil its dazzling, supreme and infinite splendor; so as to manifest Itself partly to Its creatures and permit man to meditate upon and contemplate his Deity in his thought. We have therefore to recognize in each Sephirah two aspects; one, the exterior, the negative, the body or vessel itself; the other, the interior, the positive, which is assumed to be in perfect union or affinity with the interior Unknown Essence or Divine Light. The "broken vases" which have let the Divine Light escape, are therefore spoken of. This is a view taken by both the Ancient and Modern Qabbalists.*

The writing called, the Prayer of Eliÿah† throws much light upon the subject we have just discussed, it says: "Lord of the Universe, Thou

---

* Comp. Yits-haq Luriah's *Sepher D'rushim*, Introduction. This writing may be found in the *Kabbala Denudatæ* of Baron Christian Knorr von Rosenroth; see also Moses Cordovero's *Pardes Rimonim, i. e.,* Garden of Pomegranites, fol. 21–23. Cordovero is the most logical and profound philosopher of the Modern Qabbalistic School.

† In the Tiqqooneh haz-Zohar, Pref. ii, *ad init.*

art One only, but not according to number.* 'Thou art the most Exalted of all the Exalted, the most Hidden of all the Concealed: not any conception grasps Thee; Thou hast brought forth ten forms (*tiq-qooneem*) which we call Sephiroth; in order to guide by means of them, as well the unknown and invisible, as also, the visible worlds; Thou dost Veil Thyself in them, and whilst Thou dost tarry in them, their harmony remains undisturbed; and whoever shall represent them to himself, as divided, to him it shall be accounted, as if he separated Thy unity.† These ten Sephiroth, gradually develope themselves in degrees (or gradations), one is long, the second, short, the third, between them,‡ but Thou art He who guideth them whilst Thou Thyself, be it from Above or Below, art not guided by any one.§ For these Sephiroth Thou hast prepared garments,|| which serve the human souls as points of transition.¶ Thou hast also enshrouded them (the Sephiroth), in bodies so-called in

* This refers to Ain Soph: the idea is also in Gebirol's Me'qôr Haÿ-yĭm. Comp. iv Bk. The Supreme Deity has not any number, unity of substance or inherence.

† The Sephiroth are considered only as spiritual elements of the worlds, by means of which, the Deity came in connection with the entire universe. The Sephiroth later form one potential connected whole, the Makrokosm, Adam Illa-ah or Adam Qadmon, the Heavenly or Ideal Man; through the potentiality of the Deity pervading it. It is the same wisdom, which we admire in the construction of a worm, gaze at in the revolution of the planets, and find in the highest Seraph; so it must, like the essential parts of an organism, reciprocally penetrate and complete itself in the Sephiroth as a totality. The Qabbalah teaches that each Sephirah contains, the principles of all the others, only in each separate Sephirah, a certain peculiar principle apparently preponderates. *Joel, Relig. Philos. Sohar*, p. 287.

‡ The Commentators explain this, as the principle of Mercy ('*Hesed*), the Long Suffering Divinity is the Long in Aspect; that of Fear (*Pa'had*) or Strength (*Ge'boor-ah*) the opposition to the Divine Long Suffering, is the Anger, Judgment, and Punishment, and is the Short in Visage, between these is the Harmony, the Temperate, Judgment tempered with Mercy.

§ The Deity although immanent in is yet independent and distinct from, all the Sephiroth.

|| The Lower worlds considered as shells, covers or crusts, of the Upper.

¶ The soul before it descends into the matter body, passes through these different steps of development in the Sephiroth. Comp. Joel. *Relig. Philos. Sohar*, p. 301. Comp. our Appendix. *Supra*.

comparison with the vestments surrounding them;* but in the whole totality corresponding to the members of the human shape, etc.†

Kether, the Exalted Crown, is the Kingly Crown, of which, it is said: (Is. xlvi, 10) 'Knowing the end from the beginning.' It contains, the Mystery of the Tephillin, *i. e.*, Phylacteries,‡ which obtains its true solution in YHVH, which describes the manner of development (the A'tzeel-oothic). It is the source which fructifies the (Sephirothic) Tree§ and

* As in the human organism, the Neshamah the thinking mind, which has its seat in the brain; is surrounded by the Rua'h, a spirit which dwells in the heart; and this by the Nephesh, the life spirit permeating the entire body; and finally all of these are covered with flesh, skin, bones, and then clothing, so in the construction of the universe, the Makrokosmos, in the highest Sephirothic world, the A'tzeel-oothic, is surrounded by the B'ree-atic world, that of Creation or Emanation, the Soul and expressed Will of the Deity; this by that of Ye'tzeer-ah or world of Formation, *i. e.*, the Life Force, and this finally by the world of Action, A'seey-ah, the world of Corporiety, which is the shell or cover. Joel. work cited, p. 273, note 3. Zohar i, 20*a*.

† In the text follows the connection of the Seven Lower Sephiroth, viz: the Six, called the Sephiroth of Construction with the parts of the human body, these Sephiroth being really, the representatives of the dimensions of all matter, the content of the positive and negative poles or extensions of the dimensions, Length, Breadth and Depth, together six; and the seventh as Malkhuth, *i.e.*, the Kingdom, the rest point or harmony of all, which makes the last and the complement of the decade of the Sephiroth. *Kether* is applied to the highest point of the head or brain, '*Hokhmah*, to the brain, in general; the heart as its Sephirah has *Binah*, Understanding; the back and breast, Tiph'e-reth; the arms '*Hesed* and *Pa'had*, etc. Upon these references the greatest part of the Practical Qabbalah is founded, and asserts magical effects, from the use of the Names of the Deity, as applied to the different Sephiroth. Joel. *Ibid.*, p. 303, note. Franck *La Kabbale*, p. 203. Zohar, iii, 296. Idrah Zootah. This idea runs through esoteric Hinduism. The works of Lenormant, Sayce and other Assyriologists, show that great similarities existed in the thought of the inhabitants of ancient Mesopotamia with the ideas in the Practical Qabbalah, and with the magic, angelology, demonology, etc., of the Israëlites, especially of the Jews. The great colleges of this people in Babylonia probably served to perpetuate this.

‡ In the Kether, *i. e.*, the Primordial substance, is contained the germ of all that which has been or will be in the created, whether it be spiritual or gross. Comp. Joel. *Ibid.*, pp. 217 and notes. The knots, etc., of the phylacteries partake of Chaldean Magic, see Lenormant's Chaldean Magic.

§ Joel, *ibid.*, pp. 225, 216; Zohar, ii, 42*b*.

forces the sap through all of its branches and twigs. For Thou art the Lord of the Worlds. Thou art the Foundation of all Foundations, the Cause of all Causes, Thou waterest the Tree from that Source which, like the soul in the body, spreads life everywhere. Thou Thyself hast neither Image nor Form in all that is within or without. Thou didst emanate Heaven and Earth, the Upper and the Lower, the Celestial and the Terrestrial hosts (angels and spirits.) Thou didst do all this, that the Worlds might know Thee, etc. But no one can conceive Thee in Thy Reality, we only know, that without Thee there is not any unity, neither Above or Below, and we know, that Thou art Lord of All. But beyond this we do not know anything of Thee. Each Sephirah has a destined name, after which also the angels are named, but Thou hast not any certain Name, for Thou art the One filling all Names and giving to them all value as Realities. If Thou shouldst draw back, they all would remain like bodies without souls. Thou art Wise, but not with positive Wisdom; Thou art Intellectual but not with a fixed Intellect; Thy Place (*Ma-qom i.e.*, Abode) is not circumscribed, but all these things are (said of Thee) to make known to man, Thy Power and Thy Omnipotence; to manifest to him, how the Universe is guided by means of Punishment (Judgment) and Mercy (Grace.) If therefore (as to Thy attributes) a Right or Left or Centre is mentioned, this is only done to show Thy government of the entire Universe in opposition to ordinary human actions, but not that to Thee could be imputed in Reality any attribute, one of which would be Rigor, and another, Mercy! Arise Rabbi (ben Yo'haï) see that these doctrines are unveiled through you, for to you and not to any one else has permission been given to reveal deep mysteries."

That the totality of the Sephiroth is not the Deity, is set forth in another place in the Tiqqooneh haz-Zohar. (Tiqqoon 21.) "Woe to those whose hearts are so obdurate and eyes so blinded, as to consider the Deity as the totality of Its attributes. Verily! Verily! they are like the insane one, who describes a king as the totality of his insignia. For behold a king wears his insignia, only so, that through them he may be known; Verily, so also, the King of Kings, the Concealed of all the Hidden, and the Cause of all Causes, disguises Itself in a splendid garment (*i. e.*, the entire universe), only that It may be recognizable thereby, so as to thereby, impart to the inhabitants of the earth, a conception of Its sacred nature."

We may therefore formulate as to the Sephiroth:

I. They were not created by but only emanated from Ain Soph; for by a creation, there would be a diminution of the creator, but by emanation there is not any such diminution.

II. They form together with the Ain Soph an absolute unity, and only represent different appearances of one and the same Being; just as the different rays which proceed from the sun appear different to the human eye, yet are only different manifestations of one and the same light.

III. All of the Sephiroth alike, partake of the perfections of the Ain Soph, and the latter is immanent in all of them; and whilst It, through them, emanates all the spiritually and materially made; yet the Ain Soph is transcendental to and above the totality of all of the Sephiroth and all the emanated. On the one side they partake of the No-Thing-ness of the Ain Soph, but on the other side, they emulate and keep in vitality, all the existing.

IV. As emanations from the Infinite and Perfect Ain Soph, the Sephiroth are on the one side infinite and perfect like the Emanator, yet on the other side, they are finite and through Ain Soph alone, the constitutors and preservers of all the finite, spiritual and material, Things. They are in the first condition when the Ain Soph imparts a portion of its fulness to them; in the second, when they impart the fulness Ain Soph has given to them or as broken vases, when it is withdrawn. They appear to have something like the double nature which the theologians ascribe to Christ, who is thought of as having an Infinite and Perfect Divine Nature on the one side; and yet on the other side, at the same time, is considered as having a finite and imperfect, human spiritual and fleshly nature.

V. Together the Ten Sephiroth in their manifestation, constitute and merge in an unit, and form in their totality the Celestial Adam, the Mediator; who is the content of the Name YHVH or Adonai, *i. e.*, the Lord.

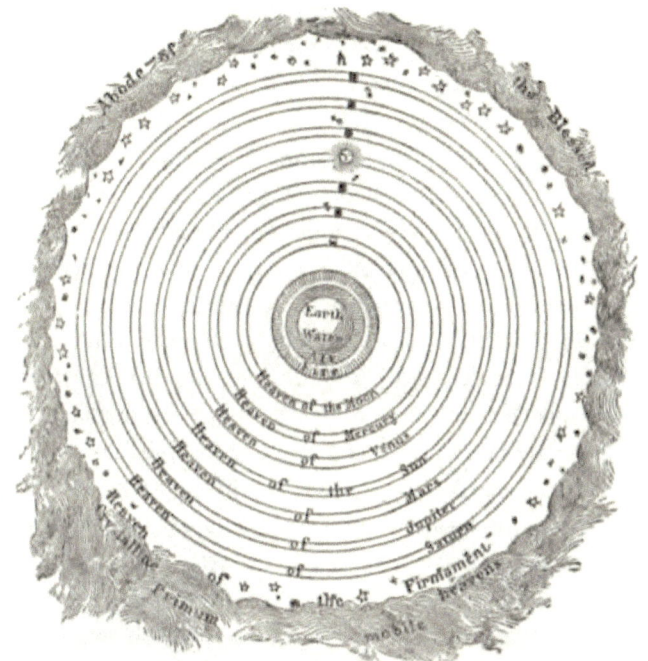

Diagram IV. The Universe according to the Ptolemaic system.

XVI.

OF THE MEANING OF THE WORDS SEPHIRAH AND SEPHIROTH. ORIGIN OF THE IDEAS AS TO THE SEPHIROTH. DECADAL DIVISION OF THE COMMANDMENTS AND THE LORD'S PRAYER.

THE derivation and meaning of the word Sephiroth; (pronounced, S'ph-e'rah, sing., S'ph-e'roth, plur.) are disputed. R. Azriel derives it from ספר *Sapheir*, to enumerate, to number;* whilst the later Qabbalists say it comes from ספיר *Saphir* brightness; (Ps. xix, 1) "The heavens declare the *glory* (*brightness*) of Elohim." Others derive it from the Greek *sphairai, i. e.,* spheres, and are not sure whether to consider the Sephiroth as principles, *árchai, i. e.,* beginnings; or as sub-

* The *Sepher Ye'sod Ha-'Hokhmoth*, p. 25, also says ; "*Sepheiros* arrives from *Sapheir* to enumerate."

stances, *hypostáseis;* or as potencies, *dunàmeis, i. e.*, powers; or as intelligent worlds (*kòsmoi noëtikoi*); as attributes; as *A'tzamoth* entities, or essences; or as *Kailem*, vessels or organs, of the Deity.

The Sepher Avodoth haq-Qadosh, *i. e.*, Holy Worship, by R. Meier ben Gubbai, fol. 16, col. 2, says: "And the author of the Book of Heaven, Whose memory be blessed! writes; From Ain Soph are derived all the Ten Sephiroth, so as to bring abundant influence upon the Lower World and that portion to which we can attain by our understanding. The singular is called ספירה Sephirah or *Narration*, from ספור Siphoor which means, *it is permitted to Narrate as to it.* For as to Ain Soph *it is not*, as we have said, *permitted to* speak (*narrate*). Or we may interpret Sephirah as something 'dazzling pure' according to Exodus xxiv, 10; 'And under His feet like a work of the whiteness of *Sappir* (Sapphir).'* Or we may say Sephirah means the end of a thing or its limit, as our Wise-men, whose memory be blessed! say: 'The city which stands on the border, Sephar.' To which (meaning) our father Abraham, peace be on him! points in the Sepher Ye'tzeer-ah, when he says: 'Sephir, Sephar and Siphur.'" †

The Sepher Ye'tzeer-ah considers a Sephirah is a number, *i. e.*, one of the ten numbers or figures (Sephiroth) instrumental in the creation of the world. These must not however be considered as identical with the Deity. It treats the *ten numbers*, as does the Zohar, as a complete totality, as *together* constituting a complete system designating the sum of all, a totality in their individual quantitative distinction forming, in comparison with the Supreme, the Mikrokosm or Adam Qadmon, the Primordial Man, the shadow or manifestation, of the invisible Makrokosm, Ain Soph, who is above all manifestation and all number to human thought; the Adam Qadmon in comparison with the terrestrial man or Adam, being the Makrokosm. The number ten, from one downwards, together constitutes the whole numerical

---

* The word Sapphir does not mean according to the Hebrew Wise-men, blue; but the color of the pearl, which is white and yet in which plays all the colors. It is iridescent. Jellinek, *Beiträge*, before cited, ii, pp. 25–26. It is like a fine opal or a crystal in the sun-light, in which all colors blend.

† Comp. Buxtorff's Works on the term Sephirah, and the 'Rabbinical Abbreviations' under ס״ת *i. e.*, Ten Sephiroth. ס״ת equal סוד *Sod, i. e.*, Secret = 70. See also John Reuchlin's and Baron von Rosenroth's Qabbalistic Writings.

system or the entities, from which all other numbers are derived *ad infinitum*. This according to the Ye'tzeer-ah is a *whole* and *as a whole* is a mathematical instrument, as it were, in the hands of the Deity in Its great work of the Creation. The Ye'tzeer-ah does not speak of *one* or *a first Sephirah*, etc., but always of the *Ten Sephiroth*, thus not admitting of any equivocation as to its proper meaning, application and intention. In the Old Testament the only place where it occurs is Psalm lxxi, 15; and there it is in the plural *Sephoroth:* the biblical Hebrew for the singular, would be *Sephorah, i. e., number* as the unit or one of *number*. The author of the Ye'tzeer-ah uses the post-biblical Hebrew *Sephiroth*, derived from *Sephirah*, numbering, numeration; which does not occur in this sense anywhere in the Old Testament, but is used in this meaning in the Talmudic literature. *Number*, as a designation of a quantity which is more than one, in the Hebrew is *mispar*, and in the Mishnah and Gemara, *minyan*. In the Talmud treatise *Kil-aÿim*, beginning, and in several other places, we find *Sephir* ספר also written ספיר, as the singular of "number," but ספירה *Sephirah* we do not find. This explains the ספירות *Sephiroth*, of the book Ye'tzeer-ah, but has not any bearing on the Qabbalistic *Divine Sephiroth*, which the Qabbalist R. Joseph Chiquitilla (or, Gikatilla) b. Abraham in the preface to his book *Sha-a'reh orah, i. e.*, Gates of Light, interprets as being called so; "On account of the purity and brightness of the Sapphire ספיר, from which this word is derived." In his preface to the *Ta-amey ham-Mitz'voth, i. e.*, Meaning of the Commandments, R. Mena'hem Reccanati, speaks of the Sephiroth as; "The attributes of the Holy One, being His own, as the flame is part of a glowing coal, and emanating from Him and thus constituting the medium, whereby he created the world (universe)." R. Isaac Euchel, (1756–1804 A. D.) rejects the Hebrew origin of the word Sephirah, and gives in its place the Greek σφαῖραι *Sphairai, i. e., sphere;* this seems to us to be the most correct, for the system of the Sephiroth is delineated in the most ancient Qabbalistic literature like the delineation of the Ptolemaic planetary system, that is in ten circles or orbits each one surrounding the other,* of which the first or outer, as the next to the Ain Soph the Endless to man's mind No-Thing, represents the *ma'hashab-ah, i. e.*, Idea or

---

* See *ante*, pp. 100, 210, and the engravings to this chapter.

I, the Ego, and the last, *i.e.*, the inmost circle, encloses Malkhuth, Kingdom. The Hebraization of σφαῖραι in the word ספירות *Sphairoth* or as we read it, Sephiroth, designating the plural; far from being an isolated example of philological license, in the Hebrew, is legalized by common usage among the ancient Rabbins, and cannot be considered as objectionable from that point of view.*

The "*Eh-ser Sephiroth b'lee-mah*" of the Sepher Ye'tzeer-ah properly means: "the ten numbers (1 to 10) without anything," physical, palpable or visible, in their nature; "*number*" as an entity and abstract idea, being formless and therefore absolutely endless, as far as man knows, as *Space*, which, viewed by mortal eye, is endless and as the real "without any-thing," the real "no-thing." Thus Job says: (xxvi, 7,) "He hangeth (suspendeth) the earth upon *b'leemah*"*:* that is, upon the absolute form, which is equal to endlessness.† In the Qabbalah for the *Eh-ser Sephiros b'lee-mah*, as applying to the "ten Sephiroth" (Spheres or Orbits, Brilliancies, Attributes) of the Infinite, we find Ain Soph, *i. e.*, the Endless, substituted for *B'lee-mah;* but both designations represent the Endless, Eternal, and therefore the Ineffable, as the Ayin or No-Thing. Job says (xxvi, 7) the Supreme Holy One "suspendeth the earth upon *b'lee-mah, i. e.*, nothing or nothingness" equal to, No-Thing and No-Thingness. Ain Soph is the Eternal but is also according to the Qabbalah, Ayin or No-Thing, therefore the Eternal No-Thing. For over seven centuries disputes have been maintained as to the meaning of the word, and the antiquity and origin of the Qabbalistic ideas as to the Sephiroth.

We are of the opinion that Sephirah and Sephiroth refer to the *maz-zol, i. e.*, influences, effluxes or the energies, emanating from and through the Spirits and Intelligences of the orbits or courses of the planets through space, and to those effluxes proceeding from the highest heavens surrounding our earth, as they were understood to exist by the Akkadians, Chaldeans, Ancient Hebrews, etc., and most of the Medieval astronomers before Copernicus.‡ R. Yekuthiel, Haÿ Gaon's brother-in-law, as to whom

---

* See many such instances given by M. Schawb in a list attached to his French edition of the Talmud Ye'rushalmi now passing through the Paris press.

† Comp. notes on Job xxvi, in Cahen's French translation from the original Hebrew.

‡ See Appendix as to the Chaldean Universe, and engravings to this chapter.

Ibn Gebirol wrote an elegy, has left some traces of his Qabbalistic knowledge which gives us some of the ideas of the Qabbalists of the time of Ibn Gebirol. He says: "The seven nuptials of the righteous are seven pearls, called by the mystics, Sephiroth, in the meaning of Sapphir, *i. e.*, pearl, 'Then went up Moses and Aaron, Nadab and Abihu, and Seventy elders of Israel; and they saw the Elohim of Israel. And there was under His feet, as it were, a paved work of sapphir stone, and as it were the body of the heaven in its clearness.' (Exod. xxiv, 9–10.) It is also found in the version of Rabbin Qesheeshi, in the punctuation of the book Ye'tzeer-ah, that the word Sephirah, has not anything in common with 'Sapheir,' *i. e.*, to number, and if thou thinkest there are ten Sephiroth out of nothing, there would not be any end of their number. As to the three (Upper), go back, be dumb, search not, for thy thoughts cannot reach them. And let the opening of thy mouth not be led astray by any Sephirah, for each Sephirah is a new world in itself and closely connected with the other one like the flame of a fiery coal. Seven pearls, with the seven mysteries of prophecies in the mirrors of the beholders, are in them; full of brightness and receiving splendor from the illuminating mirror (*i. e.*, the Godhead). Six Sephiroth are full of light, they are all turned towards each other, and occupy the same throne, except the three Supreme Ones. One Sephirah (Kether) is the Holy Inner Palace of YHVH. And the three together with the six make nine and constitute the Holy of Holies, and with the one in the middle (Kether) constitute the entire Ten."* Haÿ Gaon also says, the word Sephiroth does not come from number, but is "analogous to the mystery of the Ten Worlds, created by them." †

Some Qabbalists therefore prefer to read: the Doctrine of the Sapphire or, of the Precious Gem; or from Exod. xxiv, 10; the Doctrine of Purity or Splendor. The derivation of the name from "Spheres," is the opinion of Yitz-haq Luriah, according to Dr. Henry More in his letter on the Sepher D'rusheem, by Luriah. Dr. More says, "He almost seems to replace for the mysteries of the ancient Kabbala the Aristotelic worlds (circles or spheres) with their Intelligences."

* Jellinek's *Beiträge sur Geschichte der Kabbala*. Part ii, p. 24.
† *Ibid.*, p. 12 *et seq.*

Thomas Maurice* refers to the name Sephiroth and the offices of the Sephiroth and says; that they are called Splendors by the Qabbalists, because they issue from Ain Soph as the blinding brilliancy of light issues from the sun. In this connection we will say, that the *Or Ain Soph* or Infinite Light, is the idealized blood of the universe, in which there is the Nephesh, the Vital Soul or Life, of the entire universe. (Gen. ix, 4; Levit. xvii, 11, 13, 14; Deut. xii, 23–25.) This Light is considered as the Divine Life or Energy which at the creation and since, has always permeated by emanation, the entirety of Space; and which was thought of as an immeasurable immovable Ocean without limits. Space is termed by the Qabbalah *Maqom, i. e.*, the Place, and is a symbol of the Supreme Deity. It was in use in Philo's time.† It was thought of as the result of a contraction or centripetal movement. At that instant the Universal Prototypic Life Adam did not yet exist. To symbolize the beginning of the existence of this Life Adam or energizing Light, a germ is created, a vitalized mathematical point, the centre of which the human mind cannot grasp, a resemblance to the germ life which is the beginning of all human existence and of all vitality upon our earth. The womb of all vitality, life and existence in the Universal or the Special, is Space. By a centrifugal movement, the opposition to the centripetal, the energizing Light, the Divine Life, was projected into and filled the Void, the Space; under new conditions and under the form of an immense stream, analogous to "the waters of life which gush forth from the Throne of the Eternal."‡ This great source or fountain of the waters of life, becomes the beginning of a number of vases, the *Kailem, i. e.*, Vessels, which are the Ten Sephiroth or Splendors,§ through which, it was asserted, all the energies, forms and exterior diversities, obtain manifestation; in their totality and perfection constituting the Adam Illa-ah, the Celestial or Upper Adam.

* Indian Antiquities, etc. London, 1800. Vol. iv, p. 180 *sq*.

† See Sayings of the Jewish Fathers, by Charles Taylor. London, 1877, pp. 53 and 59 and notes.

‡ Jer. ii, 13; xvii, 13; Ezek. xlvii, 1, 5, 9; Ps. xxxvi, 8, 9. See Cahen's French Edit. note to this Psalm, verse 10. Rev. vii, 17; xxii, 1.

§ These among the Israëlites, were later thought of as attached by Twenty-two canals, the letters of the Hebrew alphabet, making together the 32 Paths.

We must note in this connection the three worlds existing in Space. I. The terrestrial world in which the material man has his power of action. II. The known or unknown astronomical world, beyond our field of action yet within our power of thought and observation. III. The undefined world in which we have power to penetrate only in our imagination, in idea, and which is beyond our direct action and our power of observation. The last may be ranked as the Neshamah, the second as the Rua'h, and the first as the Nephesh, of the Great Ideal Man, of all coming within the *intellectual conception* of the human spirit. The three were held by the Hebrew mystics as bound together. The Ladder of Jacob is an emblem of this idea.

Especially was this idea in the Primordial Adam, the content of the invisible and visible universe, the representative of the spiritual and material content of all the brotherhood of spiritual humanity; the Universal, or Upper Wisdom or Word which created all Things, the Logos of St. John which created all Things and without whom was not any Thing made that was made. (John i, 1–3.) The same idea is given by this Apostle, in the words of Jesus, in the parable of the vine. (*Ibid.* xv, 1 *sq.*)

Philo Judæus holds to the doctrine of Ayin, and that the Infinite Perfect Supreme Deity is as No-Thing, and that on the opposite side, apparently far removed, is the visible universe which is imperfect and finite. Yet that the first named fills and comprises every-Thing. He therefore, like the Qabbalists, sets forth the intervention of intermediate causes or energies which are assumed to bridge the hiatus. Philosophy had, before his time, endeavored to do the same and there existed in his period, the Platonic theory of Ideas; the Stoic, of Active Causes; the Jewish, of Angels; and the general Greek, of Daimons. Philo in his formulations used elements from all of these. He teaches, as does the Qabbalah, that before the creation of the world of the senses the Deity created perfect spiritual types, or ideas, of all Things; these were also thought of as active causes which brought disorganized matter into order. Through these spiritual powers the Deity was asserted to act in the universe. They were his ministers, the *lógoi;* by Moses termed angels, by the Greeks, daimons; but these energies of Philo, like the idea as to the Sephiroth, exist only in the Divine Thought, are the infinite powers or potentialities of the Infinite God and are an inseparable part of the Divine Existence. Yet we cannot deny that Philo also gave a personality to the λόγοι *lògoi* or συνάμεις *dunameis;* he conceived them, both as independent hypostases and also at the same time, as immanent determinations of the Divine Existence. They are therefore considered by him on the one side as identical with the Supreme, so as to make the efflux from the Infinite to the finite, and yet on the other side as different from the Supreme; so that the Deity, notwithstanding this participation, might remain transcendental to the world. Philo does not absolutely limit the number of these powers although he places the idea of the decade in a very high position. In his treatise, Concerning the Ten Commandments, he speaks of; "the perfect number of the decade, which contains every variety of number, both those which are even and those which are odd, and those which are even-odd, etc." * He also appears to have an idea of the Sephiroth.†

Philo appears to especially distinguish two powers, Goodness and Might, which go out of and merge in, the Divine Logos; which is the root from which all proceed. (Philo., Bohn's Ed. iii, 95.) The Logos is with Philo, the potentiality of the Supreme and Its vice-gerent, angel or arch-angel, which delivers the Deity's Will, the instrument by which the Supreme made the world and it is the Creative Word. The Logos is not only mediator from the Deity to the universe, but it is also from the world to the Deity. It is the High Priest who makes intercession for the world to God, but although seemingly personal, with Philo the Logos is also impersonal and neither one nor the other exclusively. The subject of the doctrines of Philo is extensive and important, both to the Qabbalah and Greek and Latin Christianity, but we have not space to go into it in this writing and we refer the student to the admirable work, A History of the Jewish people in the Time of Jesus Christ, by Dr. Emil Schürer, English Ed., before cited, 2nd Division, Vol. iii, p. 320 *sq.*, and the authorities therein cited; also to Prof. Adolphe Franck's *La Kabbale,* p. 293 *sq.*, for further investigations.

Solomon says: "Wisdom hath builded her house,
    She hath hewn out her *seven pillars.*" (Prov. ix, 1.)

---

*Comp. Bohn's Ed. iii, p. 140 *sq.*, pp. 92, 97, i, p. 12.

† *Ibid.* ii, p. 136 *sq.*, p. 159, p. 320 *sq.*, iii, 95 *sq.*, 77-8, 185 *sq.*, i, p. 180 *sq.*, p. 426, ii, p. 213 *sq.*

St. John sees, "*seven* golden candlesticks, and in the midst one like unto a son of man * * * his head and his hairs white like wool, and as white as snow. * * * In his right hand *seven* stars," which are the angels of the *seven* churches and the candlesticks are *seven* churches. (Apoc. i, 12 *sq.*) There are also "*seven* lamps of fire burning before the Throne" of the Supreme "which are the *seven* Spirits (powers or ministers) of God." *Ibid.* iv, 5, 6.) Most likely, symbols of the seven elementary and divine energies which control the movement in all Things, the seven Lower Sephiroth, the seven cords of the lyre of the universe and the seven energies of the planets.

Before the Throne is *the Great Crystal Sea*, and in the Throne, but under the Deity, the four animals; the first like a Lion, the second like a Calf (Bull?), the third like a Man, the fourth like a flying Eagle, similar to the account in Ezekiel, (*Ibid.* iv, 5–8,) and the saints sing worthy is the Lamb to receive Power, Riches, Wisdom, Might, Honor, Glory, Blessing, the seven virtues. (*Ibid.* v, 12 *sq.*) The one on the Throne has a book sealed with *seven seals*, which are successively broken by the Lamb, and when the *seventh seal* was broken, it was followed by *seven* trumpet sounds made by *seven* angels, and the *seventh angel's sounding*, produced the Eternal Kingdom (Malkhuth) of " our Lord and his Christ " upon the earth. Apoc. xi, 15, which may be termed the most wonderful and sacred text in the New Testament.

The idea of the Sephiroth of the Qabbalah, may also be found in the word, Be'resheeth, of Gen. i, which instead of " beginning ," can be read Be-raisheeth, the (Upper) Wisdom, the Word or Will. (See *ante*, p. 205 *sq.*) In the Ten "Saids" of the same chapter. Seven of which are applied to the Lower creation, and three to the Spiritual man, the Heavenly Prototypic or first Adam. The same idea as to the Word, Will, or Wisdom, is in Proverbs (viii), Psalms (xxxiii, 6), St. John i, 1–15; in the Targums of Onkelos and Jonathan ben Uzziel on the Pentateuch, and in the Targum Ye'rushalmi.*

It is to be noted that Abraham did not go below 10 when interceding for the righteous in Sodom. (Gen. xviii, 32–33.) We have already

* Compare notes and glossary to edition of the Targum, by J. W. Etheridge. London, 1865. See *ante*, p. 205 *sq.*

referred (*ante*, p. 167 and notes) to the 10 angelic divisions in the Testament of Adam, which is not later probably much earlier, than 300 A. D., and to the 10 angelic divisions in the writings of Dionysius, the Areopagite; not later likely earlier than 532 A. D. To the 10 mystical Names in Jerome (*circa* 331–420).*

The Talmud says:† "With the utterance of ten words was the world created;" also translated: "By ten sayings the world was created."‡ This refers to the statement in Genesis that the acts of creation are introduced by; "and Elohim (God) said," ten times. (Comp. Ps. xxxiii, 6, 9.) In the Yalkut, which begins with, the above quotation from the Avoth, nine occurrences, are reckoned, the tenth, it says; is implied in Be-resheeth, because it, says; "By the *Word* (Wisdom) of YHVH, were the heavens made." *Ibid.* In the Pirkey Rabba Eliezer iii, the ten *va-yomer's*, *i.e.*, "He said;" are reckoned as follows: Gen. i, 3, 6, 9, 11, 14, 20, 24, 29; ii, 18. In the Be'resheeth Rabbah, the first "saying," is implied in the word Be-resheeth of Genesis i, 1; the second, in Gen. i, 2; then follow the eight above specified up to Gen. i, 26, ending with the creation of man. In the Talmud Babli, treatise *Ha'geegah*, 12a, it is said: "Rabbi Zutrah, son of Tobiyah, said in the name of Rab (Rabbi Areka): The universe was created by means of ten words (*D'barim*), viz: 'Hokhmah (Wisdom), Binah (Understanding), Daath (Knowledge), Koah (Power or Might), G'arah (Rebuke, Admonition or authority), Ge'boor-ah (Strength), Tzad-dek (Justice), Mishpat (Righteousness), 'Hesed (Grace or Charity, Love or Compassion), and Ra'h-mim (Mercy). By Wisdom and Understanding, as it says: (Prov. iii, 19), "YHVH by Wisdom founded the Earth; by Understanding He (Hu) established the heavens." By Daath, as it says: (*Ibid.* 20), "By His Knowledge the Depths do burst forth, and the Skies drop down the dew." By Koa'h and Ge'boor-ah, as it says: (Ps. lxv, 7), "Who setteth firmly the mountains by His

---

* See also D. H. Joel, *Die Religions-philosophie des Sohar*, p. 70. M. H. Landauer. *Literaturblatt des Orients*. 1845. No 22; holds that the Zohar speaks less of the Sephiroth than other Qabbalistic writings of the time. The ten mystical Names speak for the antiquity of the Qabbalah.

† Pirkey Avoth, c. 5. Mish. 1. Hershon's Talmudic Miscel. London, 1880, p. 144.

‡ Sayings of the Jewish Fathers, etc., by Charles Taylor. Cambridge, 1877, p. 92 *sq.*

Power, who is girded by Might." By Ge'oroh, as it says: (Job xxvi, 11), "The pillars of heaven tremble, and are astonished at his Reproof." By Tzad-dek and Mishpat, as it says: (Ps. lxxix, 15), "Righteousness and Justice are the prop of Thy throne, Kindness and Truth, precede Thy presence." By 'Hesed and Ra'h-mim, as it says: (*Ibid.* xxv, 6), "Remember, O YHVH! thy tender Mercies; and thy Kindnesses; for they are from (*Olam*) everlasting."* Haÿ Gaon (997–1037 A. D.) knew of the Sephirothic symbolism of the Light and mention is made by him of 'Hokhmah, Wisdom; Ge'boor-ah, Strength; Ye'sod, Foundation; Ma'h-shab-ah, Thought, etc.† Elsewhere it is said: He created by the letter ה (Heh) the symbol of Binah, the Holy Spirit, *i.e.*, "By the breath of His mouth." (Ps. xxxiii, 6.) Sometimes בי ראשית Be-Raisheeth, *i. e.*, By Wisdom, is read; instead of Be'resheeth, Beginning (Gen. i, 1).‡

The Babylonian Talmud, treatise *Be'ra-khoth*, fol. 7a, has the following: "Rabbi Yo-'ha-nan said in the name of Rabbi Yo-seh: How can it be demonstrated that the Holy, Blessed be He! (*Haq-qadosh ba-rukh hu*), prays? From the passage in Isaiah lvi, 7: 'Even these will I bring to My holy mountain, and make them joyful *in the house of My prayer*' (*be'baith te'pheel-lathee*, properly: *My house of prayer*, but used

---

* R. Samuel Edels in his Kheddusha Haggadoth, at this passage, identifies these with the Ten Sephiroth. Comp. D. H. Joel, *Die Religions-philosophie des Sohar*, etc. Leipzig, 1849, p. 86. Lutterbeck, *Die Neutestamentlichen Lehrbegriffe*, etc. Mainz, 1852, p. 238, note 4.

† See Moses ben Schem-Tob de Leon, etc., by Adolph Jellinek. Leipzig, 1851, p. 13, note 5. S. Munk's *Mélanges de philos. juive et arabe*, p. 276, note 1.

‡ See *ante*, p. 205 *sq*. The Wise-men ('Hakhamem) of Israel have divided this word so as to read Barah Yêsh, *i. e.*, (Thou) hast created the Yêsh, the primordial essence of the existence. It is from this Yêsh, Elohim created from No-Thing, Being. Mê-aïn be-yesh. Existence comes from No-Thing. The Sepher Ye'tzeer-ah, says: "It made the No-Thing, Some-Thing" and then; "It made from the Void that which is evident to our senses," *i. e.*, It formed from To-hoo, regarded as the primitive substance, the Mammash, *i. e.*, the derived substance. Yalkut 2. Comp. Sayings of the Jewish Fathers, before cited, p. 92, note. Wisdom is sometimes identified with the Thorah and provides sustenance in a spiritual sense; thus in Proverbs (ix, 5) "Come eat of my bread, and drink of the wine (*i. e.*, Mystery, for Wine = 70 and Sod, Mystery = 70); which I have mingled." Sayings of the Jewish Fathers, by Taylor, p. 75 n., 43; p. 89 and notes.

here, and not less correctly, in the above rendering); not 'in the house of *their prayer*,' as might be expected, but ' of *My prayer*,' says God; which proves that God prayeth.

What are the words of His prayer? Rabbi Zutrah, son of Tobiyah, said in the name of Rab: (The words are:) 'Be it My Will that My mercy overcome My anger, and that My mercy manifest (itself above) My attributes, in order that I deal with My children by means of the attribute of mercy, and let them enter *within* the province of justice: (grant them indulgence above their merits).' "*

Touching the same subject the *Bo-rai-tha* (a series of books written by the ancient Jewish Doctors, after the completion of the Mishnah but probably of the same age), has the following: R. Yishma-ēl, son of Elisha, said: "Once I went into the innermost of the sanctuary (in his capacity as Highpriest. Comp. Lev. xvi) to burn incense, and I saw A-Ka THa-Ri-EL (composed of KeTHeR, *i. e.*, Crown, and EL or AiL, *i. e.*, God; the Aleph prefixed points to the Unity of the Eternal), YaH, YeHoVaH, TZe'Ba-OTH, sitting on a high and exalted throne (copied from Isaiah vi, 1), and He said to me: Yishma-ēl, My son, give Me a blessing. And I answered Him (thus): ' Be it Thy Will that Thy mercy vanquish Thy wrath, and that Thy mercy manifest (itself above) Thy attributes in order that Thou deal with Thy children mercifully, and grant them a position within the boundary of justice (*i. e.*, beyond their merits) !' Hereupon He inclined (assentingly) His head (see Canticles v, 11)."†

---

* The Talmud represents the Beth Dinn or Tribunal of Heaven, as a circle, in the centre of which, God is seated; the first places, those nearest to Him, are reserved to Divine Mercy, the second to Divine Justice.

† The Qabbalah, says Meharchah (Comp. Ein Jacob) explains; YHVH, YaH, A-KaTHRi-El, as; the Aleph of A-KaTHRi signifying Ain Soph; KaTHaR as Kether, *i. e.*, the Crown, the first Sephirah, and the words YHVH—El—YaH; as the three Ineffable Names, the three Divine Persons, the three Judges of the Celestial Beth Dinn.' See the following page. The Beth Dinn which R. Yishma-ēl sees in the Holy of Holies, was a representation of the Heavenly Beth Dinn, because the Deity was looked upon as Himself holding it, seated and judging upon the propitiatory, as He is asserted to be seated and judging in Heaven.

Samuel Edels (1565-1631 A. D.,) explains the names in this passage and the prayer itself, thus :

A-KaTHaRi-EL, YaH. The A (Aleph) points to the *Ain Soph;* (of the Sephirothic Tree)

KaTHaR (kê-ther), the *Crown*, the first of the Ten Sephiroth ;

EL, or AiL, Mighty God, Omnipotence $=$ Justice and

YaH (those letters of YHVH which signify Mercy to prevail in the midst of the other attributes).

Why are these Divine Names distinctly mentioned ? A little reflection will explain. In these Names, the prayer of the (heavenly) High-Priest is still given :

1. A (Aleph) $=$ Ain Soph ; KaTHaRi $=$ Crown, *i. e.*, Thou, oh Ain Soph, who art still the concealed love, Thy mercy overcome (*yikh-bé'shu ra-'ha'-mê-kha*) Thy wrath (*eth ka-a'sê-kha*), on account of the offended majesty in Thy Kether.

2. And Thou EL, or *AiL*, (God) omnipotent, Thy Mercy reveal itself (*yiggo-lu ra-'ha'-mê-kha*) in its entirety over Thy wrath, whilst thou art as Ail (God), also the Judge.

3. And Thou *YaH TZe'Ba-OTH*, deal with Thy Children (*tith-na-hêg im ba-ne-kha*) in the attribute of Mercy (*be' middath ha-ra-'ha-mîm*) to demonstrate Thy love in its fullness in the perfect Name of *YHVH*.

So long as we adore the Deity only in our thoughts, without the participation of the whole heart and the verification of the adoration in our deeds, our adoration is merely half (incomplete), and the Name of God is also incomplete for such worshippers. (Comp. Rashi on Exodus xvii, 16, and Ps. ix, 8.) But this Name (YHVH) shall become a complete one through the history of Israël and God's guidance of that history. Therefore *A-KaTHaRi-AiL YaH YHVH TZe'Ba-OTH* is implored thus : Thou who art sitting on the throne (*qur'saiy-yah*) high and exalted, grant Thy children a standing within the lines of Justice, deal leniently with them, not according to their deserts, but according to Thy Mercy, which is demonstrated by Thy complete Name.

"God prayeth" is explained by: "Yishma-ĕl, My son, bless me," (both of them figures of speech) thus:

Almighty love is through Its essence bound to manifest Its Mercy. It feels Itself blessed, as it were, at Its effective exercise of Mercy; when man by his piety prepares himself to receive the Love of God, *and thus actually blesses God*. Therefore God prays, *i. e.*, Wills and Desires, that man fit himself to receive directly His bounties, whereby God feels Himself blessed.*

The Talmud also says, "Seven attributes avail *before the Throne of Glory* and these are: Wisdom, Righteousness, Judgment, Grace, Mercy, Truth and Peace." (Talmudic Miscel., by P. I. Hershon, p. 117.)

St. John in the Apocalypse also says; "From him which is, and which was, and which is to come." That is the YHV in the three Upper Sephiroth "and from the Seven Spirits which are before his Throne" (i, 4). These are most probably the seven Lower Sephiroth.

The idea of the Sephirothic Tree or Scale, appears to be in Jacob's Dream of the Ladder which is set up on earth, the top of which reached to heaven; YHVH stood above it, (The Vulgate: "And the Lord (YHVH) leaning *upon the ladder*.") and the angels of Elohim ascended and descended on its rounds. (Gen. xxviii, 11 *sq.* John i, 51.)

Maurice† connects this with the idea of metempsychosis and the Mithraic rites referred to by Origen.

We find many Qabbalistic doctrines in early patristic literature, especially in such of the writings of Origen which have reached our day. This Father of the Church lived 185–254 A. D. He was Præfect of the School of Alexandria. His principal disciple was Gregory, Bishop of Neo-cæsarea, called Thaumaturgus because of his Miracles. The Hebrew teacher of Origen was Yehudah II ben Simon III known as "Rabbi." Yehudah was the first president of the Palestinian A'morä-im. Origen's teachers in philosophy were Clement of Alexandria and the asserted founder of Neo-platonism, Ammonius Sakkas. Origen held to the doctrine of emanation, that many other worlds existed prior to ours, that these had perished, that ours would also, and that after it many others would

---

* Comp. as to R. Yishma-ĕl ben Elisha, the High Priest, Yehudah Ha-Levi's Sepher Khozari. Cassell's Edition. Leipzig, 1869, p. 286 *et seq.* and notes.

† Indian Antiquities, etc., iv, p. 189 *sq.*

come into existence and be destroyed. That all souls emanated from the Divine Nature long before the foundations of the world. God was the only existence free from any species of matter. Souls had freedom of will as to good and evil and this was exercised by them before the creation of the universe; some abused this freedom and were placed in this world, some were placed as spirits of the sun, others of the moon, etc., for he held that all the heavenly bodies had spirits; other souls migrated into human bodies or into daimons. This was an imprisonment. All the souls were of an equal nature. The residence of the souls in this world was for trial and in order that the souls, by the exercise of their individual free will, might raise themselves to their original abode, heaven, and remain there. Those that did not emancipate themselves were transferred into new bodies or were punished. When all the souls had regained their original goodness the end of this world would take place and a new world be created. The world was apportioned into districts each of which was governed by a special angel, there were also ministering spirits of different grades who watched over general and special interests. Christ was begotten before all creatures and ministered in the creation. (Comp. St. Paul, Col. i, 16–18. Origen, *De Principiis*, Bk. i, c. vii.) There was an evil daimon surrounded by his own angels, whose constant aim was to lead men to sin. That the Holy Scriptures have an open and obvious meaning and also a hidden secret and recondite sense difficult to discover, which he terms, the *Soul* of the same. He holds that the Sacred Names of the Deity among the Hebrews, "*belong to a secret theology* which refers to the Framer of all Things." (Works, Vol. i, pp. 421 *sq.*; ii, 315 *sq.*) These doctrines are in the Qabbalah and the Zoharic books. There are numerous other doctrines of Origen which are in accord with the Zoharic philosophy. He holds Philo as his model as did also Clement of Alexandria. Origen and St. Paul are in many things in unison especially as to the statements of the latter in 1 Cor. xii, 8–11. Origen also says, that the dress of Adam and Eve after the Fall are our fleshly bodies, and that the word Adam is a generic name for the whole of the human race as if One Man.*

---

* *Adv.* Celsus. English Ed. Works, 1869–72. Bk. iv, c. xl. Comp. 1 Cor. xii, 12–28. See also Mosheim's Comment. on the affairs of the Christians, etc., iii, § 26 *sq.*

Origen in answer to Celsus asserts: "The Scriptures which are current in the churches of God do not speak of 'seven' heavens, or of any definite number, but they do appear to teach the existence of 'heavens,' whether that means the 'spheres' of those bodies which the Greeks call 'planets,' or something more mysterious. Celsus, agreeably to the opinion of Plato (in the Timæus), asserts that souls can make their way to and from the earth through the planets; while Moses, our most ancient prophet, says that a divine vision was presented to the view of our prophet Jacob—a ladder stretching to heaven, the angels of God ascending and descending upon it, and the Lord (*i.e.*, YHVH) supported upon its top; obscurely pointing, by this matter of the ladder, either to the same truths which Plato had in view or to something greater than these. On this subject Philo has composed a treatise which deserves the thoughtful and intelligent investigation of all lovers of truth."*

In *adv* Celsus† the latter, says Origen, quotes certain Persian mysteries as follows: "'These things are obscurely hinted at in the accounts of the Persians, and especially in the mysteries of Mithras which are celebrated amongst them. For in the latter there is a representation of the two heavenly revolutions,—of the movement, viz., of the fixed stars, and of that which takes place among the planets, and of the passage of the soul through these. The representation is: There is a ladder with lofty gates, and on the top of it an eighth gate. The first gate consists of lead, the second of tin, the third of copper, the fourth of iron, the fifth of a mixture of metals, the sixth of silver and the seventh of gold. The first gate they assign to Saturn, indicating by the 'lead' the slowness of this star; the second to Venus, comparing her to the splendor and softness of tin;‡ the third to Jupiter, being firm and solid; the fourth to Mercury; for both Mercury and iron are fit to endure all things, and are money-

---

Alger:—Doctrine of a Future Life, p. 396. Kitto Bib. Cyclop. Title, Origen. Origen's works in Ante-Nicene Library. Smith and Wace's Biographical Dict., etc. We have not space in this writing to go further into the subject.

* *Adv.* Celsus. Works, Ante-Nicene Christ. Liby., 1872, Vol. ii, p. 359 *sq.*

† *Ibid.*, 360 *sq.*

‡ We think a mistake exists here, the metal of Venus always being copper, that of Jupiter, tin.

making and laborious; and the fifth to Mars, because, being composed of a mixture of metals, it is varied and unequal;* the sixth of silver to the Moon; the seventh of gold to the Sun—thus imitating the different colours of the latter two.' He (Celsus) next proceeds to examine the reason of the stars being arranged in this order, which is symbolized by the names of the rest of matter. Musical reasons, moreover, are added or quoted by the Persian theology; and to these, again, he strives to add a second explanation, connected also with musical considerations." The arrangement given of the planets is not their natural arrangement, but the *artificial arrangement* by which they follow as the *lords of the days of the week* as we now have them, which requires that Venus and not Mercury should be placed next to the Sun. We think this is from the ancient Chaldaic system.

If one wishes to obtain means, says Origen, "for a profounder contemplation of the entrance of souls into divine things * * let him peruse at the end of Ezekiel's prophecies, the visions beheld by the prophet, in which gates of different kinds are enumerated (Ezek. xlviii), which obscurely refer to the different modes in which divine souls enter into a better world: also let him peruse, in the Apocalypse of St. John, what is related of the city of God."

Referring to certain diagrams, Origen says: "In this diagram were described *ten circles*, distinct from each other, but united by one circle, which was said to be the soul of all things (the Universe) and was called 'Leviathan.' This Leviathan, the Jewish Scriptures say, whatever they mean by the expression, was created by God for a plaything; for we find in the Psalms: 'In wisdom hast Thou made all things: the earth is full of Thy creatures; so is this great and wide sea. There go the ships; small animals with great; *there is this dragon*, which thou hast formed to play therein!' (Ps. civ, 24-26.) Instead of the word '*dragon*' the word '*Leviathan*' is in the Hebrew. This impious diagram, then, said of this Leviathan, which is so clearly depreciated by the psalmist, that it was the Soul, which had travelled through all things (the Universe)!" In the dia-

---

* We think an error is here, the usual metal of Mercury being quicksilver, that of Mars, iron. This has been supported by the discoveries in the planetary tower of Borsippa in ancient Babylonia by Sir Henry Rawlinson.

gram under the lowest circle is the word "Behemoth." The word Leviathan is inscribed on the diagram at its circumference and at its centre, thus placing the name in two separate places. The diagram was "divided by a thick black line, and this line he Celsus, asserted, was called "Gehenna, which is Tartarus." Gehenna, says Origen, is mentioned in the Gospel as a place of punishment and the Jews considered it, the name of the place "intended for the purification of such souls as are to be purified by torments." (Kitto Bib. Cyclop., ii, p. 307. Origen's Works, ii, 362 *sq.*)

Celsus says that of seven ruling daimons (angels?) "'the goat was shaped like a lion' whereas we discovered that he who is honored in the Holy Scripture as the angel of the Creator is called by this accursed diagram, Michael, the Lion-like. Again Celsus says that the 'second in order is a Bull.'" That is in the order of the seven ruling daimons, the word daimon among the Greeks being synonymous to our angel. We must not forget that the universe was supposed to have been created in the Zodiacal sign of Capricorn or of the Goat, the winter solstice sign. This second, the Bull, is called on the diagram "Suriel, the Bull-like." The third according to Celsus was "an amphibious sort of animal, and one that hissed frightfully." On the diagram it is "Raphael, the Serpent-like." Celsus said the "fourth had the form of an Eagle," on the diagram it is "Gabriel, the Eagle-like." The "fifth" according to him "had the countenance of a Bear," on the diagram it is "Thauthabaoth, the Bear-like." The sixth he says, "has the face of a Dog," and the diagram calls him "Erataoth." The seventh he says "had the countenance of an Ass, and was named Thaphabaoth or Onoel," but on "the diagram it is called Onoel or Thartharaoth, being somewhat asinine in appearance."*

* Origen's Works, Vol. ii, pp. 362–369. Compare what is said upon this diagram, in *Histoire critique de Manichée et du Manicheisme*, par M. de Beausobre. Vol. ii, pp. 63–66; also M. Jacques Matter's *Histoire critique du Gnosticisme, etc.* Vol. ii, pp. 221–237, 236–237, 242; iii, p. 9 and Plates I and D. The following book is valuable in connection with the antiquity of the Sephiroth: *Codex Nasareus, Liber Adami appellatus, syriace transscriptus, loco vocalium, ubi vicem literarum gutturalium præstiterint, his substitutus, latineque redditus, à* Matth. Norberg, etc. *Hafniæ;* tom. i, 1815, 330 pp.; *tom.* ii, 1816, 320 pp.; *tom.* iii, 1816, 320 pp., 4to. *Lexidion Codicis Nasaræi, cui Liber Adami,* etc. Matth. Norberg. Hafniæ. 1816, 274 pp.

"Now in the diagram referred to, we found the greater and the lesser circle, upon the diameter of which was inscribed 'Father and Son;' and between the greater circle (in which the lesser was contained) and another composed of two circles,—the outer one of which was yellow, and the inner one, blue,—an inscribed barrier (was placed) in the shape of a hatchet. And above it, a short circle, close to the greater of the two former, having the inscription 'Love' (Charity or Grace?) and lower down, one touching the same circle with the word 'Life.' And on the second circle, which was composed of interlaced lines and which included two other circles, with a figure like a rhomboid (entitled); 'The foresight of Wisdom.' And within their point of common section, was: 'The nature of Wisdom.' And above their point of common section was a circle, on which was inscribed 'Knowledge;' and lower down another, on which was the inscription, 'Understanding.'" Celsus says "there are between the upper circles—that are above the heavens—certain inscriptions, etc., 'a Greater and a Less' which they refer to the 'Father and Son.'" Origen attributes the formation of the diagram to the Ophites or Serpent worshippers, we have not been able, after search, to establish a connection between their doctrines and these delineations on the diagram. We are therefore inclined to agree with Beausobre (*His. des Manichians*, ii, p. 54) that it has the appearance of an ancient Jewish diagram of the Practical Qabbalah, representing some of the Ten Sephiroth, angels, etc. It certainly has the names of some of the Sephiroth such as Love or Grace, Wisdom, Understanding, and also has Knowledge and Life." (Origen, Works cited, Vol. ii, p. 376 *sq.*)

The Tree of the Sephiroth resembles, says Calmet, that diagram which they call in the Schools, Porphyry's Tree; to show the different categories of the *Ens*, *i. e.*, Being-hood.

The Sephirothic canals are usually portrayed as 22 which added to the

---

4to. *Onomasticon Codicis Nasaræi, cui Liber Adami nomen, edidit.* Matth. Norberg, etc. *Londini Gothorum*, 1817, 164 pp., 4to; and M. Silvestre De Sacy, in *Journal des Savans, a Paris*, 1819, *tom.* iii, pp. 343-364, 646-665, for a Criticism on same; also Sod, the Mysteries of Adonai, by S. F. Dunlap. London, 1861; and notes to The Book of Adam and Eve, etc. Translated from the Ethiopic, by Rev. Dr. S. C. Malan. London, 1882, for quotations from the Book of Adam.

10 Sephiroth equal 32. The Qabbalah also mentions 50 Gates of Understanding, as to which Moses only reached and passed the 49th. These 50 Qabbalistic Gates are said to have been arranged as follows:

The 50 Gates of Understanding were asserted to have 5 Chief Gates, each of which comprehended ten. The first three, included the knowledge of the first principles of the Things. At the Fourth Gate was the planetary world and all the wonders of astronomy, as far as they were then known. There we find the name of each of the seven planets and of the angel whom it was asserted directed its course. These are allotted to each of the seven Inferior or Lower Sephiroth. In Genesis it is upon the fourth day (our Wednesday?) that the planets are created for signs and seasons, so we must note that this day is among most of the civilized Eastern peoples, the day of their week ruled by Wisdom. The whole Sephirothic Tree is most likely an astronomical chart or symbol, the oldest now in the world, and has some connection with the Seven Gates erected in the Caves, used as Celsus mentions, for initiation into the Mysteries of Mithra, and also with the Sacred Tree referred to in the cuneiform texts and shown on the ancient signet cylinders of the early inhabitants of Mesopotamia, Assyria and Babylonia. The Fourth Gate was called: *Mundus Sphærarum*, *i.e.*, World of the Spheres, *i.e.*, the Sephiroth. Athanasius Kircher* gives the different Gates. That in which is the first Sphere is called by him *Cœlum Empyreum;* the second, *Primum mobile;* the third, *Cœlum firmamenti*. These are the three Upper Heavens and parallel the three Upper Sephiroth of the Fourth World. The next seven of the decade, he states, are the Spirits of the seven planets and have their names. The scheme is, according to the system of Ptolemy and is Babylonian and Chaldean, as in also that set forth in the Sepher Ye'tzeer-ah, for it will be especially noted by the scholar, that Venus is placed next to the Sun instead of Mercury. Ibn Gebirol does the same in his Kether Malkhuth. This arrangement is also necessary to make the names of the days of the week follow each other, according to the artificial system in use among us, and among most of the civilized Asiatic peoples. This artificial arrangement, we think, was Akkadian and Chaldean. Each of the planets had a presiding angel, according to the Practical Qabbalah, whose name also is apparently of

---

* Œdipi Ægyptiaci. *Tom.* ii, p. 319 *sq.*

Chaldean origin; and these probably have something in common with the ministering angels of the Apocalypse.

Besides Ibn Gebirol's Kether Malkhuth, two other prayers exist in the service of the Sephardi Jews which are Qabbalistic. One is in the Daily Service, beginning with המאיר לארץ "He lights the earth, etc."* The other beginning אל אדון El (Ail), Adon, *i. e.*, "God, Lord." †

Both of these tend to show, that the Sephiroth apply to the angels of the heavenly Spheres, the orbits of the planets, and to the Spheres above them; to the number of ten. The second, says: "The luminaries which our God created are good: for He formed them with *knowledge, understanding* and *wisdom*: he hath endued them with *power* and *might*, to bear *rule* in the world. They are *filled with splendor* and *radiate brightness*: their splendor is *graceful* throughout the world. They rejoice when going forth, and are glad at their return: and with reverential awe perform the Will of their Creator. They ascribe *glory* and *majesty* to His Name, joy and song to the commemoration of His *Kingdom*, etc." These two prayers or songs of praise, are very ancient and have special reference to the creation and nature of the sun among all the other works of the universe. They probably have come down from the Essenes or the 'Hasidim, who read the She'mah and sung songs of praise at the rising of the sun. (Comp. what is said by Josephus and Philo upon these sects.) The Zohar appears to have knowledge of the song *El, Adon* (Zohar, ii, 132*a*), which we think was in use in the Synagogue long before the time of R. Moses de Leon. ‡

One of the oldest references, beside those we have mentioned in Genesis, which is likely applicable to the Ten Sephiroth, is to be found in Isaiah (xi, 1). We do not say that this is absolute evidence of the idea of the Sephiroth having been in existence under their subsequent names, in the time of Isaiah, nor do we assert that the Qabbalists based their subse-

---

*See David Levi's Form of Prayers. London (5549) 1789, Vol i. Daily Prayers, pp. 30 *sq.*

†*Ibid.*, pp. 140 *sq.*

‡ The Talmud in *Be'rakhoth* says: the song *Ail Adon* has been made by the angel Michael and that the angels sing it every Sabbath day morning before the Lord.

quent arrangement of the Sephiroth upon it—we offer it as it stands for the opinion of the student.

Dividing the statements in Isaiah according to our idea upon the subject, we have the following result:

"But there shall come forth *a rod out of the stem* of Jesse, and *a Branch* shall grow *out of his roots*." (Comp. Zech. iii, 8, 9; vi, 12.) The rod or branch is the Sephirothic Tree, the roots of Jesse, are Malkhuth, Kingdom, the She'kheen-ah, the Presence or Glory of God, which was asserted to remain with the Congregation of Israel in the Holy of Holies.

"And *the Spirit of YHVH* shall rest upon him" (or it). This is, Kether or the Crown, the 1st Sephirah. (Comp. Is. xxviii, 5.)

"The *Spirit of Wisdom*," 'Hokhmah, the 2d Sephirah. (Comp. Wis. vii, 24–26, Heb. i, 2, 3.)

The *Spirit of "Understanding*," Binah, the 3d Sephirah.

"The *Spirit of Counsel*," עצה Eitz-ah. Tzad-dek, Justice, the 5th Sephirah.

The *Spirit of "Might*," Ge'dool-ah, Greatness, the 4th Sephirah.

The *Spirit of "Knowledge*," Daath (? Hod, Splendor), the 8th Sephirah.

The *Spirit of "Fear"* of YHVH, Ne-tza'h, Firmness also called Victory,* the 7th Sephirah.

The root as we have said is Malkhuth, Kingdom, Government; the 10th Sephirah. *The stem* of Jesse, may apply to the 9th Sephirah, Ye'sod, Basis or Foundation.†

The Talmud, treatise *Sanhedrin*, fol. 93 *a* and *b*, applies this quotation to the Messiah.

In the Apocryphal Gospel of the Birth of Mary, almost the same is repeated (c. v, 14–15). We will divide as before, viz:

---

* The Branch will answer to the Sixth Sephirah Tiph-e'reth, Beauty, that of the heart, ethics and conscience. This is the Sephirah of both the heart and of the Sun as the centre of the Makrokosm. It is put in place of the one who will judge with Righteousness. The Messiah (compare Is. xi, 3–16) is evidently referred to. He is the "Sun of Righteousness."

† See Cahen's French Bible, Vol. ix, p. x, 3 note.

"For Isaiah saith, there shall come forth *a rod* out of the *stem* of Jesse." This is the Sephirothic diagram called: The Tree. "And a flower shall *spring out of its root*," the root is Malkhuth, Kingdom. *The flower*, is Kether, the Crown, which like a lily blooms on the top of the stem.

"And the *Spirit of the Lord*, etc." That is, the Ain Soph. "The *Spirit of Wisdom*," 'Hokhmah, and the *Spirit* "*of Understanding*," Binah.

"The *Spirit of Counsel*," Ge'boor-ah, Judgment.

The *Spirit of* "*Might*," Ge'dool-ah, Greatness.

"The *Spirit of Knowledge*." Perhaps Hod, *i. e.*, Splendor.

The *Spirit of* "*Piety*." Perhaps Tiph-e'reth, Beauty or Righteousness, which is with the Hebrews, a synonym of Piety.

The *Spirit* "*of Fear* of the Lord." Ne-tza'h, Firmness. Perhaps Victory, the same Sephirah.

The *stem* of Jesse. Ye'sod, Foundation or Basis, the Support of the vitality of the Matter-World.

Here, if we are correct, are all the Ten Sephiroth and also the Ain Soph.*

"And one of the elders saith unto me: Weep not: behold the lion of the tribe of Judah, the root of David† hath prevailed to open the book, and loose the *seven* seals thereof. And I beheld, and, lo, in the midst of the throne and of the four beasts, and in the midst of the elders, stood a Lamb as it had been slain, having seven horns and *seven eyes*, which are *the seven spirits* of God sent forth into all the earth." (Revelation v, 5–6.)

The following Diagram shows a parallel decadal division of the Commandments and the Paternoster.

---

* See The Apocryphal New Testament, etc. Gebbie & Co., Philadelphia, pp. 21. Compare also verse 17. Hone's Ed. London, 1820, p. 21. Comp. Kitto's Biblical Cycl., Ed. 1876, Vol. ii, 161 ; i, 169.

† The root of David, is taken from Isaiah xi, 1. "There shall come forth a rod out of the stem of Jesse, and a branch shall grow out of his roots."

	TEN COMMANDMENTS OF THE THORAH.	TEN DIVISIONS OF THE LORD'S PRAYER.
1.	Thou shalt have no other Elohim but Me.	Our Father,
2.	Thou shalt not make any graven image (of Me).	Which art in Heaven,
3.	Thou shalt not take the Name YHVH in vain.	Hallowed be Thy Name.
4.	Thou shalt sanctify the Sabbath day.	Thy Kingdom Come;
5.	Honor thy father and thy mother.	Thy will be done on earth,
6.	Thou shalt not kill.	As it is done in heaven;
7.	Thou shalt not commit adultery.	Forgive us our trespasses and we forgive those who trespass against us;
8.	Thou shalt not steal.	Give us this day our daily bread;
9.	Thou shalt not bear false witness.	Lead us not into temptation,
10.	Thou shalt not covet.	But deliver us from evil.*

It will be observed that the first three apply more especially to the Deity, the fourth to God and man, and the last six, to mankind alone. The fifth, sixth, and seventh Commandments relate to the affections—filial, fraternal and conjugal. The infraction of which was punished by the Hebrews with death. The love of man and the sacredness of human life, is the harmony between filial piety and conjugal fidelity. The Decalogue, if we consider the eighth and ninth, inculcates honesty in thought as well as in action. As applying to man's actions in this matter-world, we therefore have a symbolical diagram in this form:

$$\begin{array}{cccc} 1 & 2 & 3 & 4 \\ & 5 & 6 & 7 \\ & & 8 & 9 \\ & & & 10 \end{array}$$

The reverse of the equilateral triangle of the sacred Tetrad of Pythagoras 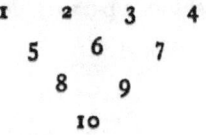 which added any way makes the holy decadic number.

* As to the Lord's Prayer and the Rabbinic writings, see Sayings of the Jewish Fathers, etc., by Charles Taylor, p. 138 *sq.*

(Comp. *ante*, 202, note.) 1, 4 and 10 are the outposts.* The 6th, the order not to kill but to love man; is in the centre; it is for the protection of human life and without life the earth would be a sterile desert.

* The numbers 1, 4 and 10 = 15 the value of the letters of יה YaH = 15. With that word it is said; "Elohim formed the worlds." See Ya'lkut ha-Zohar on; "Forming the Worlds."

Diagram V.—The idea of the universe in the Middle Ages.

Figure 30.—Hindu symbol of the Four Worlds.

XVII.

THE FOUR WORLDS. OF PRANA. OF PAN AS THE MAKROKOSMOS. OTHER IDEAS OF THE MAKROKOSMOS. ASSERTED ORIGIN OF THE IDEA OF THE FOUR WORLDS.

IN the Speculative Qabbalah, four Conditions or Worlds are enumerated. The first of these is termed, *Olam A'tzeel-ooth** or the A'tzeelatic World, the World of Emanation *par excellence.* This is the most exalted of all the Conditions and is considered as containing only the Holy Upper Ten Sephiroth; the highest round of the ladder of Intermediaries, which are nevertheless only an Unit, and are between Ain Soph, the Primal Cause of All, and the inferior emanations which develope the existences. As a totality in this Upper Condition, the Ten Sephiroth represent the operative qualities of the Divine Will, considered as the most abstract and spiritual of all the emanations of the Ain Soph. This

* It is to be noted that the names of the Four Worlds, have Sanskrit roots.

Upper World is the abode solely of *D'yooq-nah*, *i. e.*, the Image, Upper Adam, or Adam Illa-ah, the Archetypal Man; the totality of all the Sephiroth, the Protogonos, *i.e.*, first born. This condition is also known as *Olam ha-Sephiroth*, *i. e.*, World of the Sephiroth, it is considered from its nearness to and as the direct emanation of Ain Soph, as perfect and immutable, an emanation in which Ain Soph is more immediately immanent yet transcendental. It is not ever looked upon as in any way perfectly equal to the Eternal Boundless, which is concealed and hidden in Its essence from the comprehension of man.

"*A'tzeel-ooth* is the Great Sacred Seal, by means of which all the Worlds are copied which have impressed on themselves, the image on the Seal; and as this Great Seal comprehends three stages, which are three *zures* (prototypes) of *Nephesh* (the Vital Spirit or Soul), *Rua'h* (the Ethical and Reasoning spirit) and the *Neshamah* (the Highest soul of man) so the Sealed, have also received three *zures* (prototypes) namely, *B'ree-ah*, *Ye'tzeer-ah*, and *A'seey-ah*, and these three *zures* are only One in the Seal."

In this connection we present a Hindu figure, No. 31, which represents Prana, the Hindu Spiritual or Ideal Androgenic Man, who is the Life and Breath of all the existences, and evidently the Makrokosmos of the created. It is portrayed as crowned by a sun, which is to represent the subtile azothic life fire, and by two storks reaching upward for the higher breath. The stork is in India a dweller on roofs and tree tops and the tops of pillars, yet is also a water bird. It flies high and is considered to bring good fortune. Storks are considered attributes of Vayu, the wind-spirit. The remainder of the head-dress appears as if a crown with lapels falling at the sides but not covering the ears, which have ornaments like those of the Egyptian Sphinxes, and is something like the cap of the Phrygian Paris. The content of this crown, as an entirety, gives Prana a majestic appearance. It has also a curious necklace and neck pendant resembling an air tube tied at intervals. Prana supports, by its everlasting arms, the veil of Maya or Illusion; the mysterious veil of life embroidered with stars. Upon the centre of its breast is the crescent moon in the midst of the sun. In its right hand is a sceptre with 6 balls, which appear flying around as if repelled by an electrical force, probably to rep-

resent the six poles of dimension. The fingers of its left hand are held
in the position frequently assumed by religionists in blessing. The arms
and legs are winged, and the former raised as if about to fly. Around
its loins is a rich tegument composed of rhomboids, egg-like ellipses and
united circles. Its dress has four curious projections on each side over

Figure 31.

the hips. There is a kilt having three symbolical birds and lines of stars,
above and below them, portrayed upon it. The lingam is also shown
with the life-spirit as a flame united with the crescent moon, the symbol
of purity and chastity. Over its head comes down the streaming efflux
of the Upper Life. It has not visible eye-pupils, its eyes appear as cor-

ruscations of light; and streams of light and life proceed from the eyes, ears, nostrils and mouth, in all 8.* Around its navel, the seat of embryonic life, is a circular cloud united with the necklace above and the lingam life-spirit. "As the bee follows its queen so all the senses follow Prana," says a Hindu sacred book. So here we have the flying bees.† The King of the Breath of Life, stands upon the world-egg, which is surrounded by the Time serpent Ananta, and the Hindu Zodiac; from it burst five openings like the five senses of man, and from the Makrokosm, the five senses spring out as the Mikrokosm or terrestrial earth spirit or man.

Prana or the Life-spirit stands above all the creation inferior to it. It is the soul of the Universe. The Atharva-veda says: "Reverence to Prana, to whom this universe is subject, who has become lord of all, on whom all is supported."‡ Prana is also Purusha or A U M,§ and therefore the totality of Brahma, Vishna and Siva, past, present and future. The similarity of this symbol of the Makrokosm when compared to the Ze'ir Anpeen or Appayim and the Archetypal Man, of the Zoharic writings, is striking. ||

Prana was to the Hindu the Æolomorphos or Plastic Form, the Great Spirit of all Kosmic life, the hidden growth power, the content of

---

* Comp. Indian Wisdom, by Monier Williams, notes to pp. 94, 126 and 190, as to the 9 gated city of Brahma.

† Bees were a sacred symbol among some of the ancient Asiatic peoples and also with the Greeks; with the latter, new born souls were called, bees. Bees were connected with the spirit of generation and from this the name of the great nature deity *Pri-Apis*, Father Bee, may come. With the Egyptians, the sacred Bull was called *Apis*, *i. e.*, Bee. Isaiah says: "Behold, the young woman shall conceive, and bear a son, and shall call his name Immanuel (God with us). Butter and *honey* shall he eat, *that he may know to refuse the evil and choose the good, etc.*" (Is. vii, 15; comp. *ibid.* 18.) To those who wish to know more of the curious religious symbolism of, the bee; we refer to the learned statements in, The Book of God, hereafter cited, Vol. ii and iii; also to The Platonist, Vol. iv, (March, 1888,) p. 160 *sq.* See also *ante*, p. 228 *sq.*

‡ See Indian Wisdom, by Prof. Monier Williams. London, 1875, p. 40 and note.

§ *Ibid.*, 103, Barth's Religions of India. English trans., 1882, p. 71 *et seq.*

|| For a representation of the Qabbalistic Prototypic Man, the Image, see Frontispiece.

the concealed plastic and the all-pervading vital energy of the growth and existence of the created. The cause of destruction and change yet of re-creation and life, of color, light, form, texture, substance, etc., which has been going on from the beginning and will ever go on to the end.*

The Greeks crystallized this idea into the attributes of the deity whom they called Pan, who was with them the same as τὸ παν the universe, or we may say, Pan was the god of the universe.† They also identified this deity with the Egyptian god, Khem. (*Religions de l'antiquité considérées principalement dans leurs formes symboliques*, etc., by Dr. Fred. Creuzer, French ed. by J. D. Guigniaut, Paris, 1825, Vol. i, part ii, pp. 829 *sq.* *Ibid.* part i, p. 451 note, 495 *sq.* 510 *sq.* *Le Panthéon, Égyptien*, by M. Paul Pierret, Paris, 1881, pp. 39, 46.)

Orpheus in one of his poems says: All things are full of Zeus, and in him, sees the earth, water, fire, and day and night. Does he not by this intend to describe the entire universe, its head sparkling with a golden crown? Does he not describe heaven glittering with the rays of the stars? Do not the beaming eyes represent the sun and moon and the broad chest, the air? And the shoulders, prominent by the wide extent of the wings, do they not describe the velocity of winds and the rapidity shown by God in acting. This image, thus set forth by Orpheus, is almost the same as that by which in ancient times the Greeks described Pan and the Zeus who was called, the Pan παν, *i. e.*, the whole, only because he represents the *universe*, a fact proved by the symbols. The horns, as Boccaccio says, were given to him to signify the rays of the sun, moon and stars; the ruddy face means the ætherial fire, the long beard the masculine elements, the skin covered with spots, the sphere of the fixed stars, the staff with its crutch turned towards the rear, the power over things he owns and the years that ever return to him. The heptaulus, or syrinx with

---

* The scholar will find many similarities to the Speculative Hebrew Qabbalah, especially as to the four worlds and ten emanations from the Deity, in the Upanishads of the Hindu Veda's, we refer him as to this, to the Sacred Books of the East, edited by Prof. Max Muller, Vol. i, 236 *sq.* among the many places.

† The student will find a number of references, etc., upon this subject in the work, entitled The Book of God, etc., by Dr. Keneally. London. We refer to Vol. i, pp. 88, 98, 294; ii, pp. 23, 104 *sq.*, 348 *sq.*, 540; iii, pp. 188, 210, 324, 734.

seven pipes, in his left hand, expresses the celestial harmony of the planets which is shown by their motion more than by anything else. The lower limbs, rough and hairy and with ram's feet, mean only the hard, rough, rugged earth; covered with all kinds of trees, herbs and plants. The ram's feet, etc., signify the fecundity by which life in the universe is continued and preserved, in a mystical way. Both the Egyptians and Greeks sometimes represented Pan or the Lykæan Zeus, under the form of a male goat as the representative of continued creation and its preserver.

We give, Figure 32, from the learned Jesuit, Kircher, a representation of Pan or Zeus Lykæus, as the Makrokosmos. A. A ruddy face. The power of ætherial fire or heat, in the universe. B. The power of the celestial rays on those things which are under the moon. C. Masculine elements. D. Power of the year and its return and of all revolutions. E. All things are maintained by its virility. F. Power of the Firmament, the sphere of the fixed stars. G. The earth (the feminine element) teeming with plants, seeds and trees. H. Fountain of water and liquids (of the feminine element) by irrigation fertilizing the earth. I. The fields, crops and other vegetable matters. K. Harmony of the seven planets. L. Unequal and rough mountains of different heights. M. Power of fecundity. N. The cubical, or six-sided solid foundation. O. Power, energy and velocity of the winds and their rapidity of action.

Figure 32. A hieroglyphic representation of Zeus and Pan.

The ancients asserted that Pan dwelt in deserted places, so as to indicate his loneness or unity, for the universe is one and created by One. He is also clothed in the skin of a male spotted leopard or a fallow deer, to signify the beautiful variety of things and colors, seen in the world.

These doubtless have an Asiatic origin.* The Roman Church has changed the *lupercalia*, one of the festivals to Pan on February 15th, to the Procession of Lighted Candles.

In the Middle Ages the Makrokosmos was thought of as the Greek and Roman, Atlas; which was asserted, by these peoples, to support the uni-

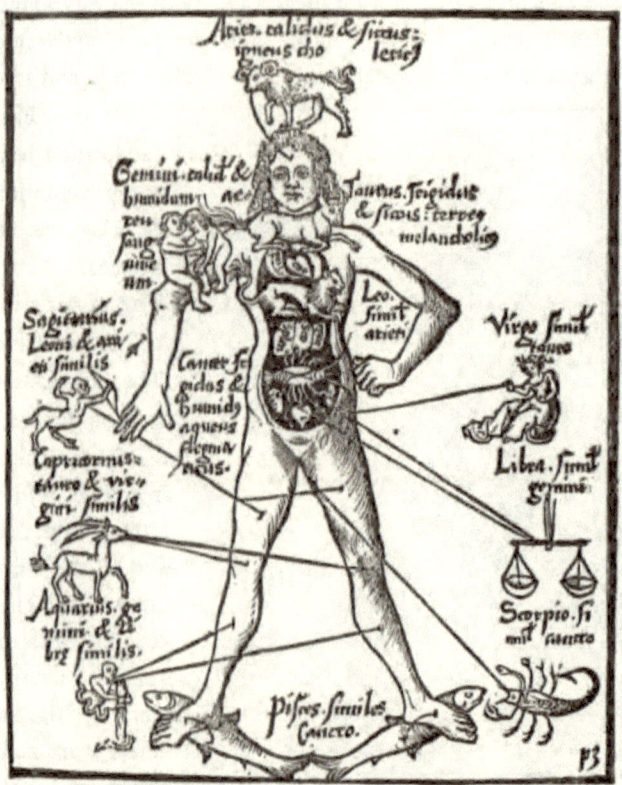

Figure 33. The Makrokosmos as portrayed in the Middle Ages.

verse. See Diagram V, *ante*, p. 319. It was also portrayed as in the foregoing plate, Figure 33, an exact copy of one made in A. D. 1503. The form and arrangement set forth in this drawing are of great antiquity. This arrangement and form have been brought down to our own day and are yet shown in the almanacs.

*Comp. *Œdipi Ægyptiaci, Tomus Secundus, c. iv, classis vi, § v, p. 427 sq. Ed. Roma 1653.*

We also give Figure 34, an exact copy of another engraving of the same date.* It is most important to all occultists as containing an important occult meaning. We may explain this in a subsequent work and will

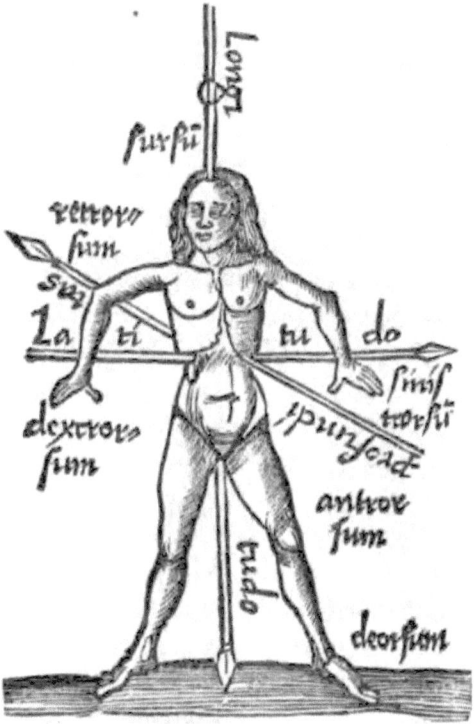

Figure 34. An occult portrayal of the Makrokosmos.

only say here, that it has much in common with the secret religious systems of the oldest peoples of the entire world, both the New and Old.

* Diagram V and Figures 33 and 34, are taken from the earliest Encyclopædia published in the Middle Ages, viz: *Margarita philosophica, totius philosophiæ rationalis et moralis principia duodecim libris dialogice complectens. Friburgi, Joannes Schotus, 1503, in 4to.*

The author was Prior of a Carthusian nunnery near Friburg. Subsequent editions were Strasburg, Grüninger, 1504, 1508, 1512, 1515 in 4to; Basle, 1535, 1583, and an Italian Ed., Venice, 1599. Panzer and Hain refer to an impression as early as 1496. We also have a copy of an Anglo-Saxon almanac, said to be 1386 A. D., which has a very similar figure to No. 33.

From the A'tzeel-oothic World, through the conjunction of the King and Queen, proceeds the World of Creation, called, the B'ree-atic or *Olam B'ree-ah* also *Qur-saiy-ah, i. e.*, the Throne. In this Condition, creation as we understand the word, begun. It is considered as the abode of only pure spirits. It also contains a continuation of the emanating rays of the Ten Sephiroth of A'tzeel-ah, as a matter of course still further removed from Ain Soph and the first Ten, but a continuation and not in any way absolutely separate and distinct from them, but nevertheless of a more limited and circumscribed potency. The purely spiritual substances which it contains have not any admixture of matter, as we understand matter; but they are inferior to the First World and superior to the following; that of the Powers, Intelligences or Angels, of the planets and celestial spheres. As *D'yooq-nah* the Prototype, occupies the First World so the great Presence Angel of the Covenant, Metatron; occupies the Second World. He alone constituting the entire World of Spirits or Angels. Metatron is "the garment," or visible manifestation of the Ain Soph, and his name = 314, is equal to Shaddai, *i. e.*, Almighty. (Zohar, iii, 231*a*.) Metatron governs the visible world, preserves the unity, harmony and revolutions of the spheres, planets and all the heavenly bodies; and is the Commander, under the Will of the Deity, of all the myriads of the angelic hosts, of the next or Ye'tzeer-atic World. These are divided into ten ranks answering to the number of the Ten Sephiroth.

Following, and also proceeding from *Olam B'ree-ah* by emanation, is *Olam Ye'tzeer-ah, i. e.*, the World of Formation. It is the abode of the Angels, the Intelligences of the Celestial planets and stars, and is also called *Mala'hay-ah, i.e.*, of the Angels. It has also Ten Sephiroth, which proceed from and are only continuations of, the Ten of the A'tzeel-atic World through the Ten of the B'ree-atic, being only extensions of the first manifestations of Ain Soph through the preceding Ten Sephiroth, but further removed. The Zohar (ii, 43*a*) says: "For the servants (Sephiroth) that serve the Holy, Blessed be He! It made the Throne (the B'ree-atic World) with four supports (pedestals) and six steps (platforms, dias) to the Throne, together ten. The whole is like a cup of blessing. That which is in it is ten words, like the Thorah which is given in ten words; and as the universe, which is the Ma'a-seh Be'resheeth, which has been created by ten sayings. The Holy, Blessed be He! affixed to the Throne legions to serve it, (the Ten Angelic Hosts, the Ye'tzeer-atic World.) These are; Malakheem, Areleem, 'Haÿ-yôth, Ophaneem, Hash-maleem, E'leem, Eloheem, Benai Eloheem, Isheem and Serapheem. And for the service of these, the Holy, Blessed be He! made Samā-el and his legions, who are as it were, the clouds to be used to come down upon the earth. And they are their horses: and above the clouds is the Merkabah, *i. e.*, the Chariot Throne, therefore it is said: (Is. xix, 1) 'Behold YHVH rideth upon a swift cloud and shall come into Misraim (Egypt).' And so the Holy, Blessed be He! rules Mitzraim." The Ten Sephiroth of this Condition or World, are still contemplated as without taint of earthly matter, or matter as man understands the word. In this World reside those intelligent and incorporeal beings, each wrapped in a luminous vestment, which are sexless and capable, by the Divine permission, of assuming a form sensible to mankind when they appear to him. They are also ministering spirits, energies or forces, which do the Will of the Deity.

The Zohar (iii, 68*a*) says: "The Holy, Blessed be He! animated every part of the firmament with a separate spirit, and forthwith all the Heavenly Hosts were standing and remained so before Him. This is meant by the Psalmist (xxxiii, 6), 'By the breath of His mouth were made all their hosts.'" The angels are of two kinds—good and bad; and they have their respective princes.

Among the angelic hosts which people the Ye'tzeer-atic World, one angel has control over one sphere, another of another sphere, one has charge of the sun, another of the moon, another of the earth, another of the ocean, another of fire, another of the wind, another of the light, another of the changes of the seasons, etc. These angels are only representatives of forces or energies, they are named after the heavenly bodies, etc., which they are supposed to rule, one is called *Nogah, i. e.*, Venus, one *Ma-adameem* (*dam, i. e.*, blood) Mars, one is *Etsem ha-Sha'mayeem, i. e.*, of the clearness (or, bone), of the heavens, (Ex. xxiv, 10, Ezek. x) one is *Uriel, i. e.*, of light, another *Nooriel, i.e.*, of fire, etc. (See Zohar, i, 42*a*, *b*; 43*a et seq.*).

The fourth and last Condition is termed; the World of Action or *Olam A'seey-ah*, the A'seey-atic World, also called *Olam Q'lippoth, i. e.*,

World of the Shells or Rinds, the Demons. It contains the actual matter of the planets or spheres (*gill-gooleem*) and what man terms matter. It is the residence of Samā-el, the Prince of Darkness and his legions. In it is our sublunary world, which is subject to matter re-birth and the dissolution of the matter forms but not the destruction of the essential atoms. It has the operative qualities of all the preceding Ten Sephiroth, but much diminished because further removed from the original source, and is merely an extension of their rays or energies to their last degree or point of cessation. The Zohar (ii, 43*a*), says: For the service of the Angelic World "the Holy, Blessed be He! made Samā-el and his legions, *i. e.*, the World of Action, who are as it were, the clouds to be used (by the Upper Spirits) to ride upon in their descent to the Earth, and serve, as it were, for their horses. Hence it is written: 'Behold YHVH rideth upon a swift cloud, and shall come into Egypt,' etc." (Is. xix, 1.)

The substances of this Condition or World, are considered to be of matter, limited by the dimensions and perceptible to the senses, by means of the multiplicity of forms. It is subject to change, birth, death, corruption and re-birth, yet not anything in it is considered as ever totally annihilated or destroyed in essence or atom. It is the abode of the Evil Spirit and his demoniacal forces.

It is a singular thing that in Genesis (i, 3–5), the production of light is mentioned five times, the first and second times the Qabbalists refer to the same light. This mention of light, four times, has been referred to the Qabbalistic idea of the four Worlds. (Conciliator of R. Manasseh ben Israel, etc. English Ed. by Lindo. Vol. i, p. 7.)

The expression "Be *Light!* and *Light* was," is referred to the A'tzeel-atic World. "Elohim saw the *light*, that it was good;" applies to the B'ree-atic World, "Elohim divided the *light* from the darkness;" applies to the Ye'tzeer-atic World, that of good and bad angels, those of light and darkness. "Elohim called the *light*, Day, and the darkness he called, Night;" refers to the A'seey-atic or Matter-world, in which, is Day and Night.

The demons, or bad angels, are considered as, the grossest and most deficient of all forms, are called the *Q'lippoth*, or mere *Shells* or *Rinds* of existence. They are thought of as energies or forces which are destructive and injurious to man. They too form Ten Degrees answering to the lowest extremity of the Ten Sephirothic emanative rays, and in these Ten lower degrees, darkness and impurity increase the further they are removed from the primordial source. Thus the first two demoniacal degrees are considered, as only the absence of visible form and organization, which in Genesis is termed; "*Tohoo W'bohoo*," which preceded the creation of the order of the Universe. The third degree is looked upon as the abode of darkness, which Genesis says at first covered the face of the earth. After this come the seven infernal halls (*Sevwah Haikhaloth*) or hells, (*Gaï-hinom,*) the abode of the demons and their princes. Here are tortured, the existences which were led astray on earth. These seven halls or hells, are divided into numerous compartments, for the different kinds of punishment apportioned for the different species of earthly sin. The Prince of the whole region is Samā-el, *i. e.*, the Angel of Venom, Poison, or Death.* He is thought of as the Satan of the Old Testament, who therein plays more the part of deceiver and accuser than that of a punisher. The Qabbalah however considers Samā-el as the Satan who seduced Eve. The Talmud holds to the same view, it says; "The evil spirit Satan and the Angel of Death, are the same." (Treatise *Bavah Bathra*, 16a.) He has a female companion, called *Esheth Zenooneem*, *i. e.*, the Harlot. They are usually represented as united under the name of 'Ha-yoh, *i.e.*, the Beast. (Comp. Zohar, ii, 255–259; i, 35*b*.) Which therefore is an assertion that the Great Power of Evil is androgenic. A dark shadow of the manifestation of the Great Androgene of Good.

"The Ten Sephiroth of A'tzeel-ooth have scintillated and brought forth the Ten Sephiroth of B'ree-ah, and from the energy of these Ten of B'ree-ah, sparkled forth the scintillations of the World Ye'tzeer-ah, and through these, the Ten Sephiroth of the World A'seey-ah were sealed, and all the Sephiroth of all the Worlds, divide themselves into fives." (*Ets ha-Haÿ-yem*, *i. e.*, Tree of Life, fol. 253, col. 2.)

Not any of the Sephiroth of the Lower Worlds are considered as of an equally divine nature as those of A'tzeel-ooth. "The *Kailem*, *i. e.*, Vessels, Vases, Sephiroth, of A'tzeel-ooth, become *Neshamah* for B'ree-ah,

---

* *Sam*, *i. e.*, Poison or Venom, and *Ail* or *El*, *i. e.*, Angel, therefore the Angel of Poison.

Ye'tzeer-ah and A'seey-ah, and these latter are not called truly divine; because even their *Neshamah* are *Kailem* and are not Lights from A'tzeel-ooth." These four Worlds form together an Unit, a single Great Man, the Makrokosm or Adam Illa-ah. (*Tiqqooneem has-Zohar. Tiqqoon,* 70, also *Sepher Kesaï Malekh,* fol. 52.)

In the philosophy of Ibn Gebirol, these Worlds can be distinguished, viz:—That of the Perfect Form or Will; that of the Simple Substances by which our creation begun; that of the Heavenly Orbits or Spheres and their Intelligences; and that of the Celestial Matter Spheres or Planets and the Elements of our Matter-world or Universe. Ibn Gebirol says; it is necessary to consider matter as having two extremities, one going upwards to the highest limit of creation, and as far as the limit of conjunction of matter with form; the other extending downwards to the point of cessation; that is the extreme inferior limit in which all form ends. The highest ascends to the Spiritual, the Will; which is above the celestial spheres or orbits, and which descends as the Unity and Simplicity, to the limit, the commencement of creation; and then, below the celestial spheres, takes a corporeal form, and as it descends, becomes more and more corporeal, until it reaches the limit of cessation.

The doctrine of the Makrokosm and the Mikrokosm, is both in Ibn Gebirol and the Zohar. Our author says: (Bk. iv, § 6 and § 44) "The Little World (man, the Mikrokosm) bears a resemblance to the Great World (the universe), through its order and construction. The substance of the intellect, which is the most subtile, simple and sublime of all the substances of the Little World, (Gebirol is referring here to the *Neshamah* or Higher Soul) is not (directly) attached to the body; because the Spirit (*i. e.*, *Rua'h*) and the Soul (*i. e.*, the Vital Spirit, the *Nephesh*); are intermediaries between the two." He then shows a similar order in the construction of the entire universe, and afterwards says; if one should wish to imagine the construction of the universe and the universal body, and the universal body and the spiritual substances which surround it, let him contemplate the construction of man, "in whom thou wilt find an analogy." The body of man corresponds to the universal body; the spiritual substances which put it in movement, to the universal substances which put in movement the universal body; among these (spiritual) substances, those which are inferior obey the superior and (successively) submit to them, until that which is movement goes back to the substance of the intellect. The intellect governs and rules (these substances), and all the substances in man's body, follow and submit to his intellect; and he says: this is their master and judge. All is disposed in the particular spirit, that of the man, as in the World of the universe, and man is a Mikrokosm. Maimonides holds to the same idea, and has said a great deal upon the subject. (Moreh Ne'boo-kheem, French Ed. by S. Munk, I. c. lxxii and notes. English Ed. I. lxxii, p. 258, 276 and notes.) The theory, that the universe was one finite system regulated by one and the same idea, was that of Aristotle, Plato and most of the philosophers of the Middle Ages.

In Isaiah the Qabbalists find a reference to the Qabbalistic philosophy as to the Four Worlds. "Fear not for I AM with thee. I will bring thy seed from the East, and gather thee from the west; I will say to the North 'give up' and to the south 'Keep not back.' 'Bring My sons from far, and My daughters from the ends of the earth; even every one that is called by My Name! For *I created* (*B'ree-ah*) *him* for *My Glory*, I *formed* (*Ye'tzar*) *him*; yea I *made* (*A'seey-ah*) *him*.'"*

A'tzeel-ah (said to be אֲצִילָה from אָצַל Atzal, to flow out†), is the World of Emanation. B'ree-ah (said to be from *barah*, to create or shape, more likely from the Sanskrit *Brih*, to expand), contains the World of pure forms or simple substances (*i. e.*, ideas). These are thought of and considered in the Qabbalah as spiritual, intelligent beings. Ye'tzeer-ah (said to be from *Ye'tsar*, to form), the world of the Celestial Spheres, of the Souls or Angels. A'seey-ah (said to be from *A'sah*, to make) the World of Matter, of objects perceptible to the senses, which come into being, grow, die and decay. (See *ante*, pp. 53, 198.)

They are also paralleled by the four divisions of Plotinus, viz: the

---

* Is. xliii, 5–7. Comp. Is. xlv, 6–7, 12. Philo Judæus in *De Somnis*, Bk. i (Bohn's Ed., Vol. ii, pp. 292–343) especially §§ iii, vii, xi, appears to refer to the Four worlds of the Qabbalah.

† See what Joel says against this in his, *Religions-philosophie des Sohar*, p. 203 *sq*. More likely it is from a Sanskrit root.

One, the *Nous* and its ideas, the Soul, and the Matter-kingdom. Neo-platonism according to Lassen (*ante*, p. 170) came from India. *

The subtile distinctions between the Neshamah, Upper Soul or Spirit, Rua'h, the Moral and Reasoning power, and Nephesh, the Vital or merely Animal Life, of man's Spiritual existence, as contained in the Qabbalah, has been quite ably set forth by C. De Leiningen in an Essay delivered, March 5, 1887; before the Psychological Society of Munich, Germany. †

* For a description of Figure 35, see The Path, New York, for March, 1887.

† See *Die Sphynx*, Leipzig, 1887; *Le Lotus*, Paris, January, 1888, p. 232 *sq*.

Figure 35.—Hindu Qabbalistic symbol of the Four Worlds.

XVIII.

EXCERPTS FROM THE ZOHAR: AS TO THE MAN WITH THE HEAVY BURDEN. VICARIOUS ATONEMENT BY THE MESSIAH. THE SHE'KHEEN-AH. A FORMULA OF THE GREAT NAMES. ORIGINAL SIN. POWER OF SATAN. FREE WILL. THE HEAVENLY MEDIATRIX BETWEEN GOD AND MAN. NECESSITY OF REPENTANCE FOR SALVATION. ETERNAL REWARD AND PUNISHMENT IN THE FUTURE LIFE. RESURRECTION OF THE DEAD IN THE BODY. JUDGMENT OF THE SOULS OF THE WICKED, ETC.

IN the introduction written by R. 'Hiz'qee-yah, which is very old, and which forms part of the Brody edition of the Zohar (i, 5*b sq.*), is an account of a journey taken by R. El'azar, son of R. Shim-on b. Yo'haï, and R. Abbah; to visit the father-in-law of the former. Whilst on the way, they meet with a man bearing a heavy burden. They conversed together upon the Ma-a'seh Be'resheeth and the origin of the Sabbath: the explanations of the Thorah, by the man with the burden, were so wonderful, that they asked him for his name; he replied: "Do not ask me who I am; but we will all proceed with the explanation of the Thorah." They asked, "Who caused thee thus to walk and carry such a heavy load?" He answered: "The letter י (Yod, which = 10, and is the symbolical letter of Kether, and the essence and germ of the Holy Name יהוה YHVH) made war, etc." "Ride on one of our mules, they said, we will carry thy burden," but he replied: "Have I not told you, that it is an order of the King, until, etc." "Tell us thy place of habitation?" finally they said to him; he replied: "The place of my abode is good and sublime to me, and it is a tower, which hovers in the air, grand and mighty, and the inhabitants of that tower are the Holy, Blessed be He! and a 'poor.' (This may refer to the Messiah, who is called 'lowly, and rideth on an ass.' Zekh. ix, 9.) That place is my residence, and we moved from there, and I carry that which is heavy * * * They said to him: 'If thou wilt tell us the name of thy father, we will kiss the dust of thy feet.' He replied: 'And why? I am not used to becoming haughty through the Thorah; but as to *my father, he had his dwelling in the Great Sea, and was a fish therein;* which destroyed the Great Sea from one end to the other, and he was great and mighty and 'Ancient of Days,' until he swallowed all the other fishes in the (Great) Sea; and after that, he produced for us, the living and existing beings, from all the best in the world; and *in his might he swims through the (Great) Sea in one moment.* And then, he brought me forth like an arrow in the hand of a powerful man, and hid me in that place, of which I told you; and *then returned to his place and hid himself in the Sea.*' R. El'azar listened to his words and said to him: ' Thou art the son of the Holy Flame, thou art the son of Rab Ham-'*nun*-ah Sabah, (the Old,)* thou art the son of the Light of the Thorah and thou goest burdened behind us!'" On page 9*b ibid.*, may be found other references to the Great Sea and its inhabitants.† The feminine Sephirah, Binah, is sometimes termed by the Qabbalists, the Great Sea. Among her divine Names are YaH and Elohim. She is called the Great Mother, the Upper Mother, the supernal ה (Heh) of יהוה. She is the Holy Spirit and the Upper She'kheen-ah. Her symbol is the brooding dove, she brooded over the face of the waters at the creation. The Great Fish is in the mythology of the Akkadians and Babylonians and is likely the Leviathan in the Qabbalah. (*Kab. Denud. Idrah Rabbah,* § 633.) Note also the invocation by the Roman Church of the Virgin and her Son, of 'Hokhmah, Wisdom or the *Lôgos, i. e.,* Word; and Binah, the Upper Mediating Mother, Universal Intellect, the Great Sea or Holy Spirit. Mary likely equals the Latin *Mare, i. e.,* Sea. According to a hymn of the Xth century sung at the Annunciation, she is;

> " Star of the Sea,
> Gracious Mother of God
> And always Virgo,
> Happy Gate of Heaven." ‡

* The *fish* in Aramaic or Chaldee is נון *nun,* pron. *noon.*

† See *ante,* p. 243 *sq.* as to the Great Sea among the Akkadians and Chaldeans, also the Fish-god. Comp. Dr. J. P. Lundy's Monumental Christianity, pp. 130 *sq.*, 368 *sq.*

‡ Rambach's Collection, i, 219.

THE ATONEMENT. "When the righteous are afflicted by illness or sufferings in order to atone for the sins of the world, it is that all the sinners of their generation (period) may receive redemption. How is this proven? By all the members of the animal (human) body. At the time when all the members (of the animal, human body), suffer through an evil illness, then one member must be beaten (operated upon,) so that all the remaining (members) may recover. Which member? The arm. It is beaten (operated upon) and the blood is drawn from it, and from this results the convalescence of all the other members of the body. So it is with the children of the world, its members stand towards each other equally, like members (of the human body) each to the other.* At the time that the Holy, blessed be He! desires to give health (sanctification) to the world, He afflicts a just (pious) one from the midst (of the world) with sickness and pain, and through him He gives health to all the world. How is this proven? It is written: (Is. liii, 5) 'And he was wounded for our transgression, he was bruised for our iniquities * * * and by his stripes (wounds) are we healed, etc.' 'By his stripes (wounds)' like the bruises (operations) made by the bleeding of the arm, are we healed; that is there is brought to us, as members of the whole body, convalescence." †

* All mankind as the descendants of Adam, are looked upon in the Qabbalah, as one great totality and brotherhood, one great united stream of life. As the great universal spiritual celestial man, the Upper Man, the Makrokosm, borne or carried in the terrestrial universal Adam, the Mikrokosm, in germ, and spiritually and still living in the flesh; by, through and from the life-giving efflux of the Makrokosm, the Adam Illa-ah, etc., as we before set forth. The Qabbalistic doctrine as to A'reekh An-peen and Ze'ir An-peen, is also here to be noted.

† Zohar iii, fol. 218a, § *Pin-'has*. (Rayah Me'hemnah) Amsterdam Ed. iii, fol. 88, col. 2, Sulzbach Edition. Zohar, Cremona Edition iii, fol. 101a, col. 402. Among the ancient Hindus, an atonement was asserted to be through the sacrifice of Purusha, the Great Hindu Universal Ideal Man. (Indian Wisdom by Monier Williams. London, 1875, p. 24. Hinduism, by the same author, pp. 36, 90.) Buddha is also reported as saying: " Let all the evils (sins) flowing from the corruption of the fourth or degenerate age (the Kali) fall upon me, but let the world be redeemed." (Indian Wisdom, above cited, p. 55 note 1.) As to the idea among the ancient people of Babylonia, etc., see *ante*, p. 240.

ATONEMENT BY THE MESSIAH. "Those souls (*Neshmosin*), which are in the lowest Paradise (*i. e.*, *Gan Eden*), hover about and look around through the world * * * and when they behold suffering, ill, or patient martyrs, and those who suffer for the unity of their Master, they return and inform the Messiah. At the time when they inform him (the Messiah) of the afflictions of Israël in Exile, and that the sinners among them do not reflect in order to know their Lord, he lifts up his voice and weeps because of those sinners, as it is written: 'And he is wounded for our misdeeds, etc.' (Is. liii, 5.) Whereupon the souls return and remain in their places. In the Garden of Eden is a palace, which is called: the Palace of the Wicked Children. The Messiah goes up into this Palace and calls all the sufferings, pains and tribulations of Israël to come upon himself. And they all come upon him. If he had not thus taken upon himself the punishment of Israël for the transgressions of the Law, not any man would be able to endure the sufferings (due for such transgressions), as it is written: "In truth he took upon himself our sickness, etc. * * * * Whilst the children of Israël lived in the Holy Land, they kept from the world, all pain and suffering by their prayers, worship and sacrifice; but now the Messiah does it, and removes them (the sufferings, etc.) from the world until the child of man departs from this world and receives his punishment."†

"The man pure of sin is himself a real sacrifice, which may serve as an atonement; therefore the righteous are the sacrifice and the atonement of the world." (Zohar i, 65a.)

THE MESSIAH AS THE SHEPHERD. The Raÿah Me'hemnah, *i. e.*, Faithful Shepherd (Zohar iii, fol.'218a, § *Pin-'has*. Amsterdam edition; Cremona Ed. ii, 100b,) also says: " This is also exemplified by the account of Job: for the Holy, Blessed be He! Seeing that the whole generation was a sinful one, and Satan coming to accuse them, The Holy, Blessed be He! said to him (Job i, 8): 'Hast thou considered My servant Job? For there are none like him upon the whole earth,' to save through him, (his) generation. This can be illustrated by the parable of the Shep-

---

* Is. liii, 4. Comp. Rom. xii, 3, 4.

† Zohar ii, fol. 212a and b, Amsterdam Ed. ii, fol. 85, col. 2, Sulzbach Ed. Cremona Ed. ii, fol. 95b. Comp. 2 Cor. v, 21; 1 Ep. John ii, 2; iv, 10.

herd, who saw a wolf approaching to tear in pieces his sheep and destroy them. What did the shepherd do? He was wise, so he gave to him (the wolf) the strongest and fattest bell-wether from all, which the flock was in the habit of following. What then did the shepherd do? Whilst the wolf was carrying this bell-wether off, the shepherd run with his sheep and put them into a safe place and then (*Ibid.*, 218*b*) returned and saved him (the bell-wether) from the wolf. In the same way does the Holy, Blessed be He! deal with a generation; He delivers a righteous man into the power of (Satan, the Wolf) the 'accuser,' for the salvation of the generation through him. But when he is as strong as Jacob, it is said by him; 'the man wrestled with him.' (Gen. xxxii, 24.) 'But he will not be able to prevail, on the contrary he will beg the righteous man to let him go' (*Ibid.*, 26) for the righteous one, chosen by the Holy, Blessed be He! is too strong for the adversary, and he (the righteous one) willingly bears the bitterest afflictions for the salvation of his generation, and is considered, as the saviour of them, and the Holy, Blessed be He! appoints him shepherd over all the flock, to feed them in this world, and to rule over them in the world to come."

THE ATONEMENT BY THE MESSIAH. "The ancient pillars of the world (the learned of Israel) differ as to the nationality of Job. One says, that he was a pious Gentile, while another takes him for a pious Israëlite, who was smitten in atonement for all the world. Once R. Hamm'nunnah met the (prophet) Eliÿah and said unto him: 'How is it to be explained, that the righteous suffer while the wicked enjoys life?' He answered him saying: 'The pious whose sins are few gets his punishment for them in this world, therefore it is that the pious suffers here, but he whose sins are many, and whose good actions are but few, receives reward for the latter in this world, this explains why 'the wicked enjoys life.' Said he to him the Judgments of the Lord of the universe are deep, but at the time when the Lord desires to forgive the sins of the world, the Holy, Blessed be He! strikes one of their arms, and so restores spiritual health to all. As a physician does, who strikes the arm of a sick man, and thus relieves all the members of the body, accordingly it is written; (Isaiah liii) 'And he was smitten for our transgressions.' " *

* Zohar § *Pin'has*, iii, 231*a*, Amsterdam Ed.; Cremona Ed. ii, fol. 106*b*. This

THE MESSIAH WASHED IN WINE. "'He washed His garment in wine.' (the Mystery?) (Gen. xlix, 11). He is 'Washing' would be more correct. But 'He washed' since the day of the creation of the world. And who is He? That is the King Messiah, Below. 'In wine' that is the Left side; 'In the blood of the grape,' that is the Left side, Below. But the King Messias is prepared to govern, (fol. 240a,) Above; over all the idolatrous nations, and break their power from Above and Below.

Another meaning of 'He washed his garment in wine,' is that wine gladdens externally, while in its nature it is ascerb, so also is the King Messiah gladdening for Israel, and is all judgment on the idolatrous nations. It is written: 'The Spirit (*Rua'h*) of Elohim hovered over the waters,' (Gen. i, 2;) that is the Spirit of the King Messiah. And from the day of the creation of the world, He washed His garment in the Upper wine. Behold, what follows (on the first quoted verse;) 'The eyes become red from wine, and the teeth white from milk, (Gen. xlix, 12, Comp. Vulgate,) this is the Upper wine of which the lords of the Thorah, drink."*

THE RELATION OF THE SHE'KHEEN-AH TO THE HOLY BLESSED. "The She'kheen-ah although she stands to the other Lights of the Creation like the soul to the body, yet she still stands to the Holy, Blessed be He! like the body to the soul, but all are one; therefore here, which is not the case with man, body and soul are one: for the body (of man) is earth (חומר 'homer, *i. e.*, clay or earth) and the soul is called שכל sekhel, (*i.e.*, reason.) The latter, is life; the former, death; but the Holy, Blessed be He! is Life and the She'kheen-ah is Life. Therefore it is

---

section or parashath, of the Zoharic writings; comprises Volume iii from fol. 213a to fol. 259b, *i. e.*, 46 folios = 92 pages, and contains many more paragraphs of the same tenor as those before cited. Therein may be the great Secret of Vicarious Atonement for the wicked. Christianity nor Aristotelianism are not referred to in the Zohar. This is a proof of its antiquity and that it is an ancient Asiatic book.

* Zohar i, fol. 239b and 240a; Amsterdam Ed. i, fol. 128b, Sulzbach Ed. Cremona Ed. i, fol. 127b. The Hebrew word סוד 4 + 6 + 60 = 70 (*i. e.*, Sod, *i. e.*, Mystery). So also does יין 50 + 10 + 10 *ya-yin*, Wine = 70. The expression "Wine of the Thorah" would mean the Secret Mysteries of the Thorah (or Law). So the above expression may mean: 'He washed His garment (covering) in the Mysteries of Wisdom '*Hokhmah Nistarah.*

written: 'She is a Tree of Life to those who lay hold upon her, etc."* (Prov. iii, 18.)†

OF THE SHE'KHEEN-AH.—" Because of (the attributes of) the Holy, Blessed be He! being concealed in the Mysteries of the Thorah (Pentateuch). By what is He known? By the Commandments which are His She'kheen-ah which is His (*D'yooq-nah*) image. As He is humble so is the She'kheen-ah, humility; as He is benevolent so is she benevolence; as He is strong, so she is the strength of all the nations of the world; as He is the truth, so is she the truth; as He is the prophet so is she the prophetess; as He is righteous (just) so is she righteousness (justness); as He is King, so she is Queen; as He is wise, so is she wisdom; as He is intelligent, so is she His intelligence; as He is the crown, so she is His diadem, the diadem of Glory. Therefore the Rabbins have decided, that all whose inner is not like the external, shall not have admittance to the *Beth ha-Midrash, i. e.*, House of learning. As the image of the Holy, Blessed be He! whose interior He is, and whose external is the She'kheen-ah; He, His interior internally, she, His exterior, externally, so that there is not any difference between she, the external, and He, the internal, as she (the She'kheen-ah) is an outflow from Him; and therefore every difference of the external and internal is obviated, and as further the inner nature of YHVH is hidden; therefore He (YHVH) is only named with the Name of the She'kheen-ah אדני *Adonai i. e.*, Lord: ‡ therefore the Rabbins say (of the name YHVH); Not as I AM written (*i. e.*, YHVH) AM I read. In this world My Name is written YHVH and read Adonoi, but in the world to come, the same will be read as it is written, so that Mercy (represented by YHVH) shall be from all sides. §

* This shows that the body and soul are not one, but that Hu, *i.e.*, He, and His She'kheen-ah together, are One.

† Zohar ii, fol. 118*b*, Raÿah Me'hemnah. Amsterdam Ed. ii, fol. 49, col. 1. Sulzbach Ed. Cremona Ed. ii, fol. 53*a*.

‡ The two names are united, merge in and form, the Unit, in the Perfect Name Adonoi or Adonai.

§ Zohar iii, fol. 230*a*, Amsterdam Ed. iii, fol. 93, col. 1. Sulzbach Ed. Cremona Ed. ii, fol. 106*a*, Raÿah Me'hemnah.

THE SHE'KHEEN-AH IS THE HIGHEST ANGEL. THE IMAGE OF ELOHIM AND ONE WITH ELOHIM. "Come, See! When Hillel, the elder, was rejoicing at that celebration (Festival of the House of Water-drawing) he said 'When אני *a'nee*, *i. e.*, *I am*, is here all are here, but if אני *a'nee I am*, is not here, who is here?' By this he signified and said: If the She'kheen-ah, which is called אני *a'nee* '*I am*' rests here, ALL are here. The place is called כ״ל *Koll*, ALL* for those who will unite themselves to her (the She'kheen-ah). But if אני *a'nee* '*I am*' is not here who is here? Because happiness is not perfect, so long as the She'kheen-ah does not rest in the Holy Land. But when the number of steers shall be completed then will come to pass, that which is written: 'Ye shall draw water with joy from the well-springs of salvation.' (Is. xii, 13.) What are they? These are the six wells, which flow in this salvation. And so the whole world shall rejoice, because the She'kheen-ah shall be liberated from the midst of the nations living in wickedness, and therefore it is written; 'The eighth day shall be a festival to you.' (Numb. xxix, 35)." †

A QABBALISTIC FORMULA OF THE GREAT NAMES, UNITY, ETC.

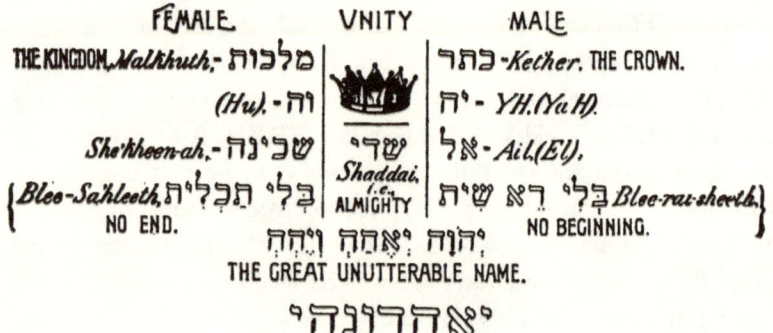

The above Diagram shows the idea of the positive (male) and negative (female) merged in the unity or harmony. The Ineffable name יהוה YHVH, divided in the Sephirothic Tree, at first makes יהו YHV of the Upper Three, the last ה (Heh), being the symbol of the seven Lower

* כ״ל = 50, that is the 50 gates of Binah, Understanding.

† Zohar i, *Hashmutas*, fol. 11*b*, Amsterdam Ed. i, fol. 16, col. 2, Sulzbach Ed. Cremona Ed. i, fol. 18*a*.

Sephiroth and more especially of Malkhuth, the Harmony of all. י (Yod) is the letter of Kether, ה (Heh) of Binah, ו (Vav) of 'Hokhmah, together, the Upper Three. Dividing the Tetragrammaton in half we have the above division, יה YH and וה VH; still further sublimated it is יה YH, this divided, is י (Yod) the letter of Kether, the Father = 10, and the first ה (Heh) the letter of Binah, the Holy Spirit or Upper She'kheen-ah, finally all take rise in the point, or י (Yod) of Kether, which emanates immediately from Ain Soph. Under the Great Unutterable Name we have placed on the Diagram, the Great Name, the Shem-Hammephorash, which the Qabbalists assert, was that pronounced in the past by the High Priest in the Holy of Holies on the Great Day of Atonement, the pronunciation of which, it has been claimed, has been lost. Those of the initiates who can read the above formula knowingly, will understand it.

The Talmud, Rashi its first commentator, and the orthodox Jewish Liturgy, hold that *Hû, i. e.*, He, is a name of the Deity. The Qabbalists hold that the Ineffable Name, יהוה YHVH, expresses a Duality in the Godhead, a He and a she, two persons in one God, the Holy, Blessed be His Name! and His She'kheen-ah. The Daily Prayers of the Orthodox in Jewish Liturgy, before putting on the Tephillin and the Tallith, are:

לשם יחיד קוב"ה ושכינתיה ברחילו ורחמו ליחד שם י"ה
בו"ה ביחודא שלים.

La'shem ye'hood qoodshah baru'k hoo ushe'kheent-ah bed'heeloo ur'heemoo l'ya'had shem יה *YH to* וה *VH b'y'hooda shlim, i. e.,* "To the One Name, the Holy, blessed be He! (Hu) and His She'kheen-ah, with Fear and Mercy, to unite the Name YH to VH, so that it shall be in a perfect Unity."*

The two, HU and YaH, form יהוה אחד, *i. e.*, One YHVH, according to the Qabbalists, One but of a Bisexual nature. The Karaites instead of יהוה write in their Litany יְיָ. The Orthodox Israëlites generally יְיָ. The former cannot be pronounced and is not communicable and is quite Ineffable.†

* Comp. the 'Tzee'nah Uree'nah. A Rabbinical Comment. on Genesis, English Ed., by P. I. Hershon. London, 1885, p. 138, note 2.

† *Ibid.*, p. 302 note.

אחד E'had, *i. e.*, the, One. א = 1, ח = 8, ד = 4. The א means the One Deity, ח means the seven heavens and the one earth, equal eight. ד signifies the four corners of the world. The Qabbalists think of this when repeating the She-mah, and pronounce the word *E'had*, One, in it, very slowly dwelling in their thoughts upon the above signification of its letters.

THE CREATION OF MAN, AND HIS PURITY AND SINNING. "' And He blew into his nostrils (Philo says, face), a breath of Life,' *l'nepesh 'haÿ-yah* (Gen. ii, 7). That is the holy soul, which has its origin from that Divine (Upper) Life. ' And thus man (Adam) became an animated חיה *'haÿ-yah living*, creature!' That is man became endowed with a holy Life (נפש *Nephesh*) from that heavenly creature חיה *'haÿ-yah*.* Which the earth brought forth, as it is written; ' The earth shall bring forth, *the living creature*, חיה נפש *Nephesh 'haÿ-yah i. e., living soul*. (Gen. i, 24.) A soul-life which is in the Divine Upper Life. Come, See! All the time that that holy soul connects itself with the son of man, he is the beloved of his master. How many keepers watch and protect him from all sides! He is the symbol for good, Above and Below, and the Holy She'kheen-ah rests upon him; and at the time man deviates from this way, the She'-kheen-ah departs from him, and the holy soul has not any longer a connection with him, and from the side of the mighty evil serpent † a spirit is stirred up, which (spirit) roams about in the world ‡ and can only find rest in the places from which divine holiness has departed,§ and thus the child of man becomes polluted and declines in flesh as well as in the whole countenance. ||

* Comp. Ezek. i, 5–27; x, 27.

† The left side the negative, destroying, female and evil side; that of Samā-el.

‡ " Be sober, be watchful, your adversary the devil, as a roaring lion, walketh about seeking whom he may devour; whom withstand." I Pet. v, 8. See Kitto's Cyclop. Biblical Lit., iii, p. 773. *sq. ibid.*, ii, p. 857.

§ Is. xxiv, 14, xiii, 21, Kitto's work just cited. iii, p. 804. *Ibid.*, ii, p. 834. Lillith, see *ante* pp. 248, 331.

|| Zohar iii, fol. 46*b*, Amsterdam Ed. iii, fol. 19, col. 1, Sulzbach Ed. Cremona Ed. ii, fol. 21*a*.

THROUGH SIN MAN LOST THE IMAGE OF ELOHIM. "'And your fear and terror shall be over all the animals upon the earth.' (Gen. ix, 2.) That is, the sublime *image of* (the) *man* until now wanting, you shall now bear. Come, See! At first it is written: 'In the *image* בצלם *b'tzalem*, of Elohim, has He made (the) man," (Gen. ix, 6;) and then again it is written; in the *similitude* בדמות *bid-mooth*, *of Elohim, He made him*. Because the *image* of man, in consequence of the sins committed, had changed from the Upper one so that its condition became such, that man feared before the beasts. In the first, all the creatures of the world trembled and quaked at the sight of *man's sublime Upper Holy Image*, but after he had committed sin, his *image* disappeared and *was changed into another similitude*, and a reverse condition, so that the child of man feared and trembled before other creatures. Come, See! The features of all those children of men, who do not sin before their Master and do not transgress His law, have *not changed* in their (original) *Upper Divine Image*, and all the creatures of the world quake and tremble before them; but in time the child of man has transgressed the words of the Thorah and their *image is changed*, and all quake and tremble before other creatures, because this *Divine Image* has changed and disappeared from them. And so the wild beasts govern over them, because they do not see the Divine Upper *Image* * as it had been before.†

THE SERPENT (SAMÄ-EL) BROUGHT DEATH INTO THE WORLD. "'And the serpent was cunning.' (Gen. iii, 1.) It is the evil spirit, it is the Angel of Death (Samā-el). And because the serpent is the Angel of Death, it caused death to the whole world. This is the mystery of what is written 'The end of all flesh has come before Me.' This is the end of all flesh, the serpent takes away the souls (*Neshamoth*) of all flesh.‡

---

* The power of Daniel over the lions the Qabbalists say resulted from his having the Divine Image.

† Zohar i, fol. 71a, Amsterdam Ed. Zohar i, fol. 22, col. 2, Sulzbach Ed. Cremona Ed. i, fol. 53a.

‡ Zohar i, fol. 35a, Amsterdam Ed. Cremona Ed. i, fol. 28a. This means, that the serpent, as the *Yetzer-ha-rah*, evil spirit or evil angel of man, causes man to sin, and causes death to their (*Neshamoth*) heavenly souls.

DEATH CAME THROUGH THE SERPENT. "R. Shim-on (ben Yo'haī) began and said: 'And they transgressed the covenant like Adam, therein they despise Me.' (Hos. vi, 7.) Who can wipe the dust out of thine eyes, O! first man? The Holy, Blessed be He! gave thee one commandment only, still thou couldst not follow it, because thou didst suffer thyself to be seduced through the slanderous words of that wicked serpent, of which it is written: 'And the serpent was cunning;' therefore thou hast caused death to thyself and to all descendants who come out from thee. Come, See! who suffers himself to be seduced by it (the serpent) and follows it even for an instant will perish through it."*

"R. Yitz-haq began and said: 'And He drove Adam out and placed him east of Gan-Eden, (Paradise.)' (Gen. iii, 24.) Come, See! The mystery of the word Adam! The letters of which signify that the object of his (Adam's) sin was at the same time also his punishment. † And caused death to himself and the entire world. And caused the Tree through which he sinned to be banished from Paradise. But Adam himself was the cause of the eternal banishment of his descendants.'"‡

MAN IS BORN IN ORIGINAL SIN WHICH REMAINS WITH HIM UNTIL DEATH. "R. Yehudah began and said: 'His angels He commanded that they guard thee in all thy ways.' (Ps. cxi, 11. Comp. Matt. iv, 6.) This verse, the companions§ explain thus: At the time when man comes into the world, at that instant appears in him the evil spirit (angel)|| which

---

* Zohar ii, fol. 106, col. 2, Sulzbach Ed. ii, fol. 262a, Amsterdam Ed. Cremona Ed. ii, fol. 115a.

† במֹה דחטא אתפס, be'Mah D'hata Athpas, *i.e., through that by which he sinned, he was punished.* The initials backwards אדם, Adam, and properly read מדא, *middah, measure,* according to the proverb: מדה כנגד מדה, *middah k'neged middah, i. e., measure for measure.*

‡ Zohar i, fol. 237a, Amsterdam Ed. ii, fol. 120, col. 2, Sulzbach Ed. Cremona Ed. i, fol. 126b.

§ The "Companions" were those who had been initiated into the Sod or Secret Doctrine later termed Qabbalah.

|| Known to the Israëlites as *Ye'tser ha-rah*, the Evil inclination or angel. It is this Evil Inclination which is referred to in the Lord's Prayer, not Satan. It is looked upon as an angel which accompanies man during his journey through this life. Comp. Sayings of the Jewish Fathers (*Pirqē Avoth*), etc., by Charles Taylor, before cited, pp. 51, 76–78, 96, 111, 112, 142–144 and notes.

always accuses him, as it is written: 'Sin lieth at the door, etc.' (Gen. iv, 7.) What is 'sin lieth'? It means ' the evil spirit' (*Ye'tzer ha-rah*). David also calls it, (the evil spirit) *sin*, as it is written 'And my sin is *always before me;* (Ps. li, 6) because he daily seduces man to sin against his Lord. This evil spirit never leaves man from the day he is born into the world. And the good spirit (*Ye'tzer ha-tob*) comes to the man from the day he becomes clean. And when does man become clean? As soon as he is thirteen years (of age). Then man connects himself with both, one on the right and the other on the left. The good spirit to the right and the evil spirit to the left. And these are the two angels which are destined to always remain by man. If man strives after sanctification the evil spirit is suppressed and the right governs the left, and then both unite to guard man in all his ways and doings, as it is written: 'His angels shall He command, etc.'"*

FREE WILL. "'And אלהים, *i. e.*, Elohim created the Man in His (Elohim's) image,' (Gen. i, 27) that is in the image of Metatron: Who is the Elohim, that created him? He is the living Elohim and King of the World. In the image† of Elohim he created him, that is, Samā-el, from whom are descended other elohim, of which it is written: 'Thou shalt have no *other* elohim beside Me.' (Exod. xx, 3.) If a man is worthy, Elohim creates him in the *image of Metatron*, the servant under his master, that is the meaning of, 'And Elohim created the Man in His image:' namely; in the *similitude* of Metatron; but if man is unworthy, he is created in the *image* of *Samā-el*, the Angel of Death,‡ who executes

---

* Zohar i, fol. 165*b*, Amsterdam. i, fol. 96, col. 2, Sulzbach Ed. Cremona Ed. i, fol. 95*b*.

† בצלם *be-tzelem*, which in the later Hebraic, the Chaldaic and Talmud, is צלם *tzelem*, a simulacrum or shadow and signifies an idol, (Comp. Daniel) that is, in the *image* (of Samā-el). The Rabbins sought to find in Gen. i, 27, a deeper meaning from the repetition therein, asserting that the first part showed the inclination of man for good or his good spirit and the repetition, that for evil, the evil spirit.

‡ Thus is the second word to be read. Samā-el has a female reflection called Lillith, as we have said before. Comp. *ante*, pp. 248, 331. United together they are called '*Hayoh*, the Beast and '*Hayoh Bishah*, the Evil or Wicked Beast. Comp. Zohar ii, 255–59. Sama-êl is considered the same as the Satan of the Old Testament, also the

under the command of his Lord, "the Judgment upon man in *gāi-hinnom* (hell) if man has not been righteous. And therefore the word וייצר *vay-ye'tzer, i. e.*, and he formed, is (written in Genesis with two '', *yodeen*. See *ante* p. 248) to show (the two-fold nature in man and) that the man created with the faculty for good (belongs) to Metatron, who also aids him by inspirations (*be'phikkoodeen* ' in the commandments,') in the study of the Thorah, (that is, 'to be a help from the Thorah, concerning the obedience to the commandments:') therefore it is written; 'I will make him a help-mate.' (Gen. ii, 18.) But if unworthy, then *Ye'tzeer-ah*, (*i. e.*, the formation,) is that of the wicked Samā-el, who is as to man *k'negdo, i. e.*, against him, and seduces man to sin, so as to condemn him into *gāi-hinnom* (hell). But both (Metatron and Samā-el) accompany the son of man (through life) in a double image." *

Nachmanides and R. Be'hai hold, the first word Elohim of the first verse of Genesis is really *e'lohim* and only meant, energies or angels, and not the Deity. That B'resheeth meant Be-raisheeth, *i. e.*, with Wisdom, one of the Sephiroth, and that through it was emanated, that, the essence of which is unknown, in three degrees or worlds: *e'lohim* (ailo-heem) representing the angelic world, and often so termed in the Divine words; *Sha-mayeem, i.e.*, the heavens, the celestial world of the stars and planets; *ha-Ah'retz, i.e.*, the earth, the elemental world, and that this is the order mentioned in Genesis. Maimonides translates the second as "angels" not "heavens," and where Job says: "the heavens are not pure in Thy sight, etc.," (xv, 15;) he says; "the *angels*, etc." This is likely from the word *Sha-mayeem*. The real meaning of *Sha-mayeem* is, that the heavens are made of ומים את, *i. e.*, *esh* fire, *mayeem* water; also *soo mayeem*, the heaven *carries the waters*. See Rashi (Gen. i, 7–8), also Tal-

---

Angel of Death, or Poison of Death. Comp. Talmud, treat. *Bava Bathra*, 16a. As to Lillith: See, Traditions of the Jews, etc., by Rev. John Peter Stehelin, London, 1742, ii, p. 110 *sq*. Of Samā-el, see *ibid.* i, p. 187 *sq.;* Allen's Modern Judaism, p. 167 *sq*.

* Zohar i, fol. 26a, § *B'resheeth*. Cremona Ed. Rayah Me'hemnah. Livorno Ed. i, 39*b*. i, fol. 25, col. 1, Sulzbach Ed. That is as the evil inclination, called the *Ye'tzer ha-rah*, and the good inclination, termed the *Ye'tzer ha-tob*. Both are considered as always present with each human being who is capable of witnessing between right and wrong. Sayings of the Jewish Fathers, *ante*, p. 346, note.

mud Babli, treatise '*Hulin, Sha-mayeem* being taken as a compound formed from אש *esh* fire, a symbol of the angels whose ministry is Severity, and מים *mayeem*, water, equally proper for the angels charged with Mercy.

METATRON IS THE FIRST OF THE CREATURES AND THE REFLECTION OF ELOHIM. "When it is said: (Gen. xxiv, 2) 'His עבדו *av'doh, i. e., servant.*' That is the servant of *Ma-qom** 'The oldest of His house,' to serve Him. And who is he? That is Metatron, who, as it has been said, is destined to glorify the body in the graves. This is as it is written; 'And Abraham said to his servant,' namely; to Metatron, the servant of *Ma-qom*. 'The oldest of His house,' because he (Metatron) is the *first of the creatures* of Ma-qom, who governs (rules) over all that belongs to Him! For the Holy, Blessed be He! has given him dominion over all His hosts. † And we have learned, said Rabbi Shim-on; that R. Yo-seh said; that Rab said; that all the Hosts of the Servant take delight and enjoyment from the pureness of the soul, and we have learned, that the Light of the soul in the coming world, is greater than the Light of the Throne, and the soul took the Light from the Throne."

THE MATRONEETHAH IS THE MEDIATRIX BETWEEN THE DEITY AND MAN. "'And the Lord drove Adam out and placed * * * the Cherubee'm * * * to guard the way to the Tree of Life.' (Gen. iii, 24) Where is the way to the Tree of Life? This is the great Matroneethah, she is the way to that Great Tree, the Mighty Tree of Life. It is written:

---

* The word *Ma-qom, i. e.*, Place, is here used as a Name of Elohim.

† Zohar i, fol. 126*b*, (Midrash Hanne-e'lam) Amsterdam Ed. i, fol. 77, col. 1. Sulzbach Ed. Cremona Ed. i, fol. 76*b*. In the recent find at Constantinople called the Didaché or Teaching of the Twelve Apostles, *ante.*, p. 116 *sq.*, Jesus is called, "the *servant* of YeHoVaH." David is also called the same. St. Luke, alone of the Apostles, uses the word παῖς = son or servant, of both Jesus and David. Acts iii, 13–26, iv, 25, 27, 30. Is. xlii, 1. Matt. xii, 18. See Dr. Philip Schaff's edition of the Didaché, New York, 1885, p. 191. The early writing called, The Pastor of Hermas, represents Christ under the figure of a *servant*, whom God has chosen and given the Holy Spirit, because of his fidelity, to inhabit the flesh; the moment of that union, he appears to have considered, to have been at the baptism of Jesus by John. *Le Pasteur d'Hermas, Paris, 1880*, p. 102.

'Behold, the bed of Solomon is surrounded by sixty valiant men from the strongest of Israël.' (Song of Songs iii, 7.) The Celestial Israël: 'They all hold swords.' If the Matroneethah takes them up, then they all take them up with her. This is that which is written; 'The Angel of Elohim which went before the host of Israël and passed behind them.' (Exod. xiv, 19.) Dost thou call her the 'Angel of Elohim?' Yea! Said Rabbi Abbah; "Come, See! so says: Rabbi Shim-on; 'The Holy, Blessed be He! has erected before Him a Holy Palace, a Celestial Holy Palace, a Holy City, the Upper (Heavenly) City! Jerusalem is called the Holy City, who enters to the King, can enter only from the Holy City, from whence alone the road leads to the King, from here the way is prepared. It is written; 'This is the Gate to YHVH, the righteous shall enter therein.' (Ps. cxviii, 20.) All the services that the King desires are attended to by the Matroneethah, and all services from here below go first to the Matronethah, and from there to the King. And by her is everything sent forth. This is what is written: 'And the Angel of Elohim which went before the hosts of Israël,' (Israël from Above.) (Exod. xiv, 19.) He is the Angel of Elohim to where it is written: 'And YHVH went before them! etc.,' (Ex. xiii, 21.) as it is explained. But is it then becoming to the honor of the King, that the Matroneethah shall carry on war and be used as a Mediatrix? Represent to thyself a King, who was espoused to an exalted Matroneethah. The King recognizing her dignity as high, above everything, thus spoke: 'All others appear like beasts in comparison with my Matroneethah, she shines above all. What distinction shall I confer on her? My whole house shall be in her hands.' And the King had it proclaimed: 'Henceforth all the affairs of the King are entrusted to the hands of the Matronethah.' What did he (further) do? He entrusted into her hands all his weapons, all the lords of war, all the precious stones of the King, all treasures of the King, saying: 'Whoever henceforth needs to speak to me, cannot speak to me until it is first made known to the Matroneethah.' Thus it is with the Holy, Blessed be He! and this on account of the great friendship and love, which He cherishes for the Superior Congregation of Israël. He delivered everything to the Matroneethah. Behold the idol worshipping nations do not find any respect from her, who is mine only one, my pious one, my dove; what shall I do for her? But this: I will deliver my whole house into her hands."*

REPENTANCE NECESSARY SO THAT MAN MAY BE FORGIVEN HIS SINS. "When does man cleanse himself from his sins? When he does repentance as it should be done. R. Yitz'haq said: 'It is when he repents before his King, Above; and prays (fol. 70a) to Him from the depths of the heart; as it is written; 'Out of the *depths* have I called to the, YHVH.' (Ps. cxxx 1.) R. Abbah said: 'Out of the depths, etc.,' that is a place hidden Above, which has the depth of a well, and out of which flows, brooks and streams for every passer by, and this depth of the deepest is called Repentance, and whoever desires to repent and cleanse himself from his sins must call upon the Holy, Blessed be He! Therefore it is written 'Out of the *depths* have I called unto Thee, YHVH.' We have learned, that if at the time man sins before his Lord, he offers a sacrifice upon the altar and the priest atones it, and he prays for forgiveness, through these the Mercy in the Holy, Blessed be He! is stirred up; and the judgments become modified and Repentance, full of blessing, flows forth like gushing springs and bestows blessing upon all the Lights, and thus man is cleansed from his sins." †

ON REPENTANCE AND CONVERSION. "R. Yehudah began and said: 'YHVH trieth the righteous, but His soul hateth the wicked and he who loveth violence (robbery).' (Ps. xi, 5.) How well ordered are the works of the Holy, Blessed be He! And all that He has done, is entirely founded on Truth and Justice! As it is written: 'He is the Rock, His

* Zohar ii, fol. 51a, Amsterdam Ed. ii, fol. 21, Sulzbach Ed. Cremona Ed. ii, fol. 22b. The Matroneethah is the She'kheen-ah, the Real Presence or Glory of the Deity, which visibly rested, according to the O. T., over the Hebrew Ark of the Covenant in the Holy of Holies. It is in Malkhuth, according to the Qabbalah, which Sephirah is the Kingdom or Government of the Deity upon our earth. Its angel is the Great Presence Angel called, Metatron, its Divine Name is the full Name Adonai. In this Sephirah is the harmony and content of all the preceding Sephiroth. Its special influence is over the Church or Congregation of Israël.

† Zohar iii, fol. 29a, Sulzbach Ed. iii, fol. 69, col. 2, fol. 70, col. 1. Amsterdam Ed. Cremona Ed. ii, fol. 32a. As to Repentance, see, Sayings of the Jewish Fathers, p. 84 note.

work is perfect; for all His ways are with Judgment; an Ail (El) of Truth and without injustice, just and right is He!' (Deut. xxxii, 4.) Come, See! The Holy, Blessed be He! did not judge the first man* until after He had first exhorted him, that his heart and will might not depart into other ways and he become unclean. But he (Adam) did not fear but transgressed the commands of his Lord. But afterwards He made known to him His judgment; yet did not judge him as he deserved, but restrained His anger for a long time, and suffered him to live one day, that is 1000 years less 70† which he gave to David, which really did not belong to him (David). Likewise He does not judge the child of man according to his evil doings, which he continually commits. If He did, the world could not exist, but the Holy, Blessed be He! restrains His anger for a long time with the just and the wicked, and waits as to the wicked a longer time than with the just, that they may do full repentance and be able to exist both in this world and in the future world; as it is written: 'Say to them: as true as אני *a'nee, i. e.*, I, live, says YHVH, etc., I have not any pleasure in the death of the wicked, but rather that the wicked turn from his evil ways and live.' (Ezek. xxxiii, 11.) That he may live in this world and in the world to come. Therefore He restrains His anger to them for a long time or also that there may shoot from them a good scion in the world, like Abraham who descended from Tarah. He was a good scion, a root and a good pearl to the world. But the Holy, Blessed be He! is always very strict with the just (pious) in all their doings, so that they may deviate neither to the right or to the left. Therefore He tries them, not for His, but their own sakes, because He knows their thoughts and power of faith and will raise up their heads, as it is written: 'And Elohim put Abraham to the test, etc. (Gen. xxii, 1.) What does the word (נסה *nis-sah*) test, signify. Raising the banner (נס *nes* standard) as it is written: 'Raise the banner' (Is. lxii, 10), 'Set up the standard.' (Jer. iv, 10.) And this is meant, that the Holy, Blessed be He! raised up Abraham's banner in the eyes of the whole world, which is hinted at in the word (נסה *nis-sah*) test, (signifying, raised the standard.)

---

* That is the terrestrial or earthly Adam.

† Adam is said to have lived 930 years.

Thus also the Holy, Blessed be He! tests the pious ones so as to raise their standards, that is their heads, in the whole world."*

THE BRINGING FORTH OF MAN AND OF REPENTANCE. "It has been taught us. At the time the Holy, Blessed be He! created the world, He also desired to create a man. He took counsel with the Thorah. She said before him: 'Thou desirest to create a man, he will certainly sin before Thee, he will certainly provoke Thee if Thou dealest with him according to his doings; the world cannot stand before Thee still less the man! Said He to her: Am I then in vain called; 'Ail, merciful, gracious and long-suffering?' (Exod. xxxiv, 6.) Before the Holy, Blessed be He! created the world, He had already created Repentance,† to whom he said: 'I desire to create man in the world, but in such a way that thou art prepared to forgive and reconcile him, when he turns from his sins to thee.' Therefore Repentance is all the time prepared for men and when men turn from their sins, she (Repentance) returns to the Holy, Blessed be He! and reconciles them all. And the judgments are all wiped out and man is cleansed from his sins." ‡

THE CHANGE NECESSARY FOR SINNERS. "Those burdened with sin need a change of place, a change of name, and a change of their doings; like it was said to Abraham; 'Go forth from thy country and thy place of birth.' (Gen. xii, 1.) Here is a change of place. And 'Thy name shall no more be called Abram, but Abraham shall be thy name.' (*Ibid*. xvii, 5.) This is a change of name. A change of doings; he changed from his former evil acts to good actions."§

THE DEITY CASTS INTO ETERNAL CONDEMNATION THOSE WHO DO NOT REPENT IN TIME. "R. Yo-seh said: Woe to the wicked, who will not do penance before the Holy, Blessed be He! for their sins, while they are still in this world, for when man repents and regrets for the sins he has committed, the Holy, Blessed be He! pardons him; and all those who

---

* Zohar i, fol. 83*a*, Cremona Ed. i, fol. 139*b*, Amsterdam Ed.

† This may be a reference to the She'kheen-ah.

‡ Zohar iii, fol. 59, col. 1. Sulzbach Ed. iii, fol. 69*b*, Amsterdam Ed. Cremona Ed. ii, fol. 31*b*.

§ Zohar iii, fol. 217*b*, Amsterdam Ed. iii, fol. 88, col. 1. Sulzbach Ed. Raÿah Me'hemnah. Cremona Ed. ii, fol. 98*b*.

tarry in their sins, and will not repent before the Holy, Blessed be He! for their sins, He will hereafter be cast into *gai-hinnom* (hell) and they can never come forth from there again." *

ON REWARD AND PUNISHMENT IN THE FUTURE LIFE. "R. Yehudah said: The time when man departs from this life, is the day of the Great Judgment, then the soul (*Neshamah*) separates from the body. And man does not depart from this world, until he has seen the She'kheen-ah; therefore it is written; 'No man can see Me and live.' (Ex. xxxiii, 20.) With the She'kheen-ah comes three angels, to receive the soul (*Neshamah*) of the Righteous: as it is written; 'And YHVH appeared to him, etc.:' as the day was hot. (Gen. xviii, 1.) That is the Day of Judgment, which burns like an oven, to separate the soul (*Neshamah*) from the body. 'And he lifted up his eyes and saw three men,' who investigate the deeds he has done and through whom, by an oral statement, he acknowledges (confesses). And when the soul (*Neshamah*) sees this, it parts from the body as far as the opening of the gullet and there waits, until it has confessed all that which the body in this world has committed with her. Then the soul (*Neshamah*) of the Righteous is glad over her deeds and rejoices that she was so faithfully preserved. We have learned, said R. Yitz-haq: The soul of the just (pious) longs for the time, when it shall leave this vain world, so as to rejoice in the future world."†

THE RISING OF THE SOUL OF THE DEAD. "Said R. Yitz-haq: At the time the soul (*Neshamah*) deserves it, and rises to her Upper place, the body lies peacefully and rests in its bed, as it is written; 'He shall enter into peace, where they shall rest on their beds; who walks in straightness.' (Is. lvii, 2.) 'What does this mean; 'Walks in straightness?' Said R. Yitz-haq: The soul (*Neshamah*) goes straight to the place reserved for her in Paradise." ‡ §

* Zohar i, fol. 66*a*, Amsterdam Ed. i, fol. 49, col. 4. Sulzbach Ed. Cremona Ed. i, fol. 51*a*.

† Zohar i, fol. 98*a*, Amsterdam Ed. i, fol 65, col. 1, Sulzbach Ed. The Midrash ha-Ne-e'lam, *i. e.*, the Hidden Midrash. Cremona Ed. i, fol. 65*b*.

‡ Zohar i, fol. 122*b*, Amsterdam Ed. i, fol. 76, col. 1, Sulzbach Ed. Midrash ha-Ne-e'lam. Cremona Ed. i, fol. 75*a*.

§ When the body is deprived of all life, the vital soul (*Nephesh*), it is called גוּף *Guff*, *i. e.*, body or corpse. The *Neshamah* is frequently called by the Rabbins: the *precious* soul, to distinguish it from the animal or vital soul.

THE RESURRECTION OF THE DEAD. "R. Yitz-haq began: 'The Dudaim (Mandrin or Mandrakes) gives an exhalation of odor, etc.' (Song of Sol. vii, 13); Our Rabbis have learned: In the future to come, the Holy, Blessed be He! will quicken the dead and awaken them from the dust, that they be no more an earthly building. For formerly they were created of real *dust* of matter, which is not lasting, as it is written: 'And YHVH Elohim formed the man (Adam) from the *dust* of the earth.' (Gen. ii, 2.) In the same time (that of the resurrection) they shall be shaken out of the dust from that building and stand into a firm building, that it shall be to them lasting. Thus it is written: 'Shake thyself from the *dust* arise captive of Jerusalem.' (Is. lii, 2.) They shall stand firm (lastingly) and rise from under the earth and receive their souls (*Neshamoth*) in the land of Israël. For at that time the Holy, Blessed be He! will spread over them all kinds of odors from the Garden of Eden; as it is written: 'The Dudaim gives exhalation of odor.' Said R. Yitz-haq: 'Do not call it 'Dudaim' but *Dodim*, (*i. e.*, friendship.)' This means body and soul (*Neshamah*) which are friends and companions one to the other. R. Na'hman says: 'This word means real Dudaim as the Dudaim bring forth love in the world.'*

So they bring forth love in the world! And what does this mean? 'They give a well-pleasing (ריח *reia'h*) odor?' That is a description of the integrity of their deeds, through which their Creator, becomes known and comprehended to their generation. 'And at '*our doors*' are all the precious fruits old with new.' (*Ibid.*) 'Our doors' that is the doors of heaven; they are open, where from, the souls (*Neshamoth*) shall descend into the corpses. 'All the precious fruits.' Those are the souls (*Neshamoth*). 'New and old,' are those, whose souls (*Neshamoth*) had parted from them many years, as also those, whose souls (*Neshamoth*) left them but a few days past, and deserve through the honesty of their actions to enter the world to come. All (these souls, *Neshamoth*) shall descend simultaneously to enter the bodies destined for them." †

* The Hebrew דודאים, Duda-im (Gen. xxx, 14) is held by many, to be the love-apple or mandragora. Comp. Kitto's Bib. Cyclop. Ed. 1876, i, 707 *sq*.

† Zohar i, fol. 134*a*, Amsterdam Ed. i, fol. 81, col. 1, Sulzbach Ed. Midrash Hanne-e'lam. Cremona Ed. i, fol. 80, col. 320.

THE RESURRECTION IN THE BODY. The Zohar holds to the Resurrection in the Body, as well as that nothing in the universe is lost. Joel* quotes; "If the naked soul is worthy to return to its former condition it will newly arise in the body, * * * from Him it is written; 'These to Eternal Life' * * * and these are the Supreme Forces of the Holy King, and nothing is lost."

"While the soul (*Neshamah*) has its sustenance from the splendor of the Above, the Holy, Blessed be He! says to that angel called, Dumah† 'Go and announce to that body, that I am prepared to make it alive (quicken it) at the time when I shall make alive the just (pious) in the future time to come. But it, the body, answers: 'Shall I have pleasure after my being decayed?' (Gen. xviii, 12.) After my being decayed in the dust and dwelling in the earth where worms and moles have eaten my flesh, shall it be able for me to be renewed? The Holy, Blessed be He! says to the soul (*Neshamah*): It is therefore written: 'And YHVH said unto Abraham, etc.,' 'Is anything difficult to YHVH?' At a time which is known to Me to revive the dead, I shall bring back to thee that body, which is entirely renewed and as it was previously, that it may be like the holy angels; and that day is destined for Me to rejoice with them; as it is written: 'The Glory of YHVH is eternal! YHVH shall rejoice in His works.'"‡ (Ps. civ, 31.)

THE FUTURE HAPPINESS OF THE RIGHTEOUS. "At that time, the just (pious) shall attain full knowledge; said R. Yo-seh; 'On the day on which the Holy, Blessed be He! shall rejoice over His works, the just will know Him in their hearts, and their understanding shall be as great as if they had seen Him with the eyes; as it is written, (Is. xxv, 9); 'And he will say on that day: Behold! *this* is our Elohim, etc.' And the joy of the soul when dwelling in the body does surpass all, because they are both constant and know and comprehend their Creator and rejoice in the splendor of the She'kheen-ah. And this is what is meant by the Good which is preserved for the just in the future to come. Thus it is written:

* *Religions-philosophie des Sohar*, p. 148 note.

† Silence, the angel which has charge of the disembodied spirits. Comp. Genesis with a Talmudical Commentary, by Paul I. Hershon. London, 1883, p. 94, *sq*.

‡ Zohar i, fol. 102*a*, Amsterdam Ed. i, fol. 66, col. 2, Sulzbach Ed. Midrash Hanne-e'lam. Cremona Ed. i, fol. 66, col. 264, and 67, col. 265.

'*Aileh tho'l-doth Yitz-haq ben Abraham* these are the generations of *Isaac* son of *Abraham*.' (Gen. xxxv, 19.) That is, these are the generations of *rejoicing* and *cheerfulness*, which at that time shall be in the world, אברהם בן *ben Abraham* son of Abraham.' That is the soul (*Neshamah*) which deserves such joy and is perfect in her elevation. אברהם הוליד את יצחק *Abraham holid eth Yitz-haq* Abraham begat Isaac! That is the soul brought forth this *rejoicing* and *cheerfulness* in the world.' Said R. Yehudah to R. 'He-yah: 'This we have learned: a feast which the Holy, Blessed be He! will prepare for the righteous in time to come. What is it?' Said he to him: 'When I came before those holy angels, the lords of learning, I had only heard this which you have heard, afterwards I heard the explanation of it by R. El'azar. This said R. El'azar: 'The feast for the righteous in the future to come, will be like this, as it is written; 'They saw the Elohim and ate and drunk.' (Ex. xxiv, 11.) And these are the foods, we have been taught. And R. El'azar said: 'In one place we have learned: 'We have rejoiced,' in another place 'We have been fed.' How do these two expressions differ?

But thus said my father (R. Shim-on b. Yo'haï) 'The just (pious) who do not deserve so much shall only *rejoice, in the reflection*, because they cannot comprehend all, but the truly righteous *shall be satiated* until they attain the fullest comprehension.'* This therefore is to be understood by eating and drinking, and this is (also the meaning of) the feast and the eating. And from where have we this? From Moses, as it is written: 'He was with YHVH forty days and forty nights, bread he ate not and water he drunk not.' (Ex. xxxiv, 28.) What was the cause, that bread he ate not and water he drunk not? It was 'he was fed by another feast, by that celestial splendor from above. And such shall be the feast of the just (pious) in the future to come.' Said R. Yehudah: 'The feast of the just (pious) in the future to come shall consist of rejoicing in His joy, as it is written: 'The humble shall hear and rejoice.' (Ps. xxxiv, 14.) R. Hunnah said, from this: 'All shall rejoice who trust in Thee, eternally shall they sing.' Said R. Yitz-haq: 'This and that shall come true in the future to come.' And we have learned, said

---

* This probably refers to a comprehension of the highest ideality of the Deity and its attributes.

R. Yo-seh: '*Wine** which is guarded and kept in the grapes from the first six days, means, the ancient mighty words that have not been revealed to man (Adam) since the creation of the world, and they will be revealed to the righteous in the future to come. And thus it is drinking and eating, surely it is so.' " †

THE SOULS OF THE WICKED. "Said R. Shemuel for R. Ya-kob; 'The souls of the wicked are given in the hand of this angel, named Dumah‡ to be led to *gāi-hinnom* (hell) and there judged. After they have been delivered to him they are not released until they are taken into *gāi-hinnom*.' " §

JUDGMENT OF THE WICKED AND THEIR PUNISHMENT. "Thus it has been taught us and thus we have heard it; that man surely departs from this world through judgment. But before he obtains entrance into the dwellings of the just (righteous) he has to present himself before the tribunal and there he is judged by that Heavenly Council. And there stands the official of *gāi-hinnom* (hell) to accuse him. Happy is he who leaves the tribunal acquitted! If not, then the official who has charge of the *gāi-hinnom* seizes him, and casts him from there, Above; to down, Below; as a stone is cast from a sling, as it is written; 'And the souls (*Nephesh*) of their enemies, them He shall cast, as out of a sling.' (I Sam. xxv, 29.) And he throws him into *gāi-hinnom*, and according to the judgment passed upon him he receives his punishment."‖

* "Wine" is the mysterious vitality and spiritual energy of (Wine = 70 = *Sod* or Secret) created Things. See *ante*, p. 340 note. The "grapes" are the created Things produced by the Deity who is likened to a vine.

† Zohar i, fol. 135a and b (Midrash Hanne-e'lam), Amsterdam Ed. Cremona Ed. i, fol. 80, col. 320.

‡ The Angel of Silence, who has charge of the disembodied spirits. Talmud treatise *Sanhedrin*, fol. 94, col. 1, Ps. cxv, 17.

§ Zohar i, fol. 124a, Amsterdam Ed. i, fol. 76, col. 2, Sulzbach Ed. Midrash Hann-e'lam. Cremona Ed. i, fol. 75, col. 300.

‖ Zohar iii, fol. 185b and fol. 186a, Amsterdam Ed. iii, fol. 75, col. 2, Sulzbach Ed. Cremona Ed. Vol. iii, fol. 89, col. 353.

XIX.

EXCERPTS FROM THE ZOHAR CONTINUED. THE HOLY, WITH THE SHE-'KHEEN-AH CREATED THE UNIVERSE. REASON OF THE EXISTENCE OF GOOD AND EVIL. OF METATRON. MESSIAH BEN JOSEPH AND MESSIAH BEN DAVID. DESCRIPTION OF, AND THE TRIADIC IDEA AS TO, THE DEITY. THE NAMES. CREATION. SOULS, SPIRITS, ETC.

THE HOLY BLESSED WITH THE SHE'KHEEN-AH HAS CREATED THE UNIVERSE. THE REASON OF THE GOOD AND EVIL. "'And Elohim said: Let *us* make a man.' (Gen. i, 26.) (The Qabbalists say, that the creation of the universe was suggested by the manifestation of the Supreme Deity, Elohim.)

'The secret of YHVH is with those who fear Him.' (Ps. xxv, 14.) Began that *Sabah d'Sabin, i. e.*, old of the oldest, and said: 'Shim-on! Shim-on! who is he that said: 'And Elohim said: Let *us* make a man?' Who is this Elohim?' Then the old of the oldest, disappeared and nobody saw him. When Rabbi Shim-on heard, that he called him. 'Shim-on!' and not Rabbi Shim-on, he said to the companions: 'It surely was the Holy, Blessed be He! of whom it says—' The Ancient of Days did sit.' (Dan. vii, 9.) It is now the time to begin with this mystery, for here there is certainly a mystery and its revelation until now has not been permitted, but now it appears, permission has been given to unveil the same.' He began and said: ' Like a King who has many buildings to build, he had a builder and this builder did not undertake anything but only with the permission of the King, as it is written: 'I was to him an architect.' (Prov. viii, 30.) The 'King' is surely the Celestial Wisdom, Above, and the Pillar of the Centre is King, Below. ' Elohim' is the architect, Above, and this is the Mother, Above. 'Elohim' is the architect, Below, and this is the She'kheen-ah, Below. It is not permissible for a wife to do anything without the consent of her husband. And all the works could only be in the way of efflux. The Father spoke through His *Amirah, i. e.*, Word, to the Mother: 'Let this or that be,' and instantly it existed; as it says: 'And Elohim said: Let light be! and it was light.' (Gen. i, 3.) 'He said' to Elohim: 'Let light be!' The Lord of the Building, He said it, and the builder did it at once. And so all the buildings arose by the way of the efflux. He said: 'Let be a firmament.' 'Let be lights.' And all has been done at once. As He appeared in the Intellectual World, the architect (Elohim said to the Master-builder, 'Let *us* make *a man* in *our image*, according to *our similitude.*' Said the Master-builder, 'It is certainly well to make him, but he is prepared to sin before Thee because he is a fool; as it is written: '*A wise son rejoices the father*, and *a foolish son is his mother's sorrow.*' (Prov. x, 1.) She replied; 'If he desires to sin, let him fall on his Mother and not on his Father, and I will create him in *my image*. Therefore it is written: 'And Elohim created the man in *his image*.' The Father did not desire to participate. In the time he (the man) sins it is written of him; 'For your transgression your mother has been sent away.' (Is. l, 1.) Then the King said to the Mother; 'Did I not tell you that he would sin?' At that time He drove him out and drove his Mother with him, therefore it is written; 'A wise son rejoices the father, and a foolish son is the sorrow of his mother.' 'A wise son' that is the Man (Adam) as the A'tzeel-atic Man, and 'A foolish son,' that is the B'ree-atic Adam, *i. e.*, the man of creation. Then the companions arose and said: 'Rabbi! Rabbi! Is there a difference between the 'Father' and 'Mother,' that man should belong on the part of the 'Father' to the efflux, and on the part of the 'Mother' to the creation? He said to them: 'Companions! Companions! This is not so; for this A'tzeel-atic Man, male-female, was from both, the side of the 'Father' and from the side of the 'Mother,' and this is the meaning of the words; 'And Elohim said; Let light be! and it was light.' 'Let light be,' on the part of the 'Father,' and 'it was light,' on the part of the 'Mother.' And this is the double-face formed Adam.* But this

* The first Adam, the Man, was an androgene and is the Primordial Ideation Adam or protoplast. Gen. i, 2; ii, 1 and 2.

(Man) had neither an image nor similitude, but the Celestial Mother had a Name (כנוי 20 + 50 + 6 + 10 = 86) whose numerical value (86) is equal to that of Elohim (אלהים, 1 + 30 + 5 + 10 + 40 = 86). Light and Darkness are contained in this Name at the same time, and on account of the Darkness contained in its Name, said the Father, it would seduce into sin, the Man (Upper Adam) of the efflux, who is the 'light' of the Upper Garment,' and this is the 'light' which the Holy, Blessed be He! created on the first day. And this *first created 'light,'* He hid for the righteous, and the '*darkness*,' which he created on the first day, He has destined for the wicked, as it is written: 'And *the wicked shall be silent in darkness.*' (1 Sam. ii, 9.) And on account of this 'darkness' which will in the future sin to the 'light,' the Father would not grant her any part in Him. Therefore Elohim said: 'Let *us* make man in *our image*,' that is in the 'Light,' 'After *our similitude*'* that is the Darkness, which is the garment of the 'Light,' as the body is the garment of the soul, as it is written: 'Thou hast *clothed me* in עור *Or, skin*† and flesh.' (Job x, 11.) Thereupon all rejoiced and said: 'Happy is our lot, that it was granted to us, to hear words, which until now, had not been heard.' Began R. Shim-on further and said: 'Behold now, that אני *a'nee* I, *a'nee*, I am, הוא Hu, *i.e.*, He, and there is no elohim with Me, etc.' (Deut. xxxii, 39, comp. 37, comp. Ex. xxxiv, 9.) Said he: 'Companions the mighty words, which permission from Above has been given to me to unveil, I shall reveal to you, who is it who says: 'Behold now I, I am He! etc.' What is He? The Above of All the Above, who is called 'the Above the Above,' Above to those Above, who not one of them can do anything till they take permission from this Exaltation, as we have explained previously the words 'Let us make a man.' 'Let US make,' surely it refers to two. He said to him above him, 'Let US make' and nothing is done without permission and saying, from Him who is above him, and He, the Highest, has not done anything till He took counsel from His companion. But the 'He' is called; the Highest of all the highest, nothing is above Him, and not anything Below,

* Simulacrum or shadow?

† עור *or, i. e.*, skin. The ע and א are sometimes interchangeable, therefore read אור *ohr, i. e.*, light, instead of עור *or*, skin. Both א and ע are vocal sounds.

resembles Him, as it says: 'To whom then will ye liken Me, that I shall be equal to him? says the Holy.' (Is. xl, 25.) He said: 'Behold now that I, I am He and no elohim is with Me,' whose advice I shall take, like of whom it says: 'And Elohim said, Let *us* make man.' Arose all the companions and said: 'Rabbi! Give us permission to say something at this place.' Said they: 'Hast thou not before explained, that the Most High, said to Kether (the Crown). 'Let *us* make man?' He said to them; 'Have your ears heard what is now spoken by your mouths? Have I not just told you *that He*, is that which is called, the Cause of Causes, *but not He*, which is called, the Cause of ALL Causes? For the Cause of ALL Causes has not any second Below from whom He shall take advice, because He is One, is *before ALL things*, and has not any partner. And therefore He said; 'Behold now that I, I am He and no elohim with Me' whose counsel He shall take, for He has not a second and no partner and not anything by which He can be counted, for instance a male and female, and of which it is said: 'But *one* I called Him.' (Is. li, 2.) But He is One, without numerical relation, (and) without a partner, and therefore it is said; 'And no elohim is with Me.' All arose and salāmed before him and said: 'Happy is the child of man, to whom the Lord, has given consent to reveal such great hidden secrets, which were not revealed even to the holy angels!' He (R. Shim-on) said to them: 'Companions! It is yet to us to explain the continuation of the verse quoted; for there are hidden secrets in that verse; 'I kill and I make alive, etc.' (Deut. xxxii, 39.) By the Sephiroth 'I make alive.' From the Right side is Life, and from the Left side is Death. If these two do not agree with the Middle Pillar, Judgment cannot be executed; for also upon these the usual legal formula has its application, which reads: 'We three in this session have unanimously concluded, etc.' Often all three agree to do the judgment. But the Right hand appears, which is always open to receive the repentant, which is *Ye-dud, i. e.*, (יהוה) *heh* הא *vau* ואו *heh* הא *yod* יו. And this is the She-'kheen-ah which is called the Right hand, from the side of Benevolence ('*Hesed*).* The Left hand, from the side of Strength (*Ge'boor-ah*);

---

* 'Hesed חסד $8 + 60 + 4 = 72$. This word contains the 72 Qabbalistic Names which issue out of YHVH.

the hand of *Ye-dud*, from the side of the Middle Pillar, (the Pillar of Harmony). If man repents, this hand releases him from the judgment. But when the Cause of ALL Causes has passed judgment, of it is said: 'And none delivers from My hand.' The three-fold mention in that verse; 'אָנִי *a'nee* I, אָנִי *a'nee* I, אָנִי *a'nee* I,' there appear in it, three אאא (*Alephs*) and three יייּ (*Yodeen*), which point to the four-lettered Name (*i. e.*, the Tetragrammaton) הא וְאו הא יוד, and there also appears in it, three ווו (*Vavin*), in the words, and none *V'en* וְאֵין and I *Va'a'nee* וַאֲנִי And I make alive *Va-a'haÿeh* וַאֲחַיֶה, which are comprehended in this Name. And with all this, that verse, which said; 'by other elohim (gods),' have the companions, explained, as it is says; 'Behold now that I, I am, He,' that is the Holy, Blessed be He! and His She'kheen-ah, whereby it is said: אֲנִי וְהוּ *a'nee v'hu* (*i. e.*, I and He); 'And no elohim with Me,' this is סמאל ונחש Samă-el and serpent.

'I kill and make alive,' 'I kill' by means of My She'kheen-ah, he who is guilty, and I 'make alive' by her, he who is pure.' 'And none can save from My hand,' that is from the hand of ידוד *Ye-dud* which is YHVH Yod, Heh, Vav, Heh, whose Name is complete, and this is כח"י במוכס"ץ כח"י. And all is *E'meth* Truth.

But what is said above of the Causes of Causes, as the Cause of ALL Causes, is a Mystery, that has not been transmitted to all the prophets and wise-men. Come, See! How many secret causes exist, which are hidden, disguised and interwoven in the Sephiroth, and the Sephiroth of the Merkabah, which in them are hidden to the conceptions of the children of man! Of them it is said; 'For a High One from above the High, is keeper, etc.' (Eccles. v, 8.) There are Lights of which some shine brighter than others, those receiving the Light from the others are darker than those above them from which they receive. But before, the Cause of ALL Causes, not any Light standeth, for all Lights darken before Him. Another exposition of the words: 'Let us make man in *our image* after *our similitude*.' This the companions have applied to the serving angels, they (the angels), said this verse. Said He to them; as they know what has been and will be, and they know that man will sin; Why did they desire to create him, and besides Aza and Azăel have slandered him at the time when the She'kheen-ah said to the Holy, Blessed be He! 'Let us make man;' said they (Aza and Azāel, see *ante*, p. 106 *sq.*): 'What is man that thou takest knowledge of him?' (Ps. cxliv, 3. Vulgate cxliii.) Why desirest thou to create man as thou knowest he will sin before thee, through the woman which is darkness? For the Light is the male, and the Darkness, the female, from this (the female) is the darkness of creation. (See *ante*, p. 242 *sq.*)

At that time the She'kheen-ah said to them: The object of your accusation is the same which will cause you, in the future, to fall, as it is written; 'And the children of Elohim (Be'nai Elohim) saw that daughters of man were fair, etc.' (Gen. vi, 2.) They lusted after them, confused themselves through them, and the She'kheen-ah cast them from their holiness! Said the companions: 'Rabbi, Rabbi! If so, Aza and Azāel have not lied in their words, for man was surely destined to sin through woman.' Said he to them: 'Thus said the She'kheen-ah; you, who are more prepared to bring complaints before me than the entire celestial host, it would be more seeming, if you were better than man in your own deeds; but if it is destined that he (man) shall sin through one woman, you will sin through many women more than the children of man, as it is written: 'The sons of Elohim saw that the *daughters* of man, etc.' It does not say, the daughter, etc., but the *daughters* of man. Besides if man is guilty, repentance is ordained which is to lead him back to his Lord, to make amends for his fault.' Said the companions to him; 'If this is so, why all this?' said Rabbi Shim-on; 'Companions, if it had not been so, if the Holy, Blessed be He! had not created good and evil spirits, (*Ye'tzer ha-tob* and the *Ye'tzer ha-rah*) which are Light and Darkness, neither purity nor guilt would have been for the *B'ree-atic* man, but created from both, (the good and evil) therefore; 'See, I have set before thee, this day life and good, and death and evil.' (Deut. xxx, 15.)* Said they to him: 'Why is all this? Would it not have been better, if they had not been created, so as not to sin and cause all this which he has caused Above, and so that there need not have been punishment or reward?' Said he to them; 'He could have so created them, but as the Thorah is created for his sake, as it is written in her (the Thorah): Punishment to the evil and reward for the just, there would have been neither

---

* That is, the opportunity to exercise Free Will.

reward to the just (righteous) nor punishment to the wicked, but for the sake of the *B'ree-atic* man, ' He did not create the world in vain.' (Is. xlv, 18.) Said they, ' We surely have heard that we have never heard before, then surely the Holy, Blessed be He ! has not created anything for which He has no need.' ' Besides the Thorah (Law) of the Creation is the Garment to the She'kheen-ah. If man, had not been created to sin, the She'kheen-ah would be without a Garment like a poor, therefore every one who sins is like one who would disrobe the She'kheen-ah of her Garment, and this is the punishment of man ; but whoever fulfills the commands of the Thorah, is like he who would clothe the She'kheen-ah in her Garment."*

METATRON THE ANGEL OF THE PRESENCE. " The Middle Pillar† is Metatron, who places peace, Above, according to the way of Tiph'e-reth.‡ His name is like the Name of his Master,§ he was created in His *image*, and after His *similitude*, for he embraces all the degrees from Above to Below and from Below to Above. He is the uniting one in the Centre, as is written : ' And the middle bolt, in the middle of the boards bolts from one end to the other.'' (Ex. xxvi, 28.) And this comprises four faces and four wings to each *haÿ-yah* and *haÿ-yah* (living ones and living ones) from Above, which are יאדרונדי.||

* Zohar i, fol. 22*a, sq.*, Amsterdam. i, fol. 26, col. 1, Sulzbach Ed. Cremona Ed., i, fol. 26*a sq.* As to the Master-builder and the architect of the world; compare, Sayings of the Jewish Fathers, etc., by Charles Taylor, p. 26, note. As to the Upper and Lower Adam, *Ibid.* pp. 64, 70, 72 and notes, also Sol. Munk's, Moreh, before cited, ii, p. 253; also English Ed., ii, p. 154. Woman regarded as the medium of temptation ; Sayings, etc., by Taylor, p. 45, note. As to the She'kheen-ah and Elohim, see the Semitic idea of the feminine reflection, *ante*, pp. 246–7, and Sayings, etc., p. 57 note ; also as to consultation with the Upper Family, *ante*, p. 246; Maimonide's, Moreh, English Ed., ii, p. 39 *sq.*; and Sayings, etc., pp. 43, 64 and notes. As to Samâ-el, Maimonide's, Moreh, English Ed., ii, p. 155 *sq.* and notes.

† The Middle Pillar or Column of the Centre, in the Sephirothic Tree represents the Harmonies and blending of all Oppositions.

‡ The Yalkut says, the highest angels must also have peace, it is written : " He makes peace in His highest regions." If peace is needed in a place where there is neither hatred nor enmity nor quarreler, how much more so here where all these passions exist.

§ Comp. Ex. xxiii, 20–31, 22–23, xiii, 21–22, xi, 19.

|| Zohar iii, fol. 227*a*, Amsterdam Ed. iii, fol. 91, col. 1, Sulzbach Ed. Cremona Ed., iii, fol. 104*b*, col. 416.

METATRON. Of the Great Presence Angel, Metatron, who alone occupies the B'ree-atic World, the Zohar says: "The letter ש Shin, in שדי Shad-daï, (i. e., the Almighty, Gen. xvii, 1,) has three branches, which hint at the three Names יהוה אלהינו יהוה, i. e., YHVH Elohainu YHVH, which are 14 letters in number. These signify the three branches of our forefathers, and in it is 14 letters which correspond to the numerical value of די daï, $4 + 10 = 14$, from the word Shad-daï. (Daï signifies, sufficiency.) And all the letters of שדי $(300 + 4 + 10 = 314,)$ which is equal to the content of מט״טרון Metatron* $(40 + 9 + 9 + 200 + 6 + 50 = 314)$ which last is the Garment of Shad-daï." †

THE MESSIAH BEN JOSEPH AND THE MESSIAH BEN DAVID. "At the time to come, when the King Messiah comes to take possession of the highest eminences,‡ and penetrate into their wings§ so as to strengthen and transpose himself into the Upper Life. From it the Messiah of David will come out on that day, and this is the secret meaning of the words: 'I will declare the decree: YHVH hath said unto me; Thou art My son, this day I have begotten thee.' (Ps. ii, 7.) I am prepared to say to that place which is called: חק hoq, law, and bring him the joyful tidings, that 'He hath said to me; Thou art My son, this day I have begotten thee.'

---

* As to the Great Angel, Metatron, see Genesis with a Talmudical Comment., by Paul I. Hershon, etc., London, 1883, pp. 23 sq., 35 sq. The Angel, Messiah, etc., by Ernest de Bunsen, London, 1880, pp. 91 sq., 101 sq., 174-5, 303. The Life of Jesus, by Ernest Renan. English Ed., 1870, p. 223. L'Eglise Chrétienne, by Ernest Renan, Vol. iv, c. ix, p. 212 sq., period 64 A. D.; Vol. vi, p. 66 sq., period 126 A.D. Beausobre, Histoire Critique de Manichée, etc., ii, p. 259 sq., period 45 A.D. Yalkut to Zechariah, by Edward G. King, p. 94 sq. Also, Traditions of the Jews, etc., by Rev. John Peter Stehelin, before cited, i, p. 213 sq., p. 272; ii, p. 92 sq. Modern Judaism, etc., by John Allen. London, 1830, p. 160 sq., 169.

† Zohar iii, fol. 231a, § Pin-'has, Raÿah Me'hemnah, Amsterdam Ed. Cremona Ed. iii, fol. 106b, col. 423.

‡ To judge the living and the dead, the seat of the Divine Court of Justice, is considered as situated on the highest eminence, as it reads, in few lines before גבעת gib'oth, heights, written defectively without ו (vav) which would read with ו, גבעות; it means, the superior height of the universe in the place of the firmaments.

§ Wings are an ancient emblem of the spiritual. See, Mythology among the Hebrews, etc., by Goldziher. English Ed. London, 1877, p. 115 sq.

On the same day He will bring forth that *hoq* from under the wings, in many lives, in many crowns, in many blessings* as it ought to be. But that *hoq*, shall not remain alone. Another Messiah, the Son of Joseph, shall join himself to it and there will he grow strong and not in another place, and while it is the lower eminence which has no life in it, so this Messiah shall be killed and remain dead, until this eminence shall gather life from the Upper eminence, and rise again." † ‡

OF THE DEITY. "We have learned, in the *Siphrah D' Tznioothah*, *i.e.*, Book of Concealment, or, Modesty; that *At-tee'kah D' At-tee'keen*,§ *i. e.*, the Ancient of the Ancients, Hidden of the Hidden, Concealed of the Concealed, prepared and arranged Himself. It may as it were be said: He is to be found and not to be found. He is not to be found, in reality, but is arranged, and He is not known because He is the *At-tee'k D' At-tee'keen*. He is known through His arrangements as a certain *Sabah D' Sabin* Oldest of the Oldest, *At-tee'k D' At-tee'keen*, Ancient of the Ancients, Hidden of the Hidden. And by His arrangements He became known and (yet) is not known.

The Lord whose dress is white and so also the appearance of the Light of His Face. He sits upon a throne of scintillations of Light that He may give Light to us. The whiteness of the Cranium of His Head is spread over 400,000 worlds, and from the Light of this whiteness, the just (pious) shall inherit in the world to come 400 worlds. Thus it is written: 'Four

---

* See II Col. ii, 3, 9.

† Zohar iii, fol. 203*b*, Amsterdam Ed. iii, fol. 82, col. 2, Sulzbach Ed. Cremona Ed. ii, fol. 94*b*, § *Baloq*.

‡ As to Messiah ben David and Messiah ben Joseph, see, The Yalkut on Zechariah, by Edward G. King, London, 1882, Appendix A. Genesis with a Talmudical Comment, by Paul I. Hershon, etc. London, 1883. The N. T. especially in the Pauline writings, refers to two Messiahs, one who had come and been executed, the other who was yet to come, in glory and full life. Justin Martyr, also speaks of the two comings of Jesus, one, to suffer, the other, to be glorious. Judgment of the Ancient Jewish Church, etc., by Dr. Peter Allix, p. 256 *sq*. Also The Jewish Repository, London, February, 1814, pp. 72, 107. Trans. Society of Hebrew Lit.; Essays on Writings of Ibn Ezra, c. ii and notes, p. 98.

§ In the words *At-tee'k, At-tee'kah, At-tee'keen*, because of the difficulty of pronouncing the ק Q, in these words, the English language, we have spelled them with k.

hundred shekels of silver, current money with the merchant.' (Gen. xxiii, 16:) In the cranium dwell every day 13,000 myriads of worlds, which rest upon It, and lean upon It. And from that Cranium drips a dew towards him who is outside (*Ze'ir An-peen*) and fills his head daily, as it is written: 'My head is filled with dew.' (Song of Songs, v, 2). And from that dew, which He shakes from this Head upon that of him who is outside, will the dead awake to the future world. As it is written: ' My head is filled with dew.' It is not written: *millethi* 'I have filled,' but *nimlah* ' is filled.' It is written: (Is. xxvi, 19.) ' The dew of lights (herbs?) is Thy dew.' The 'Lights' flow from the whiteness of the *At-tee'kah*, and from this 'dew' are sustained the holy, Above. And this is the Manna prepared for the just in the world to come. And that ' dew' drips down to the Field of the Holy Apples, (or, Sacred Fruits.) This is that which is written : ' And when the dew that lay went up, behold on the face of the wilderness lay a small round thing,' (Ex. xvi, 14). And the appearance of this dew is white like the color *b'dola'h, i. e.*, crystal stone, in which can be seen all colors, as it is written: 'And the color thereof as the color of *b'dola'h* (bdellium).' The whiteness of this Cranium shines upon thirteen different sides (surfaces) to four sides (surfaces) on one side and to four sides (surfaces) on the side of the Face, and to four sides on the side of the *a'hoor* hinder side (the back), and in one above the Cranium (*i. e.*, to the side, Above.)* And from this the length of His Face is spread to 370 myriads of worlds, and this is called ארך אפים *A'reek Apa-yeem, i. e.*, Long Faces. And this *At-tee'kah D'At-tee'keen* Ancient of the Ancients, is called *A'reek-ah D'An-peen*, and he who is outside is called *Ze'ir An-peen, i.e.*, Small Faces, in contradistinction to the *At-tee'kah Sabah Qad-dosh, i.e.*, the Ancient Old Holy, the Holiest of the Holiest, and when *Ze'ir An-peen* looks to this, all things, Below, becomes arranged, and his Face spreads out and becomes longer at that time, but not all the time like that of *At-tee-'kah*. And from that Cranium comes forth a certain white side (ray, efflux) towards the Cranium of the *Ze'ir An-peen* for the forming of his head, and from there to other craniums, Below; which are innumerable. And all the craniums reflect the whiteness to *At-tee'k Yo-men* the Ancient

---

* The Qabbalistic Figure No. 36, based on one in the Cremona Edition; iii, fol. 116*b*, may give the reader some idea of the above description.

of Days, when they are numbered under the sceptre, and opposite this is an opening towards the craniums, Below; when they proceed to the count. In the cavity of the Cranium there is an ætherial membrane of the Hidden Wisdom, Above; and this is not found and not opened. That membrane covers over the Brain which is the Hidden Wisdom and because it is covered by that membrane, this Wisdom is not opened and therefore it is called, the Hidden Wisdom. And this Brain, which is the Hidden Wisdom, is silent and remaineth tranquil in its place like good wine upon its lees. And this is what is said: An Old One, His Knowledge is Hidden and His Brain is Hidden and Tranquil. And that membrane hath an outlet from *Ze'ir An-peen* and therefore this brain is spread and goes out to 32 ways.* This is that which is written: 'And a river went forth from Eden.'" (Gen. ii, 7.) † ‡

"The Cranium of *Resha 'Hiv'rah, i. e.*, White Head, has no beginning nor end; it extends and shines as a cohesive reservoir which spreads out and illuminates. And from it the just inherit 400 worlds of delights in the world to come. From this cohesive reservoir which is the White Cranium, dew drips daily to the *Ze'ir An-peen* Small Faces, to a place which is called, *Sha-mayeem* (Heavens), and where, in time to come, the dead shall be summoned to life. It is written: 'Elohim shall give thee of the dew of heaven, etc.' (Gen. xxvii, 28.) And the head shall be filled, and from that *Ze'ir An-peen*, it drips to the Field of Apples and the whole Field of Apples (Sacred Fruits) flows from that dew. This *At-tee-'kah Qad-dosha, i. e.*, Holy Ancient, is Hidden and Concealed, and the Wisdom from Above, is hidden in that Cranium, (is found and not found. Cremona Ed.) Surely in that *At-tee'kah* nothing is revealed except the Head alone, because He is the Head of all Heads. The Wisdom Above, which is the Head, is hidden in it, and is called the Upper Brain, the Hidden Brain, the Brain which is Tranquil and Quiet, and none know

* That is, the means of knowledge and intelligence to man, looked upon as the 22 letters of the Hebrew alphabet and the decade united, as the 32 symbols by which, man has any wisdom or any power of uniting with his fellows.

† Eden or Paradise was considered by the learned of the ancient Israëlites as the place of Understanding and Wisdom, the Intellect.

‡ Zohar iii, Idrah Rabbah. Brody, Amsterdam, and Mantua Ed., 128*a* and *b*. Cremona Ed. iii, fol. 61, col. 243.

it but Himself. Three Heads are carved out, each within the other, and each above, from the other. One Head is the Hidden Wisdom which is covered up and not opened. And this Hidden Wisdom is the Head of All the Heads of the other Wisdoms. The Upper Head is the *At-tee'kah Qad-dosha* the Holy Ancient, the Concealed of all Concealed,* the Head of All Heads, a Head which is not a Head, nor does any one know nor is it ever known, what is in that Head which Wisdom or Reason cannot comprehend; and on this we read: 'Flee Thou to Thy *Ma-qom* (*i. e.*, Place).' (Num. xxiv, 11.) 'And the 'Haÿ-yoth, *i. e.*, living creatures, run and return.' (Ezek. i, 14.) And therefore *At-tee'kah Qad-dosha* the Holy Ancient, is called *Ayin*, (*i. e.*, No-Thing, or, *Non ens*) because in Him depends *Ayin* (*Non ens*). And all these locks and all these hairs come out from the Hidden Brain. † And all are even and smooth and in equilibrium and hanging over the back of the neck which is not seen in any way. Because the *At-tee'kah Qad-dosha* the Holy Ancient, is in one, entire in happiness, and does not change from Mercy forever. In Thirteen channels of Mercies is He found ‡ because that Hidden Wisdom in Him is divided three times into four-fourths (*i. e.*, a quarternary, comp. Figure 36, *supra*), and He, the *At-tee'kah* Ancient, comprises them and rules over ALL. One way is illuminated in the *middle* (the parting) of the Hair coming out from the Brain, this is the way by whose light the just are led into the world to come. It is written: 'And the way of the just is like a shining light, etc. (Prov. iv, 18.) And of this it is written: 'Then thou shalt delight in YHVH.' (Is. lviii, 14.) And from that way all the other ways which depend on *Ze'ir An-peen* are illuminated. That *At-tee'kah* the Ancient, Oldest of the Oldest, is *Kether El-yon* the Highest Crown, Above, by which are crowned all Diadems and Coronets. And from Him the Lamps are Illuminated and Lighted and they send

---

* Comp. Zohar i, fol. 147, Amsterdam Ed. The Tosephthah.

† The locks and hairs are those which cover the back of the head and nap of the neck, and in this is doubtless the hidden mystery of Ex. xxxiii, 20 *sq*. The Sphinx has lapels covering the back of the head, neck and shoulders; the priests of the Greek and Russian Church are obliged to have the back of the head, neck and shoulders, covered with their long flowing hair, and a similar arrangement is portrayed, in the ancient pictures of Christ and of the Father. Note the same on the Hindu Prana, *ante*, p. 322.

‡ Comp. Ex. xxxiv, 5–8, known to the Israëlites as the Thirteen Middoth.

forth flames and scintillate. And this is He, the Supreme Hidden Spark which is not known, and all other Lamps are Lighted and Illuminated from Him. This *At-tee'kah* the Ancient, is found in Three Heads and they are contained in One Head. (Comp. Zohar iii, 291*b*.) And He is the Upper Head, Above Above. And because *At-tee'kah Qad-dosha* the Holy Ancient, is designated by Three, so here all the other Lamps which are Illuminated from Him are included in Three. Furthermore, the *At-tee-'kah* is designated by Two; the complex of the *At-tee'kah* which is in Two, is the Upper Crown of all the Upper Heads of all the Above, the Head of all the Heads. And that which is above from this, is not known, so all the other Lamps are hidden in Two. Further the *At-tee'kah Qad-dosha* the Holy Ancient, is designated and hidden in One and is One and everything is One, so all the other Lamps become sanctified and are joined and knotted in One, are One and are ALL." *

" He (Ain Soph) is beginning and end of all degrees (in the creation). All these degrees are stamped with His image, and He can be called only One, notwithstanding the innumerable images He is still only One, surely He is so: the Above and the Below, depend on Him." †

THE SHE-MAH, TRIAD AND UNITY. "Whoever (in the שמע She-mah 'Hear O Israel, etc. Deut. vi, 4,) ‡ says, אֶחָד *E'had*, One § should pronounce the א Aleph quickly, somewhat shorten its sound and not pause on it. Whoso doeth this, his life shall be prolonged. Said they to him (R. Ilaï): He (R. Shim-on) has said: ' There are Two (חד) in conjunction with One (א) and hence they are Three, and if they are Three then they are One.' (אחד *E'had*, One.) Said he to them: ' Those two Names of the She-mah which are *YHVH*, *YHVH*, *Elohainu* connects

---

* Zohar iii, fol. 288*a* and *b*, Mantua Ed. Idrah Zootah. Cremona Ed. iii, fol. 140*a*, col. 558.

† Zohar i, 21*a*, Brody Ed. Livorno Ed. i, 36*b* and 37*a*.

‡ "Jesus answered him, *The first of all the commandments is*, Hear, O Israel; the Lord our God, the Lord is One." Mark xii, 29, New Version. This is the great Jewish Declaration of Faith used in the time of Jesus, and used by him, and now used by the pious Jews, every day, and is most probably that referred to in Daniel vi, 10, 13, and Peter, Acts iii, 1, x, 3, 30.

§ The numerical value of אחד $1 + 8 + 4 = 13$.

with them, and this is the seal of the (divine) inscription. It is Truth.*
But when these are connected together as one then they are One in
a Unity.' " †

"We have learned: In thirteen ways the knot of Truth is tied, for the
production of blessing to all, and all the *E'meth*, *i.e.*, Truth, of the Holy,
Blessed be He! is hidden in Three; therefore the Thorah is crowned in
thirteen ways." ‡

We must not assume, from the preceding and following quotations,
that the ancient Israëlites believed in a Trinity as understood in the
Christian Church; the doctrines of the latter, upon this dogma, required a long time for their formulation, and the controversies between
Arrian and Athanasius, the theologians who preceded them, and those during the Middle Ages, will evidence this to the student. The Hebrews
in common with many other of the ancient Oriental peoples, believed in
a Triadic manifestation of the Supreme Deity, who nevertheless was a
Unit. The existence of the Triadic idea in the Zoharic writings, tends
to prove their antiquity as productions of the ancient Jewish Babylonian
Schools. It is not probable that a persecuted Jew of the Middle Ages,
one of the grounds of which, was his Unitarian belief, would have forged
and placed in these writings, any thing calculated to prove the antiquity
and correctness of the dogmas of the Greek Church or the Roman Catholic Trinitarian ideas, or assist the Inquisition and the Christian Church,
in the punishment of his people.

"R. Yehudah said: 'There are two beings, one in heaven and one on

---

* This means, that the repeating of the She-mah should conclude as if with a seal to bind it, with the אמת *E'meth* Truth. When the She-mah is repeated, always before the repetition must be said in a low voice אֵל מֹלֶךְ נֶאֱמָן: "El Me'lekh ne'émon." The first letters of the three words אָמֵן *Amen*, have the same meaning as אמת *E'meth* Truth. The sentence should be repeated without a pause: I Am YHVH your *Elohainu* in Truth.

† Zohar iii, fol. 162a, Amsterdam Ed. iii, fol. 67, Sulzbach Ed. Cremona Ed. iii, fol. 77b.

‡ Zohar iii, fol. 28, col. 110, § *A'ha-rai Moth.* Cremona Ed. iii, 62a, Amsterdam Ed. In the 13 Middoth, attributes of Mercy, Ex. xxxiv, 5–7, the first three are: '*YHVH, YHVH, Ail* (God),' and the ten following are attributes pointing to the first ' of יהוה (YHVH). The just pray every day the thirteen stems.

earth, and the Holy, Blessed be He! unites them.' R. El'azar said: 'Three Lights are in the Holy Upper which unite as One; and they are the basis of the Thorah and this opens the door to All. They open the door to Truth and this is the house to All, and therefore is it called, בית *ba-is* house, because this is their house.'"*

"'Behold a people dwelling alone.' (Num. xxiii, 9.) That is, in unity without (other) mixture. All the perfect unity is so, (and is expressed in): 'YHVH Elohainu YHVH.' This is the mystery in it, that *Hu, i. e.*, He, was before the beginning of all creation,† and unites Itself at the head, at the stem, and on the way (place where it stands); 'YHVH' that is the Upper Head, in the in-itself concentrated æther.‡ 'Elohainu,' *i.e.*, our God, is the stem which is called, the 'Stem of *Yishai* (Jesse),' (Is. xi, 1); and 'YHVH' is the way, from Below. Whoever in this manner comprehends the mystery of the Unity, conceives it as it is proper."§

"The daily unity is the unity in this verse: 'Hear O Israël *YHVH Elohainu YHVH.*' They are all One: therefore it is called אחד *E'had* One. Here are three Names, how are they One? And although we read *E'had* One, how are they One? Only by the vision of *Rua'h Qaddosha, i. e.*, the Holy Spirit, is this apparent and only then, with closed eyes,‖ can we know how Three are One. And this is the mystery of the voice which has been heard. The voice is only one yet it consists of three elements, fire, air and water, and all are one in the mystery of the voice (and this can only be considered as one).¶ And so here, *YHVH Elohainu YHVH* are One, three forms and they are One, and this is in-

---

* Zohar iii, fol. 36a ξ *Shim-inee*. Cremona Ed., ii, fol. 16a, col. 61.

† The words of the text, the author takes with the meaning of chief or head (properly, *rosh tzoorim, i.e.*, top or head of rocks, representing the deity;) of creations, before the beginning of all creations, so that to Him was created *tsoor* or *ye'tsoor* a created thing, corresponding to *tsoor*. The creature is form. (Ps. xlix, (14) 15.)

‡ *Aveer-ah d'salkah* the absolute æther, appears here the same as *aveer-ah d'tsimtsum* concentrated æther, or, perhaps better, *ye'sod ha-tsim-tsum* concentrated foundation.

§ Zohar iii, fol. 203b, Amsterdam Ed. iii, fol. 82, col. 2, Sulzbach Ed. Cremona Ed., iii, fol. 94b, ξ *Baloq*.

‖ It is customary among the Israëlites to put the hands over the eyes when repeating the first verse of the She-mah, see the *Ora'h 'Haȳ-yem*, c. 61, ξ 4.

¶ *Ibid.* ξ 3. The reason for speaking the name aloud is to awaken devotion.

dicated by the voice which man must use in the expression of the prayer of unity, and put his will in unity, which is all from Ain Soph to the end, since they are all in this voice which he makes in this Three, which are One. And this is the daily (confession) of the Divine Unity which is revealed in the mystery by the Holy Spirit. And in many ways the Unity has been explained and all are true, who has done it in this way has done right, and who has done it in another way is also right. But this unity which we form, Below, in the mystery of the voice, which is one, explains the Word* in general.†

"'Hear O Israel *YHVH Elohainu YHVH* is One.' (Deut. vi, 4.) This is the One Unity and His Name is One. 'Praised be the Name of the Glory (She'kheen-ah) of His Kingdom (Malkhuth) for ever and ever.' This is the other Unity (see *ante*, p. 342 *sq.*) that His Name shall be One. And this is the secret of *YHVH Hu Eloheem, i. e.*, YHVH He, is God. And this mystery of the Unity is contained in the verse: 'YHVH is Elohim,' as it is above written, when they are conceived of in their Absolute Unity. But if it is objected: Does it not contradict the verse: 'YHVH shall be one and His Name shall be One?' (Zech. xiv, 9.) This is not so, but 'YHVH is Elohim.' For if there was written; YHVH is One and His Name, He, is One, we could agree with thee, but it is not so written, only: 'YHVH One, and his Name, One,' ought to be said like this, viz: *YHVH Hu* (He) *Hu* (He) *Elohim:* and so it would seem to be, YHVH is One, and His Name is One. But all is One when these two Names are (in an abstract manner) united, the One, in the one Unity, the other, in the one Unity, and the two Unities can be comprehended in an Absolute Unity, so that together, they express the complete conception of the Name in one Unity. And only in this way 'is *YHVH Hu Elohim*,' because each is connected with the other so to be One. But before the Unity is united they are each One considered absolutely by Itself, and the comprehension of the connection as an Ab-

---

* מלה *Millah* Word, because according to an explanation in another place (Genesis *sidrah, Vay-e'tze*) the " Word " itself comprises a triad, that is will, voice and articulated word.

† Zohar ii, fol. 43*b*, Amsterdam Ed. ii, fol. 18, col. 2, Sulzbach Ed. Cremona Ed., ii, fol. 19*b*, col. 75.

solute Unity, is not complete. This (comprehension of the Unity) is the essence of the whole Thorah. For the Thorah embraces both the written and oral: the written Thorah is this which is written YHVH, the oral Thorah is that which is written Elohim: and because the Thorah is the mystery of the Holy Name, therefore they are called the written Thorah and the oral Thorah. This (the written) is the general, the other (the oral) is the special. The general needs the special and the special needs the general, thus one unites itself with the other, that all may be One. And therefore the entire content of the Thorah is the whole content of the Above and Below, because this Name (YHVH) describes, the Above, and the other Name (Elohim), the Below. This one, is the mystery of the Higher World; the other, the mystery of the Lower World, and as to this is written: 'To thee it has been shown that thou mayest know, that YHVH *is* Elohim!' This is the essence of the ALL, and this must the son of man know in this world."*

"Come, See! The mystery of the word. There are Three degrees and each exists by Itself, and yet all are One, and are knotted in One, nor are they separated one from another."†

"' *The Ail* (or, El, *i. e.*, God) *Eloheem YHVH'diber, i. e.*, The God, God YHVH spoke and called (the) earth, etc.' (Ps. l, 1.) *Ail* is the Light of Wisdom and is called '*Hesed* (Benevolence, Mildness) *Eloheem* is *Ge'boor-ah* (Strength or Severity) and *YHVH* is the completeness of all Mercy. Hence (the words) *diber vay'iq-rah e'retz, i. e.,* He ' *spoke* and *called* (the) earth, etc.'" (is in the singular.) (*Ibid.*)

"And these are the Three degrees which are called by the name of *Din, i. e.,* Judgment, and all are knotted in One without separation." (*Ibid.*)

"' And the righteous are the foundation of the world,' (Prov. x, 25) is written. Three come out from One, One exists in Three, it is the force between Two, Two nourish One, One nourishes many sides, thus

---

* Zohar ii, fol. 161*b*, 162*a*, Amsterdam Ed. ii, fol. 111, Sulzbach Ed. Cremona Ed. ii, fol. 72*a*, col. 285.

† Zohar iii, fol. 29*b*, col. 116, letter ב, Cremona Ed. iii, fol. 65*a*, Amsterdam Ed. ‡ *A'ha-rai Moth.*

All is One, therefore it is written 'It was evening and morning one day,' the day of evening and morning joined, were one." *

THE MYSTERY OF THE THREE PARTS OF FIRE WHICH ARE ONE. "Began R. Shim-on and said: Two verses are written; 'That YHVH thy Elohim is a devouring fire, a zealous Ail (El);'† (Deut. iv, 24) again it is written; 'But you that cleave unto YHVH your Elohim, are alive, every one of you, this day.' (Deut. iv, 4.) On this verse 'That YHVH thy Elohim is a consuming fire.' This we said to the Companions; That it is a fire which devours fire, and it is a fire which devours itself and consumes itself, because it is a fire which is more mighty than a fire, and it has been so confirmed. But, Come, See! Whoever desires to know the wisdom of the Holy Unity should look in that flame arising from a burning coal or a lighted lamp. This flame comes out only when united with another thing. Come, See! In the flame which goes up are two lights: one light is a bright white and one light is united with a dark or blue, the white light is that which is above and ascends in a straight path, and that below is that dark or blue light, and this light below, is the throne to the white light and that white light rests upon it, and they unite one to the other so that they are one. And this dark light or blue color, which is below, is the precious throne to the white. And this is the mystery of the blue.‡ And this blue dark throne unites itself with another thing to light that from below, and this awakes it to unite with the upper white light, and this blue or dark, sometimes changes its color but that white above never changes its color, it is always white; but that blue changes to these different colors, sometimes to blue or black and sometimes to a red color, and this unites itself to two sides.' It unites to the above, to that upper white light, and unites itself below to the thing which is under it, which is the burning matter, and this burns and consumes always from the matter below. And this devours that matter below, which connects with it and upon which the blue light rests, therefore this eats up all which connects with it from below, because it is the nature of it, that it devour and consume everything which depends on it

---

*Zohar i, fol. 22b, col. 87, Cremona Ed. i, fol. 32b, Amsterdam Ed.

† See Herder's *Geist der Hebräischen Poesie*, Vol. ii.

‡ The blue color of Heaven and the *th'keileth, i. e.*, blue, of the Tallith.

and is dead matter, and therefore it eats up everything which connects with it below, and this white light which rests upon it never consumes itself and never changes its light, and therefore said Moses: 'That YHVH thy Elohim is a consuming fire.'* Surely He consumes. It devours and consumes everything which rests under it; and on this he said: 'YHVH is thy Elohim' not 'our Elohim,' because Moses has been in that white light, Above, which neither devours nor consumes. Come, See! it is not His Will to light that blue light that should unite with that white light, only for Israël; because they cleave or connect under Him. And, Come, See! Although the nature of that dark or blue light is, that it shall consume everything which joins with it below, still Israël cleaves on Him, Below, * * * and although you cleave in Him nevertheless you exist, because it is written: ' You are all alive this day.' And on this white light rests above a Hidden Light which is stronger. Here is the above mystery of that flame which comes out from it, and in it is the Wisdom of the Above." † See, Philo., Bohn's Ed. iv, p. 44.

THOUGHT AND THE WORD. " Come, See! *Ma'hshabah* Thought, is the first (principle) of all,‡ because Thought is, in itself hidden and not known. When this Thought began to diffuse itself, it came to the place where the Spirit rests, and when it has reached that place it is called; *Binah* Understanding, and is no more hidden like before, and although it is hidden, that Spirit spreads itself and brings out a Voice§ embracing fire, water and air, which are South, North and East, and this Voice comprises all the other *Forces*‖ (hosts, angels) and this Voice, speaks to the Word.¶ This Voice gives existence to the Word because, this Voice is

* Deut. iv, 24. Comp. Zohar ii, 226*b*. Hebrews xii, 29.

† Zohar i, 50*b*, Amsterdam and Brody Editions. Cremona Ed., i, 36*a*, col. 141. See Exod. iii, 2, 3; Acts vii, 30. Dr. Christian D. Ginsburg in : The Kabbalah, etc. London, 1865, pp. 25, 26, applies the above to the Triadic idea of the Deity. His translation of it and most of the other quotations from the Zohar, have been copied from Prof. Adolphe Franck, and cannot be depended upon. Franck has been severely criticised for his translations, by Dr. D. H. Joel in his *Religions-philosophie des Sohar*, etc.

‡ Thought, is *Kether* Crown.

§ '*Hokhmah* Wisdom, or the Word.

‖ The Cremona edition does not have this word.

¶ Comp. Is. vi, 3. The repetition is emphatic and expresses energy or force; see also II Sam. xviii, 33.

sent from the place of the Spirit and comes to speak a Word, to bring out joyous words. And when they look in the degrees, this is the Thought; this is the Understanding; 'this is Voice; this is Speech; and all are One. And this is the first Thought of All and not separated, but all are One and in One bond. This is that which is the real Thought bound in the *Ayin* and never separated, and this is 'YHVH is One and His Name One.'" (Zech. xiv, 9.)*

THE NAMES OF THE DEITY. "The secret of this word אהיה *Eh'yeh* I Am, comprises everything, when the ways are hidden and not separated and together in one place, then it is called *Eh'yeh* I am, all hidden and not revealed; but after it goes out from its defined line and that river bears in its bosom all things, then He is called אשר אהיה *Asher Eh'yeh, i. e., That* I Am, that means; I Am, prepared to bring forth all, and after He revealed and brought forth all He is called by the above Name. And after this when Moses desired to know what is the speciality of the word, He said to him, YHVH and not *Asher Eh'yeh* That I Am. * * * But after he brought everything out and put everything in its place, He said YHVH, and at this time Moses knew the secret of the Holy Hidden Name and there was revealed to him and he comprehended, that which could not be comprehended by any other of the children of the world." †

The Names of the Deity are only abstract symbols and ideas necessary to man's mind in our matter-world so as to grasp in his thought that a Deity exists. They do not describe God's essence or content. The Qabbalists found it necessary, in their subtle and abstract metaphysical investigations, to invent a Name which would describe the Deity before It created the universe, this they did by the term *Ain Soph* without end, called also *Ayin, i. e.,* No-Thing, which is nevertheless not an absolute negative or void but an unknown to man, Some-Thing. Not that in these Names any greater knowledge is contained but they point to a greater incomprehensibility of the Deity. Equaling these is the subtle and abstract Qabbalistic Name מי *Mee* Who? *Without beginning or end.* (See, *ante*, p. 129 *sq.* and Zohar ii, fol. 105*a*; i, 2*a*.) The Zohar holds that while *Ain*

* Zohar i, 246*b*, Brody Ed. Cremona Ed., i, fol. 131*a*, col. 519.
† Zohar iii, 65*b*, Brody Ed. Cremona Ed., iii, fol. 29*b*, col. 116.

Soph, Ayin and *Who?* describe the Deity, considered in Its greatest abstractness, yet the latter is united with אלה *Ele'h* These, and in this matter-world constitutes the Name אלה־ים *Eloh-im*, and therefore in the statement in Genesis of the First Emanation or Creation, the Name Elohim is exclusively used and not YHVH Elohim, as in the Second; and that this union still continues and *Mee* and *Ele'h* are still merged: (Zohar i, 2*a*); but should they ever be separated, the universe could no longer exist as after their connection. (Zohar ii, fol. 105*a*.) The *Ain Soph* received its full significance as the, No End, through Its emanation of the Sephiroth. (Zohar ii, 42*b*.) Springing out of *Ain Soph* is *Kether*, whose Divine Name is *Eh'yeh* I am, the Ego. Further considered, this is developed into *Asher Eh'yeh* that I will be, (Comp. Rashi in this place); finally it passes into reality for man, יהוה YHVH, the symbol of the Past, Present and Future. The Existence which is Creator and Preserver, yet nevertheless, for Its own wise purposes, the Destroyer of the matter-forms, but not of their atoms or essence. YHVH is contained in the manifestation called the Sephirothic Tree of Life. YHVH is הָיָה הֹוֶה וְיִהְיֶה *Hoyoh Hoveh V'ye'hyeh* He was, is, and shall be. (Rev. i, 4, 8; xxi, 6.) הֹוֶה *Hoveh* the present, may be added to וּמְהַוֶּה *u'm-haveh* causing to exist, the creating and maintaining.

Before the emanation of the universe the Qabbalists say; "He and His Name were One." Which may be paralleled in the time to come by God's Kingdom upon Earth: "In that day shall there be one YHVH and וּשְׁמוֹ *ush'mah* His Name, shall be One." (Zach. xiv, 10.) Many of the Qabbalists hold שם הויה *Shem Hava-yah* the Existing Name (*ante*, p. 342) as that embracing all the other Divine Names. Elohim is the principle emanating the universe, but is that of Rigor. YHVH is that maintaining it, and is the principle of Mercy and Harmony. In *El Shaddai* Almighty, the אֵל *El* is the principle of Grace and Mercy and is paralleled with 'Hesed; שַׁדַי *Shad-aai*, is that of Strength, and is paralleled with Ge'boor-ah; but YHVH unites both conceptions in a Harmony. Elohim is more immediately identified with Nature, and the numerical value of אלהים Elohim (86) and טבעה *Tebah* Nature (86) are the same. YHVH is Elohim and the content of both Mercy and Rigor.

Kether Crown, is *A'reekh An-peen* or *Appa-yem* Long Faces. The eight Sephiroth following are *Ze'ir An-peen* Short Faces. In *Kether* is the germ and content, in harmony, of the Sacred Form, the other Sephiroth surround it as if a rich and shining garment. In its narrowest sense *Kether El'yon* Crown of the Highest, is this garment. Note however that the word *Kether* Crown, is only used as a mere symbol of the King of All. (Zohar iii, fol. 288*b*.) It is the representative of the coalescing of the Highest with His creation and its preservation, through the efflux, to the uttermost limits of entire nature and All. A clear knowledge of the essence of *Kether* cannot be obtained by man in this world, it is to him even as if *Ayin* No-Thing. (Zohar iii, 288*b*.) The Tiqqooneem haz-Zohar says: "That degree which is called *Ayin* comprises Kether, Binah and 'Hokhmah." The entire content of the Names of the Deity applied to the respective Sephiroth are only symbols of *Ain Soph*.

The idea of the Sephiroth is like that of a builder who desires to build a great Palace. 1. He grasps in his mind the plan of the whole building. This is Kether, 'Hokhmah, Binah. 2. Then he considers the way according to which the work shall be done, that it shall correspond to the plan. This is 'Hesed, Tiph'e-reth and Ge'boor-ah. 3. He considers the means of carrying it out, this is Ne-tza'h, Ye'sod and Hod. The entire building is the Divine government of the whole world represented by Malkhuth.

MERCY TEMPERS RIGOR. "R. El'azar sat before R. Shim-on his father and said to him: 'This we have learned: that Elohim אלהים in every place is judgment, that this word is: Yod, Heh, Vav, Heh (יהוה YHVH), and it is a place which is called, Elohim; like it is written (Gen. xv, 8), 'Adonoi YHVH': (Which not read YHVH but Elohim.) Why is it called Elohim, when it (YHVH) means Mercy in every place?' Said he to him: 'So it is written: (Deut. iv, 39.) 'And thou shalt know to-day and consider it in thine heart, that YHVH is Elohim.' And it is written: (Deut. iv, 31, 35, 39.) 'YHVH is Elohim.' Said he to him: 'These words we know, that in the place of Mercy, may be sometimes, Judgment, and that sometimes Judgment is tempered with Mercy!' Said he (R. Shim-on) to him: 'Come, See! This is so, Yedud (*i. e.*, YHVH) is in all places Mercy but at the time when through sin, Mercy is changed to Judgment, then it is written YHVH but read Elohim. But: Come, See! the secret of the word (YHVH). There are Three degrees and each degree exists in itself, although all are One, connected in One and not separated One from the other."*

EMANATION OF THE UNIVERSE. "'In the Beginning' In Wisdom the King engraved forms in the clearness Above. *Botzeen-ah D' Qardinuthah, i.e.*, the brilliant inner Light, came out from the Hidden of Hidden, from the Head of the Ain Soph. A nebulous spark of matter flashed out which was not white nor black nor red nor green and not of any color whatever; but when He took the measure of the structure He made colors to light in the inner. From that *Botzeen-ah* came forth a Supreme Light from which reflected different colors Below. He stopped up its hidden point from the Mystery of Ain Soph. He opened and not opened it so its *aveer-ah* air (æther), has not been known until it came out from the power of that opening. Then he lighted a point (light) the Hidden of the Above, after that first point (light) which had not been known, and therefore that point (first point) is called *Raisheeth* Beginning, meaning the *first Word of All*." †

"The *neqood-ah qadmo-ah, i. e.*, first point, was an inner light which had no limit so that could be known, its pureness, thinness (subtility) and clearness, until it expanded itself through itself; and the expansion of this point made a palace to envelope that point. Its (the palace's) light cannot be comprehended because of its immense pureness and yet it is not so thin (subtile) and clear as that first point, which is hidden and concealed. The palace which is the garment to that hidden point, its light (is also) unlimited, although it is not so pure and clear as that first point which is hidden and concealed. That palace expands itself outwardly from its first light, and that expansion is the garment to that palace, of which its inner is subtile and clear; and from here, (each) farther spreads itself one in another, and envelopes itself, one in another, until it is found, (that) one is a garment to the other, and the other still to another; but this is, the brain (the very inner); and that, the shell," (*i. e.*, the skull, the cover of the brain, or, inner.)‡

---

* Zohar iii, fol. 65*a*, Amsterdam Ed. iii, fol. 27, col. 2, Sulzbach Ed. Cremona Ed. iii, fol. 29*b*, col. 116.

† Zohar, Cremona Ed. i, fol. 3, col. 1. Brody Ed. i, 15*a*. Livorno, i, 25*b*.

‡ Zohar i, 20*b*, Brody Ed. Livorno Ed. i, 34*a*. Cremona Ed. i, fol. 24*b*, col. 96.

"Before the world was created (the *An-peen* Faces,) did not look attentively, Faces to Faces, and the primitive worlds were made without perfect formations, and therefore the primitive worlds were destroyed. And those which were not in perfect formation are called flaming sparks, like the worker in copper or iron when he strikes on it with his iron hammer, makes sparks dash out on every direction. And these sparks which leap forth, flame and glitter, but are at once extinguished. And such are called: 'The First Worlds.' And therefore they were destroyed and did not remain, until *At-tee'kah Qad-dosha* the Holy Ancient, restored them and the Work-master went to His work. And on this we have learned in our Mathnithah; that that Ray (of Light) sent out sparks in 320 directions. And those sparks are called, 'The First Worlds;' and they at once perished. Then the Artist went to His work and He formed in male and female, and these sparks which were extinct and died at once, all remained now. From a *Botzeenah* Shining Light, of most intense brilliancy, came out a radiant strong flame as from a hammer, and brought forth sparks of the first worlds, and these were mixed with the most subtile air,* and like the *abbah* father, and *immah* mother, were mutually tempered by each other when they were merged. And this father is from the Spirit which is hidden in *At-teek Yo-men* the Ancient of Days, in him is hidden that (subtile) air, and he coalesced to that spark which came forth out of that Shining Light which has been hidden in the inner of the mother.† But when both joined together and merged one in another, was produced a large strong Cranium (the Firmament) and it expanded on its side, this on this side and that on that side. Like the *At-tee'kah Qad-dosha* Holy Ancients, in Three Heads which are found in One: (Comp. Zohar iii, 288*b*:) So ALL has been prepared under the form of Three Heads, as we have said.‡ In this Cranium drips a dew from *Resha 'Hiv'rah* the White Head, and this dew is seen in two different colors, and from it (this dew) is fed the Field of the Holy Apples (Sacred Fruits). And from that dew of the Cranium is prepared the manna for the just in the world

---

* The ætheric medium or Fourth State of Matter?

† The hidden vital energy or force, by means of which all Things exist.

‡ These are the spiritually positive or male, and the negative or female, joined together and merged through the action of the harmony.

to come, and by it the dead will be aroused to life. * * * And that subtile air contains itself in All because it is comprised from All, and All is comprised in it. Its Face expands to two sides in two lights which are comprised from All. And when the Faces look towards each other, all the *At-tee'kah Qad-dosha* is called A'reekh Appa-yem, *i. e.*, Long Faces." *

At-tee'kah Qad-dosha the Holy Ancient. The Hidden of All the Hidden is separated. It is separated from All and not separated, because All is merged in Him and He is merged in All. He is the *At-tee'kah D'Kol At-tee'keen* the Ancient of All the Ancients, the Hidden of All the Hidden. He is formed and yet is not formed. He is formed to sustain All and not formed because He is not found. When He is formed nine† flaming Lights go out from Him, from His Form; and from these Lights are emitted flames and they expand themselves out to all directions, like a lamp which spreads light to all sides. And these lights which expand themselves from it, when any (one) draweth near to know them are not found but only the lamp, alone. So is He, *the At-tee'kah Qad-dosha* the Holy Ancient: He is the Upper Lamp, the Hidden of All the Hidden and is not found, except those rays which are expanded which yet are revealed and hidden. And they are called, the Holy Name, and therefore all are One.‡

THE EMANATION OF THE ANGELS. "At the time when the Holy, Blessed be He! breathed the spirit into each of the heavenly host, all the hosts were formed and stood before Him, therefore it is written; 'With the breath of His mouth He made all the host.'" (Ps. xxxiii, 6.)§

THE SOULS OF THE RIGHTEOUS HIGHER THAN THE ANGELS. "We have found in the First Book of Adam, that all the Holy Spirits from Above, are performing messages (they have been sent to do) and all come from one place. The souls of the just (pious) from two degrees which

---

* Zohar iii, 292*a* and *b*, Brody Ed. Cremona Ed. iii, fol. 142*a* and *b*, col. 566–67.

† Franck *La Kabbale*, p. 78, incorrectly says "ten." Comp. Joel *Religions-philosophie*, etc., p. 85.

‡ Zohar iii, 288*a*, Brody Ed., Idrah Zootah. Cremona Ed. iii, fol. 140*a*, col. 558.

§ Zohar iii, 68*a*, Brody Ed. Cremona Ed. iii, fol. 31*a*, col. 122.

are comprised in one, and therefore they go higher and their degrees are higher and so it is. And those who are hidden there come down and go in their life like Enoch, of whom Death is not mentioned."*

The Qabbalists hold that the *Neshamah* soul, dwelling in us, is only a shadow or reflection of a higher and celestial, spiritual, perfect prototype, or *Zure*, which never leaves its exalted abode in the A'tzeel-atic World or World of the Sephiroth. It is thought of, as connected with the *Neshamah* of man, by an invisible thread, a *Qav Amtzaith-ah* middle cord, and is affected from Below. (Comp. Matt. x, 29–31; Luke xii, 6, 7; Matt. xviii, 10.) By inspired devotion, they say, the will of man directs his *Neshamah* to its *Zure*, Above; and the *Neshamah* endeavors to leave the body and again unite itself with its *Zure*, Above; then the higher prototypic soul becomes stirred up and, by a mystic influence, they are chained to each other. This idea falls within the higher mysticism of the Qabbalah, in which, the doctrine of ecstasy plays its part, and it is beyond the metaphysical speculation. In this is centred the idea of the union of the King and Queen; from the former, the efflux descends from the Above to the Below.

FORMING OF SOULS. "At the time that the Holy, Blessed be He! desired to create the world, it came in His Will before Him: and He formed all the souls which are prepared to be given to the children of man afterwards; and all were formed before Him in the same real form which has been prepared to be in the children of man afterwards, and He saw everyone of them: and that some of them would corrupt their ways in the world. When the time has arrived for it (to come into this world) the Holy, Blessed be He! calls to that *Neshamah* soul, He says to her: 'Go thou to that place and into that body.' She answers before the Lord of the world; 'This world in which I dwell is sufficient for me, and I do not care to be in another world in which I shall be a servant and exposed to its uncleanness.' Said the Holy, Blessed be He! to her: 'From the day thou wast created, thou wert only created for that purpose, to have thy destination in that world.' When the soul sees that it is necessary to obey, it with grief comes down, and goes in there (this body). The Thorah, which gives advice to the whole world, when she

* Zohar iii, 68*b*, Brody Ed. Cremona Ed. iii, fol. 31*a*, col. 122.

saw this, warned the children of the world, and said: 'See how much pity, the Holy, Blessed be He! has on you, a good pearl which He had He gives it to you for nothing, that you shall work her in this world.'*

EMANATION OF THE UNIVERSE. "Come, See! At the time it came up in the Will of the Holy, Blessed be He! to create the world, He brought forth from the *Botzeen-ah Qardinuthah, i. e.*, the very inner light (of the heart) a knot (or, chain) and lighted (emanated) the darkness from it and let it down Below. The darkness lighted in a hundred different ways and paths, small and great, and made the House (Tabernacle or Temple, Below. Rev. xi, 19; xv, 5, 6, 8; xvi, 1.) of the world. (The *A'seey-atic* world.) This House is the centre of all; around it are many doors, surrounding it are the holy upper places. (The *Ye'tzeer-atic* world.) There are the nests of the heavenly birds (angels) each in its kind. In it goes forth a Great Tree with strong branches which bear plenty of food for all. This Tree goes up to the heavenly clouds and it is hidden between three mountains. From under the three mountains, the Tree goes out and ascends to the Above and comes down to the Below. This House is supplied by it with drink, and there is hidden in it (that House) many hidden things Above, which are not known. This Tree is revealed in the daytime and covered (hidden) in the night. And this House rules in the night time and is hidden during the day. At the time when darkness goes up and all doors are concealed from all sides, then many spirits are flying in the air which desire to know and go into it, and they go up between these birds and they take witness and see what they see, until that darkness awakes and brings out a certain flame and hammers it with many strong hammers and opens the doors. Large stones go forth from that flame and come down out of it, and make noises in the world and awake the voices Above and Below. And then a (fol. 172*b*) herald comes forth from it and connects himself in the air and calls out. That æther comes out from the pillar of the inner cloud, and when it comes out spreads itself on the four sides of the world; thousands of thousands exist from the side which is the Left, and myriad of myriads exist from the side which is the Right, and the herald remains in his place, etc." †

* Zohar ii, 96*b* and 97*a*, Brody Ed. Cremona Ed. ii, fol. 43*b*, col. 172–3.

† Zohar i, 172*a* and *b*, Brody Ed. Cremona Ed. i, fol. 98*b*, col. 393.

25

CONNECTION OF THE ABOVE AND THE BELOW. "Come, See! When the Holy, Blessed be He! desired to create worlds He brought out a Hidden Light, from that Light came out and illuminated all the lights which are revealed, and from that Light came out and expanded itself and were made, other lights; and this is the Upper World. That Upper Light spread itself out and made again a light which does not illuminate, and it made the Lower World. And because that light which does not illuminate desires to connect itself Above and desires to connect itself Below, with that Lower knot it connects itself to illuminate in the Upper knot, and that light which does not illuminate in the Upper knot brought out all the hosts and servants of many sorts, this is what is written: 'How great are Thy works YHVH, etc.' (Ps. xcii, 5.) And everything which is Below so it is Above, and there is not the smallest thing in this world which does not depend on another thing Above, and which is not taken account of Above, and all are united one in the other."*

THE PRE-ADAMITE KINGS. "We have learned in the Siphrah D'Tznioothah: That the *At-tee'kah D'At-tee'keen* Ancient of Ancients, before He prepared His Form, built kings and engraved kings, and sketched out kings, and they could not exist: till He overthrew them and hid them until after a time, therefore it is written; 'And these are the kings which reigned in the land of Edom.' That is in a place in which all judgments exist. And they could not exist until *Resha 'Hiv'rah* the White Head, the *At-tee'kah D'At-tee'keen* Ancient of the Ancients, arranged Himself. When He arranged Himself He formed all forms Above and Below. From here we learn that the head of a nation, who has not been arranged and formed at the beginning: its people is not from this Form. * * * Before He arranged Himself in His Form, had not been formed all those whom He desired to form, and all worlds have been destroyed; therefore is written: 'And Bela the son of Beor reigned in Edom.' (Gen. xxxvi, 32.)†

"He began and said: It is written: 'And these are the Kings that reigned in the land of Edom.' (Gen. xxxvi, 31.) And it is written: 'For lo,

* Zohar i, 156a and b, Brody Ed. Cremona Ed. i, fol. 91a, col. 362. See Mat. x, 29, 31; Luke xii, 6, 7; Rev. xi, 19.
† Zohar iii, 135a, Brody Ed. Cremona Ed. iii, fol. 64b, col. 255.

the kings were assembled, they *passed by* together.' (Ps. xlviii, 4.) They 'assembled' in that place which is called the land of Edom, the place where all judgments are together. 'They *passed by* together' as it is written: 'And he died' and another 'reigned in his stead.' (Gen. xxvi, 31 sq.) 'They saw, they marveled, were troubled,' (Ps. xlviii, 5) that they did not remain in their places, because the forms of the kings had not been formed as it ought to be, and the Holy City had not been prepared."*

"*At-tee'kah D'At-tee'keen* the Ancient of the Ancients, built worlds, and formed Its Forms to exist, but they did not exist until the Supreme Grace came down and then they remained. And this is what is written: 'And these are the kings who reigned in the land of Edom.'" †

THE EMANATION OF THE MALE AND FEMALE PRINCIPLES. "We have learned: At the time when the *At-tee'kah Qad-dosha*, the Holy Ancient, the Hidden of All the Hidden, desired to arrange everything, He formed all things like male and female in the place which comprises male and female. For they could not exist save in another existence of male and female. This Wisdom comprises All, when it goeth forth and is illuminated from the Holy Ancient it does not shine except in male and female. This '*Hokhmah*, Wisdom, diffused itself and from it came out *Binah* Understanding, and it is found male and female. Wisdom is the Father and Understanding is the Mother, Wisdom and Understanding in one balance and male and female (in the other), weigh the same, and through them everything exists in male and female. If it were not for this they (things) could not exist. This beginning is the Father to all the Fathers, connects one in another and lights one in another ('*Hokhmah* Wisdom, is the Father, and *Binah* Understanding, is the Mother). It is written: 'If thou callest Binah mother;' (Prov. ii, 3:) and when they connect one with the other they bring forth and diffuse and emanate, Truth. In the sayings of R. Ye-yeva, Sabah, *i. e.*, the Old, we learned this; What is Binah Understanding? But when they connect in one another, the ' (Yod) in the ה (Heh), they become impregnated and produce a Son. And therefore it is called *Binah*, Understanding. It

---

* Zohar iii, 292a. Idrah Zootah. Brody Ed. Cremona Ed. iii, fol. 142a, col. 566.

† Zohar iii, 142a, Brody Ed., Cremona Ed. iii, 67b, col. 268.

means BeN YaH *i. e.*, Son of YaH. This is the completeness of the Whole."*

"'And Elohim said; Let the waters gather, etc.' (Gen. i, 7.) In a straight line that shall be in a straight way, that is, from the secret of that first point came out all in its concealment until it reached and gathered to that Upper Palace, and from there it came out in a straight line to other degrees, till it reached that only place where all gathered in the comprising of male and female. †

THE EMANATED SOULS AND THEIR KNOWLEDGE. "Began R. 'Heyah and said: 'That which hath been is now, and that which is to be hath already been, etc.' (Eccl. iii, 15.) This we have learned; Before the Holy, Blessed be He! created this world, He had created worlds and destroyed them, till the Holy, Blessed be He! desired in רעותיה *R'ooth-eh i. e.*, His Will, to create this world and He took counsel in the Thorah. And then arranged Himself in His conformations and crowned Himself with His Crown and created this world. And everything which is found in this world has been before, and passed before Him, and been arranged before Him. And we have learned; all the creatures of the world which have existed in each generation, before they came to this world, have existed before Him in their true *D'yooq-nah i. e.*, simulacrum or phantom of a shadow image. And so we have learned; Even all the souls of the children of man before they come down to the world have all been sculptured before Him in heaven, in that real *D'yooq-nah* that they have in this world. And all that they learn in this world they already knew before they came into the world. And we have learned; They who are pure, are true, (*i. e.*, have the true *D'yooq-nah*.) And they who are not found pure in this world, even there, are thrust away from before the Holy, Blessed be He! And they ascend into that great deep abyss, (Gen. i, 2.) and they come down into this world. And their souls know the part they will play in this world before they come down to it, and this holy part which has been given to them is thrown into that deep abyss and they take their part from there. And if they deserve it and repent before their Lord, they take that (holy) part from there." ‡

* Zohar iii, 290a, Brody Ed. Idrah Zootah. Cremona Ed. iii, fol. 141a, col. 562.
† Zohar i, 18a, Brody Ed. Cremona Ed. i, fol. 24a, col. 93.
‡ Zohar iii, 61a and b, Brody Ed. Cremona Ed. iii, fol. 28a, col. 109.

THE SOULS IN PARADISE. "At the time when the Holy, Blessed be He! descends to the Garden of Eden, all its *Neshamoth* souls, of the just, which are crowned there, all give a pleasant odor, as is said; 'And the odor of thine ointment is from all *spices*.' (Song of Songs iv, 10.) These (the spices) are the souls of the just, then R. Yitzhaq, said; 'All the souls of the just which have been in this world, and all the souls which are prepared to descend into this world, all are in the Garden which is on the earth, all remain in the *d'yooq-nah*, shadow of the *tzelem*, and *tziyor-ah* form, in which they existed in this world. And this secret has been delivered to the wise. The *Rua'h* spirit, which descends to the children of man, which is from the female side, engraves itself steadily in the engraving, like a seal. The bodily *tziyor-ah* form, of the man in this world is (Comp. Zohar i, 73*b*) shaped on the outside and the *Rua'h* is engraved in the inner. When the *Rua'h* is separated from the body, that *Rua'h* is shaped in the Garden on the earth, in the same *tziyor-ah* form and same *d'yooq-nah* shadow of the *tzelem*, of the body which it had in this world, because it (the *Rua'h*) has been always like the impression of a seal, and on this is said: 'Set me like a seal, etc.' (Song of Songs viii, 6.) As a seal is engraved in its engraving on the inside and brings out the *tziyor-ah* form, of its shape (in relief) on the outside, so here to, the *Rua'h* spirit, which has been from her (the bodily) side in this world, is engraved in its engraving on the inside, but when it separates from the body and goes up in the air of *Gan Eden* Garden of Eden, then that engraving becomes shaped on the outside, in the same *tziyor-ah* form, like the *guff* body, in this world. The *Neshamah* Soul, which is from the Tree of Life, is in there (Above) formed in the Bundle of Life, to delight in the beauty of YHVH, as it is written; 'To behold the beauty of YHVH and to enquire in His Temple.'" (Ps. xxvii, 4.)*

THE CROWNING OF THE SOUL OF THE PIOUS. "It is written: 'Thus said Ail YHVH; He that created the heavens and stretched them out; He that spread forth the earth, and that which cometh out of it; He that giveth *neshamah* soul, to the people upon it, and *rua'h* spirit, to them that walk therein.' (Is. xlii, 5.) That is what is said: 'The earth,' He 'giveth the *neshamah*' to her. Said R. Yitzhaq; 'Everything is Above:

* Zohar ii, 11*a*, Brody Ed. Livorno Ed. ii, 17*a*. Cremona Ed. ii, fol. 5*a*, col. 18.

from there goes forth the Soul of Life to this earth * * * Come, See! When the Holy, Blessed be He! created the man, he gathered the dust from all the four sides of the world and made a mark in the place where the Holy Temple stands, Below; and spread upon her a Soul of Life from the holiness Above. And this *Neshamah* Soul, is comprised in three degrees, and therefore she has three names, like the mystery Above: that is, *Nephesh, Rua'h, Neshamah. Nephesh* is as we have stated, she is the lowest from all, *Rua'h* spirit, he is appointed to rule over *Nephesh*, and he is a higher degree upon her, to remain upon her and stand upon her, as it ought to be. *Neshamah* soul, she is the highest of all and rules over all, she is the holy upper degree over all. And these three degrees are comprised in man, to those who deserve to the work of the Master. Then before had only been *Nephesh* in man, which is the holy form in which man shall prepare himself, but when man comes to cleanse himself in that degree, he is prepared to crown himself, in the *Rua'h* spirit, which is the holy degree which rests upon the *Nephesh;* that the man who deserves shall crown himself in it (the *Rua'h*). When the *Nephesh* and *Rua'h* exist in him, and he does the work of the Lord as he ought to, then rests upon him, the *Neshamah* soul, the upper holy degree; which rules over all. And then he is perfectness, perfect in all sides to deserve in the world to come, and that is the Love of the Holy, Blessed be He! as it is written; 'That I may cause those who love me to inherit substance.' (Prov. viii, 21.) Who are 'those who love me?' They are those who have the *nishmathah qad-disha* holy soul, in them."*

The *Neshamah* or upper precious or intellectual Soul, corresponding to the Spirit in the New Testament, in the Qabbalah corresponds to the *B'ree-atic World* that of Creation, and according to it inhabits the Brain. She is the last of the spiritual components to enter the man, in her fullness and perfection, at man's maturity. When death is coming she leaves her Merkabah before the appearance of death in man's face, and then remains only a resemblance of the real *Neshamah*, for the personality of man can exist with only the resemblance of the true *Neshamah*. It is here to be noted, that the *Tzelem* Shadow of the Image, acts in a magical way, from

* Zohar i, 205*b*, 206*a*, Brody Ed. Livorno Ed. i, 346*b*, 347*a*. Cremona Ed. i, fol. 113*b*, col. 460.

the first moment of conception, on the germ of human life, and gives to it a *R'shoo-mah i. e.*, designation or personality, and also imparts to it a *B'heen-ah i. e.*, essential faculty for the reception of efflux (light). In the measure that this *B'heen-ah* becomes gradually developed, the *Neshamah* appears more effectively in the man and his so-called, nature. At the instant of death, the *Rua'h* Spirit, which corresponds according to the Qabbalah, to the *Ye'tzeer-atic World*, and to the Soul in the New Testament, and which lives according to the Qabbalah, in the Heart, departs. The *Rua'h* forms, with the *Nephesh*, the actual personality of the man, which is called if he deserves, *Ye'hee-dah*. The *Nephesh* is the last of all the great Qabbalistic divisions of the incorporeal in man, which it says, is the living man in this world. It says, the *Nephesh* inhabits more especially the Liver; she is really the entire plastic system and corresponds to the Body, in the New Testament. In the Qabbalah it corresponds to the *A'seey-atic World*. She is the nearest to, and united in its lowest degree with, the actual nerve forces and energies of the bodily life of man. Her *B'heen-ah* tends to the material and sinks itself into the animal or bodily life, forming the higher spirituality of the concrete bodily and elementary existence. Even in the gross bodily existence stands the spiritual in the relation of the External to the Inner, and has in its way, a life and soul in itself, for there does not exist anything in nature without a certain spirituality and life. This elementary lower soul in man, is also called by the Qabbalists, *Nephesh*, and is the Merkabah of the spiritual *Nephesh* which controls it. As in nature there are different individual grades distinct from each other, so the nature-souls are distinguished in themselves and none are transformed into the other, but each is kept by the Deity, distinct. The spiritual *Nephesh* is the last to leave the body of man, and only fully separates from it with difficulty. The Qabbalah holds, that even after death, the spiritual *Nephesh* leaves the body only step by step and only as the body becomes decomposed. Even the dissolution and separation of, the different parts of the body is not considered an absolute separation, for that which has been one, it holds, can never be absolutely separated in its parts, one from another, but they always remain constantly in affinity with each other, as an entirety; therefore even after decomposition of the material body-form, as nothing is ever lost, it holds that a communication exists between all the several parts until the judgment of the Last Day. The innermost fundamental spiritual principle or type of the individual, it asserts, remains as a some-thing indestructible and as a *tzelem* shadow of an image, or *d'mooth* likeness or similitude, of the previous upon earth living man. This is the body of the resurrection, called by the Qabbalah *Habal D' Garmin* the elementary *Nephesh*, it can be termed, to a certain extent, the elementary man which is in the external *tzelem* shadow image, the true representative of the inner spiritual man. The elementary man the Qabbalah says; contains the three lower natural Nephesh *i.e.*, the mineral, vegetative and animal natures, and also the higher elementary *Nephesh* which as a *simulacrum*, includes the exact shape of the man as he was when existing in the body on earth. The elementary man contains four different parts, in the lowest is the mineral, then comes, the spirit of the bones, which are considered as the vegetative and as the frame-work or support of the man, and give growth to the whole and enables him to walk erect; this is followed by the *etzbon-ah d' bissr-ah*, the living atomic flesh-forming power: this with its atoms, nerves, arteries, veins, etc., etc., is the basis of the animal-feeling. And lastly, is the nature-feeling soul, etc. The Qabbalah contains much upon this subject and also upon the spiritual beginnings of life, which would surprise some of our best physiologists, but we have no space to go into the subject any further in this writing. It is to be noted, that these divisions are not considered as standing out separate and distinct, but they are considered as inextricably in affinity and connected with each other in their proper proportions, which however vary. It is also to be noted, that the *Neshamah* has three divisions, the highest is the *Ye'hee-dah*, the middle is *Haÿ-yah*, the last and third, the *Neshamah*, properly to say. They manifest themselves in the *Ma'hshabah* Thought, *Tzelem* Phantom of the Image, and *Zurath* Prototypes, and the *D'yooq-nah* Shadow of the phantom Image. The *D'mooth* Likeness or Similitude, is a lower manifestation.

THE DIVISIONS OF THE INCORPOREAL IN MAN. "The *Neshamah* of the child of man is called three different names, *Nephesh, Rua'h, Neshamah*, and all are merged one in another, and in three places are found their dwellings. *Nephesh* is found in the grave until the body is decomposed in the earth, and then it revolves around in this world to find its life and to know her trouble. The *Rua'h* ascends into the Garden which is on earth and there forms himself in the *d'yooq-nah* of the body in this world, in such a garment as they clothe there. The *Neshamah*, she ascends at once to that same place she came out from and for her sake has been lighted that lamp, Above; these (*Neshamoth* souls) do not descend to the Lower World. But before the *Neshamah* soul, ascends to connect herself in the Throne (in her place), the *Rua'h* cannot be crowned in the Garden (*i. e.*, into another body), which is on earth, and the *Nephesh* cannot remain in its place, but when she (*Neshamah*) goes up so all have rest, but when the children of the world are in trouble, and they go out to the graves (to pray); that *Nephesh* awakes and goes out and flies to and fro, and awakes that *Rua'h*, and that *Rua'h* ascends and awakes that *Neshamah*, then the Holy, Blessed be He! has pity over the world. When the *Neshamah* tarries in ascending to her place, the *Rua'h* goes and stays at the door of the Garden of Eden, and the door is not opened to him; and he (the *Rua'h*) flies to and fro and no one notices him. Then the *Nephesh* flies to and fro in the world. She sees that *guff* body, has worms in it, and she mourns over it (the body) as it written: 'Only his flesh upon him shall have pain, and his *Nephesh* soul, upon it (the *guff* body) shall mourn:' (Job xiv, 22.) and all are in punishment. Until the *Neshamah* connects herself in her place Above, and then all connect themselves in their places.*

Because all these three are one knot like the Above, in the mystery of *Nephesh*, *Rua'h* and *Neshamah*, they are all one and bound in one. (Cremona, *Ibid.*, col. 252.) *Nephesh* has no light from her own substance; it is for this reason that she is associated with the mystery of *guff* the body, to procure enjoyment and food and everything which she needs; as it is written: 'She giveth food to her house(hold) and a portion to her maidens.' (Prov. xxxi, 15.) Her house(hold) that is the body which she nourishes, and the 'maidens' are the members of that body. *Ru'ah* (the Spirit) is that which rides on that *Nephesh* (the Lower Soul) and rules over her and lights (supplies) her with everything she needs, and the *Nephesh* is the throne to that *Rua'h*. *Neshamah* (Divine Soul), goes over to that *Rua'h*, and she rules over that *Rua'h* and

---

* Zohar ii, 141*b*, Brody Ed. Cremona Ed. ii, fol. 63*b*, col. 251.

lights to him with that Light of Life, and that *Rua'h* depends on the *Neshamah*, and receives light from her which illuminates him. That *Nephesh* depends on that *Rua'h* and receives light from him and is sustained by him, and all are one bond. When the upper *Neshamah* ascends she goes to her repose to where is the *At-tee'kah D'At-tee'-keen* the Ancient of the Ancients, the Hidden of All the Hidden, so as to receive from Him, Eternity. This *Rua'h* does not go to *Gan Eden* Garden of Eden, because he is *Nephesh*, and each has its own place. The *Neshamah* Soul, goes up direct to the very inner, and the *Rua'h* Spirit goes up to Eden, but not so high as the Soul, and *Nephesh* (the animal principle, Lower Soul) remains in the grave Below."*

"This is what is written: '*Ail Elo-hāi* of the spirits of all flesh.' (Numb. xvi, 22.) It is a place where all the *Neshamoth* souls, of the world are together, and all the souls ascend and descend from there." †

THE MERKABAH AND THE CLEANSING OF THE SOUL. "And that Garden, which is from the *n'qood-ah* point, is called Eden. (This point, is what has been taken from the Mother, Above, who is hidden; from it, the point, is the *Gan Eden* on earth.) These heads of the '*Haÿ-yah* are the four faces. One of them is that of a Lion, as it is written; 'And the face of the lion to the right side.' (Ezek. i, 10.) And one is (that of) an Ox, as it is written: 'And the face of the ox to the left side.' (*Ibid.*) And one is (that of) an Eagle, as it is written; 'And the face of the eagle to the four sides.' (*Ibid.*) Man comprises all, as it is written: 'And the *d"mooth* similitude, of their faces was the face of man.' (*Ibid.*) And these are the four heads of the river which reaches to the *Qur-sāi-yah Qad-dosha* Holy Throne, and from its strength and hammering (as in a forge), it moves; and from that moving is made that river דינור *D'e-noor*, as it is written: 'The river *D'e-noor* issued and came forth from before Him, thousand thousands ministered unto him.' (Dan. vii, 10.) And the *Neshamoth* souls, when they ascend, cleanse themselves in that river *D'e-noor* and do not burn, they only cleanse themselves. Come, See! From a Salamander they make a garment,‡ and

---

* Zohar ii, 142a, Cremona Ed. ii, fol. 63b, col. 252.

† Zohar iii, 176b, Brody Ed. Cremona Ed. iii, 84b, col. 336.

‡ This doubtless refers to a species of *asbestos*.

because it is from fire, that garment can only be washed and cleansed, in fire. Fire eats up the filth in it and cleanses that garment, so here also the *Neshamah* soul, which is (of the) light (fire) which it takes from the Holy Throne, of which it is written; 'His Throne, the fiery flame.' (Dan. vii, 9.) At the time when they want to cleanse (the soul) from that defilement in her, it (the soul) is put through fire and becomes cleansed; and the fire eats up all the defilement which is in the *Neshamah* and the *Neshamah* is cleansed and becomes white."*

"It is written: 'Let the earth bring forth the חיה נפש *Nephesh 'Haÿ-yah* Living Creature. (Gen. i, 24.) That means *Nephesh* which is the Upper *Haÿ-yah* Life, and because that this *Nephesh Haÿ-yah* is holiness from Above, so when the holy earth draws up through her and is comprised in her, then she is called *Neshamah* soul. And Come, See! At all times when the child of man goes in the true way and his mouth and tongue speaks holy words, this *Neshamah* soul, cleaves to him and he is the friend of his Lord, and he has many watchers (angels) protecting him from all sides. He is designated for good, Above and Below, and the Holy She'kheen-ah rests upon him."†

THE TREASURY OF SOULS. "Before the world was created all the *Ru'hin* Spirits, of the just (pious) had been *hidden* before Him in the *Ma'hshabah* Thought, each one in his *d'yooq-nah*. But after He formed the world all have been *revealed* and remained in their *d'yooq-nah* before Him, the Supreme Above. Afterwards He put them (the souls) in a Treasury in the Garden of Eden, Above; and that Treasury never gets filled (*i. e.*, the Treasury in the Garden of Eden) (and) it always cries out: 'Behold the first things are come to pass, and new things do I declare (say).' (Is. xlii, 9.) What does this mean? It means 'I say (declare)' all by their Name, and that Treasury has not any desire and not any lust only to always accumulate the *Neshamoth* souls, there: like the *Gāi-hinnom* which has, no desire or lust, except to take the *Neshamoth* souls, to purify them, and every day it (the *Gāi-hinnom*) calls: 'Give! Give!'‡ What means 'Give! Give!' it means, Burn! Burn! And

---

* Zohar ii, 211*b*, Brody Ed. Cremona Ed. ii, fol. 95*a* and *b*, col. 378, 379.

† Zohar iii, 301*a* and *b*, Tosephthah, Brody Ed.

‡ Prov. xxx, 15. This is Lillith. Comp. Cahen's French Bible, Vol. xiv, p. 156 note.

that Treasury takes all the souls till the time they are clothed and come down to this world, and through the sin of Adam Qad'mo-ah, (the *B'ree-atic Adam*) which brought on the evil side to the world; the *Neshamoth* has to be clothed in these kinds of garments, which are the other garments."*

THE ENTRANCE OF THE SOUL INTO THE BODY. "R. Abbah, Sabah, *i.e.*, the old, stood up on his feet and said: 'Rest in peace shall be to thee R. Shim-on ben Yo'haï, that thou didst bring, back the crown, *i. e.*, the Thorah, we have learned in the *Mathneethah Qad'mo-ah;* Because the *Neshamah* Soul; is in its perfectness in the Upper Place, she has not any desire to the *guff* body, (but) only to create from it other *Neshamoth* souls, which come out from her, and she remains in her Place. Until R. Shim-on ben Yo'haï came and explained; If in this world which is vanity and the body a stinking drop, and yet the *Neshamah* goes into it; surely in the time to come when all are purified, and the body will be in its fullness and perfectness, certainly the *Neshamah* soul, will go into it with all its perfectness, Above.' Said R. A'ha; 'This very soul and this very *guff* body, the Holy, Blessed be He! is prepared in the time to come, to put in their eternal continuance, but both will be perfect in the perfectness of knowledge (so as) to reach that which they could not reach in this world.'"†

OF THAT DIVISION OF THE INCORPOREAL IN MAN CALLED, YE'HEE-DAH. "It is written: 'The silver is mine, and the gold is mine, saith the YHVH TZe'Ba-OTH, *i. e.*, of the hosts.' What means 'the silver is mine and the gold is mine'? It is like to a king who has two treasures, one of silver and one of gold, that of silver he put to his right and that of gold to his left, and said; This is prepared so that it is easy to spend it, and he has done everything in an easy way, this is what is said; 'Thy hand YHVH is become glorious in power.' (Ex. xv, 6.) If man rejoices in his portion (is contented with his lot in this life), it is good, and if not, it is said; 'Thy right hand YHVH hath dashed in pieces the enemy.' (*Ibid.*) What does this mean? Said he to him; 'That is the gold, it is written; The silver is mine, the gold is mine.' Why do they call it זהב *Zahav* gold? 'It is called *Zahav* gold, because included in it are

---

* Zohar iii, 303*b*, Brody Ed., Tosephthah.
† Zohar i, 126*a*, Midrash Ha-Ne'elam. Brody Ed. Cremona Ed. i, fol. 76*a*, col. 301.

three tributes (*middoth* measures); the ז (Zayin = 7) of the *Zahav* are seven tributes, and the ה (Heh = 5) is אחדות *A'hdoth* Unity, the ב (*Beth* = 2) means 'Hokhmah and Binah, *i. e.*, Wisdom and Understanding, and they are called *Neshamah* souls because of the last five Sephiroth. And five names has the *Neshamah*.* That is *Nephesh, Rua'h, Neshamah, 'Haÿ-yah, Ye'hee-dah.*"†

Ye'hee-dah the only one, is the *personality* of man; *Haÿ'yah* is the life in man; *Neshamah* the soul or intellect; *Rua'h* the spirit; *Nephesh* the animal soul or vital *dynameis*, the *anima*.

"In the Book of King Solomon is to be found: That at the time of the accomplishment of the union, Below; the Holy, Blessed be He! Sends a *D'yooq-nah* Phantom of a Shadow-image, like the face of a man. It is designed and sculptured in the Divine *Tzelem i. e.,* Shadow Image, and exists over this pair, and if permission was given to the eye to see, the child of man, could see above his head a *tzelem*, resembling the face of the child of man, and in that *tzelem* shadow image, the child of man is created. And so long as that *tzelem* which is sent by the Master, is not found there above his head, man is not created; therefore it is written: 'Elohim created man in His *tzelem* (shadow image).' (Gen. i, 27.) It is this *tzelem*, which is prepared to be received (by the infant) on his first entrance into this world; (and) when man enters this world it is in this *tzelem*, in this *tzelem* he developes, as he grows, and it is with this *tzelem*, again, he departs from this life, as it is written: 'Surely in a *tzelem* walketh man.' (Ps. xxxix, 60.) And this *tzelem* is from, Above. At the time when the *Ru'hin* Spirits, go out from their place, each spirit separately appears before the Holy King, invested in a sublime form, with the features in which it will exist in this world. It is from that *D'yooq-nah, i. e.,* sublime Shadow of a *Tzelem*, that the *Tzelem*, comes out, and this is the third after the *Rua'h* Spirit, and precedes it to this world and is present at the time of conception, and there is not any conception in this world in which the *tzelem*, is not present." ‡

* Which are חיִּי נֵרוֹת and these are called; the Lights of Life.

† Zohar i, 16a and b, Sepher ha-Bahir, § *Hashmutas*, Amsterdam Ed. Also Brody Ed. It belongs to Zohar i, fol. 217a. Cremona Ed. i, fol. 116b, 117a, col. 462–463.

‡ Zohar iii, 104a and b, Brody Ed. Cremona Ed. iii, fol. 50b, col. 199. Comp. Zohar ii, 150a sq.

That Image is called by the Qabbalists, *Ye'hee-dah*, *i.e.*, the indivisible principle, the personality or individuality of the man.

"Come, See! When the child of man is born there is given to him a *Nephesh*, *i. e.*, animated life, from the side of the animals, the clean side, from the side of those which are called *Auphaneh ha-Qad-dosh* the Holy Wheels. If he deserves more, there is given to him a *Rua'h* Spirit, from the side of the *Haÿ-yoth ha-Qad-dosh* Holy Lives. If he still deserves more (there) is given to him, a *Neshamah* Soul, from the side of the *Kur-saiy-ah* Throne.* And these three, are the mother, the man-servant, and the maid-servant, the Daughter of the King. If he still deserves more (there) is given to him a *Nephesh* in the way of *A'tzeel-oth* Efflux, from the side of the daughter *Ye'hee-dah* the only one, and she is called, the Daughter of the King. If he still deserves more (there) is given to him the *Rua'h* of *A'tzeel-oth* the Efflux, from the side of the Middle Pillar, and he is called Son to the Holy, Blessed be He! Therefore that is what is written; 'Ye are the children of YHVH your Elohim.' (Deut. xiv, 1.) If he still deserves more (there) is given to him a *Neshamah* Soul, from the side of *Abba* Father, and *Immah* Mother; that is what is written: "And He blew into his nostrils *Neshmoth 'Haÿ-yeem* Souls of Life.' (Gen. ii, 7.) What is '*Haÿ-yeem* Life? That is יה YH. On this we have said: 'All the *Neshamoth* Souls, shall praise יה YaH.' (Ps. cl, 6.) And in it is perfected ידוד *Yedud* (that means YHVH). If he still deserves more, is given to him ידוד *Yedud*, in its very completeness, the letters of which are Yod, Heh, Vav, Heh: Heh הא Vav ואו Heh הא Yod יוד which is (Adam) Man in the way of *A'tzeel-oth* Efflux, Above, and is called in the *D'yooq-nah* of his Lord, and on it is said; 'And have dominion over the fish of the sea, etc.' (Gen. i, 28.) And that is, he shall rule over all the Heavens and in all the *Auphaneem*, *i. e.*, Wheels, and the *Serapheem*, and over all the Hosts and Mights, from Above and Below. And therefore when the child of man deserves the Nephesh from the side of the בת יחידה *Bath Ye'hee-dah*, *i. e.*, Daughter *Ye'hee-dah*, is said by it, that 'She shall not go out as the men-servants.'" (Exod. xxi, 7.)†

---

* This is the Lower Throne. The Upper Throne is *Qur-saiy-ah*.

† Zohar ii, 94*b*, Sabah D'Mishpatim, Brody Ed. Livorno Ed. ii, fol. 160*a* and *b*.

THE MALE AND FEMALE SOULS IN THE PRE-EXISTENT CONDITION UNITED, OF THEIR REUNITING IN THIS WORLD. "Come, See! All the souls of the world paired themselves (as male and female) before Him, but after they came into this world, the Holy, Blessed be He! pairs them. Said R. Yitz-haq: 'The Holy, Blessed be He! says, that daughter to that one.' Said R. Yo-seh, 'What does that mean; it is written: 'There is nothing new under the sun.' (Eccl. i, 9.) Said R. Yehudah: 'It is written; 'Under the sun,' which I am above.' Said R. Yo-seh; 'What decree is here?' R. 'He-yah then said; 'At the very time that the son of man goes out into the world, a female partner is prepared for him.' Said R. Abbah; 'Happy are the just that their souls crown themselves before the Holy King before they come down into this world, then, so we have learned; that at the time when the Holy, Blessed be He! sends out the souls to the world all the spirits and souls collect themselves, male and female, and associate themselves like one, and they are given in the hand of one who is the official who is set over the conception of the children of man, and his name is Night, and at the time when they come down, the Holy, Blessed be He! who knows the spirits and souls, connects them together as they have been before and decrees on them, and when they connect themselves they become one body and one soul, Right and Left, as it ought to be, and therefore means that which is written; 'There is nothing new under the sun.' This union depends on his (man's) deeds and ways in this world. If he deserves and his deeds are right, he is united with that prepared for him like they were before they came out from the world Above, to this world.'" *

THE LIGHT WITH WHICH THE SOUL IS CLOTHED. "Come, See! When the soul reaches that place which is צרורא דחיי *Tz'ruroh d'hay-ah, i. e.*, Bundle of Life (see I Sam. xxv, 29) they there enjoy from that ונהרא אספקלריא *aspaq' lar-yah dinhar-ah* luminous mirror,† from that Light which comes out of the place which is above All, but if the soul was not clothed with the splendor of another garment she could not come near to see that Light. And the mystery of the word is this; such a garment as it is given to the soul to clothe itself in it so as to exist in this world, so

---

* Zohar i, 91*b*, Brody Ed. Cremona Ed. i, 62*b*, col. 247-8.

† See Philo, Bohn's English Ed. Vol. i, pp. 134, 337.

here too (Above) He gives her a garment of the splendor **Above**, so that it may exist in that world and be able to look into that *aspaq'lar-yah dinhar-ah* which proceeds from the Land of Life. Come, See! Moses could not come near to contemplate, in that (Light) which he looked at only when he clothed himself in another garment, as it is said: 'And Moses came into the midst of the cloud and went up to the mountain.' (Ex. xxiv, 18.) Which is translated 'in the midst of the cloud'; and wrapped himself in her (cloud) like one would wrap himself in a garment. And therefore it is written (afterwards): 'And Moses drew near into the thick cloud where Elohim was.' (Ex. xx, 21.) And it is written: 'And Moses came in the midst of the cloud, etc. (Ex. xxiv, 18.) 'Moses was on the mountain forty days and forty nights:' (Ex. xxiv, 18.) And could contemplate in that which he looked in. Likewise; the souls of the just in that world clothe themselves in such a garment (as Moses did), because it is only there such garments are used, and therefore they are able to look into the light which shines in the Land of Life."*

"For now we see in a mirror, darkly; but then face to face: now I know in part; but then shall I know even as also I have been known." (I Cor. xiii, 12.) "But we all with open face beholding, as in a glass, the glory of the Lord, are changed from the same image from glory to glory, even as by the Spirit of the Lord." (II Cor. iii, 18.)

The to be divisible are at their beginning contained as a unity in the Will of the Deity. When emanated and separated, they are first in the point, the *Ma'hshabah* Thought; they are then the highest sublime principles, the Upper *D'yooq-nah*, but are not yet real beings but are only the eternal *Tzurath* or Prototypic and basic beginnings of the same. The principles are first, *D'yooq-nin, i. e.*, Shadows of the *Tzelem*, the Phantom Image, more manifest, they are *Tzelem* the Phantom Image, *D'mooth* Likeness or Similitude, *Tzurah* Prototype. These are considered as the pure prototypes of the Upper *Neshamoth* or Primordial Souls of all existences. The Qabbalah considers them, as eternal principles without any concreteness in themselves and as only purely, unconsciously acting, potentialities; because, the self-acting portion of life proceeds, according to it, by incitement from Below. The Qabbalah also speaks of *B'd'mooth* in the Simili-

---
* Zohar i, fol. 65*b*, 66*a*, Brody Ed. Cremona Ed. i, 50*b*, col. 200.

tude or Appearance: and *Tab'nooth* Form. The *Tzurah* is the higher principle, which remains Above; the higher eternal principle of the continued life of the individual. The externality of all the indivisible is the Great Androgene, the Adam Illa-ah or Adam Qadmon, which includes in itself all the ideas and all the content of all the prototypes of the existences, and contains the Ye'hee-dah, 'Haÿ-yah, Neshamah, Rua'h and Nephesh, in their highest potentiality. This Adam is considered as the first distinctive beginning in the finite and therefore is the sole occupant of the *A'tzeel-atic World*, that of the Sephiroth *par excellence*.

THE SOUL IN THE PARABLE OF THE KING AND HIS SON. "The souls of the just are above all His hosts and His forces, Above. And if thou askest wherefore from so elevated a place they come down to this world, and why did they leave that place? This is like the example of a king who has a son born to him, he sends him into a village to be nursed and brought up until he is grown up and learns the usages of the king's palace. When it is announced to the king that the education of his son is finished, what does he do in his love for him? He sends the Matroneethah, his mother, after him and brings him into his palace and rejoices with him all day. So the Holy, Blessed be He! has a son born to Him by the Matroneethah. Who is he? The holy soul Above, He sends him to the village, that is this world to grow up and learn the usages and customs of the King's palace. When the King knows that his son is grown up in that village, (that is this world) and that it is time to bring him to this palace: What does He do for the love of His son? He sends the Matroneethah after him and she brings him up to His palace. The soul does not leave this world until the Matroneethah comes after her (him) and she brings her up to the King's palace and there she (the soul) remains forever. And nevertheless it is the custom of the world, the people of the village, to weep because the son of the King is separated from them. A wise (man) who was there, said to them: 'Why are you crying, is he not the son of the King and it would not be just that he should always live with you and not be in his Father's palace? So it was with Moses, he was wise, he has seen that the people of the village wept. On this said he: 'Ye are the children of YHVH your Elohim, ye shall not cut yourselves for the dead.' (Deut. xiv, 1.) Come, See! If all the just knew this they would rejoice on the day when it is their time to leave this world. And is it not the height of glory, that the Matroneethah descends in the midst of us, that she may bring us up into the palace of the King, that the King may rejoice with them a whole day, because the Holy, Blessed be He! Does not delight only with the souls of the just."*

THE WORLD EXISTS THROUGH JUDGMENT AND MERCY. "Come, See! When the Holy, Blessed be He! created the world He made it on Judgment, and on Judgment it exists, and all the actions in the world exist through Judgment, except the Holy, Blessed be He! That the world may exist and not be lost, the Holy, Blessed be He! spread out upon it Mercy, and this Mercy tempers Judgment so that the world should not be destroyed, and through Mercy the world is led and it exists through it. * * * When the Holy, Blessed be He! in His Love, has pity on the man so that He may bring him near to Him, He weakens the *guffah*, *i. e.*, body, so that the *Neshamah*, may rule over it, and the *Neshamah* rules and the *guff* body, is weakened, and when the *guff* weakens the *Nephesh* animal life soul, gets stronger, and this is the Love of the Holy, Blessed be He! as the Companions have said: The Holy, Blessed be He! gave to the just (pious man) pain in this world, so that he shall be rewarded in the world to come. But when the *Neshamah* soul, weakens and the body is strengthened, the Holy, Blessed be He! hates him, and He, does not trouble him in this world, so that he shall get all his reward in this world and shall not have any part in the future world. (Zohar i, 180*b*.) * * * R. El'azar said: 'All that the Holy, Blessed be He! does through Judgment, He only does it to purify that *Nephesh*† soul, to bring her into the world to come, and therefore He breaks that *guff* in this world, and through that purifies that *Nephesh* and therefore the Holy, Blessed be He! lets the *guff* suffer pain in this world, so that it may be clean of everything and deserve the world of life in the world to come.'" ‡

THE NESHAMAH LEAVES THE BODY OF MAN DURING SLEEP. "And Come, See! Thus we have said: Even in this world when man slumbers in his bed and the *Neshamoth* souls, find it necessary to hover around the

---

* Zohar i, 245*b*, Brody Ed. Cremona Ed. i, fol. 130*a* and *b*, col. 516–7.
† The word *Nephesh* used in this quotation really means *Neshamah*.
‡ Zohar i, 180*b*, 181*a*, Brody Ed. Cremona Ed. i, fol. 102*a*, col. 407, 408.

world, and to go out of the *guff* body, not every *Neshamah* soul, ascends to see the face of *At-teek Yo-men* the Ancient of Days, only according to man's deeds the *Neshamah* ascends, if he has not done the right he (man) sleeps and the *Neshamah* soul, goes out, and all the unclean spirits in the lower degrees which are flying around the world, connect themselves with her, but when the man is worthy, when he sleeps and the *Neshamah* soul, goes out of him, she goes out and flies up and makes herself a way between these unclean spirits and all the latter cry out: 'Make way! Make way! for her, she is not from our side:' and she goes up between the holies and they make known to her, a word of truth; and when she comes down these evil spirits want to go near her to know that word, and they make known to her other words. (Zohar i, 130a.) * * * When the *Neshamoth* souls, go forth from the body, of this world, they desire to ascend and many kinds of evil spirits are there, and if the *Neshamahoth* souls, are from their side all gather around them and transfer them to the hand of *Dumah* to bring them to *Gāi-hinnom*. Then they go up in there also, and unite with them, and they take them and they cry out: 'These are they which transgressed the biddings of the law of the Lord.' And so they fly around the whole world, and afterwards they are brought back to *Gāi-hinnom*, and so it is twelve months. After twelve months they are found in that place which is shown to them, but those souls which are worthy, go straight up and remain in their places." (i, 130b.)*

"Come, See! When man sleeps on his bed, his *Neshamah* soul, goes forth from him, and each (*Neshamah*) goes up according to its way and so it comes down, as we have said: When man lies on his bed sleeping and the *Neshamah* goes forth from him, it is written; 'In slumbering upon the bed, then He openeth the ears of men.' (Job xxxiii, 15, 16.) Then the Holy, Blessed be He! makes known to that *Neshamah* in that degree which exists in the dream, those things which He is prepared to bring on the world, or those things according to what he thinks in his heart, because man thinks of what is going on the world (during his waking hours), because they do not make known to man when he is strong in the *guff* body, as we have said; but the angels make known to the

---

* Zohar i, 130a and b, Brody Ed. Livorno Ed. i, 220b, 221a. Cremona Ed. i, fol. 78a, col. 310.

Neshamah, and the *Neshamah* makes known to man. And that dream is from Above, when the *Neshamah* goes forth from the body and each ascends according to its way."*

THE RETURN OF THE SOUL TO PARADISE. "Said R. Yehudah; 'Happy are the just! When the Holy, Blessed be He! desired to return the *Rua'h* spirit, to them and to attract (draw) that *Rua'h* into them; We have learned: At the time when the Holy, Blessed be He! desires to return a *Rua'h* to Him, if that *Rua'h* is worthy, what is written; 'And the *Rua'h* spirit, shall *return* unto Elohim who gave it.' (Eccl. xii, 7.) If it is not found worthy, Woe! to that *Rua'h*, he must cleanse himself in the fire that burns, and purify himself, so that he be prepared to go back to the *guff* body, of the King, and if he has not been prepared there, Woe! to that *Rua'h* spirit, it has to revolve like a stone thrown out from a sling. It is written; 'And the *Nephesh* of thine enemies, her shall He sling out, as out of the middle of a sling.' (I Sam. xxv, 29.) We have learned: When that *Rua'h* spirit, deserves, how many good things are hidden in the other world for him, as it is written; 'The eye hath not seen Elohim, beside Thee, what He hath prepared for him.' (Is. lxiv. 4.) Said R. Yo-seh: 'When man nears the end of his days, three days (before), the decree comes out upon him in the world, even the birds (angels) from heaven cry out upon him, and if he is worthy, these three days they cry out before the just which are in the *Gan Eden* Garden of Eden. We have learned: All these three days the *Neshamah* soul, goes forth from him every night and ascends and sees her place in that world: and the man does not know, does not give heed, and does not rule, over his *Neshamah* all these three days, as he did before. It is written: 'There is no man that hath power in the *Rua'h* to retain the *Rua'h*, etc.' (Eccl. viii, 8.) Said R. Yehudah; From the time these three days begins, the *tzelem* shadow image, of the man becomes dark and

---

*Zohar i, 183a, Brody Ed. Cremona Ed. i, fol. 103a and b, col. 412. Compare my translation of: On Dreams, by Synesios, in The Platonist, Vol. iv, April, 1888, p. 212 *sq*. Then follows Zohar i, on pages 183a and b, remarks on the dreams of Joseph, and of those by the Hebrew prophets, and of the interpretation of dreams. Also see *Ibid*. pp. 199a and b, 200a.

the *d'yooq-nah* shadow of the *tzelem*, which has been seen on him on the earth, is kept back from him."*

The Zohar further says; that the *Neshamah*, on the last seven days of man's life, goes up every night from the man, and the *tzool-mah* shadow, is no more shown on the man, and when the *tzool-mah* shadow, goes away the *Rua'h* goes with it. (i, 218a, Brody Ed. Cremona i, fol. 117a, col. 466.)

"We have learned : When the man comes near his time to go away from this world, the four sides of the world exist in strong Judgment, and there awakes Judgment from the four sides of the world, and the four sides are quarreling between themselves† and they desire to separate each to its side. And a herald goes out and cries in that world (*i.e.*, the world to come) and he is heard in 270 worlds. If the man is worthy all the worlds joy before him and if not, Woe! to that man and his lot. We have learned in that time when the herald calls out (the decree), at once, a flame comes forth from the North side and goes in and ignites the river *Dinur*, (*i.e.*, the river of fire, comp. Dan. vii, 10.) and spreads itself out to four sides of the world and burns the souls of the guilty, and that flame goes forth and comes down on the world, etc."‡

In the above pages is an account of the cock crowing thrice at the approach of death, which is evidently an explanation of Mark xiv, 30, 68, 72. Matt. xxvi, 74, 75. John xiii, 38.

"We have learned; At the time when the *Neshamah* soul, goes forth from man, all his relations and friends of that world, go with the *Neshamah* and show him the Place of Delight (Eden), and also the Place of Punishment. If he has been pure he sees his place and ascends and enjoys in the upper happiness of that world, and if he has not been pure the *Neshamah* soul, remains in this world until the body is hidden in the earth, when it is hidden, many guardians, (angels) of Judgment unite to him till they reach *Dumah*, *i. e.*, the angel of Death, and then they bring him into the dwelling of *Gāi-hinnom*." §

* Zohar i, 217b, Brody Ed. Cremona Ed. i, fol. 117a, col. 465.

† Because the *guff*, *i. e.*, body, comes out of the four sides or elements, fire, water, air and earth, and when they are to be separated they quarrel between themselves.

‡ Zohar i, 218b, Brody Ed. Cremona Ed. i, fol. 117b, col. 465.

§ Zohar i, 218b, 219a, Brody Ed. Cremona Ed. i, fol. 117b, col. 465.

The above cited pages, also give a reason for the burning of lights and candles around the body of the dead, in houses and churches.

THE ASCENT OF THE SOUL. "Come, See! The *Neshamah* soul, goes forth and ascends between separated mountains and there the *Rua'h* spirit, associates with the *Neshamah* soul, then he (the *Rua'h*) comes down, and the *Nephesh* life soul, associates with the *Rua'h;* And all come down and one connects with the other. Said R. Yehudah: The *Nephesh* and the *Rua'h* are merged one in the other, and the *Neshamah* rests in the way of the man, and she is in a hidden dwelling and her place is not known. When man comes to cleanse himself he is influenced by the *Nishmathak Qad-disha* Holy Soul, and this cleanses him and sanctifies him and he is called holy." *

From the Zohar: "When the *Neshamah* soul, goes forth from this world, she does not know which way she shall go up, then there is a way to ascend Above, to a place where the Upper *Neshamoth* souls, illuminate which is not given to all *Neshamoth*."†

From the Midrash Ha-Ne'elam. "Said R. Yehudah at the time when the soul of the just is willing to go out she rejoices, and the just is sure in his death so that he shall receive his reward." ‡

THE TAKING OF THE SOUL OF THE PIOUS, BY THE HOLY KISS. "R. El'azar said; 'Whoever studies in the Thorah in earnest does not die by the hands of the *Ye'tzer ha-rah* evil spirit, because he (the latter) is the Serpent and he is the Angel of Death, but his (the former's) death is by a Kiss, as it is written: 'Let him kiss me with the kisses of his mouth.' (Song of Songs i, 2.) This means by the mouth of YHVH; and this is the Kiss which is the connection of the *Nephesh* soul, to the trunk. And he who studies in the Thorah is strengthened in the Tree of Life and she does not leave him." §

THE RECEPTION, ABOVE, OF THE SOUL BY THE HOLY KISS. "Said that Sabah: * * * In the most mysterious and elevated part of Heaven,

* Zohar i, 62a, Brody Ed. Livorno Ed. i, 110a. Cremona Ed. i, fol. 49a, col. 193.
† Zohar i, 99a and b, Brody Ed. Livorno Ed. i, 176a. Cremona Ed. i, fol. 66b, col. 363.
‡ To be found, Zohar i, 99b, Brody Ed. Cremona Ed. i, 66a, col. 261.
§ Zohar i, 168a, Brody Ed. Cremona Ed., i, fol. 96b, col. 383.

there is a certain palace which is called *Haikhal Ahabah, i. e.*, Palace of Love, and therein are hidden profound mysteries, and the *Nasheeqin Dir'humoo, i. e.*, Kisses of the King's Love, are there; and there go all the souls of the friends of the King. When the King ascends into that Palace: it is written: 'And Jacob kissed Rachel.' (Gen. xxix, 11.) And the Holy, Blessed be He! meets there the holy soul, He advances and at once kisses her and embraces her, and caresses her* and that is what it means when it is written: 'He shall deal with her after the manner of daughters.' (Ex. xxi, 9.) Like the custom of a father to his beloved daughter, he kisses her, embraces her and gives her presents. So the Holy, Blessed be He! does to the pure soul daily, as it is written: 'He shall deal, etc."†

THE POSITIONS OF THE SPIRIT AND SOUL. "The *Rua'h* is that which stands upon the *Nephesh* and the *Nephesh* has not any existence except in the *Rua'h*, and this very *Rua'h* rests between fire and water, and from here is fed that *Nephesh*." ‡

"Come, See! There are three degrees and they are connected as one, *Nephesh, Rua'h* and *Neshamah*, and the highest of them is *Neshamah*. R. Yo-seh said; 'In every man is a *Nephesh*, and there is a higher *Nephesh* upon a *Nephesh*: and if man is worthy of that *Nephesh*, they pour upon him a crown which is called, *Rua'h*: that is what is written; 'Until the *Rua'h* spirit, he poured upon us from on high.' (Is. xxii, 15.) At once man awakes in the sublimity to look in the Law of the Holy King; if man deserves in that *Rua'h* spirit, they crown him with the holy upper crown which comprises all (three) which is called *Neshamah* soul; and it is called; the *Neshamah Elo-hai, i. e.*, Soul of God.§

The following passage shows that the *Nephesh* must associate with the *Rua'h*. "And when the *Rua'h* does not rest upon her (the *Nephesh*), she has no association with anything from Above and she does not know anything whatsoever from that world; and she is like the *Nephesh* of an

---

*Comp. Luke xv, 7, 10; Matt. xv, 21; Luke vi, 23; Rom. xiv, 17; Gal. v, 22; Heb. xii, 2; Jude 25.

† Zohar ii, 97a, Brody Ed. Cremona Ed., ii, fol. 44a, col. 173-174.

‡ Zohar i, 206a. Livorno Ed. i, 347a. Cremona, Ed. i, fol. 113b, col. 460.

§ Zohar iii, 70b, Brody Ed. Cremona Ed. iii, fol. 32a, col. 126.

animal. She is a *Nephesh* which has no rest, so she goes and flies around and awakes that official ידומיע״ם *Y'dumiam* (who has charge of the entrance to Heaven) and his servants, and they take her (that *Nephesh*) and bring her up to all the doors of *Gan Eden* (Garden of Eden, Paradise) and they show her the Glory of the just, and they call to her, her *Rua'h* spirit, and she (the *Nephesh*) connects herself in him (the *Rua'h*) and he goes in that garment (the *Nephesh*); and then she knows the things of that world. And when that *Rua'h* spirit, goes up to crown himself in that Upper *Neshamah* Above, that *Nephesh* connects herself in that *Rua'h* spirit, and illuminates from him, like the moon illuminates from the sun, and the *Rua'h* binds himself in that *Neshamah*; and that *Neshamah* connects herself into the utmost termination of *Ma'hshabah* Thought (מחשבה אין סוף *i. e.*, the inner utmost of the Thought) which is the mystery of the *Nephesh*, Above. And that *Nephesh* connects itself in that Upper *Rua'h* and that *Rua'h* connects itself in that Upper *Neshamah*, and that *Neshamah* connects herself in Ain Soph: And then this is rest of everything and the unity of everything, Above and Below, all is in one mystery and one kind, and that is the rest of the *Nephesh*, Below. And on that is written; ' The *Nephesh* soul, of my lord shall be bound in the bundle of life with YHVH thy *Ail*.' (I Sam. xv, 29.)"*

ABSENCE OF THE NESHAMAH, CREATES UNCLEANNESS. "We have learned when the *Neshamah* soul, goes out of the children of man, it leaves only the soiled body and this body soils the house, and it (the body) makes unclean everything which comes near to it, therefore is written: ' He who toucheth the dead, etc.' (Num. xix, 11.) And therefore when He takes away the *Neshamah* soul, and leaves only the unclean *guff* body, at once He gives permission to all the unclean sides (spirits) to rest upon it. * * * And Come, See! All the children of the world when they sleep on their beds in the night, and Night spreads out her wings over all the children of the world, feel the taste of death. From that taste of death the unclean *Rua'h* Spirit, hovers over the world and makes it unclean, and rests on the hands of the children of man, and makes them unclean." †

* Zohar ii, 142*b*, Brody Ed. Cremona Ed. ii, 64*a*, col. 253.
† Zohar i, 53*b*, Brody Ed. Livorno Ed. i, 94*b*. Cremona Ed. i, fol. 37*b*, col. 147.

SLEEP THE TASTE OF DEATH. "Come, See! At the time the child of man goes in the night on his bed, he must take upon himself the Yoke of the Upper Kingdom with a perfect heart, and before he (sleeps), must commit to Him the custody of his *Nephesh* soul; because the whole world (then) tastes the taste of death. Then the Tree of Death rests on the world. And all the *Ru'hin* spirits, of the children of man go out and are given under it (*i. e.*, the rule of the Tree of Death) but because they have committed the soul to Him, they all return to their places."*

MAN CAN ONLY APPROACH THE DEITY THROUGH THE INTENTION OF HIS HEART. "Because of things from Above, as well from holiness as the other (the evil) side, the child of man cannot attract the *Rua'h* from Above to Below, and can approach only with fear and through the intention of his heart and (with) a contrite heart. And then he attracts Below the *Rua'h* spirit, from the Above, and the will which is needed for it. And if he does not put his heart and will, in fear, to that (the Upper) side, then he cannot connect his will to it."†

"There are lords of the hidden Thorah, lords of attributes, which inherit the *Neshamoth* from the side of the Holy Malkhutha (Kingdom) which is comprised from the Ten Sephiroth. Who possess it and deserve it, he deserves the Ten Sephiroth without separation. Ten and not nine, because if they were separated they would only be nine, and because there is no separation in it, says the author of the Sepher Ye'tzeer-ah : 'It is ten and not nine.' "‡ The ten Sephiroth are looked upon as one and are the content of the Ineffable Name YHVH.

THE REWARD OF THE PIOUS. "When man sanctifies his substance (body) from evil, he becomes sanctified from Above, and when man sanctifies himself in the Holiness of his Lord, he is clothed in the Holy *Neshamah* which is the inheritance from the Holy, Blessed be He! and the Congregation of Israël : then he inherits everything. And they are called children of the Holy, Blessed be He! As it is written 'Ye are the children of YHVH your Ail ! (Deut. xiv, 1.)§

---

* Zohar iii, 260*a*, Brody Ed. Cremona Ed. iii, fol. 124*b*, col. 496.

† Zohar ii, 69*a*, Brody Ed. Cremona Ed. ii, fol. 31*a*, col. 121.

‡ Zohar iii, 277*b*, Raÿah Me'hemnah, Brody Ed. Cremona Ed. iii, 134*b*, col. 536.

§ Zohar iii, 24*b*, Brody Ed. Cremona Ed. iii, 11*a*, col. 42.

THE EATING OF THE FORBIDDEN FRUIT. "It is written: 'She (Eve) took from the fruit.' (Gen. iii, 6.) This we have learned: She squeezed grapes and gave it to him (Adam) and caused death to the whole world. Then this Tree, the dead rest in it, and that Tree rules in the night, and when it rules, all the children of the world taste the taste of death."*

THE POWER OF THE FLESH. "The building of the body of the child of man is thus, the *Rua'h* spirit, comes from the *Rua'h D'qudsha* Holy Spirit, the *Neshamah* soul, from that Tree of Life, and the other (the evil) side gives the flesh, and only the flesh comes from its side, and not another thing." †

"Come, See! The end of the flesh, means; his (the evil one's) whole will is only on the flesh * * * and when he rules he rules on the *guff* body, and not on the *Neshamah* soul. The soul goes to her place and the flesh is given to that (the evil) place."‡

"Over the body of the just who do not care for the pleasures of this world, the impure side cannot govern. Because they (the just) do not ever associate with them (the bad spirits) in this world, they have not the least power over them." §

OF THE INCORPOREAL OF MAN AFTER DEATH. "As soon as the body is cast off by that *Rua'h* spirit, through the hand of *Malak 'Hamoveth* the Angel of Death, he (the *Rua'h*) goes and clothes in that other body in the Garden of Eden, (which he has cast off when he came to the world. This is not in the Cremona;) and the *Rua'h* has not any enjoyment except in that body there, and rejoices that he has divested himself from the body of this world, and clothes himself in another perfect garment which is in that world, and (he) sits in it and goes and views so as to know the Secrets Above, which he could not know and see in this worldly body; and when the *Neshamah* clothes herself in that dress from the other world, how much pleasure and joy is to her there. * * * But the guilty in the world who did not fully repent to their Lord, come naked to this world and naked they go back there, and the *Neshamah* goes in

---

* Zohar i, 36a and b, Brody Ed. Cremona Ed. i, fol. 28b, col. 112.

† Zohar iii, 170a, Brody Ed. Cremona Ed. iii, fol. 81a, col. 322.

‡ Zohar i, 65a, Brody Ed. Cremona Ed. i, fol. 50b, col. 199.

§ Zohar ii, 141a, Brody Ed. Cremona Ed. ii, fol. 63a and b, col. 250-1.

shame to those others who do not have any garments, and are judged in that *Gāi-hinnom*, which is on the earth, from that fire Above."*

THE DEPARTURE OF THE HOLY SOUL. "R. 'Hiz'qee-yah begun and said: 'And when the sun was going down, a deep sleep fell upon Abram, etc.' (Gen. xv, 12.) Come, See! That day is the day of the heavy judgments, which take man away from this world. Thus we have learned: That day that man goes forth from this world, is the day of the great judgment, which obscures the sun from the moon, as it is written: 'Before the sun * * * be darkened.' (Eccl. xii, 2.) This is the Holy *Neshamah* soul, which is withheld from man 30 days before he goes out from this world, and that is the *tzelem* shadow form, which is withheld from him and is not seen. Why is it (the *tzelem*) withheld from him? Because the Holy soul, ascends and departs from man and is not seen. Thou shouldst not say, that when man dies and that *Neshamah* soul, becomes weak, she goes away from him. No! but when he is in his life and in his strength, she (*Neshamah*) goes away from him (man) and she does not illuminate any more to that *Rua'h*, and the *Rua'h* does not illuminate any more to that *Nephesh;* then the *tzelem* shadow form, goes away from him, and does not illuminate (the man). From that day all cry out upon him, even the birds of heaven (angels), because the *Neshamah* ascends from him; and the *Rua'h* does not light any more to the *Nephesh*, so that the *Nephesh* weakens, and all the desires of the *guff*, *i.e.*, body, go and pass away from him." †

"Come, See! That holy *tzelem*, *i. e.*, phantom image, in him (man), in it man goes, and in it man grows up, and it is from that *partzupha, i.e.*, plastic likeness, and *d'yooq-nah i. e.*, phantom or shadow of a *tzelem*, of him is made another *tzelem*, *i. e.*, phantom image, and they are connected as one. At the time that the two *tzulmin*, *i. e.*, merged phantom images, are found in him (man) they watch over him and his *guff*, *i.e.*, body, and the *Rua'h* spirit, rests in it. At the time when his end of days comes near they depart from him (man) and man is left without a protector, as it is written; 'Until the day break, and the *shadows* (plural) flee away.' (Song of Songs ii, 17.)"‡

* Zohar ii, 150a, Brody Ed. Cremona Ed. ii, 67b, col. 267.

† Zohar i, 227a, Brody Ed. Cremona Ed., i, 120b, col. 477.

‡ Zohar i, 220a, Brody Ed. It belongs to iii, 104a. Cremona Ed., iii, fol. 50b, col. 199, 200. Livorno Ed. i, 370b, 371a.

THE GARMENTS OF THE INCORPOREAL IN MAN. "We have learned: a thousand and five hundred odors go up every day from *Gan Eden*, which perfume the precious garments of that world which are crowned from the day of the man (time he is born). Said R. Yehudah: 'How many garments are these which are crowned (from the day he was created)?' Said R. El'azar: 'The mountains of the world (the great men of the generation) are in discussion upon it, but there are three: one to clothe in that garment the *Rua'h* spirit, which is in the Garden (of Eden) on earth: one which is more precious than all, in which the *Neshamah* is clothed in that Bundle of Life, between the angels of the King in the *purpeer-ah, i. e.*, purple, of the King:* and one outside garment, which exists and does not exist, is seen and not seen. In that garment, the *Nephesh* is clothed and she goes and flies in it, to and fro in the world." †

THE INCORPOREAL COMPARED TO A LIGHTED LAMP. "The *Nephesh* is the awakening from Below and she is the support to the *guff, i. e.*, body, and she feeds him and the *guff* unites to her and she is united to the *guff*, afterwards it (this *Nephesh*) forms and is made a throne for the *Rua'h* to rest upon, afterwards both are formed and prepared to receive the *Neshamah* and the *Rua'h* is made a throne for the *Neshamah* to rest upon him, and this *Neshamah* is the Above, Hidden of All, the Concealed of All the Concealed. Come, See! The *Nephesh* is in its awakening Below, to connect herself in the body, like the light of a lamp; the lower light, which is black, cleaves to the wick and does not separate from it, but cleaves on it and does not exist except through the wick; and when she is connected with the wick, she makes a throne to the upper light, which is white, which rests on the black light; when both are formed together, that white light is made a throne to the hidden light which is not seen, and it is not known what rests on that white light and so that light is perfect. So is the man when he is perfect in everything, and then he is called holy." ‡

* *Purpeer-ah* is also an angel who is clothed in this color because it is the color of a spark from the She'kheen-ah.

† Zohar i, 119*b*, col. 475, Cremona Ed. Livorno Ed. i, 378*b*, 379*a*, i, 224*b*, Brody Ed.

‡ Zohar i, 83*b*, Brody Ed. Cremona Ed. i, fol. 59*a*, col. 234. Livorno Ed. i, 149*a*.

THE SOULS OF THE PIOUS DESCEND INTO SHEOL TO BRING UP SOME OF THE SOULS THEREIN. Even those that do not go into *Gāi-hinnom* go down to *Sheol*, then all men: "Even the truly just go down there, but they come up at once, as it is written; 'He goeth down to *Sheol* and bringeth up again,' (I Sam. ii, 6. Comp. Vulgate I Kings ii, 6) except those guilty who never have repented. They go down and do not come up. Why do the just (pious) go down there? Because they shall take many guilty from there and bring them up Above, and those are they who desired to do repentance, but who died before they could, so the just go down purposely to bring them out from there."*

OF THE GIL'GOOL-EM, OR REVOLUTION OF SOULS. "All the souls go up into the *gil-gool-ah*, *i. e.*, revolutions or turnings, and the children of man do not know the ways of the Holy, Blessed be He! and how He judges the children of man every day and in all time, and how the *Neshamoth* souls, go up to be judged before they come down into this world, and how they go up to judgment after they go out from this world? How many *Gil'gool-em* and how many hidden doings, the Holy, Blessed be He! does with them? How many naked souls and how many naked spirits, go in that world (the other) which do not enter through the King's *pargoda*, *i. e.*, curtain? And how many worlds turn around with them, and how the world turns around in so many hidden wonders? And the children of man do not know and do not comprehend, how the souls revolve like a stone which is thrown from a sling, as it is written: 'And the souls of thine enemies, them shall He sling out, as out of a sling. (I Sam. xxv, 29.) But while it is permitted to reveal, now is the time to reveal it, that all the *Neshamoth* souls, go out from that great Tree and from that mighty River which flows out from Eden, and all the *Ru'hin* spirits come out from that other small tree. The *Neshamah* soul, comes from Above, the *Rua'h* spirit, from Below,† and unite in one like that of male and female * * * and nothing is ever lost." ‡

---

* Zohar iii, 220*b*, Brody Ed. Cremona Ed. iii, fol. 102*a*, col. 405.

† The *Rua'h* spirit, goes up to Paradise, the *Nephesh* is originated here, exists and remains here, and the *Neshamah* soul, goes up to the Supreme Place.

‡ Zohar ii, 99*b*, Sab-ah D'Mishpatim, Brody Ed. Cremona Ed. ii, fol. 45*a*, col. 177-178.

THE BODY OF THE RESURRECTION. "Said R. Pin'has; 'The Holy, Blessed be He! is prepared to beautify the body of the just in the time to come, like the beauty of *Adam Rishoun, i. e.*, the first Adam, at the time he went into *Gan Eden*, as it is written: 'And YHVH will give thee rest continually, and will fill thy soul with brightness.' (Is. lviii, 11 Vulgate.) Said R. Levi: 'The *Neshamah* when she is in her highest degree Above, she is fed from that Light from Above and is clothed in it, and when she goes into the *guff*, *i. e.*, body, in time to come, in the very same light she will go in, and then the *guff* body, will shine like the splendor of the firmament, as it is written: 'And they that be wise shall shine as the brightness of the firmament.'" (Dan. xii, 3.) *

"The just who deserve to go up to that splendor Above; his *d'yooq-nah* is carved out in that precious Throne, and so is it with all the just, that his *d'yooq-nah*, Above, is like it has been, Below; to assure that Holy *Neshamah* soul. And the splendor of the *guff* body, and the *Neshamah* soul, in that Upper Place is like the *a'yooq-nah*, they have had on earth, and that *d'yooq-nah* is fed from the enjoyment of the *Neshamah* and she is prepared in the future, to clothe herself in that substance which is left on the earth."†

* Zohar, Livorno Ed., i, 197a and b. Midrash Ha-Ne'elam. Cremona Ed. i, 69a, col. 273-274. Brody Ed. i, 113b.

† Zohar i, fol. 70a, col. 277, Cremona Ed. Midrash Ha-Ne'elam. Livorno Ed., i, 199a. Brody Ed. i, 114b.

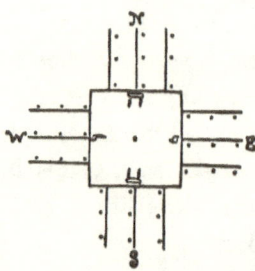

Figure 36.—An occult representation of the Ten Sephiroth, Four Worlds, Tetragramaton, etc.

XX.

STRUCTURE OF THE UNIVERSE. STABILITY OF THE OPPOSITIONS. THE LOWER WORLD LIKE THE UPPER. THE MAKROKOSM AND MIKROKOSM. THE UPPER ADAM. THE MAKROKOSM AS THE GREAT TREE, AND AS MAN. CREATION OF ADAM AND 'HAVAH. THEIR CONDITION BEFORE AND AFTER THEIR FALL. FOUR WAYS OF SEEING THE DEITY. THE PERMANENCE OF SPOKEN WORDS. LOVE AND FEAR. ENTIRE DEPENDENCE SHOULD BE ON THE DEITY WHEN MAN IS IN TROUBLE. PARADISE AND HELL. SAMÄ-EL AND LILITH, ETC. THE ANGEL OF DEATH, ETC. COMING OF THE MESSIAH AND THE KINGDOM OF THE SUPREME DEITY UPON EARTH, ETC.

STRUCTURE OF THE UNIVERSE. "R. Yehudah began, it is written: 'Elohim said: Let there be a firmament in the midst of the waters.' (Gen. i, 6.) Come, See! At the time that the Holy, Blessed be He! created the world He created 7 heavens Above. He created 7 earths Below, 7 seas, 7 days, 7 rivers, 7 weeks, 7 years, 7 times, and 7000 years that the world has been. The Holy, Blessed be He! is in the seventh of all (the millenium). He created 7 heavens Above, and in each one created stars, planets, suns, to serve in each heaven, and in all of these heavens are chariots differing one from another and one upon another, to take upon them the yoke of *Malkhutha* Kingdom, of their Lord. Some of them have six wings and some of them four wings, some of them with four faces and some with two, and some with one face, some of them are a flaming fire, and some of them are water, and some of them *ru'ha* air. This is what is written: 'He maketh his angels, spirits; his ministers, a flaming fire.' (Ps. civ, 4.) And all the heavens are one above the other, like the layers of an onion, and some Below and some Above, and each heaven trembles for the fear of their Lord: through

Him they exist and through Him they are taken away. And above all, the Holy, Blessed be He! has all in His power; so here, are 7 earths Below, they are all inhabited except those which are above and those which are below. (The Cremona Ed. says, all are inhabited, the above and below.)   *   *   *   And our companions who live in the South, have seen in the First Book and the Book of Adam, (Cremona Ed. claims the First Book is the Book of Adam), that all these earths which are Below, are like the firmaments Above, that upon that and this upon this, and between each earth, a heaven (firmament) is spread out between each other.* And each of these earths are spread out according to their names, and between them is the *Gan Eden* and the *Gäi-hinnom*, and there is in them creatures who look different one from the other like the Above; some of them with two faces, some of them with four faces, and some of them with one face, and their appearance is different one from the other; but if you object and say that all the children of the world came out from Adam, it is not so, the First Adam did not come down to all the countries, and produce children and have so many wives, but Adam has not been found at all in this world, only in that World which is the highest of all of them, which is called; תבל *Theivhel, i. e.*, the productive habitable globe, as it is written : ' He commandeth them upon the *Theivhel* of the earth.' (Job xxxvii, 12.) And that *Theivhel* is merged in the heaven (firmament) Above and is united in the Upper Name, this is what is written; 'And He shall judge the *Theivhel* in righteousness.' (Ps. ix, 8.) Surely in righteousness. Therefore the child of man who is found in that Upper Earth which is called *Theivhel,* is superior over all, like the Above. Because as in the heavens Above, there is one heaven highest above all, and Above is found the Throne of the Holy, Blessed be He! as it is written: 'As the appearance of the stone Sapphire, etc.' (Ezek. i, 26.) 'The *d'mooth* of a Throne, and upon the *a'mooth* of the Throne is the *d'mooth* of the appearance of a man upon it from above.' (*Ibid.*) So here too, in this *Theivhel,* is found the King of All. And who is he? Adam (Man), who is not found in all Below. And the Lower earths where do they come from? They are from the chain of the earth and from the Heaven Above. And there come

---

* Like the fine skin of the layers of the onion.

out from it different creatures differing one from the other. Some of them in garments (skins), some of them in shells (*Q'lippoth*) like the worms which are found in the earth, some of them in red shells, some in black, some in white, and some from all the colors. So are all creatures like these."*

THE LOWER WORLD LIKE THE UPPER. THE CREATION OF THE MAN. "And He made this world opposite to the world Above, and all that which is Above is in the resemblance of the Below, and all that which is Below, the resemblance thereof is in the sea and all is one. He created in the Above the *Ma-lakhem, i. e.*, angels, He created in this world the children of man. He created in the sea the Leviathan, as it is written: 'To join together, that it might be one.' And it is written of man: 'For in the image of Elohim He made the Man.' (Gen. ix, 6.) And it is written: 'Thou madest him to be wanting but a little of Elohim.' (Ps. viii, 5.) If the children of man are correct in their doings then the One, Above, calls them, children; as is written: 'You are children to YHVH your Ail (God).' (Deut. xiv, 1.) He calls them 'children' and they call Him, 'Father,' as it is written: 'Thou art our Father, etc.' (Is. lxiii, 16, lxiv, 8.) He chose me and I chose Him."†

THE STABILITY OF THE OPPOSITIONS. "Every *d'yook-nah, i. e.*, shadow or phantom of a *tzelem*, in which we do not find the male and female is not in the Upper *D'yook-nah*, as it ought to be, and we have so considered in the mysteries of our learning. Come, See! In every place in which is not found the male and female as one, the Holy, Blessed be He! has not put His dwelling in that place and blessing is not found, but only in the place in which is found male and female. It is written: 'He blessed *them* and called *their name Adam* on the day He created *them*.' (Gen. v, 2.) And is not written: 'He blessed *him* and called *his* name Adam.' Adam even is not named Adam except when male and female united in one, etc."‡

---

* Zohar iii, 9*b*, 10*a*, Brody Ed. Cremona Ed. iii, fol. 4*a*, col. 14.

† Zohar ii, 20*a*, Brody Ed. Cremona Ed. ii, fol. 9*a*, col. 34.

‡ Zohar i, 55*b*, Brody Ed. Cremona Ed. i, fol. 45*a*, col. 178. Comp. also iii, fol. 83*b*, col. 331.

The Qabbalah shows the existence of four Adams, or rather three continuations of the Upper Heavenly Adam. I. The Perfect Upper Heavenly Adam of the *Atzeel-atic World*, the World of Emanation. It is androgenic and the sole occupant of that world. It is thought of as a manifestation of the Deity in the Divine *D'yook nah*, or an undefined phantom shade of the *Tzelem*, which the earthly man, in the flesh, has never seen. It is a Perfect *Tzure* or Prototype, to the second and subsequent Adams. In this Upper Heavenly Man is the perfect Holy *Nephesh*, *Rua'h*, *Neshamah*, *'Haÿ-yah* and *Ye'hee-dah*, merged in combination yet existing *quasi* separately. Here is also the content of the Upper Ten Sephiroth. It answers to the Intellectual; the Brain, and is in the Upper Inner Emanated Heaven. It also answers to the Holy Upper *Neshamah* Soul.

The Second Adam is the sole occupant of the *B'ree-atic World*, the World of Creation. In this World is the *Kiseh Hakabod* or Throne of Glory. This Adam is also androgenic, is in the likeness of man, but more perfect in every respect. It is the protoplastic Adam or Makrokosm of the Terrestrial Adam, and is the Adam mentioned in Gen. i. It is the *Tzelem* phantom Image, of the First Adam, and has the First Adam's *D'yook-nah* and *D'mooth*, but in lower and much further removed degree. It is paralleled by Metatron. This Adam has the *Nephesh*, *Rua'h*, *Neshamah*, *'Haÿ-yah* and *Ye'hee-dah*, of the First Adam but in a very much less perfect degree. It is a *Tzure* to the Third Adam. It is its heel, Malkhuth; the Church or Congregation, etc., that shall bruise the head of the Serpent, *i. e.*, Satan or Samä-el. (Gen. iii, 15, 16.) It answers to the Heart, and the Ethical, also to the *Rua'h* Spirit.

The Third Adam is the Terrestrial Adam made of 'dust' and placed in the Garden of Eden or Paradise. This Adam was also an androgene. It was made in the *D'yooq-nah*, *Tzelem* and *D'mooth* of the preceding Adams, but was much further removed from both of them. It had when first created, a glorious *simulacrum* or light body, like that of the angels, and spirits, and answers to the *Yetzeer-atic World* or World of the Angels. It also answers to the *Breath* and the *Nephesh* Animated Soul.

The Fourth Adam, was the Third Adam as he was after the Fall. When he was clothed with skin, flesh, nerves, etc. This answers to the Lower

Nephesh, and *Guff*, *i. e.*, body, united. He has the animal power of Reproduction and continuance of species, and also answers to the *A'seey-atic World*, that of the Shells, but in him is some of the light of all the preceding. Together they form the Great Universal Man.

The Qabbalah also asserts the existence of Three principal emanated or created regions: two Heavens and one Earth. The Upper Heaven is called the Inner. We also note here the Qabbalistic doctrines as to the Inner, the *Panim*, *i.e.*, Face, and the External, or *A'hor;* a subject to be approached with reverence, fear and trembling, by all mortals. Even the *A'hor* is the *Panim*, for God has not any limitation, and the assertion of an apparent negativity is nevertheless that of a positive. To describe the highest externality the Qabbalah is obliged to use the terms *N'qood-ah, D'yooq-nah, Tzelem, Ma'hshabah, D'mooth*, etc.

The Qabbalah names man as the purpose of creation and the first step is the Upper Adam or Celestial Man. (Zohar iii, 48*a*.) The idea is in the vision of Ezekiel in the assertion of the existence of the human form, upon and above, the Chariot Throne or *Merkabah*. Upon this vision the Qabbalah bases the idea of the Four Worlds. *A'tzeel-ah* is the abode of the *Adam Illa-ah* or *Adam Qadmon*, *B'ree-ah* the World of Creation, that of *Metatron* and the Throne, *Ye'tzeer-ah* of the *Malakaya*, angels, and the *'Haÿ-yoth* Living Ones, and *A'seey-ah* of the *Aupha-nem* and the *Q'lippoth*. The latter World is also called *Gal'gal-lem, i.e.*, the Planetary World. The form of the Man is that which *At-tee'kah D'At-tee'keen* has chosen for Its own form. (Zohar iii, 141*b*.) The three divisions of the Sephirothic World answer to the three spiritual principles in man, *Nesh-amah*, the Intellectual World; *Rua'h*, the Ethical World; *Nephesh* the Natural World. Each of these are divided into three divisions, together nine, which with the whole content of man, constitutes the Ten.*

"Three worlds are to Him, the Holy, Blessed be He! which He has hidden in Him. The first World (the *A'tzeel-atic World*) is that Above, hidden from all, it cannot be looked at or comprehended or known, except by him who is hidden in it. The second World (the *B'ree-atic*

---

* Comp. Joel *Religions-philosophie des Sohar*, p. 303, note 2. Franck *La Kabbale*, p. 203. German Ed., pp. 147–148. Zohar iii, 296*a*. Idrah Zootah. Also the *Tiqqooneh ha-Zohar*. See the frontispiece.

World), which is connected with that Above; this is that (the World) which the Holy, Blessed be He! makes Himself known from, as it is written; 'Open to me the gates of righteousness.' (Ps. cxviii, 19.) 'This is the gate of YHVH.' (*Ibid.* 20.) And this is the second World. The third World (the *Ye'tzeer-atic World*) that is the lower World from the other, there is found in it separation, and this is the World in which the angels from Above, rest in, and the Holy, Blessed be He! is found in and not found (in that World). He is found, but when they desire to comprehend and to know Him, He ascends from them and is not seen till all enquire and ask; 'Where is the *Ma-qom, i. e.*, Place, of His Glory?' (And the others answer): 'Blessed be the Glory of YHVH from His *Ma-qom, i.e.*, Place.' (Ezek. iii, 12.) And this is the World which is not always in continuance. (Zohar, Cremona Ed. iii, 76*a*; Brody Ed. iii, 159*a*.) Like this it is said: 'In the *Tzelem* shadow image, of Elohim, He made Adam (man).' (Gen. i, 27.) Adam (man) has also three worlds: The First World, is that World which is called: עלמא דפרודא *almoh d'prudah, i.e.*, the world of separation, and man is found in it and is not found, and when they desire to look on him he vanishes from them and is not seen. The Second World is the World which is connected in that World Above, and this is the Garden of Eden on the earth, which is connected in another Upper World; and from here is known and comprehended that other World. The Third World is an Upper Hidden World concealed and not revealed and no one can know that World; as it is written; 'No eye hath seen O! Elohim, beside Thee, what He hath prepared for him that waiteth for Him.' (Is. lxiv, 4.)"*

THE MAKROKOSM. And this is what is written: 'And YHVH said; I will wipe out the Man whom I have created, from the face of the earth.' (Gen. vi, 7.) There ought to be a distinction between the *Adam D'Illa-ah* the Man Above, and *Adam D'Lthath-ah* the Man Below; and if it were not for the Man, the world could not exist, because one could not exist without the other. If it were not for the *form* (Cremona Ed. has not, 'form') of the Man (Adam) the world could not exist. This is what is written: 'YHVH by *Wisdom* hath founded the earth.' (Prov. iii, 18.) And it is written: 'And Noah (numerically = 58) found Grace (numer-

---

* Zohar iii, 76*a* and *b*, col. 302, 303, Cremona Ed. Brody Ed. iii, 159*a* and *b*.

ically = 58) in the eyes of YHVH.' And we have learned; that all the brains depend on that Brain (Wisdom) and the Wisdom comprises All. And this Hidden Wisdom in her has strength of itself, and has established the form of the Man to put All on its arrangement. Each one in its place: this is what is written: 'Wisdom strengtheneth the wise more than ten rulers. (Eccl. vii, 29.)* Which are the perfect form of the Man. And in that form of Man rests the perfection of the faith in all things; all rests upon the Throne, as it is written: 'And its *d'mooth* similitude, was like the appearance of the Man upon him from above.' (Ezek. i, 26.) And it is written: 'And I saw that he came with the clouds of heaven like a son of man and he reached unto the *At-tee'k Yo-men, i. e.*, Ancient of Days, and (he) drew near before Him.' (Dan. vii, 13.) Until here the words are hidden." †

"Because the *D'yooq-nah, i. e.*, Phantom of the *Tzelem, i. e.*, shadow Image, of the Man (said R. Shim-on ben Yo'haï), is the Above and Below, which are contained in him, and because that *D'yooq-nah* contains the Above and Below, He (the Holy One) established the *At-tee'kah Qaddusha* Holy Ancient, as His form, and the form of *Ze'ir An-peen* in that *D'yooq-nah* and form."‡

OF THE B'REE-ATIC ADAM. "It is written: 'What is His name, and what is the name of His Son?' When thou desirest to know: 'YHVH TZE'BA-OTH is His Name. § 'The name of His Son?' Israël is his name, as it is written: 'My first-born Son, Israël.' (Ex. iv, 22.) And that Israël, all the keys of Truth (Faith) hang on him, and he praises himself and says: 'YHVH said to me thou art My Son.' (Ps. ii, 7.) And surely so it is. For Abba and Immah crown him and bless him with many blessings, and said, and commended to all: 'Kiss the son.' (Ps. ii, 12.) Kiss the hand to that Son. It is like as if the Holy, Blessed be He! would give him power over all, that all shall serve him. 'Lest he be angry.' (*Ibid.* Comp. Ex. xxiii, 21.) Because they crowned him with Judgment and Mercy. Who deserves Judgment to him is Judg-

---

* The Ten Sephiroth.
† Zohar iii, 144a, Brody Ed. Cremona Ed. iii, fol. 68b, col. 272.
‡ Zohar iii, fol. 141a, Idrah Rabbah, Brody Ed. Cremona Ed. iii, fol. 67b, col. 267.
§ Jer. x, 16.

ment, and who deserves Mercy, he shows him Mercy. All the blessings from Above and Below go up to that Son and (they) crown themselves, and who prevents the blessings from that Son, spreads out sin before the Holy King (or Holy Mother). *

THE MAKROKOSM AS THE GREAT TREE. "The Male is extended to the Right and Left, by the inheritance which he received. But whensoever they are joined, it is called *Tiph'e-reth* Beauty, and the whole body is formed and made the Great Tree, strong, fair, and beautiful. 'The beasts of the field (men) had shadow under it, and the fowls of the heaven (angels) dwelt in its wings, and all were fed by it.' † His arms are Right and Left. In the Right is Life and '*Hesed* (Grace), in the Left, Death and *Ge'boor-ah* (Judgment), etc." ‡

"Also now was perfected in the earth the *Eloo-nah Qad-disha, i. e.*, the Holy Tree, like that, Above; in twelve limitations (stems) and seventy branches (nations) which were not before; and therefore the latter is complete and the first is not complete; whence the accent falleth between them, etc."§

According to the Qabbalah the soul sparks contained in Adam, went into three principal classes corresponding to his three sons, *viz:* '*Hesed*, Habel, *Ge'boor-ah* Qai-yin and *Ra'h-mim* Seth. These three were divided into 12 and the twelve into 70 species, called; the principal roots of the human race.

MAN AS THE MAKROKOSM AND THE MIKROKOSM. "With skin and flesh thou hast clothed me, etc.' (Job x, 11.) If this is so, what is the man? Is he only skin, flesh, bones, nerves? It is not so! The real man is not that, but *Neshamah* soul, and that which is said; skin, flesh, bones and nerves, together; are only the garments of the man but not the man. When the man departs (from this life), he takes off the garment which has clothed him. Yet all these bones and sinews together are in the mystery of the Wisdom, Above. Like the Above. The 'skin' represents

---

* Zohar iii, 191*b*, Brody Ed.

† Dan. iv, 12. Comp. *ibid.*, 10 *sq.*, which seems also to be a description of the Sephirothic Tree of Life.

‡ Zohar iii, fol. 296*a*, Idrah Zootah. Brody Ed. Cremona Ed. iii, fol. 144*a*, col. 574.

§ Zohar iii, fol. 138*a*, Mantua Ed. Cremona Ed. iii, fol. 65*b*, col. 260.

the firmament, like we have learned : ' Who stretchest out the heavens like a curtain.' (Ps. civ, 2.) ' Ram skins dyed red, and a covering above of badgers skins.' (Ex. xxvi, 14.) These are the garments, from Above, which cover the garments. When ' the heavens are stretched out,' these are the outer garments. The ' curtain ' is the inner garment and this is the clothing which covers up the flesh. The ' bones and nerves,' they are the Celestial Chariot, and all its *forces* which exist in the interior, '*Heilin D' Qăimin l'gou, i. e.*, the heavenly servants. And all these garments inside, is the mystery of the *Adam Illa-ah* Upper Adam, which is its inner. So here is a mystery, Below. The ' man,' he is the inner to the inner. His 'garment,' like the Above. His ' bones and nerves,' as we have said, the Celestial Chariot and its hosts ; the ' flesh ' is that which covers the hosts and the Chariots, and that remains outside. All the mystery Below, is like the Above, therefore ; ' Elohim created the Man (Adam) in His *Tzelem, i. e.*, shadow Image.' ' In the *Tzelem, i. e.*, shadow Image, of Elohim.' (Gen. i, 27.) Two Elohims are here, one for the male, and one, for the female ; and the mystery of the man, Below, is like the mystery (of the Man), Above. In that firmament Above, that covers everything, we see different figures formed by the stars and planets which contain secret things and deep secrets, and these are the signs of the stars and planets, which are in the firmament, which is covered on the outside ; so here, the 'skin' which is the cover outside of the man, which is the firmament which covers everything up ; has in it signs and lines, and they are like the stars and planets of the (heavenly) skin. All these signs have a concealed meaning, and are the object of attention for the wise who know how to read in the face of man."* (See Is. xlvii, 13.)

"Come, See! When the Holy, Blessed he He created Adam (man), He took dust from the Holy Place and built his body from the four sides (elements) of the world, that all (the sides) should give him power. After that He poured on him a Spirit of life, as it is written : ' He blew into his nostrils (*face*, Vulgate,) a *Nishmath 'Haÿ-yeem* Soul of Life. Afterwards he existed and he knew that he was from Above and Below, then

---

* Zohar ii, 75*b*, 76*a*, Brody Ed. Cremona Ed. ii, fol. 32*a*, col. 126. Comp. ii, 33*a*, col. 129.

he knew the Upper Wisdom. Like this, all the men in the world are comprised from Above and Below."*

CREATION OF THE MAN. "And YHVH Elohim formed Adam, *i. e.*, Man, therefore is written; 'YHVH Elohim, created Adam,' with the full Name, like we have stated, that he is perfect and comprises all. We have learned; On the sixth day Man was created at the time when the *Kiseh, i.e.*, Throne, was perfected, and is called *Kiseh* Throne; it is written: 'The Throne had six steps,' (I Kings x, 19), and therefore Man was created on the sixth (day) because he is worthy to sit on this Throne. And we have learned: When Man was created everything was established, everything which is Above and Below, and all is comprised in Man." †

"After He made generations, at once He called him Adam (man), it is written; 'These are the generations of Adam (man).' After He revealed the words to that upper hidden, Above; He created man, Below; it is written; 'In the day that Elohim created Adam, *B' d' mooth*, *i. e.*, in the *similitude*, of Elohim, He made him.'" (Gen. v, 1.) ‡

CREATION OF ADAM AND 'HAVAH. "Said R. Shim-on; It is written; 'And every plant of the field before it was in the earth, and every herb of the field before it sprouted: YHVH Elohim had not allowed it to rain upon the earth, etc.' (Gen. ii, 5.) 'And every plant of the field,' these are the large trees which had been small and were planted afterwards. Come, See! Adam and Eve have been created one side in the other side (means side by side). Why were they not created face to face? Because it is written: That YHVH 'had not allowed it to rain upon the earth,' and the pair have not been found in its arrangement as ought to be, but when they had been formed Below and became face to face, then they were so found Above. From whence do we know this? From the *Mishkan, i. e.*, Tabernacle; It is written: 'And Moses erected the *Mishkan* Tabernacle;' (Ex. xl, 18;) because another Tabernacle has been erected with it, and before the Below had been erected the Above could not exist, so is here (as to the man, Adam) before the Below (the Lower

---

* Zohar i, 130*b*, Brody Ed. Cremona Ed. i, fol. 78*a* and *b*, col. 310–11. Livorno Ed. i, 121*b*.

† Zohar iii, 48*a*, Brody Ed. Cremona Ed. iii, fol. 21*b* and 22*a*, col. 84–5.

‡ Zohar ii, 70*b*, Brody Ed. Comp. ii, 55*a*, Cremona Ed. ii, fol. 31*b*, col. 123.

Adam) had been erected, the Above (the Upper Adam) could not exist, and therefore till now has not been formed the Above. They had not been created face to face, and this verse shows this, for it is written: 'That YHVH Elohim had not allowed it to rain upon the earth.' And therefore what is said: 'There was not a man,' means that he (man) has not been arranged in his form; but when '*Havah* (Eve) had been perfected then Adam was perfected, but before he was not perfect. (See *Ante* p. 387) * * * (And no work has been done upon the earth, because YHVH did not let it rain upon the earth.) But what is written afterwards: ' But there went up a mist from the earth.' That means the desire of the female towards the male. (The impulse from Below to the Above.) Another explanation of why He did not cause it to rain? Because the perfect form was not found to go up from the earth (after the man had been perfected on the earth Below) so from this earth Below awakened the work Above. * * * Come, See! we have learned; went up from the earth first and a cloud awakened and all connected itself the one in other."*

"R. Yitz-haq says; Adam was created with two faces. 'He took (out) one of his ribs,' (Gen. ii, 21) the Holy, Blessed be He! parted him (it) and made two from the East and the West. (Cremona Ed. says: From the East to the West.) ' Thou hast formed me before and behind.' (Ps. cxxxix, 5.) Behind, that is the West; and before, that is the East. R. 'He-yah said: What has the Holy, Blessed be He! done? He formed that female and poured beauty all over her, and brought her into Adam * * * and it is written : ' He took one from his ribs,' that is (from) his side." †

CONDITION OF ADAM AND EVE BEFORE AND AFTER SINNING. "Come, See! Before Adam sinned he went up into and remained in the illuminated wisdom, Above, and was not separated from the Tree of Life. But when he acceded to the desire to know and to descend Below, then he followed after them (Below) until he separated himself from the Tree of Life, and knew only the bad and left the good alone, and on this is written; ' Thou art not an Ail (El) that hath pleasure in wickedness neither shall evil dwell with Thee.' (Ps. v, 4 (5). Comp. Vulgate 5, 6.)

* Zohar i, 34*b*, 35*a*, Brody Ed. Cremona Ed. i, fol. 26*a*, col. 102.
† Zohar ii, 55*a*, Brody Ed. Cremona Ed. ii, fol. 25*a*, col. 97.

Who follows the bad has no dwelling with the Tree of Life. And before they had sinned they heard a Voice from Above, and knew the wisdom from Above, (and preserved their Upper Splendor. This is not in the Cremona), and did not tremble, but after they sinned they could not stand even before the voice from Below."*

"And Come, See! When *Adam Rishoun, i. e.*, the First Adam, was in *Gan Eden, i.e.*, Garden of Eden, he was clothed in a garment like that Above, and it is the garment of the Upper Splendor. But when he was driven out of the Garden of Eden, and he needed the garment necessary to such as are in this world: What is written? 'And YHVH Elohim made for Adam and his wife כתנות *koth-nouth, i. e.*, inner garments, of עור *oûr, i. e.*, skin, and clothed them.' (Gen. iii, 21.) At the first had been garments of אור *Ohr, i. e.*, Light. Light, that is the Upper Light which served them in *Gan Eden* Garden of Eden, because in this Garden of Eden, the Upper Supreme Light which illuminates there is served by it. Therefore when the *Adam Qad'mo-ah* went into the Garden, the Holy, Blessed be He! clothed him in that garment of Light and brought him in there, and if he had not been at first clothed in that Light he could not have got in there. But when he was driven away from there he needed another garment, therefore: 'YHVH Elohim made to Adam and his wife an *inner garment of skin.*' So it has been manifested that the good deeds which the son of man does in this world, these deeds attract from that Light of Splendor, Above, for a garment to prepare himself to enter into that world to appear before the Holy, Blessed be He! And in that dress in which he is clothed he enjoys and sees the *aspaq'lar-yah dinhar-ah, i. e.*, light of the luminous mirror,† as it is written: 'To behold the beauty, of YHVH and to enquire in His palace.' (Ps. xxvii, 4.) Thus the *Nishmathah, i. e.*, souls is clothed in both worlds, so she shall be perfect in all things, in this world Below, and the world, Above." ‡

---

* Zohar i, 52a and b, Brody Ed. Compare Zohar ii, 191b. Cremona Ed. i, fol. 36b, col. 144.

† The idea of the Luminous and Non-Luminous Mirror is Philo, Vol. i, pp. 134, 337. See *Ante* 399 sq., also in the Talmud. § *Yebamoth*, 49b; *Yerushalmi* § B'rakhoth, 44; Babli § *Sotah*, 22a.

‡ Zohar ii, 229b, Brody Ed. Cremona Ed. ii, fol. 103b, col. 411-12.

THE FOUR WAYS OF SEEING THE DEITY. "The Will (Harmony, *Houram-nutha D'malkah*) of the King is seen in three colors; the first color is seen Above from afar off, and no eye can perceive it in its pureness, because it is from afar off; only when he (the man) makes his eyes see little through closing the lids by their blinking.* And on that is written; 'From far off YHVH has appeared to me.' (Jer. xxxi, 3; see the Vulgate.) The second color is seen with one eye shut, and this color could not be seen by the other eye except when that eye is shut to see little and blinking, and he could not stand otherwise its (the light's) clearness, so he shut the eye and opened it a little, blinking, so he could see this color, and this color could only be perceived through that blinking of the eye; and of that is written; 'What seest thou.' (Jer. i, 12.) The third color; that is that *zohar aspaq'lar-yah* bright luminous mirror, which could not be looked into at all, except with the rolling of the eyes (eye-balls), when they (the lids) are altogether closed, and they roll in their sockets, and there could be seen in that rolling the *aspaq'lar-yah din'har-ah* the light of the luminous mirror, and that color could not be comprehended except by him, who sees the shining of that light with the eyes shut,† and therefore is written: 'The hand of YHVH was upon me.' (Ezek. xxxvii, 1:) also 'The hand of YHVH was upon me strong.' (Ezek. xxxiii, 22.) * * * And all these things could not be seen by the true prophets except by Moses, because Moses could see that which could not be seen by others." ‡

These four correspond, to contemplation, vision, ecstacy, and illumination, which four we find with all the Mystics. The ancients also believed in four kinds of '*Furor*' as they called it. The Qabbalists considered the prophet Moses, who talked to God "mouth to mouth," (Num. xii, 6–8) as above all other prophets.

THE THREE ANGELS WHO APPEARED TO ABRAHAM. "It is written: 'And three men, etc.' (Gen. xviii, 2.) These are the three angels (messengers) which have been clothed in æther and came down to this world, and they

---

* As if looking at the sun on a clear day.

† That is in the *Ma'hshabah, i. e.*, Thought, because when the eyes are shut the contemplation becomes more intense.

‡ Zohar i, 97*a*, Sithrai Thorah. Brody Ed. Cremona Ed. i, fol. 66*a*, col. 262.

have been seen in appearance as (if) a child of man. (Comp. Zohar i, 34*a*.) And they have been three like the Above, because the rainbow is only seen in three colors: white, red and green. And surely it is so! And these are the three men; three colors, that is, a white color, red color, and green color. The white color, that is, Mikha-el, because he is the Right side: red color, that is, Gabri-el, because he is the Left side, and green color is, Rapha-el; and these three colors are those of the rainbow, because it is never seen except with them: therefore it is written: 'And YHVH appeared unto, etc.' (Gen. xviii, 1.) That is the She'kheen-ah revealed itself in these three colors. * * 'And they that be wise (intelligent, the teachers,) shall shine like זהר *Zohar, i. e.*, the splendor, of the firmament.' (Dan. xii, 3.) They shall shine a shining which shines by lighting a splendor, etc., etc. That brilliant Light which is hidden, the Spark of all the Sparks, and of All Lights, is in it invisible and hidden, hidden and revealed; seen and not seen. This shining Light came out from the Supreme Lighted Well, came out in the day and was hidden at night, * * * and this is the only thing seen, and all colors are concealed in it and it is called by the Name YHVH. From the three colors Above, have been seen three colors Below."*

THE CONTINUANCE AND ASCENT ABOVE, OF ALL WORDS SPOKEN BY MAN. "Come, See! At the time when the good deeds are done Below, *i. e.*, in this world, and man contemplates, in the service of the Holy King, that word which he makes here, Below; there is made from it a breath Above; and there is not a breath, which has not a voice which does not ascend and crown itself, Above,† and there is made from it an intercessor before the Holy, Blessed be He! And all the deeds which a man does which are not to the service of the Holy, Blessed be He! that word which he makes; a breath is created from it and goes away and flies around the world, and when the *Neshamah* soul, goes forth from that (the latter) man, that breath revolves in the world like a stone which is thrown out from a sling; As it is written, etc." See I Sam. xxv, 29.‡

* Zohar i, 98*b*, 99*a*, 100*a*, Sithrai Thorah, Brody Ed. Cremona i, fol. 89*b*, col. 355.
† Comp. *ante*, p. 124 and note.
‡ Zohar ii, 59*a*, Brody Ed. Cremona Ed. ii, fol. 26*b*, col. 104. Livorno Ed. ii, 100*b*.

WORSHIP FROM LOVE OR FEAR. "He (R. Shim-on) began and said: It is written: 'YHVH thy Ail thou shalt fear, Him thou shalt serve:' (Deut. x, 20.) and again it is written; 'Thou shalt fear for thy Ail.' (Lev. xix, 14.) Thus ought these verses to be said: Thou shalt fear thy Ail; because it is written; 'YHVH thy Ail thou shalt fear.' But what means; 'Fear *for* thy Ail.'? The mystery is from the word *m'Eloha-hu, i. e., for* thy Ail. * * * Fear conducts to Love, who serves through Love connects himself in the Upper place, Above, and in the holiness of the world to come, but it must not be supposed that to serve Him from the side of Fear is not to serve Him. Such a service from Fear is very precious, but he (such a man) cannot ascend to connect himself to the Above; but when he serves from Love, he goes up and crowns himself, Above, and connects himself in the world to come. In Love is the mystery of the Right ('*Hesed* Grace or Benevolence) and the mystery of the Unity, which is needful to them in the world to come, so as to unite the Name of the Holy, Blessed be He! and unite all different degrees from Above and Below; and to bring them all in the place of Unity, and this is the mystery which is written: 'Hear, Israel YHVH Elohainu YHVH is One.'"*

DEPENDENCE ON THE DEITY WHEN IN TROUBLE. "It is written: 'If thou faint (lose hope) in the day of adversity *thy strength* becomes small.' (Prov. xxiv, 10.) כחכה *ko'ha-khu, i. e.,* thy strength; that means if he lets up (weakens) his hand from the *Thorah,* (The Cremona Ed. says, 'The Holy, Blessed be He!) 'In the day of adversity,' this means, when he 'weakens,' so his 'strength becomes small.' What is 'Thy strength becomes small?' It means; כח כ"ה *Ko-a'h,*† then the evil is thrust outside so that it cannot come near man and cannot accuse him. But when man deviates from the Thorah and weakens from it, then the strength צר כח כה *tzar ko-a'h kaihoo, i.e.,* is the strength of the left hand, because that evil which is the Left side rules over man, and thrusts that other *ko-a'h,* (that is) the throne of Glory, away."‡

---

* Zohar ii, 216a, Brody Ed. Cremona Ed. ii, 97b, col. 387.

† The initials of הכבוד כסא *Kiseh ha-Kabod, i. e.,* Throne of Glory. The Throne of Glory is always to His Right.

‡ Zohar i, 152b, Brody Ed. Cremona Ed. i, fol. 89a, col. 354. Compare, *Ibid.*, 99b, col. 395.

THE DEITY BRINGS SALVATION TO THE WICKED. "'He goes wildly after the way of his heart.' (Is. lvii, 17.) Because the *Ye'tser ha-rah* is strong in him and therefore he goes wild and does not desire to repent. The Holy, Blessed be He! sees the way that he goes in, the evil way, He says; 'I must strengthen him under his arms.' That is what is written; 'I have seen his ways,' (*Ibid.* 18) that they go in the darkness, I need to give him a physician. Therefore it is written: 'I will heal him.' (*Ibid.*) That is the Holy, Blessed be He! puts in his (man's) heart the way of Repentance and with it He heals, the *Neshamah* soul, as it is written; 'Go and lead the people.' (Ex. xxxii, 34.) The Holy, Blessed be He! conducts him in a straight way like when one takes hold of another man's hand and conducts him out of the darkness. * * * And it is further written: 'I will lead him, and I will restore comforts unto him and to his mourners.' (Is. lvii, 18.) That means that the Holy, Blessed be He! does good to the people. From 13 years of age he places him under the charge of two angels to watch him, one to the Right and the other to the Left, when man goes in the right way (straight path) they joy in him and are happy and cry out and say: 'Give honor to the *D'yooq-nah* of the King,' but if man goes in the wrong way (crooked path) they mourn over him when they go away from him. (Cremona Ed. says: Then they go away from him.) But after, when the Holy, Blessed be He! strengthens him and leads him back to the right way (straight path), then he does Repentance; and these angels who have mourned over him, and left him, now come back to him and they joy in him and then he is surely alive; he is alive on all sides and united in the Tree of Life, and when he is united in the Tree of Life, he is called; *Ba-al Th'shubah, i. e.*, a Repentant Man."*

SAMÄ-EL AND THE FIRST SIN. From the Zohar i, 35*b*, Brody Ed.; Cremona Ed. i, fol. 28*a*, col. 110, Sepher ha-Bahir. "It is written: 'And the Serpent was more subtile than any beast of the field.' (Gen. iii, 1.) 'And the Serpent.' R. Yitz-haq said: 'That is the *Ye'tser ha-rah*.' R. Yehudah said: 'It is a real serpent.' When they came before R. Shim-on (b. Yohaï), said he to them; 'Surely it is all one, and it has

---

* Zohar ii, 106*b*, Brody Ed. Cremona Ed. ii, fol. 48*a*, col. 189, 190. Comp. Matt. vii, 13, 14. Luke xiii, 24. See Taylor's; Sayings of the Jewish Fathers, pp. 77, note 2.

been Samä-el and he has been seen on a Serpent, and his *tzelem, i. e.*, shadow image, and the Serpent, are Satan, and all are one.' We have learned; At that time when Samä-el descended from heaven riding on this Serpent and his *tzelem* was seen, all creatures saw his *tzelem* and they fled from him, and he reached to that woman with sweet words and he caused death to the whole world, surely with wisdom (subtility) he brought curses upon the world and ruined the First Tree (Adam) which the Holy, Blessed be He! created in the world."

From the Sepher'ha-Bahir § *Hashmutas* Zohar i, 12*b* in the Brody Ed. In the Cremona Edition in continuation of the above-cited page. "The *Neshamah* soul, of the male comes from Male, and the *Neshamah* of the female is from Female, and that is why the Serpent went after *'Havah* (Eve) he said (to himself), 'Because her soul is from the North, (the Left or Evil side)* I can persuade her quickly.' And the persuading has been because he came on her. The disciples asked; How did he that? Said he to them; 'Samä-el the Wicked. He conspired with all the hosts Above against his Master, because the Holy, Blessed be He! said (to Adam) You shall; 'Have dominion over the fish of the sea, and over the birds of heaven, etc.'† Said he (Samä-el) how can I make him (Adam) sin before Him; so that he shall be driven away from before Him; so he descended with all his hosts, and he sought upon the earth a companion like himself and he found the Serpent and it had a *d'mooth, i. e.*, appearance, like a camel; so he rode upon it and came to that woman: Said he to her, 'Did not Elohim say: You should not eat from all the trees of the *Gan, i. e.*, Garden.' Said she; 'We have not been forbidden only from the *Etz ha-Da-ath, i. e.*, Tree of Knowledge, which is in the Garden, and of that only, Elohim said; You shall not eat from it and not touch it or thou mayest die.' * * * What did Samä-el the Wicked, then do, he touched the Tree and the Tree *tsuva'h, i.e.*, cried out : * * * Samä-el said to her; 'Behold! I touched the Tree, yet I did not die, if you touch it you will not die.' The woman

---

* The ancient Hebrews always faced the East in worship, this brought the left side to the North. It will be noticed that, in the ancient Asiatic representations of the androgene, the woman's side is the left side. See also *Ante*, p. 120 and 142, and Fig. 36.

† The "fish" are the evil spirits, the "birds" are the angels.

touched the Tree and she saw that the *Malak Hamoveth*, *i. e.*, Angel of Death, came near to her, and she said; 'Surely I will die now, and the Holy, Blessed be He! will make another woman and give her to Adam, but I will do thus: 'I will cause him to eat with me, so if we die we shall both die together, and if we shall live we shall both live together.' So she took from its fruit and gave it to her husband. * * * So the Holy, Blessed be He! said to her; 'It is not enough to thee that thou hast sinned but thou hast brought sin to Adam too,' said she before Him; 'Lord of the World, the Serpent induced me that I should sin before Thee.' So the Holy, Blessed be He! brought all Three before Him and sentenced them with nine curses and death, and threw Samā-el and his followers down from the Place of their Holiness in Heaven, and cut the feet off the Serpent and cursed him, more than all the beasts and animals, and commanded that he should lose his skin after (every) seven years."*

THE SIN OF ADAM CAUSETH THE TASTE OF DEATH. "Come, See! If Adam had not sinned *none* would *have tasted* the *taste of death before* they ascended to the Upper World, but because he sinned so he *tasted the taste* of death *before* he ascended to the other world, and the *Rua'h* spirit, (of Adam) was separated from the *guff*, *i.e.*, body, and remained in this world; and the *Rua'h* spirit, has to cleanse itself in the river *Dinur* (Dan. vii, 10) to receive punishment, and afterwards he (the *Rua'h*) goes up to the *Gan Eden*, *i. e.*, Garden of Eden, on the Earth, and there are prepared for him other garments of light, like the *partsuph*, *i. e.*, appearance, of the *guff*, *i.e.*, body, in this world, and he (the *Rua'h*) is clothed in it and there is always his habitation." †

OF PARADISE AND HELL. "Said R. Yitz-haq; the Holy, Blessed be He! as well as He created a *Gan Eden* (Paradise) on earth so He also created a *Gāi-hinnom* upon earth, as well as He created a *Gan Eden*, *i.e.*, Garden of Eden, Above, so He created a *Gāi-hinnom* Above. He created a *Gan Eden* Below, on the earth: as it is written; 'And YHVH Elohim planted a Garden in Eden. (Gen. ii, 8.) He created a *Gāi-hinnom* in the earth: as it is written; 'A land of darkness, as darkness itself.' (Job

---

* Zohar i, 35*b*, and ¿ *Hashmutas*, 12*b*. Sepher ha-Bahir, Brody Ed. Cremona Ed. i, fol. 28*a* and *b*, col. 110, 111. Sepher ha-Bahir.

† Zohar iii, 159*b*, Rayah Me'hemnah, Brody Ed. Cremona Ed. iii, fol. 76*b*, col. 303.

x, 22.) He created *Gan Eden* Above: as it is written; 'But the *Nephesh* animal soul, of my lord shall be bound in the bundle of life with YHVH thy *Elo-hai*.' (I Sam. xxv, 29.) And it is written; 'The *Rua'h* spirit, shall return to Elohim.' (Eccl. xii, 7.) He also created the *Gäihinnom* Above: as it is written: 'And the *Nephesh* animal soul, of thine enemies (enemy) them shall he sling out as out of the middle of a sling (*Ibid.*)" *

Compare on this subject Kitto's Cyclopedia of Biblical Literature, Ed. 1876. Art. Hell, Paradise. On the Tree of Life in Paradise, etc., by Dr. Benjamin Kennicott.

OF SAMÄ-EL OR SATAN AND LIL-ITH. "The female (Lil-ith) of Samä-el was a maid-servant to the Matroneethah. And Samä-el, the other ail (el = god), was a servant to the Holy, Blessed be He! afterwards the causes (people) Below, made them to be an elohim, and the Holy, Blessed be He! is prepared to put them away from the world and entirely destroy them."†

LIL-ITH AND SAMÄ-EL. "When man connects himself in the Truth, that is in the Thorah; he needs to be tested on the same place where his father has been tested, so he shall go up perfect and come back perfect. Adam ascended but did not watch himself, but was seduced by her and sinned with, that *Esheth Z'nooneem*, *i.e.*, the Harlot, (Lil-ith) which is the First Serpent, *i. e.*, *Na'hash Qad'mo-ah*. It is written; 'And Ya-kob went from Beer-sheba, and went toward Haran.' (Gen. xxviii, 10.) 'And went towards Haran.' That is the side of the *Esheth Z'nooneem*, that is a harlot, which is a mystery. 'From the strength of Yitz-haq,' that is from the strength of judgment (Din), from the lees of old wine went out a spark which comprised male and female, and it spread itself out to many sides and paths; the male is called Samä-el and the female is always comprised in him, as it is on the Holy side so is it in the Evil side, male and female are merged in each other. The female of Samä-el which is

* Zohar i, 67*b*, col. 268, Midrash ha-Ne'elam. Cremona Ed. Brody Ed. i, 106*b*.

† Zohar iii, fol. 277*b*, Brody Ed. Rayah Me'hemnah. Cremona Ed. iii, fol. 134*b*, col. 536. Comp. as to Lil-ith, Kitto's Cyclop. Bib. Liter. ii, p. 834-5. Also *ante*, p. 248.

Na'hash, i. e., the Serpent, is called *Esheth Z'nooneem*."* Compare on this subject the Apocalypse as to the female companion of the Beast.

"Samä-el was clothed in the *d'yooq-nah* of an Ox, (whence the cloven hoofs), and Lil-ith in the *d'yooq-nah* of a Mule (which is sterile). But both are united as one." †

"The evil angry-maid, (which is Lil-ith) is the devastation of the world and she is the lash in the hands of the Holy, Blessed be He! to strike (punish) the guilty."‡

"*Lil-ith* is the mother of the *Shedim* and the *Maziqim*, i.e., the ensnarers."§

Na-amoh (Pleasure, Delight) ‖ is the mother of *Shedin*. She is considered as a very beautiful woman who drew down from heaven, the two great angels Uzza and Azaël, the principal of the *B'nai Elohim*. She has the power of assuming the form of a very beautiful woman. (Zohar i, 9*b*, 55*a*, Brody Ed.) *Aigroth* is also a great female demon. She is the daughter of *Ma'hlath* the female demon who causes sickness.

The Four Lower Oppositions to the Four Worlds, are I. The inclination of the heart towards Evil, the opposition to *A'tzeel-ah*. II. The actual thought of Evil in the *Rua'h*, the opposition to *B'ree-ah*. III. Use of Evil words, the opposition to *Ye'tzeer-ah*. IV. External Evil Action answering to the opposition to *A'seey-ah*.

If man turns his heart from the Deity, the latter turns His higher Sublime Face away, the She-kheen-ah leaves, and the *D'yooq-nah* withdraws from his *Neshamah*. If man's sin continues and he becomes hardened, Satan obtains complete control over the Divine *Tzelem* in him, and darkness and spiritual death rule over him and he has *Gāi-hinnom* in this life.

THE GREAT AND SMALLER DEMONS. "What is said: 'Let not Elohim speak with us, lest we die.' (Ex. xx, 19.) Those have been the ignorant (the mixed people) who have been with them (the Israëlites) and because they have been from the side of that Evil Serpent, of which is said by

---

* Zohar i, 147*b*, 148*a*, Sithrai Thorah, Brody Ed. i, 248*a*, Livorno Ed. Cremona Ed. i, fol. 86*a*, col. 342. *Ante*, p. 331.

† Zohar ii, 192*b*, Brody Ed. Cremona Ed. ii, fol. 84*b*, col. 336–337.

‡ Zohar ii, 190*b*, Raÿah Me'hemnah, Brody Ed. See also i, 190*a* and *b*.

§ Zohar ii, 268*a*, Brody Ed.

‖ See Dan. xi, 37, and Kitto's Cyclop. Bib. Liter. iii, Title, Nanea.

Him; 'That you shall be cursed of all the animals.' And there are many mixtures, but there are mixtures from the side of the Serpent * * * and also mixtures from the side of the *Maziqim, i. e.*, the strong hurtful demons, the souls of the guilty, they are the real *Maziqim* of the world. And there is also a mixture of the *Shedim, i. e.*, external destroying demons, and of the *Ru'hin, i. e.*, also hurtful spirits, and the *Lilin, i. e.*, children of Lil-ith, and they are all mixed in Israël, and none of them are so evil as *Amaleqh* which is the very Evil Serpent, the אל אחר 1 + 30 + 1 + 8 + 200 = 240 *ail a'hor, i.e.*, the other god.* He has been the revealer of all shame and evil things in the world, he is a murderer, and his other half is *Sam Moveth Az, i.e.*,† The Strong Poison of Death, and all are Samā-el, but it is Samā-el and Samā-el and not all are equal, but this side of the Serpent (the First Serpent) is the curse and worst of all."‡

"Come, See! To that place which is the Unclean Spirit (Samā-el), the Holy, Blessed be He! gave him dominion to rule in the world in many sides, and he can injure, and we have no permission to mock him, we must rather beware of him, that he shall not accuse us in our holiness."§

"Never shall man open his mouth to the Satan, because he is always present with man, so he will take those words and accuse us with them Above and Below." ||

"Come, See! In those evil species are *three* degrees, one above the other. The upper degree of these *three* hang in the air, the lowest degree of them, are these which laugh at people and trouble them in their dreams, because they are impudent like dogs. And there is a higher degree upon them which are from the Above and the Below, which make known to man things which are sometimes true and sometimes not true, and those things which are true they happen in the future." ¶

---

* עמלק Amaleqh 70 + 40 + 30 + 100 = 240, the same number by Gematria as *ail a'hor* also the same as מ"ר 200 + 40 = 240 *Mar, i. e.*, bitter. The initials are those of *Malak Rah, i. e.*, Evil Angel.

† This is the real Lil-ith, the mother of all the evil spirits.

‡ Zohar i, 28*b*, 29*a*, Brody Ed. Livorno Ed. i, 51*a*.

§ Zohar ii, 237*b*, Brody Ed. Cremona Ed. ii, fol. 116*a*, col. 461.

|| Zohar i, 175*a*, Brody Ed. Cremona Ed. i, fol. 99*b*, col. 396.

¶ Zohar iii, 25*a*, Brody Ed. Cremona Ed. iii, fol. 11*b*, col. 43. The Cremona Edition has not the words in *italics*.

THE ANGEL OF DEATH, ETC. "The *Malak Hamoveth, i.e.,* the Angel of Death, is at the same time the Deceiver, Satan and Accuser, what he does is the Will of the Holy, Blessed be He! Although he ought not to deceive but he does this because the Holy, Blessed be He! orders it through love to His children. This is like to a king who has an only son, and he loves him very much, and because of his love tells him not to go near evil women, because one who associates with such is not worthy to enter the king's palace, and his son promises him he would do his biddings. There was a beautiful but evil woman outside (of the palace). The king desired to test the will of his son, so he sent for this woman and said to her: 'Go and seduce my son!' She tempted the son of the king and caressed him and spoke to him sweetly with many words. If that son had been good and obeyed his father's words he would have repelled her, and his father, the king, would have been very happy and have taken him into the palace and rewarded him and given him great honor. But who would now have caused all this honor? This evil woman would have caused all this honor, and so she would be praised for it also because of the rewards to the son; so it is with the Angel of Death, because through him the just, if they do not follow the *Malak Hamoveth,* inherit all the hidden things Above; and if it were not for him, they would not (have been able to exercise their will for the good, and) have all this honor." *

"Above in the Tree of Life exist no strange *Q'lippoths* for it is said: 'With Thee dwelleth no Evil' (Ps. v, 5) but in the Tree, Below, exist the strange *Q'lippoths.*" (Zohar i, 27*a*, Brody Ed.) "Above are not any *Q'lippoth* for no one can enter in the Gate of the King in a rough (strange) garment, but the *Q'lippoth* are Below." †

BLESSINGS AND THE EVIL EYE. "That place is hidden from which all the blessings come, and therefore everything of man which is hidden, the blessings rest upon it; and all the things which are revealed that place is where judgment rests, *and he who rests upon that place is called Rah Ei-een, i. e.,* Evil Eye."‡

---

* Zohar ii, 163*a* and *b*, Brody Ed. Cremona Ed. ii, fol. 72*b*, col. 287–8.

† Zohar, Rayah Me'hemnah, Brody Ed. Joel, *Religions-philosophie des Sohar,* p. 291, note 1.

‡ Zohar i, 64*b*, Brody Ed. Cremona Ed. i, fol. 50*a*, col. 198. That in italics is not in the Cremona Edition.

"That we have said: In every place where the side of holiness rests, when the counting comes from the holy side, the blessing always rests upon it and never leaves it. From where do we know that? From מעשר *Maaser* Tithes, because this is the count to holiness so the blessing is found upon it; but all other things in the world which do not come from the holy side no blessing can rest upon it when it is counted, because the *Sith-rah a'h-rah* other side, which is the *Rah Ei-een* Evil Eye, can rule over it. * * * And when the enumeration is revealed although it is holy, also from it, *purqonah, i. e.*, remission, has to be given." *

"The Holy, Blessed be He! is prepared to expel the unclean *Rua'h* spirit, from the world." (Zohar i, 70b, Brody Ed.)

"The Righteous will be prepared to look upon the *Ye'tzer ha-rah* like an immense mountain and will wonder and say; 'How could we cross such a large mountain?' and the Evil (souls) will look upon him as if thin like a hair and they will wonder and say: 'How can we not cross over?' And both will weep. And the Holy, Blessed be He! will burn that Evil Spirit from the world so that he rule no more."†

THE COMING OF THE MESSIAH, DEATH OF ALL THE THEN LIVING, AND OF THE NEW KINGDOM. "It is written: 'I kill and I make alive.' (Deut. xxxii, 39.) That means: Till now death has been from *Sith-rah a'h-rah* the other side, but from now on 'I kill and I make alive,' that is, in that time (when the Messiah comes) all those who have not tasted the taste of death will die through Him, and He will revivify them at once. Why is this? Because nothing whatever of that pollution (the pollution of sin) shall remain in the world, and there will be a new world made by the Holy, Blessed be He!" ‡

"The *Q'lippoth, i. e.*, Shells and Evil Spirits, will not depart till the time of the Day of Resurrection, when the dead revive from the grave, then shall the *Q'lippoth* be broken and from the Brain inside, the light shall shine into the world."§

---

* Zohar ii, 225a, Brody Ed. Cremona Ed. ii, fol. 119b, col. 403.

† Zohar i, 190b, Brody Ed.

‡ Zohar ii, 108b, Brody Ed. Cremona Ed. ii, fol. 49a, col. 193. Livorno Ed. ii, 193b. Comp. Rev. xxi, 1; 1 Cor. xv, 51 *sq*.

§ Zohar ii, 69b, Brody Ed. Cremona Ed. ii, fol. 31a, col. 122.

438

We will now close, we have given but a very few of the many interesting passages of the Zohar for want of space. If a desire on the part of the public, justifies us in the attempt, we will, in the future, give many more which are of still greater value to the history of religion, theosophy and philosophy.

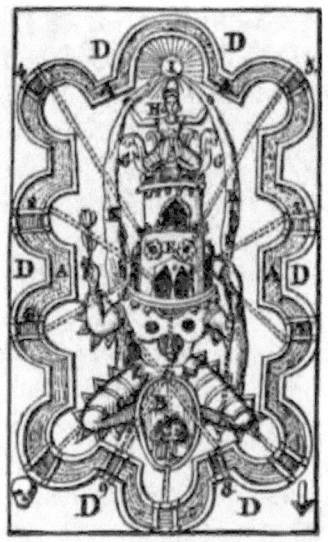

Figure 37.—A Hindu representation of the idea of the Makrokosm and Mikrokosm.

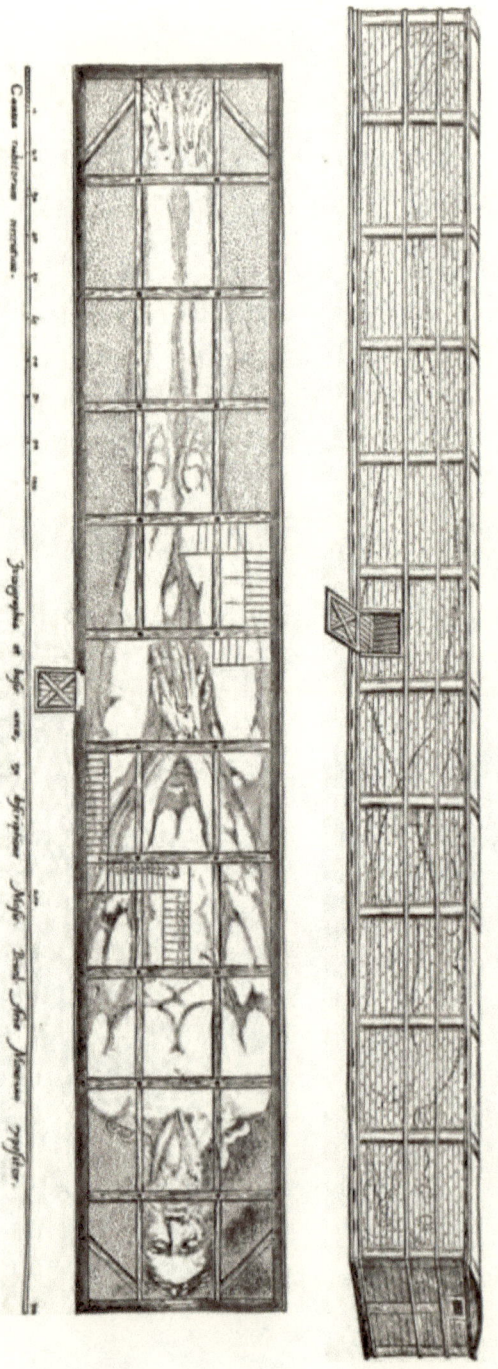

Figure 38.—A Medieval idea of the Makrokosm, in the Heavenly Zodiacal Ark.

APPENDIX A.

(First published in "The Keystone," Freemason Newspaper, Philadelphia, December 25, 1886.)

AN ANCIENT LODGE OF INITIATES.

FROM THE QABBALAH.

THE Qabbalah of the Hebrews is undoubtedly of great antiquity, a reminiscence of an ancient "Wisdom Religion" of Asia, for we find its doctrines, in germ, in the ancient Buddhist, Sanskrit, Zend, and Chinese books, also examples of its peculiar exegesis in the occult book, Genesis, and in Jeremiah. The present text-book of the Qabbalists is the *Sepher ha-Zohar*, Book of Illumination, or Splendor. This is a mystical, running commentary, on the Pentateuch or Thorah (Law), based on the *Sod, i. e.*, Secret Doctrine, and contains imbedded in it, as it were, a number of other very old writings, as is evident from their style and contents. Among these are some, asserted to have proceeded from an initiate, the Thanaite R. Shim-on ben Yo-'haī, who flourished, *circa* 110–203 A. D. He was a pupil of the great Qabbalist R. Akeeba, who was executed by the Emperor Hadrian, for participation in the Bar'ko-khab rebellion. These books are the *Siphra D' Tznioothah*, Book of Secrecy (Mystery, Retirement or Modesty), the *Idrah Rabbah*, or Great Assembly (of the Threshing-floor). This assumes the presence of the full and perfect number, ten initiates; and the continuation of the preceding two, the *Idrah Zootah* or Small Assembly, composed of the remaining seven, three having died during the giving the *Idrah Rabbah*. There is no doubt, from the Talmud, that this Thanaite had much of his time engrossed in teaching a school for the more elect, and for that reason, it is stated, was excused from the necessity of being present at all the prayers of the Synagogue. The Zohar and Zoharic writings were first made known as a totality, outside of the initiates, but written in a concealed manner, about the latter part of the thirteenth century, but many of the Qabbalistic doctrines therein are archaic, and can be traced to a very much earlier time. We find more or less of them in the Old Testament, Apocrypha, Book of 'Hanokh, New Testament, the Mishna, the early Patristic literature, in Philo, Josephus and the Hermetic books, later in the Neo-platonic school and that of Alexandria, and traces in the two Talmuds and in Gnosticism, especially the systems of Valentinus and Marcus. Also in the Dreams of St. Synesios; the writings of the pseudo-St. Dionysios, the Areopagite; the works of Saad-yah ha-Gaon, (892–942 A.D.); Sherira ha-Gaon (930–1000 A.D.); his son-in-law, R. Eliyah ha-Zaken; his brother, R. Yekuthiel; and of Haÿ Gaon, son of Sherira Gaon, (969–1038 A.D.) The latter is said to have been the first, who used the expression *Hokhmoth ha-Qabbalah, i. e.*, Wisdom of the Qabbalah; and from him, it has been said, it was borrowed by Ibn Gebirol, in the latter's *Tiqqoon Middoth ha-Nephesh, i. e.*, Adjustment of the Attributes of the (Life) Soul. Haÿ also speaks of the Sephiroth,* as do R. Azariel b. Mena'hem, Ibn Gebirol (Avicebron), and many others.

We give from the beginning of the *Idrah Rabbah*, the opening of an ancient Lodge of Qabbalists, which the learned initiates of to-day will appreciate, as its form goes back to *circa* 150 A.D., and existed likely long before, in ancient Chaldea. For the prophet who wrote on the banks of the Ke'bar, Ezekiel, is one of the greatest ancient Qabbalists, as appears from his asserted vision, which is really a Qabbalistic statement, and is a further development of Isaiah (vi, 1–8) and I Chronicles (xviii, 18 *et seq.* II Chron. iii, 8–13). The raising of the hands, appears on many of the Chaldean signet seals from 2600 B. C. down, as does also the idea of the Triad. This is especially evident in the stone Tablet found in the Temple of the Sun-god at Sipara, now called Abu Habba, and the cylinder seal of Dungi, King of Babylon, son of king Urukh.

The *Idrah Rabbah Qad-dusha*† says: "It has been learned: Said R.

---

* His language is quoted by the erudite Qabbalist, R. Moses Cordovero in his *Pardes Rimmonim*, Chapter on Splendor, § 1.

† Holy Assembly of the Threshing Floor. Cremona Edition. Vol. iii, fol. 61*a*, col. 242 *sq.*

Shim-on (ben Yo-'haï) to the Companions: 'How long shall we sit in the condition of a convivial company? It is written; 'It is time to work for YHVH, for they have destroyed Thy Thorah!' The days are short and the Creditor presses, the herald cries out daily,* and the mowers of the field are few in number, and those who are on the grounds of the vineyard (*i. e.*, humanity) do not care, and know not to what place to go as they ought to. Assemble Companions to the Threshing-floor in your breast-plates and (with) spears in your hands, be immediate in your preparation, in counsel, in wisdom, in understanding, in knowledge, in attention, in hands and in feet, make rule over you the King, in whose power is life and death, in order to determine sentences of Truth, words to which the Holy ones, Above, give heed, and delight to hear them and know them.'

R. Shim-on sat and wept, and then said: 'Woe if I reveal! Woe if I do not reveal!' The Companions who were there kept silent. R. Abbah arose and said to him; 'With the permission of the Master to reveal? 'The secret of YHVH is with those who fear Him,' and truly, these Companions here assembled are fearing the Holy, Blessed be He! They have just entered into the assembly of the House of the Tabernacle, some have entered and some have gone out.' It has been learned, that the Companions were numbered in the presence of R. Shim-on and there were found to be present, R. El'azar, his son; and R. Abbah, R. Yehudah, R. Yoseh son of Ya-kob, R. Yitz-haq, R. 'Hiz'qee-yah son of Rab, R. 'He-yah, R. Yo-seh, R. Ye-sah. They gave their hands to R. Shim-on and raised their fingers upwards,† and they entered into the field and sat down between the trees. R. Shim-on arose and offered a prayer and then sat down in

---

* Similar ideas are in Ibn Gebirol's *Kether Malkhuth*. Almost the same words are in the *Pirqé Aboth*. See Sayings of the Jewish Fathers, etc., by Charles Taylor, Cambridge, 1877, pp. 54, 55.

† See *Ante* pp. 218, 236. The initiates in the Qabbalah will understand the correct form. In this connection note the peculiar way of holding the fingers and hands by the figures, on the Akkadian, Babylonian and Assyrian cylinder signets, in the *Glyptique Orientale*, by J. Menant, Paris, 1883-1886. *Collection de Clercq*, Paris, 1885 *sq.* F. Lajard, *Culte Mithra*, also his *Culte de Venus;* Scribner's Monthly, January, 1887; and the American Journ. of Archæology, Vol. ii, No. 3.

their midst, and said; 'Let each one place his hands in my lap.'* They placed their hands and he took hold of them. He then began and said; 'Cursed be the man who shall make an idol or a molten image, the work of the hands of the craftsman, and putteth it in a secret place; and all the people answered and said, *Amen.*'† R. Shim-on began and said; 'It is time to work for YHVH.' What means 'Time to work for YHVH?' Because they have destroyed Thy Thorah (the Pentateuch, which is the Sacred Writing or Bible, *par excellence*, to the Israelite). What means 'They have destroyed Thy Thorah?' The Thorah from, Above, which will be made void, if it is not performed according to its requirements. Wherefore is this? To the *At-teek Yomen*, *i. e.*, Ancient of Days: (also called *A'reekh An-peen*, the Long Faces), for it is written: 'Happy art thou, Israël, who is like unto thee!' And it is written: 'Who is like unto Thee YHVH among the *Elim*, *i. e.*, Mighty ones!'" He called R. El-azar his son, and ordered him to sit down before him (*i. e.*, in front of him) and R. Abbah on the other side (*i. e.*, beside him R. Shim-on, the master), and (R. Shim-on) said: "We are typical of All; ‡ thus far the columns have been established. They kept silence, they heard voices, and their knees knocked together. What voices? They were the voices of the Congregation Above, which gathered together. (The spirits of the just (pious) and the She'kheen-ah or Divine Presence.) R. Shim-on rejoiced and said: "'YHVH I have heard Thy speech, I was afraid!' He said: 'There, this fear was becoming, but as to us, all depends on love, as is written: 'Thou shalt love YHVH Eloh'e-hu,' *i. e.*, thy Ail, and is written: 'While YHVH loves you,' and is written: 'I have loved you, says YHVH.'§ R. Shim-on began and said: 'He who walketh as a tale-

---

* An ancient Hebrew method of taking an oath. Gen. xxiv, 2; xlvii, 29. See Kitto's Biblical Cycl., Ed. 1876, iii, p. 348.

† The numerical value of אמן Amen, = 91, the same as the total value of, יהוה = 26 (YHVH) and אדני = 65 (ADoNaY).

‡ That is, now we represent the three columns of the Universe, the Right, Centre and Left columns of the Tree of Life, the Ten Sephiroth, or the whole universe.

§ The doctrine of Love to God is the keystone of all the true Mystics and Theosophers who have ever lived, but not goodness resulting from fear. See *Ante*, p. 429.

bearer revealeth a secret,' but the 'faithful in spirit concealeth a matter.' (Prov. xi, 13.) 'He who walketh a tale-bearer,' since is said; 'tale-bearer' why is said, 'he walketh?' A man 'a tale-bearer' ought to be said. 'Who walketh?' He who is neither sedate in his spirit nor true, the word which he has heard, is moved hither and thither as bran on the water, until the water drives it away. For what reason? Because his spirit is not a lasting spirit, but whose spirit is a lasting spirit, of him it is written: 'And the spirit concealeth the word.' The phrase 'faithful in spirit,' denotes firmness of spirit, as is said: 'And I will fasten him as a nail in a firm place.' The matter depends on secresy. And it is written: 'Suffer not thy mouth to cause thy flesh to sin.' And the world could not exist, but through that which is secret, and if with regard to earthly affairs there is need of mystery, how much more in matters the most secret of secrets in the *At-teek Yo-men* which are not even transmitted to the highest angels." (The just or righteous are considered by the Qabbalists as having more knowledge and as higher, than the angels.) Said R. Shim-on; "I will not tell the heavens to listen, I will not tell the earth to hear, for truly we now compose the columns of the world, *i. e.*, the ten Sephiroth."*

* The first Sephirah *Kether* the Crown, represents the Master; the sixth *Tiph'e-reth* Beauty, the sun; the last, *Malkhuth* the Kingdom, the moon. The first applies to the highest point of the head of the Makrokosm, the second to the heart, the third to the powers of continuing life, or perhaps soles of the feet. In this connection note: "The place of *the soles of my feet*" (Ezek. xliii, 7). Also the veneration among the Buddhists for the impression of the soles of Sakhya Mûni's feet. The Ten Upper Sephiroth as a totality, are the Qabbalistic Tree of Life, and the Adam Qadmon, or Great Man of the East, the Ideal or Celestial Adam, the Upper Makrokosm, the A'tzeel-atic Adam. Metatron is the B'ree-atic Adam, the Mediator between the Deity and His creatures. (Comp. I Cor. xv, 44–49. *Ibid.* xii, 12–27.) And in this Makrokosm, the Name YHVH, is contained; and when the Kingdom of YHVH (*i. e.* the Lord), is established upon this, our earth (see the great verse Rev. xi, 15), then; "YHVH shall be the king over all the earth; (and) on that day YHVH will be One, and His Name, One." (Zach. xiv, 9.)

Appendix B.

SYNOPSIS OF THE CHINESE QABBALAH. At a meeting of the Numismatic and Antiquarian Society of Philadelphia, held at its Hall, December 2d, 1886, I read a paper entitled: " The Chinese Qabbalah, or the Book called the Yih-King," of which the following is an abstract:

The esoteric religious metaphysics, now called Kabbalah or Qabbalah, are a reminiscence of an ancient " *Wisdom Religion*," which appears to have existed, at a most archaic period, in the Asiatic learned world. It is therefore not surprising, that its germs may be found in the ancient books of China. The oldest book of the Chinese which has reached our day is, most likely, the Yih King, *i.e.*, Book of Changes, said to have been first written 2850 B. C., in the dialect of the Akkadian or Black race, of Mesopotamia. The earliest historical antiquity of the Chinese, is with Fû-hsi, *circa* 3400 B.C., the lowest, with K'ung-Foo-Tse, *i.e.*, the Master Kung (Confucius b. 551, B. C.), about the time of the last Jewish return from Babylonia, a few years before the death of Sakhya Mûni. In the Yih, the Great Extreme is O, the two elementary forms are, male, active, ———, female, passive, ——— ———. The Yih has a system of numbers which recall the tetrad and decade of Pythagoras. Early Chinese scholars say: "In the Yih is the Great Extreme. When we speak of Yin (male), and Yang (female), we mean, the æther collected in the Great Void. When of Hard and Soft, the æther collected and formed into substance. The trigrams of the Yih contain the three powers, * * * the three powers unite and are one." * The process of change is production and reproduction. Kwei, the animal soul, is similar to the Hebrew, *Nephesh;* Shan, the intellectual soul, to the *Neshamah;* Khien, (the symbol of) heaven, is father; Khwān, (the symbol of) earth, is mother; Kan (manifests) the first application (of Khien to Khwān), resulting in the begetting of (the first) male (or undivided line), hence Kan (? Qua-in) is called the oldest son. "God

---

* Laou Tsz' had somewhat similar ideas. See *Ante*, pp. 112, 113.

comes forth in Kan (to his producing work)." This is apparently the B'ree-atic Adam or Metatron, the Makrokosm. The male numbers are, light circles and odd, 1, 3, 5, 7, 9; the female, dark and even numbers, are, 2, 4, 6, 8, 10. The light circles are Yang, vivifying energy, Thai Yang, the Great Brightness, the sun, male; the dark circles are Yin, the moon, female, plastic, called Thai Yin, the Great Obscurity. The Spiritual Light is represented by ———, the darkness by ——— ———. The numbers belonging to Heaven are 5, to earth 5. The triad or three powers are, Heaven, Man, Earth. The Man is the Great Man, paralleling the Makrokosm of the Hebrew Qabbalah. But it differs, in that the Great Universal Man of the ancient Chinese religion, is perfect, all active, nature. The perfect number is 10. The numbers for heaven, the ———, or male, are 2, 1, 6 = 9; for earth, the ——— ———, or female, 1, 4, 4 = 9; 216 + 144 = 360, (12x30 = 360.) Heaven is as the circumference of a circle, it is three times its diameter. Its number is 3. The earth is square, the circumference of a square, is four times its length or breadth, or is of two pair of equal sides. The number of the earth is 2. Heaven gives Form, the Earth is vitalized, receives Form. Life is the keeping of Form, death is the going back to Non-Form. In these, as in the Hebrew Qabbalah, is the harmony between the spiritual and material. It says, we can comprehend the invisible only through the visible. The Chinese say "God (Himself) cannot be seen, we see Him in the things which He produces." (Comp. Exod. xxxiii, 18–23.) The Yih says: "When we speak of spirit, we mean the subtile presence (and operation of God), within all things." The Chinese conception of the earth is that of a cube, and a cube has 6 sides, is a symbol of the content of all dimension, *i.e.*, length, breadth and depth; these are only grasped by the human mind through their positive and negative poles, which make 6, and with the energies of these poles, going out of and returning to the rest point, we have in the centre, the rest point, the cessation of motion or 7th day of Genesis. Khan is the lineal symbol of water, as a character, its meaning is "a pit, a defile;" so in the Qabbalah, the Deity cut into or excavated in the abyss, the face of the deep, the forms of the things. "The Superior Man," says the Yih, "in accordance with his large (nature) virtue (energy?), supports (men and) things." Khang-ze says of him: "Dwelling on high, and taking nothing from those below him, but on the contrary giving more to them, the Superior Man accomplishes his aim on a grand scale." This aim is to increase what others have, he is the life giving. "In his single person," says Lin Hsïyuan, "he sustains the burden of all under the sky * * * birds, beasts and creeping things, etc., depend on him for the fulfillment of their destined being." (Comp. Ps. viii.) The universe is a Makrokosm, humanity a Mikrokosm. (See the Yo Ki of the Li Ki § iii, 3.) Human reason is that of the Universe. The sage, the Yih says, knows the characteristics of the *anima* and the *animus*. The latter, *shan*, expands and ascends, in it the breath of life predominates in the essence of the animal soul, but the *anima* or *kwei* contracts, shrivels, goes back to earth and to non-entity. The Yih holds; everything is always in motion, expanding and contracting, similar to the *Tzimtzum* of the Hebrew Qabbalah. The Yang originates a shadowy outline, the Yin fills this outline with substance. Here is the Qabbalistic doctrine of the Balance as set forth in the Siphrah D'Tznioothah or Book of Secrecy, and the philosophical system of Ibn Gebirol, with which the much earlier writer, the pseudo-Dionysios, the Areopagite, is often in accord. The Hebrew Qabbalistic idea of the *Ain Soph*, the Without End, is stated by Wang Pi (A.D 226–249) in his Commentary on the Yih. The original of ALL appears to be the Supreme Desire, Wisdom, Reason or Word. The Hebrew Qabbalistic idea, of the first emanation or creation, being that of a point, *N'qoodah*, is the *shang* with *Tï-Shang-Tï*, the male-female, Chinese creating Deity. The point representing the *Yoni*, the inert plastic matter, is placed on the foreheads of Hindus and Japanese. With the Chinese, the creating Deity active, is expressed by 丅, when inactive 亠,* and we know that, mathematically, the centre of a geometrical point is infinitesimal. The Upper World is signified by the

---

* So in the Zohar, iii, 124*b*, Brody Edition, 1873; we have the following Figure: In the Hebrew Qabbalah these are the symbols of the Active and Passive, and they are called *Treisin*, *i. e.*, Searching, that is that either Name יהוה cannot be found alone, because one is always Mercy and the other always Judgment, but Judgment always tempers Mercy and Mercy always tempers Judgment. The Zohar asserts the world could not exist on either one, by itself.

first symbol. The dot denotes the descending heavenly scintillation. The second symbol is of the Lower World, and the ascending and returning heavenly scintillation is shown. The Chinese imagine three heavens or spheres, corresponding to those termed by the Hindus *vhü*, *vhüvar* and *svar*. The Chinese symbolize these three heavens by ☰, when they wish to symbolize the Lord of these, they cross them, with a perpendicular line 𐤅. Above this they put a dot, for the highest Deity.* We have in this the idea of the *Me'norah* or seven branched candlestick of the Hebrews. The three points in the heavens formed the holy triangle, symbolized by the Holy Balance of the Ark of the Covenant; the *She'kheen-ah* in the midst and above, the two Cherubim; one on the right, the other on the left, below. This represented the Divine Triad.

* NOTE.—Compare, the Angel-Messiah of Buddhists, Essenes and Christians, by Ernest De Bunsen. London, 1880, p. 57 *et seq.* Theolog. of the Chinese, W. H. Medhurst, Sen. Shanghæ, 1847, p. 198 *et seq.*

Figure 39.—Brahma Viraj, the Hindu androgenic first manifestation, of Brahman (*neuter*).†

† See my Article in, The Path, New York, 1886, p. 251 *sq.*

APPENDIX C.

CONSTRUCTION OF THE AKKADIAN, CHALDEAN AND BABYLONIAN, UNIVERSE.

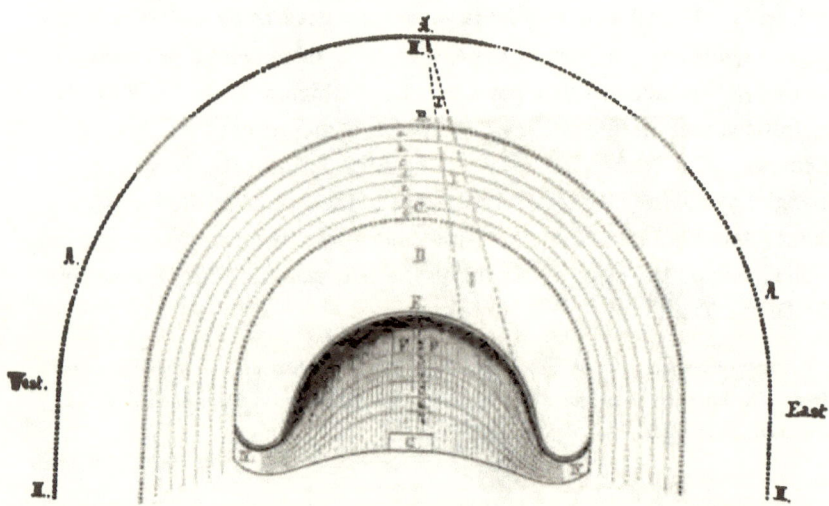

Diagram VI.—Represents a half section, divided perpendicularly, of the inverted bowl-shaped universe, which was the shape in which our universe was thought to exist, by the ancient Akkadians, Chaldeans, Babylonians, Assyrians, Hindus, Hebrews, and most of the very ancient peoples, and by many even in Medieval times in Europe, before the time of Copernicus; there being exceptions as we have mentioned (*Ante*, p. 139 *sq.*).

A, REPRESENTS the Zodiac. It was in Space and the Great Celestial Ocean. This Great Ocean or Sea was called the Deep and the Abyss. *T'hom*, the Great Dragon of this Great Sea was also called *Tiamat* or *Tiavat*. In Akkadian it was termed *ap-su* or *ab-zu*, *i. e.*, the dwelling place of knowledge. It was also termed *Zi-kum* or *Zi-gareem* the Heaven or Deep, which was considered as extending above the *firmament of heaven*: it was really the primordial Abyss out of which both heaven and earth proceeded. Subsequently it was called *Bahu*, "the Great Mother," and earlier, "the pure wild heifer." This was the *Bohu* of the Hebrew Genesis, and the *Baau* of the Phœnicians. *Bahu* was the plastic existing subtile chaotic matter, the azoth or æther mass, out of which, *barah*, *i. e.*, was scooped, the universe. *Thohu*, was the active energy, *Bohu* resisting energy. *Zi* or *Zi-kum*, *i. e.*, the spirit of the deep. (see *Ante*, p. 243 *sq.*) The Upper firmament was between A and C, from C to E was the Lower firmament. E represents the convex hollow earth shell. F F, the hollow concave under-world with its seven Zones, answering, as shadows, to the orbits of the seven planets. G was that part of the underworld called the *Nadir* (or Root) a word which has been anglicized. In it were "the waters of life." Below it were the 21 hells, the abode of demons. Extending beyond these upwards and around to an unknown distance, was the Great Crystal Sea, from or in which, the universe visible to man, was formed. B in Akkadian was *E'zara*, the zone of the fixed stars. A to B was the zone of *Ana* or *Ziana* the spirit of the heavens, called by the Semites *Anu*, also *Baal Sha'mayeem*. *Anu* means in Sanskrit an atom, and from this word probably comes our *annual*, and the Latin *anus* a circle. B to C was *ul-gana*, the lower part of the upper firmament. This was the zone of the planets, *i. e.*, *lubat* or *lu-bad*, also called, "the seven bell-wethers." They were "sheep," "wanderers," "watchers." It was the zone of lightning and thunders, and was ruled by *Bel* or *Baal:* the lower part was said to be ruled by him in common with *Ea* or *Hea* Wisdom.

The planets, in the Assyrian *bibbu*, were arranged by the Chaldean astrologers, as follows:

	Planet	Metal	Color	Symbols on the Boundary Stones.
1. *a.*	Saturn	Lead	Black.	Tortoise or Camel's head and neck.
2. *b.*	Jupiter	Tin	White, sometimes orange, or purple.	Bent horns arranged in a pyramidical shape.
3. *c.*	Mars	Iron	Red.	Spear head.
4. *d.*	Sun	Gold	Yellow or gold color.	Pointed star.
5. *e.*	Venus	Copper	Green or Yellow Green.	Wedged shaped symbol. (*Yoni ?*)
6. *f.*	Mercury	Quicksilver	Blue.	Erect serpent alongside of bent horns arranged in a pyramidical shape.
7. *g.*	Moon	Silver	Silver or silvery white.	Crescent.

Venus is placed next to the sun. This arrangement is required to produce the artificial sequence of the planetary names of the days of the week, as we now have them. It is one of the proofs that these came to us from the people of Archaic Babylonia. C to E was the zone or firmament of the atmosphere, of winds, storms and clouds. In it poured forth the rain through *ganul, i. e.*, gutters. This zone rested upon the convex Earth-shell E. The Earth-shell was called, "the countries." Its spirit was *si-ki-a*. F, F, was under E, the Earth-shell. It was the realm of the king of the ghost-world, the king of the dead, *Mul-lil* or *Mul-ge*. It was also at one time thought to be especially ruled by *Ea* or *Hea*, the deity of Wisdom. It was thought to contain seven zones. (*Ante*, p. 415 *sq*.; Is. xiv, 15.) The dead were said to be awarded positions in the different zones dependent on their sins when alive, but this point is not settled among Assyriologists. The good who died may have gone at once to the "land of the Silver Sky." F, F, was called *Ge*, note the *Gāi* of *Gāi-hinnom*, also the place of *El-im*, and of *Mul-ge* or *Mul-lil*, its king. It was the realm of *Nin-ki-gal* or *Allat*, queen of *Hea* or of *Mul-ge*. She was queen of "the Great Country;" "the country from whence none return;" "the land of no-return;" "the tomb;" "temple;" and of *ekur-bat*, "the temple of the dead." In some respects it was like the Hebrew *Sheol* (Is. xiv.) G, was the Nadir, the opposite of this, was (*nuz-ka*) perhaps the Zenith. It was also "the foundation of the whole universe," and in it, was the throne of *Bahu* or Chaos, near which were "the waters of life." I, was *Kharzak-kurra*, the mountain of the East or, of the world. The ark was said to have rested upon it. The gods lived upon it like the Hindu deities did on Mt. Meru, and the Greek deities on Mt. Olympus and Mt. Atlas. It supported the firmament, and by some of the texts, it may be thought of as rooted in the Nadir. (Comp. Is. xiv, 13-14.) The Old Testament several times speaks of a Holy Mountain of God. The cuneiform texts imply it was used by the gods, like Jacob's Ladder, to go up and down on. (See *Ante*, p. 245.) It widened at the top and upon that they lived. It may have some reference to the polar star and the apparent revolutions of the heavens around it. II, is the Great chaotic Crystalline Sea, *abzu-arra;* or *arra* the river, surrounding the Earth-shell, and extending an indefinite distance. III, *Nuz-ka* was on the top of the World-mountain. It was the pivot of the starry vault. IV, are the gates or entrances controlled by porters, to the underworld, the abode of *Allat*. A place for the ghosts of the dead, also for punishment. In it were held the "waters of life" a parallel perhaps to the Tree of Life.

An idea of the Egyptians and Hebrews, was, that the universe was depicted by the layers of an onion; (see *Ante*, p. 415 *sq*. The former considered in early times, that vegetable, as too sacred to be eaten.) The Mohammedans and Russians, from the onion-shaped domes of their sacred buildings, seem to have a similar idea as to this vegetable. Through the gloomy regions of the underworld the ancient peoples of Babylonia and Chaldea, thought the nocturnal journey of the sun took place. All the stars, planets, etc., revolved around *Kharzak-kurra*, the Mountain of the World, as to which the idea is pre-historic. It was the central shaft around which the heavens and earth were built, perhaps was referred to the North star, around which the Dipper appears to float. This pivotal point, the top of the world-mountain, was not thought of as the zenith for that was immediately above the land of Akkad, but the mountain which was the pivot upon which the firmament revolved, was to the North East of the land of the Akkadians and Babylonians. Beyond this mountain was the land of Aralli, rich in gold* and inhabited by the blessed spirits and the gods. It was from the under-world F, F, that the demons of death and disease came, but they were subject to the control of the heavenly gods, and as we have said, it is not certain that the Akkadians and archaic Babylonians considered F, F, as the place inhabited by the dead of mankind, they may have been placed in the yet lower abodes, and F F have been considered the place occupied by the Evil Spirits, Gnomes, etc.

The *Maskim*, *i. e.*, ensnarers, who are also mentioned in the Zohar, (As *Maziqim*. See *Ante* p. 434 *sq*.) obey the command "which comes from the midst of Heaven, the evil destiny which issues from the depths of the Abyss." One of the cuneiform tablets says:

"They are the productions of the infernal regions,
On high they bring trouble, and below they bring confusion."

They penetrate everywhere:

"Doors do not stop them,
Bolts do not stop them, they glide in at the doors like serpents."

Each part of the body had a demon to affect it, *Idpa* was the fever, *Namtar* the plague, *Utug* held the forehead, *Alal* the chest, *Gigim* the bowels, and *Telal* the hand.

* Comp. Zohar i, fol. 132*a*, col. 526. Brody Ed. i, 249*b*, 250*a*.

The people had great fear of darkness, as did the ancient Hebrews, and the old and modern Hindus.

The images of the spirits were amulets and talisman, and were cut on stone and worn suspended from the neck; magic knots and bands, enchanted waters, magic numbers, especially seven, and the supreme ineffable name, known only to Ea;* were especially sacred. The figures of the winged bulls with human heads, *Sed*, *Alap* or *Kirub* (cherub), placed at the portals of palaces, were talisman which were supposed to contain invisible genii which were bound to the door posts as long as their images remained there; the Jews to this day, place amulets, *Me'zuzzah* (*Ante* p. 67), in the door posts of their houses and use the *Phylacteries*. Some of the genii, *e.g.*, *Nergal*, had a lion's body with a man's head, sometimes a man's body and a lion's head, *Nattig* an eagle's head, *Ustar* a human likeness.† On the cylinder signets are representations of, the good and evil, light and darkness, a solar myth and the spirit of chaos and disorder, fighting.‡ These signets were not only talismans, but the impression of the intaglio was supposed to preserve the objects impressed, from the influence of evil spirits. In the poem of the Descent of *Ishtar*, the infernal regions are divided into zones like those in the Zohar and parallel the poem of Dante, and the magic tablets mention, "seven doors and seven fastenings of the world" controlled by porters.§

The main entrance to the Underworld was in the West, near the Mountain of the West (or, South-West). The "great porter" of this gate was *Negab*, the "porter of the world," this gate would be in opposition to the Mountain of the East or North-East, the abode of the gods and the blessed.‖ In the west the sun disappeared beyond the waters of the Great Ocean. This gate was asserted to be guarded by two human-headed bulls or genii, one on each side, inside were twelve gods of bronze sustaining the bronze inclosure. In the Underworld were, "seven gods

---

* See, Descent of Ishtar to Hades, as to the word given by Ea to the Phantom.

† Comp. Ezek. i, 10–14. Records of the Past iii, 121. F. Lenormant's Chal. Magic, pp. 39, 47, 121.

‡ Smith's Chald. Genesis, pp. 62, 95–96, 102, 174, 239. *Ante* p. 237 *sq*.

§ See, The *Hakhailoth*, *i. e.*, Palaces and Dwellings. Zohar i, 38a to 45b, Brody Ed.

‖ Trans. Soc. Bib. Arch. ii, p. 188. Chald. Magic, p. 167.

sons of the lord of the infernal regions, *Eni-mesari* or *Nin-a-yu*, Darkness (Assyr. Dis., Smith, 199), who dwell in flame." Inside of the bronze inclosure another genii was invoked. The demons of disease "came forth from Hell" and were "the productions of the tomb." The plague, *Namtar*, was the favorite son of *Mul-lil* or *Mul-ge* the king of the demons, by his queen *Nin-ki-gal*. *Mul-ge* was the father of seven evil spirits who warred against Heaven and the Moon. The nocturnal Sun, *Nin-dara*, was his child, it fought against the demons and plagues, and when hidden from the Chaldeans it was thought to be combatting the Darkness, the demon *Tiamat;* as it also was said to have done on the first day of the creation. It triumphed by its rising. The demons were especially inhabitants of the desert,* but they also entered into and took possession of man and diseased him.† Then there were frightful ghosts, the *Innin*, the *Uruku* a hobgoblin, and larva, the worm that dieth not.‡ *Alal, Gigim, Telal, Mazkim* (Maziqim?) the Phantom, Spectre, and the Vampire and Lil-ith. The latter two attacked man, the two named previously to these, only frightened him. Then there were the *Incubus*, *Succubus* and the *Nightmare*. These were a few of the frightful productions of the fearful mythology of the early Semitic inhabitants of Mesopotamia, Chaldea and Babylonia, which they had received from the Black race, the Turanian Akkadians.

The sorcery of the Chaldeans was of two kinds; one, came from the power of the gods constraining the action of the demons, which partakes of the characteristics of a religion, and may be termed White Magic: the other sought to propitiate the demons. The latter is witchcraft and devil worship, it is necromancy or negromancy, Black Magic.§ Along with the priests of the gods, witches and wizards legally flourished to an enormous extent. They were both feared and hated. (Chald. Magic, p. 60.) Their great enemy was the light, the sun ; their sorceries were therefore

---

* Chald. Magic 31. Isa. xxxiv, 13-14.

† Chald. Magic 20-21, 32-33. Trans. Soc. Bib. Arch. ii, 56. The Thrones and Palaces of Babylon, Newman, 116.

‡ Isa. lxvi, 24. Mark ix, 44-46, 48.

§ Comp. Tylor's, Primitive Culture, also his, Researches into the Early Hist. of Mankind.

prepared in the darkness of night. The spell or charm was, "that which acts, that which is bad, that which is violent." The formula of the wizard was called "the Work;" the incantation was, "the Word;" the Philter; "the Mortal Thing." The sorcerer caused "the Evil Eye;" the "Unlucky word;" and the demons became subject to him, and he sent them against persons and countries. He could even kill if he wished, and do this by making images of wax, etc., such as were afterwards used by the Medieval sorcerers of Europe.* The most potent form with the sorcerer was "the Imprecation," by this he was supposed to gain power over the protecting spirit of the individual.† Above these and above the world-shell, were the angels, the *Ideds* and *Igigi*, the celestial; and within it, the *Anúnaki* the gnomes, and the terrestrial, spirits.‡ The archangel of the Abyss was *Anúnna-ge*.§

When we come to investigate the kosmos of the Siphrah D'Tznioothah, Idrah Rabbah and Idrah Zootah, of the Book Zohar; we find a remarkable similarity, which tends to show the Chaldean kosmos in these oldest books of the compilation called the Zohar. In A B, B C, C E, and E G we have similarities to the Four Worlds. The three great heavens answer to the Upper Three Sephiroth. I. That of the Father, Abba, or *Kether*, the Crown, to *Anu* afterwards *Ana;* the place of the æther or highest sublimated air or atmosphere. II. The Son, Bel, El or Baal, the sublimated fire, answering to '*Hokhmah*, Wisdom. III. The Mother, Immah, to Ea the sublimated water, to *Binah*, the comprehending Intellect. Above all of these is *Ao*, *Ilu* or *El*, the unknown ideal deity; which parallels the *Ain Soph*, Endless to man's comprehension No-Thing. This unknown ideal deity, held the highest place in the Chaldean Mythology. Under these were the seven planets in their seven orbits, or spheres; the probable germ of the idea of the Sephiroth, or media between the Highest and Lowest worlds. The Tower of Borsippa (Babel?) parallels the Mt. Meru of the Hindus; each of its seven stories was devoted to a

---

* Chald. Magic, pp. 5, 43, 61–63.

† *Ibid.* pp. 68, 64.

‡ Chald. Magic, pp. 138, 148, 122. See, Book of Enoch, c. 68–77.

§ Chald. Magic, p. 164. Comp. on the subject of Magic; Rydberg's, Magic in the Middle Ages.

planet, a metal, and a color, as Sir Henry Rawlinson discovered and has written upon.

The connection between the Ten Sephiroth and the orbits of the planets, may be a solution of the puzzle of the learned for over 800 years, and may show that the seven-storied Tower of Solomon's Temple, Mt. Meru, the Tower of Borsippa, Jacob's Ladder and the Holy Mountain, (Ezek. xxviii, 14, xx, 40; Ps. lxxxvii, 1 ; Is. xi, 9, lvii, 13, lxv, 11) have a great similarity between themselves and refer to seven storied planet towers, and so have a connection with the Seven Lower Sephiroth. The curious heretofore unexplained craniums or skulls, etc., of *A'reekh An-peen*, the Long Faces, and of *Ze'ir An-peen*, the Small Faces, would be similar to the skull shape of the divisions of the Chaldean universe. The eyes of the latter, white, red and black, may be the sun in its different phases; these eyes are like those of fishes, not having lids; they are in the Great Crystalline Sea:* the hairs of the head and beard are the effluxes or emanations flowing from the Highest, and bringing down the " Dew of Life " which "supports the existing and resurrects the dead." The universe as this Great Head, has ears to hear, witness, sound; eyes to see, note the rays of the sun ; and its mouth throws out the breath of vitality upon all. In the Book of Enoch ('*Han-okh*) we have descriptions which appear to have as a foundation, the plan we have shown.† In the Chaldean Universe is; the Mountain whose point reaches to heaven, the Water of Life, the Great Sea, into which the sun sinks in the West and from the East side of which it rises; there is the place of the departed spirits, " the Great Darkness," *Sheol*. The Nadir is also mentioned, as " the great corner stone of the earth," the "four pillars of heaven," etc. The watchers, in Enoch, are the planets. (Compare Enoch 93–104–105, c. xviii, 24; c. xxii, 9 ; also c. vii, § 2 and viii; and Tobit vi, 13.)

* *Ea* the Deity of Wisdom, is " the great fish of the ocean " or " the sublime fish." Chald. Magic, p. 156 *et seq.* He is *Oannes*, the Chaldean Fish god.

† Schodde's Enoch, Andover, 1882, p. 89.

Appendix D.

THE MYSTIC THEOLOGY OF DIONYSIOS, THE AREOPAGITE.

CHAPTER I.

A DESCRIPTION OF THE UNKNOWN DEITY WHO IS IN THE DARKNESS.

To Timothy:

SECTION 1. Triad above all substance, super-divine and above the Good, guide of the Christians into the Divine Wisdom,* conducting us to that above agnosy, *i. e.*, the unknowable, to the highest clearness and the super-eminent height; in which the simple, absolute, and immutable mysteries of theology, are to be discovered in the bosom of the super-luminous obscurity,† by a silence, which is initiator to the arcana:— obscurity which, in the thickest darkness, shines forth with the greatest splendor, and, under a perfect intangibility and invisibility, overfills with charms above beauty, the eye of the intellect.

Behold this my prayer:—

Do thou, my friend Timothy, exercise thyself without relaxation in the mystical pageant, departing from the side of the senses and intellectual operations, the wholly sensual and intelligible, the entire being and non-being; and by means of the agnosy (*i. e.*, knowledge not obtained from the material) elevate thyself, as far as possible, to a union with that which is above all substance and gnosis, (*i. e.*, materialistic knowledge.)

Because it is through that free, sincere and pure ecstasy, outside of thyself and of all (the material;) that, renouncing the same and disen-

---

* " For the knowledge of the Divine Intelligence, study not the existences through the existing, for It is in Itself and through Itself, Its own quality and cause.   *   *   *   The Gnosis of all, in place of considering each thing in its idea, perceives and conceives all under its embrace as one cause,   *   *   *   the Divine Wisdom, in Itself knowing, comprehends All." Dionysios on, the Divine Names, c. vii, § 2. "He *made darkness His Secret Place*, His pavilion around about Him were *dark waters* in cloudy skies." Ps. xviii, 11, Comp. Ex. xix, 9; II Sam. xxii, 10, 12; I Kings viii, 12; II Chron. vi, 1.

† Faith *is the substance* of things *hoped for,* the *evidence of things not seen.* Heb. xi, 1.

gaging thyself from all, thou wilt elevate thyself to the super-substantial splendor of the Divine obscurity.

SECTION 2. Preserve as to all of this, that which should not be understood by the profane (multitude), that is, (keep it) from the men who, plunged into the material, imagine that above it there is not anything super-substantial; and believe they understand by their own knowledge, that which has taken the darkness for Its retreat.

But if the divine mystagogy goes beyond their capacity, what shall we say of those men still more profane, who, representing the super-eminent Cause of All by the last of the existences; pretend that the Deity does not excel anything above the atheistic and multiform phantoms of their own fabrication.*

Whilst we ought to bestow on the Deity, by affirming as in It, all the compositions of the existences, since of ALL, the Deity is the Cause (Acts xvii, 28), or, better still, by denying them all; because the Deity is ruler above ALL; and having in our thought that these negations do not contradict those affirmations, but that, so much as it is, through the excess of priority above the privations, the Deity is above all division and all composition.†

SECTION 3. It is then with this meaning in his mind that the divine Bartholomew says: That theology is at the same time ample and brief, and that the Gospel, though vast and developed, is nevertheless concise.

It has seemed to me supernaturally understood, that the good Cause of All expresses Itself in many words, in a few words, and also without words, there not being for It either speech or intellection, because, It is super-substantially superior to all (words and intellectuality;) and that the Deity manifests Itself, in openness and in truth, only to those who, traversing all impurity and purity, leaping over the height of the most sublime sanctity, and putting aside henceforth all the divine lights, all sounds, and all celestial words; to by so doing swallow themselves up, as it were,

---

* Rom. i, 23.

† The Deity is pure action, essentially existent, containing essentially all the perfections in their greatest absoluteness and simplicity, yet we cannot bind or limit It by asserting any of Its qualities. Comp. also Aristotle, Metaphysics, Bk. iv, c. xxii.

in the darkness, in which in reality, as the oracles (*i. e.*, the Scriptures) teach, is the Deity which is above All (the created.)

So it was not without a motive that the divine Moses received the order to at first purify himself,* and then separate himself from the impure† that, the purification accomplished, he (might) understand the various sounds of the trumpets, and might see the multiplied fire which threw out numerous and limpid rays; and who, in short, departing from the multitude, ascended with his chosen priests‡ as far as the summit of the Divine ascensions. At the same time Moses had not any conversation with God, no more than he could perceive God, because *God is unperceivable;* he saw only *the Place* (*Ma-qom*) in which the Deity was. This signifies, in my view, that the most divine and sublime objects in the visions or intellections, are in some way, only the insinuative expressions of the attributes of the Deity, who exceeds all: expressions which indicate Its presence, above all intellection; passing over the intellectual summits of the most holy places. (Comp. Prov. iv, 18, 19.)

And then (the man,) delivered as much from that which is seen as from that which sees, penetrates into the true mystic obscurity and darkness of the agnosy; in which, he lays aside all the conceptions of knowledge (the gnosis), so as to find himself in the intangible and invisible under all its affinities, entirely the object above all, no longer in himself or others; united, in a most excellent manner, to the absolute agnosy through the inaction of the gnosis, and, through that he understands No-thing, knowing all that is above intelligence. (Exod. xx, 21.)

* Exod. xix, 10. *Ibid.*, iii, 5.
† Exod. xix, 12.
‡ Exod. xix, 24.

APPENDIX E.

THE DOGMAS IN THE NICENE CREED AND THE QABBALAH.

IT will be observed in three of the Diagrams or Qabbalistic Trees of the Sephiroth which we have given, that 'Hokhmah Wisdom, or the Son, the Greek, *Logos* or Word; proceeds as No. 2 directly from *Kether*, Crown, the Abba or Father, and that *Binah* Understanding, the Upper Mother or Holy Spirit is placed No. 3. Those who are interested in the subject of the relation of the *Logos* to the Father, should compare the doctrines of the New Testament with those of Philo, and the Early Fathers of the Church, prior to the Council of Nicæa, of which the Roman Catholic theologian, Hefele,* has given a resumé.† There is warrant in the Zohar for asserting that No. 2 should be *Binah* and No. 3, '*Hokhmah*, but most of the Diagrams make the Son proceed directly from Abba. The Creed adopted by the Council of Nicæa (325 A. D.) as given in the English edition of Hefele (the Italics are by us), is:

"We believe in one GOD, the Father Almighty, Creator of all things visible and invisible; and in one Lord JESUS Christ, the *Son* of GOD, *only-begotten* of the Father, that is, *of the substance* of the Father, GOD of GOD, light of light, very GOD of very GOD, *begotten, not made*, being *of the same substance with the Father*, by whom all things were made in heaven and in earth, who for us men and for our salvation came down from heaven, was incarnate, was made man, suffered, rose again the third day, ascended into the heavens, and He will come to judge the living and the dead. And in the Holy Ghost. Those who say; There was a time when He was not, and He was not before He was begotten, and He was made of nothing (He was created), or who say that He is of another hypostasis, or of another substance (than the Father), or that the Son of God is created, that He is mutable, or subject to change, the Catholic

---

* A History of the Christian Councils, from the original documents, to the close of the Council of Nicæa, A. D. 325, by Charles Joseph Hefele, D.D., etc. English Trans. Edinburgh, 1881. Book ii, c. i, § 18, p. 231 *sq.*

† See also History of Christian Doctrine, by Prof. Henry C. Sheldon. New York, 1886, Vol. i, p. 53 *sq.* Especially p. 63 *sq.*, p. 194 *sq.* Schaff's Creeds of Christendom, etc., hereafter cited, Vol. i, p. 24 *sq.*

Church anathematizes."* The student will find very interesting thought in comparing ante-Nicene Patristic Literature and the Nicene Creed, with the early religious philosophy contained in the Zohar.

APPENDIX F.

THE ANTIQUITY OF THE HEBREW VOWEL POINTS.

WE will not be able, for want of space, to give our views in full upon the antiquity of the Hebrew vowel points. We have examined the Zohar thoroughly upon the subject and in several places some of them may be found named, but there are not as many as are now found in the Hebrew grammars. The Phœnician and early Hebrew alphabets are quite similar, and most likely both are from a common source. The Arabic probably came through them, and although the Greek and Latin alphabets are Aryan and have a Sanskrit basis, yet there are certain similarities in them to the Phœnician and the Hebrew. The reader should consult the writings of Isaac Taylor and François Lenormant on the Alphabet in this connection. In the Greek, the letters *A alpha, E ep'silon, H e'ta, I iota, O om'ikron* and *Y u'psilon,* were used as vowels. In Hebrew the nearest approach to vowel sounding letters are א *a'leph,* ה *heh,* י *yod,* and ע *ayin.*

The Pentateuch Rolls used in the Synagogues by the Jews are never vowelized. The Gaon Natrunai ii, b. Hilai, of Sora (859–869 A. D.); says; "And you enquire of me whether it is permissible to punctuate the Pentateuch. We have not any punctuation in the Pentateuch and

* Hefele's, History of the Christian Councils, etc., pp. 293–5. The original Greek is also given. Sheldon, History of Christian Doctrine, etc., before cited, gives a different reading, see his Vol. i, p. 201. John Fulton, D.D., Index Canonum, etc. New York, 1872, pp. 118–119, gives the original Greek and an English reading, differing from that of the above cited writers. Compare also: The Creeds of Christendom with a History and Critical notes, by Philip Schaff, D.D., LL.D. New York, 1877, Vol. ii, pp. 57–60; Vol. i, pp. 28, 29. Dr. Schaff gives the Greek, also a Latin and an English translation.

the punctuation was not given on Sinai, only the wise-men ordered it for a sign."

We would here say that there are two forms of Hebrew vowel pointing.

I. That of Babylonia now termed the Assyrian, in which it is above the letters. II. That of Palestine or that from the School of Tiberias, in which it is below the letters. The general opinion of the Jewish learned men of the Middle Ages was, that the pointing went back to the epoch of the writing by Ezra although many Jews held that it went back to Moses. The former, was the opinion of Ibn Ezra, Yehudah ha-Levi, and also of the Buxtorfs, Raimundi Martin, Perez de Valentia, Nicholas de Lyra, John Calvin and Martin Luther, indeed one of the Synods of the Swiss Protestant Church, declared the inspiration of the vowel points of the Hebrew Old Testament an Article of Faith. In the XVI century, based on the writings of Elias Levita, b. 1469, d. 1549; called by the Jews the Grammarian, a contrary opinion arose. Levita was the teacher of Hebrew to Cardinal Ægidio de Viterbo, Sebastian Munster, Paul Fagius and other illustrious Christian Hebraists of the Renaissance. Louis Cappel (Cappelus) of Saumar (1585–1658) in 1624; Jean Morin in 1669, and François Masclef in 1716, adopted similar opinions. Indeed the opposition went so far, that in 1732–3, C. F. Houbigant and his followers, asserted that not only was the vowel notation very recent but that the Tradition to the Reader, upon which it is based, had not any foundation. A third view was intermediate, it held, that the present *written* designation of the vowel points was not very old but that it represented an ancient *oral* tradition, sufficiently exact, of the ancient pronunciation, and had taken the place of a still more ancient and rudimentary system. This is the view now generally accepted. It was first proposed by J. H. Hottinger (1620–1667) and he has been followed, with some modifications, by John Prideaux in 1648, A. Schultens (1686–1750) also by Michaëlis and Eichorn. François Lenormant holds, that Ezra wrote the Old Testament in the ancient Aramaic alphabet, which approaches the writing termed Rabbinic, and not in the present square character, which he says was not in use until about 100 B. C., and that Ezra did not use diacritical signs for the vowels. Isaac Taylor agrees with him as regards the square character. In the Targums we see the first traces of the vowel notation. The age of the Targumim is in dispute. The Zohar says, that of Ounqelos, was from the disciple of Hillel the Babylonian, *circa* 60 B. C.* It was undoubtedly known in the II century. The other that of Yonathan ben Uziel, is apparently after that of Ounqelos. It is said earlier examples than those in the Targumim exist.† The Talmudim also mention certain signs. When the Jewish nationality and undoubtedly also books, were destroyed by the Romans, the learned priests feared that the ancient oral tradition of reading the Holy Writings would be lost, and this would also have caused a loss of the true meaning of the Thorah, therefore they sought to fix and preserve the traditional pronunciation as it had come down to them, intact and as it were in an inflexible matrix. This they did by revealing the secret oral system through a written symbolism and so established a notation of pronunciation, but it must be said, the pronunciation fixed at Tiberias was that used by that School. This object is indicated by the precept in the *Pirqé Aboth* c. i, § 1.‡ "Make a fence to the Thorah." So we also have in the Talmud§ "The children of Yudah have carefully cultivated their language, and have placed below, the signs of pronunciation, so they have preserved their Thorah in their hands. The children of Gallilee have not carefully cultivated their language, and have not placed below (the letters) the signs of pronunciation; so they have not guarded their Thorah between their hands." That is, the Talmud attributes to the unfaithfulness of the Gallileans to the Mosaic law, the corruption of their language and forgetfulness of the true pronunciation of the Thorah, because of the absence of the proper vowel signs. The Massoretic doctors of Tiberias directed their attention more to a criticism of the text than to a study of grammar, and the *invention* of the vowel points did not naturally or necessarily enter into their work. The view of Yehudah ha-Levi‖ was, that the Massorites only put into writing and gave a

---

* Comp. McClintock and Strong's Cyclop. of Biblical Liter. x, p. 123. This evidences the antiquity as stated in the Zohar. It holds Ounkelos was about the time of Jesus.

† See, On Mankind, their Origin and Destiny. London, 1872, chap. ii.

‡ Comp. Chas. Taylor's, Sayings of the Jewish Fathers. London, 1877, pp. 25, 68 and notes. Renan *Hist. des langues sémitiques*, 1st Ed., p. 160.

§ Treatise *Nedarim*, fol. 53.

‖ Khuzari. Part ii, § 80; iii, §§ 28, 31, 35.

form to, the Secret Oral Tradition given at Sinai, which Ezra had not dared to transcribe. We assert that it was not by one man nor in a short time, that the symbolic signs of the traditional pointing and accenting were formulated, it took a long period and many learned men of different epochs.* The Zohar, On the Song of Solomon, says: "The vowel points proceeded from the same Holy Spirit which indited the Holy Scriptures, and that far be the thought to say; the Scribes made the points, since even if all the prophets had been as great as Moses, who received the Thorah direct from Sinai; they could not have had authority to alter the smallest point in a single letter, though it be the most insignificant in the whole Bible." † The Massorites applied, wrote and propagated, the vowel points in existence at their time, according to the pronunciation in the School of Tiberias, they did not invent them. ‡

In the Middle Ages some of the learned men, as we have said, made the institution of the vowel points we now have, go back to Adam, to Moses, or at least to Ezra.

In a writing attributed to the Greek, Demetrius of Phalereus (b. *circa* 345, d. 284 B.C.) § lxxi, it is said: "In Egypt, the priests celebrate the praises of the gods through the seven vowels, which they repeat one after the other." The first Hebrew Grammarians, among whom is Ibn-Ezra, equally adopted the seven vowels. These, grouped in a certain way, offered some resemblance to the 7 letters of the word YeHoVaH, but it is not improbable that they signified 7 methods of chanting or 7 liturgical formulas. However we must here note that Josephus says of the Name YHVH that it was written in vowels.§

Eusebius|| cites some verses to the Name of the Deity, from a Grecian

---

*The accents were undoubtedly in existence and revealed, before the time of St. Jerome and the Talmud. See in the Talmud, Treatise *Be'rakhoth*.

† See, The Massoreth ha-Massoreth, of Elias Levita, being an exposition of the massoretic notes of the Hebrew Bible, etc., by Christian D. Ginsburg, LL.D., London, 1867.

‡ Pinsker, Sepher *Licquté Qadmoniyoth i. e.*, The First Gatherings, Vienna, 1860.

§ Whiston's Ed. Wars, Bk. v, c. v, § 7.

|| *Preparat. evangel.*, v, c. xiv, xi, c. vi.

sage: "The seven vowels celebrate Me, Myself that am the imperishable God, the indefatigable Father of all the Beings."*

The Karaites believe the vowel signs make such an integral part of the sacred text, and Yehudah Hadessi (of Odessa? *circa* 1148 A. D.) considered them, without doubt in the name of his predecessors, as a Siniatic revelation, of that, which had existed from the time of Adam. †

All languages written solely in consonants, such as the Hebrew, Syriac, Aramaic, and Arabic, require to be vivified by the addition of vowels, otherwise the consonants are dead symbols. The earliest historical evidences of the existence of written vowel points, are to be found in the Syriac. The Syrians sought to adapt to their written language, the Greek vowels *A, E, H, O, Y,* and abridged and slightly changed them into vowel signs. These first signs they called by almost the same names we now find in the Hebrew and Arabic, but they changed them to accord with the Syriac pronunciation, and they were the equivalents of the Hebrew letters ק Qoph, ב Beth, ו Vav, and צ Tza'dhe. It is well to add that these letters became long before א Aleph, ו Vav, and י Yod, which are known among the ancient Hebrew grammarians, as the "Mother vowels." The Arabs appear to have obtained their written vowel system from the Syrians, therefore the names of the vowels in Arabic, Hebrew and Syrian, are very similar. Buxtorf held that the Hebrew vowel points, as we now have them, were anterior to the Massoritic doctors and as old as the Hebrew language, and although his views were vigorously opposed by Cappelus, yet Buxtorf has had followers, among whom we mention, the Rev. John Gill, an English Baptist divine, who wrote a book upon the subject.‡ The Massorites noted peculiarities in the use of the vowel points, of the *dagesh* and the *mappik*, and the accents, which Buxtorf claims, is evidence that they did not invent the diacritical marks which indicate the vowels and accents, for had they been the inventors of them, they would not have noted anomalies and errors but would have corrected or removed them. At the most

---

* See, Mankind their Origin and Destiny, by an M. A. of Balliol College, Oxford. London, 1872, p. 36 *sq.*

† Comp. Steinschneider's Hist. of Jewish Liter., p. 323 n. 23. Also, *Actes de la Société Philologique, Tome, vii, p. 197.*

‡ A Dissertation concerning the Antiquity of the Hebrew Language, letters, vowel points and accents, London, 1767, to which we refer the reader.

they only gave the pronunciation of the School of Tiberias, as it existed therein in the VI century. This differed from that of the time of the Septuagint translation made in Alexandria, and most probably from that in use in the Babylonian Schools, now called the Assyrian, and perhaps still more from that of the ancient Hebrews, which is now most likely entirely lost.

Other scholars following Schultens, although believing in the modern institution of the points now used, held nevertheless, that the Hebrews had at all times, certain signs distinguishing the vowels, but that these marks were different from those we now have, and that the Massoritic doctors substituted the latter for the more ancient. This they held because of the indispensable necessity of vowels, to fix in the reading, a sure pronunciation and meaning of words or expressions, in a tongue, which like all language had a tendency to continual change, written wholly in consonants.

Perhaps those who think the points arose in the VI century A. D. may be able to explain Hebrew xi, 21, where the author of that Epistle has interpreted the text he quotes from Gen. xlvii, 31, very differently from that to be found in the Tiberian pointed and accented Hebrew text. With the points it reads: "And Israel bowed himself upon the bed's head," but the author of the Epistle to the Hebrews, reads: Jacob "worshipped leaning on the top of his staff," reading מַטֶּה *mate*, instead of מִטָּה *mita*, a difference wholly resulting from the use of a vowel point. Jacob's death is not spoken of till the next chapter, consequently the version in the Epistle is by far the most probable. Matt. v, 18, has also been cited to show that the Thorah in the time of Jesus was written in the square character, as the י *Yod* of the ancient Hebrew alphabet is as large a letter as א *Aleph*. The tittle probably refers to the *tag-in*, *i. e.*, crowns, which the final letters were provided with. St. Jerome and the Talmud both speak of these.

In the Syriac as early as the III century A. D. are to be found traces of a Massorah upon the version of the Holy Scriptures. The Abbe Martin in his erudite writing upon the Syriac Massorah and pointing,* treats

---

* *Histoire de la Ponctuation ou de la Massore chez les Syriens*, in the *Journal Asiatique*. Paris, 1875. Tome v, p. 82 *sq*.

of the early phonetic points in the Syrian literature during the epoch of St. Ephraim (d. *circa* 378) and traces them down to the VI century A. D. H. A. Ewald, the great German biblical scholar, has written upon the same subject.* He is of the opinion that both the Syriac and Hebrew systems of pointing, were derived from a common but also sole and unique source, that we can consider both as different and independent developments of one system, and that the least complicated features of this are to be found in the Syriac writing. It would seem that a distinction must be made between the first Punctuators and the Massorites. The Jewish doctors who gave to Hebrew philology the written points, took for their model the Syriac pointing or at the very least a common source, they rather inhabited Babylonia than Palestine, and appear to have been those called Saboraim and not those called Massorites.† If we admit, as indeed we must, that a system of vowel points existed among the learned of the Syrians in the time of St. Ephraim (d. 378) they preceded the Massorites. M. de Vogue‡ has shown that points to ר *Resh* and ד *Daleth* were used in the II century A. D., in the writing of Palmyra. Points were also used in the Pehlevi on coins.

Before the period in which James, Bishop of Edessa, invented or perhaps only wrote down, the first Syriac method of marking the vowels in a complete and perfect manner; his compatriots already used a method of vowel notation, which consisted in placing a point *above* the consonants, so as to reader the vowels a, o and u, short; and *below* them, to render e, i and u long.

When the Hebrew was a language generally spoken and written, by the people of Palestine; it is extremely probable that it was only necessary to present the articulations, that is the consonants, and sight was sufficient to indicate the suitable vowels to each word; but when the Hebrew tended to become an extinct spoken language, the learned thought was necessary to make symbols which should if possible, indelibly fix the sounds or vowels and the signs which should mark the pauses, and prevent that

---

* *Zeitschrift für die Kunde des Morgenlandes*, Vol. i, 206 *sq.*, and *Abhandlungen zur orientalischen und biblischen Literatur*. Göttingen, 1832.

† See also as to Luzzatto's opinion, M. Steinschneider's Hist. Jewish Liter., p. 325.

‡ *Revue archéologique*, April, 1865, p. 3.

change which all language is continually undergoing. So it is said chanting and singing were also precedent to musical notation. The books of the old Hebrews, as indeed are many to-day, were issued without pointing: as this also to this time is maintained in the Rolls written on skin for use in the synagogue. As to them they claim to have preserved through the oral tradition the ancient custom of reading without the points. The method of reading is: the person to read studies at home carefully, the portion to be subsequently read in the Synagogue; the portion to be read is then read in the Synagogue under the supervision of two men, one on each side of the reader, and the latter marks his progress by means of a small rod terminated by a small hand with the index finger extended. The Rolls do not contain any orthographic signs, except certain mysterious superior points, which appear to have been intended to fix the attention of the reader and answer to our italics. A tradition, which goes back to the time of the redaction of the first Midrashim in the I century A. D., attributes to Ezra, the Massoretic points placed above certain letters of the Rolls which were considered as doubtful. In the Midrash Bamidbar Rabbah, c. iii, are these singular words attributed to Ezra; "If the prophet Elias (Eliÿahu) should come to me and say: 'Wherefore hast thou written these letters?' I would respond to him that I had already noted them by the points; and if he should say; ' Thou hast well made the writing,' I would only efface the points." These were only used to denote to the reader a hesitation or partial stop when he pronounced these letters.

The points according to the views of many were taken from ordinary books; the ancient grammarians, says Derenbourg,* first "applied their system of pointing to the Targumim, before borrowing that profane usage so as to apply it the sacred text." The Talmudim show an ancient and complete system of vowel accents or טעמים *Ta'amim* fully in use. Philoponos *circa* 610 A. D. cites in transcribing into Greek, a verse of Genesis (i, 26) exactly reproducing the present pronunciation. In the VIII century, differences of pointing may be noticed, giving a different pronunciation between the Jews of the Schools of Babylonia and those of Palestine. In the X century the version of Saad-yah ha-Gaon of Fayum and

---

* *Journal Asiatique*, 6th series, Tom. xvi, 469 and note.

the Greek translations, other than the Septuagint, which are in the Library of St. Marco in Venice; are made from a text the pronunciation of which is nearly similar, this is also the case with the most ancient pointed Hebrew MSS. of the Holy Writings which has come to our day. This was formerly at Odessa but is now in St. Petersburg, and bears a date corresponding to 916 A. D.* The points are no longer placed above, as was usual in the Babylonian pointing, but below, the letters.

The Zohar containing the content of an ancient Secret Tradition, it is not wonderful that it should have had in it, the early knowledge of the Secret Tradition on pointing. It is very singular that Elias Levita, the great exponent, in Judaism, of the modern invention of the vowel points, should use these strange words. "If any one shall prove to me, by clear evidence, that my opinion is opposed to that of our Rabbins of blessed memory or *is contrary to the genuine Qabbalah of the Zohar, I will readily give in to him and declare my opinion void.*" This was first noticed by Azzariah Min ha-Adomin, or dei Rossi, of Mantua (b. 1513, d. 1577) in his *Sepher M'ohr Enaÿim, i.e.*, Enlightenment of the Eyes.† Dei Rossi holds that the vowel points are indicated in the Babylonian Talmud, Treatise *Nedarim* 37, g, the corresponding passage in the Ye'rushalmi Gemarah, Midrash Be'resheeth Rabbah and the books Bahir and Zohar. The cognate tongues Syriac, Chaldaic, Arabic, Persian, all have vowel signs, and the genius and spirit of the Hebrew tongue absolutely presupposes the ancient existence of points in books intended for general circulation. Those who believe in the modern invention refer to St. Jerome's letter to Evagrius, in which speaking of Enon near Salim, Jerome says; "It matters not whether it be called Salem or Salim, since the Hebrews seldom use the vowel letters in the middle; and the same words are pronounced with different sounds and accents, according to the pleasure of the readers and variety of country."‡ This only tends to show that St. Jerome's

---

* Pinner in 1845, published a *fac-simile* of this MSS. at Odessa.

† Vienna, 1829, p. 286*b*–292*a*, especially 287. Comp. Kitto's Cyclop. Bib. Litera. s. v. Rossi.

‡ *Hieronymous. Ed. of Paris, Vol. i, p. 1062, Ad. Evagrium. Epist.* cxxvi. *Epistola ad Evangelium Monachi Ed. Martianay*, tom. ii, *p. 574.*

Rabbinical Master did not reveal to him the secret method of punctuating, which was likely noted on the Hebrew Secret Rolls in the possession of the Jewish sacerdotal caste. The Buxtorfs used Levita's remark against him.* Another thing is to be noted, the names of the vowel points and especially the tonic accents, are not Hebrew but Chaldaic, and if their origin is Hebraic their exterior form is at least Chaldean or Syro-Chaldean. These names have then been composed by men to whom the Hebrew tongue in its purity was not familiar, and who possessed of it only a mixture of barbarous words, similar to the language of the Talmud and the period succeeding it.

The Zohar says:† "It is written; 'The wise shall shine.' (Dan. xii, 3.) That is the letters and points; 'Like the brightness.' That is the modulations of the accents. 'The wise shall shine' like the moving of the accents (in the tone of the modulations of the accents) and in their tone *athvoun, i. e.*, the letters, and *n'qood-ahs, i. e.*, points, move after them, like an army after their king. (See, *Tiqqoonim* 24.) The letters are the body, and the points are the *ru'hin, i.e.*, spirits. All (the letters and points) move after them (through that tone) but when they stop they do not move but remain standing. And 'The wise shall shine' (guide) the letters and points, like the light of the singing of the tones of the accents. 'And they who bring many to righteousness.' That means the stopping of the accent, that is, they stop in their words, (pause) so that their words shall be understood." See also, the Vulgate, Deuter. xxxi, 19; Nehem. (ii, Esdras) viii, 8, 9; *Ibid*. xiii, 24. King James version. *Ibid*. It was the institution of the written vowel points which prevented the absolute death of an idiom, then nearly dead, even for the learned; and they were the means not only of its resuscitation but were the efficacious means of the subsequent intellectual and moral development of Judaism. The following are a very few of the words which can

---

* *Commentarius Massoreticus, c. ix, p. 74 ed. Basel. 1620.* Not in the Sulzbach Ed.
† Vol. i, fol. 3, col. 2, Cremona Ed. Brody Ed. i, 15a.

be given, the consonants of which are exactly alike, and the pointing of which is necessary to give the true meaning:

עַם	people	שָׁם	there	רִמָּה	worm
עִם	with	שֵׁם	name	רָמָה	throwing
שָׁנָה	year	רַק	only	קֵרֵחַ	bald
שֵׁנָה	sleep	רֹק	spittle	קֶרַח	ice
שָׁנִי	crimson	רַץ	fragment	קַל	swift
שֵׁנִי	second	רָץ	runner	קֹל	voice
		רָעָה	evil		
		רֵעָה	friend		

FINIS.

INDEX.

A

Abba, Father, 194, 256, 262, 382, 387, 398; the Father, and the Will, in Ibn Gebirol, 199.

Abbah. Rabbi, of the Zohar, a Babylonian Jew, 52; to write the teachings of R. Shim-on b. Yo'haï, 51 note, 52. See also 441–2.

Abd-er-Rahman al-Nasr, 5.

Abendehut, 9.

Abn Becr Mo'hammed Ibn Ya'hya, usually called, Ibn Badja. See, Ibn Badja.

Above and Below. Connection between a very ancient idea, 210; resemblances in, 386, 417.

Abraham. The three angels who appeared to, 427.

Abraham Ha-gaon, 46, 53; his commentary on the Siphrah D'Tznioothah, 53.

Abravanel. R. Yehudah, also called, Abarbanel, 9.

Abu-'Ali al-'Hoséin ben-'Abd-Allah Ibn Sina. See, Ibn Sina.

Abulafia. R. Abraham b. Samuel, 10, 38.

Abulafia. Todros b. Joseph ha-Levi (or **Hallevy**), 12, 38.

Abu-Naçr al-Farâbî. See Al-Farabî.

Abyss. The, according to the Akkadians, etc., 243, 448; See, Great Sea, 235.

Adam. See also, Man; 346 note; 418, 419, 420 *sq.;* all the people of the world do not descend from the First, 139, 416; an androgene, 122, 360 *sq.;* the A'tzeel-atic, 360 *sq.*, 418 *sq.;* the B'ree-atic, 360 *sq.*, 396, 418, 419; the Celestial, 224, 280, 300; the Celestial, affected by the Fall of the Terrestrial, 183; clothed in skin, 265; Conflict of, 167 note; creation of, 360 *sq.;* creation of, and covering with skin, etc., 423; creation of the dust body of, 423 *sq.;* of dust, 273; D'Illa-ah, 420; D'Lthath-ah, 420; and Eve. Creation of, 424 *sq.;* the First, 414; the First, clothed in Light, 423, 426 *sq.;* the First and Second, 114; the head of the Heavenly, reaches to Heaven, 202; the Heavenly or Upper, 128 note; the Highest, the Sole occupant of the World A'tzeel-ah, 401; Illa-ah, 138 note, 419; length of years, 352 note; male-female, 417; men do not all descend from, 139, 416; the Nephesh in, 273; the Primordial, 138, 301, 415 *sq.;* Qad'mo-ah, 396, 415 *sq.;* Qadmon, 114, 125, 128 note, 138 note, 280, 281, 415 *sq.*, 419; Qadmon, the Bolt which unites the visible and invisible, 114; Qadmon, the Celestial Man, 181; Qadmon. The Sephiroth applied to, 292 note. See, Frontispiece; Rishoun, 414; the son of God, 247; the Terrestrial, 114; Testament of, 167 note; the Universal Prototypic Life, 300; the Upper, 273, 278, 337 note, 419, 421; the Upper, in the World A'tzeel-ooth, 321; Upper and Lower, 365 note.

Adams. The Four, 418 *sq.*

Adam's knowledge of the Qabbalah, 165; body at first a Light Body, 205. See, Eden.

Adelard of Bath, 162.

Adonai or **Adonoi,** *i. e.,* YHVH, 128, 129, 175, 272, 341, 342.

Ægidius of Viterbo. Cardinal, largely influenced by the Hebrew Qabbalah, 171.

Æons of the Gnostics, 231.

Æther. Absolute, 373 note; Concentrated, 373; Luminiferous, 186.

Agrippa. Henry Cornelius, favors the Antiquity of the Hebrew Qabbalah, 11, 171.

Aigroth, 434.

Ain, 127.

Ain Soph, 110, 127, 128, 181, 195, 251, 253, 298, 371, 378; Chinese idea as to, 446; the Creation by, 211, 212; emanation of the created, from, 231; in Ibn Gebirol, 199; Light of, the idealized blood of the universe, 300.

Akkadian idea of creation, 242, 448 *sq.*

Akkadians and Chaldeans, 235, 236 *sq.*, 448 *sq.* See, Chaldeans, and, Hebrews.

A'keebah. Rabbi, The Master of R. Shim-on b. Yo'haï, 439.

Alain of Lille, 162.

Albensubrun or Ibn Gebirol, 9, 162.

Albert the Great, 162, 163.

Al-Farabi called Alpharabius, 163.

Algebra, hidden for 300 years, 177 note.

Al-Ghazali, 164.

Al-Kendi, 163.

Al-Kuti. Chefez, 5.

Allen. John, 11.

Allix. Rev. Dr. Peter. Favors the Antiquity of the Zohar, 64.

Almighty. See, Shaddaï.

Alphabet. Arabic, 460; the Celestial, 422, 423; the Hebrew, origin of, 460; Phœnician, 460.

Alpharabius. See, Al-Farabi.

Al-Shefa. The, of Ibn Sina, 164.

Altars in the Ancient Temples, 241.

Amaleqh. The Great Demon, 435.

Amen, meaning of, 442 and note.

Ancient of the Ancients, to be distinguished from the Ancient of *All* the Ancients, 136 note. See, At-tee'k-ah D' At-tee'keen and At-teekah D'Kol At-tee'keen.

Ancient World. Knowledge in the, 177; methods of the, 175.

Androgene. The, 122 *sq.*, 417 *sq.*

Androgenes, 138 and notes.

Androgenic Man, 123. See, Adam.

Angels with the Babylonians equal, 10, 237, 238; called Birds, 217; Chaldean, 454; emanation of the, 329, 383; Good, the building up, forces or energies, 126; names of the, 249, 329; different Species in the Kether Malkhuth, 192; composed of a Species of Matter, 191; and Evil Spirits. The names of the angels from Babylonia, 249; world of the, 280, 328, 348, 349; oppose the creation of Adam, 106 *sq.*, 363 *sq.* Below the Pious, 383, 401, 409.

Angelus bell, 167 note.

Animals. Fear of man, 345.

An-pen or An-peen. Ze'ir. See Ze'ir An-peen.

Arabian philosophy. The authors of, not Arabs, 163 *sq.*

Arabs in the Zohar, 69, 70, 71; did not believe in the Revolution of the Earth on its axis, 140.

Aramaic in the Zohar, 53, 54; Aramaic requires vowel points, 464 *sq.*

Architect of the World, 365 note.

Archetypal Church, 116; Man, 45 note.

Appayeem, *i. e.*, Faces, 323.

Aquinas. Thomas, 162, 163.

A'reekh An-peen, *i. e.*, Long Faces, 182, 258, 368 *sq.*, 379.

A'reekh Appayeem, *i. e.*, Long Faces, 323, 368, 379 *sq.*

Areopagite. Dionysios, the, His Ideas in accordance with much in the Qabbalah, 127, 128, 167 note, 440, 456. See, St. Dionysios, also, Dionysios.

Aristotle's *De Mundo*, 8; opposes the idea of the Revolution of the Earth, 139, 140.

Ark. In the Babylonian Temples, 240.

Asbestos or Salamander, 394.

A'seey-ah. Olam ha-, 228, 321, 329 *sq.*

A'seey-atic World, 198, 330 *sq.*

Asher b. Meshullim b. Yacob, 9.

Asher. R. Be'haï b. Asher. Favors the antiquity of the Zohar, 64 note.

Assyrian language and Hebrew language, 228; methods of vowel pointing, 461, 465.

Astronomy. First, by the Akkadians, 240 *sq.*, 448 *sq.*

Atonement. The, 337 *sq.*

At-tee'k, *i. e.*, the Ancient, 257, 367 *sq.*

At-tee'kah D'At-tee'keen, 127, 134, 135, 136, 253, 367 *sq.*

At-teekah D'Kol At-tee'keen, 383.

473

At-tee'kah Qa'dosha, 253.
At-tee'kah Sabah Qad-doshah, 368 *sq.*
At-tee'k Yo-men, *i. e.*, the Ancient of Days, 257, 368 *sq.*
A'tzeel-ah, 228.
A'tzeel-atic World, 198.
A'tzeel-ooth. Olam ha-, 110, 320 *sq.*
Aupha-nem, 329, 419.
Avicebrol, is Ibn Gebirol, 162.
Avicebron, is Ibn Gebirol, 1, 8, 162.
Avicembron or Ibn Gebirol, 162.
Avicenna. See, Ibn Sina.
Avempace. See, Ibn Badja.
Avendoth. Jean, 162.
Aven-Pace. See, Ibn Badja.
Averroes. See, Ibn Roschd.
Ayin, 118, 127, 136 note, 181, 253 *sq.*, 275 *sq.*, 378 *sq.;* in Philo, 301. See, Ain Soph.
Aza and Azäel, 107 *sq.*, 363 *sq.*, 434.
Azäel, 107 *sq.*, 363 *sq.*
Azariel or Azriel, ben Mena'hem, 283, 284 *sq.;* his Explanation of the Ten Sephiroth, 284 *sq.;* quoted, 284.
Azriel, 9. See Azariel; and Ezra, 38; Commentary on Canticles, 49; opinion on Thought as the first emanation of Ain Soph, 192; on the power of the Sephiroth, 289, Colors in the Sephiroth, 259, 261, 262, 269, 270, 271, 288.

B

Babylonian Jews. The Qabbalah with the, 46 *sq.*, 51, 52; philosophy, esoteric, 237; Rabbins captured by the Moors, 5; Talmud. See, Talmud and Talmudim; Temple Towers, 240, 241.
Back. Of the, of the Deity, 53, 226, 419.
Bacon. Sir Francis, studied the writings of Dr. Robert Fludd the Rosicrucian and Qabbalist, 171.
Balance. Doctrine of the, 118, 126, 137 note, 185.
Baptism, 229.
Barnabas. Epistle of, 167.
Bartolocci (de Celano) Giulio, 11.
Barukh. Apocalypse of, 167.
Basic element of most of the Ancient Religions, 108 *sq.*
Basnage de Beauval. Jacques, ascribes the doctrines of the Hebrew Qabbalah, to the Egyptians, 10, 171.

Bdellium, 134.
Beast. The, Samä-el and Lil-ith, 331, 347 note. See, Samä-el, Lil-ith.
Beäuval. Jacques Basnage. See, Basnage.
Beer. Dr. B., On the comet in the Zohar, 82 *sq.*
Bees. Symbolism of, 229, 323 and note.
Be'hai's R. Exposition of the Thorah, 73 note.
Bell. The Angelus, 167 note.
Below and the Above, connection between, 108 *sq.*, 386.
Below a weak copy of the Above, 108 *sq.*, 386, 417.
Be'nai Edom, means Christians, 73. See, Edom, Rome, Children of Yishmaël.
Be'nai Elohim, 106 *sq.*, 364, 434.
Benamozegh. Elia, one of the greatest Qabbalists now living, favors the antiquity of the Hebrew Qabbalah and the Zohar, 173.
Be'resheeth. Ma-a'seh. See, Ma-a'seh, Be'resheeth.
Berger. Paul, ascribes the origin of the Hebrew Qabbalah to the Chaldeans, 172.
Bernard of Chartres, 162.
Bêrôssos, Views of the ancient Chaldean historian, 242, 243.
Be'tza leel, said to have known the combination of letters by which heaven and earth were made, 160 note.
Bhagavad-gitâ. Qabbalistic ideas in, 170.
Binah. Holy Spirit, 182; Sephirah, 192, 193, 199, 260 *sq.*, 292 note; produces a Son, 387 *sq.;* sometimes called, the Great Sea, 336.
Black Races of Mesopotamia, 238, 239.
Blue of the Heaven and blue of the Tallith, 376 note.
Bo-az. See, Ya-kheen.
Body called *Guff, Guph* or *Gupha*, 354 note.
Body of Man only a Garment, 205 and note.
Body of the Resurrection, 355 *sq.*, 410 *sq.*, 414, 437.
Böhmen, Bohme or Behmen. Jacob, was largely influenced by the Hebrew Qabbalah, 171.

Bohu or Primeval Space, 235, 243, 244, 448 *sq*.
Bolt. Adam Qadmon the, between the two Worlds, 190, Nebo, the, 206, 235, 242 *sq*.
Borsippa. The Planet Tower of, 206, Colors of, 449.
Botz-rah means Rome, 75.
Brahma, etc., 45 note. See, Description of Plates.
Brahman *neuter*, 45 note. See, Description of Plates.
Brain. The, Upper, 369 *sq*.
Bread. Reason of the use of, 230.
B'ree-ah. Olam ha-, 228, 321, 328.
B'ree-atic world, 198.
B'ree-atic Adam, 360, 396, 421. See, Adam; also, Man.
Bretschneider. C. G., thought the Hebrew Qabbalah originated with the Persians, 172.
Bride. The Mystic, 117. See, Malkhuth.
Brucker. Johann Jakob, his writings on the antiquity of the Hebrew Qabbalah exhibit but little knowledge of the subject, 172.
Buddæus. Rev. John Francis, favors the antiquity of the Hebrew Qabbalah, 11, 171.
Buddha, Bo, Fo, etc., 206, 337 note; and the Tree of the Sephiroth, 187; representations of, with woolly hair, etc., 239. See, Sakhya Mûni.
Bull. The, 228, 259, 394; of St. Luke, 45 note; symbol of the Sephirah 'Hes-ed, Grace, Spiritual water, hence Baptism, 229; symbol for water, 229; Zodiacal sign of, 228, 240, 452. See, Ox.
Bruno. Giordano, 162.
Bunsen. Baron von, quoted. Introd. x.
Burgonovensis. Archangelus, favored the antiquity of the Qabbalah, 171.
Buxtorf. The Elder, 10; the Younger, 11.
Buxtorfs. The, on the Hebrew vowel pointing, 469.
Byzantium in the Zohar, 72.

C

Cahen. Samuel, 10.
Candlestick. The seven-branched, 447.
Canopy. Supreme, 136.
Capnio. See John Reuchlin.
Cappelus. Lewis, 10, 172, 461.
Cardan. Jerome, 45 note, 46 note, 171.
Cardinal Ægidius of Viterbo, 11.
Carmoly E'liacin, on the antiquity of the Zohar, 56 *sq*.
Categories. Ten, of Ibn Gebirol, 160.
Cause of all Causes, 362 *sq*. N.B.—In the Zohar, this phrase generally translates, Destiny of all Destinies; First Efficient, 144 *sq*.; the Primal Cause, in archaic times, 174.
Celestial Adam, 125. See, Adam; also, Man. Adam in the N. T., 115; Hierarchy like the Ten Sephiroth, 167 and note.
Chaldea. Different Captivities of the Hebrews in, 228; protecting Genii in, 227, 237 *sq*., 448 *sq*.
Chaldean Cylinders, Signets, etc., Method of holding the hands shown on, 440; Thought, its influence upon the Jews, 228; Universe. Description of the, 448, *sq*.
Chaldeans and Hebrews, 221, 226, 227, 228, 234 *sq*. See, Hebrew, also, Akkadians.
Chariot. Spiritual World, a, 220 note.
Chariot Throne, 220 note. See Ma-a'seh Merkabah, 227.
Chartres. Amaury de, 162.
Chasm. The, between the Real and Unreal, 277.
Cherub or Kirub, 227, 237 *sq*., 448 *sq*.
China. Principles of the Tao-teh-King, 111 *sq*.
Chinese believe, that each created being or thing has a double, 113; the Great Azure Dragon of, 235; Makrokosm, 112; Qabbalah, 444 *sq*.; Spiritual ideas of the, 444, 446; symbolism, 445 *sq*.; knew of the Tetrad of Pythagoras, 203 note; Writings and the Qabbalah, 112 *sq*., 444 *sq*.
Christ the male; the female, the Bride, the Church, 117; Symbolic color of the robe of, 262.
Christian Qabbalah, claims of the Roman Catholic Church to the possession of a, 232.
Christianity. By whom Formulated and kept alive, 178, 179; and the Hebrew Qabbalah, 174, 230; Hebrew and Jew-

ish, Secret Doctrine in, 174; value of the Secret Doctrine to, 179. See, Introduction.

Christians. Celebration of the Mysteries of the Faith, by the first, accompaniments of, 230.

Church Fathers' idea as to the Ayin or No-Thing, 127.

Cicero's idea of the invisible God, 114.

Clean and Unclean animals in ancient Babylonia, 240, 241.

Cock. The crowing of the, three times, a secret, 405.

Color of Binah, blue, 203, 261; Blue, 261 and note; of Christ's robe, 203; of the Virgin Mary's robe, 203; of 'Hesed, 269; of Hod, 270; of 'Hokhmah, 262; of Kether, 259; of Malkhuth, 203; of Ne-tza'h, 270; of Pa'had, 269; and Sound, 277; of Tiph'e-reth, 270; of Ye'sod, 271.

Colors. The ancient Babylonian astrological, in the Tower of Borsippa, 206, 449; emanation of the, 195; the mystical, 229; the seven, 277; the white, red and green, 427 *sq.*

Comet in the Zohar 77 *sq.*; statements as to the, in the Zohar, incorrect, 83 *sq.*

Commandments. The Ten Commandments and the Lord's Prayer, 318.

Companions, the name given by the Qabbalistic initiates to each other, 346 note; names of the, of R. Shim-on ben Yo'-haï, 441.

Compass. The points of, in Azriel, 284; Four, points of, in the Zohar, 216.

Composite animals, 452 *sq.*

Conceptualism, Introd. xii, xiii.

Conflict of Adam, 167.

Connection of the visible and invisible, 115, 386, 417.

Contemplation. Inner, Introd. xii.

Cranium. The Great, 133, 134, 367, 368, 382 *sq.*; of the Makrokosm, the Firmament, 118 note.

Creating Deity with the Akkadians, 242, 247.

Creation. Account of the, 122; of Adam and Eve, 421 *sq.*; Assyrian account of, 245; the present preceded by another, in the Assyrian account of, 246; the same statement in the Zohar, 137, 386; according to the Chaldean historian Bêrôssos, 243; only a Copy of the Eternal Idea, 115; or Emanation of the Universe, 135, 359 *sq.*; Quotation from the Siphrah D'Tznioothah, 232, 233, 234; with the Semitic peoples, 242; termed by the Qabbalists, the Shadow of the Upper World, 256.

Creed. Nicene, 459 *sq.*

Crollius. Oswald, largely influenced by the Hebrew Qabbalah, 171.

Crown. The, Highest, 370 *sq.*; or Kether, 256 *sq.*

Crusades, said to be mentioned in the Zohar, but this is doubtful, 69, 70; time of, 69 note.

Crystal, 134.

Cube. Chinese conception of the earth as a, 445.

Cuneiform Tablets, content of, and the Hebrew Qabbalah, 234 *sq.*, 448 *sq.*

Cusanus (Cusani). Cardinal Nicolas, largely influenced by the Hebrew Qabbalah, 171.

D

Da'ath, *i. e.*, Knowledge, 260, 261.

Dante. Hebrew Qabbalism in the writings of, 171.

Darkness. Fear of, 452; Kingdom of. See, Kingdom of Darkness.

Daud Ibn, 9.

Daughter. The, with the Qabbalists, the Church or Congregation of Israël, 117.

David. R. Abraham b. (of Posquieres) or **Rabad**, 9, 38.

David Luriah's Sepher Kadmooth ha-Zohar, 40-54.

David and Solomon had great knowledge of the Qabbalah, 166.

Death. The Angel of, 347, 348, 432, 436; and Life, 362 *sq.*; Malakh Hamoveth, the Angel of, 410, 432, 436; what happens at, 354; an advantage to the Pious, 436; results from the Sin of Adam, 432.

De Causis. The Book, 9, 162.

De Leon. R. Moses Shem-Tob, claimed to be the author of the Zohar, 56 *sq.*; writings by, 60 *sq.*; Ibn Gebirol's knowledge of the Zoharic philosophy, 250 years before the time of, 188.

Del Rossi's opinion on the antiquity of the vowel points, 468.

Deity can only be Approached through the Intention of man's heart, 409; to whom can you Compare the, 277; cannot be Defined, Introd. xiii; dependence upon, when in trouble, 429; has a Form and yet not a Form, 274 *sq.;* may be considered in Four points of view, 128; Existence of the, 254; the Four ways of seeing the, 427; creates Good and Evil, 126; cannot in Its Highest essence be described, 127, 136 and note; perfect Ideas as to, cannot be grasped in the human intellect, 456 *sq.;* Immanent in everything, 195; incomprehensibility of, 274 *sq.;* Hebrew, male-female, 175, 342 *sq.;* our Knowledge of, 136 and note. See Appendix, Mystic Theology of Dionysios; leaves man when he sins, 434; cannot be seen by man, whilst he is in the flesh, 181. See Introduction. Views of Moses of Cordova and Maimonides on the Essence of, 266, 267; without Matter, 191; Names of, 378 *sq.;* according to the Qabbalistic Symbolism, the Deity manifests Itself through a *N'qood-ah*, 127; the Deity *neuter*, 125 note; of the Conformations of, 367 *sq.;* brings Salvation to the wicked, 430; distinct from the Sephiroth, 291; the totality of the Sephiroth, not the Deity, 290 *sq.;* is always enshrouded in Its She'kheen-ah or Glory, 181; alone is pure Simplicity, 212; Supreme, produces through the Absolute Idea, Thought, or Perfect Paradigmatic Form, 181; Supreme, the only Real and True, 181; Supreme. The entire Universe not the Content of the, 181; according to Qabbalistic Symbolism, manifests Creation as if on a Veil, 127. See, Maya, Name, Names.

Demons. The, 433 *sq.;* of the Akkadians, Chaldeans, etc., 452, 453 *sq.;* the destroying forces, 126; Great and Small, 434, 435. See, Samä-el, Lil-ith, Q'lippoth.

D'i-noor or Dinur. The Fire river, 394 *sq.*, 405.

Description of Plates, xix.

Desire or **Will.** The creator, 191, 194.
Diagrams. Qabbalistic, mentioned by Origen, 311, 312, 313. See, p. xxiv.
Dimant. David de, 162.
Dimension. 200.
Dimensions. The, 137 note, 268 note, 292 note.
Din. Abraham Ab-Beth-, 38.
Din. The Sephirah, 200, 269.
Dinur or D'i-noor, the **Fire-river**, 405.
Dionysios, the Areopagite (St. Denis), 46 note, 127, 128, 167 note, 440; Mystic Theology of, 456 *sq.* See, St. Dionysios.
Dior. Ben, 9.
Disciplina Arcana. The Ancient, 177 and note. Introd. viii.
Divine Assistance granted Man if he will call for it, 183; Love, 111; Mediator most likely symbolized in the Qabbalah, by the Sephirah 'Hohkmah, Word or Wisdom, 182; Names in St. Jerome, 168 and note, 169. See also; Name, Ineffable Name, etc.; Power. How it weakens, 211; Qabbalistic Name, Who? 128 *sq.*
Doctrine. Secret. See, Secret Doctrine.
Dove. The brooding, 336.
Dragon. The, 233-235, 243-245; Great Sea, 448 *sq.;* Tiamat of the Chaldeans, etc., 243, 448 *sq.* See, Great Sea, also, Harmony.
Dravidian races of India, 239.
Dreams, 403, 404 and note; Demons act on man in his, 435.
D'Tznioothah. Siphrah, quotations from, 232, 233, 234.
Duality. The, in the Deity, 175, 342, 343, 373 *sq.*
Dudaim. The, 355.
Dumah. The Angel of Silence, 403, 405, 406.
Duns Scotus, 162, 163.
Duretus. Claude, favors the antiquity of the Hebrew Qabbalah, 171.
Dust and Ghost forms, 247, 248.
D'yooq-nah, 388 *sq.*, 411, 414, 417, and many other places.

H

Ea or **Oannes,** 235. See, Fish-god, also, Hea and Oannes.

Eagle, 45 note, 244, 394; the meridian sun, 240; and Scorpion, 259; of St. John, 45 note; Symbol for air, perhaps æther, 229, 244; Symbol of the Sephirah Tiph'e-reth, the spiritual æther or air, hence voice and sound in worship, 230; eagle-headed deity, 452.

Earth, Qabbalistic, Chaldean, Chinese and Egyptian ideas as to its Revolution, 139, 140 and notes; One, 419; its Revolution on its axis, believed in by some of the Greek philosophers, 140; ideas as to its Revolution by Arya-bhata, an ancient Hindu, 140; the Revolution of, in the Zohar, 139 *sq.*

Ecstasy in the Mystic Theology of Dionysios, 456 *sq.*; Theory as to, 158, 427.

Eden, 45 note, 404, 405, 408, 416; the Garden of, 273, 412; or Paradise, 369 note. See, Garden of, and, First Sin. Ibn Gebirol upon, 205; the Upper, 205.

Edom. Children of the Christians, 70–73; Christian Rome, 71, 72; kings of, 118, 135, 137. See, Pre-Adamite kings and, Kings of Edom; Pagan Rome, 71 *sq.*

Ego, I. 127, 259; and Non-Ego, 256; the Zohar says, this was the Light which created everything, 128.

Egyptians. Views of the Ancient, 239; Ineffable Names used by, 237. See, Description of Plates.

E'had, One, 344.

Eh'yeh or **AIH'YeH,** *i. e.,* I Am, 127 *sq.,* 182, 378.

Elders. The Seventy, 221.

Eleh, *i. e.,* These, 129 *sq.*

Elements. Four, in the Zohar, 216, 229.

El'hanan. Rabbi, 5.

Eliyah. Prayer of, 290 *sq.*

Ellenberger. Heinrich, on the Antiquity of the Zohar, 56.

Elohim, the Hebrew for God, 128, 175, 379; the Deity in Nature, 175; Be'nai, 364 *sq.*; according to some Hebrew writers, means *e'lohim, i. e.,* energies or angels, 348; translated in the English Bible, God, 129. See, She'kheen-ah.

El Shaddai, *i. e.,* the Almighty, 379.

Emanation of the **Universe,** 135, 195, 363 *sq.*, 381 *sq.*, 385 *sq.*

Emden. Jacob (Yabetz), 11. See, Yabetz.

Enoch or **'Ha-nokh,** mention of, in the Zohar, 98, 99; Book of, 167.

Ens. A two-fold, 152, 153.

Esdras. Books of, 167.

Esh Nogah, 68.

Etheridge. J. W., 11.

Eunuch. Explanation, from the Zohar, of the word, Eunuch; as used in the New Testament, 92 *sq.*

Eunuchs. Disciples of the Wise, called, Eunuchs, in the Zohar, 92.

Evangelists. Symbols of the, 45 note.

Evil angels in New Testament and in the Zohar, 106 *sq.* See, Demons.

Evil Eye. The, 436 *sq.*, 454.

Evil exists for the wise purposes of God, 184; and Good, created by the Deity, 126; Inclination, *i. e.,* the *Ye'tser ha-rah,* 346 and note; Necessary to the Good, 184, 185; Spirits or Q'lippoth, 126.

Ex nihilo. Creation, 124, 276.

Expansion and Concentration, 110. See, Tzimtzum.

Eye, the closed, 200; degrees and coatings of, Ancient ideas as to, 215, 216; the Evil, 436 *sq.*, 454; metaphor of Sight through the, 213, 214; of Providence, always open, 118.

Ezekiel or Ezeqiel; the Four Faces of the Chariot Throne of, 45 note, 229, 394. See, Merkabah. The Visions of, and those of Isaiah, Daniel, 227; a great Qabbalist, 166; Vision of, 45 note, 242. See Vision; Vision of and the Apocalypse of St. John, 303.

Ezra and **Azriel,** 38. See, Azariel.

Ezra re-wrote the Old Testament in the Aramaic alphabet, 461.

Ezra Ibn. On Ibn Gebirol. See, Ibn Ezra.

Ezra. Moses Ibn Jacob ben, 160.

Ezra the Qabbalist. See, Azariel and Azriel.

F

Faces. The Partzupheem or Faces, 211, 283, 382 *sq.*, 394 *sq.* See, Partzupha; also, A'reekh An-peen and Ze'ir An-peen.

Falaquéra. Shem-Tob b. Joseph Ibn, 8, 10. See, Ibn Falaquéra.

Father. The. Symbolized in the Qabbalah by Kether, 182. See, Abba.

Fear and Love. Worship through, 429.

Female and **male** principles, 118, 137, 185, 387 *sq.*, 399, 417. See, Adam.

Feminine deity among the Semites, a reflection of the male, 246, 247, 342, 373 *sq.*; reflection of the Supreme Deity, with the Qabbalists, 247.

Ficinus. Marsilus, largely influenced by the Hebrew Qabbalah, 171.

Fifty Gates of **Understanding,** 247, 314, 342.

Fire and Incense, 230; the mystery of the three parts which are one, 376 *sq.*; river, 394 *sq.* See D'i-noor and Dinur; and Water, 348, 349.

First Sin. The, 410, 425 *sq.*, 430 *sq.* See, Adam, Grapes.

Fish. The, 336. See, Fish-god.

Fish-god, 234 *sq.*, 243 *sq.*, 336 note, 448 *sq.* See, Oannes, also Ea, and Hea.

Flesh. The, from the Evil side, 410; of Moses was red, according to the Zohar, 93. See, Moses. Power of the, 410.

Fludd. Dr. Robert, 11, 171.

Fons Vitæ, 8, 9, 162.

Forbidden Fruit. Eating of the, 410, 425, 430. See, Grapes; also, First Sin.

Form. Chinese idea as to Non-form and, 445; the Idealized, 181; Universal, 143 *sq.*

Four animals in early Christianity, 230; animals of the Merkabah in the Apocalypse, 230; figures in the Vision of Ezeqiel, 45 note, 229, 394 *sq.* See Ezeqiel; Worlds, 198. See, Worlds, Eagle, Ox, Man, Lion.

Franck. Prof. Adolphe, thought the Hebrew Qabbalah originated with the Persians, 11, 172, 173; errors in his translations from the Zohar, 377 note.

Franck. Jacob, 11.

Free Will, 347, 348; Ibn Gebirol's views on, 197; in Man, 126, 183, 194.

From nothing, nothing comes. The Qabbalah opposes this maxim, 124.

Fruit. The Forbidden, what it was, 410. See Grapes.

Fû-hsi, 444.

Furor. Ancient ideas as to, 427.

G

Gabalas. Count de, Poem of the Rape of the Lock, by Alex. Pope, based on 171.

Gäi-hinnom, 358, 395 *sq.*, 403, 405, 411; who calls his fellow-man Wicked brings him to, 105 *sq.*; the Wicked cast into, 353, 354; in the Zohar, 99. See Hell.

Galatinus. Peter, favors the antiquity of the Hebrew Qabbalah, 171.

Gale. Theophilus, largely influenced by the Hebrew Qabbalah, 171.

Gan Eden. See Paradise, Eden, Garden of Eden.

Garden of Aromatics, by Ben Ezra, 160.

Garden of Eden, 204, 205. See, Eden and Paradise.

Gebirol. Ibn. Attributed a Species of matter to all the created, 191; held that the Deity was immanent in everything, 195; on the Neshamah, *i. e.*, Soul, etc., 196; opinions upon Ibn Gebirol and his writings, 161; on the influences between the Superior and Inferior Worlds, 189; his philosophical system resembles that of the Zohar, but it differs in its method of treatment, 7. See, Ibn Gebirol, and Me'qôr 'Haÿ-yim.

Ge'boor-ah. The Sephirah, 200, 269, 375.

Gedal-yah Ibn Yachia b. Don Yosef, on the antiquity of the Zohar, 61, 62.

Ge'dool-ah. The Sephirah, 200, 269.

Geiger. Dr. Abraham, opposes the antiquity of the Hebrew Qabbalah, especially the Zohar, 10, 172.

Genesis. Key to the first chapter of, 122, 123.

Genius. What is, 138.

Ghost-world. Mul-lil, Lord of the, 247.

Gill. John, 11, 464.

Gil'gool'em. The revolving of the Incorporeal, but not Metempsychosis, 198, 330. See Revolution.

Ginsburg. Dr. Christian D., 10; opposes the Antiquity of the Zohar. His objections, 65 *sq.*; on the statement in

the Sepher Yu'hasin, 56; his objections answered, 65 sq.
Gnomes, 238; Chaldean, 454.
Gnostics and the Qabbalah, 170; Æons of, 231 and note.
God, the Hebrew Name of is Elohim, 129; His love and mercy acts in the Advancement of humanity, 180; seeing God, 226, 427.
Gods. Babylonian; The sacred number of many of the, 238; of the Heathen not to be reviled, according to the Zohar. See also, Qur'ân, 93.
Good and **Evil,** in Chaldea, 242; and Evil, created by the Deity, 126; and Evil, not considered by the Qabbalah as two independent powers, but both under the Supreme Deity, 184; inclination or *Ye'tzer ha-tob*, 348 note.
Grace or **Love.** The Sephirah of. See 'Hes-ed.
Graetz. Dr. Hirsch, opposes the antiquity of the Hebrew Qabbalah and especially the Zohar, 10, 37, 56, 172; his hypothesis against the antiquity of the Qabbalah, 39.
Grapes, 358, 410, 430 sq.; simile of the Bunch of, 217.
Great Sea. The, 233-235, 243, 244. See, Bohu; Serpent of the Great Crystalline Sea is Leviathan, 233-235.
Greek idea of the Oppositions, 186; vowel letters, 460, 464.
Groddeck. Gabriel, 10.
Guillaume de Auvergne, 162, 163.
Gunsalvi. Dominic, translated into Latin the Me'qôr 'Haÿ-yîm, 162.

H

Habal D'Garmin, *i. e.*, the Body of the Resurrection, 392. See, Resurrection.
Habel and **'Hes-ed,** 422.
Hamburger. J. Favors the antiquity of the Zohar, 64 note.
'Hannanel. Rabbi, 5.
Hands. Qabbalistic methods of holding the, 440, 441 note. See, the Description of the Plates.
'Ha'nokh. Rabbi, 5.
Harmony is represented Symbolically, by the Serpent with its tail in its mouth, 186. N.B.—This is likely Leviathan. In Hindu Symbolism it surrounds the Universe; and Oppositions in the Zodiac, 186.
Harmonies in the Sephiroth, 203.
Haÿ Gaon, 47; knows of the Sephiroth, 160.
Ha-Levi. Abraham b., attacks the writings of Ibn Gebirol, 161.
Ha-Levi. Yehudah, has ideas similar to those Ibn Gebirol, 161.
'Haÿ-yah. The, 392.
'Haÿ-yîm. The **Me'qôr,** 3, 142 sq., 188, sq. See Ibn Gebirol.
'Haÿ-yoth ha-Qadosh, *i. e.*, the Holy Living Creatures, 259.
He or **Hu,** 175, 342, 373 sq.
Hea or **Ea,** a Babylonian deity, 241 sq., 448 sq. See, Ea, also, Oannes.
Head of all Heads, 369 sq.
Head. White, 369, 382, 386. See, Resha 'Hiv'rah, also, Cranium.
Heads. The Three, which are One Head, 369 sq., 382 sq.
Heaven. The coming Kingdom of, 202, 203 and notes.
Heaven of **Heavens,** the Highest Ideal World, 277.
Heavenly Adam, 202. See, Adam.
Heavenly Family. The, with early Semites, 246. See Introduction xiii; Ideal of the Visible, in the Old and New Testaments, 189.
Heavens. Two, 419; Like the layers of an onion, 415 sq., 451.
Hebrew Alphabet, origin of, 460; Ancient, pronunciation of, likely lost, 465; Old Testament. The naturalness of, is merged in the Greek idealization of the New Testament. Introd., xi; Square Character. Antiquity of, 461; Square Character, not used by Ezra in rewriting the O. T., 461; Square Alphabetic Characters used in the time of Jesus, 465; and Syriac vowel pointing, from the same source, 466; vowel letters, 460; vowel points, 66, 460. See, Vowels, also, Vowel Points.
Hebrews, Origin of in Chaldea, 228.
Hegel. Georg Wilhelm Friederich, influenced by the doctrines of the He-

brew Qabbalah, 171; views as to the Deity, 255; his Opinion on the existence of Good and Evil, 184.
Hell or Gäi-hinnom, 348.
Hell and Paradise, 432 *sq.* See Gäihinnom and Eden.
Hell or the Underworld. The Chaldean, etc., 450.
Helmont, Franz Mercurius van, favors the antiquity of the Hebrew Qabbalah, 171.
Hermas Pastor. See Pastor of Hermas.
Hermes Trismegistus, 167.
'Hes-ed. The Sephirah, 200, 268 *sq.*, 292 note, 375. See, Sephirah, Sephiroth.
Hindu deity never Winks, 214; heavens, 447; Idea as to Non-annihilation, 124 note; representations of the Figures of the Chariot Throne, 45 note; belief in the Revolution of the Earth, 140; Symbols of the Four Worlds, 320, 334. See, Description of Plates; Symbolism, 127 note; Veda's and the Qabbalah, Introd., xiii, 324 *sq.;* representation of the Four Figures in the Vision of Ezeqiel, 45 note.
Hierarchies. Spiritual, of the Akkadians, 246 *sq.*, 448 *sq.;* Angelic, 167 note; of the Roman Catholic Church, 167 note.
Hiram Abiff, of Tyre, 185.
Hispalensis. Joannes, 9; Aria Montano, 241, xxiii.
Hod. The Sephirah, 201, 270, 271.
'Hokhmah Illa-ah, *i. e.*, Heavenly Wisdom, 258; Lashon, 220; Nistharah, 220, 221; The Sephirah, 192, 193, 261, 292 note; the Son or Logos, 182; Theosophy, 220; the Sephirah, is Wisdom, the Logos or Word, 199; the Word, called by the Qabbalists, the Son of God, 199; Yavonith, *i. e.*, Grecian Wisdom, 220. See, Logos, Word, Wisdom, Sephiroth.
Holy of Holies. In the ancient Temples of Babylonia, 240, 241.
Holy Kiss. Reception of the Soul by the, 406, 407.
Holy Spirit. The, 260, 336; with the Qabbalists, is the Mother, the Church is the Daughter, 117.
House of the World, 385. Comp. 245.

Hu, *i. e.*, He, 175, 342 *sq.*, 373, 374.
Human Face, the symbol of St. Matthew, 45 note.
Human Race. Roots of the, 422.
Humanity considered in the Qabbalah, as a Great Universal Brotherhood, 181.
Humiliation and Prayer. Days for, in ancient Babylonia, 240.
'Hushiel. Rabbi, 5.

I

Ibn-al-Çayeg. See, Ibn Badja.
Ibn Badja, 164.
Ibn Ezra. Abraham, on Ibn Gebirol's writings, 160, 161; on the Four Worlds of Ibn Gebirol, 198.
Ibn Falaquéra. Shem Tob, says, the Me'qôr Haÿ-yim, of Ibn Gebirol, contains Ancient Learning, 161; Shem Tob appreciated the writings of Ibn Gebirol, 161.
Ibn Gebirol. Solomon b. Yehudah, Life and Writings, 1 *sq.;* on the Soul, by, 4; on the Will, by, 4; on the Makrokosm and Mikrokosm, 4; Poems of, 4; Grammar, by, 4; Choice Pearls, by, 4; Tiqoon Middoth ha-Nephesh, by, 4; cause of the forgetfulness of his philosophical works, 161; considered an Arab in the Middle Ages, 163; considered a Christian, 163; influence of his writings on the scholastic philosophy, 162; the first so-called, Arabian philosopher, in Europe, 164; ideas influenced the Mediæval Mystics, 163; Moses Maimonides does not mention him, 164; the Qabbalistic philosophy the predominating influence shown in, 219; poem on the 32 Paths, 218; similarities between his writings and the Zohar, 188; writings have similarities to the Zoharic, 188, his Me'qôr 'Haÿ-yim, 142 *sq.*
Ibn Roschd or, Averroes, 164.
Ibn Sina, called by the Scholastics, Avicenna, 161, 163, 164.
Ibn Tofail. Abû-Becr-, 164.
Ideal Man. See, Adam Qadmon, and Adam Illa-ah.
Ideas, of the early thinkers, 113; in the ancient world of thought, 276 *sq.*

481

Idrah Rabbah. Translation from the beginning of, 440 *sq.*
Ilu. Babylonian Supreme Deity, 238, 242, 454.
Image. Divine. Man in the, 345.
Immah, *i. e.,* Mother, 398. See, Abba.
Immah Illa-ah, *i. e.,* Upper Mother, 199, 260. See, She'kheen-ah.
Importance of the investigation of the relations of man to the Primal Cause, 174.
Incense and **Fire,** 230.
Incorporeal compared to a lighted lamp, 376, 412; divisions of the, 392 *sq.;* in man after Death, 410 *sq.* See, Nesh-amah, Rua'h, Nephesh, 'Haÿ-yah, Ye'hee-dah.
Incubus, Succubus, etc., 453.
Ineffable Name, 175, 341, 342, 343; not used by Eve or Satan, 124. See Name, also, Tetragrammaton and YHVH.
Initiates. An Ancient Lodge of, 439 *sq.*
Intellect. Universal, 144.
Invisible to be comprehended only through the visible, Introd. xi; the idea of a Perfect Invisible and an Imperfect Visible, among the Primitive ideas of mankind, 111; reached through the visible, 114, 174, 189.
Isaac or **Yitz-'haq of Acco,** a Practical Qabbalist, 58; quotations from his Sepher Yu'hasin, claimed, by Dr. Graetz *et al.,* as proof that R. Moses de Leon wrote the Zohar, 56, 57, 58, 59 *sq.,* 60.
Isaiah. Book of the Ascension and Vision of, 167.
Isaiah had knowledge of the Qabbalah, 166, 198, 315 *sq.*
Ishmaëlites or Yishmaëlites, named in the Zohar, 49, 69-73.

J

Jacob's Ladder. Explanation of, by Ibn Gebirol, 204.
Jannes and **Jambres.** An account of, 95 to 98.
Jellinek. Rev. Dr. Adolph, 10; Introduction to German edition of Prof. Adolphe Franck's *La Kabbale,* 11; his favorable remarks as to the antiquity of the Qabbalah, 39; statement as to the Comet, in the Zohar, 80 *sq.;* began in opposition to the antiquity of the Hebrew Qabbalah and the Zohar, his quotations however, favor their antiquity, 172; his opposition to the Zohar, 38.
Jerome. St. His letter to Marcella mentioning the Ten Divine Names, translated, 168 note. See, St. Jerome.
Jesus. Time of the birth of, 87 and note, 88; Three conceptions of, in the N. T., 119; the religion of, 230; uses the She-mah, 371 note.
Jewish Church called, the Daughter of YHVH, in the Zohar, 94; Deity, male-female, 175, 247, 342 *sq.; Disciplina Arcana.* Value of the, Introd. viii; knowledge from Chaldea, 228. See, Thought, and, Secret Doctrine, 174.
Joel. Rev. Dr. D. H., 11; favors the antiquity of the Zohar, 64.
Johannic. The. theology, 119.
Josephus, 167, 463.
Jost. Dr. I. M., favors the antiquity of the Hebrew Qabbalah, 172; on the Qabbalah and Zohar, 11, 61, 65, Introd. xiv.
Jourdain, cited, 162.
Jubilees. Book of, 167.
Judgment. Divine Power of, 126; and Mercy. The World exists through, 402, 446 note; the Pillar or Column of, 282; the Place of, of the Living and Dead, 366 and note; of the Wicked, and their punishment, 358.
Just. The. See, Pious.

K

Kallem. See, Vessels, and, Sephiroth, 279 *sq.,* 300, 331.
Kan (Qa-yin or **Cain),** 248, 444.
Kepler upon the Constellations at the coming of Jesus, 87.
Kether. Sephirah, 127, 128 note, 190, 199, 256 *sq.,* 283, 292 note; is A'reekh Anpeen, 283; clear Knowledge of, cannot be obtained by man in this world, 380 *sq.;* represents the Brain and the Neshamah, *i. e.,* Soul, 282; called, the Father, 182; is the Unity in Number, 282.

31

Kether El-yon, *i. e.*, Highest or, Upper, Crown, 370 *sq*.
Kether Malkhuth, cited, 2 *sq*., 66, 195–198.
Kernel and **Shell**. Description of the Universe as, 191.
Khosari, Kusari or **Cosri**. Ideas in this writing, similar to those in the Me'qôr 'Haÿ-ylm, 161.
Khunrath. Henry, largely influenced by the Hebrew Qabbalah, 171.
King and **Queen**. The union of, 110, 203, 283.
King. The. and his son. The Parables of, 401, 436.
Kingdom. The great text as to the coming Kingdom of the Righteous on earth, 202. Compare 437; of Darkness, has injured the Ancient tradition, 180; the Ideal Perfect, 201, 202.
Kings of **Edom**. The Pre-Adamitic, 118, 135, 137, 138 and notes, 185, 236, 386 *sq*.
Kircher. Rev. Athanasius, 11, 65; ascribes many of the doctrines of the Hebrew Qabbalah to the Egyptians, 65, 171; favors the Antiquity of the Hebrew Qabbalah, 171; a figure of Pan or Zeus Lykæus, from his works, 325.
Kiseh ha-Kabod, *i. e.*, Throne of Glory, 418. See, Throne of Glory.
Kiss. The Holy, taking of the Soul of the Pious by, 406, 407.
Kleuker. John Frederick, on the Hebrew Qabbalistic philosophy, 172.
Knowledge, in Hebrew, Da-ath, 260, 261; in the ancient World, 177.
Ko-a'h Kis-eh, *i. e.*, The Throne of Glory, 418, 429. See, Throne of Glory.
Konitz. Moses b. Me'na-a'hem Mendel, 20 *sq*.; has written in favor of the antiquity of the Hebrew Qabbalah, 20, 172 *sq*.
Kosmic Mystery, in the book, Teaching of the Twelve Apostles, 116 *sq*.
Kosmogony of the Zohar, 139, 415 *sq*.
Kosmos. The. with the Qabbalists, 117; of the Zohar and that of Chaldea, 139 *sq*., 454 *sq*. See, Universe, also, Makrokosm.
K'ung-Foo-Tze, or, Confucius, 444.

L

Lactantius on the Revolution of the Earth, 139.
Ladder of **Jacob**, 301, 308.
Landauer. M. H., 10, 11.
Lange. Joachim, ascribes the origin of the Hebrew Qabbalah to Gentile philosophy, 172.
Language, Introd., xi, xii; Ancient, 175 *sq*.
Laou Tsz'. Philosophy of, 111 *sq*.; his Tao-teh-King, 113; a Qabbalah in his asserted writings, 170.
Lassen. Christian, believes Neo-platonism came from India, 170.
Law. The. See Thorah.
Law. The Common. a species of Qabbalah, 232.
Learning. Secret. See, Secret Learning.
Leibnitz. Baron, interested in the study of the Hebrew Qabbalah through Baron Knorr von Rosenroth, 171; concealed his scheme of Differential Calculus, 177 note.
Length, Breadth, Depth, 137 note, 200, 292 note. See also, Dimension and, Dimensions.
Leo Hebræus, 9.
Leon R. Moses b. Shem-Tob de, 7, 10; not the author of the Zohar, 41 *sq*. See, Moses de Leon.
Letters, numbers and **proportions**, bind man's thoughts in matter symbolism, 181, Introd. xi.
Levi. Abraham b. David ha-, 5.
Levi. Abraham b. ha- (the Elder), 9.
Levi. Eliphas (Abbe Alphonse Louis Constant), 11; on the Qabbalistic idea of the Deity, 254, 255.
Leviathan, 234, 235. See, Serpent.
Levita. Elias, on the antiquity of the Hebrew vowel points, 468. See, Vowel points.
Light. The Zoharic, 428; body of Adam, Ibn Gebirol's writings upon the, 205; in which the Soul is clothed, 399.
Lightfoot. John, 11.
Lil-in. The, 435.
Lil-ith, 248, 347 note; the wife of Adam, 248; and her companion, Samä-el, 433 *sq*.

Lion, 45 note; symbol for fire, 229; symbol of Force, Energy, Fire, also of Ge'boor-ah, Spiritual Fire, 229; of St. Mark, 45 note. See, Ezeqiel, Vision of Ezekiel, Four Animals.

Life and Death, 362 *sq.*

Life. Entrance into, of the Soul, 396 *sq.*; Source of. See, Me'qôr Haÿ-yim; Tree of, 204, 235, 236. See, Tree.

Living. All, to die and be at once revivified, at the coming of the Messiah, 437.

Lodge. A Qabbalistic, and the arrangement of, 442, 443 note.

Loescher. Valentine Ernest, 11.

Logos. The, 301, 302, 336, 459; the Creative, 137. See, Word, also, 'Hokhmah.

Lord. The, is given in the English Bible as the equivalent for YHVH, 129; or Adonaï, 175.

Lord's. The, Prayer, end of, Qabbalistic, 202 note; Divisions of, and the Ten Commandments, 318.

Lost. Nothing ever, 124, 125.

Löw. Dr. Leopold, favored the antiquity of the Hebrew Qabbalah, 11, 172.

Lower man or Adam, 114; World, a copy of the Upper, 108 *sq.* See, Adam, also, Man.

Love. The Divine, 111; and Fear, Worship through, 429; to God, 442 note.

Lully. Raymond, agreed with the Hebrew Qabbalists, 11, 171.

Lupercalia. The, 326.

Luria or **Luriah. David.** Analysis of his book in favor of the antiquity of the Zohar, 11, 40 *sq.*; wrote in support of the Antiquity of the Hebrew Qabbalah, 40–54, 172 *sq.*

Lutterbeck. Joh. Ant. Bernh., 11.

Luzzatto. S. D., 10.

Lyra. Nicholas de, adopted the four Jewish methods of interpretation of the Old Testament, 105.

M

Ma-a'seh Be'resheeth, 162, 220.

Ma-a'seh Merkabah or Chariot Throne, 44 *sq.*, 162, 220, 227; Interdictions as to teaching, 222, 223. See, Ezekiel or Ezeqiel; Vision of; Four Animals.

Magic. Black and White, 47 note, 453 *sq.*; different meaning of, in Ancient times, from that in the Middle ages, 47 note.

Ma'hshabah, *i. e.*, Thought, 128 and note, 377, 395, 400, 408.

Maimonides an **Aristotelian**, 161; holds that the Earth is round and revolves, 140; does not mention the Name of Ibn Gebirol, 164; favorable to the Speculative Qabbalah, 39 *sq.*; not favorable to the philosophical ideas in the Writings of Ibn Gebirol, 161.

Makrokosm, 4, 46, 118 note, 121, 128 note, 144, 147, 150, 156, 157, 160, 181, 231, 316 note, 332, 333, 337 note, 420, 443 note; The Chinese, 112 *sq.*, 445 *sq.*; the Great Man seen by Nebuchadnezzar, 216; as the Great Tree, 422; usually represented as an Immense Man, sometimes as an Immense Head, 118 note; Maimonides on, 333; and Mikrokosm, 296, 422; Termed by the Qabbalah, son of Elohim, *i. e.*, God, 231.

Makrokosmos, 115, 225, 292 note; as Atlas, 319, 326; Engraving of, as portrayed in the Middle Ages, 326, 327; the Greek, 324 *sq.*; the Hindu, 321 *sq.*

Makroprosopos, 182.

Malakh Hamoveth, *i. e.*, the Angel of Death, 432, 436; Rah, *i. e.*, Evil Angel, 435 note.

Male and Female principles, 387 *sq.*; All exists through, 193, 199; principles on Solomon's Temple, 117; Souls in the Pre-existent condition, 399. See, Preexistence.

Malkhuth. Deity in, 128; Kether Malkhuth, 2 *sq.*, 9; represents the Nephesh, 282; called, the Queen, Daughter, Matroneethah, Matron, the She'kheen-ah, etc., 203, 283; the Sephirah, 201, 202, 203, 272; Symbolized by the Moon, 282. See, Colors, Sephirah, Sephiroth, Kingdom.

Man. The Androgenic; 281; the Angelic, symbol of the Sephirah Malkhuth, the Kingdom, the Spiritual Earth, hence the Products of the Earth, Wine and Bread, 230; as the Zodiacal Aquarius, 259; in the Body, cannot raise the Veil absolutely, 181, Introd. xi; the bringing forth of, 353. See, Adam. The Man with the Burden, 335; the Celestial, 419. See, Adam. Not considered in the Qabbalah as Autonomic, 180; Creation of, 106 *sq.*, 417; Creation of, his purity and his sinning, 344, 345, 424; his Creative power, 183, 184; Danger to, from the Unclean Spirits which surround him, 225; can only approach the Deity through the Intention of the Heart, 409; in the flesh, is always subject to Dissolution and Death, 184; the Earthly, 231, 232; Feared at first by all the Animals, 345; cannot attain his lost Felicity through his unaided powers, 181, 182; whilst in the Flesh cannot See the Deity, Face to Face, 181; in the Flesh can only See the Back of the Deity, *i. e.*, the Visible Universe, 181; the Form of the, 400 *sq.*, 415 *sq.*, 420, 421; Garments of the Incorporeal in, 412; the Great Man, 147. See, Makrokosm. Incorporeal in Man after death, 410 *sq.*, 412; the Inner, desires a Worship from the Heart, Introd. ix; the Mystery of, 414 *sq.*, 422, 423; of the present, his hopes and fears, 183; The Real, is the Inner Spiritual not the outside, 184, 422; partakes of two opposing Regions, that of Goodness and that of Evil, 184; gives a portion of his Spirituality to his Works, 138; of to-day, only a Concatenation of the Being-hood of all precedent human life, 183; Upper, Everything in the, 114; in the vision of Ezekiel (Ezeqiel), 45 *sq.* and note; Words, all spoken by, Continue in the future, 428. See, Adam, Makrokosm, Mikrokosm.

Man's Works, a part of himself, 138, 139.
Manichæans and the Qabbalah, 170.
Ma-qom, *i. e.*, Place, 300, 420.
Mars. The planet, 329, 449.
Mazkim. The, 249, 451, 453. See also, Mazikim and Maziqim.
Massorah. The Syriac in the III century A.D., 465 *sq.*
Massoritic Doctors only substituted for the more ancient symbolism of the Vowels, a more modern, 465; points in the Synagogue Rolls, 467; Doctors; their duties, 462 *sq.* See, Vowels, Vowel pointing.
Materialism and **Formalism.** The dangers of, Introd. viii, ix, x.
Matroneethah, 76, 128, 203, 401; The, the Mediatrix between the Deity and man, 349, 350, 351 and note, 401.
Matter. The Deity without, 191; Different kinds of, 145, Ibn Gebirol on, 142 *sq.*
Matter. Jacques, 11; thought the Hebrew Qabbalah originated with the Persians, 172.
Matter, always in Motion, 135 note; no Absolute Matter, 152 note; Universal, 143 *sq.*
Maurice. Rev. Thomas. Favors the antiquity of the Zohar, 64.
Maya or **Illusion,** 276 *sq.*, 321. See, Description of Plates.
Maziqim, 434, 435, 451, 453. See, Mazkim.
Maz-zol, the Influences, 298.
Mediator. Among the ancient Babylonians, 241; a Divine, a necessity to man, 181, 182.
Men. Zohar speaks of, as not all descending from Adam, 139, 416.
Me-qôr 'Haÿ-yîm, by Ibn Gebirol. Analysis of, 142; Influences in the Formation of the, 142, 143; a Resumé of, 143 *sq.;* contains an Ancient System, 10.
Mercy and **Judgment,** 446 note.
Mercy. The Pillar of, 281; tempers Rigor or Severity, 380 *sq.;* the Sephirah 'Hesed, sometimes called, 269.
Merkabah, 45 note, 227, 419; in early Christianity, 230. See, Ma-a'seh Merkabah. The, and the cleansing of the Neshamoth, 394.
Merodach or **Marduk,** 241, 244.
Mesopotamia ancient, Civilization of, its progression, 237; the Population of Ancient, 237 note.
Messer Leone Hebreo, 9.
Messiah. The, 335; Atonement by the, 337, 338 *sq.;* the Coming of the, 85 *sq.*, 437; Ibn Gebirol on the time of the coming of the, 217; ben Joseph and the Messiah ben David, 366, 367 and note;

as the Shepherd, 338, 339; Star of the, 88; Time of His coming, Kepler upon, 87; Time of the coming of, in the Zohar, 88 *sq.;* Washed in wine, 340; in the Zohar, 77 *sq.,* 85 *sq.*

Metals. Four, in the Zohar, 216.

Metatron, 116, 128, 174, 228, 272, 347, 350, 366 and note; the B'ree-atic Adam, 418, 419; the first of all Creatures and the reflection of Elohim, 349 and note, 351 note; the Presence Angel, 365, 366; in the Second World, 328; the Servant of *Ma-qom,* 349; his name equals that of Shaddaï, the Almighty, 328, 366.

Metempsychosis, 197, 308. See, Revolution.

Mexican Androgene, 157.

Meyer. Johann Friederich von, 11.

Me'zuzzah. The, 67, 452.

Michäel Archangel identified in the Pastor of Hermas, with Christ, 116.

Middle Pillar, 281 *sq.*

Middoth. The Thirteen, 372 note.

Midrash Va-yiqrah Rabbah, 73; Ye'-rushalmi, 48.

Midrashim. Ancient, 167.

Might and **Mysticism,** 217.

Mikrokosm, 4, 46, 121, 128 note, 134, 144, 147, 150, 156, 157, 160, 181, 198, 231, 232, 265, 332 *sq.,* 333, 337 note; and Makrokosm, 422. See, Makrokosm, Adam, Man.

Mikrokosmos, 225.

Mikroprosopos, 182.

Millennium, 233.

Minir. Isaac Ibn, 12.

Miracles, 193, 194.

Mirandola. Prince Giovanni Pico della, 9, 11.

Mithras. Quotation from Origen on, as to the metals, etc., 310, 311.

Mohammedans say the First thing created by God was a pen, 115; not necessarily mentioned in the Zohar, 72 *sq.*

Molitor. Franz Joseph. Favors the antiquity of the Zohar, 11, 65.

Month. Names of the Jewish, from Babylonia, 249.

Moon. The Spirit of, 242.

More. Dr. Henry, favors the antiquity of the Hebrew Qabbalah, 11, 171.

Morin. Jean, 10, 172; on the Hebrew vowel pointing, 461.

Moses. Book of the Assumption of, 167; an Egyptian General, 94; and Eliÿahu, in the Zohar, 99; Face red like the face of the sun, 93; his Father was Amram, 94; asks to see the Glory of the Deity, 226; knowledge of the Qabbalah, 166; name of has a connection with that of the Babylonian sungod, 239, 240; buried on the Wisdom Mountain, Mt. Ne'bo, 206.

Moses of Cordova, cited, 266, 267.

Moses. Rabbi, 5.

Munk. Salomon, 8, 11; favored the antiquity of the Hebrew Qabbalah, 172.

Musical notes. The seven, 277. Compare, 325, 463.

Mystæ, 177.

Mystery or **Sod,** 166, 305, 340 note.

Mystical colors, 229.

Mystics. The greatest, influenced by ideas similar to those in the Qabbalah, Introd. ix.

Mysticism. The Higher, of the Qabbalah, 384; termed Might, 217.

N

Na-amoh, the beautiful Demon, 434.

Nachmanides or **Ben Na'hman,** 39.

Nagid. Josef ha-, 4 *sq.*

Nagréla. Samuel ha-Levi b. Josef, 4, 5, 6.

Name. Hidden, 3, 237 *sq.,* 342.

Name. The Ineffable, 202, 203 and note, 263, 274, 341; the reversed, Ineffable, 446 note. See, Ineffable Name, Tetragrammaton, YHVH.

Name of, 72, 202 and note. See, Tetragrammaton; also, Ineffable Name.

Names of the Deity, 378 *sq.;* Divine, Secret, 237; Divine, in St. Jerome, 168 and note; Great, Qabbalistic formula of the, 342; Ineffable, with the Babylonians, Egyptians, etc., 237, 247. Construction of the Chaldean Universe. See Appendix, also Name.

Nazir. Jacob. (of Lunel), 38.

Ne'bo, 241, 242; the Wisdom deity of ancient Babylonia, his planet Mercury, 241, 242; the bond of heaven and earth, 206.

Negations, Introd. xii, xiii. See, Ayin.

Ne'hunyah, the Pious, knew of the Zohar, 48.

Neo-platonicians in Italy cite from Ibn Gebirol's philosophical works, 162.

Neo-platonism probably from Hindustan, 170.

Nephesh, *i. e.*, animal soul, 147, 153, 155, 196, 200, 203, 232, 282, 292 note, 321, 332, 354, 390 *sq.*, 402, 411, 412, 418, 419, 433 *sq.*, 444; in Adam, 273; of the Great Ideal Man, 301.

Ne'qood-ah Pe'shoot-ah, *i. e.*, Smooth Point, 257; Rishoun-ah, *i. e.*, Primordial Point, 257.

Neshamah, Intellectual Soul, 147, 153, 155, 160, 196, 200, 203, 232, 282, 292 note, 321, 331, 332, 354 *sq.*, 384 *sq.*, 390 *sq.*, 402, 410, 411, 412, 413, 414, 418, 419, 422, 423, 428, 429 *sq.*, 444; Absence of the, Creates Uncleanness, 408; leaves the Body of man during sleep, 403 *sq.*; of the Great Ideal Man, 301; return of, to Paradise, 404; Rua'h, Nephesh, Zohar on, 197; the Upper, 190.

Ne-tza'h. The Sephirah, 201, 270.

Newton, Sir Isaac, studied the writings of Jacob Böhmen, 171; influenced by the Hebrew Qabbalah, 171; hid his invention of Infinite Series, 177 note.

New Testament. The Apocryphal, 167; and the Secret Doctrine, Introd. viii, 440; a fusion of Hebrew and Hellenic thought, Introd. xi.

Nicene Creed. Dogmas of and the Qabbalah, 459 *sq.*

Nistaroth, *i. e.*, Mysteries, 36.

Noa'h and **'Hen**, *i. e.*, Grace, 420, 421. See, Description of Plates.

Non-form. Chinese idea as to, 445.

Nothing. Creation from, 213; is ever lost according to the Zohar, 124; from nothing nothing can come, 230.

No-Thing. The Absolute, 148; the No-Thing, 275 *sq.* See, also, Ayin and, Ain Soph. Ideas of the Great Church Fathers as to, 127; Qabbalistic idea as to, 125; the Universe created from, 305 note.

Number, etc. God doeth all things in, 230.

Numbers. Chinese, of Heaven and Earth, 445; Male and Female, 445; views as to, in connection with the Universe, 141 and note.

Numerals and **letters**. The 32 Paths of Wisdom, 204.

Nut. Comparison of the Universe to a, 190.

O

Oannes, 244. See, Fish-god.

Odor of the Righteous, 355.

Olam Gal'gal-im, 419; Gil-gooleem, 280; Mala'khay-ah, 280.

Olam ha-Moor'gash, *i. e.*, the Moral or Sensuous World, 200, 270.

Olam ha-Moos'kal, *i. e.*, the Intellectual World, 200, 263.

Olam ha-Mut-bah, *i. e.*, the Natural World, 201, 271; ha-Sephiroth; Q'lippoth; A'tzeel-ah; B'ree-ah; Ye'tzeer-ah and A'seey-yah. See, those Titles.

One or E'had, 344; composed of Three, 372 *sq.*

Onion. Sacredness of the, 451; roofs shaped like an onion, 451; Universe in layers like an, 415.

Open Eye, 118.

Oppositions and the **Harmony**, 117, 118, 185.

Oppositions, the stability of, in male and female, 417; to the Four Worlds, 434.

Oral instruction in ancient times, 178 *sq.*

Oral teaching. The value of, 178.

Origen, on the Secret meanings to be found under the words of the Old Testament, 103, 104 *sq.*; Qabbalistic ideas in the writings of, 308 *sq.*

Original Sin. Man born in, 346, 347, 432.

Osiander, Andreas, agrees with Kleuker as to the antiquity of the Hebrew Qabbalah, 172.

Otto, Julius Conrad, favors the antiquity of the Hebrew Qabbalah, 171.

Ounqelos, 98, 207.

Ox. The, 45 note, 259.

P

Pa'had. The Sephirah, signifying, Fear, 200, 269 *sq.*, 292 note.

Palace used to indicate the different degrees of expansion of the Sephiroth,

191; used to signify, the Supreme Canopy or Veil, 136.
Pan. The Greek, 324 *sq.*; represented as clothed in a spotted skin, 325 *sq.*
Paracelsus. Philippus Aureolus Theophrastus, Bombast of Hohenheim, usually known as, was largely influenced by the Hebrew Qabbalah, 171.
Paradise or Eden, 273, 369 note; Paradise and the Garden of Eden. The distinction between, 204, 220; Ibn Gebirol's explanation of, 204; and Hell, 432 *sq.*; return of the Soul to, 404; the Souls in, 388 *sq.* See, Eden, Garden of Eden, Souls, Spirits, Gaï-hinom.
Partzupha, 411.
Partzupheem, 211, 253.
Partzuphin or Faces, 118.
Pastor of Hermas cited, 116, 167.
Patristic Literature and Ideas as to the No-Thing, 127 note; Literature and the Qabbalah, 167.
Pentateuch Rolls not pointed with the Vowel Symbols, 460 *sq.*
Persian idea of the Oppositions, 186.
Pfeiffer. Augustus. Favored the antiquity of the Hebrew Qabbalah, 11, 171.
Pharisees, destroyed the Inner Spirituality of the Hebrew Sacred Writings, 174, Introd. viii, ix.
Philo Judæus, 167; his ideas as to the intermediaries, 301, 302.
Philosophical systems as to intermediate causes, 301.
Philosophy and Religion ought not to be separated, Introd. x.
Phœnician alphabet, 460.
Phylacteries or Th'pheelin. Antiquity of 95, 452; worn constantly in ancient times by the Jews, 95.
Physiognomy, 45 note; 47.
Piety of the Qabbalists, 63, 64.
Pigs and Reptiles, Unclean in ancient Babylonia, 241.
Pillar of the Centre, 282; of the Right, that of Mercy, 282; the Left, that of Judgment, 282. See, Diagrams.
Pious. Atonement by the, 337, 338, 339; the Deity, very strict with the, 352, 353; future happiness of, 356, 357, 358, 389 *sq.*, 406, 409. See, Righteous; also, Just.

Place, *i. e.*, Ma-qom, 118, 278, 349.
Planetary World called Gil'gooleem or Gal'gal-im, 280, 419.
Planets created on Wednesday, 206; each was thought to have a presiding angel, 314; their colors, metals, and symbols, in Chaldea and Babylonia, 449 *sq.*; World of the, 330.
Plato. His doctrine as to Ideas, 113, 276 *sq.*; his idea of the invisible God, 114.
Poetry Jewish, in the Middle Ages, 1, 2.
Point. The, 280, 281; the Chinese, 446 *sq.*; the first, is the Sephirah Kether, *i. e.*, Crown, 127; the first, called, *ne'qood-ah qadmo-ah*. Emanation of the Universe from, 136, 381 *sq.*
Points on the Pehlevi coins, 466; to the *Resh* and *Daleth*, in the II century A.D., 466.
Poison. The Angel of, 435. See, Samä-el Lil-ith.
Pope Nicholas III, 81 *sq.*
Pope Sixtus IV. Largely influenced by the Hebrew Qabbalah, 171.
Porphyry's Tree, like the Tree of the Sephiroth, 313.
Postel. William of. Favored the antiquity of the Hebrew Qabbalah, 171.
Power of Judgment, 126.
Powers of Philo, 231. See, Philo.
Practical Qabbalah among the Babylonian Jews, 51 and note. See, Qabbalah.
Prana. The Hindu, 321, 322, 323, 324.
Prayer of Eliyah, 290 *sq.*
Prayer. The Lord's. End of the, 202 and note; and the Ten commandments, 318.
Prayer at Night before going to bed, 409.
Prayers. Two Qabbalistic, in the daily service of the Sephardi Jews, 315.
Pre-Adamite Kings, 118, 137, 386 *sq.* See, Kings of Edom.
Pre-existence of Souls, 196. See, Souls.
Priests and Prophets. Ancient, of the Hebrews, 221.
Priests originally not a distinct class, Moses confined them to the Sons of Levi, 221; orders of, among the Akkadians, etc., 240.
Primal Cause, 174.
Primordial Point, 257. See, Point.

Principles. Male and Female, 387 *sq.* See, Male and Female Principles, Adam, Man, Kings of Edom.

Procession of Lighted Candles, 326.

Proclus, 162.

Pronunciation of the ancient Hebrew probably lost, 465.

Prophets called, *Nabiu*, or *Na'bee*, 206; The last, 222; originally not a distinct class, Moses changed this to the initiates, 221; come prominently forward in the time of Samuel, 221; as a profession. Time of the cessation of the, 222.

Prototype. Elohim the, R. Moses Cordovero on, 212. See Tzure, Tzurath, The, in the First World, 328. See, Adam also, Makrokosm.

Prototypes Above, 109 *sq.;* 418, Lower World, 190.

Providence. An uninterrupted, in government of the universe, 193.

Punishment of Sinners who do not repent, 353.

Purpeer-ah, an angel, 412 and note.

Purusha, 323, 337 note.

Pythagoras, 444; Tetrad of, 202 note, 318; believed the Universe has been made through the proportions of Numbers, 141.

Pythagoreans. Opinions of as to Ideas, 113; favor the idea of the Revolution and Rotundity, of the Earth, 140.

Q

Qabbalah. Ancient doctrines of. The Books which contain them, 166, 167; Antiquity of the, 165, 180, 218; in the Apocrypha, New Testament, etc., 166, 167, 440; and Assyriology, 235 *sq.*, Introd. xiii; among the Buddhists, and the Dravidian races of India, 170; Christian, 232; in the Common Law, 232; in the Cuneiform Writings, 218; Difficulty of studying, Introd. xiii, xiv, 179 *sq.;* the Dogmatic or Positive, 226; called '*Hen, i.e.*, Grace, 221; the Hebrew, its origin, 219; Hebrew, the problems it seeks to solve, 223; Hebrew Speculative, 161; Hebrew, bases itself on the Hebrew Sacred Writings, 224; Hebrew Practical, 224; Hebrew, cardinal doctrines of, 225; and Hindu Aryan thought, 438, Introd. xiii; Investigation of, almost wholly ignored by the writers of this Century, Introd. vii; how a Knowledge of it was obtained by the Egyptians, according to the Qabbalists, 166; considers Humanity as an Universal Brotherhood, 181; and Massorah, 221; the Modern views of Luriah and Cordovero, on the potential activity of the Deity in Nature, 193; in Old Writings, 440; Origin of, 221; the Practical, 226, 227; Practical, in ancient Babylonia, 237; in India, Introd. xiii; Qabbalah early called a Science, 36; a continuation of the Secret Doctrine, 179; in the Septuagint Translation of the Hebrew Sacred Writings, 166; the Speculative or Metaphysical, 179, 226, 236; nothing of it written, until the time of Shim-on b. Yo'hai, 166; the Symbolical, 226; the Theoretical, 226; Theories of, proceed from the lowest to the highest, 225, 226; traced to the Jewish Universities in Babylonia, 39; Value of the study of, Introd. vii; Value of to the truly spiritual and inner man, Introd. ix; in the Vedas, especially their Upanishads, 170; Introd. xiii, 324 note, 439; the Wisdom of, mentioned by Haÿ Gaon and Gebirol, 440; in the Zend writings, 170.

Qabbalistic Formula of the Names, etc., 342, 343; Tree of Life of the Sephiroth, with the Divine Names attached, 169. See, the Diagrams.

Qabbalists and Ibn Gebirol, drew from the same source, 161; the names of Ancient, 440.

Qadmon. Adam, 3, 4, 181, 190, 231, 281. See, Adam Qadmon.

Qa-yin and Ge'boor-ah, 422.

Qimchi. R. Joseph Ibn, 8.

Q'lippoth, 126, 436 *sq.;* Olam ha-, *i. e.*, World of the Shells, 329, 330.

Queen. Malkhuth called, 203; the She'-kheen-ah called, the, 341, 401.

Qur'ân, prohibits cursing strange gods, 94.

R

Rabbins. Capture of the Babylonian, 5.

Recanati. R. Mena'hem di, 12, 226, 289.

Rekhabites. The, 227.
Repentance necessary before man is forgiven his sins, 351, 352; created before the World, 353.
Resha 'Hiv'rah, *i. e.,* White Head, 133, 258, 369 *sq.* See, Head.
Resurrection. The, 354; of man in the body, 354, 355, 356, 414; and existence after death, believed in, by the Semitic Chaldeans, 246. See, Body of the Resurrection.
Reuchlin. John (or Capnio), 11, 171.
Revised versions of the Holy Scriptures, Introd. xiii.
Revolution of the Earth, in the Zohar, 139 *sq.*; of the Earth, a fallacy according to the Church Fathers, Lactantius and Augustine, 139. See, also, Earth; of Souls, 413. See, Gal-gal-im.
Rhenford or **Rhenferdius. Johann,** favors the antiquity of the Hebrew Qabbalah, 171.
Ricci. Paul, favors the antiquity of the Hebrew Qabbalah, 171.
Righteous. The souls of the, higher than the angels, 383 *sq.* See, Pious; also, Just.
Rising of the Soul of the dead, 354 *sq.* See, Resurrection.
Rittangel. John Stephen, favors the antiquity of the Qabbalah, 171.
River of Fire. See, Dinur.
Rivers. The Four, of Paradise, 216.
Rolls of the **Synagogue.** The method of Reading the, 467. See, Vowel Points.
Roman Catholic Church and its hierarchy, 167 note; claims to be the possessor of a Christian Qabbalah, 232.
Rome, in the Zohar, 71 *sq.*
Rose. Romance of the, Hebrew Qabbalism runs through the poem of, 171.
Rosenroth. Baron Christian Knorr von, Favors the antiquity of the Zohar, 11, 65, 171.
Rosicrucian Society, largely influenced by the Hebrew Qabbalah, 171.
Rossi. R. Azzaryah Min Ha-adomim dei. Believed in the antiquity of the Zohar, 64.
Rua'h, *i. e.,* Spirit, 147, 153, 160, 196, 200, 203, 232, 282, 292 note, 321, 332, 390 *sq.*,
404, 410, 411, 412, 413, 418, 419, 432, 433; of the Great Ideal Man, 301.
Rua'h ha-Qadosha, *i. e.,* the Holy Spirit, 260.
Rûm Ma-aleh, *i. e.,* Inscrutable Height, 258.

S

Saadyah Gaon mentions the Ten Sephiroth, 160 note; on the Sepher Ye'tzeer-ah, 159.
Sabah's (the Old Man's) words, 124.
Sabah D'Sabin, 367.
Sachs. Dr. Michael, opposes the antiquity of the Hebrew Qabbalah, especially the Zohar, 172.
Sacrifices in ancient Babylonia, 240.
Sakhya Mûni or Buddha, 187, 239, 443 note, 444.
Salamander, 394 *sq.*
Salvation to the Wicked, from the Deity, 430.
Sam Moveth Az, the Demon, 434.
Samä-el, 330, 344, 365 note; The Angel of Death, 347, 348; and his Companion, Esheth Zenooneem, 330, 331; brought Death into the World, 345; Dangerous to mock, 435; the Evil Serpent, 344, 345 and note, 346; and the First-Sin, 430 *sq.;* and Lil-ith, 433 *sq.* See, Lil-ith.
Samson's riddle, 229.
Saracens, 71 *sq.*
Sarcognomy, 45 note.
Satan, the Accuser, but an angel of the Deity, 242; not to be Cursed, 93, 94; a Necessity, 186. See, Talmud.
Satanow. J., Favors the antiquity of the Zohar, 64 note.
Sabbath, perhaps our Sunday, kept by the ancient Akkadians, etc., 240.
Scaliger, 10.
Schelling. F. W. J. von, quoted as to the importance of the Hebrew Qabbalah and the Zohar, 173, 174; influenced by the doctrines of the Hebrew Qabbalah, 171.
Schiller-Szinessy. D., favors the Antiquity of the Hebrew Qabbalah, 172; favorable to the antiquity of the Zohar, 63; translation of a passage of the Zohar by, 106 to 108.

Schœttgen. Christian, 11, cited, 114; Works of, recommended, 115 note.
Schopenhauer. Arthur, influenced by the Hebrew Qabbalah, 171.
Schultens. Albert, on the Hebrew vowel pointing, 461 *sq.*
Sea, the Great Crystalline, 233, 234, 235, 257, 336, 448 *sq.*
Sea. The Great Crystal in the Apocalypse, 303; Symbolism of the, in the formation of the Sephiroth, 279.
Secrecy by the ancient wise men, 178.
Secret Doctrine, 166, 179; in the time of Jesus, 174; or Learning, not to be found in the Talmuds, Introd. vii, viii; called; Sithrai Thorah, Sodoth ha-Thorah, 'Hokhmah, Pardes, *i. e.*, Paradise, etc., 220; Reason of the Secrecy, as to, 222; of Genesis, 123; Learning, 161; Learning in the New Testament, Introd. viii; Learning, mentioned in the Talmudim, 54, Learning. The Teachings in the, 222; meanings contained in the words of the Thorah and of the Old Testament, 102 *sq.*, 105; Science, 52; Science or Qabbalah among the Jews in Babylonia, 53; Wisdom, 284.
Sepher Arugath ha-Bosem, 160; Bahir, called Ye'rushalmi, 48; Bikku-reh Ha-eettim, 93; B'rith Me'nu-'hah, 54; Dibreh Hayoumim L'Moshch, 94, 98; Emeq ha-Melekh, 110 note; Ha-maggid, 54; Ha-mishqal, 60; ha-Qabbalah, 5; ha-Rimmon, 60; ha-Shem, 60; ha-Sodoth, 60; Mash-mee-ah ye'shoo-ah, 75; Mathnoth Ke-hun-hah, 73; Ma-ye'nai ye'shoo-ah, 73; M'bo Shé-arim, 110 note; Matzreph l'keseph, 64; Migdal Oz, favorable to the antiquity of the Zohar, 42; Quotations from Maimonides, favorable to the antiquity of the Qabbalah, 40; Mishkan Ha-edooth, 60; Nephesh Ha-'hokhmah, 60; Ne-tza'h Yisraël, 73; Qadmooth ha-Zohar, in favor of the antiquity of the Zohar, 40; Sha-ar ha-Shemoth, 60 note; Sha-ar ha-Tzinoroth, 60 note; Shalsheleth ha-Qabbalah 62; Shee-oor Qo-mah, 44; She-qel Ha-Qodesh, 60; Shepathal, 110 note; Shushan Ha-edooth, 60; Sublime Faith. Abraham b. David Ha-Levi in this book, attacks Ibn Gebirol, 161; 'Tzee'nah Uree'nah, 343 note; Ye'tzeer-ah, 218; Ye'tzeer-ah. Antiquity of, 39; Ye'tzeer-ah on Ayin, 256; Ye'tzeer-ah, cited, 126; Ye'tzeer-ah, Known to be Ibn Gebirol, 159, 203; Ye'tzeer-ah, quoted, 305; Ye'tzeer-ah, on the meaning of Sephirah, etc., 296, 297, 298; Yu'hasin. Disputes as to the correctness of the versions of, 55, 56, 62.
Sephirah, Sephiroth. Meaning of the words, 295 *sq.*; Triad in each, 281.
Sephiroth. The, 156; of Construction, 200; as to the Deity and between themselves, 289; Delineations of like those of the Ptolemaic planetary system, 297, see, Plate, p. 295; Form the Adam Qadmon, 182; Formulations as to, 294; Ibn Gebirol's idea, as to the, 209, 210; known to Haÿ Gaon, 160; Heavenly spheres, 314 *sq.*; Idea of, in the Apocryphal Gospel of the Birth of Mary, 316 *sq.*; Idea of in Isaiah, 315 *sq.*; the Maz-zol, 298; names of, in the Zohar, 280; Olam ha-, 321; Origin of the Idea of the, 302 *sq.*; Idea of, like that of one who desires to build a palace, 380; in Philo, 160 note; see, Philo. Quotations from the Talmud, as to, 304, 305; known to Saadyah Gaon, 160 note; The Seven Lower, 292 note; Spheres or orbits, 191 note; Symbolical description of the forming of the, 277 *sq.*; The Ten, 251 *sq.*, 409, 421 note, 442 and note, 443 note; The Ten, action of, 193; Ten, in Ibn Gebirol, 160; The Ten, together, compose the Adam Qadmon, and are the content of the Ineffable Name, 231; the Ten, perhaps in the hierarchies of Dionysios, the Areopagite, (St. Denis) and, The Testament of Adam, 167 and note; The Ten, triadic, 281; The Tree of, with the Akkadians and Chaldeans, 235; The Voices Seen, not heard, 100.
Sephirothic Diagram in circles, 100; Tree, like Porphyry's Tree, 313. See, Diagrams.
Serpent, 204; brought death into the World, 346; of Eternity, 45 note; The Evil, 435; The Evil. See Samä-el. The

Great, has Seven heads, 235; the Great; the bond which was thought to hold together, the Heavens and the Earth, 235; the, of the Great Sea, 233, 234, 235, 243; the great Subtility of, and the reason of this, 235. See, Leviathan, also, Samä-el.

Seth and **Ra'h-mim**, 422.

Seth's knowledge of the Qabbalah, 165.

Seven kings of Edom, 118, 246, 386. See, Pre-Adamitic kings; also, Kings of Edom. Lights in early Christianity, 230; a number sacred to the Ancient people of Babylonia, 240, 448 *sq.*; Planets, 235; Seven-headed Serpent of the Great Sea, Leviathan, 233-235; Spirits before the Throne, 308; Stars of the Great Bear, 235; Value of the number in ancient times, 277, 302, 303, 317; Divisions in the Universe, 415.

Seventh Thousand year of the World, 233.

Sex in the deities of the Semites, 246. Comp. *Hu*; also, Feminine.

Shaddai, *i. e.*, the Almighty, 272. See, Metatron.

Shaddaï. El. At first probably triadic, 175.

Shadow. The created made from the *D'yooq-nah*, *i. e.*, Shadow, of the Light of the Deity, 211.

Shafruth. Yitz-'haq Ibn, 38.

Shalsheleth Ha-Qabbalah, 64.

Sha-mayeem, *i. e.*, Heavens, 348 *sq.*, 369.

Shaprut. R. Chasdai ('Hasdai or Chisdaï), Ibn Shaprut ben Yitz-'haq b. Ezra ha-Nasi, 38.

Shedim, 434 *sq.*

Shedin, 434.

She'kheen-ah, 116, 128, 175, 340, 341, 342, 349-351 note, 401; part in the Creation of the Universe, 359 *sq.*; and Elohim, 365 note. See, Queen; also, Matroneetha.

She-mah. The, 371 *sq.*

Shemaryähu. Rabbi, 5.

Shem Ha-me'phorash. See Ineffable name; **Hava-yah**, *i. e.*, the Existing Name, 342, 379 *sq.*

She'reerah (Gaon). R., 38; on Physiognomy, 45, 46, 47.

Shesheth. Jacob b., 38.

Shim-on b. Yo'haï's School, 48. See, Yo'haï. Shim-on b.

Sibylline Oracles, 167.

Side. The other, or Evil, 437.

Silence or Death. The Angel of, 403, 405. See, Death.

Simon. Richard, ascribes the origin of the Hebrew Qabbalah to the Chaldeans, 172.

Sin. The First, 430 *sq.*; Original. Man born in, 346, 347, 432. See, Adam, Man, First Sin.

Sinners. The necessary change for, 353.

Siphra D'Tznioothah. Beginning of, cited, 118; a Zoharic book, 13.

Six thousand years of the World, 233.

Sixtus IV. Pope, influenced by the Qabbalah, 171.

Sleep, the taste of Death, 409; the soul leaves the body during sleep, 402 *sq.*; dreams, 403.

Smooth Point, 257. See, Ne'qood-ah, also, Point.

Sod or Mystery, 6, 220, 340 note. See, Mystery, Wine, Secret, 358, 346 note.

Solomon Engraved on the walls of his Temple, likenesses of the male and female principles, 117; The Psalter, of, 167; the Temple of, 185; Book of, 397.

Son. The, of God, 194, 199; The Only Begotten, 262; Production of the, 387 *sq.*; The Upper Adam, the, 421; The, or Word, 459. See, Logos, Word, Messiah, Metatron, Mediator.

Son of God, an angel, 116; Ideas as to in ancient Babylonia, 247; the Thorah, 116.

Sorcery among the Chaldeans, 453 *sq.*

Soul. Abode on earth a means of education and trial, 197; Animal. See, Nephesh. Ascent to the bosom of the Deity, 111, 406; a Chariot, 220 note; entrance of, into the body, 396 *sq.*; effect as to purity or uncleanness, according to Ibn Gebirol, 198; the Light in which it is clothed, 399 *sq.*; departure of the holy, 411; manifestation of through the light of the eyes, 215. See, Neshamah for the Upper Soul, Nephesh for the Animal or Vital Soul. Soul of the

Pious. The crowning of, 389 *sq.*; Pre-existence of, 196; the Prototypic Higher Soul, 190; Reminiscence in the, 196; Return of to Paradise, 404; passes through the Sephiroth, 291 note; and Spirit. The positions of, 407 *sq.*; Writings upon the Divisions of, 334.

Souls. The souls above, 388 *sq.*; Descent of, 388 *sq.*; Descent of the souls of the pious into Sheol to bring up souls which are therein, 413; all existed at first, in the Divine Idea, 196; Divisions of the, 196, 390 *sq.*; Emanated and their prior knowledge, 388 *sq.*; Emanation of, through the Right and the Left, side, 110; Forming of the, 384 *sq.* See, Neshamah, Rua'h, Nephesh and, Soul. In Paradise, 389 *sq.*; Doctrine of the Pre-existence of, 190 and note; in the Pre-existent condition, 399; The Revolution of. See, Gil-goolem. Revolution or Revolving of the, 413; of the Righteous, higher than the angels, 383 *sq.*; The Three, 200; Treasury of the, 395 *sq.*; of the Wicked, 358; The Coming down to this World of the, 384 *sq.*

Sound and Color, 277; Eternity of Sound, 124 note, 428; sound in Worship, 230.

Space. Infinite, 231; Qabbalistic ideas upon, 300, 301; Three Worlds in, 301.

Spaces. The Two, 146.

Spark. The emanation of the Nebulous, 195. See, Point; also, Ne'qood-ah.

Speculative Qabbalah, 230.

Spencer. Herbert, cited, 113.

Spinoza. Barukh or Benedict, influenced by the Hebrew Qabbalah, 171.

Spirit. The Evil, 346 and note, 347. See, *Ye'tser ha-rah*, and Samä-el. The Holy, considered by the Qabbalah as in the Sephirah Binah, 182. See, Rua'h.

Spiritual Elements of the worlds, or, *Ru'hoth ye'sod ha-Olam*, 193; in Man or Adam, 114. See, Adam.

St. Augustine did not believe in the Revolution of the Earth on its axis, 139.

St. Dionysios, the Areopagite, 45 note, 167 note, 440, 456; Mystic Theology of, 456. See, Dionysios.

St. Ephraim used vowel pointing in the Syriac, 466.

St. Jerome, on the Ten Divine Names, 168, note.

St. Jerome's knowledge of the Hebrew vowel points, 468, 469.

St. Paul refers to the Celestial Adam, 114, 115; says, we live and move in God, 114; holds that the Visible declares the Invisible, 114. See, Introduction xi.

St. Synesios, on Dreams, 46, 115 note, 440.

Steiger, confesses the importance of an investigation of the Hebrew Qabbalah, 172.

Steinschneider. Dr. Moritz, 11; says, the true history of the Hebrew Qabbalah, has not been written, 172.

Stern. Ignatz, favors the Antiquity of the Hebrew Qabbalah, 11, 172.

Stork. The, 321.

Strunz. Fred, 10.

Sun. Eclipse of, in the Zohar and the Kether Malkhuth, 198; the Nocturnal, 453; Parallel of the light of the Sun, by Ibn Gebirol, 149.

Subjective and objective, 193.

Superior and Inferior. As Male and Female, 189.

Symbolism. Hindu, 127 note; of Language, 175 *sq.* See, also, Introduction xi *sq.*; of writing, 178. See, Colors.

Synesios of Cyrene shows a knowledge of the Qabbalah, 46 note. See, St. Synesios.

Syriac and Hebrew vowel pointing from the same source, 466; Massorah in the III century A.D., 465 *sq.*; Vowel pointing, 465 *sq.*

T

Tab'nooth. The Form, called, 401.

Tag-in. The, 24, 202; mentioned by St. Jerome and the Talmud, 465.

Talisman and amulets, 452.

Talmud. Early name of, 48; opposes the cursing of Satan, 94; when and where edited, and the content of, 48.

Talmidai 'Hakhameen or Disciples of the Wise, 92.

Tantras. Hindu. Qabbalistic ideas in, Introd. xiii, 170.

Tao. Principles of the, 111 *sq*.
Tao-teh-King, by Laou Tsz', 113.
Targums. Age of, 461, 462; are Mystical, 53.
Teacher and Pupil. In the ancient world and to-day in India, 177.
Teaching of the **Twelve Apostles** cited, 116 *sq*.; curious statement as to the Kosmic Mystery, 116 *sq*.
Te-bah, *i. e.*, Nature, and Elohim, 379.
Tel-loh. Wonderful discoveries at, 237 note, 238 note, 239.
Temple of Solomon, 185; Solomon's and the Babylonian, 240, 241; Towers, 240, 241. See, Solomon.
Temples. Angles of the ancient Babylonian, 240.
Temptation through woman, 365 note. See, First Sin.
Ten Angelic Hosts, 167 and note, 329; Of the number Ten, 302 *sq*.; the number, in ancient Babylonia, 240; ten 'Saids'. The, 122; The Ten Words, 328, 329.
Tennemann. Wilhelm G., agrees with Brucker, 172.
Terrestrial Man, 123 *sq*. See, Man; also, Adam.
Testament of Adam, 167 note; of the Twelve Patriarchs, 167.
Tetrad of Pythagoras, 202 note, 318.
Tetragrammaton, 263. See, Ineffable Name.
Thanksgiving days, existed with the ancient people of Babylonia, 240.
Theivhel. Of, 416.
The'na-im. The, 48.
Theosophy. Jewish, at Sora in Babylonia, 52. See, Babylonian Jews.
These, *i. e.*, Eleh, 130 *sq*.
Thirty-two ways of Wisdom, 199, 204, 369 note.
Thohu, 243, 244, 305 note, 448 *sq*. See, Bohu.
Tholuck. Augustus, opposes the antiquity of the Hebrew Qabbalah, especially the Zohar, 10, 172.
Thorah. Creation of, 135; Secret meanings in the words of, 102, 103.
Thorah's. The two, 375.
Thought, *i. e.*, *Ma'hshabah*, 128 and note, 297, 298, 377 *sq*., 408; Most of the Ancient has perished, 178; Waves of, pass through Humanity, 180; and the Word, 377 *sq*. See, Ma'hshabah.
Three Degrees of initiation in Ancient Babylonia, 249; of Initiation in the early Christian Church, 249; the three Dimensions, 137 note. See, Dimensions. Are One, 371 *sq*.; Parts of Fire which are one, 376; Upper Sephiroth form YHV, 186.
Throne. The, 280, 424; Kiseh ha-Kabod, *i. e.*, Throne of Glory, 429 note; Kursai-yah, the, 328, 394.
Tiberias. The School, and the vowel points, 465.
Tiph'e-reth. The Sephirah, 200, 201, 203, 270, 282, 283, 292 note. See, Sephiroth; also, Colors.
Towers. Sacred, 240, 241.
Tradition. Antiquity of, 175, 176; Oral and Written, 176. See, Introduction.
Transmigration of Souls, 90 *sq*.; St. Jerome upon, 91. See, Revolution, Gil-goolem, Metempsychosis. Origen upon, 91.
Tree of Death, 409, 410.
Tree. The Great, 349 *sq*., 385, 422; The Holy, 422; of Knowledge, 204, 431 *sq*.; of Life, 205, 252, 253, 349, 406, 436; of the Sephiroth, 235, 252 *sq*., 314; The World, 235.
Triad, 259, 281; very Ancient, 212, 213; with the Chinese, 444 *sq*.; with the Israëlites, 372; in Ibn Gebirol, 212; in the Holy of Holies, 186; in each Human being, 200; She-mah and the Unity in the, 371 *sq*.; in each Sephirah, 281.
Triadic deities of the Akkadians, 246, 247; Idea, 263, 264, 265, 266, 267, 268, 372 *sq*.; Idea in the Zohar, 182, 183, 200; Representations on Signets and Amulets, 249, 250; symbolism in the Qabbalah, 182.
Trinity, 208; in Judaism, 372.
Trisagion, in early Christianity, 230.
Trismegistus Hermes. See, Hermes Trismegistus.
Tritheim. The **Abbot Johannes**, largely influenced by the Hebrew Qabbalah, 171.

Trouble. When in, man should depend on the Deity, 429.
Truth, the Seal, 372 note, one of the foundations of the Universe, xix *sq.*
Tzelem, 347 note, 390 *sq.*, 404 *sq.*, 411 *sq.*
Tzim'tzum. The Qabbalistic theory of, 201, 211, 231, 446.
Tzool-mah. The, 405.
Tzurah. The, 401.
Tzure, *i. e.*, Prototype, 384 *sq.*
Tzurath, Prototypes, 392, 400.

U

Understanding. See, Binah, Sephirah and Sephiroth.
Underworld. The Chaldean, etc., 450 *sq.*
Unity, Triad and She-mah, 371 *sq.*
Universal Form of Ibn Gebirol, 199; and Matter, 143 *sq.*; Intellect, 144.
Universali. The, **De Materia,** 8.
Universe. Construction of the Akkadian, Chaldean and Babylonian, 448; Emanation of, 135, 195, 381 *sq.*, 385 *sq.*, called the Garment of God, 280; in the Middle Ages. Diagrams of, 295, 319, 448; formed from an Indivisible Point, 136; Qabbalistic ideas as to the construction of, 415 *sq.*; Present, before its Creation, to the Holy One, in Idea, 127; created by the Deity and His She'kheenah, 359 *sq.*; went forth from the Will, 127.
Upper and **Lower,** connection between the, 386; Deity and Lower Deity in the religious system of the Akkadians, 247; Family. As to consultation with the, 246, 365 note, Introduction xiii; and Lower Deity of the Qabbalah, 247; and Lower Worlds, 256; Man or Adam, 114; Universe of which the Lower, is a copy, 108 *sq.*
Us. Let, make Adam, 360 *sq.*

V

Van Helmont. John Baptist, 11; Franz Mercurius, 11.
Van Helmonts. The two, largely influenced by the Hebrew Qabbalah, 171.
Veil. The, cannot be raised in the matter world, Introd. xi; on which Creation was Portrayed, 127, 135 and note, 136. See, Maya or, Illusion, and, Description of Plates.
Venus. The Planet, 329; placed next to the Sun instead of Mercury, 314.
Vessels. The, the Sephiroth, 210. 211. 279 *sq.* See, Sephiroth, also, Kailem.
Vicarious Sacrifices, in Ancient Babylonia, 240.
Villars. Abbe de, author of the Count de Gabalis, 171.
Visible. Through it we obtain knowledge of the invisible, 109, 113, 174. See, St. Paul, and the Introduction.
Vision of Ezeqiel. Animals of, in Chaldea, 45 note, 227, 228.
Visions. The, of Ezeqiel, Daniel, Isaiah, 45 note, 227.
Voice. The, 136, 137; and Sound in Worship, 230; The, and the Word, 377 *sq.*
Voices, seen not heard, 99, 100.
Vincent de Beauvois, 163.
Virgin Mary. Hymn to the, 336; Symbolic color of, 261 note.
Vowel Accents in the Talmud, 467.
Vowel Pointing. Antiquity claimed for it, 461 *sq.*; An Example to show antiquity of Vowel pointing, 465; was not Invented at one time, 463 *sq.*; Syriac and Hebrew from the same source, 466.
Vowel Points in 610 A.D., 467; Assyrian and Palestinian, 461; from the Babylonian Saboraim and not the Massorites, 466; Buxtorf believed them to be ancient, 464 *sq.*; in the VIII Century A.D., 467; in the X Century, 467 *sq.*; Dr. John Gill on the antiquity of, 464; The Great value to Judaism, of the establishment and making known with certainty, of the, 469; Hebrew, 460 *sq.* See, Hebrew vowel points. In the Hebrew, first applied only in ordinary books, 467; names of, not Hebrew, 469; Opinion of the Karaite Jews upon the, 464 *sq.*; only give the Pronunciation as it existed in the VI Century in the School of Tiberias; Reason of their having been made known, 462 *sq.*; not on the Hebrew Synagogue Rolls, 467; St. Jerome's knowledge of, 468, 469;

pointing in the Syriac, 465 *sq.;* Syriac gives the earliest historical knowledge of, 464 *sq.;* in Syriac, Chaldaic, Arabic and Persian, 468; points in the Syriac quite perfect in the time of James, Bishop of Edessa, 466; System of, among the Syrians in 350 A.D., 466; Reasons for the introduction of a more permanent and known System of vowel points, 466 *sq.;* Words showing the value of, 469, 470; in the Zohar, 468, 469.

Vowels. In the Aryan languages, 175; the Hebrews asserted to have always had, 465; Necessity of vowel points in the Hebrew writings, 465; The Seven, 277; Seven in Egypt, 463; Seven, among the Greeks, 463 *sq.;* Seven, among the Hebrews, 463 *sq.;* Written, not in the Semitic languages, 175.

W

Wachter. John George, ascribes the origin of the Hebrew Qabbalah to Gentile philosophy, 172.
Wakkar. Yoseph b. Abraham Ibn, 12.
Water-Basins. In ancient temples, 240.
Ways. The Thirty-two, 300, 313, 314, 369 note.
Wednesday. The day of Ne'bo, also the day of Buddha and the day of Mercury, 206.
Week. Names of the days of the, 449.
Weigel. Valentine, Largely influenced by the Hebrew Qabbalah, 171.
Weight, Measure, Number. God doeth all things, in, 230.
What? and, **Who?** 128, 129 *sq.*, 378. See, Eleh.
Wheat. The Parable as to, from the Zohar, 101.
Where? Meaning of, 275.
White Head. The, 133. See, Resha 'Hiv'rah.
Wicked. The Deity, restrains His anger as to the, 352, 353; The Souls of the, 358; the Judgment and Punishment of the, 358, Salvation of the, 430.
Wieseler upon the Comet at the time of the Birth of Jesus, 87.

Will of Ain Soph, 231; Creation by the, 135, 137; Creative, Logos or Word, 137; The Divine, 143 *sq.*, 193, 194; Divine, does not abolish Free Will, 194; the Sephirah Kether, 190; as the Source of Life, 196; a Triad yet a unit, 204; the Will as an active agent in the Creation of the Universe, 3, 191; Universe Engraved in the, 195.
Williams. Dr. S. Wells. His Middle Kingdom, cited, 113.
Winder, 10.
Wine. Reason of the use of, 230; and Sod, 358. See, Sod.
Wings, an ancient emblem of the spiritual, 366 and note, xix.
Wisdom, 125, 262 *sq.;* the Wisdom, Above, 368, 369 *sq.;* The Akkadian Deity of, 243-244; Deity of, among the ancient Chaldeans, 241, 242. See, 'Hokhmah. Creating Power. Views of Proverbs, St. Paul, etc., upon, 205; Religion, 221; St. Paul on, 208, 209; Upper and Lower, 206, 207; the Upper Paradise, 205 and note; or the Word, created the Universe, 205-209. See, Logos, and Word.
Wolff. Rev. John Christopher, ascribes the origin of the Hebrew Qabbalah to Gentile Philosophy, 11, 172.
Woman. Regarded as the Medium of temptation, 365 note; Looking out of the Window, a Parable from the Zohar, 104, the Evil, 436. See, Lil-ith 'Havah or Eve, Na-amoh, First Sin.
Wool. White and Pure, an Oriental symbol for the efflux of Wisdom and Vitality, 118 note.
Word. The, 125, 262 *sq.*, 336, 377 *sq.;* The Creative, 137, 301; Doctrine as to the, in Different Nations, 205; The, the First-born brother of Satan, 116; The, First Word of All, 381; and Logos, 262. See, Logos, 'Hokhmah, Wisdom.
Words. All spoken by man continue and ascend, 428; in the Abstract Sciences only have a partially definite meaning, Introd. xi; Creation by Ten Sayings or, Words, 304; The Ten, 328, 329. See, Logos, Wisdom, Word, Ten.
World. The Ancient, and its Methods,

175; Angelic, 348; Exists through Judgment and Mercy, 402; the Inferior is the Female, 189; The Intellectual, 200, 262; The House of the, 385; Lower like the Upper, 417; the Material, 201; the Moral or Sensuous, 200; the Mountain of the, 450 *sq.;* The Natural or Matter-World, 201; The Planetary, 280, 419; of Separation, 420; the Superior, Male, 189.

Worlds. Derivation of the names of the, 320, 333; the Four, 198, 216, 280, 292 note. 320, 418 *sq.;* the Four, in Isaiah, 333; Four Oppositions to the, 434; the Four, paralleled by the four divisions in Plotinus, 333, 334; Prior, to ours, 386, 387; the Four Worlds, with Ibn Gebirol, 332; Superior and Inferior, influences between, 189; The Two, 190; the Three Worlds in the Sephiroth, 281 *sq.*

X

Xenophon's idea of the invisible God, 114.

Y

Ya-betz, 21 *sq.* See, Yaqob b. Z'vee and, Zohar

YaH. The world said to have been formed through that Name, 319 note.

Yakar. Yehudah b., 38.

Ya-kheen and Bo-az, 185.

Yang, Yin, Yih, 444 *sq.*

Ye'dud, *i. e.*, YHVH, 398.

Ye'hee-dah or Personality, 391 *sq.*, 396 *sq.*, 401.

Yekuthiel. R., on the Sephiroth, quoted, 38, 298, 299.

Yesh. The, 305 note.

Ye'tzer ha-rah, *i. e.*, the Evil Inclination, 126, 346 and note, 364, 430, 437; not the Devil. Introd. xiii; is the Serpent and the Angel of Death, 406. See, Evil Spirit.

Ye'tzer ha-tob, the Good Inclination, 126, 348, 364.

Ye'tzeer-ah. Olam ha, *i. e.*, World of Formation, 228, 321, 328 *sq.*

Ye'tzeer-ah. Sepher, very old, 159, 160; in the Talmud, 159, 160; and Zohar. Differences between the, 159.

Ye'tzeer-atic World, 198.

Ye'rushalmi Talmud. See, Talmudim.

Ye'sod. The Sephirah, 201, 271. See, Sephirah, also, Sephiroth.

Ygg-drasil of the Norse Mythology, 235.

YHVH in English Bible translated Lord, 129; YHVH, 128, 379 *sq.* See, Ineffable Name, Tetragrammaton, Name, etc.

Yih King. The, 170, 444.

Yih, Yin, Yang, 444 *sq.*

Yishmaëlites, the Bedawee Arabs, 69 *sq.;* Children of, not necessarily the Mohammedans, 69–73.

Yitz-'haq, the Blind (of Beaucaire), 38, 283.

Yo'haï. R. Shim-on ben, 7, 10, 17 *sq.*, 166, 439 *sq.*

Yotma or Yotna, an Engraving of, 228, 229.

Z

Zaqen. Eliÿah ha-, 38.

Ze'ir An-peen, 134, 138 note, 182, 258, 368 *sq.*, 380.

Zi-kum, 242–244.

Zodiac, 137 note; Ancient Mexican Signs of, 157; Assyrian Account of the creation of, 245; The Chaldean, etc., 448 *sq.;* has the Symbols of the male, female and harmony, 186.

Zodiacal Constellations, Ancient, 248, 249, 259; Constellations at first, Ten, 248. See, Description of Plates. Signs and the Animals of the vision of Ezeqiel, 228; Signs, Scorpio, Virgo, and Libra, 118. See, Description of Plates.

Zohar, 7, 8, 10; R. Abraham Gaon on, 53; Account of the Zoharic writings, 439; The Ancient, in Fez, 47; On the Angels in the, 192; Antiquity of, 12, 41 *sq.*, 55; Antiquity of from its definition of Eunuch, 92; The Aramaic language in, Introd., 50, 51; Claimed to have been forged by R. Moses de Leon, 56 *sq.;* Content of, 12, 13; and the cuneiform terra-cotta tablets, 232, 233 *sq.;* the Directions of R. Shim-on as to writing down the, 51 note; the Divinely mystical in, is concealed, and to be only learned orally, 53; the, Early acceptance of, 7; Editions of, 13 *sq.;* Excerpts from, 335 *sq.;*

Dr. Ginsburg, opposes the Antiquity of, 65 *sq.*; Dr. Graetz opposes the Antiquity of, but admits the early existence of, The Mysteries of R. Shim-on b. Yo'haï, 37; Ideas in, prior to the redaction of the Talmuds, 49; Illumination by the, 428; Introduction to the Cremona edition, 14 *sq.*; Jellinek's Introduction, 11; Analysis of Konitz's book in support of its Antiquity, 20 *sq.*; on the Messiah, 77 *sq.*; Morin's opposition to, 21; names of, 11; not by R. Mosheh (Moses) de Leon, 50 *sq.*, 58 *sq.*; opposed by Dr. Jellinek, 38; originally a Camel's load, 47; Predictions in, 49; Quoted, 25 note, and in many other places; Refutation of Yabetz's opposition to, 21; on the Repetition of, YHVH YHVH, evidencing two Worlds, 190; sets forth the Revolution of the Earth on its axis, 139; on the Superior and Inferior Worlds, 189; on Thought as the First Principle, 192; Time of the Composition of, according to David Luriah, 50; contained the Ancient Secret Tradition therefore that as to the Vowel Points, 469 *sq.*; Comparison of the Universe to a Nut, 190; on the Universe as the Kernel and Shell, 190, 191; Quotation from, as to the Vowel Points, etc., 469; Ya-betz speaks highly of the Zohar, 35, 36; R. Yaqob b. Z'vee, of Emden (Ya-betz), his opposition to, 21, 35, 36; called Ye'rushalmi, 48; Quoted, as to the Children of Yishmaël, 73–75. See, Yishmaël, Edom, Rome, Ma'hshabah, De Leon, etc.

Zoharic Idea, that the Deity has given definite laws to Nature and it follows these, 193; Parables, 101, 104, 436; Philosophy and the Chaldean systems, 454, 455; Writings, sometimes grand in thought, at others, puerile, 54.

Zorzi Franc Giorgio (Franciscus Georgius) surnamed Venetus, largely influenced by the Hebrew Qabbalah, 171.

Zuckermann on the Comet in the Zohar, 77 *sq.*, 81 *sq.*

Zunz. Dr. Leopold, opposes the antiquity of the Hebrew Qabbalah, especially the Zohar, 10, 172.

Z'vee. Yaqob b. (of Emden). See also, Ya-betz and, Zohar, 21 *sq.*

ERRATA.

Unimportant and easily to be recognized errors, are left to be corrected by the intelligent reader. For Haÿ-yim or 'Hayyim always read, '*Haÿ-yim;* for Hesed read, 'Hes-ed'; for Pirkeh or Pirkey Avoth read, *Pirqé Aboth;* for She'keen-ah read, She'kheen-ah ; for K'lippoth read, Q'lippoth ; for Yits-'haq or Yitz-haq read, Yitz-'haq ; for Ezekiel read, Ezeqiel; for Ya-kob or Jacob read, Ya-qob ; for Akeebah read, A'qee-bah.

Page 5, l. 9, r., 'Hanannel.
" 13, l. 15, r., Mishpatim.
" 14, l. 13, r., Naphthali.
" 16, l. 15 and 31, r., *P'tha'h-yah;* l. 20, r., *P'tha'h 'Enaÿim.*
" 19, note * l. 1, r., *Me'na'hoth;* l. 2. r., Qoheleth.
" 27, l. 8, r., *Mitzreem;* l. 11, r. *Mitz-rayim.*
" 29, l. 1, and 9, r., *Hal* for *Hall;* l. 21, r., Qametz.
" 38, l. 11, r., ha-Zaqen ; l. 14, r., ha-Nasé for, ha-Nazi.
" 39, l. 4, r., *'Hokhmah.*
" 41, l. 14, r., *Ha-'hokhmah;* l. 15, r., *Ha-Mishqal.*
" 48, l. 7, r., *Me-arobee.*
" 60, l. 11, r., *Ha-'hokhmah,* also in note r., *Tzinoreth.*
" 62, l. 23, r., Yehudah.
" 64, l. 11, r., *Matzreph;* l. 9. r., *'Enaÿim.*
" 65, l. 24, r., *Bo-tzeenah Qadoshah.*
" 66, note, r., *Licqute Qadmoniyoth.*
" 75, l. 6 and 7, r., Botz-rah ; l. 15, r., *Ze-ba'h.*
" 82, l. 12, r., Tzema'h.
" 85, l. 8, r., *Agoodoth Me'shee-a'h.*
" 88, l. 5, *dele* "perishing in the north," insert, will fall; l. 6, *dele* " dominion (palaces)" insert, daughter.
" 93, l. 3, r., *Biqoo-reh Ha-eetim.*
" 94, l. 19, r., *Ha-youmim;* in note, r., *Qe'du-sheen.*
" 95, l. 3, from bot. for " Mareh " r., Mamreh.
" 98, l. 4, r., *Ha-youmim;* l. 20, r., *Ounqelos.*
" 99, l. 1, r., Noa'h.
" 99-100, for "Sephiroth" r., letters of the Thorah.
" 105, note, r., *Qe'dusheen 28a, Ke'thubboth.*
" 107, l. 4, r., Azza.
" 108, l. 2, r., Azza ; in note, r., Siphrah; notes† and‡, r., *Va-yet-zeh, 156b.*
" 110, l. 20, r., Zee-vug; in note, r., *Emeq ha-Melekh.*
" 117, l. 14, r., *v-the'tha-in.*

Page 125, note †, add : Comp. Franck's *La Kab-bale,* p. 216.
" 126, l. 18, r., *Q'lippoth.*
" 131 and 132, wherever it is " *Ele'h* " r., *Eleh.*
" 133 and 134, for " hivrah " r., 'Hiv'rah.
" 135, note, r., Mantua Ed. iii, 135*b.*
" 137, l. 21, r., Hadar ; l. 23, for " Ghost" r., Spirit.
" 138, note after " Ed." r., iii.
" 147, l. 24, r., *ha-qaton;* l. 27, for " spirit " r., soul.
" 150, l. 10, r., *ham-dabbereth ;* l. 19, r., *su-geem.*
" 168, note, l. 4 fr. bot., for " Ezer " r., Asher.
" 171, l. 20, r., Spinoza.
" 182, l. 13, r., Abba.
" 183, note † r., *She'la'h.*
" 189, note, r., *Va-yet-zeh.*
" 192, l. 14, r., *Va-yeeq'rah.*
" 193, l. 25, 26, r., *Ru'hoth ye'sod ha-Olam.*
" 194, l. 20, r., Abba ; l. 26, for " *chay* " r., 'Hai.
" 195, note, after " fol.," r., 3, col 1.
" 196, l. 5, fr. bot., r., for " spirit," soul ; for " soul," spirit.
" 197, l. 17, for " Neshamah " r., Rua'h ; l. 18, for Rua'h r., Nishmatha.
" 198, l. 4, r., *qe-tzeph ;* l. 7, r., 99*b.*
" 199, l. 6, r., Abba.
" 200, l. 19, for 188, r., 288; in note, l. 3, r., '*haÿ-yah.*
" 201, l. 5, for " *Moota'bo* " r., *Moot-bah ;* l. 21, for *te-bang* r., *te-bah ;* l. 21, for " *Mool-bang,*" r., *Moot-bah.*
" 203, l. 15, for " Spirit" r., Soul ; l. 16, for " Soul " r., Spirit.
" 204, l. 25, for " Havvah " r., 'Havah.
" 207, l. 7, for " Onkelos " r., Ounqelos
" 211, l. 5, r., Partzupheem.
" 212, l. 21, r., *Niqood.*
" 213, l. 3, fr. bot. r., *'Hephetz.*
" 215, l. 23, r., *K'thoneth.*
" 217, l. 26, r., 'Hadash.

Page 220, l. 1, r., Razé; l. 21, r., חכמה.
" 226, l. 28, r., Notariqon.
" 232, l. 2, fr. bot. r., ha-shama'yem; l. 4, r., D'Tznioothah.
" 234, ult., for "Bava" r., Babha.
" 248, l. 20, r., Qa-yin.
" 252, note ‡ r., 'Enayim.
" 253, l. 14, r., Elon, the Tree; l. 3, fr. bot. r., Qa-disha.
" 254, l. 4, r., Ohr for "Or."
" 256, l. 3, r., A'harai; l. 4, r., 'Hadash; l. 17, r., Emeq; l. 20, r., Hadreth; ult. r., Abba.
" 257, l. 20, r., Risho-nah; l. 3, fr. bot., dele "the Ancient of the Ancients."
" 265, l. 10, fr. bot., for, "spirit," r., soul; for, "soul," r., spirit; in note, r., Sheqel.
" 266, l. 6, r., 'Heereq.
" 267, note, r., ha-'Hasaqah.
" 268, note, l. 5, r., P'ree Etz ha-'Haÿ-yim.
" 269, l. 14, r., Din.
" 271, l. 3, fr. bot., for "mutbang" r., mutbah, same line r., ha-Moot'bah.
" 280, l. 8, fr. bot. r., D'yooq-nah; l. 6, r., Kur'sai-yah; l. 5, r., Malakhaÿ-ah; l. 4, r., Gil-goolem.
" 281, ult. r., Sitrai Yemeen-ah amoodah D'Hes-ed.
" 282, l. 4, r., Dismalah; l. 9, r., Ra'hmim; l. 12, for, "Spirit" r., Soul, for, "Soul" r., Spirit.
" 284, l. 11, for, "Or" r., Ohr.
" 291, l. 3, r., ti-qoonen.
" 300, l. 4, r., Ohr Ain Soph.
" 303, l, 30, r., Ounqelos.
" 304, l. 13, r., Pirqé; l. 21, r., Koa'h.
" 305, note, l. 1, r., 'Hidusheh.
" 307, l. 4. fr. bot., r., Kur-sai-yah.

Page 328, l. 3, r., Kur-sai-yah.
" 329, l. 3, for, "Ophaneem" r., Auphanem; for Hash r., 'Hash; l. 9, r., Mitzraim.
" 332, l. 5, r., Kiseh Melekh.
" 334, l. 6, for "has" r., have; in note, r., Worlds.
" 343, l. 20, for, יחיד r., יחור
" 344, l. 8, for, "l'nephesh 'haÿ-yah" r., nishmath 'Haÿ-yim, and l. 10 for "ה׳יה haÿ-yah living, creature;" r., l'nesphesh Haÿ-yah.
" 345. l. 4, r., b'tzelem in note r., 71b.
" 348, l. 3, r., vayeetzer; in note, l. 2, for 39b, r., 52b.
" 349, l. 6, r., ab'doh for "av'doh.
" 366, l. 18, r., 'hoq.
" 367, l. 3, r., 'hoq.
" 368, l. 27, r., Qa-dosha.
" 379, l. 29, r., Shad-dai.
" 380, l. 10, r., Tiqooneh.
" 382, l. 18, r., Abba.
" 394, l. 26, r., Kur-sai-yah; l. 28 and 31 r., D'i-noor.
" 395, l. 11, r., 'Haÿ-yah.
" 410, l. 12, r. Malakh Hamoveth.
" 414, l. 16, r., d'yooq-nah.
" 416, l. 5, fr. bot., r., d'mooth.
" 417, l. 21 and 23, page 418, l. 5 and 20, r., D'yooq-nah.
" 429, l. 6, r., m' Elohe-khu.
" 432 and 436, top, and l. 19, r., Malakh Hamoveth.
" 437, l. 21, r., Sit-rah; l. 3 fr. bot. for "grave" r., dust.
" 440, l. 14, r., 'Hokhmath; ult. r., Qad-disha.
" 442, l. 25, r., Elohe-khu.
" 444, ult. Qa-yin.

www.ingramcontent.com/pod-product-compliance
Lightning Source LLC
Chambersburg PA
CBHW021132230426
43667CB00005B/82